IS THERE DIETARY TREATMENT FOR ARTHRITIS?
HOW CAN A CHAMOMILE POTION BE USED TO TREAT STOMACH ULCERS?
WHAT IS THE IMPORTANCE OF VITAMIN B1 IN PREVENTING CANCER?

◀ ◀ ▶ ▶

In the thousands of Life Readings given by Edgar Cayce, he stressed the unity of the body, the soul, and the Universal Force that all of us share. Good physical health was vital, and Cayce often gave revolutionary, detailed medical diagnoses to people for whom he knew no more than a name and address. Since his time, many of Edgar Cayce's astounding recommendations have been borne out by modern research—and more and more people today are recognizing the importance of diet, exercise, stress management, and nontoxic medicines as part of overall good health. With treatments for everything from acne to Alzheimer's disease, complete with case histories and natural formulas, the *Edgar Cayce Encyclopedia of Healing* is a lasting, important book for better health.

◀ ◀ ▶ ▶

EDGAR CAYCE
ENCYCLOPEDIA OF HEALING

S0-BRK-456

Books in
The Edgar Cayce Series

Published by
WARNER BOOKS

EDGAR CAYCE

ENCYCLOPEDIA OF HEALING

BY REBA ANN KARP

WARNER BOOKS

A Time Warner Company

PLEASE NOTE:
The Edgar Cayce Encyclopedia of Healing is documentary and must not be interpreted as a guide for self-healing. If you wish to follow any of the Cayce suggestions, do so only under the supervision of a medical doctor.

WARNER BOOKS EDITION

Cover design by Karen Katz

Warner Books, Inc.
1271 Avenue of the Americas
New York, N.Y. 10020

Visit our Web site at
http://warnerbooks.com

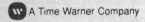 A Time Warner Company

Printed in the United States of America

First Printing: June, 1986

Reissued: May, 1988

15 14

A special thanks to the research staff of the Heritage Store...

Tom Johnson

Carol Baraff

Linda Keener

Barbara Salerno

Lise Stryker

Earendil Spindelilus

Steve Borgardus

Jane Gilbert

Bob Fears

Table of Contents

FOREWORD

Everyone who is ill wants to be healed. This book gives the reader an encyclopedic picture of how Edgar Cayce—the twentieth century's outstanding mystic and seer—sees healing come about in the human body.

Cayce died in 1945, but his legacy of more than 14,000 readings continues to be researched and worked with academically and in clinical practice. And this information tells us that man is an eternal being, spiritual in nature, creative and building through the powers of the mind, and utilizing a body in this dimension that is the product of his mind working with spiritual energy.

It is perhaps appropriate that Reba Ann Karp has entitled this book *The Edgar Cayce Encyclopedia of Healing*, for she indeed has covered a multitude of subjects, concepts, problems, therapies and case studies.

My own experience has told me over the past three decades that there is truth in the way Cayce saw the human body. He talked about functioning systems and organs within the body fulfilling their mission to maintain life so that we can be active and fulfill a destiny and purpose in this world we live in.

Cayce's approach was fundamental. If we can bring about a coordination of these functions—the assimilation, elimination, circulation, respiration, regeneration, etc.—then the healing must come about. The emotions, attitude, beliefs, responses to life's situations all play a part in instigating or worsening an illness of the body, but a therapy designed to balance and bring into attunement the functioning body, the mind and the spiritual reality spells health in the majority of cases.

Sometimes a very simple therapy program will do wonders when it is directed toward helping the body. Very recently, a patient of mine—a man in his thirties—developed a hepatitis. Before we could determine from the laboratory which type it was, a course of therapy involving rest, special diet, castor oil packs over his abdomen and a positive frame of mind brought high enzyme readings back to normal, his icterus following suit, and he was back to work feeling normal within three weeks.

You will enjoy reading *The Edgar Cayce Encyclopedia*, for it will give you a head start in thinking about your body in a new way—a way that will allow you to have more control over your own health, for healing does indeed come from within. And you should have control.

                                                  William A. McGarey, M.D.

Edgar Cayce:
A Brief Biography

In presenting a brief summary of someone's life, it is usually best to start with the beginning—or the day of birth. However, when trying to construct enough of the salient facts surrounding the life of Edgar Cayce to introduce him to readers, starting at the beginning may be a problem.

Edgar Cayce was a psychic born on March 18, 1877, in Hopkinsville, Kentucky. He died on January 3, 1945, in Virginia Beach, Virginia.

That much is statistical. However, according to one of his sons, the late Hugh Lynn Cayce, his father came into this life to introduce psychic ability to the age, and his ability to do so, or to function under trance conditions, was something he had carried over with him from a past incarnation.

Hence, that which made Edgar Cayce the psychic began long before March 18, 1877.

However, staying within that relatively short span of time, between 1877 and 1945, we find a man who began

1

his life on a farm in Kentucky, the only son of Leslie and Carrie Cayce. Later in his life, Edgar's father was to be elected justice of the peace, a position which earned him the title of Squire but limited the time he had to spend with his sensitive growing son.

Deeply attached to his mother, Edgar also developed a close relationship with his Grandfather Cayce, who was the county's dowser. After his grandfather died, Edgar claimed he came back to talk with him in meetings which were as real to him as the imaginary children he said came to play with him.

Unenthusiastic about studies, Edgar accidentally found, during a grueling spelling session with his father, that he could absorb or learn a subject by sleeping on the book. Not much time was required either; just a little nap would accomplish the task. Thereafter, he found he fared better in school.

One Sunday afternoon, stirred by a particular sermon at church, he slipped off into the woods to read the Bible and pray for a chance to heal the sick, during which time he was visited by a radiance which told that his prayers had been heard and that he would have the opportunity to heal the sick if he remained faithful to his prayers.

Hugh Lynn Cayce noted that many people attributed his father's psychic ability to being hit with a baseball in the spine when he was fifteen years old. After the accident, his normal quiet reserve was shattered by his obvious inability to control himself. He became noisy and quarrelsome, talking loudly and throwing things. When the Squire came home, he put his son to bed, where he subsequently drifted off into a coma, during which time he told his astonished parents that a poultice mixed with special herbs and chopped raw onions must be placed at the base of his brain if he was ever to be normal again.

After the poultice was applied, Edgar fell into a normal sleep, and when he woke in the morning, he had regained his personality.

Despite his bouts with the paranormal as a child, Edgar's psychic ability didn't really surface until he reached adulthood. The specific event that triggered it was a paralysis of the throat muscles which threatened to cause him the loss of his voice and his job as a salesman. Since medical doctors were unable to correctly diagnose the cause, he consulted a hypnotist. Under a subsequent trance condition, Edgar was able to correctly describe the cause: nervous stress, which was forcing a tightening and contraction of nerves and muscles throughout his body.

Following the diagnosis, Edgar requested that the hypnotist, in turn, suggest to him under a hypnotic state that the circulation in his vocal cord area was increasing. A few minutes later, Edgar's neck flushed red, and upon awakening he was able to speak normally once again.

Afterward, he found that his ability could be put to use to help other people, thereby fulfilling the promise made in the woods many years ago when the radiance told him he would have the opportunity to heal the sick if he remained faithful to the promise.

What followed were many years of helping people while in a self-induced state of unconsciousness, during which time Edgar had access to information on virtually any subject imaginable. The readings were conducted over the next forty years, with the assistance of his wife, Gertrude, and secretary, Gladys Davis Turner. At first the readings were limited to medical problems. Later, as the scope of his psychic ability expanded, such topics as meditation, dreams, reincarnation, and prophecy were included.

Among the predictions yet to be fulfilled and which are the expectations of many now living are the slipping of portions of Japan into the ocean; the rise of the continent of Atlantis, which supposedly disappeared into the ocean in 1530 B.C.; an end to communism in Russia, which event will make that country become "the hope of the world"; and a tilt in the earth's rotational axis, which will cause a reversal of climates.

Today there are over 14,000 readings on file at the Cayce Foundation—the Association for Research and Enlightenment, located between Sixty-seventh and Sixtyeighth streets in Virginia Beach. Among those 14,000 readings, 8,976 of which are devoted to medical subjects, are 900,000 pages—14 million words—of notes transcribed while Edgar Cayce was in a self-induced trance.

The ARE, as it is known today among its membership, is under the leadership of Cayce's grandson, Charles Thomas Cayce, who is its president. The ARE's aim is to advance the study and research of Cayce's psychic readings, or as Hugh Lynn Cayce explained: "I think we are in a new age of man's discoveries. Man is discovering new space within himself. We are part of this—we're aiding and abetting."

The original Cayce hospital, which is situated on a hill overlooking the Atlantic Ocean, was built in 1928 by the Association of National Investigators. Following the 1929 stock market crash, the headquarters were to part from the Cayce family, only to be returned in 1956 when they were once again purchased by the Cayce association. During the interim, the building served as a gambling house, a beach club, and, during World War II, a quarters for nurses.

On Easter Sunday, March 30, 1975, the ARE opened its newest addition, the ARE library and conference center, a 20,000-foot library which contains one of the world's largest collections of writings on subjects such as telepathy, precognition, and ESP.

In addition to the library–conference center, the ARE facilities include a therapy department open to members only, in which treatments that were most often discussed in the readings—massage, steam baths, colonic irrigation, and whirlpool baths—are administered. The Therapy Department is staffed by registered nurses and massage therapists. Additionally, the ARE headquarters presents week-long conferences to help participants discover a new level of physical and spiritual fulfillment. Topics focus on dream interpretation, healing, and the mysteries of ancient Egypt and Atlantis, to name a few.

Then, too, there is the ARE camp, located in the Appalachian Mountains of Virginia. Here, under the direction of the ARE Youth Activities Department, the camp applies the philosophy of the Cayce readings for children, youth, and families. Activities include workshops, wilderness hikes, group dream work, swimming, and meditation.

The ARE Clinic, Inc., in Phoenix, Arizona, is the only holistic treatment center in the world where Edgar Cayce's health principles and remedies are applied to augment traditional medical and surgical practices. The clinic was formed in 1970 under the direction of Drs. William and Gladys McGarey.

Also an integral part of the ARE are its study groups. In 1956, when the ARE repurchased its headquarters, there were only 140 such groups; today the number is in excess of 1,500. During these sessions, participants have the opportunity to develop psychic abilities, rediscover God, as well as explore other areas of the spirit via the concepts presented in the Edgar Cayce readings.

Last but not least are the Circulating Files, collections of readings on both physical and metaphysical subjects. The files make the study of a particular illness (e.g., arthritis) easier and eliminate hours of reading through hundreds of complete readings in order to obtain specific information. Currently, there are 360 Circulating Files, and more are in preparation. For the convenience of its members, the ARE keeps a list of physicians and other health-care professionals who have expressed a willingness to help implement the treatments suggested in the Cayce readings.

As Cayce explained: "The cycle has rolled to that period when the individual entities again in the earth's experience gather together for a definite work" (254-47).

Cayce's Theory of the Causes of Disease

In all of the Cayce readings for illnesses, there is deliberate emphasis placed on locating the root cause of each malady, which accounts for Cayce's focus on establishing new and more constructive habits and attitudes rather than on simply alleviating symptoms.

Since the majority of the readings were given for specific individuals, results must be studied and evaluated under the care of physicians willing to experiment with the Cayce therapies. Dr. William A. McGarey, director of the ARE Clinic (4018 North Fortieth Street, Phoenix, Arizona 85018), has studied the readings and has applied some of the treatments suggested to his own practice. (A list of referral doctors who will follow some of the Cayce treatments is available to ARE members.)

The difficulty in analyzing the readings is due to their complex nature. Also, it is apparent that many of the readings were given to individuals who had other disorders as well as the one being discussed. This very complexity contributes to the problem of interpretation, making it difficult to match the many treatments recommended for any individual to a single, specific disease.

Readers will note that there are apparent common denominators in the causes suggested by Cayce for disease—poor assimilations and poor eliminations, inadequate diet, improper acid-alkaline balance, spinal subluxations and lesions, imbalance-incoordination of the nervous system, imbalance-incoordination of the circulatory system, glandular malfunction, stress, overtaxation and overexertion, karma, attitude, and infection.

Despite the similarities of the causes, the treatments were prescribed specifically for those disorders, individually tailored for the person and, of course, his complaint.

The following is a short discussion of the causes as mentioned in the readings.

• Poor Assimilations—proper assimilation provides a full and constant supply of building materials and energies needed for the continual construction of new cells and tissues. Poor assimilation occurs when even one chemical element needed for rebuilding is not supplied to the body through diet and digestion or is not efficiently utilized and converted into specific nutrients necessary for each different kind of cell. Disease attributed to poor assimilation involves nutritive deficiency and results in cellular degeneration.

• Poor Eliminations—the fact that poor eliminations are the most cited cause of disease in the Cayce readings indicates the fundamental importance of proper elimination in the maintenance of physical balance and health. When the processes of elimination are impeded in some way, any number of disease symptoms can ensue. The readings concur with medical science in describing several excretory systems which, in a state of balance and coordination, act to remove all unwanted substances from the body efficiently and completely. These systems are the intestinal tract, the kidneys and bladder, the pores of the skin, and the lungs. When an imbalance occurs in any of these systems, slowing down the excretory processes, the result is a buildup of poisonous wastes (toxins) which can endanger any of the components and systems of the body, down to the cellular level, by impeding the rebuilding process itself.

• Diet—almost every one of Cayce's nine thousand physical readings include dietary advice. This wealth of information gives a clear message that eating habits are either a vital source of health or an inevitable cause of bodily imbalance and disease. Although he discouraged becoming "extremist" or "a slave to a set diet," Cayce did often recommend constant and respectful attention to diet. What the body needs are nutrients—carbohydrates, proteins, minerals, vitamins—in forms that are most complete, are easily digested and assimilated, aid efficient eliminations, maintain systemic balance, and provide materials for cellular rebuilding. Cayce especially praised fresh fruits and vegetables as fulfilling these requirements, while he included candy and cake among those "things that hinder the body": foods that lack nutrients, are hard to digest, impair eliminations, and unbalance the metabolism.

• Improper Acid-Alkaline Balance—the whole body participates in a constant effort to keep a biochemical acid-alkaline balance. In order to maintain health and life itself, each cell must retain a proper relationship between acidity and alkalinity in its composition. In the fluid between cells, this dual composition is a basis for the transmission of positive-negative electrical impulses from cell to cell, which occurs, for example, in the transference of nerve impulses between the brain and body. Electrical energy is released by the oxidation of both nutritive and toxic materials in the intercellular fluid. An excess of acidity or alkalinity impedes these chemical processes, resulting in higher levels of toxicity, increased susceptibility to disease, and lowered energy levels over the whole body.

• Spinal Subluxations and Lesions—a spinal subluxation is a partial or incomplete dislocation of one or more vertebrae of the spine. A spinal lesion is a spinal injury that damages tissue and is usually associated with a subluxation. Subluxations and lesions can have similarly detrimental effects. Since the vertebrae house nerve impulses to virtually every part of the body, a mechanical trauma of either kind will exert pressure either on the autonomic ganglia or directly on the nervous return from the extremities. This will block the nerve impulses to specific areas of the body fed by those nerves. The results may include the prevention of proper drainages, a gradual slowing of the circulation, and both local and sympathetic or reflex pain. Subluxations and lesions can therefore be the cause, as well as the result, of undue physical stress. Typical causes given in the readings were injury and strain.

• Imbalance-Incoordination of the Nervous System—the body relies upon a smoothly operating nervous system for the impulses and energies that control both conscious movements and unconscious functions. These functions include breathing, heartbeat, circulation of blood and lymph, the proper functioning of the glands, digestion, assimilation of nutrients, and elimination of waste—all the aspects of metabolic rebuilding required by every living cell. In turn, the nerve cells themselves depend upon these processes for their own efficient functioning. Vital to a healthy nervous system are the assimilation of certain necessary nutrients and the secretion by the glands of substances needed by all the cells of the body to reproduce themselves, including nerve cells.

The nervous system as a whole has three main subdivisions: the cerebrospinal, autonomic, and sensory systems. The cerebrospinal system controls conscious movements and includes in its makeup the brain and spinal cord and such consciously controlled organs as the vocal cords. The spinal column includes, from top to bottom, seven cervical vertebrae, twelve thoracic, or dorsal, vertebrae, five lumbar vertebrae and the sacral and coccygeal fused segments. Each vertebra is the site of ganglia governing nerve impulses to specific areas of the body. The autonomic system "automatically" regulates the organs of the body which function without conscious control. Dr. McGarey calls it "the nervous system of the unconscious mind," while Cayce termed it the "sympathetic" nervous system. Medical science divides this system into two more subdivisions: the sympathetic and the parasympathetic. These together act as a check-and-balance system to help the body respond in a balanced manner to extreme internal and external demands. The sympathetic part of the system has an excitatory effect (by activating the adrenal glands, for example), while the parasympathetic prevents the body from accelerating to extremes.

The sensory (or voluntary) system receives information from all parts of the body, including the sensory organs of sight, smell, hearing, taste, and touch, and relays messages to the brain. It also conveys messages from the brain to the motor nerves, which operate the muscles. One motor nerve and its branching fibers may have control over thousands of muscle fibers. In short, the harmonious functioning of the three nervous systems is central to the maintenance of physical (and psychological) well-being.

• Imbalance-Incoordination of the Circulatory System— the flow of blood throughout the system performs the function of supplying nutrients to the tissues and organs and removing waste material. An impaired circulatory system occurs when the blood is unable to flow freely to all parts of the body, interfering with the proper functioning of the affected areas. Control of the circulatory system as a whole lies in the sympathetic, or autonomic nervous system. Its functions include balancing or coordination between the deeper and superficial circulation; maintenance or control of the platelets, which regulate clotting; and the production of substances which control the integrity of the walls of the veins and arteries.

Cayce found that a number of factors could lead to circulatory imbalances. These included an accumulation of toxins or waste materials in the liver, spleen, or pancreas which could lead to a reabsorption of some of these substances into the bloodstream, resulting in toxemia; disturbances of the hepatic circulation itself, or of the combined interaction of liver and kidneys, which could create numerous other interrelated causes; an improper diet, which could impede the functions of the excretory system as well as fail to supply needed nutrients; physical or mental overtaxation, resulting in sluggish or impeded circulation; and misalignment of the vertebrae in the spine due to injury, stress, or other factors—pressures, subluxations, or lesions in any area of the spine can impede both the nerve impulses and circulation to some part of the body.

• Glandular Malfunction, Imbalance, and Incoordination—a gland is any organ that separates certain elements from the blood and secretes them in the form of either a substance for the use of the body, such as adrenaline, or a substance for the body to discard, such as urine. Some glands have ducts and empty into an organ; others are ductless, or endocrine glands, and pass their secretions directly into the bloodstream. Cayce identified seven endocrine glands in all, some being the gonads, the cells of Leydig, and the thymus and pineal glands.

In an esoteric sense, Cayce singled out the endocrine centers as the seat of soul memory and as the bearers of karma, or lessons needed for soul growth. Accordingly, he considered these glands the centers of energy generation and control in both spiritual attunement and physical equilibrium. Hence, their big role in health and balance at many levels.

A vital function of the glands is to secrete substances needed for cells to reproduce themselves. Interference with this function can occur from several causes, each of which creates a predisposition toward certain types of imbalances. According to Cayce, glandular imbalance can be attributed to shortages in the body of minerals and nutrients. These include a short supply of iodine, a mineral particularly needed by the thyroid gland; a shortage of gold, which can lead to a deficiency in a hormone necessary for the proper functioning of the nerves; and a lack of vitamins, which have an activating effect on glandular tissue.

• Stress, Overtaxation, and Overexertion—Cayce cited overtaxation of the body as a primary or contributing cause in several mental and physical disorders. Generally, physical overtaxation implied overwork, while overexertion suggested insufficient sleep and opportunities to relax. Understandably, if the system was already depleted due to poor diet or some already existing physical imbalance, overtaxation could easily occur. When the stress was of mental origin, emotions such as worry, anxiety, and anger were those most frequently cited. Negative emotions could lead to extreme fatigue, tense muscles, and problems with the digestive and excretory processes.

Subsequently, the body would become weak and depleted and eventually toxins created by the glandular system would flow into the lymph circulation, causing a blockage to the eliminating channels and creating congestion and further acidity. In this condition, the body's resistance would be lowered, making "dis-ease" practically imminent.

• Karma, Attitudes, and Emotions—the Edgar Cayce readings give a clear message that the causes of disease and the sources of health extend beyond the physical to the mental and spiritual aspects of the self. Mental attitudes, emotions, and the Law of Karma affect mind, body, and spirit.

A central concept of the readings is that each human being embodies a spirit or soul, a part of the Source of all life and health. The readings used several terms to describe that Source: the Creative Force, the Universal Forces, or God. Each individual for whom a reading was given was described as an "entity"—a being existing as a trinity of body, mind, and spirit. Just as the readings define physical health as harmonious, balanced cooperation between the constituents of the body, so do they emphasize the need for harmony between the three aspects of self in order to create and preserve health and to alleviate disease:

> The body, the mind, the soul are one within the physical forces; for the body is indeed the temple of the Living God. In each entity there is that portion which is part of the Universal Force, and is that which lives on. All must coordinate and cooperate. (1593-1)

One of the remarkable implications of the above message is that the soul is as integral a part of our physical existence as are the material organs of the body. It is equally remarkable that a part of each of us is also a part of the infinite and divine Universal Force, that which creates all life. "That which is brought into materiality is *first* conceived in the spirit" (3395-2).

Cayce held that the body and mind come into being for the purpose of manifesting the soul in the realm of materiality, not just once but through successive lifetimes. The experience of different minds and bodies enables the soul to become more and more attuned with the spiritual Source.

According to Cayce, the Law of Karma refers to the causes and effects of thoughts, emotions, and actions, especially those that carry over from one lifetime to another: "Karma is that brought over, while cause and effect may exist in one material experience only" (2981-21). Until an entity achieves full attunement with God, the principle of karma operates from moment to moment, hour to hour, and from lifetime to lifetime. All experience in material life can create karma, which Cayce also termed a "constant meeting of self." As a further explanation of karma, Cayce often cited the biblical passage from Paul: ". . . for whatsoever a man soweth, that shall he reap."

Through the "constant meeting of self" and from reaping what is sown, actions and disturbances of mind and spirit create physical disease. The effects of attitudes and emotions on the body are often obvious. Anger brings on headaches or indigestion; depression results in general weariness; emotional turbulence triggers asthmatic conditions. Cayce found numerous examples of the direct effect attitudes and emotions have on the body:

> To be sure the attitudes oft influence the physical condition of the body. No one can hate his neighbor and not have stomach or liver trouble. One cannot be jealous and allow anger of same and not have upset digestion or heart disorder. (4021-1)

Within the past century, the relationship of mental attitudes and emotions to bodily disease has been gradually recognized and studied by medical science. Science terms this relationship "psychosomatic," from the Greek words *"psyche,"* meaning mind, and *"soma,"* body.

The Cayce readings state that glands secrete according to impulses from the emotional and nervous system. Anger, resentments, contention, hate, self-condemnation, animosity, and related nervous tensions release poisons from the glandular system into the lymphatic circulation, deplete bodily energies, block eliminations and generally create a condition which predisposes the system to disease. In this view, attitudes and emotions, which are nonmaterial, involve nerves and glands as the material "conductors," as the organic connection between the nonphysical aspects of self and the physical body. The readings describe emotions as "electronics," as the "glow" of life itself coursing through the body in the nervous system and acting as the vibratory communication between mind, body, and spirit.

> As the sensory forces or nerve centers are the passage from the finite to the infinite, why not attune the body-forces of self to the beauties of the infinite and show thyself approved unto God, a workman not ashamed? (3697-1)

Within the indissoluble trinity of body, mind, and spirit, any illness involves all three aspects of an entity in a "meeting of self." Even that most common and universal disease, the cold, requires mental and emotional change and a spiritual lesson to be learned:

> Thus you can take a bad cold from getting mad. You can get a bad cold from blessing out someone else, even if it is your wife.

> Instead of snuffling, blow! Instead of resentments, love! (288-44)

Perhaps included along with karma should be reference to congenital defects. According to the readings, a number of disorders were attributed, at least in part, to congenital defects or weaknesses in the body. In many of these cases, Cayce found injury to be at fault, occurring either during gestation or during labor and delivery. A small number of readings traced the damage to poor nutritional care of the mother or poor attitudes held during gestation.

In other cases, the terms "congenital defect" and "karma" were used interchangeably, suggesting that all congenital problems merit consideration and treatment as karmic situations. Viewed in this manner, this concept could help free parents of the guilt usually associated with a child born with birth defects, because it would imply that the child (and parents) chose the situation for a special purpose, which always involved cultivating the love, patience, and selfless service needed in caring for an "exceptional" child.

• Infection—this is simply explained as communication of a disease from one organism to another or the presence of single-celled microorganisms, bacteria, or fungi in the body of a host. Once contracted in a weakened state, infection can spread rapidly unless checked. An example of how the common cold is contracted illustrates how resistance can be lowered and the body made susceptible to what Cayce termed "infectious forces."

In a cold, the factors are often poor diet in combination with strain and overexertion, which leads to fatigue and a feeling of not being up to par. Negative attitudes and emotions indulged in this state lead to a further depletion of the vital energies. The acid-alkaline balance of the system is disturbed, the body becomes overacid, and a cold results. Without proper care, the body is susceptible to potentially more serious disorders, such as pneumonia and tonsillitis.

Similar cause-and-effect sequences could also predispose the body to other problems, according to Cayce. For instance, Cayce traced some causes of colitis to colds, congestion, and intestinal flu, which in turn resulted in a lymphatic disturbance. Syphilis was attributed to a spirochete organism, pyorrhea to a particular "bug," and athlete's foot to a fungal infection. Infection of the skin was also regarded as one of the root causes of scleroderma.

Frequently, in cases where an infection had been cured, Cayce noted that aftereffects persisted, often in the form of a particular weakness which had not existed previously. And since weaknesses could increase susceptibility to illness, the readings emphasized the importance of thoroughly eradicating the effects of an infection from the system.

The Encyclopedia—
from Acne to Xeroderma

The following section is devoted to brief examinations of the more than nine thousand medical readings on file at the Association for Research and Enlightenment (the Cayce Foundation) in Virginia Beach, Virginia. It is very important that those interested note that the studies contained in this volume are not meant to be comprehensive. Those wishing more information are encouraged to consult and study the Circulating Files at the ARE, P.O. Box 595, Virginia Beach, Virginia 23451 (Atlantic Avenue at Sixty-Seventh Street); and before attempting any therapy, to consult a medical doctor.

Additionally, the case histories which follow the individual medical write-ups were taken from the readings themselves and are frequently incomplete due to lack of follow-up data. However, this does not imply that there were no beneficial results obtained—only an inability to keep in contact with those who received the readings. The case histories are intended to give examples of typical readings for a specific disorder.

However, data from recent case histories, received from those who have successfully applied the advice found in the Circulating Files, are included elsewhere in the book.

Also, it should be noted that Cayce gave readings on most conditions, but that "new" diseases are being diagnosed and named almost daily.

Additionally, due to time limitations, not all diseases that Cayce gave information on are included in this book. Those wishing information on these may contact the ARE.

Acne

Acne is a skin disease characterized by eruptions, pimples, and blackheads on the face, appearing at times even on the neck, shoulders, and back. Although this condition is commonly identified with the period of adolescence, it often persists through adulthood if not taken care of when it first develops. One of the unfortunate features of acne is that it can leave scars and often deep pockmarks on the skin, even when it is cleared up.

Edgar Cayce gave thirty-seven readings on acne for twenty-nine people, most of whom were in their teens and twenties.

Cayce consistently determined that acne was caused by either poor eliminations (eighty-seven percent of the cases), or nervous and/or glandular incoordination which directly affected the eliminations. Poor circulation or deficiencies in the blood, such as a lack of iron, were also noted in nearly twenty percent of the cases.

The following is one of his explanations for acne and its causes: "Through the reactions in the blood supply we find disturbing factors in which there is a lack of a balance in the chemical reactions through the system for proper assimilation and proper elimination of used energies. Some are destructive in their reactions—as is indicated in the manner in which there is a disturbance in the eliminations such as to cause poisons to attempt to be eliminated through the perspiratory system; or the abrasions, the pimples, the blackheads that form on that portion of the system'' (1691-1).

Cayce believed that acne was a symptom of a chemical imbalance in the body, where blockages or disturbances of the proper channels of elimination led to attempts to eliminate waste through inappropriate channels in the glands in the skin.

Treatment

Cayce's treatments focused mainly on establishing proper nutritional habits, and he suggested dietary guidelines in over seventy percent of the cases. Most often suggested were plenty of alkaline-reacting foods, such as citrus fruits and their juices, green vegetables and vegetable juices, fish, fowl, lamb, whole wheat bread and whole-grain cereals, and milk. Foods to be avoided included red meat, pork, fried or greasy foods, starchy sweets, chocolate, white potatoes, and white bread. Some were advised to drink a glass of milk or tomato juice with yeast twice a day.

Spinal manipulations to ensure balanced nerve coordination were recommended for over half of the individuals. These were to be administered twice a week at first. Also recommended as often were various forms of electrotherapy to establish better equilibrium among the body forces. The method most frequently suggested was low diathermy, which was usually to be given in conjunction with spinal manipulations. Use of the Violet Ray was also at times suggested.

Nearly forty percent of the individuals were prescribed herbal preparations with ingredients such as tincture of stillingia, essence of burdock root and yellow dock root. Yellow saffron tea, a digestive aid, was recommended in two cases.

Massage was considered an important factor in treatment for about thirty percent of the individuals. Instructions were to gently massage the entire body, giving special attention to the area along the spine. Various combinations of oils and other substances, such as olive oil mixed with tincture of myrrh and lanolin, mineral oil mixed with rose water, and spirits of peppermint and distilled water, were frequently part of the massage routine.

Recommended for twenty-five percent of the individuals were topical applications for blemishes. These included Cuticura soap and ointment, Black and White creams, stearate of zinc powder with balsam (mainly for skin irritation), and camphorated oil.

Case History

Only six individuals receiving readings indicated that they had followed Cayce's advice, but all six reported either remarkable improvements or a complete cure.

Case 5218 was a thirty-five-year-old man who had spent twenty-two years trying unsuccessfully to cure his serious acne condition, which Cayce noted stemmed from poor eliminations and glandular malfunctioning.

Treatments began with a mixture composed of a table-spoon each of sulfur, Rochelle salts, and cream of tartar. A teaspoon of this mixture was to be taken in water each day until the mixture was used up. To correct conditions in the third, fourth, and sixth dorsal and in the third cervical and lumbar vertebrae, twelve osteopathic adjustments were to be administered on a twice weekly basis. A diathermy treatment was to be given just prior to each adjustment.

Following the series of adjustments, the man was to resume taking his sulfur–Rochelle salts–cream of tartar mixture and then repeat the diathermy and adjustment cycle.

Chocolates and pastries were to be avoided; however, an occasional glass of noncarbonated Coca-Cola was permit-ted, as Cayce considered it beneficial in cleansing the kidneys.

Later 5218 reported remarkable improvements in the

condition of his skin, even though he had not completely followed the treatments as prescribed.

Alcoholism

According to Edgar Cayce, alcoholism was a condition that contained both physical and psychological factors. He believed if it was not corrected, both factors perpetuated themselves and each other to the increasing detriment of both the mind and the body. Cayce held that a generalized outline for treatment of alcoholism wasn't possible, "for each individual has [his] own individual problems" (606-1).

His readings, however, emphasized the importance of tailoring treatments to individual needs, while pointing to a few general ways of making it easier to cope with the problem.

A total of twenty-seven readings were given for twenty-three individuals who were alcoholics. These cases were notable in two respects: one being that most of them took place during Prohibition; the other that most of the subjects were male and the majority of the readings had been requested by another person, often a wife.

An individual asked Cayce about the future of Prohibition in America and was told that it had already failed because, "No one may ever legislate goodness in the heart or soul of anyone" (3976-8).

As explained, Cayce viewed the causes of alcoholism as having both physical and psychological dimensions. Physically, the need for alcohol was exaggerated by specific disturbances such as adrenal imbalances and spinal lesions which were centered in the dorsal area. As long as the appetite for alcohol was stimulated by a physical condition, it was difficult, if not impossible, for the will to gain control. Typical symptoms of the physical strain were overtaxed nerves; poor assimilations and eliminations; glandular imbalances; a reduced resistance to infection; disturbed circulation between the heart and liver; strain on other organs such as the pancreas, spleen, and kidneys; toxins in the blood; and diabetic tendencies.

Cayce placed as much importance on the psychological causes of alcoholism as on the physical. He frequently warned against overindulgence in stimulants, and at times viewed these overindulgences as karmic in nature, a need carried over from a past life.

Treatment

Several specific types of treatment dominate the readings on alcoholism, although many of the individuals had other physical problems as well. As expected, the treatments were both physical and mental-spiritual in nature.

To help restore the physical balance, the consumption of alcohol had to be discontinued, usually entirely. This was made easier by Cayce's "gold cure," which consisted of small doses of gold chloride, usually combined with bromide of soda and taken in water according to specific cycles. The gold cure was said to produce a nauseous reaction if any alcohol was consumed.

The instructions for taking the gold cure varied. A simple cycle of taking gold chloride alone was suggested in reading 845-4 and entailed taking one drop in water for two days, two drops for two days, three drops for two days, two days of rest, and then a repeat of the cycle. Cayce predicted that the nauseous reaction would be apparent by the end of the second round. Reading 2010-1 also suggested only gold in strength of one grain per ounce of distilled water. This cycle consisted of one drop in half a glass of water daily for five days, two drops for five days, three drops for five days, and four drops for five days. After a five-day rest, the cycle began again.

For those prescribed soda and gold, a wide variance in the dosage is noted.

There was another antialcohol medication suggested in a few readings, which was said to produce a similar effect. The ingredients varied somewhat from reading to reading but were combined in capsule form. The dose prescribed for case 845 was a combination of about one drop of oil of eucalyptus, one-half drop of oil of turpentine, and one-half of compound tincture of benzoin. Other combinations included eucalyptol, tincture of benzoin, tincture of valerian, rectified oil of turpentine, benzol, and codeine. These capsules were usually to be made one at a time and would keep for only a short time.

Also suggested in a number of cases were electrotherapy treatments. Most often suggested was the Wet Cell with gold chloride. This was believed to help rebuild the nerve connections and introduce gold vibrationally into the system. In a few instances the Radio-Active Appliance was suggested. The readings warned against taking any alcohol during treatment periods, explaining that "electricity and alcohol don't work together. It burns tissue and is not good for any body" (323-1).

Other physical treatments mentioned were spinal manipulation, diet, hydrotherapy, exercise, body-building stimulants, and various methods of cleansing the system. The dietary guidelines emphasized fruits and vegetables, fish, fowl, and lamb, and meat juices or broths. Beef, pork, and large amounts of foods that were acid forming or alcohol forming were to be avoided.

The hydrotherapy treatments were usually to take the form of sweats and colonics. Also recommended were exercising in the open and stimulants to help build resistance, such as Atomidine and vitamin supplements.

Treatment at the mental-spiritual level was given as much importance as physical measures. First, for any treatment to be successful, it was believed absolutely necessary for the individual to want to change. At times, entering an institution where the cure could be supervised was viewed as the best and easiest first approach. A change in environment and companions was often suggested.

Once the decision was made to stop drinking, it was then implemented by replacing a negative thought pattern with a more constructive one. One suggestion was to refrain from negative emotions such as anger, hate, and self-condemnation. Another was to cooperate and actively participate in the physical treatments suggested. Creative visualization was seen as contributing even further toward building the positive expectancy of a healthy mind and body. Additionally, Cayce believed the key to healing was in the cultivation of a more spiritual attitude toward life. Prayer was particularly important. Some were counseled to devote thought to the self and its relationship with the universe and God. To reinforce the spiritual perspective, Bible reading was advised. Specific passages repeatedly mentioned were Genesis 1:5–6; Exodus 19:5; Deuteronomy 30; and John 14–17.

Finally, those who were close to alcoholic individuals and who truly desired to help them were given similar attitudinal counseling. Cayce repeatedly suggested persistent prayer and a constructive, noncondemning attitude.

Case History

Case 2161 was a thirty-eight-year-old alcoholic whose reading noted that his predisposition for addiction was mental as well as physical. Mentally, he lacked willpower to control his physical appetites. Physically, his blood was affected and his glands were becoming more involved. The general strain had caused a subluxation of the sixth and seventh dorsal area of the spine, impeding nerve impulses to the digestive functions and exaggerating the appetites.

The treatments concentrated on counteracting the desire for alcohol and restoring balance to the system. Spinal adjustments were recommended twice a week until eight to ten had been taken, correcting the subluxation of the dorsal area and coordinating this with the fourth lumbar, the upper cervicals, and the rest of the spine.

Also during this period, one drop of one-grain-per-ounce gold and two of three-grain-per-ounce soda, taken in half a glass of water in the morning and evening for five days, was prescribed. After five days rest, he was to begin Radio-Active Appliance treatments with approximately four-grains-per-ounce gold in the solution jar. Applications were to be made for twenty minutes each evening for ten days. Following a rest period, the gold-and-soda doses were to be resumed, continuing the above sequence of treatments until there was no more desire for alcohol.

The diet emphasized raw vegetables, such as carrots, celery, lettuce, and tomatoes, as well as cooked vegetables. Fish, fowl, and lamb were recommended rather than beef. The man was warned that alcohol was to be completely avoided, for after a series of adjustments and gold treatments, it could cause illness.

Psychologically, Cayce counseled the man to strengthen both his will and his spiritual purposes.

One month later, the man's mother reported that her son was following Cayce's advice and had become a new man from the first week. At the time of her communication with Cayce, her son was back at work and feeling good.

Subsequent reports indicated that he had been cured of his drinking problem.

Alzheimer's Disease

Alzheimer's disease is presenile mental deterioration associated with cortical cerebral sclerosis. It involves a decrease in or loss of mental faculties, reasoning power, memory, and will, which is believed to be due to organic brain disease. Characteristic symptoms include confusion, disorientation, apathy, and stupor of varying degrees.

The causes of Alzheimer's disease are unknown, and medical treatment is usually unsuccessful.

Incoordination between the sympathetic and cerebrospinal nervous systems was found by Cayce to be a main cause of Alzheimer's disease. In one of the two readings which discussed this disease, Cayce attributed the disorder to a shock to the system which was of such a nature that the reflexes from the cerebrospinal centers themselves created a condition that prevented coordination.

Treatment

In both of the cases, the Wet Cell Appliance was recommended to normalize and strengthen the nerve forces of the body. Also in both cases, the Wet Cell was to be followed by a gentle massage along the cerebrospinal centers, using equal portions of olive oil and tincture of myrrh.

Case History

The causes of Alzheimer's disease recorded for case 5204 were incoordination of the nervous system and blood clots.

Cayce's first suggestion for therapy was the daily use of the Wet Cell Appliance, followed by a massage along the cerebrospinal area. The massage formula suggested was equal portions of olive oil and tincture of myrrh. Cayce believed that if his advice was followed "regularly and prayerfully," it would bring back memory and coordination between cerebrospinal and sympathetic systems.

The woman's husband, however, felt that he could not properly apply the treatments prescribed, and her condition gradually worsened until she died.

Amyotrophic Lateral Sclerosis

This is a chronic progressive disease characterized by deterioration of the nerves and muscular system, with onset usually between the ages of forty and sixty years. Symptoms are often weakness and wasting of the extremities, mainly the upper extremities, and progressive muscular atrophy. Life expectancy after the first symptom is about three years.

Although there was only one case of ALS in the Cayce readings, he attributed it to common causes such as poor assimilations and destruction of the nerve sheaths through chemical imbalances. Problems with attitudes and emotions were also viewed as underlying causes.

Treatment and Case History

The one case of ALS in the Cayce readings was that of 5019 and involved a thirty-four-year-old man whose prob-

lems began with a slight limp. His condition gradually
deteriorated to where one arm was beginning to atrophy
and he could not walk without the use of crutches. In his
diagnosis, Cayce centered on a deficiency of gold in the
body chemistry which had caused undernourishment and
weakened the nerve sheaths in the spine. Additionally, his
afflictions were attributed to an unspecific karmic situation.

Cayce recommended the thirty-minute-daily use of the
Wet Cell Appliance, with alternating solutions of Atomidine
and spirits of camphor. When using Atomidine, the copper
plate was to be attached to the man's lumbar axis; when
using camphor, the plate was to be placed over the brachial
center or in the area of the first and second, or third and
fourth dorsal vertebrae.

The treatment also included a peanut-oil-and-lanolin
massage for thirty to forty-five minutes following each
Wet Cell treatment. Cayce also recommended small doses
of gold chloride and bromide of soda, which were to be
taken in distilled water. Starches and alcoholic foods and
beverages were to be avoided. The patient was encouraged
to read the Bible, especially Chapter 19:5 of Exodus and
Chapter 30 of Deuteronomy.

No follow-up was recorded in this case.

Anemia

The term anemia broadly refers to any condition in
which the number of red blood cells in the body falls
below the normal count, although there are several types
of anemia. Insufficiency of red corpuscles is one, as is an
insufficiency of hemoglobin or even a diminution in the
amount of blood in the body. Typical symptoms include
shortness of breath, pallor, lassitude, and lack of energy.

Fourteen individuals, ranging from four to fifty-four
years, received a total of fifteen readings from Edgar
Cayce detailing anemia.

Noted by Cayce in thirteen cases of anemia was an

imbalanced circulation, which was associated with metabolic imbalances. Various types of digestive disturbances would frequently interfere with the production of blood cells, resulting in a low red count and at times a low white count as well.

Mentioned in eight cases as a major contributing factor to anemia was poor elimination, which could lead to a toxic buildup, overacidity, and infection, all of which would adversely affect the assimilations and circulation. Spinal misalignments, mentioned in eight cases, could also add to the problem by deflecting proper nerve impulses to the digestive organs and impeding the circulation. A closely related factor in seven cases was incoordination between the cerebrospinal and sympathetic nervous systems. Other contributory problems which were occasionally involved included glandular imbalances, infection, injury, and prenatal factors.

Treatment

A primary treatment recommended by Cayce for all but one of the individuals was a change to a more balanced diet, which was to fortify the system. Fresh vegetables, citrus juices, liver, seafood, beef juice, milk, whole grains, and other nerve- and blood-building foods were strongly suggested. Fried foods, carbonated drinks, and white bread were not allowed.

Also suggested in nine cases were electrotherapy treatments, with the intent to stimulate the circulation. The Radio-Active Appliance and the Violet Ray were most often recommended. Readings for over half of the cases advised spinal manipulations and frequently focused on the lower half of the spine, coordinating other areas as needed. Recommended as often were blood-building nutritional supplements such as Codiron, Adiron, and Ventriculin.

Colonics, enemas, and laxatives such as milk of magnesia were suggested as stimulants to the eliminations. Massages of the spine and/or abdomen, using olive oil, peanut oil, and other substances, were also advised in six instances. Other occasional suggestions included herbal tonics, inhalants, and Atomidine taken internally.

Case History

Although there were no follow-up reports in the majority of cases, thirty percent noted improvements in health, and some felt the improvement was complete.

An example was case 1796, a sixteen-year-old male who received one reading for anemia. Cayce found that lesions throughout the nervous system had caused circulatory deflections in the dorsal and cervical areas, which resulted in improper eliminations and poor assimilation of foods. This caused a deficiency in the circulatory system which led to his anemia condition. A catarrhal condition had also developed which was affecting the sensory organs.

The first treatment for the youth was a series of ten to fifteen osteopathic adjustments which were to aid in setting up proper drainages so the system would be cleansed of toxins and the eliminations would become more normal. Also recommended for similar reasons was a tablespoon of milk of magnesia at least three times a week.

The Violet Ray, using the bulb applicator, was to be applied when the third or fourth adjustment took place. Additionally, two or three times a week at bedtime, gentle massages were to be given along the spine, also using the Violet Ray. These were to be three minutes in duration and cover the areas from the base of the brain to the end of the spine and around the front of the throat and chest.

One drop of Atomidine in half a glass of water before breakfast for five days, followed by a five-day rest period, was suggested. After two more rounds of the Atomidine routine, a three- to four-day rest period was advised, followed by Adiron taken with each meal for at least two to three weeks.

Blood-building foods were strongly advised, including broiled liver, fish, and lamb. Also highly recommended were yellow foods such as carrots, yellow peaches, and yellow corn. Fried foods were not allowed.

The youth followed Cayce's instructions and reported improved health and greater vitality.

Aphonia

Aphonia is the loss of voice due to disease or injury to the throat or vocal cords.

Sixteen people received a total of twenty-one readings on this subject. The first of these was Edgar Cayce himself, who began his psychic career in hypnotic trance, during which time he was able to diagnose and suggest a treatment for his own severe case of laryngitis.

The most frequent cause of aphonia noted by Cayce was incoordination of the nervous system brought on by stress, overtaxation, or poor spinal alignment. At times, minor paralysis of the larynx or another organ of speech was also a contributing factor.

In approximately thirty percent of the cases, excess acidity in the body produced cold and congestion which attacked the organs of speech. In twenty-five percent, poor eliminations and toxemia were involved, at times occurring in conjunction with congestion.

An interesting factor discussed in another fourth of the cases was psychological in origin—a repression of fears and anxieties which manifested itself in the loss of voice. At times, this involved psychic imbalance as well, a condition termed "psychophonesia."

Treatment

Establishing and maintaining good nerve coordination throughout the body was emphasized by Cayce in treating aphonia. Spinal manipulations, especially of the cervical vertebrae in the neck, were recommended in over sixty percent of the cases, with frequency of treatment not often specified.

To rid the body of accumulated toxins, colonics and

eliminants such as Eno salts or olive oil were mentioned in nearly sixty percent of the cases.

Internal therapies such as diet or natural medicinal compounds were each recommended in over forty percent of the cases to restore the normal acid-alkaline balance in the body. Foods such as fruits, vegetables, and seafood were recommended, while sweets and starches were to be avoided.

Finally, a fourth of the readings suggested body massage as a means of stimulating the circulation and promoting relaxation.

Case History

Good reports were received from three individuals, one of which was Edgar Cayce himself. The other thirteen given readings on aphonia did not report on the results or on whether the treatments were ever carried out.

Case 294 was that of Edgar Cayce, whose career as a psychic diagnostician began when he realized he was able to diagnose and prescribe treatments for illnesses while in a self-induced trance state.

His first reading on aphonia was the result of a session with a hypnotist which he had after he suffered for a year from severe laryngitis. He was thirty-three years old at the time. His unconscious dissertation, which was given in normal voice, described a condition of nervous stress which had caused a tightening and contraction of the nerves and muscles throughout his body. This had impeded the circulation in the larynx and resulted in his inability to speak. Cayce suggested that the hypnotist, in turn, suggest to him that the circulation in the area of his vocal cords would increase. The hypnotist did this, and a few minutes later, during which time Cayce's neck flushed bright red, the hypnotist suggested that the circulation return to normal. When Cayce awoke, he was able to speak normally once again.

Stress along with overtaxation was again responsible for the loss of his voice when he was forty-seven years old.

The reading this time suggested that he maintain good circulation and eliminations and use positive suggestions to effect a cure. However, the fatigue which Cayce was known to be subjected to periodically, due to the demands for his readings, introduced another condition of aphonia four years later. This time, his reading recommended osteopathic manipulations every other day to promote drainages and stimulate eliminations.

Cayce's last reading for himself on aphonia, given when he was fifty-five, attributed the loss of voice to poor eliminations and toxemia. Suggested were strict adherence to a well-balanced alkaline diet and alternate doses of milk of bismuth and milk of magnesia, followed by a dose of phenolphthalein to flush out the system.

Each time, Cayce followed his own recommendations for treatment until he was cured, although he suffered frequent relapses due to his dedication to giving readings. In later life, his aphonia seemed to be his body's way of insisting that he take a short vacation.

Apoplexy

Edgar Cayce devoted forty-three readings for thirty cases of apoplexy, more commonly known as "stroke," although these readings did not refer to heart attack particularly. A stroke can either be due to blockage of a blood vessel, or due to hemorrhage or a blood vessel that has become occluded.

A stroke may result in cerebral hemorrhage, partial or complete paralysis, and in some instances, death. Symptoms can reach a peak within seconds, minutes, or hours. Symptoms for lesser grades of stroke include disorganized speech, thought, motion, sensation, and vision.

The common denominator in Cayce's readings for apoplexy was poor circulation, accompanied by the weakening or destruction of cells in the blood vessel walls, leading to the formation of clots. Poor elimination was a critical factor in about thirty-five percent of the cases. It was often found in conjunction with nervous stress, overtaxation, and tension, and at times with poor nerve coordination associated with spinal subluxations or lesions. That such complications were consistently noted in all of these cases seems to suggest that Cayce felt that the cause of strokes was related to chemical and metabolic disturbances which ultimately react upon the heart and circulatory system.

Treatment

Cayce focused his treatments for individuals afflicted with stroke primarily on restoring the well-being of their bodies and on establishing new health habits for the prevention of future strokes.

Physiotherapy and electrotherapy were most frequently recommended. Daily gentle massages of the body, especially of the spine and back muscles, limbs, and areas afflicted with paralysis, were advised in approximately seventy-five percent of these cases. Often suggested in the massage were peanut oil, pine oil, olive oil, or combinations of these oils. More stimulating massage compounds included such ingredients as oil of cedar wood, oil of wintergreen, compound tincture of benzoin, oil of sassafras, oil of mustard, and oil of cedarwood. To help relax the muscles and promote good circulation, the use of a gentle electric vibrator was at times considered beneficial.

Various types of electrotherapy were recommended in about forty percent of these cases. In the majority of instances, the use of the Wet Cell Appliance was encouraged. These treatments were to be administered from fifteen to thirty minutes daily, using a solution of gold chloride, at times alternating solutions of gold chloride with spirits of camphor. Cayce also recommended the use of the Radio-Active Appliance, although treatments were not specific or consistent enough to be explained.

Since chemical dysfunctions which resulted in poor eliminations were noted, Cayce outlined a balanced, highly alkaline diet in almost forty percent of the cases. The diet included an abundance of green vegetables, vegetable juices and soups, and citrus fruits and their juices. For the more severe cases—those involving complete or partial paralysis—a liquid or semiliquid diet of juices and meat broths and their juices was suggested. Pork, red meat, large amounts of starches, and combinations of starches were to be avoided.

Since Cayce diagnosed poor nerve coordination and nerve stress as causes or contributing factors in apoplexy, osteopathy was prescribed in over twenty percent of the cases. Massages were to follow the treatments.

In nearly twenty percent of the cases, various eliminants were recommended to relieve toxic buildup. Zilatone, Sal Hepatica, olive oil, and enemas and colonics were methods mentioned.

Complete rest and relaxation and abstention from work during the recovery period was emphasized.

Case History

Case 1187, a woman of fifty-seven, had suffered a paralytic stroke which Cayce attributed to a breakdown in the walls of the circulatory system, brought on by overtaxation and stress. In addition, he noted subluxations in the ninth dorsal and lumbar axis centers, which produced a number of sympathetic disturbances.

The woman received five readings which outlined a series of treatments. The legs and feet were to be massaged with a mixture of mutton tallow, spirits of camphor, and spirits of turpentine. The massaging motions were to be away from the trunk of the body in a downward direction. Enemas were suggested to remove pressures in the colon and alimentary canal, along with spinal manipulations (excluding the cervical vertebrae).

Improvements were noted by the second reading, which advised that the massages and enemas be continued. However, the massage area now included the spine, limbs, and left side, and the lotion consisted of a combination of Russian white oil, olive oil, tincture of myrrh, oil of cedarwood, oil of wintergreen, and compound tincture of benzoin.

In other readings, 1187 was advised to have additional osteopathic adjustments in the lumbosacral area. Her diet was to focus on highly alkaline foods, with the emphasis on vegetable and fruit juices, beef juices, and proteins balanced with starches.

The woman made improvements and was gradually able to take moderate exercises. Few adjustments were required as her recovery progressed. Massages were to be continued to maintain good circulation, and the use of the Violet Ray was found to be beneficial.

Much to the amazement of her doctors, 1187 experienced a complete recovery and lived to the age of seventy without further apoplectic distress.

Appendicitis

Appendicitis is the inflammation of the appendix. It is frequently experienced in its acute form, with a rapid onset of severe symptoms, which include pain in the right lower abdomen, anorexia, and nausea, followed by low fever and elevated white blood cell count.

At least fifty individuals received readings concerning appendicitis or tendencies toward the disorder, as well as other related discomforts. The following summary is based on thirty-four readings which were given for twenty-six individuals with appendicitis.

Although Cayce did not cite causes in all cases, poor elimination, often chronic, was mentioned as a factor in more than half of them and was regarded as central to the development of appendicitis. Cayce held that poor eliminations led to engorgement and a building up of toxins in the appendix, cecum, and upper-colon area which would eventually lead to inflammation and severe discomfort.

Poor circulation and spinal subluxations were the two other most frequent causes mentioned, with other factors varying from case to case. In most instances, a combination of two or more factors was involved.

Treatment

Cayce's treatments for appendicitis ranged from eliminants to surgical removal of the appendix. Despite the fact that doctors had recommended an operation in many of the cases, Cayce found that surgery would not be needed in all but three cases if his treatments were followed immediately and faithfully. Cayce's treatments were designed to help the system absorb and eliminate the inflammation, allowing the intestines to return to normal. However, he did caution several individuals to watch their temperature carefully as an operation would be advisable if there was any increase.

Cayce's treatments centered primarily on methods of increasing eliminations, correcting diet, applying packs, and administering massage and spinal manipulation.

Laxatives, colonics or enemas, and sometimes both, were prescribed to stimulate the eliminations and were recommended in twenty-two cases. Specifics varied, but the laxatives most often recommended were olive oil, Castoria, milk of bismuth, and ragweed-based laxatives. The olive oil could be taken in small, frequent doses throughout the day or taken in large amounts (half a cup was typical). Ragweed, which was almost a specific for the appendix, was generally prescribed in tonic form, with ingredients and instructions varying with each individual.

For many individuals with a history of poor eliminations, colonics or enemas were prescribed. These were at times to be used along with laxatives and at times alone. Salt and baking soda were often to be added to the water used. (It is important to note that many physicians feel that any stimulation of the eliminations should be expressly avoided when appendicitis is suspected.)

Corrective dietary measures were recommended in over sixty percent of the cases. A liquid or semiliquid diet was advised for those with a more acute situation, and consisted mainly of beef juice, fruit juice, and vegetable juice. Recommended twice were grapes and grape juice. To avoid adding to the strain already upon the body, light diets were to be continued until the discomfort subsided. After ward, the emphasis was placed on soft, alkaline, easily digestible foods, with the gradual addition of liver and other body-building foods as the strength increased. Meats and fats were not advised in large amounts. Fried foods and pork were to be avoided, frequently for as long as six months to two years.

In nine cases, the use of various packs was also recommended. Most frequently suggested were packs of castor oil or Epsom salts and grape poultices. The castor oil packs were intended to relieve congestion in the entire gastrointestinal area. Their purpose was to "relieve the tension in the area and act as a counter irritant to the properties added internally" (562-1).

Grape poultices, to be applied over the same area, were prepared by crushing Concord grapes and then placing the result at least a half inch in thickness between pieces of cloth. The poultices were to be left on for at least two hours a day, with one change of poultice during that time. (It is important to note that many physicians feel that any application of heat to the abdomen should be expressly avoided when appendicitis is suspected. Castor oil packs may be applied without a heating pad if heat is felt to be undesirable.)

Spinal adjustments were suggested in almost half of the cases. Although a general manipulation was at times suggested, most adjustments were to focus on the lumbar and dorsal regions; the fourth lumbar and eighth and ninth dorsal vertebrae were often specified. Rest was also fre-quently advised.

In several instances, massages or rubs were recommended, with instructions tailored to individual needs. Sites of application were either general or in specific areas of the body. Substances to be used in the massage included grain alcohol (over the spine to reduce temperature) peanut oil, and a combination of olive oil and tincture of myrrh.

Case History

There were many favorable reports received from individuals with symptoms of appendicitis who followed Cayce's treatment instructions carefully. Eight experienced a complete recovery without having to resort to surgery, and four others reported relief from symptoms. Those who needed an operation apparently recovered afterward.

A typical case was 1003, a twenty-five-year-old man who requested a reading due to severe pain in his right side. Cayce found what he termed an engorgement in the ascending colon which was producing toxins, which in turn accumulated in the system. This was evidenced by rashes, streaks, and spots on various areas of the man's body. A contributing factor was pressure in the coccygeal area, which was produced by a misalignment of lumbar vertebrae. The reading cautioned that the inflammation in the cecum (beginning of the large intestine) was the most dangerous of the conditions present, but that it could be alleviated if the treatments were correctly followed.

To relieve pain, Cayce recommended painting the lower cecum and ascending colon areas with a three-to-one mixture of tincture of laudanum and aconite. These applications were to be followed by castor oil packs for a four- to five-hour period. A high colonic irritation was also advised. The treatments were to begin immediately and were to be repeated the next day. Other recommendations included osteopathic adjustments in the lumbar, sacral, and coccygeal areas, a light diet consisting mainly of fruit juices and a little beef juice, and one-half cup of olive oil taken internally to stimulate eliminations. Rest was also strongly advised.

The reading warned the man that if his temperature increased, it would indicate sufficient inflammation was present to require an operation. However, this did not occur, and the day following the reading, case 1003 was free of pain. Four days later, he returned to work and no recurrence of the condition was reported.

Arteriosclerosis

Arteriosclerosis accounts for most forms of degenerative arterial disease, and it is commonly characterized by the gradual narrowing and ultimate occlusion of the arteries. It is more prevalent among people over forty, particularly men.

Edgar Cayce gave a total of thirty-three readings for twenty-eight individuals who ranged in age from forty-eight to sixty-nine years and who suffered either directly from arteriosclerosis or from related conditions.

Mentioned as a major cause in seventy-five percent of the cases was poor circulation, which was associated mainly with the hardening of the walls of the arteries and high blood pressure. In about half of the cases, poor eliminations were involved, causing toxins to build up in the blood supply. A sluggish circulatory system contributed to the toxin buildup.

Noted in six cases were spinal subluxations of the dorsal and cervical regions, which created additional imbalances in the body. Other contributing factors mentioned were physical overtaxation, poor diet, and poor attitudes.

Treatment

Treatments prescribed by Cayce for arteriosclerosis were massage, electrotherapy, and dietary improvements, each being suggested in about half of the cases.

Cocoa butter massages along the spine from the head downward were recommended, and at times an herbal tonic was also advised to help stimulate the system. In several cases, to help relieve the body of accumulated toxins, hot packs with Epsom salts were to be used after the massage.

The types of electrotherapy advised were the Radio-

Active Appliance, the Wet Cell, usually with gold, and the Violet Ray. An increase in B vitamins, particularly B_1, was frequently recommended. Foods high in iron, silicon, and phosphorus were also suggested. Fried foods and most meats were to be avoided.

In twelve cases, spinal manipulations were suggested. These most often were to focus on the fifth, sixth, seventh, and ninth dorsal and on the first and second cervical areas. To assist in the cleansing of the system, in seven cases colonics were advised. In a few cases, gold-and-soda doses and hydrotherapy were mentioned.

Case History

As in other serious illnesses, many of those with arterio-sclerosis who requested readings from Cayce had advanced stages of the illness and had exhausted orthodox medical approaches. However, in thirty percent of the cases, partial to complete restoration of health was experienced by those who followed the advice given in their readings.

A particular case of interest was 1049, a sixty-three-year-old woman who received one reading for arteriosclerosis. Cayce attributed the condition to poor eliminations which had prevented the proper flow of circulation to various parts of her body. Calcium deposits further contributed to her condition.

She was advised to use the Radio-Active Appliance for a week or more at a time, depending on the severity of the symptoms. At two- or three-day intervals, the Violet Ray with the bulb applicator was to be used. The light was to be applied over the entire cerebrospinal area, beginning with the cervical area, moving downward over the dorsal and lumbar regions, and at times continuing to the extremities as well. This was to be administered for eight to ten minutes, three to four times a week.

Massages were also to be administered, using pine oil, olive oil, or a combination of pine oil and tincture of myrrh. The massages were to be followed by an alcohol rubdown using only grain alcohol.

Dietary advice was also given and included foods rich in silicon and iron, such as pears, which would help produce the glandular activity necessary to eliminate toxins and regulate the circulatory flow. Foods high in iodine were also suggested.

After following Cayce's advice, the woman reported that she had experienced an improvement in her condition.

Arthritis

There are about one hundred different types of arthritic diseases recognized by American rheumatologists, for the term is used to cover a wide range of illnesses that affect the musculoskeletal system. Basically, however, arthritis refers to inflammation of the joints, and the most common form is osteoarthritis, or degenerative joint disease. Less common, but more disabling, is rheumatoid arthritis, which is more painful and usually manifests itself as a chronic, progressive disease.

Although there are instances of temporary remission, modern medicine has not yet found a cure for arthritis. The most common drug prescribed by doctors to alleviate the symptoms of arthritis is aspirin, which, in addition to its analgesic properties, acts to suppress inflammation. Cortisone is also prescribed for arthritis sufferers, but despite the fact that it is effective, extended use has shown side effects. These include interference with the functioning of the adrenals, thereby impairing the body's ability to withstand stress. Additionally, there is a tendency for the symptoms to intensify when the cortisone is withdrawn.

The most encouraging aspect of Cayce's treatment for arthritis is that it involves no drugs—only natural methods, such as diet, hydrotherapy, and massage. Another interesting aspect of the readings is that they tend to incorporate treatment of the mind as well as the body, and suggest psychosomatic factors in arthritis.

The causes of arthritis as researched in the Cayce readings were limited to seven categories: poor assimilation and elimination, impaired circulation, glandular malfunction, karmic and psychological causes, previous treatments, spinal subluxations, and injuries.

Poor assimilation and elimination were noted as a first cause in seven percent of the cases. In another one percent, intestinal imbalance was mentioned as a factor, and included in this category were arthritis symptoms attributed to malfunctions of the liver, kidney, and/or gallbladder.

According to Cayce, there was a pattern of improper eliminations which began with the production of excess stomach acid, a condition often triggered by suppressed anger and other stress-related emotions. The excess acid tended to decrease the function of the lymphatic system, and the liver became less active and did not produce the enzymes needed in the digestive process.

Occurring less frequently was poor assimilation, which decreased the rebuilding forces normally needed to stimulate regular eliminations. According to Cayce, some foods actually became poisonous in the system due to their inability to be utilized property. Constipation usually resulted.

Waste materials not entirely eliminated were picked up by the circulation, further aggravating digestive problems and creating a physically debilitating cycle.

Cayce believed that the disturbances in the body that developed at this point were related to the type of imbalance present before the eliminations were first disturbed.

Although mentioned as a contributing factor in forty percent of the cases, poor or impaired circulation was noted as the first cause of arthritis in only one percent of the cases in the readings.

In eight percent of the cases, glandular malfunction was considered to be a first cause for arthritis. In another twenty-nine percent, it was mentioned as a contributing factor. At times specific glands were mentioned, including the thyroid and adrenals. Glandular incoordination between the liver and kidneys was also mentioned. Frequently, the glands, glandular forces, or glandular systems were referred to in general terms.

Perhaps the most intriguing cause of arthritis noted by

Cayce had to do with karma or psychological reasons. This type accounts for three percent of the first causes of arthritis. It was mentioned in a total of fifteen percent of the cases. Karma, or cause and effect, is neither positive nor negative, although illnesses may be viewed as the result of negative karma.

The spiritually oriented counseling found in the readings was an attempt to heal the whole person by providing therapeutic directions for the mind as well as the body. In reading 3196-1, the holding of resentments was found to be a major factor in the development of arthritis. And case 3365 was advised that if he could actively trust in God as the healer, holding no grudge toward anyone, he would feel better.

Another cause occasionally noted by Cayce was previous treatments, either for arthritis or for another disturbance, which had only aggravated the distress. In the case of arthritis, harmful treatments were noted as the first cause in ten percent of the cases.

An example of a previous treatment having negative results was noted in case 1619, a fifty-two-year-old man who had had "preventive" injections (immunization shots?) years before his reading. He was told those injections had disturbed his circulation, resulting in arthritic symptoms.

In a few readings, Cayce recognized the need for relief from the pain associated with arthritis and gave instructions for preparing an aspirin substitute. Typical active ingredients were tincture of benzoin, rectified oil of turpentine, Canadian balsam, and oil of eucalyptus. However, there was a warning given in reading 120-3 against using the substitute on the same day aspirin was taken. Cayce further noted that this formula was not to be taken indefinitely, but was to be gradually decreased as other treatments took effect.

Another first cause of arthritis cited by Cayce was spinal subluxations and injuries or misalignment of the vertebrae. This was mentioned as first cause in four percent of the arthritis readings and as a factor in another two percent. Most of the readings mentioned the coccyx (base of spine) or the lower portion of the spine as the source of the disturbance.

Other contributing factors in arthritis, mentioned less often as causes, were frequently found as part of treatment. They are diet, exercise, and attitude.

According to Cayce, certain foods and other substances, e.g., excess alcohol, cane sugar, were harmful or inadequate to meet the nutritional needs of the body. Exercise was to be conducted in moderation, for a system already under stress could be easily overtaxed by too much physical activity. And finally, negative attitudes were regarded as unhealthy, especially if they were internalized and not expressed.

In reading 2768-1, given for a forty-four-year-old man, the primary cause noted for arthritis was an unbalanced condition in the assimilating, or digestive system, which was combined with an inability to properly eliminate poisons from the system. Additionally, there was a lack of coordination between liver and kidney functions. Sedatives and certain applications taken to alleviate the condition had contributed to the poisons and toxemia which had built up in the system. This resulted in pressures that inhibited the body's movements and slowed the circulation, putting strain on the heart. Accumulations became crystallized, especially in the extremities, followed by pain and a general lowering of physical resistance.

Treatment

Cayce's treatments for arthritis were designed to restore the body's capacity to function normally and, as a consequence, began by gently stimulating the natural efforts of the system to heal itself. Methods of relieving pain were viewed as secondary in importance because they focused only on symptoms of the illness without treating the causes.

Treatments that will be discussed are diet, massage, Atomidine, colonics, enemas and laxatives, Epsom salt baths, Epsom salt packs, spinal manipulation, proper attitudes and emotions, fume baths, electrotherapy, gold and soda, and exercise.

The most frequently recommended treatments in the readings were Atomidine, Epsom salt baths, colonics, massages, spinal adjustments, and diet.

Special emphasis was placed on diet, and foods to be avoided were white flour and its products (white bread, pasta, etc.), fried foods (with the exception of very crisp bacon), carbonated drinks, beer, and hard liquor (an occasional glass of red wine was permitted), and white potatoes (an exception was potato skins). Combinations of foods to be avoided were starches and sugar (including many desserts), coffee or tea with milk or cream, and citrus fruits or juices with cereals or dairy products.

A typical diet for arthritic individuals based on the readings placed emphasis on vegetables and fruits, whole grains, and light proteins. Frequently advised was a decrease in meats and starches, with meat being occasionally excluded from the diet completely for a period of time. In severe cases, a liquid or semiliquid diet was advised to help avoid strain on the digestive system.

Massage, indicated in sixty-three percent of the case readings, in most cases was to be administered following another treatment such as Epsom salt baths. Occasionally a massage was recommended following a steam bath or use of the Wet Cell Appliance.

Cayce recommended special oils for massage and at times an osteopathic massage routine, which included gently moving the body's joints through their full range of flexibility and making adjustments in less flexible areas during the course of the massage. Initial rubs with a towel after Epsom salt baths were also suggested. The most commonly recommended oils for arthritis were peanut oil; equal parts of olive oil and a tincture of myrrh, prepared by heating a small amount of olive oil and then adding the myrrh; or equal parts peanut oil and olive oil.

It was suggested that the oils be used freely, as much as the body could absorb. Other massage ingredients include lanolin, mineral oil, oil of pine needles, sassafras oil, witch hazel, oil of wintergreen, cedarwood oil, mustard oil, kerosene, and tincture of benzoin.

Cayce also recommended warming the massage formula prior to use. This was supposed to increase the rate of absorption into the skin. Reading 4358-3 advised a massage with olive oil, sponged off with a solution of baking soda, and followed by a rub of equal parts of the herbs life everlasting and hydrastis (goldenseal).

Massage was to be administered in a firm but gentle rotary motion, not pinching the muscles, but drawing the circulation by moving the hands smoothly over the skin. Special attention was to be directed to the areas along the neck and spine, and to specific areas of the body where there was pain and discomfort. Contrary to suggestions found in other readings, where the massage was directed toward the heart, the reverse was suggested in six out of seven arthritic cases where direction was specified, i.e., from the trunk of the body toward the extremities.

The frequency with which the massages were to be administered was not always specified, but the most common treatment schedules mentioned were once weekly, once monthly, and three times weekly.

Atomidine as part of the treatment for arthritis was mentioned in forty-two percent of the readings. It was also recommended in fifty-four percent of the cases where only glandular involvement was mentioned, and in forty-eight percent of the cases describing glandular and organ involvement and in thirty-eight percent of the cases where the glands were not mentioned.

Due to its high iodine content, Atomidine was to be taken only under the supervision of a physician and only in very specific dosages and treatment cycles. Cayce warned that excess iodine in the system could overstimulate the thyroid gland and result in harmful effects on the body. Atomidine was never to be taken in conjunction with thyroid medicine or other drugs, as the drugs could neutralize each other or overstimulate the system.

According to Cayce, the most common dosage for arthritis was one drop daily for five days, followed by a five-day rest period, then one drop daily for another five days. Before resuming the cycle, another rest period of at least five days was recommended. Daily dosages ranged from one drop daily for five days to as high as eight drops daily. It was suggested that Atomidine be taken in a half glass of water in the morning before eating. Frequently, Atomidine was coordinated with Epsom salt baths and massage, with the baths being administered during the rest periods and immediately following an Atomidine sequence.

The readings recommended various methods of directly stimulating the elimination process in a total of about thirty-seven percent of arthritic cases. The most frequent were castor oil packs, seventy-nine percent; enemas, seventy-nine percent; colonics, twenty-one percent; and Eno salts, three percent.

Body-temperature water was to be used for a colonic, which was to be followed by a rinse containing an antiseptic such as a tablespoon of Glyco-Thymoline to a quart of water. Enemas and Eno salts were also recommended. To help restore equilibrium to digestion and elimination, warm castor oil packs applied over the abdominal area in conjunction with internal doses of olive oil were advised.

When the reaction to colonics and enemas was too severe, emphasis was placed on gentler methods, such as Epsom salt baths, steam baths, and a diet rich in natural laxative foods.

Epsom salt baths, which were to be taken during the rest periods between cycles of Atomidine dosage, were recommended in thirty-four percent of the readings on arthritis. To further stimulate circulation, massaging or rubbing the extremities of the body while in the bath was frequently recommended. Additionally, the readings advised having an attendant regulate the bath, performing the rub while the individual was in the bath, and rubbing the body with a towel afterward. However, before the massage, the residue from the salts was to be rinsed from the skin.

The procedure for the bath was to submerge as much of the body as possible in a tub full of water for twenty to thirty minutes, adding as much hot water as necessary to keep the temperature constant or to raise it gradually. The water was to be hot as bearable without causing weakness. One reading suggested 110 degrees. An ice bag or cold wet cloth was to be placed on the head. Hot Epsom salt baths were to be taken with caution by those with high blood pressure or cardiovascular disease. The proportion of salts to the water varied, but the most common ratio was one pound of Epsom salts for each two gallons of water.

Epsom salt packs were advised in fourteen percent of the readings for arthritis and were to be applied when needed over areas in extreme pain and prior to osteopathic adjustments in order to relax the cerebrospinal system. The packs could be placed over the affected areas as often as once daily.

Recommended in twenty-seven percent of the readings on arthritis was spinal manipulation, which was used as a system of therapy to manually manipulate the vertebrae of the spinal column. The method most frequently recommended was osteopathy, although chiropractic and neuropathy were at times suggested.

In reading 1158-31, Cayce claimed that there was no other mechanical therapy as closely in accord with the natural attempts of the body to heal itself as spinal manipulation. In another statement made in reading 110-4, Cayce noted that general manipulation serves to facilitate natural adjustments by breaking up congested areas and helping ganglia under strain adjust so that proper drainage and a stimulated circulation to the organs will take place.

The instructions regarding the treatment procedure varied and were at times atypical of the context of the readings in general. For instance, the most typical direction for treatment was from the upper to the lower end of the spine, while several readings recommended the reverse order. Instructions given in several readings were to begin with the extremities and work toward the central portion of the body.

Cultivating a mental attitude conducive to healing was suggested in almost a fifth of the readings on arthritis.

Cayce believed that positive thinking prevented further consequences from emotional stress and opened the body and mind to the Source of all healing—that which is spiritual and unitive in nature.

Cayce reminded individuals seeking physical relief that the "mind is the builder" of health as well as of illness, and that only the self stood in the way of healing. A demonstration of faith, for example, was to be "consistent and persistent" with treatments.

Fume baths were suggested in nineteen percent of the readings on arthritis. These baths were supposed to relax the body and stimulate the perspiratory system so that it could throw off toxins and waste accumulations through the pores of the skin. Various substances were added to the evaporating water, but the substance most frequently advised was witch hazel. Suggested at least once were Atomidine, pine oil, Epsom salts, and combinations of witch hazel and iodine, pine and wintergreen oil, or pine oil and tincture of benzoin. Cayce advised that treatments with steam baths should be monitored by an attendant. To help avoid strain, an ice bag or cold cloth placed on the head was advised.

Fume baths were frequently suggested in conjunction with other treatments, such as those involving hydrotherapy. In almost all instances, a massage with oils was to immediately follow the sweat.

Various methods of electrotherapy were recommended in over forty percent of the readings for arthritic patients. These included the Wet Cell, seventeen percent; the Radio-Active Appliance, nine percent; the Violet Ray, nine percent; and the ultraviolet light, seven percent. Generally, the Wet Cell was to be used in more severe cases. The readings considered it a "low form of electrical vibration," designed to stimulate the nerves in all parts of the body and thereby helping to revive depleted physical energies.

During treatment, the positive and negative plates were placed in contact with specific regions of the body. The most typical placement of the negative was over the umbilical area, and the usual area for the positive plate was over the fourth lumbar vertebra and the ninth dorsal vertebra, or occasionally over one of the extremities.

The Wet Cell was found to be most beneficial directly following hydrotherapy treatments, such as Epsom salt baths. Generally, it was to be used for about thirty minutes in the evenings during rest periods between cycles or other treatments. A massage with oils prior to retiring was usually to follow. Cayce stressed that individuals should employ meditation and constructive thoughts along with the administration of the Wet Cell.

The Radio-Active Appliance, also referred to as the Impedance Device, was also generally recommended to stimulate a more balanced circulation of bodily energies. As with the Wet Cell, positive and negative plates were attached to specific areas of the body, preferably at the wrist and opposite ankle, although the placement could be altered when solutions were added. One such solution was gold.

Treatments with the Radio-Active Appliance were to be twenty minutes in duration and were to be given in cycles of four or multiples of four. Again recommended were meditation and devotional thoughts during application.

Another method of electrotherapy was the Violet Ray, a hand-held device which generated static electricity into a detachable glass applicator. Basically, the Violet Ray was to be applied along the spine and over the areas afflicted with arthritis.

The Violet Ray was also recommended in conjunction with other treatments, specifically with internal doses of chloride of gold and bromide of soda taken before the Violet Ray treatment, and in one instance, oil rubs with salt packs.

The ultraviolet light or ray was another electrotherapy treatment recommended by Cayce to relax the body, energize the nerves, and supply additional oxygen to the main portions of the body. It was to be particularly applied over the spine and lower limbs, at times in conjunction with other therapies and other appliances. Treatment time varied from one and a half to thirty minutes and daily to once every two weeks. An alternative to the ultraviolet light was sunbathing.

Internal dosages of gold-and-soda solutions were advised in fourteen percent of the readings on arthritis. Most frequently suggested were minute amounts of chloride of gold and bicarbonate of soda in a half glass of water, although one-third suggested bromide of soda alone.

Gold-and-soda was always recommended in conjunction with other treatments, especially massage and electrotherapy. (Gold can be toxic to the body and should be taken *only* with the advice of a physician.)

Exercises were recommended as part of the treatment in five percent of the cases, although the readings cautioned against overtaxing the body and participating in the wrong types of exercise, which could cause stress and strain on the nervous system and result in permanent injury. One reading suggested covering the body with sand from the seashore for the beneficial effects of the sea and the trace amounts of gold found in the sand. In one case, swimming in the ocean was specifically advised.

Arthritis: Rheumatoid

Rheumatoid arthritis is a chronic systemic inflammatory disease of unknown cause. Although rheumatoid arthritis may begin at any time, the usual onset is between the ages of twenty and forty. There is characteristically symmetric joint swelling with associated stiffness, warmth, tenderness, and pain.

Edgar Cayce gave a total of nineteen readings for eleven individuals with rheumatoid arthritis. They ranged in age from twenty-two to seventy-two years.

Glandular incoordination, mentioned in seven cases, was a major factor in the cause of arthritis, in that the lack of proper hormone secretions contributed to problems with the circulation, the blood and calcium levels, and the absorption of minerals from food. In six cases, improper eliminations, which would lead to a buildup of toxins within the body, were cited. This, in turn, would eventually lead to such a strain on the systems that an arthritic condition resulted.

Mentioned in four cases was spinal misalignment, especially in the lower spine. Poor assimilations were mentioned as a contributing factor in three cases.

Treatment

The treatments suggested by Cayce for individuals with rheumatoid arthritis were consistent. Ten individuals received dietary advice, with the emphasis on alkaline-reacting foods. Cayce advised plenty of raw vegetables, especially cabbage, watercress, celery, carrots, and lettuce. These could be served in any combination for one meal a day. (He also suggested that for variety these could be shredded into gelatin.) Leafy vegetables were preferred over the pod or tuberous variety. Strongly advised were food sources containing specific minerals such as magnesium, silicon, sulfur, and iodine. Foods containing these minerals are lobster, shrimp, mushrooms, onions, tomatoes, pineapple, scallops, garlic, pears, citrus fruits, egg yolks, spinach, almonds, walnuts, rye, whole wheat, grapes, barley, cherries, gooseberries, oats, prunes, shredded wheat, apples, unpolished rice, brussels sprouts, cauliflower, kale, mustard, radishes, and blueberries. Also recommended were lamb and fowl, but red meats, fried foods, and starches were to be avoided. In two instances, wild game was mentioned as an acceptable source of meat.

Nine individuals received instructions for massages, which frequently were to involve the use of oil combinations based on olive oil and peanut oil. The limbs, joints, and extremities were to receive special attention.

Various forms of electrotherapy were suggested in seven instances, and in serious cases where there was evidence of nerve deterioration, the Wet Cell was advised to aid rejuvenation. The Violet Ray and Radio-Active Appliance each received two recommendations.

Hydrotherapy was recommended in five cases and most frequently took the form of Epsom salt baths. This treatment was to relax the body and relieve pain.

Four individuals received instructions for internal doses of Atomidine to improve glandular incoordination. Also suggested in four cases was gold chloride, once by itself, and in three readings combined with either bromide or bicarbonate of soda in water. This was intended to aid the nervous system.

To help relieve pain in the afflicted joints, Cayce advised the use of locally applied packs in some cases. Receiving two mentions was Epsom salts and one recommendation each for castor oil and Glyco-Thymoline.

Sedatives were advised in three cases, in the form of aspirin, cobra venom (to be administered by a doctor versed in this field), and a capsule consisting of eucalyptol, rectified oil of turpentine, and benzosol.

Recommended in two cases were Kaldak tonic and stimulants for eliminations. Adjustments to the entire spinal column were suggested in four cases.

Case History

Only three of those receiving readings for rheumatoid arthritis definitely followed its instructions. Two reported beneficial results, and the third noted no improvement.

One of the two who noted an improvement in her condition was case 120, a seventy-two-year-old woman who received seven readings for rheumatoid arthritis. According to Cayce, spinal pressures in combination with poor eliminations slowed the circulation and affected the nerves leading to the afflicted joints, resulting in arthritic symptoms.

Her first reading suggested a change of surroundings, although no specific area was mentioned. Also discussed was diet, which was to include foods especially rich in magnesium, silicon, and sulfur.

She was to begin osteopathic adjustments along the entire spine, with general and corrective treatments given on alternating days. A sinusoidal treatment was also to be given for three minutes at a time, especially in the brachial center and lower lumbar center.

The woman's second reading recommended treatments with the Violet Ray, to be applied at least every other day or more often for relief. One and a half to two hours before each Violet Ray treatment, she was to take small doses of sodium-bromide-and-gold-chloride solutions. Instructions noted that while a solution containing one grain of gold chloride per ounce of distilled water was prepared, another containing ten grains of soda was to be placed in an ounce of distilled water. She was to take two drops of the gold solution and four of the soda solution in a half glass of water.

At this time, the manipulations were to be administered only once a week, in conjunction with wet heat. In place of aspirin, Cayce advised a compound of eucalyptol, rectified oil of turpentine, and benzosol in simple syrup for pain. To help relax the body, sweat baths using witch hazel were recommended.

The third reading advised hot packs saturated with Epsom salts. These were to be applied directly to the painful joints and limbs. Also recommended at this reading were the use of the Wet Cell Appliance and regular exercise outdoors so that the woman could benefit from the ultraviolet rays of the sun.

The fourth reading advised the woman to discontinue taking the eucalyptol compound, and the fifth reading recommended the use of the Radio-Active Appliance with iodine.

The sixth reading suggested specific neuropathic treatments in which the extremities were to be gently massaged along the nerve pathways leading toward the central nervous system. A continuation of this type of massage was recommended in the seventh reading.

Asthenia

Edgar Cayce recognized that asthenia, a condition characterized by lethargy and exhaustion which is not improved by rest, could be induced by both psychological and organic factors.

Contributing to the condition psychologically are depression, anxiety, and cardiac neuroses. Organic causes include anemia, endocrine and metabolic disorders, and excessive use of sedative drugs, just to name a few.

Cayce gave eleven readings on asthenia for seven men and women. For all, the causes were apparently related to injuries or pressures on the spine, which in turn produced stress on various organs of the body.

The parts of the body most frequently affected were the glands, circulation, and elimination.

Additionally, Cayce noted that exhaustion, both mental and physical, could help develop asthenia. He believed that in many cases both were responsible for the weakening of the nervous system, which contributed to the condition.

Treatment

No two treatments for asthenia were exactly alike in the readings, although Cayce emphasized in almost every case manipulation and massage of specific areas of the spine, usually to be administered with peanut oil or witch hazel. In the two cases involving spinal damage through injuries, spinal adjustments were recommended at least twice a week until improvements were noticed.

However, outlined in almost each reading was a series of treatments specifically suited to the individual.

Diet was important to recovery in five cases. Emphasis was placed on vegetables, fruits, fish, wild game, and foods high in various minerals. Restricted from the diet were acid-reacting foods such as pastries, cake, white bread, potatoes, and fried or greasy foods.

In four of these cases, the readings also established the need for good eliminations. Recommended laxatives were Castoria, syrup of figs, and Eno salts. Cayce also suggested colonics at times.

To rebuild the nerves and provide a needed stimulus to the body in general, electrotherapy was recommended in three cases—the Violet Ray, shortwave ultraviolet light, and the Radio-Active Appliance.

Herbal remedies were suggested in two cases of asthenia.

Case Histories

Case 119 involved a seventy-two-year-old man who complained of low vitality and slowed responses. Cayce's diagnosis revealed a past injury to the seventh, eighth, and ninth dorsal centers. The damage produced disturbances in digestion and eliminations. Also, the man's condition bordered on diabetes due to an overproduction of sugars.

He was given two readings. One advised resting from all work for two or three months. Treatments included a series of spinal manipulations every other day, making structural corrections once each week. To assist his digestion, he was advised to add ambrosia (ragweed) to his diet in the form of tea. The diet emphasized alkaline-reacting foods high in calcium and sodium and the avoidance of all starches and sweets.

Cayce estimated that the man could be restored to good health within 90 to 120 days if he followed the recommended regime. He subsequently entered the Cayce hospital for the prescribed treatments, and later case 119 reported a "complete recovery."

Case 5522 was a thirty-four-year-old woman suffering from physical weakness and feelings of anxiety. Her poor eliminations and assimilations were said to have been caused by extreme nervous tension and nervous incoordination.

Her treatment consisted of a twenty-six-day series which included daily spinal manipulations and massage and frequent doses of an herbal tonic, a mixture of simple syrup, wild cherry bark, compound syrup of sarsaparilla, tincture of stillingia, syrup of rhubarb, sassafras oil, elixir of calisaya, tincture of capsicum, balsam of tolu, and grain alcohol.

A diet of alkaline-reacting foods as well as meat juices or broths for body building was recommended, as was an occasional colonic as needed to cleanse the intestinal tract.

Daily use of the Radio-Active Appliance was also considered helpful when used for a period of thirty minutes to an hour each night before bedtime.

Reports following the first series of treatments indicated improvements in her condition.

Asthma

Asthma is a lung condition characterized by a widespread narrowing of the air passages, which can vary spontaneously over short periods of time. Allergy may be a contributing factor in this condition.

Symptoms include cough, mucoid sputum, generalized wheezing, and bronchial obstruction. Symptoms may occur in varying degrees of severity—from mild to life-threatening.

A total of seventy-three readings were given for twenty-three individuals for asthma.

During the course of the readings, Edgar Cayce found asthma to have its origin in neurologic stimuli which were touched off by either lesions and adhesions in the bronchi and larynx or by pressures exerted on the autonomic ganglia and their connections with the cerebrospinal system. In other words, he believed that spinal problems were generally involved, occurring mainly in the dorsal or cervical area, although these may or may not have been the result of actual subluxations.

Cayce further believed that poor spinal alignment combined with certain precipitating factors, such as stress or poor diet, would cause the bronchi to constrict, bringing on an asthmatic attack. Frequently, congestion would result, and toxins, not fully eliminated from the lungs, would cause a sympathetic reaction in both the kidneys and liver. Glands associated with assimilation would also frequently become sympathetically involved. In some cases, poor elimination and/or toxemia were involved with the general breakdown of the body.

Treatment

Treatments for asthma generally began with a series of specified spinal adjustments designed to relax the body, break up lesions, and correct subluxations. The adjustments were to relieve the pressures and relax the bronchial tubes.

Certain dietary restrictions were offered, and the most frequent injunction was to avoid "sweets," or foods containing sugar. One woman was advised that "any sweets will aggravate the condition" (3046-1). Heavy foods such as beef, fried foods, and large amounts of starches were to be avoided, as were certain acidic food combinations. Cayce advised a body-building diet consisting mainly of vegetables, fruits, and seafood.

To help open bronchial passages and expectorate mucous, an inhalant, which was usually alcohol based, was frequently suggested. Inhalant ingredients generally included oil of eucalyptus, compound tincture of benzoin, turpentine oil, Canadian balsam, pine needle oil, and tincture of tolu balsam. Instructions were to shake the inhalant well before use and to inhale the fumes through the nose and mouth as needed. Also suggested at times was a steam inhalant which was prepared by boiling water and adding small amounts of eucalyptus and benzoin and then inhaling the fumes.

In instances where a glandular imbalance was noted or where there was a need to supply calcium or iodine, Cayce recommended small internal doses of these elements. Atomidine or Calcidin (calcium iodate) was recommended for those lacking iodine.

Several readings mentioned the need to stimulate eliminations, and methods suggested were colonics and laxatives. Also occasionally recommended were treatments such as electrotherapy, massage, hydrotherapy, and herbal tonics.

Cayce noted in several readings that a change of climate would be helpful and suggested a drier, warmer climate, or ocean air or a high altitude. He also occasionally mentioned psychological factors and commented in some readings that a more positive attitude would speed and assist in recovery.

Case History

Three readings were given in response to a request made by a mother of an eleven-year-old girl, case 3053, who had asthma attacks since the age of three. In diagnosing her condition, Cayce noted a subluxation in the second, third and fourth dorsal centers which he felt was the source of the asthma. The subluxation had affected the nerve impulses to the trachea, bronchi, and glands involved in the assimilation process. As Cayce noted: "These are the sources of that disturbance, physically, that causes the activity to be slowed; so that accumulations as of lymph or of mucus in the area of the bronchi, larynx, as well as upper portions of the lungs are produced by this slowing of coordinated activity in the glands of the body—as related to assimilation."

According to Cayce, the lack of proper assimilation tended to produce constipation, which, combined with the lack of proper elimination of wastes from the blood supply through the respiratory system, produced a backup of toxins in the blood which also affected the liver.

To help relieve this condition, Cayce first recommended a series of relaxing osteopathic adjustments. After the adjustments were completed, and to help stimulate body and glandular activity, one drop of Atomidine in a half glass of water was prescribed. This dosage was to be taken each morning before eating for a five-day period. This was to be repeated at the same time each month.

To help keep the body alkalized, internal doses of Glyco-Thymoline were suggested. The doses were five to six drops in a half glass of water, three times a week.

To assist eliminations, two laxatives—one made of senna and pumpkin seeds in an alcohol base, and the other

Caldwell's Syrup of Pepsin, another senna-based laxative—
were prescribed.

To ease breathing during asthma attacks, a steam inhalant was suggested. This solution consisted of a teaspoon of
eucalyptus oil and a half teaspoon of compound tincture of
benzoin added to boiling water. The procedure was to
cover the head with a towel and breathe in the fumes
slowly and carefully from a croup cup. Cayce believed that
this would be beneficial in relaxing the spasmodic reactions in both the bronchi and the throat.

The child's diet was to be both body building and
alkaline reacting. Sweets were to be avoided and special
attention given to food combinations. Seafood was to be
eaten at least twice weekly; fowl and lamb only occasionally. Raw vegetables were to be included in at least one
meal each day. Highly recommended were tuberous vegetables, especially in a combination, or two underground
vegetables to one leafy green vegetable.

In response to a question regarding a change in climate,
Cayce felt it would not benefit the child, unless the change
was to a very high altitude such as Asheville, North
Carolina. However, he did note that if his suggestions
were followed, not only would the child's condition be
relieved, but the basic disturbances would be corrected also.

Reports from the mother one year later indicated that her
daughter had recovered and that she was no longer subject
to asthmatic attacks. Ten years later, 3053 reported that
she had not had an asthma attack in years.

Athlete's Foot

There are two forms of athlete's foot—acute and chronic. The former is characterized by small blisters on the
sides of the feet and between the toes, accompanied by a
patchy redness of the skin. Bacterial infection of the
blisters is common, with fissures and a softening of the
infected tissues occurring as well. The latter is typified by
scales which form on dry red areas.

Some people appear to be more susceptible to athlete's foot, probably so termed because it can be easily contracted in a damp locker room. The factors that seem to predispose individuals to athlete's foot are closely spaced toes which do not spread on standing and excessive sweating of the feet. The current standard treatment involves antifungal soaks and the removal of dead or contaminated tissue after soaks and baths. Recurrences are common in strongly predisposed individuals.

Nineteen readings were given for thirteen individuals with athlete's foot, five of whom were women. In all of the cases, athlete's foot was only one of the problems under consideration and usually not the central one. The readings highlighted three major predisposing factors—spinal misalignments, poor diet, and poor eliminations.

Spinal problems were noted in at least ten cases. In one instance, Cayce said that "persons having athlete's foot would almost always be found to suffer from an underlying osteopathic lesion or 'impingement' which is disturbing the normal physiology of the lower extremities" (477-1). This resulted in poor circulation in the legs and feet, thereby reducing the resistance to infection.

Cayce frequently recommended changes in eating habits, suggesting that a poor diet could contribute to the onset of athlete's foot by lowering resistance. Cayce stressed that excessive acid-forming foods, which included meats and starches, or which contained sugar or alcohol, were to be avoided.

A history of injury to the spine as well as complaints of backaches, particularly in the lower spine, could indicate an underlying spinal lesion, according to Cayce. The lumbosacral and coccygeal areas were most frequently involved in these cases. But at times, secondary problems were evident in the upper spine as well.

Treatment

There were five general areas of treatment based on the underlying causes described in the readings—spinal manipulation, dietary corrections, improved eliminations, electrotherapy, and topical applications. Each treatment procedure was individualized and based on the specific patterns of imbalances and incoordination.

In twelve cases, topical applications applied nightly were recommended to complement the treatment of basic imbalances. Ray's Ointment and Ray's Solution were frequently mentioned. (Other solutions that are no longer available were also suggested.)

Various massage preparations for the treatment of feet and ankles were recommended in a few cases. For two individuals, Cayce prescribed a mixture of equal parts olive oil and tincture of myrrh. His instructions included heating the oil before adding the myrrh. It was to be thoroughly massaged into the toes, across the instep, and onto the soles of the feet.

Soaking the feet in a mild, warm antiseptic solution such as Absorbine Jr. or saltwater was recommended in several cases, and one reading suggested applying mullein stupes to the feet and limbs.

Spinal manipulation was recommended in ten cases. The corrections were to be made in a gradual series of treatments designed to restore normalcy to the spine. Emphasis was frequently placed on the lumbar, sacral, and coccygeal areas, although the spine as a whole was treated.

Changes in diet were suggested for eight individuals. Stressed were alkaline foods such as vegetables and fruits, both raw and cooked. The most frequently recommended "meats" were fish, fowl, and lamb. Beef was to be eaten only rarely, and pork avoided completely. Also to be largely avoided were dried legumes, such as dried peas and beans, potatoes, and heavy combinations, such as macaroni and cheese. Other detrimental food combinations included citrus and cereals, and coffee or tea with milk or cream. Excessive sweets, fried foods, beer and ale, and carbonated beverages were to be completely avoided.

In four cases, colonics, enemies, and a laxative diet

were prescribed. Suggested with the same frequency were forms of electrotherapy—especially the Violet Ray—used to stimulate the circulation generally and in specific areas.

In summary, the Cayce readings suggested that approaching an apparently minor skin problem such as athlete's foot also provided the opportunity to discover and treat chronic physiological imbalances involving the spine, diet, and eliminations.

Case History

Few follow-up reports dealing specifically with athlete's foot were received. However, three individuals reported that after following Cayce's suggested treatment, the condition was "cured."

Case 219, a nineteen-year-old male, received one reading for athlete's foot, which was compounded by several other disorders. Spinal subluxations in the dorsal area caused by an injury were said to be the primary cause of athlete's foot. A secondary factor was general debilitation. Also involved were glandular imbalances, poor assimilation and elimination, poor circulation, and toxemia.

To create a better balance internally, Cayce prescribed a well-balanced diet. To correct the spinal problems, a series of eight to fifteen adjustments was suggested. To stimulate the eliminations, Cayce recommended that the young man take ragweed tea, Simmon's Liver Regulator, and digestive aids. As a massage for the feet, a combination of Russian White Oil, witch hazel, sassafras oil, and kerosene was recommended.

It was later reported that the parents of 219, who were chiropractors, administered the recommended treatments, and the young man recovered completely. It was felt that "he would never have made it, mentally or physically, if his mother had not gotten the reading for him and followed the advice."

Atrophy

Muscular atrophy is a disorder in which there is a wasting away or arrested development of muscular tissue and related nerves. This condition can be hereditary or acquired and is often one symptom of a larger disease category, such as progressive muscular atrophy, myasthenia gravis, or various forms of tonic muscular spasm. The progressive form of systemic muscular atrophy can lead to paralysis and death.

A total of twenty-one readings were given for seventeen individuals with muscular atrophy and related conditions, whose ages ranged from seventeen to seventy. In ten of the cases, the muscular atrophy was found to be more of a symptom than a disease in itself. Diagnoses, which varied from case to case, included mention of conditions such as muscular dystrophy, arthritis, paralysis, and osteochondritis.

Cited in five cases was spinal misalignment, which involved a slowing of nerve impulses to the muscles, eventually leading to atrophy. A closely related factor cited in five cases was poor circulation. Karma was also noted as a cause in five cases.

Mentioned in three cases was poor assimilation. This condition would cause a shortage of nutrients in the system, which in turn contributed to a breakdown of nerve and muscle tissue. Spinal subluxations were involved in the same number of cases. Infections directly affecting the bones and muscles were cited in two instances.

Treatment

Massages were the most frequent recommendation, and readings for thirteen individuals suggested a variety of oil combinations for this purpose and included a combination of oils, such as olive oil, peanut oil, and lanolin.

In eleven instances, electrotherapy treatments were advised, and the method most frequently recommended was the Wet Cell to help restore damaged nerve connections. The Radio-Active Appliance and a variety of other devices were also at times mentioned.

Eleven individuals also received dietary advice. Foods

high in vitamins, such as fresh fruits and vegetables, were especially emphasized. Beef juice was recommended for its blood-building benefits. Also mentioned were nutritional supplements such as Calcios and vitamins.

Spinal manipulations to help remove blockages to the nerves were advised for eight individuals. The adjustments were intended to improve the flow of nerve impulses to the muscles, thus helping to reduce the atrophy.

To help relax the muscles in three cases, hydrotherapy treatments such as fume baths and Epsom salt baths were suggested. Two individuals also received advice on digestive aids, packs, herbal tonics, and exercise.

Case History

Four of the ten individuals who gave feedback on the outcome of their treatments reported improvements in their condition. The others did not follow the advice in their readings or did so only partially.

One of those who followed Cayce's advice, with positive results, was case 849, an adult male who received one reading for muscular atrophy. His condition involved a slow atrophying of the muscles in his right leg and thigh. Cayce noted the cause to be excessive treatment of a knee injury which had created a circulatory imbalance in the body. Thus, his leg became "lacking in certain hormones necessary to prevent atrophy in the cellular forces."

Immediately advised were spinal manipulations, which were to be applied to the sacral, coccygeal and lower dorsal vertebrae. Additionally, the limbs, feet, and the lumbar and sacral areas were to be massaged, using a combination of mutton suet, spirits of turpentine, spirits of camphor, compound tincture of benzoin, and sassafras oil. Afterward, heated flannel was to be placed over any painful areas.

The reading further advised an alcohol-free diet of blood- and body-building foods, supplemented by Ventriculin without iron, a gastric stimulant.

Regular treatments with the Radio-Active Appliance were prescribed on a regular basis of two weeks usage alternated with two weeks off the appliance. This was to improve the circulation in general. The use of the Radio-Active Appliance was the first treatment applied, and it had such a positive effect on the subject's nervous system that he then began to follow his entire reading.

When case 849 reported on his progress, he noted that "there was immediate relief from the system of treatment outlined in my last reading. The leg, which was rapidly atrophying, has put on flesh. . . ."

Baby Care: General

The eighty-five Cayce readings on baby care deal with problems and questions most commonly encountered by parents during the first year of child rearing. These readings were for thirty-one children, ranging in age from one day to five years, who were suffering with such ailments as colds, fever, indigestion and colitis, teething problems, and skin rashes.

Whether the question concerned colic, indigestion or colds and fever, more than half of the readings on infant illness attributed the discomfort or illness to poor feeding habits or lack of vital nutrients in the foods. Almost all of these ailments resulted from overacidity in the system, and in cases of colic or indigestion, Cayce frequently noted that the baby was being overfed as well as undernourished. Therefore, he placed a great deal of emphasis on diet and eating habits, as well as on maintaining good eliminations to prevent the buildup of toxins.

In twenty-six cases, recommendations for diet and feeding were specific. Babies were not to be fed more than they wanted at any time. Meals were to be in the morning, afternoon, and evening, allowing a midmorning and mid-afternoon snack to keep the appetite even. Diets rich in alkaline-reacting foods were outlined as follows: Fresh fruits, excluding apples and bananas, were encouraged, although in the early months fruit juices, especially small amounts of orange juice, were preferable. Citrus juices and cereals were not to be served at the same meal. Highly recommended were cooked breakfast cereals—especially oatmeal made from rolled or steel-cut oats. Also suggested at times was whole wheat or graham bread, preferably toasted with butter, and coddled egg yolks.

Recommended vegetables were those that grow above the ground, either well cooked or prepared as juices or in soups. Also permitted were potatoes, turnips, and beets and their juices. Meat juices were also recommended, especially in cases where the babies were not receiving sufficient nourishment in their diet. With the exception of fish, fowl, and lamb, meats were to be avoided, as were sweets and fried and greasy foods.

Cayce placed emphasis on the need for silicon, iron, iodine, and calcium in the diet of the growing baby. Calcium, a fundamental element in the growth and development of bones and teeth, was noted to be best supplied by milk.

In addition to mother's milk, dried milk, buttermilk, evaporated milk (Carnation), and Bulgarian milk were most frequently mentioned in the readings. In cases in volving a deficiency in the mother's milk, Cayce advised substituting Mellin's food in the baby's diet.

Good eliminations were also very important in the readings on baby care. Therefore, Cayce was very specific in outlining detailed instructions for the use of gentle eliminants. In most cases, he advised the use of Fletcher's Castoria and, occasionally, Syrup of Figs, syrup of pepsin, or milk of magnesia.

Cayce suggested that the baby receive a few drops of Castoria every half hour or hour until a good bowel movement was produced. This was to be followed by a few drops of Glyco-Thymoline in a teaspoon of water a few times a day until the odor of the same could be detected in the stool. Cayce believed this twofold treatment would serve first to clear the alimentary canal and then to cleanse and alkalize the digestive tract. In some cases, to prevent acid buildup in the body, Cayce suggested giving the baby a few drops of Glyco-Thymoline in water or milk a few times daily. Finally, five readings recommended enemas using warm or cool water and a drop or two of Glyco-Thymoline to further promote the eliminations.

To help prevent gas and assist in digestion, several readings suggested the use of diluted cinnamon water and limewater solutions. The usual dosage was several drops of each in a teaspoon, added to a bottle of milk or glass of juice. Also suggested at times was a teaspoon of straight limewater added to the milk.

Body massages and rubs were prescribed in twenty-three of the cases and were to be administered following the evening bath with various substances—cocoa butter, peanut oil and olive oil, olive oil and tincture of myrrh, or a combination of equal parts mutton tallow, spirits of turpentine, and spirits of camphor. The rubs were supposed to promote good circulation and relaxation. To help reduce fever, a rub along the spine with grain alcohol was advised to follow the evening bath.

The readings mentioned a variety of nutritional supplements as aids to health and body building. As a calcium supplement, Cayce at times suggested Calcios twice a week, spread on a slice of whole wheat bread or on a cracker. Other body-building tonics rich in essential elements, such as Calcidin, Ventriculin, and cod liver or halibut oil, were also at times suggested—both to build up the baby's resistance to illness and to help overcome an existing cold.

To reduce congestion and relieve irritated areas of the skin, Cayce prescribed topical applications in seven readings. Carbolated Vaseline, camphorated oil, and camphor ice were recommended to soothe either cold sores, skin rashes, or abrasions. In addition, a powder containing stearate of zinc, preferably with balsam, was highly recommended for prickly heat and other types of skin rashes. Suggested to relieve congestion was a liniment consisting of equal parts camphor, turpentine, and mutton tallow.

Finally, painful teething was a concern expressed by the mothers in five cases. Most often mentioned was Ipsab, a gum remedy, which was to be rubbed on the sore gums with a cotton swab a few times weekly. In addition to supplying the needed relief, Ipsab would provide the salivary glands with salt, calcium, and iodine, substances necessary to the teething process, according to Cayce. In addition to Ipsab, Cayce sometimes advised that a weak salt-and-soda solution or a piece of ice be rubbed on the gums. A peeled raw carrot for gnawing and chewing was also considered useful for teething.

Case Histories

Case 324 was a thirteen-month-old girl with an advanced cold and serious congestion which had affected membranes in her ear, throat, and lungs. The cause given for the infection was improper diet, complicated by poor digestion and poor eliminations.

The first reading was concerned with reducing the baby's fever. Cayce prescribed five to eight drops of Syrup of Squill every three or four hours and a nightly massage of the chest, throat, spine, and the soles of the feet with equal parts mutton tallow, spirits of camphor, and spirits of turpentine, followed by wrapping these parts of the body with warm flannel cloth. Sipping a glass of water containing a small quantity of Calcidin was suggested to ease the irritation produced by a croup cough.

Shortly afterward, the parents of 324 reported that the fever had been reduced. However, some months later a glandular infection flared up, affecting the right ear. To relieve the ear infection, Cayce advised a few drops of a warm oil in the ear twice a day for two days. For the eliminations, small intermittent doses of Fletcher's Castoria containing a teaspoon of senna were to be given several times daily for a few days. Massage of the feet and limbs with olive oil and myrrh was also suggested to improve the circulation.

About six months later, the acidic condition of the

baby's body had developed into whooping cough, which Cayce explained as an inflammation of the throat glands caused by excess acids in the system. He advised establishing alkalinity in the body through dietary measures. Sweets and other acidic-reacting foods were to be avoided. Daily rubs of the throat, back, and spine were to be administered with the mutton tallow combination. To ease throat irritation, gargling and swabbing the throat with Lavoris or Glyco-Thymoline were advised.

The parents of 324 followed the reading and later reported that the recommended treatment "worked like a charm" in curing their baby of whooping cough.

The parents of case 2752, a girl of six weeks, brought their child to Cayce. They were concerned over loose bowel movements, rawness of the rectal area, and an irritating skin rash. Cayce attributed the child's discomfort to lack of nutrients in the mother's milk. It was later determined that the mother had been a heavy drinker, even during pregnancy, and did not drink milk. As a consequence, Cayce advised that the baby be given immediately ten drops of milk of bismuth and, in place of her mother's milk, be put on diluted evaporated milk with pectin. Several hours later, a few drops of Castoria were to be given every few hours until a bowel movement was produced. Following this, one or two drops of Glyco-Thymoline were to be added to the feeding until its odor was detectable in the stool. Also advised was an enema with warm or cool water containing a drop or two of Glyco-Thymoline.

For relief of rawness in the rectal area and for skin rash, Cayce advised external applications of carbolated Vaseline or camphorated oil.

Several weeks later, improvements in the skin condition were noted. In a later reading, Cayce prescribed a daily massage of cocoa butter and, to prevent scalp dryness, olive oil, peanut oil, and cocoa butter.

In two check readings for 2752, given for the child when she was two years old, Cayce reinforced his original instructions for an alkaline diet by excluding sweets and pastries, although natural sweets such as honey were allowed. For healthy teeth, Calcios once a week was recommended.

In the majority of the cases, follow-up reports to the readings were never received. However, in ten cases the parents did report "excellent" results upon following the treatments prescribed by Cayce.

Balding

There are seven different types of baldness which can affect both men and women. Statistics note that over seventy-five percent of the male population experiences varying degrees of baldness and ninety-five percent of the individuals in this group suffer from a type known as male pattern baldness. The primary cause of this disorder is said to be hereditary, but contributing factors to hair loss include hormonal deficiencies, diet, stress, anemia, medication, and hair treatment.

Edgar Cayce gave ninety-two readings for sixty-five individuals concerned with loss of hair. These readings generally included advice on how to reverse hair loss or prevent it.

About a third of the individuals who were concerned about balding were told that a lack of glandular activity, related particularly to the thyroid, was causing their hair loss. In one case, the reading explained that improper coordination of the activities in the inner and outer glandular force as related to the thyroid was responsible for the loss of hair. Another reading, given for a thirty-two-year-old woman, stated that there was "an upsetting of the glandular system by the activities in the body that destroy the effect of these glands, producing such elements in the thyroid glands, especially; thus destroying the oils that were a portion of the activity in the sympathetic nervous system as related to the epidermis" (4086-1). Over one-fourth of the readings indicated that poor circulation, either alone or combined with glandular imbalance, was a cause of hair loss.

In over ten percent of the cases, the readings suggested that a more positive attitude would be beneficial.

Treatment

The treatments for individuals concerned with hair loss varied. Often these were determined by the extent of the hair loss and by what had initially caused the condition. Recommended in most cases were local applications and changes in diet or other internal remedies.

The most popular external applications recommended (in over one-third of the cases) were twenty-percent-grain-alcohol solutions, white Vaseline, and crude oil. Although the alcohol solutions could vary in strength, the mixture most frequently consisted of twenty percent pure grain (not rubbing) alcohol to eighty percent distilled water. White Vaseline is what is commonly available today, and Cayce's crude oil was the pure, unrefined product as it is extracted from the ground.

A typical treatment consisted of massaging small amounts of crude oil into the scalp for thirty to forty minutes. This was then to be rinsed out, using the grain-alcohol solution, followed by a small amount of white Vaseline massaged into the scalp. If desired, the individual could stop with the alcohol, which would cut the crude oil, and then shampoo. Or use only the crude oil or only the Vaseline, followed by the alcohol treatment. Other external applications occasionally suggested were hog lard and kerosene.

Listerine was recommended in several cases of dandruff. The most frequently recommended shampoos were pine-tar shampoo or equal parts olive oil and pure castile shampoo.

To help stimulate the circulation of the scalp, the Violet Ray was recommended eight times and an electric vibrator twice. An indirect treatment mentioned in a considerable percentage of the readings was spinal adjustment (and occasionally massage).

The internal treatment most often mentioned was Atomidine, recommended to stimulate sluggish glandular activity and, thus, sluggish hair growth as well. A typical dosage was one drop in half a glass of water before breakfast each day for five days, followed by five days without Atomidine, then a resumption of the dosage for another five days and then discontinuation of the medication for two weeks. The cycle could be repeated in this manner for as long as six months, in coordination with other treatments, depending on how the condition improved.

Diet was another source of iodine. Most often mentioned were peelings from Irish (regular white) potatoes, and/or the water in which these potatoes (or peelings) had been cooked. This was recommended for restoring hair color as well as for stimulating glandular activity and hair growth. Seafood was also highly recommended for its iodine content, and carrots (perhaps not an iodine source) were also suggested in a few cases. Herbal tonics and hydrotherapy were each mentioned in a few cases and probably had only an indirect bearing on the problem of loss of hair.

Case History

Case 1467 received a series of nineteen readings between the ages of thirty-two and thirty-nine, several of which touched on his problem of hair loss. According to Cayce, the condition was one of the effects of an injury to and pressures from the third dorsal to the second and third cervical vertebrae, which resulted in poor circulation to the scalp. There was also a buildup of toxins in the superficial circulation due to the system's inability to eliminate through the proper channels, as well as a lack of glandular activity, especially in the thyroid.

To correct the initial cause of the condition, spinal manipulation was suggested. Manipulations were to be given two to three times each week for two to three weeks. After a two-week period, the entire series of treatments was to be repeated.

For the scalp, Cayce suggested massages with Vaseline, followed by a rinse with thirty-five-percent-grain-alcohol solution. Afterward, small amounts of Cuticura ointment were to be rubbed into the hair and scalp to heal the skin and promote hair growth. When the hair continued to fall out, supplemental topical applications were suggested, including the alternation of alkaline and acid antiseptics, such as Listerine and Fitch's Scalp Tone. Massaging the scalp every ten days with plain soap and water followed by shampooing with a shampoo containing quinine was later suggested for scalp stimulation. For hair conditioning, olive oil shampoo was later recommended.

To stimulate thyroid activity, a body-building diet and Atomidine were suggested. The Atomidine was to be taken five days at a time, adding one or two drops to half a glass of water before the morning meal. Diet was also to play an important role in treatment. Seafoods were highly recommended, as were raw vegetables, citrus fruits, and laxative foods such as prunes or figs.

Although there were subsequent readings given for this individual, there was no indication as to whether the treatments were followed or hair growth restored.

Bedsores

Bedsores are ulcerations caused by impaired blood supply and tissue nutrition from prolonged contact with bedding, generally occurring in those confined to bed for long periods of time.

Edgar Cayce gave one reading each for seven individuals with this discomfort.

The major cause, cited by Cayce in six instances, was poor circulation in the ulcerated area due to contact with the bed. In one case, poor elimination was also cited as a cause.

In five cases, external applications were suggested. Ichthyol ointment was most frequently recommended, with camphorated oil and Iodex also being mentioned.

Massages were advised in two instances to help increase the circulation around the affected areas. Oil combinations such as tincture of myrrh and olive oil were to be used.

Also recommended in two cases were spinal manipulations which were to concentrate on the cervical, dorsal, and lumbar areas.

Case History

Only one report was received on the outcome of the readings. Case 585, a forty-seven-year-old woman, received spinal manipulations and applied Ichthyol ointment, which eventually cured her bedsores. The woman received one reading in which it was noted that adjustments were to be given over the upper dorsal and throughout the cervical areas in two series of six adjustments each, and were to be administered three to four months apart. Ichthyol ointment was recommended as an external treatment.

The report on the outcome of the reading stated that "the bedsore remedy was wonderful; my patient never had any more trouble from sores."

Bedwetting

The term bedwetting, or eneuresis, is generally a problem involving children, who though they may well have bladder control during the day, continue to urinate in bed at night. In most cases, this is an unconscious phenomenon inasmuch as the child has not learned to be awakened by the urge to urinate. Bedwetting is believed to have more psychological than physical causes.

Edgar Cayce gave seven readings for six children with this problem. These youngsters, both male and female, ranged from one to twelve years. In no case was bedwetting the only focus of the reading, nor was it often the major one. Actually, one case, that of a one-year-old child, did not have a real problem so far as Cayce was concerned. In this instance, he believed the child was still young enough that bedwetting was a natural consequence of the child's growth and development.

Cayce attributed bedwetting mainly to psychological causes, regarding it as the result of an incoordination between conscious and unconscious volition. This was given special emphasis in the case of 2779, an eleven-year-old boy who had reverted to bedwetting. In this case, the condition was noted as being karmic; the child was experiencing the consequences of a past lifetime where, as a minister in early America, he had once condemned psychic children to "ducking." In the instance of case 3165, another eleven-year-old boy had an emotional dependence on his mother which she had fostered.

Other cases had more physical aspects. Case 674 was a twelve-year-old boy suffering from bronchial asthma and diabetes. Cayce attributed his bedwetting problem to pressure on the ninth and tenth dorsal vertebrae, which was making the kidneys overactive. A less typical case was that of 3289, a seven-year-old girl suffering from a severe kidney infection and whose lack of bladder control was attributed to irritation.

Treatment and Case Histories

Positive suggestions were recommended in four cases, and generally these suggestions were to be made by parents just as the child began to fall asleep. Cayce cautioned that their tone should be positive and constructive and that they should avoid negative references.

In the karmic instance, Cayce recommended that a hypnotist make the nocturnal suggestions instead of the parents. In the case of the child who was emotionally attached to his mother, the mother was to give suggestions not only for kidney and bladder control but also advice as to how the child's entire life could be guided toward moral, mental, and material aspirations.

In two cases, spinal adjustments were suggested—in one instance, to be given twice a week in the ninth and seventh dorsal areas. These, Cayce found, would "relieve a great deal of the pressure from the kidney—or the activity to the pancreas reaction; as well as the general condition in the relationships between the sympathetic and cerebrospinal responses in the body'' (679-2). In the other case, periodic adjustments would be generally helpful.

Follow-up indicated that Cayce's suggestions were followed in every instance but one. Three of these children were reported as "cured" of bedwetting, and another experienced at least partial improvement. No final report was received in the case of the child with the kidney infection.

Bladder: Stricture

An abnormal narrowing of a canal, duct, or passage caused by the formation of scar tissue or by the deposit of abnormal tissues is referred to as stricture of the bladder.

Edgar Cayce gave only two readings on the subject, one for a sixty-five-year-old woman who was not told the cause of her condition other than a reference to general debilitation; the other subject received numerous readings on various ailments, five of which were related to bladder strictures.

In the main, Cayce attributed stress and strain from other ailments, along with anxiety, poor eliminations, and previous treatments, as the main causes of bladder stricture. These conclusions were reached during the numerous readings given to case 2504, a sixty-three-year-old man.

Treatment

In treating bladder strictures, the two cases mentioned by Cayce received different regimens. Reading given for case 1746, the sixty-five-year-old woman, put the emphasis on diet, which was an integral part of her therapy. Jerusalem artichokes were to be eaten two or three times weekly. Diluted Atomidine was to be applied to the affected areas. Importance was placed on finding a bladder specialist for this individual.

For case 2504, a sixty-three-year-old man, Cayce suggested

castor oil and mustard packs. In addition, a pea-sized piece
of resin was to be slowly chewed or allowed to dissolve in
the mouth. A combination of hog lard and turpentine was
to be used as a hot poultice and placed over the area above
the neck of the bladder. In another reading, enemas were
suggested to help ease the eliminations. Epsom salt packs
were recommended to help reduce swelling.

Case History

After case 2504's initial readings, he received another
which indicated that prostatitis was also a complication. It
was recommended at this time that previous treatments be
continued. Nine days later, he received another reading
which indicated that he had not made good progress and
that poor eliminations were causing the trouble. The Radio-
Active Appliance was suggested for balancing the system
and increasing his eliminations. In the last reading given
for the sixty-three-year-old man, continued use of the
Radio-Active Appliance, along with massage, sweats, and
good eliminations, was recommended.

In follow-up reports, case 1746 was said to have received "no help" from her reading. Although case 2504
received extensive treatment at the Cayce hospital, there
are no indications of whether his bladder problems were
alleviated.

However, there was a positive report on the use of resin
from case 264, who, seeing the suggestion made for case
2504, gave it to her father, who was having difficulty
urinating. Prior to the resin, even catheterization could not
get his kidneys to act; afterward it was said he voided one
to two quarts.

Blepharitis

Blepharitis is a chronic inflammation of the eyelid mar-
gins which is often accompanied by smarting, burning,
and itching. Edgar Cayce at times referred to it in the

readings as an inflammation of the eyes and at other times as a glandular condition appearing on the lid and/or around the eyeball. Three-quarters of the readings on this topic were researched, amounting to eighteen readings given for fourteen individuals with blepharitis.

Blepharitis is often conventionally attributed to infection by bacteria or viruses or to allergic sensitivity to dust, pollens, or molds. However, Cayce consistently regarded the infection as primarily a side effect of other internal disorders, usually arising from more than one causative factor. Typical "first causes" were pressures in the cerebrospinal system (caused by injury in one case), nerve imbalances, digestive imbalances, poor eliminations, and blood conditions such as acidity, toxicity, or low vitality. Another reading described the cause of the eye problem as partly prenatal, and another was attributed, in part, to inhalation of fumes at work.

In a reading given for a seventy-six-year-old woman, case 774, Cayce noted pressures in the upper dorsal and cervical areas of the spine, which restricted the circulation to and through these portions of the body. The consequence was an accumulation of toxic substances in the system until the eyeball itself became infected, with accumulations also taking place in the lachrymal duct area, hindering the natural reactions of the lids and retinas.

In still another reading, case 2577, a fifty-one-year-old man had developed a form of infection in his blood supply due to an inflammation in his system. Additionally, the normal flow of eliminations from the eyes was blocked by pressures in the dorsal and cervical areas, where coordination was made between the central nervous system and the sensory system.

Improper eliminations through the circulatory system and toxic forces arising from acidity throughout the assimilating and eliminating systems were the causes of eye disturbances explained in case 1772 for a fifty-eight-year-old man. This disturbance had resulted in a general impoverishment of the organs and of the sensory system, made most acute in the eyes due to subluxations in the cervical and vagus centers.

Treatment

Spinal pressures were mentioned so frequently in the blepharitis readings that it is not surprising that the treatment most often recommended—in all but two of the cases studied—was spinal manipulation or massage, particularly in the area of the cervical vertebrae. The primary application for local inflammation, mentioned almost as often as spinal treatment, was a poultice of scraped white potato applied over the eyes with a gauze covering for varying periods of time. Since the purpose of the poultice was to draw out and absorb infectious material, a fresh one was to be prepared for each application, or even more often. Regular cleansing of the eyes with a mild antiseptic solution, such as boric acid, was also frequently advised.

The Violet Ray was recommended in half of these cases, with the advice to apply it over the spine or eyes, or in both areas according to specific instructions. In four cases, these treatments could begin at any time, while readings in two other cases specified waiting until after a series of adjustments lasting two and three to four weeks had taken place. Use of the Radio-Active Appliance was recommended twice.

Methods of stimulating drainages and assimilations were at times part of treatment. Mild laxatives, colonics, enemas, and herbal tonics were all occasionally recommended. Attention to the balanced diet advocated throughout the readings was sometimes stressed, with emphasis on alkaline, laxative, body-building, and easily assimilated foods.

Based on follow-up, six individuals derived partial benefit from following Cayce's suggestions. In three cases, it seemed difficult to completely eradicate the eye trouble, although the condition of the eyes was definitely improved. In the other three cases, the eye trouble completely, or almost completely, cleared up. Success from the use of the potato poultice was reported in seven additional cases.

Case History

Case 1963 was a man in his sixties whose blepharitis was compounded by general debilitation, neurasthenia, and toxemia. Cayce described his condition as nerve exhaustion, with pressures produced by the presence of toxins throughout the system. Pressures in the upper dorsal area of the spine were the primary source of the eye inflammation.

Cayce recommended that the man begin with a colonic every three to five days to remove the effects of toxic forces remaining in the system. Plenty of Glyco-Thymoline, an alkalizer and antiseptic, was to be used in the last water. At these times, a gentle manipulation of the spine was recommended to stimulate the nerves.

At least twice daily, potato poultices were to be applied over the eyes for thirty minutes to an hour at a time. When the poultices were removed, the eyes were to be cleansed with a weak antiseptic solution, such as Glyco-Thymoline or boric acid.

When there was no longer any indication of mucus in the colon, actual osteopathic adjustments were to begin, stimulating the eliminations and making corrections in the lumbar and sacral areas.

Initially, the diet was to consist mainly of liquids and semiliquids, with plenty of beef juice and chicken broth, a little fish, and all the vegetables that could be easily assimilated. Jerusalem artichokes were suggested as a natural source of insulin.

Follow-up here indicated that the man was impressed with the reading and followed it with good results, later reporting that his health had improved and that the inflammation of his eyes had been "cured."

Blindness: Loss of Vision

Edgar Cayce gave fifty-three readings on this subject for a total of twenty-nine individuals suffering from varying degrees of vision loss.

Vision loss was generally found by Cayce to be precipi-
tated by the same variety of physical imbalances involved
in other types of eye problems. Typical contributory causes
were nerve impingements caused by spinal pressures, poor
eliminations, poor or depleted circulation, toxins or infectious forces in the system, and improper diet.

Also noted was a correlation between blindness and
previous treatments which resulted in more harm than
good, and prenatal and karmic conditions.

Treatment

Cayce believed at least partial sight could be restored in
cases where the optic nerve had not been completely
atrophied, or wasted away. Therefore, probably the most
hope existed where the loss of vision was not yet complete.
Treatments in these cases were widely divergent, varying
with the nature of the companion ailments that were often
present.

The treatment mentioned most consistently—in three-
fourths of the cases—involved adjustments and massages
of the spine. These treatments focused on the dorsal and
cervical areas. Electrotherapy was recommended almost as
often, most typically in the form of the Wet Cell with
gold, or the Violet Ray over the spine or eyes. Also
mentioned were electric vibrator treatments, the Radium
Appliance, and various other devices.

Dietary changes were made in a little over a third of the
cases, with special emphasis on balance and alkalinity.
Other miscellaneous recommendations included laxatives,
enemas, sweats, herbal tonics, potato poultices, and mild
antiseptics to cleanse the eyes.

Treatments were not especially different in cases that
were karmic or prenatal in origin.

Case History

The majority of those receiving readings concerning loss
of sight did not follow their instructions or did not report

on the results. Several, however, experienced general improvements, but little or none in vision.

Of the three individuals who did report improvement in vision, one case is especially significant. This was case 4061, a young child with infantile glaucoma, which was considered completely incurable. After a month of treatment, it was noted that his condition steadily improved. Approximately five weeks later, the child had become much calmer, and his eyes had changed from hard to normally soft. He had developed some sight and was "improving by leaps and bounds."

The second reading reported that he had gained ten percent of his vision in the right eye and fifteen to twenty percent in the left. Follow-up indicated that during the next few years, he continued to steadily gain light, object, and color perception.

Blindness: Tendencies

Cayce gave twenty-three readings for seventeen individuals who were experiencing progressive deterioration of their vision. It was evident in all of these cases that if preventive measures were not taken, they would eventually lose vision in one or both eyes.

Cayce believed that tendencies toward blindness were caused by a combination of factors, the main ones being physical debilitation, inadequate elimination of toxins, and spinal pressures which created strain on the nerves. In only three out of twenty-three instances was injury partially responsible for the deteriorating vision.

Reading 148-1, given for a fifty-six-year-old man, found hindered eliminations and an attack on the system by toxins deposited in various parts of the body. Eventually specific organs had become affected—the sensory system in particular. The taking of properties (unspecified) into the body had exaggerated the condition, irritating the digestion to such an extent that pressures were produced throughout the cervical region of the spine, creating more toxins in the system. The facial and optic nerves reacted to this situation, resulting in a weakening of vision. Cayce defined this condition as an external strangulation of the optic nerve rather than an internal atrophy. Also noted in conjunction with the "strangulation" was an irritation of the optical cavity and a film over the eyes themselves.

In another case, that of an eight-year-old boy, prenatal influences were involved. Weakness in the body of the mother during gestation had caused the child, case 545, to be susceptible after birth to weakness and strain. As a result, the nerve impulses were insufficient for the proper development of vision. The muscles which normally hold the eye in the correct position were weakened, creating a misalignment which impaired his vision.

Four readings were given for a thirty-two-year-old woman, case 2348. In this instance, Cayce diagnosed that poor eliminations in conjunction with nerve disturbances and subluxations in the dorsal and cervical ares of the spine had hindered the nerve and blood supply to the sensory organs, particularly the eyes. This had resulted in a tendency toward inflammation of the optic nerve and of areas behind the eyes.

Congestion and the nonelimination of bacteria, which settled in the weakest part of his system, were said to be responsible for the visual deterioration experienced by case 3740, an adult male. The combination produced strain on the nerves of the sensory system, particularly the optic nerve, and resulted in a strangulation of the optic nerve from outside. An atrophy or wilting of this nerve was not involved in his condition, but Cayce noted that it would result if the strangulation was allowed to continue.

Treatment

The primary treatment recommended by Cayce for impaired vision was spinal manipulation—either adjustments or massages or both were advised in every case but one of this aforementioned group.

Additionally, various types of electrotherapy were

mentioned in over two-thirds of these cases. Most often recommended was the Erlanger method, in which low electrical currents were applied to the area of the eyes. In a few cases, the Radio-Active Appliance and Wet Cell were suggested.

For almost a third of these individuals, the importance of a properly balanced and body-building diet was emphasized. Eye operations and Glyco-Thymoline packs on the spine were recommended twice.

Cayce believed that in most of the cases, the deterioration of vision could be arrested, and often reversed, if his treatments were followed.

Case History

Unfortunately, most of the individuals mentioned either did not follow the suggestions given in their readings or did not follow up with the results. However, of the five who definitely took the advice of Cayce, all reported improvement in vision, and at least one's vision was one-hundred percent improved.

The treatment prescribed in case 2558-1 for a fifty-year-old woman suffering from iritis was typical. Spinal manipulations were to be administered about twice a week for six weeks and thereafter on an occasional basis. These were to focus on the last dorsal, the vagus center, and the cervical area, making specific corrections in these areas every other time.

After twelve adjustments, Erlanger treatments were to be administered twice weekly for at least four to five weeks, followed by a rest period of one to two weeks. Then there were two to four more treatments, another rest period, and more treatments. These were to be applied directly to the optic nerve, eye socket, and the pupil itself. A mild eyewash was to be used following each treatment.

Special attention to the eliminations was needed throughout the course of treatment. Dietary instructions were also given. Emphasis was placed on foods high in vitamins B_1,

C, and A, found especially in foods which are yellow in color, such as squash, corn, peaches, and carrots.

Meats were to be eaten only in moderation. Fish, fowl, and lamb were permitted, provided they were not fried. Raw vegetables were also recommended, including carrots, lettuce, celery, fresh alfalfa stems, and watercress.

Boils

A boil is an extremely painful inflammatory swelling of a hair follicle that forms an abscess. Typical symptoms include redness, swelling, and tenderness.

A total of thirty-eight readings were given for thirty-one individuals with boils and similar conditions. Their ages varied from twenty-one months to sixty-eight years. In over eighty percent of the cases, the major factor in the development of boils was poor eliminations. In general, this implied that toxins that were not being eliminated properly were creating a localized infection. Improper drainage from the liver, colon, and kidneys contributed to the toxic buildup.

Related causes in fifteen percent of the cases were poor lymphatic and hepatic circulation. A contributory cause found in five cases was an infection due to such things as the bite of a mosquito and to various types of "germs." In three cases, Cayce cited an unbalanced diet as contributing to the development of boils. Too much fat in the diet had contributed to poor eliminations, which in turn produced irritation and poisons in the body.

Treatment

Treatments in twenty cases advised changes in diet. Fats, sugar, fried foods, and most meats were to be avoided, while vegetables, fruits, body-building foods, and plenty of water were recommended.

Various methods of increasing the eliminations were suggested in sixteen cases. One frequent recommendation was the use of a laxative compound and blood purifier containing equal parts of cream of tartar, Rochelle salts, and sulfur. Also suggested were other types of laxatives, such as Syrup of Figs and enemas and colonics, and in five cases herbal tonics were recommended.

To relax the body and improve the general circulation, spinal manipulations were advised in fourteen cases. These were to focus on the lumbar axis, the ninth dorsal vertebra, and the cervical area.

In ten cases, various typical solutions were suggested, usually for the purpose of drying the boils. These recommendations included plantain ointment, Epsom salt solutions, mercury bichloride, iodine compounds, and spirits of camphor.

Massages and rubdowns were also suggested for ten individuals. Typical substances used were olive oil with tincture of myrrh and cocoa butter.

In nine cases, various forms of electrotherapy were suggested to help improve the general circulation. These most often took the form of the Violet Ray, the Radio-Active Appliance, or the electric vibrator treatments (sponge applicator) applied along the spine.

In four cases, hydrotherapy in the form of sweats and baths was suggested to help improve the circulation and help eliminate toxins. In three cases, the application of packs over the site of the infection was suggested, using ice, Epsom salts, or Glyco-Thymoline after the boils had been lanced.

Case History

Reports indicate that about half of the individuals receiving readings on boils followed the advice given and were relieved of the discomfort of their boils.

One case that reported a "complete cure" with no further problems was 1747, a thirty-four-year-old woman who received one reading on boils. Cayce noted the origin of her discomfort as excessive toxins in the system due to improper eliminations. This produced inflammation between the lymph and the general circulation, which then led to the development of boils.

She was prescribed twice weekly osteopathic manipulations and weekly hydrotherapy. Additionally, about twice a month, she was to receive high colonics in conjunction with fume baths, using either pine oil or wintergreen. Afterward, a rubdown with salt rum was to be given. In later rubdowns, alcohol was to be used.

Her diet was to consist of body-building foods such as green vegetables and fish, fowl, and lamb for protein. Large amounts of starches and heavy meats were to be avoided.

To treat the open sores resulting from the boils, an ointment made from plantain was advised.

Brain Tumors

A tumor is an abnormal mass of cells which enlarges and grows independently of its surrounding structures. Edgar Cayce gave sixteen readings dealing with brain or intracranial tumors—six of these for the same individual.

Cayce most frequently attributed brain tumors to a sluggish circulation which prevented portions of the brain from receiving enough oxygen. The inadequate circulation also interfered with the proper elimination of cellular by-products and the transmission of disease-fighting lymphocytes.

Nervous incoordination, glandular imbalances, poor eliminations and assimilations, psychological factors, and inadequate diet were cited as related causes.

Treatment

Recommended treatment in approximately half of the cases was massage. Four readings stressed a rubbing motion away from the head and toward the lower extremities. The types of massage oil suggested varied; two readings mentioned a combination of equal parts of olive oil and tincture of myrrh. Other treatments mentioned were proper diet, heliotherapy, and electrotherapy (by means of the Wet Cell or Radio-Active Appliance).

Case History

The treatment for case 673, a twenty-five-year-old woman, is, in many respects, representative of the treatments specified in the readings for the majority of individuals with brain tumors.

Her initial symptoms, which began suddenly, were double vision, nausea, severe headaches, and dizziness. After a two-week stay in the hospital, the woman's condition was diagnosed as an inoperable and incurable brain tumor. In a few months, she had lost the use of her left arm and leg.

Cayce found that her tumor was caused by a serious complication of conditions for which little could be done physically without extreme patience and persistence. She had experienced a loss of confidence and faith in a friend. This disappointment, complicated physically by toxic forces in the system, had caused a nervous breakdown, making emotional control impossible at times. Additionally, the woman's toxic blood condition created a lymph inflammation and stiffness in the tendons. Other contributing causes to the physical incoordination were an overuse of drugs and hypnosis, which had added to the buildup of toxins.

Cayce treated the psychological aspects of the woman's illness by stimulating her spiritual awareness. This included awakening the will to free herself of obsessions so that she could live a purposeful life. To treat her physically, Cayce prescribed a daily dose of one-quarter grain of animated ash, followed by heliotherapy using ultraviolet light and quartz light. Each evening before retiring, massage was to be administered over her entire cerebrospinal system, using a combination of equal parts olive oil and tincture of myrrh. Attention to diet was also stressed.

Later reports indicated that she had been discouraged from following the reading and was under the care of a neurologist.

Bronchiectasis

Bronchiectasis is a chronic dilatation of the bronchial tubes due to pulmonary infection or bronchial obstruction. It may be marked by bad breath and sudden and intense coughing spells, with the expectoration of matter containing both mucus and pus.

The two readings given for individuals with bronchiectasis showed differences in both causes and treatment suggestions.

In case 3220, a woman in her thirties, a major cause given was negative attitudes and emotions. The physical cause in this case was a chemical burn which had irritated the throat, larynx, and windpipe.

In case 1467, the bronchiectasis of a thirty-nine-year-old male was attributed to the effects of poor assimilation and poor elimination.

Treatment

Treatment for case 3220 involved the use of an inhalant four or five times a day and once or twice at night. The inhalant consisted of thirty drops oil of eucalyptus, ten drops rectified oil of turpentine, forty-five drops compound tincture of benzoin, thirty drops rectified creosote, and twenty drops tolu, added to a four-ounce grain-alcohol base.

Recommended additions to the diet were a teaspoon of beef juice daily, vitamin B complex tablets nightly before bed, and large amounts of seafood. Additionally, gentle massages using cocoa butter were to be given once a week, extending from the ninth dorsal to the base of the brain.

For her negativity, Cayce advised a reshaping of attitudes and emotions. She was told to use her body and mind in the service of God.

For case 1467, an occasional osteopathic adjustment was suggested for times when the digestion was upset or when there were headaches or acute pains in the body. Also suggested were massage and eliminants—alternating between vegetable compounds and mineral salts.

Bronchitis

The inflamed throat, lungs, and bronchial tubes which is known as bronchitis is characteristically marked by fever, difficulty in breathing, and extended coughing spells accompanied by acute chest pains. In addition to being a localized toxic condition of the respiratory system, bronchitis is, according to the Edgar Cayce readings, the result of toxic conditions and imbalances throughout the body.

There are forty-five readings in the Cayce files on bronchitis. These were for thirty-one individuals who sought Cayce's assistance in combating the respiratory illness.

A typical cause noted for the general toxemia associated with bronchitis was the poor elimination of toxins by the lungs and the organs along the alimentary canal, combined with circulatory imbalances. Frequently related causes were lack of coordination between the sympathetic and cerebrospinal nervous systems, poor assimilations, and spinal subluxations.

Typically, the spinal problems would impoverish the nerve supply to the lungs and excretory system, further toxifying the circulation in the lungs. These organs would be unable to effectively oxidize the blood, impairing the hepatic circulation. At this point, an incoordination between the circulation of blood and lymph would develop, compounding the elimination problems and in many cases interfering with the assimilations as well.

In only a few cases did Cayce attribute bronchitis

directly to cold, flu, or congestion in the lungs, although these were often accompanying symptoms.

Treatment

Cayce's treatments for bronchitis were both local and internal. Most of the readings prescribed some type of inhalant to stimulate the circulation and act as an antiseptic and expectorant to relieve the congestion in the lungs.

Dietary instructions also predominated in almost every one of the cases. While the infection was draining, a diet that was both cleansing and body building was stressed. A liquid or semiliquid diet, with an emphasis on fruits, fruit and vegetable juices, and water, was recommended. Body-building measures included beef juice (rather than meat), vitamins A and D, small amounts of alcoholic stimulants, and light proteins (cereals, nuts, seafood).

Cayce also emphasized stimulating the eliminations and alkalizing the system. Cleansing measures most frequently mentioned were enemas, colonics, laxatives, and, at times, antacids. Massages with olive oil, peanut oil, and lanolin were important for improving the circulation and muscle tone. Often suggested as an adjunct to or as a separate form of massage was the use of an electric vibrator. This was particularly for use along the spine. Also mentioned, but with somewhat less frequency, was spinal manipulation, recommended to correct problem areas, improve the nervous coordination, and assist the eliminations.

Electrotherapy was occasionally mentioned—most frequently being the Violet Ray. It was to be applied over the cervical area of the spine and/or the head, neck, and chest, using the sponge applicator over delicate areas.

Case History

A forty-five-year-old woman, case 4252, requested a reading to help relieve not only her bronchitis but her asthma and gallbladder problems as well.

In diagnosing her condition, Cayce explained that poor

eliminations were the cause of her problems, with involvement of the cerebrospinal system and various organs of the excretory system. The complications in the respiratory system were caused by spinal subluxations and poor oxygenation of the blood due to the poor eliminations.

Two types of inhalation therapy were recommended. The first, apple brandy in a charred oak keg, was kept warm so that brandy fumes would be produced within the keg. These fumes were to be inhaled at least twice daily, acting as healing agents for the throat, lungs, and larynx, and as a tonic for the blood.

The second type of inhalant was alcohol based, a solution shaken well and inhaled through the nose and mouth. When used for cleansing the nostrils alone, the solution was to be poured into boiling water and the fumes inhaled while a towel was draped over the head.

The woman's diet was based on foods that were both blood building and alkaline reacting in nature. Fruit juices, nuts, and beef juice were suggested as beneficial for the system. Salt rubs were to be administered to increase the circulation, followed by gentle osteopathic manipulation. All treatments were to be given daily for three weeks.

Reports indicated that some progress was evident but was accompanied by periodic relapses, as the woman did not fully follow Cayce's advice. Nevertheless, she requested another reading at a later date and lived in good health until her death forty-three years later in 1974.

Burns

There were seven readings given by Edgar Cayce for burn victims. Three were for children and one for an adult—all of whom had suffered major burns through accidents with hot metal, fire, or boiling water.

There was a high level of consistency in the treatments suggested in the readings, for Cayce's approach was for the total person and involved not only care of the burned tissue but of the whole body so that it would be aided in its attempt to restore normalcy to the system.

In three out of the four cases, Cayce emphasized the necessity for maintaining proper eliminations so that burned and destroyed cell tissue, as well as toxins produced by the burn, would not coagulate in the body. For this, Cayce recommended frequent doses of such eliminants as Fletcher's Castoria, Alophen, or Phenolax. Also noted as important in providing body-building nourishment was diet. Highly recommended were fruits, whole-grain cereals, whole wheat bread, and foods containing iron, such as meat juice. Sweets and excessive starches were to be avoided.

Keeping the burns properly dressed was emphasized, and it was suggested that this be done under the supervision of a physician. Between daily dressing of the wound, Cayce at times advised rubbing Unguentine into the burn and applying camphorated oil around the area of the burn. This was to prevent the dressing from adhering to the skin.

One reading suggested the application of an ointment containing burnt alum or heated powdered alum, spirits of camphor, and mutton tallow around the area of the burn before applying the dressing. The burned area itself was to be cleansed with an antiseptic solution. Unguentine and camphorated oil were also noted as beneficial in reducing or removing scar tissue.

Case History

Case 487 concerned an eight-year-old boy who had slipped into a blazing fireplace, receiving severe burns on his left side from his ankle to his hip. Cayce emphasized the need to assist the eliminations in the first two readings. He suggested taking small daily doses of Calomel, Alophen, or Phenolax, followed by broken dosages of Castoria. Treatment of the actual burn involved a doctor changing the bandages daily.

Cayce also advised following the cleansing of the burn with an application of Unguentine or a very mild mercury bichloride antiseptic solution. To prevent the skin from adhering to the dressing, an application of camphorated oil around the skin of the burn was recommended.

The diet recommended was plenty of fruits, beef, chicken, fish, milk, and blood-building foods; the consumption of sweets and candies was discouraged.

By the third reading, improvements in the boy's condition were noted, as well as a toxic buildup in the blood, indicating a need for better eliminations. Cayce advised continuing the prescribed treatments and following them with a moderate dose of a saline laxative as well as massaging the spine in the evenings.

Three months following the first reading, the boy was off crutches and able to move freely again without pain. He even regained full use of his left leg without the need for further treatment.

Bursitis

Bursitis is an inflammation of one of the fluid-filled membranes that are interposed between moving parts of the body such as tendons, ligaments, bones, and joints.

Fourteen individuals, ranging from twenty to seventy-one years old, were each given one reading for bursitis and related conditions.

In general, Edgar Cayce considered bursitis the result of a chemical imbalance in the body, which was associated with metabolic conditions. Such an imbalance was regarded as responsible for the irritating accumulations in the bursas.

In more than sixty percent of the cases, Cayce cited poor elimination as the primary cause. This imbalance would lead to a buildup of toxins in the general circulation and an accumulation of calcium or other substances in the bursas, causing friction at the joints and, hence, inflammation. A frequently repeated factor mentioned in over forty percent of the cases was poor circulation, which could be either a cause or a result of the problems associated with the eliminations. As a consequence, the circulation in the extremities would become slowed, further impeding eliminations.

Another contributing factor mentioned several times was poor assimilation, cited at times in conjunction with overacidity. Other factors mentioned in two cases each were spinal subluxations in the dorsal and cervical regions, general overtaxation, and an injury, which at times was the result of overexertion, as mentioned in the case of a tennis player who played too long and too hard.

Treatment

Cayce's treatments for individuals with bursitis were basically designed to restore the balance of the body as well as relieve pain until it became less acute. Readings in sixty percent of the cases advised changes in diet, stressing alkaline-reacting foods such as fruits and vegetables and their juices.

Also recommended were moderate amounts of foods such as whole grains, milk, soups, broths, and beef juice. Meat was to be eaten in extreme moderation and then only in the form of fish, fowl, or beef liver. Red meats, fried foods, grease, sugar, and white flour products were to be avoided.

Also especially recommended were eliminants to rid the body of toxins and excess acids. Colonics and a variety of laxative substances were suggested for this purpose. Massage was recommended in over forty percent of the cases, to be administered in some instances with peanut oil and other substances. The massages were intended to improve the circulation and eliminations and relieve irritation in the bursas.

In almost thirty percent of the cases, Cayce recommended hot packs placed over the affected areas to help relieve pain. Three individuals were advised to use Epsom salt packs, while one was told to use Glyco-Thymoline packs. Also recommended in thirty percent of the cases were hydrotherapy treatments. These were to be in the form of fume baths or other specially prescribed baths and showers.

Spinal manipulation and electrotherapy were each advised for two individuals; and Atomidine and Acigest, an alkalizer and digestive aid, were prescribed for two people.

Case History

About one-half of the fourteen individuals receiving readings for bursitis reported marked improvement, including case 3012, a fifty-one-year-old woman who received one reading from Cayce. Her condition was found to be due to an accumulation of calcium in the joints, which caused considerable pain in her extremities.

At first the woman was advised to take Atomidine internally—one drop in half a glass of water each morning for a ten-day period. During this time, she was advised against drinking any carbonated beverages or alcoholic drinks.

Upon completion of the ten-day Atomidine course, she was to begin hydrotherapy treatments—fume baths with witch hazel, and after each fume bath she was to take a hot and cold needle shower, followed by a thorough rubdown with a combination of peanut oil and pine-needle oil. These treatments were to be administered once a week for a minimum of six weeks. At least one colonic irrigation was recommended during that time period.

At the conclusion of hydrotherapy treatments, she was to resume the Atomidine doses, this time for periods of five days each, alternated with five days without Atomidine. In the diet, vegetables were to be included with meals as often as possible. Meats and greasy or fried foods were to be avoided.

After following the treatments prescribed in her reading, the woman reported that she had regained her health and the full use of her body.

Cancer: Lung

Edgar Cayce gave readings for seven individuals with lung cancer, who ranged in age from ten to sixty. Common symptoms of the disease were shortness of breath, exhaustion, and acute pain in the lungs and chest.

In five cases, Cayce did not elaborate upon the cause of the cancer but referred to the existence of germs in the blood or system, or bacilli of a destructive nature. He did not clarify their origin or method of introduction into the body, except in two instances. One involved a young girl who had accidentally inhaled a brass pin which was causing destruction of the respiratory system. The other case involved a severe cold which had caused respiratory inflammation and the subsequent collection of fluids in the lungs.

In almost all cases, the respiratory activities were severely affected, creating reflex conditions throughout the body. The inability of the lungs to oxidize the blood supply contributed to a feeling of extreme weariness and lack of vitality. Some individuals also had poor eliminations, which further reduced the ability of the body to rid itself of the bacteria.

Treatment

To assist the respiratory activity, Cayce prescribed the use of inhalants in six readings. Most frequently recommended was the inhalation of fumes from apple brandy, with instructions to fill a charred oak keg half full of apple brandy and keep the keg near heat so that fumes would collect in the empty portion of the container. According to Cayce, inhaling the fumes two or three times a day would assist the respiration and help the body eliminate toxins.

Another inhalant recommended at times consisted of small amounts of such ingredients as rectified oil of turpentine, pine-needle oil, and eucalyptus oil, added to a grain-alcohol base. Half of these individuals were advised to take one-eighth grain of animated ash daily and to follow this dosage with the application of either the ultraviolet light or Violet Ray, usually over the portion of the back opposite the lungs. Cayce believed the light of the rays would allow the animated ash to react in the bloodstream and promote the destruction of cancerous cells. Application of the rays was usually not to exceed a few minutes and was believed most effective within minutes of taking the animated ash. In one case, a rubdown over the afflicted area with an ointment of Iodex mixed with animated ash was recommended to relieve pain.

Dietary advice was given to one-third of the individuals. Typically recommended were foods that would help the eliminations and promote proper assimilation, such as leafy green vegetables, fish and fowl, liver, gelatin, and dark breads. Only small portions of red meat were advised, and pork was forbidden.

Those individuals whose conditions were in the advanced stages were encouraged to pray and to set their minds to healing themselves by adopting positive attitudes. Cayce advised one person that "the consciousness, the awareness of the Divine must be aroused within self if destructive forces would be put to rout."

Case History

In four cases, there were either no reports or reports indicated that the readings were not followed. Although two individuals with serious conditions died soon after their readings were given, it was reported that they had shown some signs of improvement after Cayce's treatments were administered.

One case that involved a woman who faithfully carried out her treatment noted remarkable improvements which enabled her to work and function in a normal manner, in spite of the fact that her condition was serious.

Another case, which did not produce positive results, was that of 1070, a forty-eight-year-old male. Cayce attributed his cancerous condition in the lungs to infectious agents involving the soft tissue in the throat, lungs, and other parts of the body. The man's respiration was severely impaired, as was the functioning of the pancreas and liver, which affected the eliminations. Doctors had diagnosed this case as terminal.

Treatment was to extend over a twenty-six- to thirty-six-day period. One-eighth grain of animated ash was to be taken with water every day, and every other day, the ultraviolet light was to be applied three to five minutes after ingestion of the animated ash. Use of the shortwave mercury or quartz lamp was also recommended and was to be held thirty-six to forty-two inches from the body. Cayce advised exposing the cerebrospinal area over the lungs to the rays for one and a half to two and a half minutes.

Once treatment with the animated ash and ultraviolet light was initiated, the man was advised to frequently inhale the fumes from apple brandy in a charred oak keg, with the capacity approximately three times the volume of the brandy. In order to generate more fumes, Cayce advised keeping the keg near heat and closed with a stopper at all times.

To assist eliminations, colonic irrigations were recommended when needed. Although case 1070 was urged to have a second reading following the first thirty-six days of treatment, it was reported that he gave up hope and did not pursue his treatment.

Cancer and Tumors: Breast

Edgar Cayce gave fifteen readings on cancer of the breast and ten on breast tumors. In view of the close similarities in cause and treatment of both conditions, the data have been summarized together.

Diagnoses for six of the thirteen women revealed the presence of toxic elements and destructive "humors" in the blood. Due to poor eliminations, prevalant in most cases, the toxins accumulated in the lymph glands, especially the mammary glands. A hormone deficiency was noted as a cause for tumors or cancerous growth in the breasts in two other cases, and twice Cayce found a chemical imbalance in the blood—attributed in one case to excessive potassium, which he considered responsible for the formation of breast tumors.

Treatment

Although no two treatments for either condition were exactly alike, a definite treatment pattern emerges. Special emphasis was placed on diet, electrotherapy, and topical applications.

The diet was to be rich in alkaline-reacting foods in ten cases of breast cancer or tumors. Foods to be avoided were starches, fatty or fried foods, and all meats, except for occasional seafood or chicken in certain cases. Brazil nuts and almonds were highly recommended, as they were reported to contain elements vital to the prevention of cancer.

The use of light and electrotherapy, especially the ultraviolet light, was viewed as important to treatment. The usual instructions were to swallow one-eighth grain of animated ash with water about fifteen minutes before exposure. The light was to be kept at a distance of thirty-eight to forty inches from the body. To prevent reddening of the skin, the use of green plate glass placed about eighteen inches from the body was recommended. In some cases, other forms of electro-therapy were recommended in conjunction with the ultraviolet light.

In six cases, Cayce suggested a variety of topical appli-cations which were to be gently massaged in and around the breast on a daily basis. The most common ointments were cocoa butter or a mixture of animated or carbon ash with Iodex. The need to maintain good eliminations was emphasized in four cases.

To stimulate the glands, Atomidine, taken in water in varying doses once or twice a day, was recommended in three cases.

Case History

Cayce gave five readings for case 4438, who had a noncancerous tumor in her left breast. The reading revealed that an excess of potassium in the blood had caused a chemical reaction in the glands which triggered the accumulation of wastes in the lymph glands of the breast.

Use of the ultraviolet light three times a week was

prescribed in the first reading. This thirty-minute treatment was to begin after the woman had taken a quarter grain of animated ash with water. Using the heavy lamp, the recommended distance was from thirty-eight to forty inches (with the smaller hand lamp thirty-four inches), with exposure specifically directed to the area of the third, fourth, and sixth dorsal vertebrae. It should be noted that this light was almost always to be directed at specific areas of the cerebrospinal system and not at the breast.

To purify the glands, eight drops of Atomidine were to be taken in a glass of water twice a day for ten days, followed by a five-day rest period, and then resumed at these intervals for a three- or four-month period.

A mixture of one-quarter ounce of Iodex and one-quarter grain of animated ash was prescribed as a topical ointment. A gentle daily massage was to be followed by covering the breast with a gauze cloth and then rabbit fur, if available.

It was crucial in this case to maintain a well-balanced diet, for if excess fats and proteins were not reduced in the blood, a harmful chemical reaction could result through the absorption of the Iodex-ash ointment into the system. A strict diet high in leafy green vegetables and nuts was encouraged. No meats, fats, or oily foods were allowed, and tuberous vegetables were to be eaten sparingly.

In the second reading, Cayce cautioned the woman that she was not following the treatments thoroughly or consistently enough.

Just prior to the third reading, the woman's husband reported that his wife was feeling better, but that the breast was swollen and draining through small cracks in the skin. Again Cayce stressed the importance of maintaining complete consistency in all phases of treatment, which was lacking in this case. He advised extending the light treatment for another ten to fifteen minutes, preceded by the taking of animated ash. The strength of the ointment was to be increased by mixing three-quarters grain of animated ash to one-half ounce of Iodex. Additionally, an herbal cathartic consisting of podophyllum, leptandrin, sanguinaria, cascara sagrada, and senna was recommended.

In the third reading, the woman reported the appearance of a painful lump under her left shoulder joint which was hindering movement of the arm. Cayce explained that this was due to the movement and accumulation of sarcoma which had lodged in the lymph nodes under the arm. He prescribed a compound of plantain leaf and root cooked with butterfat or thick cream, to be gently rubbed into the lump.

In the fifth reading, it was advised that surgery would be necessary if improvements did not occur soon. No further follow-up reports are available in this case.

However, of the thirteen women who sought Cayce's assistance with breast tumors or cancer, five did not report on their progress and two reportedly did not follow their readings. But the six women who followed Cayce's advice obtained good results, including two who reported a "complete recovery" from breast cancer and/or tumors.

Cancer: Skin

Eight cases of skin cancer were discussed in seventeen readings. The majority of these individuals noted irritation, rash, or blisters around the head and face, or open, painful sores.

Of all types of cancer, skin cancer is the most common and the most easily cured. There are three major types of skin cancer: basal cell cancer, squamous cell cancer, and malignant melanoma, which accounts for up to five percent of all cases of skin cancer.

Causes for skin cancer cited by Edgar Cayce were different in each instance. Poor eliminations, unbalanced thyroid functioning, infections, and mercury poisoning were all mentioned as causative factors. In each case, the resulting internal disturbances ultimately affected the superficial circulation and glandular secretions in the skin layers. In yet another case, the skin cancer was caused by an old injury to the lips which had damaged the lip muscles, causing the development of altered skin cells which were harmful to the surrounding normal tissues.

Treatment

Recommendations for treatment of skin cancer were just as varied as its causes. Readings in four cases recommended electrotherapy, in the form of the Radium Appliance, the infrared light, the ultraviolet light, and the Violet Ray. The latter two were to be used after swallowing small doses of carbon or animated ash.

Diet in three cases emphasized a strict, highly alkaline diet, which included fruits and vegetables, occasional fish, fowl, and lamb, whole wheat bread, and cereals. Red meats, sugars, fried and fatty foods, and large amounts of acid-reacting foods in general were to be avoided.

Plantain cream, made with chopped plantain leaves cooked in cream, was prescribed in two cases as a salve to be applied directly to the cancerous skin. Also suggested in two cases were back and spinal rubs using various kinds of oils. The rubs were to stimulate and relax the muscles and nerves. Additionally, mullein tea and laxatives were advised in two instances.

Case History

In the majority of the instances, there were no follow-up reports received. However, in one case improvement was noted, and in another (case 4907) the condition was recorded as completely cured.

This particular case involved a seventy-seven-year-old man who suffered from cancer on his lips. Cayce recommended that he treat this condition by taking an eighth grain of animated ash each day with water and then applying the Violet Ray to the upper portion of the body for from three to five minutes. The man was also advised to include more alkaline-reacting foods in his diet and to avoid all forms of heavy starches.

The man followed Cayce's advice and reported that his condition was cured.

Cancer: Stomach and Intestines

Cancer is a general term used to indicate various types of malignant, abnormal tissue growths, most of which invade surrounding tissues and eventually spread to several sites. Carcinoma of the stomach includes upper gastro-intestinal symptoms with weight loss in persons over age forty, as well as anemia and blood in stools.

Twenty-five readings were given by Edgar Cayce for thirteen individuals suffering from cancer of the stomach and intestines.

In treating the cancerous growths, Cayce prescribed a combination of healing regimes. Most frequently, due to the advanced stage of the cancer, the reading would clearly state that the treatments outlined were not designed to cure, only to extend the life span and reduce the pain.

Poor eliminations were cited as either the main cause or as a contributing factor in a third of the cases. One-fourth of the individuals were told that poor assimilations, often in combination with poor eliminations, were the cause of the condition. Overacidity was central to the cancer in a few cases.

Unfortunately, the common denominator in all cases was that the cancer was in its advanced stages by the time the reading was requested. Twelve of the individuals died within six months of their last reading, and one person was informed that death was imminent at the time of the reading.

Only one individual was reported to be in good health three years later.

Treatment

In over one-half of Cayce's readings for cancer of the stomach and intestines, animated ash, often combined with the use of the ultraviolet light, was suggested. This was to stimulate the release of oxygen into the system, enabling the blood supply to revitalize the system to a degree. Dosage for the ash varied between one-eighth to one-quarter grain, to be taken orally with a glass of water twice daily. The ultraviolet light was to be used thirty minutes later for two to three minutes.

In one-half of the cases, principally where poor eliminations were involved, dietary changes were usually mentioned. Generally stressed were predigested or easily assimilated foods and beef juices. To increase eliminations, one-third of the readings suggested the use of enemas, laxatives, or colonics. Castor oil packs, used either alone or in combination with Epsom salt packs, were also recommended in several cases to aid eliminations.

Spinal manipulation or massage was recommended in one-fourth of the cases, and various herbal prescriptions in two-thirds. Elm water and/or saffron tea were suggested in five cases for their antiseptic and soothing qualities in the stomach. Both recommended twice were bismuth and chalk compounds, also to ease digestion, and a combination of limewater, cinnamon water, bromide of potassium, and iodide of potassium to relieve vomiting and nausea.

Visualization, prayer, meditation, and the laying on of hands were suggested in the readings as a way of prolonging life.

Case History

Two readings were given over a period of eight days for 2512, a woman who had had a malignant growth removed from her rectum eight months earlier. Her first reading explained her feelings of exhaustion and shortness of breath as reflexive reactions to the toxic condition in her system. The toxemia was the result of blocked eliminations due to mucus throughout the colon. This, in combination with a liver disturbance and the lack of gall duct activity, had produced an imbalance in her hepatic circulation.

To relieve the condition, hot castor oil packs were to be

placed over the liver and right side of the abdominal area for a period of one hour each day for three days. To help stimulate eliminations, on the evening of the third day, two tablespoons of olive oil were to be taken internally. The next day, a general hydrotherapy treatment was to be administered, including a colonic. Following a rest period of ten days, the process was to be repeated every ten days until there was no indication of mucus in the colon. Cayce's dietary recommendation included fresh green vegetables, especially those high in vitamin B_1.

The woman's second reading was given in response to specific questions concerning the cause, cure and condition of the cancerous growth. This reading described the primary cause of her condition as a chemical imbalance which had become localized and, due to unspecified influences, had led to the malignancy.

The reading recommended continuing hydrotherapy treatments in conjunction with the ultraviolet light using the green glass. Colonics consisting of a weak salt-and-soda solution were also suggested. Beef juices, citrus fruits, B vitamins, and yellow vegetables were advised; and if needed, narcotics were to be taken to ease pain.

At the end of the reading, Cayce explained that the treatments suggested would not cure, only help prolong life. Reports afterward indicated that case 2512 died seven days after her last reading.

Cancer: Uterus

Of the six cases of uterine cancer mentioned in the Edgar Cayce readings, only three discussed causes, which were attributed to "destructive forces" or harmful organisms which invaded the uterus and pelvic area, destroying healthy tissue and creating destructive cells. There were a total of twenty readings on cancer of the uterus, the majority of which were for women who did not approach Cayce until a malignant condition had already been established. Consequently, the discussion of the causes was generally omitted and attention focused on providing relief, if not a cure.

Treatment

The majority of recommendations centered on electrotherapy treatments, utilizing the X-ray and ultraviolet light, which were mentioned in two readings each. Also discussed were the Radium and Radio-Active Appliances. Length and intensity of exposure depended on the severity and the condition.

Frequent douches with diluted Atomidine, Glyco-Thymoline, Creolin, or Lysol were suggested in four readings. The usual dilution of Atomidine or Glyco-Thymoline was one teaspoonful to one quart of warm water; dilutions of Lysol and Creolin were much weaker.

Hot packs were advised to relieve localized pain. Hot Epsom salts, hot salt, or a poultice of plantain leaf applied over the abdomen or uterine area or on the base of the spine were recommended.

Dietary recommendations were made in two cases, with the emphasis on easily digestible, body-building foods. Laxatives were suggested twice.

The importance of a positive attitude was also at times stressed. Patients were encouraged to adopt a cheerful disposition and not to dwell on their problem, for "the dread of the condition and the outcome brings as much suffering as the condition itself" (4741-1).

Case History

Since, in the case of 468, the cancer had already progressed to a terminal stage, Cayce's efforts were directed toward providing comfort and relief from pain.

Under a physician's supervision, he advised a daily medication consisting of small amounts of oil of eucalyptus, rectified oil of turpentine, Canadian balsam, and codeine. To prevent further spread of the disease, every other day the woman was to take one-quarter grain of animated ash several minutes before application of the Violet Ray, which was to be placed over the upper dorsal vertebrae for two to three minutes.

Occasional douches with one to three drops of Lysol, or three to ten drops of Glyco-Thymoline added to a quart of water were to be used to help keep the vaginal area free from infection.

No follow-up report is available.

Canker Sores and Herpes Simplex (cold sores)

Edgar Cayce gave sixteen readings for thirteen individuals with canker sores and single readings for two individuals with cold sores or herpes simplex. The former is characterized by painful ulcerations, usually around the mouth or lips. Herpes simplex is a viral infection characterized by recurrent lesions which can occur anywhere but most often occur on the lips, mouth, and genitals. Since these disorders are similar in symptoms, they are summarized together.

In all cases involving canker sores and herpes simplex, Cayce noted other physical problems which had predisposed the body to the facial irritations. Generally, Cayce considered such sores the body's way of circumventing potentially more serious conditions by acting as an early-warning signal.

He believed all were experiencing digestive problems and poor eliminations, which contributed to excess acidity in the system. In ten cases, the facial sores were specifically attributed to the regurgitation of excess acids from the stomach to the throat and mouth, where the acids irritated the membrane lining.

Spinal subluxations or lesions which produced an incoordination, especially in the hepatic area, were cited as a major cause of the initial digestive trouble in seven cases. In four other cases, toxic conditions in the blood and poor eliminations were described as initial causes of the digestive disturbances. Congestion was also noted in some of the cases.

Treatment

Changes in diet were recommended in eleven cases. This was to incorporate more alkaline-reacting foods such as raw and cooked leafy greens and citrus fruits, as well as fish, fowl, and lamb and whole-grain cereals. Foods containing fats and starches and those which were acid producing were to be avoided.

Readings in ten cases prescribed relaxing manipulations and/or massages and rubs administered mainly around the back and spine to correct the spinal incoordination and promote eliminations. Various substances were to be used in the massage. Suggested twice to relieve congestion was a combination of mutton tallow, spirits of turpentine, and spirits of camphor. In addition, readings in three cases recommended specific osteopathic adjustments to correct spinal subluxations and lesions.

For local relief, seven readings advised rinsing the mouth with an alkaline antiseptic such as Lavoris or diluted Glyco-Thymoline or Atomidine. Also recommended were applications of carbolated Vaseline, Ipsab full strength, a laudanum-aconite combination, and camphor.

Cayce also suggested internal alkalizers, and those recommended included minute amounts of Glyco-Thymoline in water, Bisodol, and Al-Caroid. In six readings, Cayce gave advice on methods of assisting eliminations. Most often suggested were Castoria, colonics, and specially prepared compounds, some of them herbal in nature. These were to be administered at various intervals to stimulate the necessary drainage of toxins from the system. Hydrotherapy was suggested in three cases, also to promote eliminations and stimulate circulation. Suggested as frequently as hydrotherapy were abdominal packs, using castor oil, Glyco-Thymoline, and vinegar and salt, respectively.

Case History

Case 2462 was a thirty-four-year-old man whose canker sores Cayce ascribed to overacidity in the system. He noted the primary cause as spinal lesions in the dorsal area and lower spine, which deflected impulses to the circulation and resulted in an overtoxic system.

The treatment prescribed included osteopathic adjustments within a ten-day time period. Specific reference was made to the fifth, sixth, eighth, and ninth dorsal vertebrae and to the coccygeal and sacral areas. After the third adjustment, he was to have a full hydrotherapy treatment, including a cabinet sweat, colonic, hot and cold shower, and a thorough massage along the spine using peanut oil followed by alcohol. A series of six more adjustments was to follow ten days of rest.

After eating his heaviest meal of the day, he was to take half a teaspoon of Al-Caroid in water, followed by two full glasses of water. Once a month, he was to drink some lithia water.

The diet was to include raw vegetables at least once a day. Carbonated drinks, fried foods, and pastries and cake were to be avoided, although fruit pie was occasionally allowed. As a local application, he was to use an alkaline antiseptic such as Glyco-Thymoline or Lavoris.

A follow-up noted that 2462 reported improvement, although at the time his condition had not entirely cleared. No further report was available.

Carbuncles

A carbuncle is an inflammation of the skin resembling a boil but larger in size. In reading 270-41, Edgar Cayce described a carbuncle as "a breaking of cell tissue that allows the accumulations within same." Five individuals received twenty-four readings concerning this and other conditions.

At least a contributing factor in almost all of the readings was a disturbance in the glands of assimilations; and two readings specified that carbuncles arise from a chemical imbalance affecting the glands. In fact, in reading 270-41, Cayce noted carbuncles "may be said to be the effect of the thyroid activity."

Treatment

Treatment prescribed for carbuncles was fairly well-rounded and concerned diet and physiotherapy as well as topical applications.

Salves and ointments for the relief of pain associated with carbuncles were prescribed in all cases. Combinations recommended most frequently were liquefied mutton suet, spirits of turpentine and spirits of camphor, and Iodex and animated ash. Instructions were to rub in the ointments until absorbed into the carbuncle. This was to be done at least once a day. Lancing or surgical removal of the carbuncle was recommended in three cases, as well as postoperative treatments to be continued at home.

In three cases, general massages and rubdowns with pine oil, olive oil, or an electric vibrator were suggested, with special attention to be given to specific areas of the back and spine. Two readings emphasized the necessity of an alkaline-reacting diet to assist in establishing good eliminations.

Case History

The following is a general case history given for a forty-five-year-old woman. Although she later decided on surgery, a similar treatment for case 1325 obtained "excellent" results.

Ten readings were given for case 303, a woman with painful carbuncles on her back and legs. Cayce attributed this problem to glandular distress, complicated by poor circulation and poor eliminations.

For immediate relief, she was advised to use an ointment consisting of a small amount of Iodex mixed with one-half grain of animated ash. She was to receive a massage every evening before bedtime for approximately two weeks. This was to be administered with an electric vibrator around the base of the brain, as well as around the throat, face, and head. To aid eliminations, Cayce recommended an alkaline-reacting diet.

Pain from the carbuncle persisted by the third and fourth readings due to poor circulation in the affected area. The strength of the ointment was at this time increased to fifteen grains of animated ash mixed with an ounce of Iodex. This was to be massaged into the carbuncles twice each day. Also suggested was an herbal tonic of spirits of frumenty, elixir of calisaya, yellow dock root, fluid extract of poke root, essence of stillingia, and tincture of capsicum. This was to be taken several times a day.

By the sixth reading, the woman complained that her clothing was irritating the carbuncles. Suggested were nightly back and leg rubs with Iodex and animated ash ointment. This was to be followed by application of a gauze pack treated with a compound of mutton tallow, spirits of turpentine, and spirits of camphor. By the final reading, 303 decided on surgery, to which Cayce agreed. No further reports were received.

In summary, in three cases where reports were received, improved conditions were noted as a result of following Cayce's suggestions.

Cataracts

A cataract is the partial or complete opacity of the crystalline lens of the eye or of its capsule. As the cataract matures, it allows steadily less light to reach the retina. The degree of vision loss corresponds to the density of the cataract.

Cayce gave a total of twenty-six readings for nineteen individuals with cataracts.

Edgar Cayce found that cataracts were caused by uneliminated materials accumulating both around the eyes and in reflex centers to the eyes. Over a period of time, the accumulation could be sufficient to cause the formation of an obstructing film.

He said the accumulations were the end results of two major causes. The first, and by far the most predominant, involved the nonelimination of what were described as "refuse forces" created in the course of normal use of the eyes. Since every movement of muscle in the body expends energy, it thereby produces some waste material which must be removed by the system. Consequently, he believed the gradual buildup of waste in a system with poor or depleted circulation was inevitable.

The second major cause was often linked to spinal pressures, which could impair the nerve impulses to the entire sensory system. Other causes were congestion or inflammation of the mucous membranes and external injury to the eyes, both mentioned only in a few instances.

Treatment

Cayce's research found cataracts to have common origins which were easily treatable, provided the optic nerve itself had not yet atrophied. These treatments were consistent.

The most frequent recommendation—made in almost three-fourths of the cases—was attention to the spine in the form of manipulation, massage, or at times a combination of the two. Various forms of electrotherapy were suggested in half of the cases. Most often mentioned were the Violet Ray—applied to the spine and/or to the eyes—the low electrical vibrations of the Erlanger method applied directly to the eyes, and the ultraviolet light.

A balanced diet was suggested for about one-third of the individuals. Hydrotherapy was also suggested at times, as was the use of potato poultices when needed.

Operating to remove the cataract was recommended in only three instances. In these cases, timing and preparation were considered highly important. Treatments concentrated on strengthening the body and reducing pressures, which would facilitate a full recovery. In two other cases, Cayce found that an operation was best avoided, and his treatments were directed toward dissipating the toxins through absorption and the natural eliminating channels. Treatments were designed to gradually remove the pressures, stimulate the circulation, and set up drainage throughout the system.

Case History

Seven readings were given for case 5451, an adult male. Osteopathic adjustments were advised, giving special attention to the first and second dorsals, the third, fourth, and fifth cervicals, and drainage areas in the upper sides of the face.

Fume sweats were recommended prior to the manipulations to thoroughly relax the body.

In addition, the ultraviolet light was to be applied over junctions of the sympathetic and cerebrospinal nerve systems in the dorsal and cervical regions for three to five minutes at a time, alternated on different days with Violet Ray applications of two to seven minutes. The eliminations were to be increased as necessary. Potato poultices were to be used as a cleanser when needed. Eye exercises were recommended after further drainage had taken place.

Regrettably, most of the individuals who requested information on cataracts either did not follow their readings or did not report on the results. Two individuals, however, reported impressive results.

One was case 2178, a three-year-old girl who had accidentally thrust a can opener into her eye, leaving a metallic particle that was producing irritation. The reading found that the inflammation resulting from this puncture would eventually cause a coagulation of mucous membranes in the form of a cataract.

Cayce noted, however, that treatments suggested would probably dissipate the particle, thus avoiding the necessity of an operation. A follow-up report noted that Cayce's instructions did help to eliminate the possibility of a cataract forming in one eye. After only a few days of treatments, the condition of the eye had been improved.

Another individual, case 1861, a man in his mid-thirties who had been born blind, sought Cayce's help. Through treatments recommended in a series of readings, he was eventually able to see well enough to read with the use of heavy lenses.

Charcot-Marie-Tooth Disease

Charcot-Marie-Tooth disease is a rare disorder characterized by clubbing of the feet and progressive muscular atrophy. This disorder, which is due to cell degeneration of the lower part of the spinal column and the nerves governing locomotion, begins in the muscles supplied by the peroneal nerves on the outer sides of the legs and progresses slowly to involve the muscles of the hands and arms.

Symptoms usually begin before twenty years, but may be delayed until forty or fifty.

Only one person receiving a reading was specifically diagnosed by a physician as having Charcot-Marie-Tooth disease. This was case 1122, a twenty-year-old woman who had lost voluntary use of her left hand and was also beginning to drag her left leg. The condition was attributed to a fall while roller-skating at the age of fourteen. This accident had created pressures in the sacral and coccygeal areas, with reactions in other parts of the spine which were impeding proper nerve impulses to and from the brain and interfering with movement.

Treatment

Typical treatments for paralysis and muscular atrophy included spinal manipulation, massage with oils, electrotherapy, dietary changes, glandular stimulants, and positive attitudes and prayer. However, emphasis centered on spinal manipulation, which was to reestablish proper coordination between the sympathetic and cerebrospinal nervous systems. Also recommended were sinusoidal ray treatments. Additionally, positive suggestions for healing were to be given while the woman was falling asleep. Apparently this was to augment other metaphysical teachings in which the woman was involved.

Case History

Although there were no follow-up reports in case 1122, positive results have been attributed to Cayce's treatments in similar cases. One involved a seventy-five-year-old woman whose legs, at the time she requested a reading, had been paralyzed for sixteen months.

Specific instructions were given for making adjustments in the lumbar and sacral areas. A balanced diet and massage were also advised.

After six months of treatments, the woman completely regained the use of her limbs. Consequently, the doctor who had treated her was amazed at the recovery, especially in view of her age.

Chicken Pox

Chicken pox is a contagious disease caused by a virus; it is primarily contracted by young children. This disease is not generally dangerous and is characterized by symptoms such as a low-level fever and skin ulcers. As with several other common childhood diseases, contracting it once generally immunizes the victim's body against future exposures.

Edgar Cayce gave one six-year-old boy a reading for an acute case of chicken pox. He noted that the treatment measures being taken were appropriate, although they were not specified. The only suggestions made by Cayce were basically to maintain good eliminations and to ensure that the child did not catch cold. Therefore, the system was to be kept alkaline, and acid-forming foods were to be avoided.

There was no further report.

Child Training: Behavioral Problems

Parents frequently came to Edgar Cayce with questions about their children. Although the most frequently cited cause for consultation was irritability, the problems that prompted these requests were varied, ranging from disobedience to chronic lying.

Six children received one reading apiece dealing with behavioral problems, and a seventh reading was requested for children in general in response to requests on how to best teach and train young minds so that they might achieve their full potential.

The causes of these children's problems as cited by Cayce were varied. In seven cases, there was some degree of nervous imbalance, which generally involved a problem in the cerebrospinal nervous system. Two children suffered from glandular imbalances, and two had poor circulation. The problems in one case were almost completely attributed to karma, although the details of the child's karmic history were not given. Karma was also cited as a contributory factor in one other case.

When discussing the reasons for behavioral difficulties, Cayce frequently suggested alternative ways of viewing them and suggested that they be perceived as natural reactions to the given circumstances rather than as abnormal or dysfunctional conditions. For instance, while the behavior of 566, a six-year-old girl, was regarded as abnormal, the child was found to be simply reacting to "existing pressures" (emotional?) and "existent physical forces."

Cayce encouraged the parents of the children to try to see beyond the inconvenience of a behavioral problem and to view it as a necessary expression of forces operative in the child's development. Regarding the chronic lying of case 566, Cayce noted: "These [lies] to the body are *real;*

not as untruths. If the body is continued to be harassed by what seems to others as an untruth, it builds ... self-preservation, not understanding, and the body *will* become more and more stubborn, more and more feeling it is not understood, more and more feeling that it *must* exaggerate, it *must* expand, to be considered at *all* in the scheme of things!" (566-7).

Another instance concerned a child who was rebellious and forgetful. The parents were told that the reason most people forget is "something within themselves, all their inner consciousness, has rebelled, and they *prepare* to forget" (5022-1). In other words, Cayce viewed this type of behavior also as a direct response to the conditions surrounding the child and not just as a random phenomenon.

Treatment

In his discussions on how to deal with behavior problems, Cayce recommended a holistic approach which involved physical treatments as well as the emotional-mental-spiritual aspects of the situation. The most common physical treatment, recommended in four out of six cases, was a daily bath to relax the body and open the pores, followed by a daily spinal massage using cocoa butter, olive oil, or a mixture of peanut oil, olive oil, and lanolin.

A general description of the most frequently recommended massage procedure follows:

1. Apply a small amount of oil to the entire surface of the back. Then, starting on one side of the body with the hands perpendicular to the spine, push one hand forward across the back. As you pull that hand back toward you, start the other hand pushing forward, creating a simultaneous push-pull motion. Follow this procedure up and down one side of the spine and then move around to the other side.

2. Using the thumbs or fingertips, rub in small circles along *either side* of the length of the spine (not directly on the spine itself). Use a clockwise motion on the right side and a counterclockwise motion on the left. Work from the top of the spine to the base.

3. Finish the massage by standing at the child's head.

Place both hands, with fingers spread, on the shoulders at the top of the back. Then slide the hands down the length of the back to the top of the hips, letting your thumbs run along the sides of the spine. Use some pressure, as though you were squeezing something from the back.

In many instances, Cayce insisted that the parents perform the massages, as opposed to a nurse or physical therapist. The reason given for this was that the children's problems were not to be viewed as belonging solely to them, but also served as lessons and opportunities for parents and children to work together.

In one case, the parents were told that "[the conditions] are very much dependent upon the application of the wills of those about the entity, and the obligations as well as opportunities others have toward [the] entity. And those responsible . . . should parallel their experiences, showing those opportunities and those obligations with this entity. For, with such a paralleling, there will be a much greater comprehension of purposes, as come into the experiences of those who oft are inclined to pass off such disturbances as chance, or as conditions that are unavoidable" (2153-2).

Other physical treatments occasionally suggested were spinal manipulation, use of the Radio-Active Appliance, and use of castor oil packs. A California psychiatrist associated with the ARE noted "incredible" benefits from using castor oil packs on disturbed and handicapped patients. A study conducted by the ARE recommends using castor oil packs five times a week.

To help create a sense of inner harmony for the children, in four out of six cases Cayce advised the parents to give their children presleep suggestions. At times, he advised that this be done concurrently with a massage or a castor oil pack, as he believed that both of these treatments were conducive to relaxation and sleep.

Cayce explained the benefits of this procedure in the following way: "In that state when the body loses consciousness in sleep, the soul . . . may be impressed by suggestions that will be retroactive in the waking [state], or in the physical normal body. [The mind] becomes then retentive and will retain same as the ideas and ideals of every element of the body's activities" (5747-1).

The suggestions were to be given just as the child was falling asleep. The parents of one child were told to give the following affirmation as they prepared to conduct the suggestions: "Father God! In thy mercy and in thy love, be thou present with us now, as we seek to guide the body and mind of this, thy child, in becoming a better channel of service to thee at this time."

They were told to mention the name of the child and then the following suggestions: "Thy inner-self, thy subconscious self, thy superconscious self will react to the will of the Father-God; that ye may be a better channel for His service in the earth" (4058-1).

Since presleep suggestions can be effective, Cayce believed it was important that those giving the suggestions maintain a loving and positive attitude. Generally, parents were told to rephrase their suggestions and modify them to suit their individual needs. Cayce's use of presleep suggestions was not an attempt to directly influence behavior. They were only to serve as reminders to the inner being of its spiritual nature.

Additionally, the parents of one child were advised to record his dreams, although there was apparently no effort made to interpret them. This was simply to keep track of them during the course of treatment in order to detect changes in inner feelings and attitudes. Cayce warned that the parents should not let the child know that his dreams were being recorded, but he offered no explanation for this advice.

Cayce discussed parental attitudes in all of the readings on children's behavioral problems. Patience, gentleness, and understanding were advised. He recommended that the parents be sincere and willing to "meet" themselves in the situation and to consider the child's problem as if it were their own. To serve as inspiration, the parents were advised to read biblical passages such as Exodus 19:5 and

20; Deuteronomy 30; and the stories of Hannah and Elkanah.

Case History

Only one set of parents submitted a progress report, and it noted remarkable improvement in the child. Additional information on the effectiveness of Cayce's recommendations was obtained from the psychiatrist in California who noted considerable improvements from the use of castor oil packs. The ARE study, which involved a twenty-eight-day regimen of castor oil packs, spinal massage, and presleep suggestions, also noted favorable results. Though the reports varied greatly from one to another, all indicated improvements in the child's behavior.

General Recommendations for Parents

In the reading for parents in general, 5747-1, Cayce broadly outlined the attitudes and ideals which he felt should accompany the rearing of children. He emphasized the importance of aligning oneself as a parent in service to the "Great Teacher," and noted that preparations for parenthood should ideally begin before conception.

When asked for the best approach to the education of children, his response was, "First and foremost teach, train and *impress* the developing mind that it is expected to be in accord with that inner self that seeks expression in the relationship with its Maker, and when one trains a mind, a child, in the way it shall go, when it is old, it will not depart from same."

Further, Cayce's advice for stimulating a child's curiosity and interest was to take a holistic approach, using creative suggestion rather than compulsion.

Cayce advised using nature as a tool for teaching children about God: "the grasses, the flowers, the birds," were an "expression of the Creative Energies in its activity."

Cayce held that the most important aspect of learning for a child was the development of the "imaginative forces, rather than the material or objective." The readings warned against segregating children according to their respective educational and spiritual development. Cayce cautioned that to group children with this consideration would hinder their progress and result in combativeness.

Among the universal advice found in the readings concerning being a parent is the following quotation: " 'Unless ye become as little children, ye shall not enter the kingdom of heaven.' Be able then, of thine own consecration, to be one *with* them in their problems, for in the tot that has just begun to think *their* problems, to them are as great as thine own, yet how easily are they forgotten—as yours should be! Train in the way as a child, and when old, they will not depart from laying troubles aside."

Chorea

The term "chorea" is derived from the Greek *"choreia,"* which means "dancing," and accordingly the condition is characterized by involuntary muscular twitching and spasms of limbs or facial muscles. Appropriately, Sydenham's chorea has been tagged St. Vitus' dance. There are other types of chorea as well, such as Huntington's.

Edgar Cayce gave a total of five readings for three young males with chorea. Various effects were noted, such as poor appetite, impaired vision, tension, brittle teeth, and nervous strain.

In the case of 1225, Cayce attributed a poor diet lacking in vital nutrients as the cause of the condition. A specific lack of calcium in the diet was noted. This deficiency in calcium, which is critical to nerve and muscle function, produced an imbalance in nervous and muscular coordination, which in turn contributed to an overall glandular disturbance.

The other two cases of chorea, 2780 and 5428, were attributed to injury and trauma sustained at birth in the lumbosacral area of the spine, which triggered an incoordination in the sympathetic nervous system and subsequently in the glands. These individuals, age nine and four, respectively, were noticeably underdeveloped for their ages and exhibited unnatural nervousness and tension.

Treatment

Treatment for case 1225, a young man of eighteen, required a total restructuring of diet toward more alkaline-reacting foods. Sweets could be taken in a more natural form, such as the cocoa bean, but cane sugar products were to be avoided. A general cleansing of the circulation by means of an herbal tonic administered four times daily and teaspoons of milk of magnesia twice daily was advised. The young man was also advised to get plenty of sun and fresh air. Additionally, placement of the electric vibrator over the back and along the spine was also suggested.

For the two other cases, 2780 and 5428, Cayce recommended osteopathic manipulations to help correct spinal misalignments, coordinating the lumbosacral area with the cervical. The manipulations were to be administered two or three times a week in the first case, for a series of three to four weeks. In the case of 5428, a four-year-old child, the treatment was to begin gradually in view of his age, working up to once weekly. Applications of the Radio-Active Appliance for one hour daily were also suggested for the four-year-old, as well as hot baths to promote relaxation. Cycles of doses of mayblossom bitters in water, beginning with two drops daily for five days, then three drops for five days, were also recommended.

After following Cayce's advice, cases 1225 and 2780 reported a complete cure. The four-year-old, case 5428, died shortly after surgery.

Cirrhosis

Cirrhosis is a chronic, progressive disease of the liver characterized by atrophy of the cells and an increase of connective tissue.

Edgar Cayce gave six readings for a total of five individuals with this disorder. Most or all of them were in their fifties and sixties.

A common cause of cirrhosis, cited by Cayce in all of the cases, was poor eliminations, a condition which, in some instances, had deteriorated into incoordination between all of the organs of elimination. Anemia was an accompanying symptom in three cases, and toxemia was mentioned twice. The other symptoms and related problems varied from case to case.

Treatment

Cayce's treatments for cirrhosis took two distinct forms. Three readings recommended basically similar methods of improving the eliminations and stimulating the liver, centering on the use of castor oil packs, doses of olive oil, colonics or enemas, and proper diet. In two cases, spinal manipulation was also advised. Accompanying treatments varied.

For two individuals, the entire treatment consisted of internal doses of two herbal preparations, which differed in each case. The formula in one was an herbal tonic similar to that suggested in the "spring tonic" reading (5450-3) and a version of clary water. The other reading gave a different herbal-tonic formula and also suggested a laxative formula containing senna, cascara sagrada, licorice compound, and yellow saffron.

Case History

Case 1648, a fifty-eight-year-old woman, requested a reading due to several physical disturbances. Her liver disorder was accompanied by incoordination of eliminations, toxemia, uricademia, dermatitis, shortness of breath, intestinal mucus, puffy eyes, insomnia, and headaches. Cayce viewed all the symptoms as being related to or the result of cirrhosis. Her condition was attributed mainly to the aftereffects of flu, which through fever had affected the upper hepatic circulation, creating a tendency for hardening or spots on the right lobe.

Cayce recommended nightly massages, extending from the lower ribs to the groin area and using a combination of equal parts of mutton tallow, spirits of turpentine, and spirits of camphor. Additionally, he recommended castor oil packs two evenings a week, upon retiring, for about two weeks. These were to remain on the body for at least an hour or two each time.

After the third of fourth pack had been applied, the woman was to take two tablespoons of olive oil. Two days later, osteopathic manipulations were to begin, focusing on the upper dorsal and cervical areas. These treatments were to be administered either two days apart or twice a week. Abdominal massages, to help drain the colon, were also suggested at these times. Following three treatments, a colonic irrigation was to be administered. This was to be followed by a rest period of two weeks, and then the entire sequence of treatments was to be repeated, this time adjusting the lumbar and sacral areas as well as those already indicated.

Dietary suggestions were also made, and emphasis was placed on fruits and fresh and raw vegetables. Fried foods, large amounts of starches, and meats were to be avoided. Nuts for protein were to be added to the diet later. To counteract insomnia problems attributed to nerve conditions, Cayce recommended the Radio-Active Appliance.

A few days after her reading, the woman reported that Cayce had described her symptoms perfectly and that she was beginning the treatments suggested. A few weeks later, she wrote, saying she was halfway through the treatments and already felt like a new person.

No further reports were received.

Colds

A cold is an infection of the upper respiratory tract caused by a virus which often follows exposure to cold temperatures, dampness, or drafts.

Cayce dealt with the common cold in 279 readings, given for 152 individuals who ranged from six weeks to seventy-four years old. He described numerous causes and associated symptoms and suggested a wide variety of treatments. Although his prescriptions were quite individualized, a number of recommendations were repeated so frequently that together they constitute a generalized approach to treatment.

Primary causes in 138 cases were infection, congestion, and/or inflammation. Generally, the congestion developed in the mucous membranes of the face, head, throat, bronchial tubes, and lungs, resulting in difficulty in breathing, headache, watery eyes, and sore throat. Readings in eighteen cases mentioned additional sites of congestion, including the lymph and blood, the nerve plexes, and the digestive system.

Cited as a direct cause in eighteen cases was poor eliminations. This condition would lead to a buildup of toxins in the system, predisposing the body toward overacidity, slowed circulation, and congestion. A contributing factor in inadequate eliminations was poor circulation, mentioned in fifty-nine cases. Poor circulation was also evident in poor assimilations, mentioned in thirty-seven cases.

In forty-five cases, Cayce noted overtaxation of the nerves and the entire body, which would lead to a state of low resistance or general debilitation. Spinal subluxations and lesions were involved in twenty-seven cases, and nervous incoordination, which often coincided closely with spinal problems, was cited in twenty-three instances.

In sixteen cases, dietary imbalances were found to be a major cause of colds. Improper food combinations, too many sweets and starches, and too much meat contributed to an overacid condition in the body. Overacidity was mentioned as an important contributing factor in thirty-five cases involving colds.

Noted in fifteen cases were negative attitudes and emotions, an interesting statistic inasmuch as Cayce found

climate and cold temperatures and drafts responsible for
colds in a total of sixteen cases. Other factors contributing
to colds that were mentioned by Cayce were glandular
incoordination, twelve cases; pre- or postnatal factors,
three cases; injuries in later life, twelve cases; blood and
lymph disorders, nine cases; toxins and bacilli, four cases
each; and smoking stress, poor resistance, and damp feet,
two cases.

Treatment

Dietary changes were suggested as treatment in 115
cases, with the focus being on developing a diet as
alkaline-forming as possible. While meat juices were often
suggested as blood and body builders, meat was to be
avoided, although small amounts of fish, fowl, wild game,
or mutton were permitted. Citrus fruits and juices, whole
wheat toast, cereal, and milk (avoiding citrus and cereal or
milk combinations) were often to be included as part of
breakfast. Leafy green and other raw vegetables such as
carrots, celery, and parsley were especially advised for
noon meals. Regarded highly as blood purifiers were
vegetables such as lettuce, celery, and kale.

Eggnog with spirits of frumenty and red wine with dark
bread were at times suggested for midafternoon snacks.
Cooked vegetables were often to be a major portion of the
evening meal.

Cayce's formula for those especially ill or for those who
wanted to recover rapidly was small meals eaten often,
with a concentration on liquids or semiliquids. Fruits and
juices, beef juice and other meat broths, malted milk,
eggnog, gruels, groups, soft-boiled eggs, and hot lemon-
ade all fell into the semiliquid diet.

To be avoided during recovery from colds were fried
foods, meat fats, combinations of two different starches,
citrus and cereal combinations, sodium benzoate (a
preservative), large amounts of starches, heavy meals,
and, for some, all sweets except honey and natural fruit.

Coffee and tea were usually permitted in small amounts, as were some desserts such as ice cream.

Cayce considered drinking large amounts of pure water an important method of purifying and cleansing the system. To assist the digestive process, Cayce recommended that all foods be thoroughly masticated before swallowing. Finally, a positive attitude, the natural companion of a good meal, was considered a must. Cayce stated on several occasions that it was better not to eat at all than to eat when angry or upset, when extremely tired, or when rushed.

It is evident that controlling the type and quantity of food eaten was part of Cayce's plan to help clear the alimentary canal, making it easier for the body's normal excretory forces to remove accumulated toxins and wastes. Additional treatments were intended to keep the eliminations moving, relieve muscle tension, and assist such processes as digestion, respiration, and expectoration of mucus, so that the body could fully mobilize its capacity for healing.

Another major treatment, mentioned in ninety-two cases, involved massages and rubs on various parts of the body, using a number of different substances to lubricate the skin and benefit the deeper tissues. The preparation most frequently advised to relieve congestion was a combination of equal parts mutton tallow, spirits of turpentine, and spirits of camphor. Other massage compounds included substances such as camphorated oil, musterole, tincture of myrrh and olive oil, cocoa butter, grain alcohol (in cases of high fever), compound tincture of benzoin, peanut oil, kerosene, witch hazel, and pine oil.

Receiving high priority on the treatment list were aids to elimination, which were mentioned in ninety-one cases. Keeping the eliminations open would facilitate cleansing the system so that congestion could be more effectively reduced. Methods recommended were both internal (laxatives) and external (colonics, enemas) or both. Generally Glyco-Thymoline was to be added to the water used for colonics and enemas. Most frequently recommended as an internal laxative was Fletcher's Castoria. Often prescribed were doses of about half a teaspoon every hour (for an adult), sometimes until the whole bottle had been taken. Other types of laxatives suggested included Syrup of Figs, milk of magnesia, milk of bismuth, and Simmon's Liver Regulator, a ragweed-based product. At least one person was advised to avoid using the same laxative repeatedly.

The two next most common treatments—each recommended in eighty instances—were spinal manipulation and tonics and other similar miscellaneous prescriptions (not including digestive aids).

The adjustments were basically intended to relax the body and relieve areas of tension so that the circulation and eliminations could function more freely and congestion could be more quickly relieved. Some were advised to begin their adjustments gently for the first two to four treatments, with a deeper series following a short rest period. The frequency of treatments suggested varied from two or three times monthly to as often as three to even five times weekly, for limited periods of time.

Generally to strengthen the body and aid its natural healing process, tonics and other internal prescriptions were suggested. The most popular prescription, which was recommended in twenty cases, was some type of cough syrup or expectorant formula. To relieve one individual's chest congestion, Cayce advised a formula consisting of honey, water, grain alcohol, syrup of wild cherry bark, syrup of horehound, syrup of rhubarb, and elixir of wild ginger. To relieve another case of sore throat, Cayce suggested a combination of water, honey, apple brandy, syrup of horehound, syrup of ipecac, and chloroform.

A formula prescribed to aid the alimentary canal as well as soothe the mucous membranes of the throat and head consisted of distilled water, wild ginseng root, dried Indian turnip, elder flowers, yellow dock root with beet sugar dissolved in water, tincture of stillingia, tincture of capsicum, and grain alcohol.

For a rough throat and fever in another case, the tonic

suggested consisted of simple syrup, syrup of horehound, syrup of ipecac, syrup of senna, and apple brandy.

Calcidin, a calcium-and-iodine supplement, was recommended for thirteen individuals; olive oil was to be taken internally in eleven cases; and aspirin was recommended in just nine cases. Less orthodox suggestions included juice from steamed onions, Syrup of Squill, Calcios, and quinine preparations.

Additionally, Cayce recommended the application of various packs for forty-seven individuals. Generally, the pack was to consist of three to four folds of cloth saturated with desired ingredients, although there were a few readings which called for different procedures.

Packs were typically to be applied for specific periods of time, which ranged from half an hour to overnight, depending on both the type of pack and individual needs. At times, a heating pad was required to keep a pack, such as castor oil, warm; at other times, as with grape packs, the material was applied at room temperature and was to be removed after a specific period of time.

There was no particular pack favored among the readings on colds. Castor oil packs over the abdomen (followed by a baking-soda-water rinse) were advised for eight individuals. Antiphlogistic (inflammation reducing) packs and decongestant packs using mutton tallow, spirits of turpentine, and spirits of camphor were each suggested in seven cases. Packs of chopped onion and yellow cornmeal were recommended for six individuals and Glyco-Thymoline for five.

Packs of hot salt and Epsom salts were each advised in four cases. Other pack ingredients occasionally mentioned included mustard or musterole, Ben-Gay, ice, and Atomidine. Sites of application depended on both the individual needs and the type of pack suggested and included the face and throat, the abdomen, and the base of the spine.

Electrotherapy or heliotherapy, hydrotherapy, and digestive aids were each suggested for forty-three individuals. Heliotherapy treatments, suggested in over half of these cases, included the ultraviolet light, the infrared light, or sun lamp applied for brief periods. Electrotherapeutic devices included the Radio-Active Appliance, the Wet Cell, and electric vibrator treatments. In some cases, more than one type of electrotherapy was suggested.

Hydrotherapy was a general term applied to several types of treatment involving water. Hot-water baths were advised in twelve cases, sweats in eleven, and hot mustard-water baths, foot soaks, and sponge baths in eleven others. Five individuals were advised to "bathe" themselves in various kinds of fumes, such as those from witch hazel. Sitz baths, "dry" baths of warm air, and cold-water baths (to reduce fever), were also occasionally recommended. This type of treatment was intended to increase the circulation and help cleanse the system by increasing eliminations through the pores of the skin.

The various digestive aids suggested were basically intended to help the overtaxed intestinal tract digest foods and assimilate nutrients. Many of these substances were alkalizers as well, helping the system to become sufficiently alkaline so that cold germs could no longer flourish in the system. The digestive aids which received the most recommendations were baking soda in water (twelve cases), citrocarbonate (nine cases), and saffron tea (seven cases). Other substances occasionally advised for this purpose included elm water and pepsin-containing preparations.

To help ease breathing and relieve other cold symptoms, thirty-one individuals were advised to use various types of topical preparations. Among those suggested were Ben-Gay, cocoa butter, and Coco-Quinine, and the mutton tallow, turpentine, and spirits of camphor combination. Eight individuals were advised to gargle with antiseptic solutions such as Glyco-Thymoline alternated with Listerine; four to apply Ichthyol or Mono-Ichthyolate over congested portions of the face; and two to apply a few drops of olive oil in aching ears.

To help relieve breathing difficulties associated with nasal or bronchial inflammation, Cayce recommended various inhalation therapies in twenty-eight cases. The inhalant solutions were typically based on pure (not rubbing) alcohol, to which small amounts of expectorants were added, such as eucalyptol, benzoin, balsam of tolu, rectified creosote, rectified oil of turpentine, and Canadian balsam. Instructions were to keep these solutions in a dark glass container and to inhale the fumes with a breathing tube. Another method was to add the solution to very hot water and to inhale the fumes this way. Sprays made from inhalant solutions also received occasional mention, as did the use of vaporizers.

When substances such as narcotic pain killers or dangerous drugs like strychnine and chloroform were recommended, the subjects were advised to have treatment under a doctor's supervision. Eighteen individuals received this recommendation. Basically, medical supervision was advised whenever conditions were sufficiently serious or specialized treatments were necessary.

Among the other treatments recommended by Cayce for cold sufferers were rest of body and mind, in forty-seven cases; light exercises in seventeen cases; and keeping the body, especially the feet, warm was advised in twenty-three cases. Sixteen individuals were advised to keep the feet dry.

Additionally, seven individuals were urged to spend more time outdoors, three to avoid night air or cold air, and three to avoid crowds. Two individuals were advised to move to a higher altitude, two to have a change of scenery or climate, and two to spend more time in the sunshine. Moderate smoking was allowed in two cases, and deep breathing encouraged in another.

Seventeen individuals were advised to maintain or change to a more constructive attitude, and another was told to pray and study. Cayce's practical spirituality was evident in his advice to one person to "keep an equal balance between thought and physical acts" (826-7), and to another to "be good, and be good for something" (1683-10).

Case History

Only seventy of those receiving readings for colds reported on the results. Of these, fifty-six noted an improvement in their condition, while another ten did not follow Cayce's advice and two had either neutral or negative results.

Among those who noted an improvement in their condition upon following Cayce's advice was case 759, a young boy who received four readings concerning colds while he was between one and fourteen years. Among his symptoms were sinus congestion, sore throat, and swollen glands. Poor eliminations were apparently the main cause of the colds each time Cayce was consulted.

The first reading, given when the child was one year old, noted that teething and a liver condition were partially responsible for the cold. At this time, it was suggested that osteopathic adjustments be administered to increase eliminations through the alimentary canal. To help relieve congestion, doses of Syrup of Squill and an antiphlogistine or a hot onion poultice were suggested. Also prescribed were a few drops of Castoria to be taken a half hour apart. It was reported that these instructions were followed with positive results.

The second reading, given when the boy was one and a half years, attributed his cold to atmospheric conditions created by a change in climate and to incomplete manipulations of the spine previously. Suggested at this time were more adjustments of the cervical and upper dorsal and Syrup of Squill. Milk of magnesia was also to be given to help cleanse the system and increase eliminations. To help lower his temperature, an ice pack was to be applied.

The third reading, given two months later, attributed the congestion and infection in the system to stress and incomplete adjustments during the previous treatment. Once again, Syrup of Squill was recommended, along with a narcotic pain-relieving medication, which was prescribed by a physician. This was to help the body rest and recuperate more rapidly.

The fourth reading, which was given when the boy was fourteen years, recommended two doses of Simmon's Liver Regulator to improve eliminations, a colonic or enema to further flush the colon, and massages to further stimulate the eliminations. Bed rest was strongly recommended following the piercing of the tonsils, which was done to relieve pressure due to pus and high temperature and infection. A liquid or semiliquid diet was strongly suggested. This was to be followed by a normally balanced diet when the congestion and cold were relieved. Kaldak was recommended as a dietary supplement.

For painful throat glands, Cayce advised massaging the area each evening with a combination of equal parts mutton tallow, spirits of turpentine, and spirits of camphor. At bedtime, a cloth or piece of gauze was to be soaked with this same mixture and placed around the throat and then covered with a dry cloth.

A report received six weeks later indicated that the boy's condition had improved.

Colic

Colic, or abdominal pain, is usually found in infants under three months old. Typical symptoms are regular bouts of extended crying, most often in the evening; abdominal distention; and large amounts of flatulence or gas. Emotional as well as physical factors are suspected in this discomfort.

Edgar Cayce gave a total of twenty-three readings for sixteen children with colic. They ranged in age from six days to eighteen months, though the majority were three months old or younger. The most frequent cause of colic found in these cases was poor assimilation due to an improper diet. There were both breast-fed and bottle-fed babies in this group.

Often the problem was simply that the food provided did not supply the necessary nutrients. In the case of the breast-fed baby, the mother's diet was at fault. Another problem cited was the combination of certain foods which reacted adversely together, such as orange juice and milk, which can cause indigestion and inflammation of the intestinal tract.

Another important thought in the readings on colic was that the emotional climate at mealtimes greatly affected the body's ability to assimilate foods. Cayce noted that this was true for adults as well as children.

According to Cayce, improper diet usually resulted in poor elimination, which would in turn trigger an imbalance between the digestive and excretory systems, often resulting in a buildup of waste products in the system. Toxins would be produced, causing inflammation of the colon and, on occasion, skin rashes.

In a third of the readings, various infections in the systems contributed to the condition. Examples were colds and congestion, which were said to cause an imbalance in the digestive system which later developed into colic.

Treatment

Most of the treatments suggested were somewhat similar. Diets consisting of easily assimilated foods were advised for each infant. Mothers who were breast-feeding their babies were advised to eliminate gas-producing foods, such as cabbage, and heavy spices from their diets. Of course, for these mothers a well-balanced diet was regarded as a necessity.

The formula prescribed for bottle-fed babies was Carnation milk (presumably canned). Until these babies were at least five or six months old, orange juice was to be avoided. Oatmeal and carrots were foods mentioned as being easily digestible in one case. Sources of certain vitamins and minerals, which varied from case to case, were often suggested.

In all but two instances, some type of mild internal medication was prescribed. The most frequently recommended was one or two drops of Glyco-Thymoline in water. This was to help balance the activities of the colon and alkalize the system. Castoria was also frequently suggested and was to be taken in minute doses during the course of the day to aid the digestive system and gently assist the eliminations. In nine cases, limewater, a mild antacid, was to be added in small doses to the baby's formula. Occasionally, cinnamon water and other digestive aids were to be added as well. Yellow saffron tea was also recommended for the digestion in the small number of cases where skin rashes were a factor.

For seven babies, massages were recommended to help relax the body and equalize the circulation. The substances most typically used in the rubs were cocoa butter and camphorated olive oil (used separately). These were to be gently massaged along the spine and over the diaphragm and shoulders. In cases where a skin rash was involved, Cayce suggested a variety of soothing applications, including oint-ments and body powder containing zinc and balsam.

As in many other disorders, Cayce stressed the importance of maintaining positive attitudes and emotions when caring for young children; he believed that when the emotions of the parents were positive, the treatments would have a beneficial effect upon the child.

Follow-up reports indicated that more than half of the readings were followed by the parents, who noted a great deal of improvement in the condition of their children.

Case history

Case 928 was a three-week-old baby girl suffering from colic. Her reading attributed the disorder to an incoordination between assimilation and elimination, which resulted in a shortage of enzymes needed for digestion.

The first treatment recommended a teaspoon of limewater diluted in water following each nursing. In addition, half a drop of Glyco-Thymoline, also diluted, was to be given once daily following a feeding. Castoria was also recommended in minute doses.

Additionally, once or twice daily spinal massage with cocoa butter was suggested. The abdomen was to be kept warm using a band of flannel covered with a combination of equal parts mutton suet and sweet oil (olive oil).

It was later noted that the parents followed the reading and the colic disappeared.

Colitis: General

Colitis is an inflammation of the colon during which the body loses its ability to assimilate foods properly. Diarrhea forces food through the intestines so rapidly that there is no time for digestion to occur, and the body becomes weak and depleted.

Six individuals, ranging in age from one month to sixty-five years, each received one reading dealing with colitis. In four of the cases, congestion of the intestinal tract, twice referred to as intestinal flu, was found to be the first cause. The body would become feverish and the colon congested and inflamed. The resulting strain and irritation of the intestinal tract would hinder the processes of both assimilation and elimination and cause colitis to develop.

Other first causes, each mentioned once, were an injury to the stomach and liver area which produced an excess of mucus throughout the alimentary canal, and spinal subluxations which caused nervous incoordination and hindered the assimilations. A depleted blood supply was involved in three cases, and spinal problems which affected the nerves in two.

Treatment

Edgar Cayce's treatments for colitis were fairly consistent, and in each case dietary restrictions were an important part of the treatment. The parents of the two children who received readings for colitis were advised to underfeed them for a while to ease the strain on the intestines and to promote cleansing.

Other guidelines for diet included foods which were body building, such as fruits, fruit juices and vegetables, and small amounts of lighter meats, and beef juice taken as a medicine.

In five cases, spinal manipulations were advised, and to stimulate the organs of elimination, the adjustments were generally to be made along the entire cerebrospinal system. Based on Cayce's information on the causes of colitis, the eighth and ninth dorsal vertebrae would probably merit special attention.

To help normalize the intestinal tract, herbal tonics were advised in three cases. Ginseng was an ingredient in each of the preparations. Other digestive aids were occasionally suggested as well.

Additionally, packs, massages, and eliminants were mentioned three times. Recommended in two cases was a grape poultice, which was prepared by placing a thick layer of crushed Concord grapes on a layer of gauze and placing it over the abdomen for several hours. A Glyco-Thymoline pack over the abdomen was suggested in a third case.

The massages were to be administered along the spine in two cases and over the abdomen in the third. Substances recommended included olive oil and peanut oil. The massages were designed to relax the body and help the system recover its vitality. The aids to elimination frequently took the form of enemas or colonics and were intended to help cleanse the colon of congestion and irritants.

Case History

A typical reading involved a fifty-year-old woman who received one reading for colitis. Cayce attributed her condition to intestinal flu, which had infected the lymph circulation throughout the alimentary canal. Further, her colon and lower portion of the jejunum were inflamed, causing her temperature to rise at times. Anemia further debilitated the body.

Cayce's first recommendation for case 5057 was an herbal tonic consisting of a fusion of wild ginseng, fusion of wild ginger, lactated pepsin, and grain alcohol. This preparation was to be taken ten days on and five days off until all the preparation had been taken.

A poultice of crushed grapes was to be applied over the entire abdomen at least once a week. The grapes were to be placed over gauze in a layer one-inch thick and allowed to remain until dry (about four hours).

When cramping was felt through the alimentary canal and colon, a tonic consisting of alum root, simple syrup, and grain alcohol or rye whiskey was to be taken. Two or three days after the tonic, a colonic was recommended.

The woman was advised to avoid consuming large amounts of starches. Recommended were small amounts of seafood, freshwater fish, fowl, and lamb, along with a few tuberous vegetables. Osteopathic adjustments were to be administered in a manner conducive to relaxation.

The woman followed her reading and it is uncertain whether the reading was effective. However, the treatments suggested were used with success by four individuals who reported good results. Additionally, it is reported that the advice in this particular reading had been followed by other individuals who noted great improvement in their conditions.

Colitis: Ulcerative

Ulcerative colitis is an inflamed condition of unknown causes characterized by bloody diarrhea with lower abdominal cramps, fever, and weight loss. Constipation, however, may occur instead of diarrhea. Ulcerative colitis has a tendency for remission or exacerbation.

Cayce gave eight individuals one reading each for ulcerative colitis and related conditions. They ranged in age from twenty to sixty years. He generally attributed the colitis to an overactive lymph circulation, which would create an excess of mucus in the intestinal tract, causing irritation and inflammation. In one-half of the cases, intestinal flu was cited as the cause of this condition. Poor elimination was more often an effect than a cause of the colitis, and frequently the stomach would be so upset that very few nutrients could be assimilated from the diet.

Spinal subluxations and nervous imbalances contributed further to the upsetting conditions in two cases each.

Treatment

Cayce's treatments for colitis were quite consistent. Recommended in each case were varied versions of a special type of herbal tonic which was designed to stimulate the organs of assimilation. The most typical prescription was a combination of wild ginseng, wild ginger, and elixir of lactated pepsin, with stillingia at times an added ingredient.

Dietary changes which would assist healing were advised for seven individuals. Generally, the readings emphasized alkaline-forming foods which could be easily assimilated, such as meat juices, raw vegetables, fruits, and at times special preparations such as malted milk, junket, and arrowroot. Sweets, fats, and most starches and red meats were at least temporarily banned because of their acid-forming qualities.

In three cases, spinal manipulations were advised to stimulate the excretory and circulatory systems and relax the body. Corrections generally focused on the midspine area. Eliminants such as colonics were suggested in three cases to cleanse the intestinal tract of mucus and toxins. Neuropathic massages, in one case using olive oil and myrrh, were suggested twice.

Case history

Four of those receiving readings on colitis followed the treatments and reported on the results, with three noting definite improvements.

One of those reporting improvements was case 5215, a fifty-one-year-old woman who received one reading for chronic colitis. According to Cayce, intestinal flu had created a disturbance in her alimentary canal which led to improper eliminations throughout the system. This condition caused the colon to become inflamed, and colitis resulted. Poor elimination also resulted in neuritic and arthritic conditions in the extremities.

Cayce's first treatment involved the use of an herbal tonic to aid in soothing the intestinal system. This consisted of a fusion of wild ginseng and wild ginger to which elixir of lactated pepsin and alcohol were added.

Additionally, a series of sixteen to twenty-four osteopathic manipulations was recommended. The adjustments were to be administered in a relaxing manner, making corrections through the lumbar and sacral areas and coordinating the sixth dorsal vertebra with the brachial and the cervical centers.

Her diet was to consist of foods that were alkaline and easily digested, with a minimum of sweets. Vinegar was to be especially avoided due to its acidic quality.

To further aid eliminations, Cayce suggested colonics containing water, salt, and soda initially and then Glyco-Thymoline in the rinse as an intestinal antiseptic.

She noted improvements after one month of treatment.

Colon: Impaction

An impaction of the colon is characterized by a buildup of waste in the intestinal tract, which can lead to more serious disorders such as diverticulitis and general systemic toxicity.

A total of forty-two readings dealing with colon impactions were given for thirty individuals, ranging from six to seventy-five years. The primary cause of this disorder, mentioned in a majority of cases, was poor elimination, which resulted in a buildup of waste in the colon, causing congestion and toxicity. In fifty percent of the cases, improper circulation in the intestinal area was a contributing factor which weakened the colon and led to a further slowing of the eliminations and an increased buildup of toxins.

Another causative factor mentioned in thirty percent of the cases was spinal subluxations and/or incoordination between the sympathetic and cerebrospinal nervous systems. This was, at times, attributed to prolonged stressful emotions such as nervousness and worry. With almost the same frequency, the toxic buildup was attributed to poor assimilations, brought on by improper eating habits.

Glandular problems were involved in twenty percent of the cases; other contributing factors occasionally mentioned included intestinal flu and other infections, spinal misalignments, poor attitudes, and overtaxation of the entire system.

Treatment

The treatment recommended in eighty percent of the cases was the gentle stimulation of the eliminations to relieve the immediate distress. Also recommended almost as frequently were cathartics as well as colonics and enemas. Both methods were often included as part of overall treatments. The cathartics frequently suggested included Castoria, ragweed-based preparations, olive oil, and saline laxatives. In some instances, vegetable- and mineral-based laxatives were to be used alternately.

In seventy-five percent of the cases, dietary changes and precautions were advised. The typical diet was to be primarily composed of alkaline-reacting, easily assimilated foods. Liquids and semiliquids were frequently advised until the intestinal distress had been alleviated. Also offered were suggestions concerning drinking large amounts of water and warnings against overeating.

In over fifty percent of the cases, manipulations of the spine were recommended, with advice to give special attention to the mid- to lower spine or the dorsal and lumbar areas.

Also suggested frequently were abdominal packs to help relieve lower bowel tension. Those most often suggested were castor oil and/or Epsom salts, in order of frequency.

In thirty percent of the cases, massages were recommended, using a variety of substances. These included cocoa butter, a combination of peanut oil, olive oil, and lanolin, and a combination of pine oil and wintergreen oil. At times the massages were to focus especially on the abdominal muscles.

Hydrotherapy was suggested in over twenty percent of the cases, with sweats and fume baths most frequently mentioned. In the three cases where the pain was acute, Cayce suggested the application of a combination of laudanum and aconite tinctures over the abdomen until the other treatment measures had time to act. Additionally, electrotherapy was advised in four cases, rest in three, and the use of Calcidin and herbal tonics in two.

Case History

There was no information received on the outcome of Cayce's treatment in over half of the cases. However, twelve of the thirteen individuals who did report noted positive results.

One of these cases involved a forty-eight-year-old man, case 644, who complained of a number of symptoms, including shortness of breath, abdominal pain, pain in the heart area radiating down his arm, and soreness in his face, head, and throat.

Cayce found this man's major problem to be poor eliminations due to impingements upon the cerebrospinal system at the eighth and ninth dorsal plexes. This impingement caused an unequal blood supply to the upper and lower portions of the body. The slower impulse in the lower body led to impactions in the cecum, the transverse colon, and the ascending colon. This, in turn, created an acute condition in the activity of the liver ducts and even slower circulation and poor elimination through the alimentary canal. Additionally, the spinal pressures caused slowed digestion and a feeling of fullness in the stomach, regardless of the food intake.

Cayce's treatment began with the man taking a small amount of olive oil (one-quarter to one-half teaspoon) every two hours for three days. The oil was intended to act as a lubricant for the intestines as well as food for the gastric juices. Following the first three-day cycle, castor oil packs were to be applied over the cecum and liver area for three to four hours each day for three or four days. This treatment was intended to reduce inflammation and help the system heal itself.

To help increase the flow of lymph and stimulate the

eliminations without producing irritation to the cecum and the other ducts and glands, Cayce recommended that the man take Simmon's Liver Regulator. After taking this preparation three or four times daily for two or three days, a high enema was to be administered.

In order to relieve pressures on the face, head, and throat, Cayce advised a series of three to six osteopathic adjustments in the dorsal area to be coordinated with the cervical area. During this time, a diet of semiliquid foods that were alkaline reacting was recommended along with another cycle of doses of olive oil. This was to be taken for two or three days, discontinued for two or three days, and then repeated. The reading noted that it would be beneficial to continue this type of olive oil cycle indefinitely.

A report of the man's condition stated that he had "followed his reading and received 100% results... [as] symptoms disappeared just as predicted."

Color Blindness

Color blindness is the inability to detect or differentiate between all or some of the seven primary colors.

There was only one individual seeking help for color blindness in the readings, and these three readings were given for case 820, a twenty-five-year-old man who experienced an unspecified version of color blindness since birth. Although Edgar Cayce attributed this defect largely to karmic factors, several physiological deficiencies were also involved.

Cayce believed the inability to distinguish colors to be a "deflection" in nerve impulses from the vagus nerve, located in the second, third, and fourth dorsal vertebrae, to the optic nerve, located in the cervical vertebrae, which controls the circulation around the eyes. This "deflection" created a buildup of toxins in the eyes which, along with the continued use of the eye muscles, was overtaxing the entire sensory system.

As Cayce explained, the color blindness was "the effect

from the lack of the flow of blood and nerve energy from those basic nerve ends that emanate from the cerebrospinal and sympathetic system in the upper dorsal and cervical area'' (820-2). As a result of the impeded circulation, irritation and swelling had occurred in the lids and portions of the eyeball, affecting what was actually seen in the retina, or ''the character of that which is reflected in the lens, iris, and in the response to the optic center itself'' (820-2).

Treatment

The treatment involved two to three osteopathic adjustments each week for two to three weeks for correction of first the dorsal vertebrae and then the first and second cervicals. To stimulate the nerves, application of the Violet Ray to both areas of the spine was to follow each adjustment. The Wet Cell with gold was to begin at regular (unspecified) intervals during the rest period from the former treatments. The copper plate was to be placed at the fourth dorsal and the nickel plate between the first and second cervical vertebrae. Treatment with the Wet Cell was designed to help make corrections between the cervical area and the brain centers and to strengthen other nerve impulses to the head and neck as well. Treatments were to be given in cycles of two to three weeks, alternated with three weeks, until improvements were noted.

Cayce also recommended a diet rich in citrus fruits, green and raw vegetables, and whole wheat bread. Few meats and potatoes were allowed, although potato peelings could be eaten. Bananas and raw apples were discouraged.

There are no follow-up reports for 820.

Complexion Problems

Edgar Cayce gave helpful comments on care of the complexion for at least fifty individuals. These comments mainly concerned existing skin problems, prevention of future problems, and the best soaps, lotions, etc., to use.

The general philosophy of the readings regarding cosmetology was that the condition of the skin was a reflection of internal health. This applied to all aspects, including color, texture of skin—dry or oily—and facial blemishes. Treatments for problem skin would therefore often be directed internally, although external measures were frequently suggested as well.

Of paramount importance in general skin care was a well-balanced diet and strongly emphasized was an alkaline, easily digested diet consisting of fruit and fruit juices (cooked apples, orange or lemon juice) and vegetables (carrots, squash). Many of the foods mentioned were yellow, a source of the B vitamins that Cayce found so beneficial for the skin. Fish and fowl were suggested in place of red meats and whole grains in place of white-flour products. Sugar and fried foods were to be strictly avoided.

Eating two or three almonds a day was said to have benefits for the skin and was mentioned in more than one reading. A reading for an eleven-year-old girl claimed that "if ye would take each day, through thy experience, two almonds, ye will never have skin blemishes" (1206-3).

Skin problems such as blemishes and dryness were basically attributed to the system being overtaxed. The primary cause cited most frequently by Cayce was poor elimination, poor circulation, or both. Cayce believed that skin eruptions occurred when waste materials in the blood were not eliminated through their normal channels, forcing the system to attempt to excrete them through the pores of the skin.

Also an important contributing factor to skin dryness, blisters, superfluous hair, and other complexion problems was glandular imbalance.

Treatment

Internal cleansing and stimulation of the circulatory system were Cayce's prime treatment suggestions for individuals with skin problems. Colonic irrigation once every month or two, or even more frequently, was the usual method suggested. Also highly recommended for this purpose was the three-day apple diet. During this three-day span, only apples were eaten, along with plenty of water. To complete the cleansing of the intestines and prevent the formation of gas, on the evening of the third day, between one tablespoon and two ounces of olive oil were to be taken internally.

The most frequently suggested methods for improving circulation were exercise and massage. Daily exercises, especially walking, preferably outdoors, and weekly massages of the spine, extremeties, etc., were advised. To improve the general texture of the skin (and prevent arthritis), massages using pure peanut oil were occasionally recommended. Another massage formula suggested by Cayce for the hands and body was a combination of peanut oil, olive oil, rosewater, and lanolin. This was to be applied following a fifteen- to twenty-minute tepid bath taken with any good soap.

In addition to massage, the readings occasionally suggested general manipulations to relax and coordinate the entire spine. These were intended to improve the nerve impulses to the body and thus benefit the general circulation as well. Hydrotherapy, in the form of sweats, fume baths, etc., was another type of general stimulation suggested to help keep the pores cleansed.

External applications were to be applied gently, without interfering with the normal functions of the body. The readings mentioned several brands of soap, including ivory, Camay, and Sweetheart, but the most highly recommended was castile soap, which at the time contained olive oil and sodium hydroxide. As for the use of deodorants, Cayce believed that "the use of pure soap is preferable to any attempt to deodorize" (2072-9).

Case History

Reports dealing *specifically* with the complexion were apparently received in only one instance. Case 1968 was a young woman whose facial dermatitis was "completely cured" as a result of following Cayce's advice, in which a central recommendation was massage. Another individual, whose reading was not specifically for complexion problems, reported, "Face entirely clear—has been for some time—doesn't look like I am the same person."

Also, an interesting report was received from a Canadian concerning the peanut oil-olive oil-rosewater-lanolin lotion Cayce prescribed for case 1968. The Canadian reported that it not only stopped his sensitive skin from peeling as a result of exposure to the sun, but also acted as an extremely effective insect repellent. When sunbathing with friends in black fly and mosquito country, all were quickly "beleaguered by literally thousands of them and bitten awfully, *except* a friend and myself. We were also covered with them, but with dead ones. Not one bite. The moment they come in contact with this lotion, they die."

A case involving a combination of complexion problems was that of a twenty-year-old woman, who complained of rash, blackheads, acne, and enlarged pores. Cayce's diagnoses for case 2154 revealed poor eliminations through the alimentary canal, which caused blotches all over her skin at intervals as the perspiratory system attempted to eliminate excess toxins. Additionally, spinal subluxations in the second and third cervical and the third and fourth dorsal vertebrae, were accompanied by a glandular imbalance, and had slowed her digestion.

Cayce suggested two or three general spinal adjustments, giving special attention to the coordination of the dorsal and cervical areas with the lumbar axis. A series of hydrotherapy treatments was also advised. These were to be dry-cabinet sweats followed by thorough massages with oil and hot- and cold-water applications. Treatments were to take place once weekly for four to five weeks, and about once every eight weeks, a colonic was recommended.

Additionally, a teaspoon of Eno salts was to be taken each morning before breakfast in a series of five days on and five days off. This was to continue for the duration of the adjustments and hydrotherapy treatments.

To supplement her diet, at least one ounce daily of raw vegetable juice, such as that from lettuce and carrots, was recommended. In place of the heavier meats and fats and fried foods, fish, fowl, and lamb were recommended. White bread and potatoes were to be avoided.

Coronary Thrombosis

Coronary thrombosis is caused by clotting of blood in the coronary arteries of the heart, leading to a sudden, complete occlusion of the narrow segment. It generally occurs in an artery involved with arteriosclerosis.

A total of forty-three readings were given for individuals with coronary thrombosis or tendencies toward this disorder. This report deals with twelve individuals, ranging in age from thirty-eight to sixty-four years, who received a total of twenty readings dealing with this condition.

The major cause of thrombosis among this group of individuals was attributed to poor circulation stemming from an overtaxed circulatory system. In each case, Edgar Cayce found a disruption of the circulation between the heart and liver, which, as one reading explained, was "producing a thrombosis; that is, a hardening of the walls of the arteries that direct the flow of the vein blood from the liver to the heart.

"This is engorging one portion of the heart, and draining the other valve" (1187-12).

According to Cayce, in sixty percent of the cases, poor eliminations contributed to the unbalanced condition, and in the majority this was due to improper functioning of the colon, which resulted in uneliminated toxins accumulating and causing pressures on the circulatory system.

Pressures on the spine were also involved in thirty percent of the cases. These were usually in the dorsal and cervical regions, but at times were noted in the lower spine as well.

In a few cases, poor assimilation in the digestive tract prevented the body from receiving the nutrients it needed. Instead of being digested properly, food taken into the body would cause dyspepsia and indigestion. Contributing to the problem was overtaxation.

Treatment

Treatments for coronary thrombosis focused on reducing body toxicity. In each case, a change of diet was advised. Meats, especially beef, and fried foods and fats were discouraged. Most frequently recommended were fish and fowl, vegetables, and fruits and fruit juices.

In seventy-five percent of the cases, osteopathic adjustments were suggested to help relieve tension in specific areas. Those areas mentioned most often were the fourth, fifth, sixth, and ninth dorsal and the second and third cervical vertebrae and the lumbar and sacral regions.

Colonics and enemas were suggested in seventy percent to facilitate drainages. Typically, saline and soda solutions were used as a primary cleanser, with Glyco-Thymoline added to the rinse water.

Massages were recommended for forty percent. These were to be administered when needed for relaxation and were to improve body functions. Compounds such as olive oil with tincture of myrrh and compound tincture of benzoin were prescribed to stimulate the body. To stimulate the circulation, electrotherapy was mentioned in the same percentage of readings. Most often recommended was the Radio-Active Appliance. The need for rest was emphasized in four cases, and hydrotherapy was suggested twice.

Case History

In cases with follow-up reports, forty percent of the individuals noted experiencing either great improvement or a complete recovery.

An example was a fifty-five-year-old man, case 1141, who received one reading on coronary thrombosis. After experiencing shortness of breath and indigestion, along with other feelings of pressure in the body, the man consulted a heart specialist who subsequently diagnosed his condition as coronary thrombosis.

Cayce, however, diagnosed his symptoms as being connected to improper eliminations, which had caused an engorgement in the colon and a buildup of toxins in the bloodstream. This in turn caused the pressure on his heart.

Cayce immediately advised high enemas and colonics. Salt and bicarbonate of soda were to be added to the water, adding Glyco-Thymoline to the rinse water. Eight days after the first colonic, 1141 was to receive another one and twenty-four days later, a third. The last colonic was to be given thirty days after the third.

The man was advised to take small quantities of Al-Caroid after meals for two to three days and then only following the evening meal. After this regimen, Caroid and bile salts (a laxative) were to be taken on nonconsecutive days.

Following the above treatments, the Radio-Active Appliance was to be used daily for an hour before bedtime. Osteopathic adjustments were also recommended. These were to focus on the dorsal and cervical areas, also making corrections in the lumbar and coccygeal regions and the sacral and ileum plexes. In diet, white bread, Irish potatoes, and dried beans were discouraged. Fruits, fruit juices, and vegetables were highly recommended.

After following Cayce's advice, case 1141 reported that he had experienced a "complete recovery."

Cystitis

Cystitis is an inflammation of the bladder which usually involves the urethra (the tube that empties the urine from the bladder). The main symptoms are frequent urination and incontinence. Acute cases are characterized by tenderness, pain associated with urination, and a constant desire to pass water. The urine is acid and may contain large amounts of blood and some pus. Cystitis is more prevalent in women than in men, and there is a high rate of recurrence.

A total of thirty-six readings were given by Edgar Cayce for twenty-seven individuals with cystitis. The group ranged in age from seven to seventy-two years.

According to Cayce, the fundamental cause of cystitis, cited in twenty-three cases, is improper elimination. When the liver and kidneys fail to eliminate wastes and toxins properly, the normal count of bacteria in the bladder increases to a level that allows infection and inflammation to develop. Poor circulation in the liver and kidney areas was a related factor mentioned in ten cases.

Mentioned in seven cases were spinal problems, with lesions and subluxations in the lower spine contributing to the problems with eliminations. In six cases, poor assimilation was involved, and in five individuals, colds and infections had led to the disorder by lowering resistance.

Treatment

The major treatment for cystitis, suggested in fifteen cases, was dietary advice. The readings placed special emphasis on eating large amounts of fruits and vegetables, especially those which are sources of B vitamins. Eating whole grains, such as steel-cut oats, and drinking more water were also highly recommended. Fried foods and large amounts of starches were to be avoided.

Spinal manipulations were suggested for twelve individuals. When a location was specified, the dorsal and lower lumbar areas were those most often noted as needing special attention. In ten cases, massages were suggested, using a variety of substances including olive oil and a combination of mutton tallow, spirits of camphor, and spirits of turpentine. Colonics and enemas or various laxative substances were advised for ten individuals.

Also suggested was the use of packs, most often made with hot salt. The packs were to be placed over the bladder area and right side when pains were acute.

Several other recommendations were made in three cases. These were douching with a weak solution of Atomidine or Glyco-Thymoline, various methods of hydrotherapy, and watermelon-seed tea and other digestive aids.

Case History

Case 2462 was a thirty-four-year-old man who received one reading for cystitis. Cayce found that he had lesions in the mid to lower portion of the spine which caused improper nerve impulses to the organs of elimination. This had led to toxicity, acidity, and, eventually, cystitis.

To treat this condition, three thorough general adjustments were advised, focusing on the upper and ninth dorsal vertebrae and the coccygeal and sacral areas. After the third adjustment, full hydrotherapy treatments were recommended, including a cabinet sweat, colonics, and hot and cold showers. These treatments were to be followed by thorough massages along the spine with peanut oil, and then rubdowns with alcohol.

The man was advised to rest for ten days after these treatments before receiving six more adjustments with a similar hydrotherapy routine. Following the heaviest meal of his day, he was advised to take a little Al-Caroid with water, and once a month a glass of lithia water.

His diet was to include raw vegetables once daily. Carbonated drinks and fried foods were prohibited; pastries and cake were allowed only in moderation.

Case 2462 followed his reading and reported good results. He wrote: "Treatments have been very satisfactory though there is still room for improvement . . . [and] the functioning of the elimination system shows signs of becoming normal."

Reports were received from eleven of the twenty-seven individuals given readings for cystitis. Ten reported benefiting from the advice they were given.

Cysts

A cyst is generally a sac with a distinct wall containing fluid or other material. It is found either just beneath the surface of the skin or in some internal area of the body.

Edgar Cayce gave a total of thirty-three readings for twenty-four individuals with cysts, two-thirds of whom were women.

In about one-half of the readings devoted to cysts, Cayce attributed the cause to lymph accumulations which formed into pockets in different areas of the body. In one-fourth of these cases, poor eliminations and poor circulation were seen as contributing factors in cyst formation. A third were warned that surgery would be required if the cyst were to begin to put too much strain on the system as a whole.

Treatment

In one-half of the cases, the readings consistently recommended some form of local massage. For skin cysts, a combination of castor oil and baking soda was to be massaged directly onto the affected area. For cysts occurring at the base of the spine, a combination of one ounce Iodex to five grains of animated ash was recommended as a rub. For lymph accumulations and fatty cysts, a combination of mutton tallow, camphor, and turpentine was suggested as a rub following a hot bath.

Osteopathic adjustments were recommended in one-third of the cases to help stimulate the eliminations and circulation and to assist in the correction of other disorders that were present. Various forms of hydrotherapy and colonics were suggested with less frequency throughout the readings, depending on the condition of the system as a whole.

Diet was seen as a major factor in overcoming cysts. Leafy raw vegetables were often the main part of the diet. Seafoods were also highly recommended. Red meats, pork, and starches were to be avoided.

Case History

Two readings were given for a thirty-eight-year-old woman, case 3247, who had requested a reading due to chronic cystitis and previous operations which had caused her bladder and stomach to adhere to each other.

The first reading explained that the operations had left scar tissue in which cysts had formed. Due to the amount of scar tissue involved, the reading suggested that another operation could be necessary if the treatments outlined were ineffective. In addition to the cyst formations on the scar tissue, subluxations in the eighth and ninth dorsal and in the third cervical vertebrae were found to have affected the general circulation and caused disturbances in the excretory system.

Weekly hydrotherapy treatments, including a mild sweat followed by a fume bath, hot and cold shower, and a rubdown, were suggested. After the woman began this treatment, a series of six spinal adjustments were to be administered. Afterwards, the abdomen was to be massaged with an equal combination of olive oil and peanut oil. It was also suggested that the affected area be massaged with an ointment consisting of two pinches of baking soda added to a teaspoon of castor oil. However, this was not to be used until all the other treatments had been completed.

The second reading noted that there were continuing disturbances throughout the entire abdominal area. Castor oil packs were to be administered four to five days each week, with each pack followed by a massage of the abdominal area.

At the end of each series of packs, small quantities of olive oil were to be taken internally about three to four times each day. (Hormone injections of theelin and estrogen were to be discontinued, as it was noted that these would tend to create deposits in the system.) At this point, the operation was still a strong possibility.

This was the last reading given for 3247, and due to the lack of correspondence from the woman, the results were not known.

Cysts: Ovarian

An ovarian cyst is a thin-walled cavity or sac containing fluid or semifluid developed on or attached to the ovary. Abdominal pain and cessation of the menstrual period may develop, depending on the type of cyst and where it is located.

There were twelve readings given for six women, ranging from twenty-eight to fifty-four years old, who had cystlike conditions within the ovaries and fallopian tubes.

Disorders mentioned in sixty percent of the readings for ovarian cysts were poor elimination, congestion, and nervous system imbalances. Generally, poor eliminations would develop into a toxin buildup within the system and in the pelvic region in particular. Under certain conditions, the bacteria would spread throughout the pelvic organs, infecting the ovaries and causing the cyst to develop. Neuralgia was a related factor in three cases, and nervous incoordination in another.

Treatment

Edgar Cayce's treatments for ovarian cysts varied considerably, depending on the nature of the disorder and on its severity. Mentioned most frequently for the relief of pain, congestion, and local infection were douches and the application of packs. Five women were advised to douche with diluted solutions of Atomidine, Glyco-Thymoline, or both used alternately.

The application of the hot abdominal packs was also advised in five cases. The substances most often recommended for the packs were castor oil, Glyco-Thymoline, and a combination of mutton tallow, spirits of turpentine, and spirits of camphor.

Other treatments, each recommended in half of the cases, were diet changes, spinal manipulation, eliminants, and massage. Although specifics varied, the diet was to be alkaline, body building, and easily digested. The manipulations were recommended to improve the nervous system coordination, with emphasis on the hips and lumbar area. Colonics were most often suggested as aids to eliminations, and the massages were designed to relax the body and improve the circulation, the latter administered with a variety of substances.

Additionally, electrotherapy treatments using the Violet Ray received two recommendations, and exposure to the sun was advised in a third case. Another woman was advised to consult a gynecologist, and another to go to the hospital if her condition worsened.

Case History

Reports on the outcome of the readings were received from five women, who noted that they had benefited as a result of following the advice given by Cayce.

Case 5270, a thirty-seven-year-old woman, received one reading dealing with a cyst on her right ovary. According to Cayce, her condition was caused by a subluxation in the spine, which centered in the third and ninth dorsal vertebrae as well as in the lumbar area.

Cayce's treatment involved the application of Glyco-Thymoline packs over the lower abdomen and pubic areas. These were to be placed daily for half an hour for a period of one week.

At the end of this period, three weekly osteopathic adjustments were to begin, focusing on the ninth and upper cervical vertebrae and in the brachial and mastoid areas. Following six or eight adjustments, mild diathermy treatments over the lumbosacral area were to be given twice a week along with the adjustments.

Also at the same time, the woman was to douche using Glyco-Thymoline and Atomidine solutions on alternate days. Two tablespoons of Glyco-Thymoline were to be combined in a quart and a half of water at body temperature. The Atomidine solution consisted of one teaspoon to a quart and a half of water at body temperature.

To assist in strengthening the body, Cayce advised dietary improvements which included foods high in vatamins B_1 and B_2, niacin, and phosphorus. Additionally, a teaspoon of Zyrone was to be taken each morning.

Although the woman's doctors had concluded that nothing further could be done for her, following Cayce's advice brought about significant improvements in her condition. Within a month, the discharge from the cyst had totally ceased.

Cysts:Pilonidal

Pilonidal cysts appear around the coccyx or anal area, accompanied by small growths of hair. Cayce gave readings for three individuals with this condition.

Two of the three cases will be discussed—that of a twenty-year-old man with pilonidal cysts near the anus and that of a twenty-seven-year-old man with pilonidal cysts and cold sores in the mouth.

Treatment

Readings 661-1, -2, -3, and -5 were given for a twenty-year-old male with pilonidal cysts near the anus which occurred as the result of an injury to the lower end of his spine. As a topical solution, Cayce prescribed a compound consisting of an ounce of Iodex mixed with two grains of animated ash, applied on a strip of gauze and onto the cyst. Frequent cleansing of the cyst area with a weakened solution of bichloride was also advised.

A series of ten (twice daily) spinal manipulations was also recommended to correct poor alignment of the spine.

Also prescribed was a glass of water containing a half teaspoon of milk of bismuth and six drops of lactated pepsin, which was to be taken internally after meals for two days in a row, every other two days.

The subsequent readings suggested a series of Atomidine treatments to balance the glands. For five days the young man was to take a half glass of water containing a drop of Atomidine twice daily. After a rest period of one day, the dosage was increased to two drops in water taken for five days. This was to be followed by a rest period, after which the entire treatment was to be repeated.

In order to correct the condition of the spine, Cayce recommended ten or more osteopathic adjustments. These were to be followed by treatments with the Violet Ray.

In reading 661-5, given approximately three years later, Cayce found that the young man's diet was too rich in fatty and acid-producing foods, which was causing an outbreak of blemishes around the chin and face. Additionally, the cyst had been aggravated by lack of proper attention. Several corrections to the cerebrospinal system, with special reference to the coccygeal and the ninth and tenth dorsal vertebrae, were recommended. Diathermy treatments were required once a week to relieve the condition, as well as small daily quantities of elm water and saffron tea. An ointment consisting of a quarter grain carbon ash to one ounce Iodex was recommended for application to the cyst. Fried and greasy foods, sugar, butter, and meats were to be avoided.

Since 661 reported he was having difficulty locating an osteopath to administer the diathermy treatments, no major improvements were noted in this case.

The next case, reading 670, was that of a twenty-seven-year-old man suffering from pilonidal cysts and cold sores in the mouth due to a hyperacidic condition. Osteopathic adjustments, given every two or three days, were intended to correct poor alignment of the spine, thereby relieving the cyst problem. Additionally, Cayce prescribed a compound of sulfur, cream of tartar, and Rochelle salts for better elimination.

No follow-up report was received.

Cysts: Skin

A cyst is a closed sac with a distinct membrane which forms on the surface of the skin and is usually filled with fluid or semifluid matter.

Edgar Cayce gave a total of nineteen readings for fifteen individuals with skin cysts and related conditions.

The basic cause for skin cysts, noted by Cayce in sixty percent of the readings, was poor elimination and improper circulation. Cayce believed the disturbance began with the circulation being impeded in some way and, as a result, slowing excretory functions. Toxins then began to build and pass into the bloodstream, and cysts would form on the skin. In one reading, Cayce, commenting on the formation of cysts, noted: "These, as we find, have to do with the separation of the lymph circulation and the emunctory activities from the deeper circulation. And when cellular forces become so aggravated, either by bruising or lack of elements in the system to keep continuity of life force, they set up within themselves. Thus they draw upon the system, becoming . . . originally, and oftentimes . . . malignant in their nature" (1013-1).

Some form of glandular incoordination was a contributory factor in thirty percent of the cases. Usually this was associated with an overproduction of lymph due to the concentration of toxins in the system.

Improper assimilation, poor diet, and spinal problems were mentioned as factors in nearly twenty-five percent of the cases. An overly acid-forming diet containing too many meats, sweets, and starches would cause a slowing of the eliminations. Spinal subluxations and various other sources of pressure upon the nervous system would further disturb the circulatory and excretory functions of the body.

Treatment

Dietary guidelines and spinal manipulations were the two types of treatment suggested most frequently by Cayce— each in sixty-five percent of the cases. Maintaining an alkaline diet and abstaining from eating large amounts of sweets, starches, fats, fried foods, and heavier meats (beef and pork) were advised. The most highly recommended foods were citrus and other fruits, raw and cooked vegetables, whole grains, eggs, milk, and fish, fowl, and lamb in moderation.

Spinal manipulations were advised to help restore normal circulation, making corrections where pressures on the nervous system existed. Additionally, manipulations were to encourage relaxation, which in turn would help the system to detoxify itself.

Massage, external applications, and electrotherapy were suggested in about forty-five percent of the readings. The massages were to assist general relaxation; the external applications to help dissolve the cyst; and electrotherapy to help heal and strengthen the circulatory system.

External ointments consisted of a combination of substances such as castor oil and baking soda; Iodex and animated ash; and mutton tallow, spirits of camphor, and spirits of turpentine. Electrotherapy was to be administered by the Radio-Active Appliance and the ultraviolet light, both of which were mentioned twice by Cayce.

Assisting the eliminations by means of enemas, colonics, or laxatives such as olive oil was advised in four instances. Three individuals were also advised to take small doses of Atomidine to help correct glandular imbalances.

Case History

Reports were received in only about half of the cases. However, all of those who reported noted benefits from following Cayce's suggestions.

Although there is no follow-up on the outcome, a typical case history was a twenty-seven-year-old woman who received one reading dealing with cysts. Cayce attributed their formation to an imbalance between the physical, mental, and spiritual selves. On the physical level, this manifested itself in poor assimilation, which in turn led to an "inefficiency of the replenishing forces, by the activity of the glandular system to supply the elements necessary for the bodily functions." Because of the unbalanced "vibrations," case 1436 had accumulations in certain areas which formed into cysts.

To cleanse and stimulate the glands, especially those of the digestive system, Cayce advised case 1436 to take one drop of Atomidine daily, three days a week for three weeks. Thirty-minute use of the Radio-Active Appliance was recommended, and meditation during this period was strongly advocated.

After three weeks of the treatments, osteopathic adjustments were to begin, focusing on the coccygeal, the ninth and last dorsal, and the upper dorsal and cervical vertebrae. These were to be administered twice weekly for three weeks followed by a month-long rest period and then three or four more treatments.

Her diet was to consist of a daily balance of two meals of cooked foods and one of raw. Meats were to be avoided, although fish and fowl could be eaten occasionally. The morning meal was to include citrus juices or cereals, but not both. Well-cooked whole wheat or a mixture of rye and barley were possible cereals.

Additionally, the cyst areas were to receive gentle massages, using a combination of mutton tallow, spirits of turpentine and spirits of camphor.

Deafness: Nerve

Nerve deafness is hearing loss which is due either to a nerve disorder or to conductive deafness from fluid in the middle ear.

Eleven individuals, ranging from six to seventy years,

received a total of thirteen readings dealing with nerve deafness and related disorders.

The major cause, cited in almost seventy percent of the cases, was poor eliminations. This would cause general congestion and at times a catarrhal condition in the body which would localize in the eustachian tube, producing pressure upon the sensory nerves and leading to a degeneration in hearing.

In fifty percent of the cases, a contributing cause was nervous incoordination due partially to spinal misalignments which would hamper the sensory nerves in general and the auditory nerves in particular. Poor circulation of the lymph and blood supply was also a contributing factor in thirty-five percent of the cases. Infection of the inner ear and mental and emotional conditions were each mentioned in two cases.

Treatment

Edgar Cayce's major treatment for nerve deafness, recommended in seventy percent of the cases, was massage. This treatment was designed to stimulate the circulation around the spine and/or the facial area and over the eustachian tubes. In about sixty percent of the cases, spinal manipulations, concentrating on the cervical and dorsal areas, were advised. Electrotherapy was recommended approximately forty percent of the time, most frequently in the form of the Wet Cell Appliance with gold chloride.

Dietary advice was given for about thirty percent of the individuals, with an emphasis on easily assimilated, alkaline-forming foods such as fruits and vegetables and their juices. Colonic irrigations were recommended in two cases to assist the cleansing process.

Maintaining a positive attitude was considered highly important in treating the whole person. To one individual, Cayce gave the following advice: ''He who doubts that the best will come to him with doing of that which is correct is already defeated. Don't blame others for what has happened or may happen. Do right yourself, physically, mentally, spiritually, and the best will come to you'' (5203-1).

Case Histories

Reports were received from four of the eleven cases. Three individuals reported good results, while the fourth apparently did not follow his reading. Two of the four cases reporting are summarized below.

Case 1090 was a six-year-old boy who received one reading for nerve deafness. At the age of five months, he had contracted whooping cough, and as he grew older he had difficulty in hearing and his speech failed to develop. At the time of the child's reading, he had visited twenty-three medical doctors, each of whom claimed that the nerves in the boy's ear had been destroyed due to the strain caused by whooping cough and that he would never hear properly again.

Cayce, however, gave the child a different and more encouraging prognosis. The child had already received chiropractic treatments, and Cayce noted that with these and other therapies he could realistically hope to recover his hearing.

The reading given for the child cited congestion in the lacteal duct centers of the abdomen as the root of the deafness. To relieve the congestion, hot castor oil packs were to be applied over the lacteal duct area three or four times weekly for two to four weeks (or the area was to be massaged with castor oil on the same schedule). The adjustments were to be continued up to four weeks, followed by a rest period of two or three weeks, and then another four-week series was to begin. A diet of foods that were blood building and easily assimilated was also advised.

After the treatments had been followed for a period of time, the boy's chiropractor made the following report on his progress: "After several weeks [of] treatments, [the] patient could hear sounds and repeat words while turned away from me, so as not to read lips."

Another case, that of 5132, a seventy-year-old man, received one reading for nerve deafness which attributed the hearing loss primarily to a catarrhlike condition which had attacked the eustachian tube and caused pressure upon the nerves, resulting in deafness and head noises.

To treat the condition, Cayce recommended the Wet Cell Appliance with gold chloride. In conjunction with each Wet Cell application and to assist in breaking up the congestion, a massage was to be given along the entire spine.

The man apparently followed Cayce's advice and reported that he had experienced general improvement, although some head noises still continued.

Deafness: Prolapsed Eustachian Tube

A prolapsed eustachian tube is a condition characterized by a collapsed or "fallen" eustachian tube, causing loss of hearing. Edgar Cayce gave a total of thirty-two readings for this condition for twenty-three individuals from twenty-four to seventy-five years.

The major cause mentioned by Cayce in sixteen of the cases was poor or impoverished circulation. He noted that many of these individuals had anemia and/or poor lymphatic circulation. Also frequently involved were inflammation and mucosity in the ear, which weakened the eustachian tube and eventually caused its collapse.

In ten other cases, improper assimilation was found to be the primary cause of the condition, resulting in hyperacidity and leaving the body open to infection which ultimately involved the ear. Poor elimination contributed to the over acid condition in almost as many instances. Also occasionally involved were spinal subluxations and nervous system incoordination. One reading gave the following view of the origin of the ear condition: "These effects in the circulation again show a subluxation in the upper dorsal and cervical area, affecting the auditory circulation. This produces the collapsing of tissue in the head, the eustachian tube, the antrum, the soft tissue in face becoming involved, so that all portions of the sensory organism are at times involved in this circulatory condition" (685-1).

Mentioned in four cases was an infection or eczema, which created an irritation in the eustachian tube. This led to inflammation and ultimately to the collapsed tube.

Treatment

The main treatment for this condition, recommended by Cayce in twenty-one cases, was a form of local manipulation called "finger surgery." This was to aid in breaking up the adhesions within the eustachian tube itself. An osteopath specially trained in this technique was necessary for proper results. General adjustments were also frequently involved.

To improve circulation and strengthen nerves, readings for fifteen individuals suggested electrotherapy treatments, which, depending on need, took various forms. Those most often recommended, in order of frequency, were the Violet Ray, the Radio-Active Appliance, and the Wet Cell Appliance.

Nine individuals were given dietary advice which strongly emphasized alkaline-forming foods such as fruits and vegetables. Heavy meats were not advised; however, occasionally beef juice was suggested as a tonic.

To relieve excess acidity and eliminate excess toxins, digestive aids and eliminants, such as Eno salts and soda preparations, were recommended in ten cases.

Massages, focusing especially on the cervical and dorsal areas, were suggested for three individuals. This was to aid in relaxing the nerves and muscles and to stimulate circulation. Recommended as often was the use of warm Glyco-Thymoline packs. These were to be applied to the base of the ear to encourage drainages. To help the body to regain the balance necessary to fight the infection, relaxation and meditation were also recommended in a number of instances.

Case History

Follow-up reports were received in only six of the cases. Three individuals reported little or no improvements, while three others noted beneficial results.

One case in which improvements were noted was 3105, a seventy-five-year-old woman who received one reading for deafness in both ears due to prolapsed eustachian tubes. Cayce regarded the primary cause as a disturbance in the nerve impulses to the sensory system, which was the result of subluxations in the third and fourth dorsal vertebrae. The circulation was impeded, the ears became inflamed, and the eustachian tube subsequently collapsed, according to Cayce.

The main treatment advised was osteopathic finger surgery to break up the adhesions within the ears and restore hearing. Also recommended were daily Glyco-Thymoline packs. These were to be prepared by soaking three or four thicknesses of cotton cloth in Glyco-Thymoline and then applying the packs at the base and sides of the ears for a period of one hour. Following the packs in the evening, electric-vibrator treatments using a sponge applicator were to be applied over the face, neck, and ears and in the dorsal area of the spine. Additionally, the Radio-Active Appliance was to be used daily, while the woman meditated on the Bible.

This individual reported improvements after following the treatments prescribed in her reading.

Dermatitis

Dermatitis is an inflammation of the skin characterized by redness, swelling, and itching. Many forms of dermatitis appear to be an allergic reaction, having either an internal or external source.

The Edgar Cayce readings given on this subject suggested that this skin condition was usually caused by poor eliminations, forcing intestinal toxins to be carried by the circulatory system and eliminated through the skin. In each case, diet was cited as the cause of poor eliminations. The reading given for case 1573 noted that diet, "as has been indicated, is a greater part of the disturbance." In only one case was the skin disturbance caused by a psychological rather than a physiological reaction.

Treatment

Cayce directed most of the corrective action toward balancing the system through the alimentary canal. The diet was basic: red meats, sweets, salt, fried foods, fats, and most fruits were to be avoided; seafood, fowl, lamb, green vegetables, whole grains, and broths were to be included.

To stimulate eliminations, Eno salts or laxative tablets were to be taken; also, enemas or colonics were recommended. Externally, in four cases the affected areas were to be dusted with a body powder containing stearate of zinc and balsam.

In some readings, spinal manipulation was recommended, with the seventh through the ninth dorsal and the cervical centers receiving special attention. In all cases, it was stressed that the treatments would not be beneficial unless the diet was followed.

Case History

Cayce explained in four of the readings given for case 480, a twenty-two-year-old woman, that her body was attempting to throw off excessive toxins through her respiratory and perspiratory systems.

He further noted that the rash, "as we find, comes from food values that have been, and are, of improper natures in the system." Attention, therefore, focused on diet. Alkaline-reacting foods were encouraged, while red meats, sugar, and fats were discouraged. The affected areas were to be dusted with a powder of stearate of zinc with balsam to relieve itching.

The follow-up report indicated that the woman followed the advice given for diet and her rash and itch lessened.

Detached Retina

Detached retina is the separation of the retina from the choroid of the eye and should be referred immediately to an opthalmologist. During transportation, the patient's head should be positioned so that the detached retina will fall back with the aid of gravity. The main symptom is blurred vision in one eye which becomes progressively worse. Approximately eighty percent can be cured with one operation; ten percent need a second operation.

Four readings were given for three individuals with detached retinas. However, causes of the disorder were related in only two cases.

In one reading (679-1), he found impingements in the cerebrospinal system which prevented the proper functioning of bursas and ganglia along the spine. Nerve impulses to the excretory system were cut off, causing a buildup of toxins in the blood. Impingements in the centers governing the lymph circulation, blood supply, and nerve energy to the sensory system caused the impairment of vision. Cayce found that in this case the retina was not truly torn, but that the waste materials in the system had caused the formation of a lip hanging over the eye.

In another reading (1132-1), he described a stiffening of spinal segments in the cervical area which caused subluxations, formed lesions in the eyes, and deflected proper nerve incentives. This, in combination with pressures in the superficial circulation, impoverishment of the blood and astrological influences during the period of gestation, had brought about the eye disturbance.

Treatment

Treatments varied for those seeking help due to conditions believed to be a detached retina. In one case (679), the spine was to be massaged daily with a combination of Russian White Oil, oil of cedarwood, carron oil, witch hazel, oil of sassafras, kerosene or coal oil, and tincture of benzoin. On the third day, osteopathic adjustments were to follow each massage, gradually making corrections in the cervical, dorsal, and coccygeal areas.

A highly alkaline diet was recommended. The morning meal was to consist of citrus juices, whole wheat toast, and coffee (without tannin) or a cereal drink. The noon or evening meal was to consist entirely of raw vegetables, such as lettuce, celery, tomatoes, carrots, spinach, onions, and peppers, garnished with oil or mayonnaise dressing. The other meal was to feature well-cooked vegetables, in the proportion of three grown above the ground to one grown below, with whole wheat, rye, or sour (not white) bread.

Proper eliminations were to be maintained through the alimentary canal during this period. After several months, the massages were reduced to two or three times weekly.

For another individual (1132-1), osteopathic corrections were recommended, especially in the cervical area. Treatments by an eye specialist were advised to break up the eye lesions. Shaded lenses of rose or amber were to be worn.

Diarrhea

Diarrhea is an increase in the frequency and fluidity of bowel movements. It was discussed in five Edgar Cayce readings given for four individuals.

Cayce described diarrhea as a condition characterized by an overactive circulation through the digestive tract. Poor digestion and poor assimilation were cited as major causes.

In two cases, the diarrhea was an after-effect of surgery. Other contributing factors were laxative substances, bad teeth, nervous incoordination and tension, dietary indiscretions, and toxins in the system.

Treatment

Although Cayce's treatments for diarrhea varied, emphasis was placed on aiding the digestion, rebuilding vitality, and improving circulation. Stressed in the diet were foods that were alkaline, body building, and easily assimilated, such as fruits and fruit juices (pears, citrus), raw and cooked vegetables and light proteins (conch soup, fish, fowl, and beef). One reading counseled against too much starch and another against sugar-and-starch combinations, fried foods, and carbonated beverages and hard liquor.

Additionally, other ways of improving the digestive process were mentioned. These included saffron and chamomile tea, alum root—chewed (both before meals); Al-Caroid (with meals); and olive oil. Mentioned in two readings was a combination of elixir of lactated pepsin and milk of bismuth taken in water. Aids to assimilations and eliminations in the form of colonics and castor oil packs were each mentioned once.

Adding easily assimilated iron to the diet was at times recommended. One reading mentioned a supplement known as Adiron and another, Codiron. Dietary sources mentioned were beef juice and certain fruits, such as pears and citrus. As a source of phosphorus, one reading recommended conch soup.

Spinal adjustments and massage were two methods of improving circulation and generally relaxing the body and were mentioned by Cayce twice. Frequency of adjustment ranged from occasionally in one case to a series of at least three to four in another. The massage was to be part of a general hydrotherapy treatment, including hot and cold water applications in one specific case.

Maintaining positive attitudes was suggested twice. One woman was told to be cheerful, and another was advised to concentrate on being helpful to others.

Case History

Case 2085, a sixty-seven-year-old woman, contracted diarrhea as a result of dietary indiscretions. Too many starch-and-sugar combinations had adversely affected the blood pressure, heart, liver, gall duct, pancreas, and kidneys. The improper diet, in conjunction with other conditions of overtaxation in the system, had resulted in digestive upsets which Cayce viewed as only temporary if proper measures were taken.

As treatment, Cayce first prescribed a diet of mainly fruits and fruit juices for the first day or so. Emphasis was placed on citrus fruits and other foods that were easily assimilated. Foods recommended in the general diet were Jerusalem artichokes (cooked in Patapar Paper three times weekly), raw vegetables and cooked vegetables (beans, lentils, leafy greens), and light proteins (fish, fowl).

Castor oil packs placed over the liver area for an hour at a time, two or three days a week, were also advised. To help improve the eliminations and relax tensions between the liver and heart, three or four spinal adjustments were recommended. These were to pay special attention to the lower cervicals and upper dorsals.

As an aid to assimilations, Cayce suggested daily doses of a teaspoon of milk of bismuth with ten drops of elixir of lactated pepsin mixed together in water.

Disks

In each of the three readings given by Edgar Cayce on disks, the individual had incurred injury to the spinal disk which was responsible for a variety of sympathetic disorders throughout the body. In view of the specific nature and effects of each injury, two of the readings are summarized as case histories.

Case History #1

Case 2805 was a thirty-two-year-old man who complained of tautness and discomfort in the limbs and shoulders and a dull aching feeling throughout his body. Cayce found a circular spinal lesion in the coccygeal region and a lateral spinal lesion in the third and fourth dorsals.

The pressure in the coccyx and along the upper lumbar axis was affecting the cerebrospinal nerve impulses to the glandular system. Additionally, as a result of poor glandular functioning, the blood count of red and white cells varied from time to time, and this incoordination caused disturbances in many organs.

A hydrotherapy routine was specified for a period of six to ten weeks. Hot and cold showers were to be followed by a fume bath using one teaspoonful of Atomidine to one pint of boiling water in the steam cabinet. For the first few times, treatment required placing a thick towel dipped in a saturated solution of Epsom salts on the coccygeal area, followed by a gentle massage with equal combinations of olive oil and tincture of myrrh.

To aid eliminations, a diet including fruits and vegetables was advised. Mild exercises in the evening, such as stretching and swinging the limbs, were also advised.

In summary, the man expressed confidence in the reading and preferred Cayce's advice to that of the doctors he had consulted—so much so that he eventually recommended that his brother obtain a reading from Cayce.

Case History #2

Case 4020 was a thirty-eight-year-old policeman who told Cayce that his job was in jeopardy due to back pains experienced while working. In his case, doctors at the Mayo Clinic had diagnosed a slipped disk, which differed from Cayce's opinion that poor eliminations and assimilations were weakening the locomotory nerves and muscular forces at the extremeties.

Cayce recommended hydrotherapy treatments consisting of a mild fume bath and thorough massage once a week for three weeks, followed by a three-week rest and then resumption of treatments. Application of shortwave therapy in the upper dorsal and lumbosacral areas was also suggested.

The dietary menu included seafood, fowl, and lamb and raw vegetables. To help correct the improper assimilation of sugar, Cayce recommended Jerusalem artichokes, cooked in their own juices, about once a month. Candies and artificial sweets were discouraged, although natural sweets such as honey were permitted.

Although the policeman reported that his condition had improved following Cayce's treatments, he preferred the diagnosis made by the physicians at the Mayo Clinic and said that he felt Cayce's diagnosis had been incorrect.

Diverticulitis

The clinical manifestations of diverticulitis vary with the extent of the inflammatory process and may include pain and cramping in the left lower abdomen, chills, fever, and signs of peritoneal irritation. Diverticulitis is a complication of diverticular disease, which becomes more frequent with advancing age and may be entirely asymptomatic.

Edgar Cayce gave a total of five readings on diverticulitis for three individuals in their fifties.

Diagnosis in all of the cases reviewed by Cayce seemed to revolve around problems with the lymph circulation, such as excessive mucus production and inflammation. In two cases, this condition was attributed to an accumulation of toxins in the system which irritated the intestinal wall and caused mucus to build up. In one case, the poor elimination was the cause; in another, the disease was the result of problems in the cerebrospinal system.

Treatment

Cayce's treatments for diverticulitis were fairly consistent. Special dietary advice was given for all three. Readings for the two other individuals placed strong emphasis on raw vegetables and fruits, along with juices of all kinds. (This advice, incidentally, is in direct contrast with orthodox medical treatment for the condition, which usually stresses the avoidance of all raw foods and other sources of roughage.)

Also recommended in every case were gentle enemas and colonics to cleanse the intestines of toxins and remove accumulations from the diverticulum. For two individuals, massage was recommended to relax the body and stimulate the circulation. This was to be especially over the lower half of the spine. A peanut-oil-and-olive-oil combination was specified in one case.

Twice recommended were ultraviolet light treatments over the spine, beginning with very brief applications and with the light placed about thirty-eight inches from the body. Packs over the abdomen and small of the back were also recommended twice, using castor oil and Glyco-Thymoline, respectively. In the most acute case, a solution of tincture of laudanum and aconite was to be applied over the abdomen to relieve pain until conditions improved.

Case History

Two of the three receiving readings on diverticulitis reportedly followed their readings and experienced good results.

One of these, case 3079, a fifty-five-year-old man, received three readings on the condition. His symptoms included swelling in the abdomen as well as other discomforts.

In the first reading, Cayce found that tension and stiffness had been produced in the lumbar and lower dorsal areas of the spine due to toxic accumulations in the blood and from a lack of sufficient elimination from the colon. A lymph inflammation had resulted through the lower abdomen, back, and extremities which had presumably led to the diverticulitis.

The first treatment was one drop of Atomidine taken in a half glass of water before breakfast for two weeks. At the end of this period, the man was to take a gold-and-soda solution for the next ten evenings. During this entire period, colonic irrigations were to be administered once a week, and the entire spine (but especially the sacral and lumbar areas) was to be massaged every evening with a combination of peanut oil and olive oil.

Also prescribed was a special six-day juice fast in which only watercress juice was to be taken the first day, carrot and lettuce juice the second, beef juice the third, celery and lettuce juices the fourth, fresh apple juice the fifth, and fresh grape juice the sixth. Following this, the diet was to include the juices of seafood and stew broths two or three times a week. Also recommended were plenty of corn bread and a little fowl, such as chicken, with the soft bones being chewed. White bread was not advised.

Cayce noted an improvement in the man's condition during his second reading, but he cautioned against overtaxing the body. Glyco-Thymoline packs were recommended, to be placed over the small of the back to help reduce the pressures.

The third reading advised the man to reduce the amount and frequency of his gold-and-soda dosage and that he return to his Atomidine dosage during the rest periods from the gold prescription. The other treatments previously suggested were to be continued.

During the course of the readings, 3079 experienced a steady improvement in his condition, and his last report noted that he was feeling much better and had no further swelling or pain.

Ears: Abscessed

Edgar Cayce's treatment for an abscessed ear, a localized collection of pus formed in either the inner or outer portion of the ear, focused on internal disorders which he felt produced the discomfort. Contrary to traditional medical treatments, which consist of internal antibiotics combined with local applications directed at controlling the infection, the Edgar Cayce readings treated ear infections as symptomatic of deeper disorders.

Most of the cases of abscessed ears in the readings were attributed primarily to a buildup of toxins in the system, which in turn were caused by poor eliminations. However, Cayce noted, before the infection settled in the ear, poor eliminations produced more generalized disturbances. In nine out of the sixteen readings, the abscessed ear was related to poor circulation, which was attributed to a lack of coordination between the lymph system and the blood supply.

Additionally, in almost half of these cases, the problem could be traced to poor assimilations, a condition Cayce closely related to both poor eliminations and poor diet. Three other individuals had problems directly involved with the coordination between the autonomic nervous system and the cerebrospinal nervous system. In three cases, there was a basic upset in the acid-alkaline balance of the body.

Treatment

Cayce's approach was to treat the abscessed ear locally and at the same time eliminate its causes by suggesting ways of improving the general health of the individual.

Specific treatments were suggested. One individual was told to massage the outer ear with sweet oil or camphorated oil in the mornings and castor oil in the evenings.

Cayce advised another individual to cleanse the ear with a mixture of St. Jacob's Oil and a mild antiseptic to remove the infectious forces.

And for still another, an eighteen-month-old child with an infectious right ear and a tendency toward contracting colds, Cayce prescribed one part sweet oil to two parts St. Jacob's Oil. One drop of this warmed combination was to be placed into the outer ear of the child when he was ready for bed; upon awakening the next morning the child was to have its ear washed with an alkaline antiseptic. (Since the original formula for St. Jacob's Oil has been altered by the omission of one ingredient, it should *not* be used in the ears today.)

Case History

An example of Cayce's whole-body approach to treating illnesses is found in reading 3116-1, which was for a thirty-three-year-old woman who had a running ear and was close to deafness due to the aftereffects of a high temperature. According to Cayce, the woman was suffering from poor digestion and a lymph infection caused by drainage from the nose, ears, and throat into the alimentary canal, which was undermining her central nervous system and general circulation.

Following an initial colonic irrigation, she was advised to undergo hydrotherapy for one week, which was to consist of fume and sitz baths and needle showers. This was to be followed by a general massage. After the second week, another series of colonics, hydrotherapy, and massage was suggested.

Cayce also recommended that the woman see an osteopath who specialized in ear, nose, and throat problems and receive a series of osteopathic adjustments to the dorsal and cervical regions.

The woman was advised to keep a proper dietary balance and to consume acid and alkaline foods rich in B vitamins.

Eczema

Eczema is an acute or chronic, noncontagious inflammatory disease of the skin, usually characterized by varying combinations of itching sores. The itching may be severe and prolonged, frequently leading to emotional disturbances.

Edgar Cayce gave a total of fifteen readings for eight adults suffering from eczema. Ages ranged from the twenties to the forties.

Cayce attributed eczema to an incoordination of the organs of elimination which had caused overacidity in the intestinal tract and forced excess toxins into the bloodstream, making it necessary for the body to eliminate the toxins through the perspiratory system and pores of the skin.

Frequently compounding the situation were factors such as incoordination of the deeper and superficial circulation, spinal subluxations, and glandular imbalances. In more than one case, Cayce attributed eczema to hot weather and allergic reactions. As an example, the rash on the hands of case 2516 was partially attributed to the prevalence of aluminum dust in the factory where he was employed.

Treatment

Cayce's treatments for eczema were consistent in many respects. Stressed in seven out of eight cases was diet. The guidelines he offered largely followed those in the readings as a whole, with an emphasis on alkaline, body-building, and laxative foods. Three individuals were advised against drinking beer and carbonated beverages, which Cayce believed contributed toward physical incoordination.

Spinal manipulation was recommended in five cases, and was designed to correct subluxations contributing to eczema. Other treatments focused mainly on the assimilations and eliminations and on treating eczema externally.

Suggested as a digestive aid in four cases was saffron tea. Mullein was mentioned as frequently, both as a tea or tonic and as an external solution in the form of a wash or stupe. The treatment for three individuals suggested doses of an herbal tonic, and two of these readings advised a tonic made from yellow dock root, burdock root, snake root, buchu leaves, podophyllin, green ragweed, elder flower, rye whiskey, and balsam of tolu.

To further assist eliminations, colonics were advised in half of the cases. A laxative powder described as a blood purifier was suggested three times. This consisted of equal parts sulfur, cream of tartar, and Rochelle salts. Also mentioned were various other laxatives.

Several types of external applications were also found helpful in keeping the skin from drying and cracking excessively. Palliative substances mentioned twice were Cuticura soap, Ray's Ointment, Glyco-Thymoline, and a powder containing stearate of zinc and balsam.

Case History

Case 2332, a forty-four-year-old woman, had athlete's foot as well as eczema when she came to Cayce for a reading. Her problem was attributed to a "deflection" (possibly a blockage in the nerves or circulation), resulting from subluxations in the lumbar, sacral, and coccygeal areas. This condition was combined with disturbances of the glands, especially the adrenals. The deflection in the lower limbs had led to inflammatory strep and problems in the superficial circulation, which in turn resulted in eczema and athlete's foot. Her eliminations were poorly coordinated, there were toxins in the system, and the nervous system and circulation had been affected.

Cayce recommended a series of at least six to eight adjustments, focusing on the lower spine. Adjustments were also to be made in the first cervical and third and ninth dorsal segments every other treatment. Mullein tea was to be taken in small amounts (one to one and a half ounces) each evening before retiring. The instructions for preparation were to steep two ounces of the fresh leaves in a quart of water. Any remaining tea was not to be kept any longer than two days. In the diet, fried foods, potatoes, white bread, and beef were to be avoided. Recommended were plenty of vegetables, especially squash, carrots, and okra. Dried beans, bulbous vegetables, and fruits were to be included infrequently (though fruit was found beneficial in other cases).

The reading also advised against mixing different types of food acids, such as peaches and tomatoes. Ale, beer, and carbonated beverages were to be avoided, although Coca-Cola syrup in plain water could be taken for the kidneys. Additionally, a combination of equal parts of olive oil and peanut oil was suggested as an emollient for the affected areas.

According to follow-up reports, both the eczema and athlete's foot had been described as "cured."

Edema

Edema is characterized by an excessive accumulation of clear, watery fluid in the tissues and cavities of the body, which results in swelling in these areas.

Edgar Cayce gave a total of twelve readings for nine individuals with this condition. The subjects ranged from thirty to seventy-four years.

Improper circulation, mentioned in six of the cases, was the major cause, according to Cayce. In each case, the improper circulation had different results with symptoms that included high blood pressure, varicose veins, poor lymph flow, and an enlarged heart.

Five individuals suffered from poor eliminations, which could have been the result of circulatory problems. In four cases, neuritis and nervous incoordination were both mentioned as contributing factors. Noted in each case was a buildup of toxins in the circulatory system, leading to excessive fluid retention.

Treatment

Suggested for the treatment of edema, or dropsy, as it was referred to in the readings, was the use of a homeopathic remedy known as Cimex Lectularius and consultation with a homeopathic physician. The readings noted that this medication could be used as an alternative to atropine, a prescription circulatory stimulant.

To help rid the body of excess fluids and toxins, colonics and enemas were suggested in five cases. Also recommended, in one case each, were herbal teas made from mullein, senna, and watermelon seeds to help improve the circulation and stimulate the liver and kidneys.

Dietary advice was given in four cases, with special emphasis being placed on easily assimilated foods. These included vegetables and fruits and their juices as well as beef juice, seafood, and yogurt. To be avoided were large amounts of fat and meat and fried foods.

To help stimulate elimination of excess fluids and to coordinate the cerebrospinal and autonomic nervous systems, Cayce recommended spinal manipulations to three individuals. Generally, the entire spine was to be treated, although certain areas were always to receive special attention.

Additionally, in three cases, various kinds of electrotherapy were recommended, and in two instances massage was recommended.

Treatment

Four of those receiving readings on edema followed Cayce's advice and later reported on their progress. All noted improvements. One case in particular was that of a sixty-three-year-old man, case 420, who had received one reading for dropsy (edema). He reported difficulty in sleeping and suffered from neuritis and chest pains.

The man was advised to consult a homeopathic doctor. Colonic irrigations, to cleanse the system of toxins, were also suggested. Osteopathic adjustments were to be administered twice weekly, with special attention given to the upper dorsal, cervical, sacral, and lumbar areas. Watermelon-seed tea was suggested to help cleanse the body of excess fluids. The diet was to consist of vegetables, fruits, and seafood. Fats were to be avoided.

Case 420 followed Cayce's advice and reported positive results. His symptoms diminished and gradually disappeared.

Emphysema

Emphysema is a condition characterized by the abnormal presence of air in body tissues. The usual symptoms are wheezing, weakness, shortness of breath, and chest pains. Cough is frequently aggravated by intercurrent respiratory infection.

Edgar Cayce gave three readings dealing with emphysema for one individual who requested them between the ages of thirty-one and thirty-three. Nervous imbalances were involved in the onset of his condition, with a "sap-

ping of the vitality through the pulmonaries," according to
Cayce.

Treatment and Case History

Cayce's first treatment was medication to aid the lungs
and relieve pain. The preparation, to be taken over a
five-day period, consisted of Canadian balsam, rectified
oil of turpentine, benzosol, and heroin. This reading also
recommended massages of the cerebrospinal system, using
a combination of olive oil and tincture of myrrh. The diet
was to be light and consist mainly of predigested foods or
that which could be easily assimilated.

Following his first reading, 5642 reported that the heroin
was unobtainable, but that he did have the massages and
noticed improvements. The second reading advised a grain
alcohol-based inhalant for the lungs, containing eucalyptol, creosote, balsam of fir, tincture of benzoin, turpentine
oil, and tolu. An herbal tonic containing wild cherry bark
and several other ingredients was suggested as a digestive
aid. Enemas were advised when necessary, and the massages were to continue. The diet was to include plenty of
vegetables.

The third reading basically advised a continuation of the
previous treatments. The subject followed Cayce's advice
and experienced excellent results, later reporting, "In all
ways I am much better."

Encephalitis

Encephalitis, which is caused by a virus, is an inflammation of the brain marked by fever, malaise, stiff neck,
sore throat, and nausea and vomiting. Also present, in
later stages, may be stupor, coma, and convulsions.

Four children and one adult received readings from
Edgar Cayce on encephalitis. Frequent convulsions and
fever were common symptoms noted.

Three cases of encephalitis were directly attributed to

injuries, although in two instances this was not obvious due to a delayed onset of the disease. For example, case 3401, a fifteen-year-old girl, had no apparent warning; she was healthy one day and feverish and unable to get out of bed the next. Case 2999, a one-year-old boy, did not show signs of stress until five months following two falls in close succession. Case 2042, a twenty-two-year-old woman, was still unconscious seven months following an accident.

In four of the five cases, spinal misalignment was seen as a major cause of the physical disorder. The general problem areas were the first through fourth cervical, the lumbar-coccygeal, and occasionally the dorsal centers. By deflecting the normal nerve impulses to various parts of the body, these misalignments would produce an incoordination between the cerebrospinal and sympathetic nervous systems in a manner which would result in pressure on the brain. In two of these cases, glandular imbalances were also involved.

In these four cases of encephalitis, there was a definite prognosis for improvement. The fifth case, however, was seen differently. Case 3555, a two-year-old girl, had been illness-prone since birth. The reading described this case as a karmic situation for all concerned, and a condition which physical treatment could not alleviate.

Treatment

To relieve pressures and restore the proper nervous coordination, spinal manipulation was recommended in four cases, at frequent intervals. In the case of the woman who was unconscious following an accident, Cayce recommended manipulations in the first and second cervicals and lower lumbar to bring a return of consciousness.

For the one-year-old boy, case 2999, Cayce suggested "magnetic" healing treatments, given in conjunction with the adjustments and whenever there were tendencies for convulsions. (This is described in more detail in the case history.) Suggested twice to give stability to the nerves was the use of the Wet Cell with gold. A third reading noted that use of the Wet Cell could begin later, provided the convulsions had stopped.

Applying Glyco-Thymoline over the spine was suggested twice—in one case by means of a gentle massage and in another in the form of packs applied over the lacteal area, the neck, and the upper spine. Cocoa butter was also recommended for massage in one case, with instructions to apply it along the spine, moving away from the head.

Diet was mentioned in two readings, with emphasis on blood- and nerve-building foods.

In the karmic situation, Cayce noted that the only treatment that could possibly aid the child would be an injection of one-sixteenth grain of atropine into the lower spine. This was to deter water from gathering about the brain. However, he warned that the injections would cause harmful lesions unless extraordinary preventive measures were taken, so he advised that it was probably best not to attempt any treatment.

He stressed the importance of prayer for two individuals. One parent was warned: "Don't pray about the body one way and act another way to somebody else's neighborchildren" (3401-1), and the mother of another child (161) was told to "pray like thunder!"

Case History

The reports accompanying encephalitis indicate that in two cases the readings were not followed and that in one case definite improvement was noted.

Case 2999 was a one-year-old boy whose early development was normal. At the age of three months, he had two falls in close succession, with no apparent injury. Two months later, however, it was noted he was uncomfortable, and a week later, he was quite ill and unresponsive. He was taken to the hospital, where he exhibited symptoms of pneumonia and spinal meningitis, accompanied by convulsions and high temperatures. After several months of serious illness, the child's condition had improved, but he was still far from normal. Visits to a chiropractor had been of some help.

Cayce's reading attributed the illness to the injuries and described their effect as the shattering of the nerve plexus in more than one center along the spine. As a reflex action, incoordination had arisen between the cerebrospinal and sympathetic nervous systems, causing voluntary responses to become involuntary in the ganglia, especially in the lumbar axis in the first to the fourth cervical vertebrae.

Cayce's treatment included massaging the spine in the evenings before bed with all the Glyco-Thymoline it would absorb. Each morning after the bath, another massage was to be administered, this time using cocoa butter, working it in circular motions away from the head as far as the ninth dorsal and then from the base of the spine toward the same area. Also recommended were spinal adjustments given every three to five days.

The second reading found that there was some improvement as well as some apparent aggravations as the system attempted to normalize. Cayce recommended that treatments were to be continued, with the adjustments to focus especially on the part of the spine related to the lacteal area. Additionally, at the beginning of each convulsion, Cayce suggested holding a wet cloth at the base of the brain. The Wet Cell was to be used later if the convulsions ceased.

An unusual type of treatment advised was a series of "magnetic" healing sessions which were described as follows: "Place the right hand under the right side of the body, and the left hand over the same on the upper side of body. Also we would d apply the magnetic treatment though the area where the secondary nerve forces to the sensory forces are associated with the cerebrospinal system. This will aid in quieting the body. The right hand would be placed between the shoulders, and the left hand on or over the breast bone."

For best results, Cayce suggested keeping the hands very clean and rubbing them thoroughly together before giving a treatment, as the object was to "let the vibration from the body pass through the child's body." This form of "laying on of hands" was to be administered for a few minutes at a time several times a day, whenever there were tendencies for convulsions, such as during adjustments. It was found that the mother could do the treatments only part of the time, as they tended to be enervating.

The child responded well to the treatments, his coordination improved dramatically, and the convulsions practically ceased. Although the child had become virtually blind and deaf, Cayce seemed to feel that this could be treated over a period of time.

However, no further readings were requested.

Enteritis

Enteritis is a chronic inflammatory disease which generally occurs in young adults and may be marked with mild to severe complications. The disease is characterized by exacerbations and remissions, with symptoms including abdominal pain in the right lower quadrant, bouts of diarrhea, and low-grade fever.

Three readings were given by Edgar Cayce on enteritis.

Although the precipitating cause of enteritis was different in each case, the main causes in all three were attributed to poor eliminations, circulatory imbalances, and incoordination of the sympathetic and cerebrospinal nervous systems. Two cases also noted spinal subluxations.

For case 533, the initial cause of enteritis was a blow to his side which had caused internal injuries. In reading 805-1, the sepsis poisoning was attributed to the aftereffects of an operation. Lesions had formed which compartmentalized the large intestine and blocked eliminations. Case 562's enteritis was the result of a nerve condition in the excretory organs which caused spasms in the large intestine and resulted in constipation and an inflamed intestinal tract.

In all three instances, poisoning of the circulatory system would occur, as the putrefaction process caused toxins to be reabsorbed into the system. This would compound the elimination problem and eventually even affect the spinal column, causing lesions which would result in nervous incoordination.

Treatment

In each case, treatments for enteritis stressed the importance of a proper diet. Highly recommended by Cayce was maintaining a balance of eighty percent alkaline to twenty percent acid-forming foods in diet, and drinking six to sixteen glasses of water daily.

Recommended to help build the body were eggnog, egg in beer, beef juice, and fruit juices. To improve the circulation and relax the body, massage was suggested in all three cases, while spinal manipulation was recommended twice. To encourage eliminations, gentle enemas and small doses of olive oil were advised in two readings. Also recommended twice were castor oil packs and/or Epsom salt packs to break up the adhesions or lesions in the intestines.

As a relief for pain, two readings suggested painting the abdomen with a combination of laudanum and aconite tinctures prior to applying the packs. An alternative application advised in the third reading was bathing the abdomen with olive oil and tincture of myrrh. Also emphasized in two cases was proper rest while the body recuperated its energies.

Case History

Case 633, a twenty-three-year-old man who developed enteritis as a result of an injury from a plow handle which jabbed him in the side, received a series of readings. His injury had eventually produced a tendency for the colon to adhere to the peritoneum (the membrane surrounding the digestive and excretory organs), which caused intestinal inflammation. He was in a "run down" condition and complained of severe pains in his side. Doctors were convinced that an operation was needed.

To help relieve pain, Cayce suggested that laudanum and aconite tinctures in the ratio of three to one be painted over the right side and over the transverse and descending colon. This was to be followed by alternately applying castor oil packs and Epsom salt packs on the left side to improve the kidney and bowel eliminations. However, after three applications, the castor oil packs were to be used only on the right side.

Forty-eight hours after therapy began, Cayce advised a series of thirty-six spinal adjustments in order to begin to coordinate the sympathetic and cerebrospinal nervous systems and to relax the body. The man was to maintain a semi-liquid diet. Arrowroot and junket were prescribed as easily digested foods. Eggnog (egg yolk, spirits frumenti, and milk) was mentioned as an aid to digestion and to stimulate the circulatory system. Cayce also recommended that the young man drink six to fourteen glasses of water daily and get ample rest.

The man's second reading found that although the laudanum and aconite were no longer needed, the castor oil packs should be continued. Enemas were now suggested to aid the eliminations. Beef juice and citrus juices were to be added to the diet.

The third reading noted considerable improvement and suggested light exercise in the open air. The castor oil packs were to be reduced in frequency to two or three a week. Cayce added vegetable juices along with whole raw egg mixed in beer to 633's diet and noted that in ten days solid foods could be included in accordance with a normal highly alkaline diet.

Cayce's last reading for the young man noted continued improvement and warned not to revert to old eating habits. The only additional suggestions were to take olive oil internally and to have an occasional massage. A balanced diet, including roughage, was once again stressed.

In a report to the June 1934 Congress of the ARE, Dr. Richardson, the young man's physician, said that positive results had been obtained by his patient and that lesions had been corrected.

Epilepsy: Children

Edgar Cayce gave twenty readings for four children with epileptic symptoms such as uncontrollable jerking and poor muscular coordination. Two children were unable to talk due to the extent of incoordination between the brain and the vocal cords, and all were prevented from leading normal lives.

In all the cases, the causes of the condition was directly related to a malfunctioning of the nerve system, which resulted in incoordination between the nervous and muscular systems. Cayce made specific reference in two cases to "engorgement" of the pneumogastric and perineurial nerves which occurred at the onset of seizures.

Two children had suffered pre- or postnatal damage to the brain, one as the result of a difficult breech birth and the other from neurosurgery which had been performed in the child's third year. In the third case, spinal lesions were found in the cervical and dorsal vertebrae, and in the last case, incoordination between the hypogastric, pneumogastric, and perineurial nerve was a causative factor.

Treatment

For epilepsy symptoms, Cayce most frequently gave specific instructions for administering spinal manipulations to afflicted areas of the spine on the average of twice a week for varying lengths of time. Electrotherapy was advised in three cases, two of them referring to the Wet Cell battery. Fifteen-minute massage of the spine, given by hand or by electric vibrator, was also recommended in three cases.

Important to the child's development in almost all cases was exercise in fresh air and sunshine. Parents were advised to use their own discretion to determine whether a physician should be consulted in conjunction with the treatment.

The parents of three children were encouraged to give helpful and positive suggestions to their youngsters when the latter were in a relaxed state.

Cayce recommended the use of passion flower fusion as a mild sedative in two cases, which was reported given with excellent results in case 146.

Case History

Cayce gave five readings for case 161, an eleven-year-old boy who suffered grand mal attacks and was unable to talk due to the extent of nervous incoordination arising from undue pressure upon the pituitary. Cayce made vague reference to damage incurred to the brain as a result of an operation and injection which had been performed on the brain at the age of three. Subsequent nerve incoordination had contributed to the disturbance in the lymph and blood circulation and poor assimilations. In addition, the child suffered from asthmatic breathing.

Treatment called for daily use of the Wet Cell Appliance for thirty minutes, with the positive anode attached to the base of the brain and the negative to the umbilical area.

Spinal manipulations were also recommended on a daily basis, as well as outdoor exercise. To ease the disturbance in assimilations, the child was to take a combination of milk of bismuth and pepsin.

In the fourth reading, Cayce noted that the treatments were not being administered as prescribed. The parents were further instructed to sponge the child along the spine with warm water and then alcohol.

By the fifth reading, Cayce noted improvements in the youngster's body. However, six years later it was reported that the treatments were not followed any further and the boy died at the age of seventeen. Despite the fact that the outcome of this case was not positive, good reports were received from other persons who followed the treatments as recommended by Cayce in their readings.

Epilepsy: General

Epilepsy, a chronic nervous disorder, has been classified as everything from demon possession to insanity. Epilepsy, however, is a brain disorder characterized by periodic seizures during which a wide variety of explosive discharges of electrical brain activity occurs.

The usual symptoms include motor, sensory, and mental dysfunction. A loss of consciousness and convulsions may occur, with headaches following the seizures.

Edgar Cayce gave over 250 readings for individuals with epilepsy and related disorders. The following study is based on 84 readings given for thirty-seven individuals with epilepsy, ranging in age from twenty months to sixty-two years.

Although Cayce attributed epilepsy to a variety of causes, the factor most frequently mentioned was glandular imbalance, which implied adhesions or lesions in the lacteal area of the intestines. In a few cases, other glands were involved, particularly the pineal. He mentioned the presence of a "cold spot" in the lacteal area as being an indication of epilepsy, and in one reading explained that "from *every* condition . . . of true epileptic nature there will be found a cold spot or area between the lacteal duct and the caecum" (567-4).

In another reading, Cayce explained how such an abnormality in the lacteal duct area, here found in conjunction with preexisting nervous system imbalances, could lead to epileptic seizures.

"Partially, as we find, this has been a prenatal condition, that has affected—or did affect—the nervous system of the body, which, combined with those reactions caused in the lacteal duct—in the right side, has caused those reactions to the sympathetic system as to prevent at times the perfect balance or coordination between sympathetic and cerebrospinal system. Thus there is caused the spasmodic reaction at the base of the brain, or through those

connections where these systems each enter the brain"
(2153-1).

In sixteen cases, spinal subluxations and lesions were
found to be a direct cause. Although the vertebrae in the
lower spine opposite the lacteal duct area were frequently
involved, these misalignments could originate in any part
of the spine. These misalignments created pressure on the
upper cervical vertebrae, which would interfere with the
proper nerve impulses to the brain and result in seizures.
Frequent contributing factors to the misalignments were
injury or prenatal conditions.

Injury, which was mentioned in sixteen cases, followed
a particular pattern—beginning with the original damage in
either the cervical or the lumbar area, with a reflex effect
on the upper spine. Whether the injury occurred at birth,
as it did in four cases, or in later life, the result was
long-standing adhesions and misalignments which affected
the brain.

Also mentioned as a cause was poor eliminations, which
tended to increase the severity of the disorder in eleven
cases. Cayce believed a sluggish excretory system would
lead to an overabundance of toxins in the system, causing
irritation to the nerves and glands. Cited in ten cases were
disorders in the nervous system, which most frequently
involved an incoordination between the cerebrospinal and
sympathetic nerve impulses, including those leading to the
brain. Frequently, part of the problem was spinal misalignments.

In nine cases, Cayce found the epileptic condition to be
at least partially of karmic origin, implying that the
physical predisposition toward epilepsy was present, or
occurred, at birth for the purpose of soul development.

The presence of prenatal factors was mentioned in eight
cases and involved such conditions as the mother's poor
diet. Subsequently, Cayce at times reminded the parents
that the epileptic child was a karmic situation for them as
well, and was best met by caring for the child themselves
as much as possible.

Treatment

Treatments recommended by Cayce for these individuals were fairly consistent, and dietary observances and precautions were outlined in a total of twenty-five cases. The emphasis was placed on light, alkaline-reacting foods which were high in minerals and vitamins and would be easily assimilated. The recommended list included fruits and vegetables and their juices; to be eaten in moderation were whole grains, nuts, milk products, seafood, and the lighter meats. Due to their reaction upon the nervous system and the heart, fried foods and heavy meats were to be avoided.

In twenty-six cases, Cayce suggested spinal manipulations, generally in the form of osteopathic adjustments. The areas specified as needing attention varied but frequently were the first, second, and third cervical vertebrae, which directly control nerve impulses to the brain. Cayce believed the adjustments would eventually break up spinal lesions and restore proper alignment and coordination to the nervous system. Hence, a lengthy series was frequently prescribed.

To aid in breaking up the lesions in the lacteal duct area and relax the nerves, Cayce recommended packs, usually of castor oil, to twenty-one individuals. Generally, the packs consisted of a few layers of flannel soaked in warm oil. They were applied daily over the abdomen for an hour and were kept warm with an electric heating pad. Internal doses of olive oil often accompanied the use of the packs, which were to be followed by a rinse with a solution of bicarbonate of soda in water.

Also recommended to help restore coordination in the nervous system and to improve circulation were various types of electrotherapy or heliotherapy treatments, suggested in fourteen instances. Most frequently recommended were the Wet Cell and the Radio-Active Appliance; occasionally mentioned were the Violet Ray and ultraviolet light.

Internal doses of a tonic or tea made from the passion flower herb (also referred to as maypops, mayblossom, bitters) were prescribed for thirteen individuals. The tonic was to strengthen the nerves, restore nervous coordination, and act as a sedative. The tea or infusion was most frequently recommended. Typical instructions for preparing the infusion were to add one gallon of the dried passion flower herb (including blossom and fruit) to two gallons of distilled water. The combination was to simmer in a glass container until there were two quarts of the liquid when strained. To this liquid, one pint of ninety-proof grain alcohol was to be added. The dosage prescribed was three tablespoons daily, taken at mealtimes.

Massages were recommended for fifteen individuals and were to be administered over the spine and other areas to relax the body and help reduce the lesions. Active ingredients to be rubbed into the skin, where such was specified, included formulas with peanut oil, olive oil, and/or cocoa butter.

To cleanse the system and reduce the pressures on the spine, eliminants were prescribed in sixteen instances. Most commonly recommended were enemas and colonics or mild vegetable laxatives such as Castoria and olive oil.

Two unusual treatments, mentioned only twice, involved salt and ice. The first was to place a pinch of salt on the individual's tongue to relax the body and help prevent the occurrence of seizures. The ice was to be applied at the base of the brain and was to reduce the severity of the seizures. (The ice treatment was used with considerable success.)

Case History

Considering the seriousness of epilepsy and the complications which frequently occur, Edgar Cayce's reported success rate was extremely high. Nearly one-half noted either a complete cure or considerable improvement. The others either did not report on the outcome or did not follow Cayce's advice completely.

One case history that noted improvements was 2153, a young girl who had received twelve readings for epilepsy between the ages of twelve and fourteen. The cause of her disorder was found to be a lesion on the spine, which affected her lacteal area and impeded the proper nerve impulses to the brain, causing the attacks. The lesion appeared on the spine during prenatal development, according to Cayce.

In her first reading, Cayce advised the application of hot castor oil packs over the liver area. This was to help establish proper eliminations and aid in breaking up the lesions. At this time, a tablespoon of castor oil was to be taken internally, followed by a tablespoon of olive oil later in the day. Massages, using a combination of peanut oil and olive oil, were to be given once a week over the entire spine area. Before sleep, a pinch of salt was to be placed on the tongue.

Dietary recommendations included fruits and vegetables and foods high in vitamins B, B_1, A, C, and D. Sweets were to be avoided.

The second reading advised the continued use of the packs, afterward sponging off the abdomen with a lukewarm solution of bicarbonate of soda in water.

Osteopathic adjustments were to begin, making corrections throughout the spine. To soothe the nerves and reduce the severity of the seizures, Cayce recommended a passion flower tonic made with water, the passion flower, and fruit and grain alcohol. Whenever a seizure seemed imminent, as a preventive measure, ice was to be placed over the first, second, and third cervical vertebrae.

Further dietary instructions were given in this reading. Soybean milk and fruit were to be eaten at breakfast, a fresh salad at the noon meal, and fish, fowl, or lamb with cooked vegetables at the evening meal.

The next eight readings basically recommended continuing the treatments, maintaining a positive attitude, and having faith that the outcome would be for the best. At various times, deeper massages and a more alkaline diet were suggested.

The girl's eleventh reading recommended that a masseuse give the massages. Petrolagar was recommended to help eliminate the toxins which had accumulated in the body and emphasis was placed on the continued avoidance of sweets and carbonated drinks.

The final reading suggested the use of the Wet Cell with spirits of camphor. Additionally, massages—using salt and pure apple vinegar—over the knees and lower limbs were recommended. These were to further aid the nervous system in breaking up the lesions.

After following the suggested treatments during the two-year span of the readings, many improvements were noted. The child had a more positive outlook on life, and the frequency of the attacks had decreased.

Erysipelas

Erysipelas is an acute inflammation of the skin caused by a streptococcus infection. Symptoms may include pain, malaise, chills, and moderate fever. A bright red spot is noted frequently near a fissure at the angle of the nose or on the cheek.

Edgar Cayce gave seven readings on erysipelas for three individuals.

Although Cayce's explanations on how erysipelas originated varied, there were common denominators noted. For case 409, he attributed excretions from the skin infection itself as poisoning the entire body and subsequently affecting the eliminations and other body functions.

In the 1014 readings, Cayce diagnosed cold and congestion of the lungs and other organs as responsible for a depleted blood and nerve supply, explaining that, as the body attempted to restore balance in the various systems, its resistance to disease was lowered, allowing the infection to take hold. The poisons from the disease contributed to a degeneration of the organs of assimilation and elimination.

The central problem in the case of 5479, a ten-year-old girl, was described by Cayce as an incoordination between the brain and the rest of her body. Cayce found that this incoordination was partially due to the aftereffects of the drug digitalis, which had been prescribed by a physician. The symptoms of erysipelas had thus been produced in a body which would probably never be completely restored to normal.

Shared symptoms in all three cases were poor eliminations, poor assimilations, and circulatory imbalances. Infection was another common factor in the first two cases.

Treatment and Case History

Cayce's treatment for erysipelas varied from case to case. His treatment for case 1014 involved dietary measures, oil enemas, an herbal tonic, and massage.

Treatment for case 5479 also recommended massage and an herbal tonic, along with doses of Syrup of Squill as a cardiac stimulant and the use of the Radio-Active Appliance with gold.

The four readings given for case 409, a twenty-one-year-old woman, noted that the disease had worked its way into the muscular tissue of her legs, impairing her ability to walk. The poisonous excretions from the skin lesions had circulated throughout her body, affecting the eliminations and hindering the circulatory system. The poor circulation subsequently caused stomach inflammation, which was responsible for poor digestion.

Cayce's initial treatment for erysipelas, along with treatments previously suggested, was to increase her daily recommended dose of animated ash to one-half grain. After some improvement was noted, the woman requested a second reading. Along with the animated ash, Cayce recommended mullein stupes placed twice weekly over her upper legs, where the erysipelas had retarded capillary circulation. Daily massages were also recommended, using a combination of equal parts olive oil and tincture of myrrh, with the instructions to rub toward the trunk of the body to help eliminate toxins and improve the circulation. Instead of manipulations, an electric vibrator was to be used over the entire spine. Emphasis was placed on a balanced and cleansing diet and on spending time outside.

Her third reading noted an improvement, and the wom
an was advised to continue the same treatment regimen
with the added use of the Violet Ray and exercises taken in
the mornings and evenings. The woman's condition apparently improved temporarily, but she returned to Cayce for a
fourth reading on the subject when her erysipelas returned.
Cayce attributed the relapse to the woman's indiscretions
and internal weaknesses. He recommended the treatments
previously given, along with watermelon tea to improve
eliminations through the kidneys and bladder. The tea was
to be prepared by steeping one-half ounce of the crushed
seed in eight ounces of water thirty to fifty minutes. One
tablespoon was to be taken three or four times a day for
two or three days.

Eyes: Puffy

Five individuals, ranging in age from forty to seventy-
seven years, consulted Edgar Cayce regarding problems
with puffy eyes, and received a total of six readings. In all
cases the puffiness was regarded as symptomatic of internal imbalances which could be corrected.

According to Cayce, pressures on the kidneys would
interfere with the circulation and nerve supply to the eyes,
resulting in a puffy appearance. The pressures could be the
result of spinal misalignments, kidney infections, glandular imbalances, liver-kidney incoordination, or any combination of these problems.

Treatment

Cayce's treatment regimen was to correct the internal
distress, giving special attention to the kidneys. Although
these treatments varied with the individual nature of each
condition, there were several consistent factors.

Recommended in four cases were spinal adjustments in
the form of either osteopathy, chiropractic, or neuropathy,
with special focus on the lumbar vertebrae. Readings for

the same number of cases recommended hot packs over the lower spine, using either a mutton tallow–spirits of camphor–spirits of turpentine combination or Glyco-Thymoline. These were to be kept warm with a heating pad or a dry pack of hot salt. The frequency of application, when specified, was one hour daily for five days in succession.

In three cases, dietary advice was given, with instructions to eat Jerusalem artichokes, drink plenty of water, and eat plenty of raw vegetables. To flush toxins from the system, Eno salts were suggested in two readings. Also recommended in two readings was electrotherapy in the form of the Wet Cell and Radio-Active Appliance. Suggested in one reading was watermelon-seed tea, a kidney stimulant. As a direct application for the area around the eyes and the rest of the face, one reading recommended an astringent.

Case History

Reports were received in only two of the cases. One was sketchy but indicated improvement. Impressive results were experienced in the case described below.

Case 987 was a forty-nine-year-old woman who Cayce found was suffering from poor assimilations, poor circulation, and spinal lesions, among other problems. Her first reading attributed her puffy eyes to pressures on the lumbar axis to which the kidneys were reacting, affecting the circulation to the eyes.

In treating this condition, osteopathic adjustments were advised. These were to be given in two series of two or three times weekly for two or three weeks, alternated with a rest period of equal duration. After that, they could be taken occasionally as needed. Massages were also advised. Her diet was to be kept highly alkaline.

To improve the circulation and general vitality, use of the Radio-active Appliance was suggested. To improve eliminations, enemas with oil or a saline solution were recommended.

Later the woman reported that she did not follow the

reading completely but noted that the adjustments had helped her and that she would follow the other suggestions if she felt in need of them. Two months later, she requested another physical reading, this time for a kidney infection which was causing puffy eyes and red splotches on the skin. Cayce warned that her condition would become more serious if it was not attended to right away.

To combat the infection, Glyco-Thymoline packs were to be placed over the kidney area and covered with a heated, quilted bag of iodized salt. The packs were to be applied for one hour daily for five days in succession. On the following day, or after a day of rest, one-half ounce of watermelon-seed tea was to be taken daily. The tea was to be prepared by pouring boiling water over a level teaspoon of crushed seed and steeping for thirty minutes.

Her diet was to consist of raw vegetables, eaten as a meal at least five times a week. This could include carrots, lettuce, celery, watercress, and mustard greens with an oil dressing. At other times, they were to be prepared with gelatin, preferably lemon. Foods that were to be avoided included meat, wine, and carbonated drinks.

A few weeks later, the woman reported that the reading had pinpointed her condition, adding, "It is possible that you saved my life." After more weeks of following the treatments, she reported feeling infinitely better. For the next twenty years, she continued to lead an active life with no serious health problem.

Facial Tic

A facial tic is characterized by an uncontrollable twitching in the muscles of the face. The principal cause found by Edgar Cayce in all three was incoordination between the sympathetic and cerebrospinal nervous systems.

A latent cause in two of the cases was spinal subluxations. One reading also mentioned poor assimilations and eliminations, circulatory imbalances, and an improper acid-alkaline balance. Another reading noted that nervous tensions was a factor.

The dominant treatment in all three cases was spinal manipulation to coordinate the nerve impulses and restore normal equilibrium throughout the body. One reading also suggested dietary measures, electric vibrator applications along the spine, and Wet Cell treatments. Another suggested hot and cold packs to stimulate circulation.

Case History

The facial tic suffered by case 4480, a fifty-seven-year-old man, was attributed to several internal causes. According to Cayce, poor eliminations had created too much acid in the lower portion of the digestive system, causing stresses in certain nerve centers which resulted in poor assimilations. These imbalances depleted the body's energy reserves. The weak and depleted circulatory system, in turn, brought taxation and strain to the cardiac and cervical nervous centers, affecting the respiratory system and resulting in the facial tic.

Cayce's treatment suggestion in this instance was a gentle massage and rest and recuperation in mountain or salt air in order to cleanse and rebuild the blood. Also recommended was osteopathic manipulation in the cervical and upper dorsal areas to help maintain normal equilibrium throughout the body.

Feet: Calluses

A callus is a thickened, hardened area of the skin, most often appearing on the palms of the hands or the bottoms of the feet. Seven complete readings discussed the causes and treatment of calluses on the feet, and approximately ten additional readings provided further suggestions regarding treatment.

In five of the definitive readings on the subject, Edgar Cayce noted several common causative factors, with the two major ones being subluxations or impingements in the spine and poor circulation through the lower limbs and feet. In three cases, problems in the spine and circulation were cited, and in two cases Cayce attributed the calluses to tight-fitting shoes, which reduced the circulation to the feet and produced irritations, eventually forming calluses.

Treatment

Treatment for foot calluses usually included a topical solution, although Cayce usually emphasized a holistic approach which treated all disturbing symptoms within the body, including the calluses.

To assist digestion and eliminations, an alkaline-reacting diet of fruits, vegetables, and their juices was suggested in six cases. To be avoided were starches, fried foods, carbonated drinks, and all meats, except for occasional lamb or seafood.

In five cases, a variety of formulas was suggested to be massaged daily into the feet, and in three cases these formulas were to be massaged into the limbs and spine. The three combinations for massage mentioned most frequently were equal parts of olive oil and tincture of myrrh (also recommended for back rubs); bicarbonate of soda dampened with spirits of camphor; and a combination of melted mutton tallow, spirits of turpentine, and spirits of camphor.

In three cases, weekly spinal adjustments were advised, and in two other cases thorough massages of the back and spine with olive oil and myrrh or with peanut oil were suggested.

Other treatments included an occasional colonic to help remove excess wastes in the digestive tract, and daily foot soaks to help soften calluses, consisting of a warm saltwater or soda solution.

Case History

Many of the individuals receiving readings for their calluses reported obtaining good results, especially from the use of local applications. One woman who reported good results was case 2555. This elderly person suffered from painful calluses on her feet and toes, as well as other disturbances throughout her system.

Her condition was diagnosed by Cayce as being caused by a disorder in the lumbar axis which deflected the circulation and created undue pressure on her feet. He referred to the disorder as a "dis-ease" in the body, which was reflected in several of its disturbances.

The woman was advised that by correcting the distress in the lumbar axis, she would be helping to relieve the pain caused by her calluses. Spinal manipulations and massages were advised, as well as the application of hot and cold packs to the spine, especially to the ninth and tenth dorsal, the lumbar axis, the sacral vertebrae, and also to the area from the third through the fifth dorsal. These were to be administered by a doctor. Following application of the packs, a massage over the back and the lumbar plexus area was advised using a combination of equal parts mutton tallow, spirits of camphor, and spirits of turpentine, followed by the application of heat to those areas.

Also suggested was a nightly foot massage using equal parts olive oil and peanut oil, after which the feet were to be wrapped in a light cloth. She was also advised to follow an alkaline-based diet which was to include Jerusalem artichokes, cooked in their own juices, once a week.

Feet: Weakness, Swelling, Etc.

Edgar Cayce was consulted for a number of problems involving the feet and lower limbs, which have been grouped here under the broad heading of weakness and swelling. Nine individuals, who ranged from twelve to seventy-two years, received a total of ten readings which dealt with disorders of the feet.

The problems involved in these cases included swelling, bunions, corns, soreness, and calluses. Cayce noted that the causes could be internal, external, or both. The basic

cause in four cases was poor elimination, which led to the
retention of fluids in the feet, ankles, and lower legs. Poor
circulation was also a factor in several cases. The most
prevalent external cause was shoes that did not fit properly
and which would restrict the circulation and cause calluses
to form.

Treatment

Cayce's treatments were centered on restoring normal
circulation to the feet. Readings in six cases recommended
massage, either of the feet or lower limbs, as well as in
other areas of the body. To help relieve swelling and
discomfort, various substances were to be massaged into
the affected areas. These differed in each case.

Foot baths, using various solutions, were suggested in
three cases. Spinal manipulations were recommended as
often and were designed to improve the circulation to the
legs and feet and generally relax the body. Other advice on
the care of the feet was occasionally offered. These suggestions included keeping the feet dry and out of drafts and
avoiding shoes that did not fit properly, including those
that restricted the feet as well as those with high heels.

Case History

A typical case was that of 623, a woman who received
one reading for swelling in her lower extremities. Cayce
found her discomfort to be due to spinal pressure, poor
eliminations and digestion, and a sluggish liver.

Cayce advised a foot massage using a combination of
mutton tallow, spirits of turpentine, and spirits of camphor.
General spinal manipulations to help improve the circulation to the lower limbs were to be administered twice a
week until fifteen adjustments had been given. A well-
balanced diet was also recommended, with an emphasis on
alkaline foods.

While there was no report received on the outcome of
this case, reports were received from five others, and four

of them noted improvements in their condition upon following the advice given in their readings.

Flu (Influenza)

Flu is an abbreviated term for influenza, an infectious disease caused by a virus. Common symptoms include fever, chills, coughs, headaches, muscle aches, and occasionally nausea.

Edgar Cayce gave a total of twenty-three readings concerning flu-related disorders for thirteen individuals, ranging in age from three to seventy-five years.

In all of the cases, some type of viral infection was the immediate cause of the illness. Further descriptions of causes in the readings concerned factors that lowered the person's resistance sufficiently to allow the flu virus to take hold in the body.

Mentioned in eight cases were imbalances involving the circulation and eliminations. Usually congestion in the hepatic and lymphatic systems caused by circulatory problems would lead to pressures and irritation in the mucous membranes. This would cause excess lymph production, infection, and fever.

A closely related problem, which would lead to a toxin buildup in the colon and bloodstream, was poor eliminations. The body would subsequently become congested and the circulatory system overtaxed. Poor assimilation and spinal misalignments were also contributing factors. When these factors combined, they created a situation conducive to the growth of bacteria, which would lead to fever and a variety of other flu-related symptoms.

Additionally, bacteria would invade the throat and chest areas, causing respiratory problems such as nasal and lung congestion and coughing.

Treatment

Treatments prescribed by Cayce for individuals with flu were basically aimed at reducing congestion and helping the body fight infection. Dietary suggestions were given in every case but two, and stressed liquid and semiliquid foods in an effort to place the least possible strain on the system until the worst of the infection had passed. Diet for these individuals consisted almost entirely of fruit and fruit juices (especially citrus), vegetables and vegetable juices, beef juice, and eggnog consisting of egg yolk, a little alcohol, and milk.

In less severe situations, other easily assimilated, body-building foods could be included as long as the diet was kept sufficiently alkaline. In these cases, the diet included whole-grain cereals, liver, seafood, and eggs. Foods to be avoided were other meats, grease, and large amounts of sweets and starches.

To help decongest the system and cleanse it of excess toxins, various methods of stimulating the eliminations were suggested in eleven cases. Most often prescribed were enemas or colonics and Castoria. Typical Castoria instructions were to take small doses at frequent intervals throughout the day until results were obtained.

Six individuals were advised to have spinal manipulations to balance the circulation and help stimulate drainages from the kidneys and colon. These were usually general in nature, with the focus being on the dorsal and cervical areas. Massage, which received almost as many recommendations, was also to balance circulation and stimulate drainages.

To reduce congestion, rubbing the feet and lower limbs with a combination of mutton tallow, spirits of camphor, and spirits of turpentine was advised in two cases.

Various types of inhalation therapy were recommended for five individuals. These included alcohol-based inhalants, sprays, and fumes from a ''croup cup,'' all of which were suggested as expectorants and were intended to relieve congestion and reduce coughing. Herbal prescriptions to relieve coughing and promote expectoration of mucus were suggested in two cases, and two other individuals were advised to take a mixture of egg whites, lemon, honey, and glycerine.

Hot packs applied over various parts of the body were suggested in four instances. In one case, Epsom salt packs were to be placed over the abdomen, and in another, at the small of the back. Also recommended were onion poultices placed over the throat and chest in one case, and over the neck, back of the head, and pit of the stomach in the other. The poultices, which were to stay on the body at least two to three hours, consisted of raw onions ground up and placed in a thickness of one-quarter to one-half inch in a cloth sack. Following the treatment, the body could be bathed.

Hydrotherapy was suggested for three individuals, twice in the form of hot mustard-water baths for the feet and lower limbs to stimulate circulation. Various other treatments received occasional mention and included Calcidin, saffron tea, electrotherapy, and bicarbonate of soda in water.

Also occasionally recommended were bits of common-sense advice, which included keeping warm and staying out of drafts, keeping the feet warm and dry, and getting plenty of rest until fully recovered.

Case History

Case 431 was a thirty-one-year-old man who received one reading for flu, cold, and congestion. His condition was attributed to improper eliminations and poor drainage from the duodenum, which caused an acidic condition in his digestive system and had weakened the body's resistance to the flu germ.

Since the digestive tract was involved, Cayce prescribed a liquid diet of fruit juices. A high enema, using salt and soda in the water, was recommended to increase eliminations and remove toxins from the system. Also suggested to aid eliminations were small doses of Castoria taken every twenty to thirty minutes until the stomach was eased. Alka-Seltzer was recommended as an alkalizer, which Cayce felt would have a calming effect on the stomach. One tablespoon was to be taken after two or three doses of Castoria.

An osteopathic adjustment was also suggested to help regulate eliminations, and to help the liver function more effectively, Cayce advised Zilatone be taken on the evening of the day the adjustment was administered.

The man apparently followed Cayce's advice and a few days later reported that his condition had improved.

Flu: Aftereffects

Influenza is characterized by an abrupt onset of fever, chills, malaise, cough, and weakness. It can have a debilitating effect on the body which can delay a full recovery for some individuals.

Edgar Cayce gave a total of twelve readings for eleven individuals who were suffering from the aftereffects of the flu. The main problem, noted in ten of the cases, was a disturbance in the hepatic circulation, which disrupted the production of lymph, a process that had already been weakened by the initial bout with the flu.

Poor eliminations, which allowed toxins to increase in the body, were mentioned in all but three of the cases. A related factor in seven individuals was poor assimilation. In its weakened state, the body could not derive the proper nutrients from the diet, thus leading to further physical weakening.

In four cases, spinal subluxations further contributed to the problem. Lesions and pressures in the dorsal and cervical areas were impeding proper nerve impulses and causing further disturbances in the circulatory system.

Treatment

Cayce's treatments were primarily aimed at strengthening the body's resistance. Dietary advice was given in ten cases and included body-building and alkaline-reacting foods such as fruits and vegetables and their juices. Whole grains, egg yolks, seafood, and the lighter meats were also recommended, while pork, large amounts of starches, white bread, and fried foods were to be avoided.

Intestinal cleansing to remove accumulated toxins and waste products was recommended in eight cases. Colonics and enemas were most frequently recommended, although laxatives also received occasional recommendations.

Suggested in seven cases were spinal manipulations, primarily to help relieve pressures in the area of the liver and kidneys. Readings for two individuals specified osteopathic massages to relax the entire body.

To stimulate circulation, electrotherapy was recommended in four cases. The Radio-Active Appliance was suggested in half of the cases.

Herbal tonics also received four recommendations. The tonics, which were to stimulate assimilations and generally strengthen the body, contained digestive aids such as wild ginseng, wild ginger, and stillingia. Other types of digestive aids, such as Acigest, received three recommendations. Hydrotherapy, massage, exercise, and Calcios were each suggested twice.

Case History

Case 2580 was a man of unspecified age who received one reading following a bout with a cold and the flu. The illness had left him with digestive disturbances, a weakened lymphatic circulation, and a prolapsed colon. He also had blood pressure irregularities and experienced dizziness and headaches.

To cleanse the colon of toxins, Cayce recommended two colonics be given during the first ten days of treatment. Following this, osteopathic manipulations were to begin, making corrections in the sixth and seventh dorsal vertebrae, the lumbar axis, and the area from the third and fourth dorsals to the first cervical. Eight to ten such adjustments were to be administered, followed by a one-week rest period and then another series of manipulations.

Fats and heavy meats were to be avoided, although fish, fowl, and lamb could be eaten in moderation. Carbonated drinks were also not advised. Fruit, fruit juices, and raw vegetables and their juices were especially recommended.

To aid digestion, two herbal remedies were suggested. The first, elm bark, was to be chewed once or twice a day and the resulting liquid swallowed. The other was a mild tea prepared from American saffron, which the patient was to drink once a day.

Although the man expressed satisfaction with his reading, he did not follow its advice due to personal reasons. In summary, only three of the eleven individuals receiving this type of reading reported on the outcome. Two, upon following the advice, fully recovered.

Fractures and Sprains

Fracture and sprains are injuries to the muscles, ligaments, and bones in the body. Fractures range in severity from small cracks in the bone to compound fractures in which the bone protrudes through the skin. Sprains are the result of a wrenching or twisting of a joint, with a partial rupture of its ligaments. A bluish or red discoloration, which is a result of ruptured blood vessels, may appear.

Edgar Cayce gave a total of forty-seven readings on various kinds of fractures and sprains for thirty-four individuals who ranged from fourteen to eighty-three years old.

Treatment

Treatments for fractures and sprains were fairly consistent throughout the readings. The major treatment, recommended in twenty-three cases, was to massage or pack the injured areas. Frequently used for the packing was a solution of apple cider vinegar and salt, which was to be applied by means of cloths soaked in the solution and placed on the injured areas.

Also frequently recommended was a combination of olive oil and tincture of myrrh and other oil-based combinations. Reading 326-5 gave a general-purpose massage formula which Cayce stated would be good for backaches, sprains, strains, and bruises: "To one ounce of olive oil add two ounces Russian White Oil, a half ounce of tincture of benzoin, six ounces of coal oil [kerosene], a half ounce of witch hazel and 20 minims oil of sassafras."

In twelve cases, to accelerate healing of the injured area, various forms of electrotherapy were suggested, and most often mentioned were the Violet Ray and at times the ultraviolet and infrared lights.

Ten individuals were given advice regarding foods that would help supply needed elements for healing. Often recommended was an increase of foods containing an abundance of minerals, especially calcium, iron, and phosphorus. Blood-building foods, including fresh fruits and their juices, celery, lettuce, and carrots, were also advised. Beef and fried foods were strongly discouraged.

In seven instances, spinal manipulations were advised to aid in coordinating the body and stimulating its natural healing ability. Also recommended were topical applications such as bichloride of mercury and iodine in four cases. Recommended as often were eliminants such as enemas and milk of magnesia and local packs using substances such as mullein. Surgery was advised in two instances. Both rest and exercise were also occasionally advised, suggesting that care must be taken in these particular cases to maintain a healthy balance between the two.

Case History

The follow-up reports made in these cases were exceptionally positive, with seventeen individuals noting beneficial results due to following the advice given in their readings.

One case of interest (case 1771) involved a twenty-four-year-old woman who received two readings concerning an injury she sustained through an accident which fractured her kneecap and sprained her knee.

Cayce's first suggestion was to apply wet heat once or twice a day to the damaged limb. He also advised massaging the knee, using a salt-and-apple-vinegar solution. If massage was too painful, on the second or third day, infrared light treatments were advised. The reading also cautioned against overexercising the knee.

During the woman's second reading, Cayce suggested the use of an oil compound which was to be massaged into the knee each morning. The oil mixture was to consist of four ounces of peanut oil, two ounces of oil of pine needles, one ounce of oil of sassafras, and one tablespoon lanolin.

The woman followed Cayce's advice and later reported that the pain had subsided and that the knee was healing nicely.

Gallbladder Disorders

The gallbladder, a pear-shaped organ situated under the surface of the right lobe of the liver, is used for the storage and secretion of bile and mucus. Most gallbladder disorders, including gallstones, are the result of the formation of cholesterol or cholesterin crystals and other elements found in bile.

Poor digestive processes and poor eliminations are the primary causes of gallbladder disorders, according to Edgar Cayce, who cited incoordination in both the nervous and circulatory systems as the secondary causes. Generally, disturbances in the pancreas, spleen, and gall duct were said to be a result of an inadequate nerve and blood supply.

Treatment

Eleven of the fourteen readings recommended small doses of olive oil taken at frequent intervals throughout the day, coordinated with the application of castor oil packs several times a week. This was to stimulate eliminations, help shrink and pass the stones, improve absorption through the lacteal ducts, and aid the entire hepatic circulation. In nine cases, spinal adjustments were suggested in order to coordinate the nervous systems. The same number of readings suggested colonics or enemas to aid the eliminations and to speed removal of toxins from the system.

Additionally, dietary changes were frequently suggested, with an emphasis on liquids. In four cases, various forms of massage were suggested. In only one instance was an operation recommended.

Case History

In the case of 1857, a thirty-eight-year-old woman, Cayce attributed her gallbladder problems to "lesions in the last dorsal and first lumbar—these have been the sources of the disturbances with this body, combined with the inflammatory condition which existed at childbirth—causing, with those activities in the system, an adhesion in the right portion of the abdominal area."

This adhesion, Cayce felt, was causing disturbances in the gall duct and liver area, as well as through the cecum, colon, and pelvic organs. The reading indicated that surgical measures were not needed if steps were taken that would break up the adhesions as well as create the proper reactions in the liver, gall duct, pancreas, and spleen.

A major treatment was castor oil packs applied for one hour a day, three times each week for three to four weeks. These were to be placed over the lower portion of the liver area. On the day following each session of three packs, two teaspoons of olive oil were to be taken as an internal aid to eliminations. Colonics were also to be given on the same day to prevent the cecum and ascending colon from becoming engorged.

Massages, using equal parts of olive oil and peanut oil, across the abdomen and diaphragm areas, as well as the rest of the body, were advised for those days when the castor oil packs were not applied.

After the prescribed number of castor oil packs were applied, osteopathic adjustments were recommended to assist in breaking up the lesions and in emptying the gall duct. Jerusalem artichokes were specifically recommended as part of her diet.

One year later, the woman reported that she had benefited from the application of the castor oil packs. Thirty years later, however, she reported that her gallbladder had been subsequently removed, but she felt that if she had continued the treatments outlined in her readings, surgery would have been avoided.

Gaucher's Disease

There are two cases of Gaucher's disease in the Edgar Cayce readings. It is a genetic disorder caused by a deficiency of a specific enzyme and is characterized by enlargement of the spleen, discoloration of the skin, and/or acute anemia.

Cayce attributed one case of Gaucher's disease to an incoordination between the sympathetic and cerebrospinal nervous systems (due to anxiety), and the other to spleen and pancreas problems and disturbances in the bone marrow which affected assimilations.

Treatment

The treatments suggested for the two cases of Gaucher's disease were similar in some respects and different in others. One recommended the combined treatment of proper diet, X-ray treatments, Atomidine, colonics, massages, and ultraviolet light. The other involved diet, spinal manipulation, and the use of the Radio-Active Appliance.

Case History

Case 4019 involved a forty-eight-year-old man whose symptoms were severe enlargement of the spleen and severe anemia. A primary cause suggested by Cayce was a chronic disturbance in the bone marrow which had caused an imbalance in the number of red and white blood cells. This had resulted in the engorgement of the spleen and in a disturbance in the functioning of the pancreas. Related symptoms were general weakness and poor assimilations.

Cayce first suggested two X-ray treatments for the spleen to be given a week apart. A rest period of five days was to be followed with five days of Atomidine dosage, taking one drop daily in water thirty minutes before breakfast. This was to be followed by a series of daily massages to stimulate the circulation. Using cocoa butter, the massage was to be administered in a circular motion along both sides of the spine, especially in the areas where the ribs joined the spine. This series, consisting of at least eight to ten treatments, was to be followed by a series of ultraviolet light treatments, with the instructions to place a sheet of green glass between the light and the body. The treatments, lasting between one and one and a half minutes, were to be given three times a week. Cocoa butter massages over the ribs and extremities were to follow. Dietary instructions were to include fruits and vegetables to control eliminations, beef juice, and rare broiled liver.

Follow-up reports indicated that case 4019 used the treatments suggested, and although he was not cured, he noted that as a result his general health improved.

Glaucoma

There are two types of glaucoma, the second leading cause of blindness. The more common is wide-angle glaucoma, which is characterized by increasing tunnel vision. The other is acute, or narrow-angle, glaucoma, which is characterized by pain and blurred vision.

There are seventeen readings on glaucoma in the Edgar Cayce files. These were given for fourteen individuals with varying stages of the eye disease.

The causes most frequently cited by Cayce for glaucoma

were glandular dysfunction, especially adrenal; toxins or "infectious forces" in the system; the deflection of proper nerve impulses to the eyes, usually due to spinal misalignments; poor circulation and impaired eliminations; kidney and liver imbalances; and a general depletion of energy in the system. The glaucoma in two cases was said to be partly karmic, implying an inborn predisposition toward the disease.

According to Cayce, any of the above conditions, either singly or combined, could result in a lack of nutriments, circulation, and/or proper nerve impulses to the eyes, causing distress, sometimes inflammation, and a progressive deterioration of vision.

Treatment

The treatments suggested in cases of glaucoma were particularly consistent. Spinal manipulation, as often by massage as by osteopathy, was recommended in every case but one. These treatments were to focus on the cervical and dorsal areas, sometimes following heat applications.

Hydrotherapy treatments were recommended in about half of the cases. These included heat (usually wet) applied over specific areas of the spine; cabinet sweats (dry heat, at times adding fumes by placing a pan of boiling water in the cabinet); steam (fume) baths using substances such as Atomidine and witch hazel; colonics; and hot and cold needle showers.

Various forms of electrotherapy treatments were recommended in about a third of these cases, to be taken according to specific instructions. Most often mentioned were the Radio-Active Appliance, Erlanger treatments, and the Wet Cell Appliance, or at times simple "low electrical vibrations." Attention to diet was stressed frequently, with special emphasis on carrots and other vegetables served both raw and cooked.

Case History

The reading given for case 698, an adult male, offers a typical treatment. A steam bath with Atomidine, and the temperature no hotter than 101 degrees, was recommended at least once monthly. This was prescribed to aid the eliminations, reduce pressures, and improve glandular conditions in the system. Later eucalyptus, wintergreen, and oil of pine needles were to be used in the steam.

Each steam bath was to be followed by a massage using a combination of Nujol, witch hazel, tincture of benzoin, and sassafras oil, giving special attention to the cervical, upper dorsal, and lumbar areas. High enemas were to be included with each hydrotherapy treatment to help reduce the blood pressure.

The diet was to be highly alkaline, free of heavy or red meats, and high in foods containing phosphorus, gold, and silicon, such as carrots, salsify, squash, skins of white potatoes, and okra.

Treatments with the Radio-Active Appliance were also part of the therapy.

No follow-up reports were made.

Goiter

A goiter is the abnormal enlargement of the thyroid gland, located at the base of the throat. In many parts of the world, simple goiter is due to lack of iodine.

In reading 3797-1, Edgar Cayce defined the general condition as "the clogging of the glands by secretions not eliminated through their proper channels, and by the lack of stimulation to the center governing this circulation."

Eighteen readings on this condition were given for thirteen people.

In nine of the cases, the condition was attributed to poor blood circulation. Generally, Cayce did not explain the circulatory problems in detail, but in some cases he did attribute subsequent nervous and glandular disturbances to faulty blood circulation. In case 850, improper oxidation of blood in the lungs caused a nervous disorder resulting in glandular imbalance. Similarly, in case 4600 improper metabolism in the blood set off a nervous reaction which created an imbalance in the glandular functions. Five readings cited poor eliminations and four others mentioned lack of elements such as iodine, calcium, and iron as causative factors.

Treatment

In treating goiter, adjustments of the spine to restore normal nerve coordination were prescribed in almost each case. Electrotherapy was recommended for eleven subjects, usually in the form of the Violet Ray or the Radio-Active Appliance, and in two cases by means of the Wet Cell Appliance.

Dietary advice was given in two-thirds of the readings. This generally included fruits, raw and cooked vegetables, and the lighter proteins. Eating fried foods and pork was discouraged, as well as eating two or more starches at the same meal, such as potatoes, white bread, and spaghetti. In a few cases, Cayce specified that only iodized salt be allowed in the diet. Additionally, Atomidine was prescribed for six subjects in varying amounts in order to purify and balance the glands.

In three cases, Cayce referred to the need for the individuals to heal themselves by proper attunement mentally and spiritually to healthy vibrations within and without the body.

Case History

Due to an iodine deficiency and an excess amount of potassium in the blood, the thyroid of a fifty-year-old woman had become enlarged. Symptoms of case 813 were indicative of a hypothyroid condition—weariness, lack of vigor, slowed nerve coordination and sensory distortion were indicated.

Treatment began with a drop of Atomidine in a half glass of water in the morning and evening, increasing the dosage by one drop a day, up to ten drops to be taken on the tenth day. A rest period of three days followed, during which time Cayce recommended use of the hand Violet Ray, applied each evening to the areas around the throat and collarbone.

After the second series of Atomidine and Violet Ray treatments, deep osteopathic manipulations three times a week were prescribed. These were to set up drainage in the cervical and upper dorsal vertebrae and to stimulate better eliminations through the alimentary canal. Following the second week of manipulations, a one-week rest period was specified, after which the manipulations were to be repeated at the same intervals. Although Atomidine treatments could continue during the manipulations, use of the Violet Ray was forbidden at this time.

Regarding diet, Cayce advised 813 to include foods rich in iron, iodine, and silicon and to avoid sweets and starches.

In follow-up reports, case 813 noted she did not believe that the treatments had contributed to her "complete recovery," which she felt was due to the chanting and meditation exercises which she began after she started treatment. It is interesting to note, however, that three other individuals reported a complete recovery from goiter after following Cayce's recommendations.

Gonorrhea: Female

Gonorrhea is a contagious inflammation of the genital mucous membranes. It is transmitted primarily through coitus. Symptoms may include pain and burning during urination and a discharge of mucus. Other complications such as vaginitis may occur.

Twelve readings were given for five women with gonorrhea. Four of them were told that their condition was due, either in part or completely, to their poor attitudes or negative emotions. For example, in a reading given for case 272, Edgar Cayce stated that "the causes are both physical and psychopathological.'' The reading described the physical development of the disease and its strong relationship with negative attitudes.

In about half of the cases, the blood contained bacilli which should have normally been eliminated through the alimentary canal, but in the cases of gonorrhea, the bacilli had spread into the circulatory system, causing complications such as engorgement of the liver as well as overacid kidneys.

Treatment

Treatment of gonorrhea as mentioned in the readings generally consisted of a series of douches and sitz baths, dietary restrictions, and changes in attitudes. Operations (the type was usually unspecified but was probably dilation and curettage) were considered as an alternative in about one-half of the cases if the disease threatened to become more virulent. However, most consistently advised was douching. Creolin (highly diluted) was recommended as an antiseptic for douching in four out of five of the cases. In one-half, diluted Atomidine douches were suggested for their antiseptic qualities. Some women were advised to alternate douching solutions for both cleansing and alkalizing the vagina.

Sitz baths were suggested in seventy-five percent of the cases. The bath solutions generally consisted of tincture of myrrh boiled with either sweet gum, tolu, or aloes in water. As a glandular stimulant, oral doses of Atomidine were suggested in about one-half of the cases. In two instances and to encourage healing, use of the Violet Ray was suggested. The recommended diet was well-balanced and alkaline reacting in nature. Meats, fats, and seafoods were to be avoided, and intake of sweets and starches reduced.

Case History

Eight readings were given by Cayce for a thirty-two-year-old woman with gonorrhea who had requested a diagnosis as well as a confirmation of her suspicions that her husband and sister were having an affair.

The first reading for case 272 focused on her condition and explained that her mental attitude was instrumental in causing her present state: "Here we find from the greater amount of distress, for from there being stored in the mental forces of the body those of aggression, discontent, the holding of the disorders against individuals, had produced much as has been stored as of detrimental influences." Subluxations in the fourth lumbar had accentuated this imbalance by accelerating the discharge from the pelvic organs.

The woman's treatment included the advice to change her attitude, to become more forgiving. An herbal tonic was prescribed to calm and balance her nerves as well as to change the vibratory forces in her system. osteopathic adjustments were to be administered in the cervical, upper dorsal, and lumbar regions.

Her second reading suggested douching twice daily with either Lysol (highly diluted) or an antiseptic with similar properties. To relieve the discharges, the Violet Ray was to be applied over her lower spine and pubic area. At this point, her herbal tonic was changed to one that would help purify the system. Dietary restrictions were given concerning meats, fats, and greasy foods. Vegetables were recommended for the main part of diet, particularly pod or leafy ones.

Subsequent readings given by Cayce suggested curettage to help relieve the condition. Douches using Creolin (a half teaspoon to a gallon of water) and then Atomidine (one ounce to ten ounces of water) were to be given to help eradicate the infection. Internal doses of Atomidine were also suggested. This was to be taken twice daily, five to eight drops in one-half glass of water. Laxatives were also occasionally suggested.

Later reports indicated that the woman's health gradually improved, and her last letter indicated that there had been a dramatic change toward a more positive attitude.

Gonorrhea: Male

Gonorrhea, a venereal disease, is the contagious inflammation of the genital mucous membrane. In males, it is characterized by burning on urination and a serous or milky discharge. A few days later, the pain is more pronounced and the discharge becomes yellow and profuse, at times tinged with blood.

Edgar Cayce gave eighteen readings for nine men with gonorrhea, most of which focused mainly on treatment. He generally diagnosed the symptoms as stemming from an infection in the genital area. In many instances, the genital infection was found to have introduced toxic substances into the blood and lymph glands, which contributed to digestive disturbances and incoordination between the cerebrospinal and sympathetic nerve centers. Problems with eliminations would also occur due to painful urination and stricture of the urethra or bladder opening.

Treatment

The most prevalent treatment, mentioned in seven cases, was penile douches using a urethra syringe. Recommended several times weekly, the douches were intended to cleanse the bladder and prostate area and prevent stricture of the urethra. The most typical solution consisted of Atomidine diluted in distilled water. The usual strength was seven to ten drops of Atomidine to one ounce of distilled water.

In most cases, strict dietary rules were specified. Not advised were beef or pork, fats, and starches such as white bread, white potatoes, and rice. Highly recommended were fruits and leafy green vegetables. Smoking and alcoholic beverages were also discouraged during treatments.

Massages and rubs using such substances as peanut oil, olive oil, and alcohol, as well as sweat baths were suggested in many instances to relax the body and aid in the elimination of body toxins.

In four readings, Cayce prescribed various herbal tonics consisting of yellow dock root, buchu leaves, burdock root, mandrake root, and balsam of tolu. Taken in small doses a few times daily, the tonics were to assist in the general purification of the body as well as aid digestion.

Attitude was cited as a critical factor in the relief and prevention of gonorrhea. Cayce advised 849 that good health could be restored "by following the clean living, *physically, mentally,* and the application of self to introspectiveness... [and] keeping self pure and unspotted from the world."

Case History

Case 2317, a thirty-five-year-old man, was suffering from poor health as a result of gonorrhea. His blood had been affected, producing irregularities throughout the circulatory and nervous systems, and an imbalance between the cerebrospinal and sympathetic nervous systems was producing stress throughout the body.

For treatment, Cayce recommended daily penile douches using one teaspoon of Atomidine to two ounces of distilled water. Additionally, three drops of Atomidine in water were to be taken internally each morning. Cayce also prescribed an herbal tonic which, taken four times daily a teaspoon at a time, would help cleanse the system of infection. The tonic contained yellow dock, burdock root, prickly ash bark, dog fennel, mandrake root, buchu leaves, elder flower, and balsam of tolu. Colonic irrigations were advised on an occasional basis to cleanse the colon of toxins released by the tonic.

While there was no report from case 2317, another case, that of 391, who had six readings, reported that his symptoms had cleared up following Cayce's recommendations.

Halitosis

In the eight cases receiving readings, Edgar Cayce found halitosis—bad breath—to be caused by poor eliminations, circulatory imbalances, poor assimilations, and spinal subluxations. Incoordination of the nervous system and poor diet were cited as related causes.

According to Cayce, the condition began with poor eliminations, often associated with spinal subluxations. Circulation would subsequently become slowed and the blood contaminated by a buildup of toxins, impeding the distribution of nutrients through the system. The result was a digestive backup of which offensive breath was a symptom.

Treatment

Cayce's treatment of halitosis was consistent, for in six out of eight readings he recommended spinal adjustments to coordinate the sympathetic and cerebrospinal centers and to improve the flow of nerve impulses. Recommended just as often were various kinds of eliminants, including laxatives, colonics, and enemas. In three cases, massage was suggested to stimulate the circulation. Other detoxifying treatments mentioned were sweats and mud packs. In another reading, the Violet Ray was suggested to coordinate the sympathetic and cerebrospinal nervous systems, thus improving the circulation.

Case History

Case 2461, a forty-seven-year-old man, complained of restlessness, slight headaches, fatigue, and bad breath. Cayce believed the primary causes of his distress were poor eliminations combined with tension in the lumbar and sacral areas. As a consequence of poor eliminations, the circulation was impeded, the blood toxic, and the blood pressure unbalanced. His condition was further aggravated by alcohol abuse. The man's toxic state was causing overacidity and creating disturbances in the digestive system, lungs, and liver. The breath odor was caused by the system attempting to eliminate the poisons through the lungs.

Cayce's first treatment involved Eno salts, which were to be taken as an eliminant each morning before breakfast for a ten-day period, followed by a week's rest and then taken for another ten days. The cycle was to be repeated until the toxic condition was relieved.

After the first ten-day period, the man was to undergo general hydrotherapy treatments, including sweats, massages, and rubdowns, administered once a week for ten weeks. During this period, two colonic irrigations were also to be given. Following this, the subject was to have a series of six to eight osteopathic adjustments, with special attention given to the lower spine and dorsal areas. To further purify the system, changes in diet were suggested. The normal Cayce guidelines were to be followed, with emphasis on drinking plenty of water. Once a week, a glass of lithia water was to be taken.

Hay Fever

Hay fever is an acute allergic reaction to pollens or other irritants. Frequently the cause of repeated colds in children, symptoms include nasal discharge, watery itching eyes, and attacks of sneezing. Asthmatic attacks may also occur.

Eight individuals, who ranged from five to sixty-four years old, each received one reading concerning hay fever.

Edgar Cayce found the most prevalent cause of hay fever, discovered in seven of the eight cases, was spinal misalignments or subluxations, usually located in the dorsal or cervical areas of the spine. These disorders would disturb the mucous membranes of the throat, nasal passages, and lymph circulation, making the body "very susceptible to inflammation as a result of pollens, dust, and odors for it accentuates the olfactory and the lymph circulation" (5039-1).

Other contributing factors involved were poor circulation, mentioned in four cases and which lowered the body's resistance to infection, and poor assimilation, which could weaken the body by reducing the supply of available nutrients.

Treatment

The treatments were consistent for individuals with hay fever. In seven cases, the use of an inhalant was suggested whenever the hay fever symptoms were severe. These inhalants had a grain alcohol base, to which small amounts of various stimulating expectorants were added, such as oil of eucalyptus, rectified oil of turpentine, tincture of benzoin, oil of pine needles, and tolu balsam.

To alleviate subluxations and lesions and to relax the nerve centers, spinal manipulations were advised in six cases. These were to focus on the dorsal vertebrae in almost each case, coordinating the alignment of other areas.

Dietary advice was also given for six individuals, and recommended were foods that were alkaline, easily digested, and body building. On the menu were fruits and vegetables and lighter proteins (fish, fowl, and lamb) in moderation. To be avoided were starches and sweets. Further, colonics were suggested in two cases and a change of climate in one.

To help build immunity to pollen, one individual was prescribed doses of a tonic made from ragweed that was prepared in the springtime by simmering a pint of tender young leaves in a pint of distilled water. When half of the water was cooked off, the remainder was to be strained and grain alcohol (fifteen percent) added to act as a preservative. The dosage advised was half a teaspoon a day during the months of July and August.

Case History

Follow-up reports were received in only two of the cases, with one individual noting beneficial results due to following the reading, and the other, who did not follow Cayce's suggestions, noting no improvement.

Although there was no follow-up for case 5196, a man of forty-five years who suffered from hay fever, Cayce found that the allergy was due to a spinal problem which caused a strain on the muscles and nerves supplying the entire sensory system. The bronchi and trachea had become taut, and the respiratory system was subsequently sensitive to certain substances in the environment.

To provide temporary relief and aid expectoration, Cayce recommended use of a grain-alcohol-based inhalant containing eucalyptus, turpentine, oil of pine needles, and benzoin. When the inhalant had been used for a week, two to three times daily, osteopathic adjustments were to begin and were to concentrate on the brachial centers, coordinating the upper cervical, lower dorsal, and lumbar vertebrae. Wet heat was to be applied over the spine before each treatment.

The man's diet was to contain large amounts of raw vegetables and all fruits except raw apples. Fish, fowl, and lamb could be eaten in small amounts. Sweets, starches, and especially fried foods were to be avoided.

Headaches: General

Fifteen individuals with a tendency toward headaches received a total of seventeen readings. Excluding migraines, the three most common causes cited by Edgar Cayce were nervous incoordination, disorders of the digestive system, and blood deficiencies.

Seven readings attributed an incoordination between the sympathetic and cerebrospinal nervous systems as the cause. This incoordination was seen by Cayce as being due to spinal subluxations or lesions which blocked the nerve impulses to certain areas of the body and thereby resulted in headaches.

Six diagnoses focused on digestive disturbances, but only insofar as these disorders directly affected either the circulation to the brain or the coordination between the cerebrospinal and sympathetic nerve systems. In all six cases, toxins and mucus were present in the digestive tract as the result of poor digestion or assimilation. The toxins were absorbed into the bloodstream, causing headache discomfort.

One case had an overtoxic circulation due to hyperacidity in the digestive and assimilative tracts which was being absorbed into the bloodstream. This subject also had a tendency toward anemia. In another instance, a toxic condition was produced in the stomach due to the abnormal positioning of the pyloric end of the stomach, where digestive juices ferment. Thus the headaches were not solely the result of poor circulation, but of digestive disturbances which directly affected the circulation.

Anemia was cited as the cause in four readings. In some cases, the anemic condition had created an overall lack of vitality, resulting in poor circulation in the head, which in turn resulted in headaches.

Treatment

The most frequent methods of treatment for headaches were diet, spinal manipulation and massage, and colonic irrigations. Dietary recommendations were typical of those found in the readings as a whole, with an emphasis on balance, alkalinity, and body building.

In over half of the readings, Cayce suggested osteopathic adjustments to alleviate the spinal conditions. Spinal massages using a combination of peanut oil and olive oil were also advised in five cases, at times with the use of electric vibrators to stimulate the circulation.

Recommended in almost half of the readings were colonic irrigations. These were to cleanse the intestinal tract of mucus and toxins. Additionally, in three cases Cayce advised Al-Caroid as a means of increasing alkalinity in the system.

In some readings, Cayce also emphasized the need for a healthy outlook on life in overcoming physical distresses.

"Do keep the spiritual and mental in the creative activities. All arise from the spiritual attitude. The mental is the builder" (5147-1).

Case History

Case 2045 was a fifty-eight-year-old woman who had anemia and a tendency toward toxicity in the blood. Cayce found that the pyloric end of her stomach was dropping, allowing for fermentation of the digestive juices and the formation of toxins. He also detected a spinal lesion in the upper dorsals which hampered normal blood circulation in the head.

A series of spinal adjustments, administered twice weekly, was recommended for a period of twelve to fourteen weeks, along with a diet stressing vegetables such as Jerusalem artichokes and the oyster plant (salsify). Colonics were suggested on an occasional basis. Cayce also advised the woman to take two to four Caroid and bile salt tablets at meals once a week until her eliminations improved.

A follow-up report noted that the woman did not follow through with the adjustments recommended by Cayce, and at a later date her gallbladder had to be surgically removed. However, she did follow some of the treatments mentioned and at age seventy-seven was reported to be "in excellent health."

Heart: Leakage

Edgar Cayce gave readings for four adults and two infants in which he mentioned problems with leakage or valvular disturbances in the heart or major arteries. Three of the readings contained warnings that such conditions were imminent, while the remaining three cases actually showed the disorder.

Common symptoms related to this problem included head and limb pains, fatigue, and dizziness. Most cases were accompanied by other disorders, some of which were generated by the same cause. While each case was unique in its manifestation, there were similarities in the causes and treatments cited in the readings. Nearly all the cases were considered curable.

The most common cause of heart leakage, cited in five cases, was insufficient or imbalanced circulation. Specifically implicated in several instances was the hepatic circulation. Poor eliminations were evident in four of the cases, which in turn affected the circulation by virtue of the toxins present in the blood supply.

Three of the six were suffering incoordination in their nervous systems, typically between the sympathetic and cerebrospinal systems. This incoordination was expressed in disorders of the spinal cord in two cases, one having lesions and the other having an engorgement around the coccyx.

Incoordination in the liver and kidneys was cited twice and was said to be the primary cause of the disorder in one case. Two cases involved inadequate assimilations, though it is unclear whether this was causative or a result of other disturbances. Two cases mentioned problems on the mental-spiritual level, one related to fear and the other explaining it as "part of the development of the entity."

Treatment

Cayce's treatment for heart leakage was fairly consistent. All six readings contained references to diet, five of which advocated a standard alkaline-reacting diet with fresh raw vegetables and fish, fowl, and lamb as meats. Fried foods, refined flour, and sugar were to be avoided. One man was advised to follow a semiliquid diet during the course of his treatment.

Eliminations were the next most frequently targeted area, being mentioned in four readings, three of which advocated colonics or enemas; the other suggested the use of Eno salts. Massage, often around the cervical and dorsal areas of the spine, was also cited four times. This was to be administered using a variety of oil compounds, most of which contained peanut oil, among other ingredients. One woman was advised to have spinal manipulations in the dorsal areas instead of massage.

Packs were recommended twice, one using Glyco-Thymoline at the base of the brain, the other using castor oil over the liver and gall duct area. Two others were advised fume baths with Atomidine; one was to use witch hazel in addition to the Atomidine. Electrotherapy was advocated twice, once in the form of the Violet Ray and once with the Wet Cell Appliance. Exercise was also recommended twice, and three readings contained attitudinal advice. For example, case 2952 was told to follow the advice in his reading with persistence and consistency and was given the affirmation: "I am His-God's. He is mindful of me. And in applying His nature, His service, I may better serve my fellow man to the glory of Him who gives me life, light, and immortality."

Case History

Follow-up reports were received from three of the six receiving readings, and all three noted positive results.

An interesting case was 3036, a sixty-six-year-old man who received two readings for dizzy spells and fatigue. While this man didn't actually show signs of heart leakage, Cayce warned that such a condition could develop and lead to a stroke.

The subject's primary cause was cited as poor assimilations; poor eliminations accounted for the presence of "poisons" in the blood. According to Cayce, these disorders, in turn, affected the nervous system, hampering locomotion and mental capacities.

Cayce recommended that the man "keep away from sedatives and drugs as much as practical." Also advised was an alkaline-reacting diet. Cayce also cautioned against taking in "too great a quantity of bulk," which would adversely affect the digestive and eliminative processes.

To help stimulate proper eliminations, Eno salts were advised. The man was to take a teaspoon in a glass of water each morning before breakfast for three to five days, discontinue for five to six days, and then resume the Eno salts again.

Mild fume baths, using two teaspoons of Atomidine to four ounces of water in the fume cup, were recommended to help stimulate the circulation, to aid in eliminating toxins from the system, and to help relax the subject. The weekly fume baths were to be followed with a thorough rubdown using three parts pine oil to one part olive oil.

Case 3036 reported that his condition had improved after following Cayce's advice, but a recurrence of dizzy spells caused him to solicit another reading. In the second reading, Cayce advised him to continue the fume baths and massages and to "be patient, be understanding. Use the abilities constructively, if he would keep improving."

Heart: Tachycardia (Paroxysmal)

Paroxysmal tachycardia is the forceful and rapid acceleration of the heartbeat and pulse, occurring at sudden intervals. In the twenty-six readings given to sixteen individuals with this problem, a variety of accompanying symptoms was noted, almost all of which involved circulatory and/or nervous disturbances.

In at least five cases, the cause was linked to poor eliminations which had caused toxicity in the blood. Five other readings noted the presence of spinal subluxations or lesions which produced an imbalance in the coordination of nerve impulses to the heart. Anemia was found in three cases, and in two other cases severe nervous stress had resulted in irregular heartbeat and pulsation.

Treatment

Treatments were fairly consistent in all cases, with the major emphasis being on dietary improvements, which were advised in nine cases. Foods that Cayce recommended were fruits, vegetables (especially raw), fish, fowl, and lamb. Other meats and fried foods were to be avoided.

Eight cases required a series of at least three or four spinal adjustments to relieve pressures in the spine which Cayce felt contributed to the rapid heartbeat and other accompanying disorders.

Massage was suggested in seven cases to promote relaxation and stimulate healthy circulation. Peanut oil was mentioned in two cases as a desirable massage oil, and in a few cases an electric vibrator was to be used as part of the massage therapy.

Readings in seven cases recommended the use of electrotherapeutic devices, especially the Radio-Active Appliance and shortwave diathermy, mentioned in two cases each. Specific recommendations as to the frequency and duration of usage were generally absent in these readings.

To treat poor eliminations, Cayce prescribed a variety of eliminants in six cases. Colonic irrigations were advised at regular intervals, ranging from a few times weekly to once every six weeks. Additionally, frequent doses of psyllium-seed tea, olive oil, or milk of bismuth combined with milk of magnesia, were advised in some instances to assist eliminations.

Finally, in three readings hydrotherapy was advised, including sweat and fume baths and rubdowns. These were to improve the eliminations through the skin.

Case History

A total of five individuals reported good results upon following the advice given in their readings, including one woman who had only partially followed Cayce's advice. In the remaining cases, two confirmed that they had not adhered to the advice in the readings, while the others did not register a response.

Cayce gave eight readings for case 279, a man of thirty-one who suffered periodic spells of tachycardia. His diagnosis revealed an anemic blood condition and subluxations in the spine, both contributing factors to the ailment.

It was also noted that case 279 experienced perpetual anxieties and worries which increased his apprehension about the sudden attacks of rapid heartbeat.

By the time the man had his first reading, he was already receiving osteopathic treatments. Cayce added to this a series of colonics to be given every other week for several weeks. Weekly hydrotherapy, including sweat baths followed by a thorough rubdown, was prescribed. In diet, 279 was advised to eat more fruits, cereals, vegetable soups, and broth as well as fish, fowl, lamb, or beef (never fried).

Improvements were noted by the second reading, and subsequent readings encouraged continuing the osteopathic adjustments twice a week. Occasional colonics were to be continued until a sense of physical well-being was established. Mentally, Cayce discouraged unnecessary worry over business matters, which in the past had greatly contributed to the man's discomfort. Psyllium-seed tea, taken on an occasional basis, was part of a treatment to relieve digestive discomforts which had developed from the original disturbances.

After following the advice contained in his reading, case 279 reported that he was feeling much better. However, he did not adhere to the prescribed diet and subsequently gained weight, which later caused other health complications.

Hemophilia

Hemophilia is a disorder of the blood, characterized by prolonged bleeding after an injury or following surgery. It is due to a chemical defect in the blood which inhibits effective coagulation.

Although hemophilia is largely considered to be the result of hereditary factors, Cayce did not cite heredity as a cause. In the two readings given for individuals with hemophilia, the disorder was simply attributed to poor assimilations caused by a chemical deficiency, or to "the lack of those elements in the blood supply to build the walls, and resistance necessary in the walls of the arteries and veins. . . . So, with bruises or injuries to the body, there is the formation of blood spots, or clots'' (2769-1).

Despite the view today that hemophilia is usually congenital and familial, Cayce approached the condition as being curable and prescribed two specific, though distinctly different, treatments in these cases.

Treatment and Case Histories

The first reading was given for a ten-month-old boy who developed large black-and-blue marks following slight bruises. Treatment included adding small quantities of blood pudding, made from calf's liver, to the diet and using the Wet Cell Appliance. Wet Cell treatments were to be administered for twenty minutes, daily alternating solutions of gold chloride, spirits of camphor, and Atomidine, as well as altering the plate attachments accordingly.

Reports indicated that the reading was not followed, as the child's father felt that Cayce's advice was not valid.

Case 2832 was a thirty-year-old woman. Her treatments included weekly hydrotherapy with fume baths, followed by a thorough massage with a mixture of olive oil, peanut oil, and lanolin. Instructions were to administer four or five weeks of treatment and then discontinue them for three or four days. Then there followed a series of osteopathic adjustments to relieve spinal pressures which had developed as a result of the condition.

Outdoor exercise and a well-balanced diet rich in citrus juices, raw vegetables, fish, fowl, and lamb; vitamins A, D, and B_1 and iron were also recommended.

There was no follow-up report in this case.

Hemorrhoids

Hemorrhoids, enlarged veins in the tissue inside or around the rectum, can be attributed to straining to evacuate hard, dry stools or to pregnancy and pressure caused by

an enlarged uterus. Liver disorders can also contribute to
the condition. The most common symptoms are pain and
discomfort, accompanied by itching and at times bleeding
from the rectum.

Edgar Cayce gave a total of 126 readings for ninety-four
individuals with symptoms of hemorrhoids. They ranged
in age from seventeen to seventy-eight years. The main
factor, mentioned in sixty-seven cases, was found to be
poor eliminations. The readings frequently attributed the
onset of hemorrhoids to a disturbance in the colon which
raised the level of toxins in the body and produced hyperacidity. Poor circulation, also a result of the toxic conditions, was cited as a related cause in twenty-five cases.

In eighteen instances, spinal problems, mostly in the
form of subluxations, were found to have contributed to
the development of hemorrhoids. Poor assimilation was a
contributing factor in fifteen cases, and glandular imbalance, often involving the kidneys and/or liver, was found
in nine of the hemorrhoid cases. The glandular imbalance
could lead to an enlarged prostate gland in men and
increased pressure upon the veins in the rectal area, according to Cayce.

Mentioned in seven cases were general debilitation and
the aftereffects of injuries centered around the lower spinal
regions. Emotional upsets contributed to the disorder in six
cases.

Treatment

Treatments for hemorrhoids were extremely consistent
throughout the readings. To relieve pain and swelling,
some type of topical application was suggested in sixty-
five cases. Most frequently recommended was a compound
known as Tim, which included iodine, benzoin, butterfat, and tobacco. Suggested in another seventeen readings
was a combination of carbolic acid (phenol), mineral oil,
and glycerin. Additionally, a product known as Pazo Ointment received six recommendations, while a combination

of aconite and laudanum was to be used in a few cases when the pain was severe.

In fifty-two instances, dietary changes were advised. Special emphasis was placed on increasing the amount of raw fruits and vegetables in the diet because of their laxative qualities. Also highly recommended were alkaline-reaction foods, along with body-building foods such as whole grains and beef juice.

Stimulating the eliminations was advised in nineteen cases. Methods mentioned were colonics, enemas, and mild laxatives such as olive oil, castoria, and Eno salts.

To help restore the circulation and nerve impulses to normal, spinal adjustments were advised in thirty-four cases and were often to focus on the lower spine.

Massages were suggested in twenty-five cases to improve the circulation and stimulate the internal organs. Oil combinations such as lanolin, olive oil, and peanut oil, or olive oil and myrrh were to be applied in many instances.

Cayce recommended exercise in twenty-three readings, and all but three outlined the following procedure: In bare feet, stand erect, gradually stretching hands over head and at the same time gradually rising on the toes. Then bend forward with hands reaching toward the floor and touching it if possible.

Most readings suggested following this exercise for two or three minutes each morning and evening while undressed. Cayce explained the effectiveness of the exercise by noting that the exercise would aid in raising the internal organs sufficiently to eliminate a great deal of pressure in the lower abdomen.

Twenty individuals were advised hydrotherapy to aid both the circulation and elimination through the pores of the skin. Most often recommended for this purpose were fume baths and sitz baths.

Various forms of electrotherapy were suggested for nineteen individuals. Most frequently advised was the Violet Ray, at times with the rectal or rod applicator.

Also, for nineteen individuals digestive aids such as elixir of lactated pepsin, Acigest, and saffron tea were frequently mentioned to increase the body's ability to assimilate nutrients.

Although various packs were recommended in sixteen cases, only six were targeted specifically for the hemorrhoid condition; the others were prescribed for problems accompanying hemorrhoids. Of these six, four readings mentioned Epsom salt packs placed across the lower back, and two instructed that ice packs be applied to the rectal area. The packs were to enhance the circulation and promote relaxation.

Case History

Forty-five of the fifty individuals giving reports on following Cayce's advice noted that they obtained good results.

One of these was case 98, a thirty-four-year-old woman who received two readings for hemorrhoids. Cited as the major factors in the development of her hemorrhoids were improper eliminations, spinal lesions in the dorsal area, excess anxiety, and too much standing on her feet.

The first treatment advised was osteopathic adjustments to the dorsal vertebrae, to be given about once a week. Since the changes brought about by these corrections could be detrimental if they occurred too quickly, Cayce suggested that every other treatment consist of a gentle massage. Sinusoidal ray treatments were also recommended for the spleen and liver.

Dietary recommendations included whole grains and oysters and fish, as these carry essential nutrients without excess starch or sugar. Vegetables high in phosphorus and silicon were also recommended. Coffee and tea were to be avoided, although Ovaltine and cocoa were occasionally permitted.

The woman's second reading advised internal doses of olive oil to reduce swelling. It was also suggested that the Tim compound be applied topically for the same reason.

Hepatitis

Hepatitis, an inflammation of the liver caused by an infection, may be transmitted in various ways, including contaminated food or blood transfusions. Symptoms include loss of appetite, nausea, fever, tenderness around the liver, and enlargement of the liver. If the condition persists, jaundice may develop along with rapid loss of weight and strength.

Although there are two distinct types of hepatitis, there is no easy way now of deducing from the readings which types were involved.

Edgar Cayce gave fourteen readings for thirteen individuals with hepatitis. They ranged from one to sixty-eight years in age. Cited as a cause in five cases was poor elimination, which would frequently result in a torpid liver, which would in turn lead to hepatitis. Cholecystitis, or inflammation of the gallbladder resulting in improper assimilation, was given as a cause in four cases. Infection from other sources was another cause in two cases. Deficient circulation around the hepatic region was mentioned in one case and glandular imbalance in another.

Treatment

The most common treatments involved stimulants for the eliminations and various packs, with each being recommended eight times. Both were intended to help cleanse the liver area of excess toxins. Castor oil packs were recommended most frequently, with mullein packs being mentioned once. Both were to be placed across the lower abdomen and across the kidney area. Advised as aids to eliminations were colonics or high enemas with various measures of combined salt and soda to be followed by one teaspoon of Glyco-Thymoline to one quart of water as a final cleansing for the colon. Also suggested at times were laxatives and tonics. One of the eliminants recommended was "sufficient Castoria to act thoroughly: one-half teaspoon every half hour until the upper bowel has acted thoroughly."

Dietary reforms were recommended in six cases and alkaline-reacting foods, especially fruits, vegetables, and their juices, were stressed. Consumption of meat was to decrease and at times be avoided, with the exception of beef juice. In some instances, predigested food was suggested and was to be consumed until the body could better assimilate at a regular rate.

Six individuals were advised body massages with a variety of substances including cocoa butter and oil combinations. The massages were intended to help stimulate circulation around the liver and to cleanse the liver and surrounding organs of toxins.

Case History

Five of the thirteen receiving readings for hepatitis reported favorable results due to following their readings. There were no unfavorable reports received.

An interesting case was 3670, a sixty-year-old woman who received one reading for hepatitis. Cholecystitis, or inflammation of the gallbladder, was cited as the major cause: it resulted in a lack of proper assimilation, which deprived the body of energy.

Cayce recommended that hot castor oil packs, made of three to four thicknesses of saturated flannel, be placed over the gallbladder and liver for an hour at a time—morning, afternoon, and evening—until the condition had improved. An electric heating pad was to be placed over the flannel to keep it hot.

A gentle massage, given neuropathically or osteopathically, was to be given after each pack. This was not intended as a correction, but a massage to relax the body. This was to be followed by a gentle cocoa butter massage over the abdomen and gall duct area.

A half teaspoon of olive oil was to be taken after the first pack. This was to be repeated every hour during the time the woman was awake. The procedure involving the packs, massage, and olive oil was to continue until the body had cleansed itself.

Her diet was to consist of body-building foods, which included vegetable and chicken soups and beef juice. Rice was not to be eaten, but barley could be used in the chicken soup if desired. Potatoes, carrots, and beets could also be used in soups. Beet juice was recommended, and coffee and tea were permitted, but not in combination with milk.

Several follow-up reports were received which noted that the woman and her family had followed all the suggestions made by Cayce and that she had experienced a complete recovery from the gallbladder inflammation and subsequent hepatitis.

Hernia: Abdominal

The abdominal hernia—an abnormal protrusion of all or part of an organ through the wall surrounding the abdominal cavity—is generally thought of as being either congenital or acquired as a result of weight, strain, or the aftereffects of an operation.

Edgar Cayce delivered twenty-one readings for individuals with abdominal hernias, through which he explained how a sometimes complex series of abuses to the body can weaken the abdominal wall.

Cayce believed that the initial weakening of the abdominal wall was due to a gradual buildup of toxins in the system. He attributed this toxic state to poor eliminations and a condition which was at times due to lesions in the lumbar area of the spine. The resultant toxic accumulation also created an imbalance in the lymph and blood circulation and a lack of coordination between the cerebrospinal and the sympathetic nervous systems. Because of the impeded nerve impulses, the digestion would be weakened and hormonal secretions impaired.

In view of the contributing factors, Cayce believed it would take little, if any, external strain to rupture the

abdominal wall and cause the hernia. In only a few cases
for which there were readings was the hernia due to real
strain or overexertion.

Treatment

As usual, Cayce's treatments were directed toward restoring a balance between the various systems of the body,
creating optimal conditions for healing. Stressed was the
importance of positive attitudes and emotions.

In most cases, it was recommended that a truss or
support be worn to aid the gradual healing process.

A strict acid-alkaline diet was found to play an important role in healing the rupture. The diet was to contain
little or no meats, whereas vegetables, to help rebuild the
weakened structure, were strongly recommended.

Cayce also suggested spinal manipulations, especially in
the lumbar vertebrae or the area of the spine opposite the
abdomen. Colonics and enemas were advised to get rid of
body toxins. Massage and other forms of physiotherapy
were suggested to aid in the eliminations of toxins and to
generally prepare the body so that the spinal adjustments
would be most effective.

Case History

In the readings for a fifty-one-year-old man (case 333),
Cayce noted a lack of coordination in eliminations and in
the glandular system which weakened the structural portion of the abdomen, including the bones and the spine.
The incoordination between the cerebrospinal and sympathetic nervous systems created an insufficient blood supply,
which over the years thinned the walls of the colon. A
painful protrusion of the colon through the abdominal
walls occurred.

For the glandular imbalance, Cayce recommended Atomidine. The dose suggested was three drops in a glass of
water each morning, followed by three drops in half a
glass of water each evening. This procedure was to contin-

ue for five days, but the Atomidine was to be discontinued for the following five days. On the eleventh day, the dosage was to be increased to five drops in the morning and evening for five more days and then discontinued for another five days, followed by a repeat of the three-drop dosage. The complete cycle was to be repeated five times. Additionally, six general spinal adjustments were required, as were high enemas to stimulate the eliminations. Epsom salt baths, coupled with massages using a stimulating liniment, were recommended twice weekly in the evening during the Atomidine cycles.

In a follow-up letter to Edgar Cayce, case 333 wrote: "The reading brings me closer than ever to a consciousness of God's love and his ministry through the Master. You have saved me from a future of much misery and physical and mental suffering." He also reported that he had become conscious of a need for service and love for his fellow man.

Later, obviously due to his becoming lax in his treatments, the man's discomfort returned. The hernia had slowed the peristaltic movement through the colon, causing an engorged condition. As a result, poisons were accumulating in the system, causing circulatory disturbances, nervousness, and restlessness.

In order to better equalize the circulation and remove some of the strain, Cayce recommended a new course of treatment. This included general osteopathic adjustments three times weekly, morning and evening massages, dietary precautions, and the wearing of a truss.

Apparently due to failure to adhere to Cayce's dietary instructions, the man began to experience frequent dizzy spells and constant fatigue. A third reading indicated further problems with toxemia due to the hernia. In this reading, Cayce suggested osteopathy once a week for five weeks, a refitting of the truss, and improvement in mental attitudes (confidence), and Bible reading. Reports of improvement in the condition followed.

Three years later, case 333 experienced another recurrence of the hernia problem. In the reading that was subsequently requested, Cayce indicated that the lymph in the patient's system was overflowing and accumulating in the bloodstream, causing the distress. The recommended treatment included regular hydrotherapy and colonic irrigations to be followed by massage. Additionally, a deep osteopathic adjustment was recommended twice weekly. The man was cautioned against eating sugar and fats in excess and against smoking too many cigarettes.

Three months later, the man's condition intensified, and he feared he was becoming susceptible to a stroke. Cayce's reading on the condition found that toxic forces had accumulated throughout the body, causing pressures in the abdominal area which resulted in dizziness and swelling. The recommended treatment consisted of a thorough colonic irrigation, followed by the application of heat to the solar plexus area and then a thorough massage.

Three weeks later, case 333 reported an improved physical condition, though some dizziness remained. Cayce's subsequent reading noted that there was now an imbalance between the lymph circulation and the superficial blood circulation. The lymph was forming pockets in the throat which could result in the need for an operation.

The pressures from wearing a truss, as well as the hernia itself, prevented normal eliminations through the alimentary canal, and the consequent treatments included more colonics, osteopathic adjustments, and massage. The diet was to include beef juice (but no beef), seafood, raw leafy vegetables, and vegetable soups.

No additional feedback from case 333 was recorded.

Herpes Zoster (Shingles)

Herpes zoster is characterized by pain along a nerve course followed by painfully grouped vesicular lesions. It usually occurs in adults, and with rare exceptions one attack usually confers lifelong immunity.

Edgar Cayce gave a total of eleven readings for ten individuals with herpes zoster.

He attributed herpes zoster to an infectious virus and warned that in elderly or debilitated persons, it could be fatal. In each case but two, he cited poor eliminations as a major cause. Mentioned in six instances was poor circulation, and incoordination between the sympathetic and cerebrospinal nervous systems was mentioned as a cause in three cases.

Treatment

The most frequent treatment recommended was to stimulate the eliminations. The methods suggested included watermelon-seed tea; sweet spirits of niter; olive oil; a blood-purifying combination of Rochelle salts, cream of tartar, and sulfur, as well as other laxative preparations. Colonics were also suggested in three cases.

Various topical applications were also suggested, and a frequent recommendation to help soothe irritations was a body powder containing stearate of zinc and balsam. Its use at times was to be preceded by the application of ice packs or warm soda water placed over the lesions. A variety of other solutions was also suggested.

In six cases, an alkaline, easily digestible diet was advised. A typical diet for this condition would consist mainly of fruits, citrus juices, and raw and cooked vegetables and their juices. To be avoided were sweets, alcohol, meats, citrus-cereal combinations, and apples.

In five cases, Cayce recommended spinal manipulations to be centered in the dorsal and cervical areas, coordinating these parts with the lower spine. Two to six adjustments over a period of several weeks were usually advised. Massages were also recommended at times. These were to be administered once or twice a week.

Case History

There were many follow-up reports in the cases, but most were inconclusive. Although the majority reported only partial or no success the treatments were not followed fully or correctly.

One case which did respond to treatment was that of 322, a sixty-year-old man who received one reading for a case of shingles. His condition was attributed to poor elimination and poor circulation.

Treatment involved an alkaline diet. To be avoided were sweets, alcohol, meat, and especially apples. Spinal adjustments were suggested in the upper dorsal area. To assist eliminations, Cayce recommended small doses of sweet spirits of niter (three to five drops two to three times a day). A powder containing stearate of zinc and balsam was to be applied over the skin irritations.

The man followed Cayce's instructions and noted a successful recovery. He was so pleased with his diet that he encouraged some of his friends, who also had shingles, to follow it. One, a woman, tried the diet and noted improvement until she ate some applesauce, suggesting that the apples had a direct effect on the skin disorder.

Hirsutism or Unwanted Hair

Cayce gave one reading each for nineteen women, most of whom were in their twenties and thirties, on excessive growth of facial or body hair.

Shaving and depilatories, which remove the hair by breaking down its composition, and epilatories—waxes, electrolysis, etc—are all external methods of dealing with excess hair. Cayce's approach, however, was internally oriented. In fifteen cases, the major cause was said to be from an imbalance in glandular secretions, resulting in the overstimulation of hair growth. His diagnosis focused on both overactivity and underactivity of the thyroid gland. The former condition was limited to one case, however.

In the remaining four cases, Cayce attributed the excessive hair growth largely to karmic conditions, although he did not explain the particular lessons to be learned. Poor circulation was also listed as a possible cause.

Treatment

Since the predominant cause of unwanted hair, according to Cayce, was glandular disorders, he prescribed various treatments to stabilize the glandular system, which would, when balanced, act to decrease the growth of and gradually remove the unwanted hair.

In seven cases, various dietary recommendations were made. These emphasized raw and cooked vegetables and foods high in iodine, such as seafood and potato peelings.

In six cases, Atomidine was recommended to help regulate and cleanse the glandular system. A typical dosage was one or two drops of Atomidine in a half glass of water, which was to be taken before breakfast.

Hodgkin's Disease

Hodgkin's disease is characterized by enlarged, firm, nontender regional lymph nodes. It is a localized process that tends to spread to contiguous lymphatic structures. Symptoms such as fever, excessive sweating, and fatigue, usually appear late.

Cayce frequently attributed the disease, discussed for six individuals, to a glandular imbalance or malfunction affecting the lymph and excretory circulation. Three subjects had suffered youthful or prenatal injuries to the spine, which Cayce felt disturbed neural coordination as well as the glands. In other cases, according to Cayce, a chemical imbalance involving the lymph system contributed to the overproduction of lymph tissue.

Treatment

Cayce's treatment for Hodgkin's disease varied considerably. The most consistent recommendation, however, was spinal adjustments or massage for those who had suffered spinal injury. These were to benefit the nervous system. Use of the ultraviolet light, in one case with green glass, was suggested for two individuals in order to stimulate the spleen to produce more red blood cells.

A diet high in iron and protein to help rebuild the blood's vitality was recommended in two cases. Foods and supplements mentioned included citrus fruits, beef, iron and wine tonics, beef juice, and liver juice.

The importance of attitude was stressed. Positive attitudes were essential in assisting the body to rebuild and restore itself.

Case History

Five readings were accompanied by follow-up reports from those afflicted with Hodgkin's disease. Two individuals reported improvement after beginning treatments, but these individuals and two others died not long afterward. One man did not show any improvement, although it is not clear whether he had followed the prescribed treatments.

It should be noted, however, that most who sought Cayce's assistance were already in the advanced stages of Hodgkin's disease. Treatment seemed to delay, not prevent or cure, the deteriorating effects of the disease.

One particular case history involved a thirty-year-old man who came to Cayce with a case of pernicious anemia which was rapidly developing into leukemia. Cayce's reading for case 2621 disclosed that a chemical imbalance had triggered a chemical reaction in the body which affected the glandular functions. The effects produced in the glands and lymph were those of Hodgkin's disease.

Cayce's treatment included taking a teaspoon of beef juice every two hours and adding liver-juice extract or liver pudding in the diet. A five-minute application of the shortwave ultraviolet light, directed through a sheet of green glass, was prescribed daily. Weekly hot and cold showers and sitz baths were also advised.

To stimulate the glands, a drop of Atomidine in a half glass of water was to be taken once daily, increasing the dosage by one drop each day up to five drops, discontinuing for five days, and then starting again with one drop.

Cayce explained that the treatments could help improve the condition ''if there is kept by the body, and those about the same, that prayerful, expectant attitude of using the strength, the abilities of the body, in a spiritually, mentally constructive way and manner in dealing with others'' (2621-2).

Although 2621 eventually died of Hodgkin's disease, he corresponded with Cayce on many occasions during which he reported feeling better as a result of the treatments.

Homosexuality

In the almost nine thousand Cayce medical readings, only nine cases deal with homosexuality. It is not surprising, however, for the readings were given between 1926 and 1944, at a time when homosexuality was very much ''in the closet,'' partly due to its being considered a mental illness and partly because homosexual self-help organizations were still several years in the future.

Eight of the individuals receiving readings on the subject were male. Seven of the eight knew that they were homosexuals, and as a consequence had low self-esteem. In their cases, there were often attendant physical problems to be treated, which the readings indicated had been brought on entirely or had been aggravated by their anxiety and guilt.

The other male, a child of only one month, was noted by Cayce as having strong tendencies toward homosexuality. His parents were counseled specifically as to the diet, physical environment, and emotional climate that should be maintained for the child so as not to augment these tendencies. Unfortunately, there is no data as to whether or not Cayce's advice was followed.

In the sole case involving a woman whose visit to Cayce was to determine if she was a lesbian, Cayce, in telling her she was not, explained her feelings as being related to a previous life experience, which had triggered a mistrust of men's sexual intentions and that it was this fear of men she was interpreting as latent lesbianism.

Cayce's advice was, "Then study to show thyself approved until God, a workman not ashamed, rightly stressing each phase of the experience, keeping self from condemnation; not condemning self, not condemning others" (3685-1).

Then, in the case of 479, who wrote Cayce, asking, "Must I live so that my conduct would, were it generally known, win general approbation, or may I safely conduct myself to my own moral satisfaction?" Cayce's reply was direct and compassionate.

"That there are physical defects . . . that are prenatal in their basic forms is too often condemned by the entity . . . [and] that which is often counted as sin or error is for the mercy to a soul from an All-Wise and beneficient Father. . . . For, in His mercy He has given to all that which is the desire of every heart in a material plane—to seek companionship in a manner that there may be the exchange of experience in whatsoever sphere the body-soul may find itself. . . . Then, let the acts of thine body, the temple of thine soul, be kept clean in thine own consciousness" (479-1).

Case History

The most exhaustive reading on homosexuality was for case 1089, for it covers thirteen years of association and correspondence. It was also one of the few where the karmic cause was specified rather than simply alluded to, for the man was told that when he had lived in France in the pre-revolutionary court, he had drawn cartoons satirical of certain homosexuals, while at the same time inwardly harboring desires for such activity. The result was that he became homosexual in this life, experiencing the ridicule and intolerance he had shown others.

Cayce advised the man, "Condemn not, then, that ye may not be condemned. For indeed with what measure ye mete it will be measured to thee again. And that thou condemnest in another (yea, every man—every woman), that thou becomes in thine self!'' (1089-1).

Revealing the ignorance of the thirties in regard to sexual matters, case 1089 felt his homosexuality had been triggered by overindulgence in masturbation. Cayce's subsequent letter to him was specific on the relationship between the sexual and the spiritual.

"Sex, of course, is a great factor in everyone's life; it is the line between the great and the vagabond, the good and the bad; it is the expression of reactive forces in our very nature; allowed to run wild, to self-indulgence, becomes physical and mental derangement; turned into the real influence it should be in one's life, connects man closer with his God, and that is the use you should put it to."

In an earlier reading, counsel was given that is universally applicable. "Look into self, and those eccentricities of thine own activity; and these may be studied better by studying nature, by studying the soil, the products of same, the varied activities as in things growing, as in the birds and the bees, as in the flowers, as in the trees, as in those things that live or act about thee.

"Keep *alone* for periods at a time. Let thy self make a study of these. And let much of the time be spent in meditation and prayer. Read (not until they become as rote, but as living words) the last word, the last message as He gave, as the Master gave, 'In my father's house there are many mansions; if it were not so I would have told you' '' (1089-3).

Hydrocephalus

Five readings were given for four individuals with hydrocephalus, three of whom were infants and children fourteen years and under. Commonly referred to as "water on the brain," hydrocephalus is characterized by the excessive accumulation of fluid which dilates the ventricles in the brain. In infants, this accumulation is manifested in a bloated, enlarged head.

Edgar Cayce generally attributed hydrocephalus to a defect in the cerebrospinal system or to a prenatal defect which he described in one instance as "lack of coordination in the centers where there are the greater patches of the lymph, where the central and cerebrospinal nervous systems coordinate" (3208-1).

Treatment

Cayce's treatments for hydrocephalus varied with the unique nature of each case. The most consistent suggestion was spinal manipulation, which was advised in three cases to improve neural coordination. Swedish massages to improve drainage were suggested in the fourth case, that of an eight-year-old boy.

The only adult, a forty-two-year-old woman, was advised to have surgery to remove harmful scar tissue on the spine and to use hot castor oil packs over the abdomen. She was sent to an osteopathic sanatorium for treatment, as Cayce had suggested.

The eight-year-old boy was advised to have diathermy treatments over the lacteal and solar plexus areas, and another, a five-year-old girl, was advised to have an injection of atropine at the base of the spine. Cayce also recommended a neuropatch to correct a tailbone malfunction.

No follow-up reports were received from these individuals.

Hyperthyroidism

Hyperthyroidism is a condition caused by excessive secretion, or overactivity of the thyroid glands. Symptoms and signs include restlessness, irritability, and unexpected weight loss despite a good appetite.

Edgar Cayce gave fourteen readings for nine individuals with overactive thyroids.

In the majority of readings on hyperthyroidism, Cayce's

findings disclosed a chemical imbalance of elements in the blood, which produced an imbalance in the glandular system. In three of these cases, the imbalance was specifically related to an excess of potassium and a deficiency of iodine. In three other instances, spinal subluxations or injuries caused the condition because the lack of proper nerve impulses affected the glandular system.

All of the subjects suffered from various physiological disturbances as reflex conditions resulting from the hyperthyroid activity. Most common were stress on the nervous system, which affected the eliminations and assimilating functions; and circulatory problems affecting blood pressure and blood toxicity. Where spinal injuries or subluxations were responsible for the glandular disorder, the circulation and eliminations were also heavily affected.

Treatment

Spinal manipulation and /or massage to ease pressure on the nerve centers were suggested in the majority of readings. In seven cases, specific dietary recommendations were made in which Cayce emphasized raw and cooked vegetables, citrus fruits and juices, and fish, fowl, lamb, brains, and liver.

To cleanse the glands, Atomidine was recommended in over half of the cases. The usual dosage was one drop daily in a half glass of water taken for five days, discontinued for four or five days, and then resumed.

To stimulate the glands, electrotherapeutic appliances—such as the Wet Cell, ultraviolet light, and the Radio-Active Appliance—were suggested in four of the readings.

Due to digestive problems, three individuals were advised colonic irrigation or enemas to clear the colon and intestinal tract once or twice monthly.

Cayce also gave spiritual advice in some of the readings. Reading 726-1 suggested that ''within self must be found that which may be awakened to the *building* of that necessary for the body, mentally and physically, and spiritually, to carry *its* part in this experience.''

Case History

Case 2568 involved a fifty-nine-year-old man whose condition of hyperthyroidism had caused a growth on his face. Cayce diagnosed an excess of potassium in the blood, which was causing overactivity of the thyroid and metabolism and contributing to a disturbance in the hepatic circulation and in the circulation between the heart and lungs. Spinal subluxations were found between the fourth and sixth dorsal vertebrae, causing an incoordination of the nervous systems and hindering eliminations.

Cayce prescribed osteopathic adjustments of the dorsal and lumbar areas and weekly fume baths with witch hazel and oil of pine needles, followed by massage. To aid eliminations, two colonics during the first month of treatment were prescribed. The subject was also advised to maintain a diet emphasizing fruits and vegetables, and fish, fowl, and lamb and avoiding fried foods.

The follow-up report came from a friend of 2568 who noted that after treatment the man lived a number of years in good health.

Hypoglycemia

Hypoglycemia is low blood sugar and is approximately the opposite of high blood-sugar levels which are associated with diabetes. The two conditions are closely related, however, and hypoglycemia can precede diabetes.

Among the symptoms of hypoglycemia are fatigue, depression, nervousness, headaches, rapid heartbeat, vertigo, anxiety, and irritability.

Edgar Cayce gave five readings for four individuals with various symptoms of hypoglycemia. They ranged from five to fifty-nine years old. The major cause, cited by Cayce in two of the cases, was a disturbance in the blood circulation. An infection in the bloodstream, improper assimilation, and a prostate gland disorder were each mentioned once as contributing factors.

Treatment

Dietary reforms were suggested for three of the individuals. Fresh fruits and vegetables were recommended because of the natural sugars they contain. Processed sugars were to be avoided. Vitamin B_1 was to be added to the diet of one individual.

The remaining treatments varied widely, depending on individual needs. They included colonics, electrotherapy, massages, a prescription using animated ash, exercise, and fresh air.

Case History

A sample case history was that of 440, a twenty-three-year-old male who received one reading for hypoglycemia. According to Cayce, imperfect blood coagulation caused by urea in the man's hemoglobin was the cause of his hypoglycemia.

A change in diet was recommended. He was advised to drink a glass and a half of water the first thing each morning. This was to be so hot that it could only be sipped. After this, citrus and grape juices and toast, buttered or dry, were to be eaten. Fresh or stewed fruits and eggs were to be occasionally part of the breakfast meal.

A green salad was suggested for the noon meal, and the reading stressed that it should be well chewed. Milk was to be drunk either before or after the meal.

The evening meal was to include well-cooked vegetables. Meat, preferably fowl or lamb, could be part of this meal. He was advised against eating beef, although beef juice was recommended. Vegetable soups were also recommended.

Sweets made with either beet sugar or saccharin were

permitted as between-meal snacks. Chocolate, creams with chocolate, or nut candies could also be eaten as snacks.

Additionally recommended were the Radio-Active Appliance, to help correct the circulatory balance, and colonics, to help rid the body of toxins.

No report was received concerning the outcome of the treatments.

Hypothyroidism

Hypothyroidism is the lack of thyroid hormones which may affect virtually all body functions. Symptoms include weakness, fatigue, constipation, anemia, and dry, yellow puffy skin, among others.

Edgar Cayce gave ten readings on hypothyroidism for eight individuals. Seven cases were attributed to an imbalance of chemicals in the blood, most frequently an excess of potassium and a deficiency of iodine. Cayce emphasized the importance of iodine as being "one of the four principles necessary to be present in the activity of a normal body" (2072-6). Iodine was seen as essential to the proper functioning of the thyroid gland.

In the majority of cases, physiological disturbances were produced in the body as responses to the malfunctioning gland. These responses included poor eliminations, incoordination of the nerve forces, poor circulation, and respiratory and digestive disorders. The physical problems tended to place stress on the nervous system, causing nervous and emotional sensitivity.

Treatment

Electrotherapy was recommended in six readings, and most often suggested was the Violet Ray, which was prescribed to stimulate glandular activity in the region of the throat.

Five individuals were given dietary advice that stressed

plenty of raw and cooked vegetables, fruit and vegetable juices, citrus fruits, and fish, fowl, and lamb.

In more than half of the readings, Cayce suggested osteopathic adjustments or spinal massage with peanut oil and olive oil for relaxation of nerves and muscles. Half of these individuals were advised to take Atomidine as a thyroid stimulant. Typical instructions were to take it daily for five days, discontinue, and then resume prescribed dosage, which was usually one drop daily in a half glass of water taken before breakfast. Thyroid extract, to be taken under a physician's supervision, was recommended in two cases.

In many cases, cultivation of a better attitude toward self and others was an important element in treatment.

Case History

Case 1247, an adult female, suffered from poor eliminations and constant physical exhaustion. Cayce described her condition as an imbalance in the potassium-iodine content of the blood, which contributed to incoordination between the cerebrospinal and sympathetic nerve reflexes and a disturbance in the hepatic circulation. Resulting strain upon the adrenal glands, which assist in the functioning of the spleen, caused trouble with both her assimilations and eliminations. Her lack of vitality was attributed to low metabolic rates caused by the deficiency of certain elements in the blood.

Cayce recommended the use of the Wet Cell Appliance with gold chloride for two periods of twenty-eight days, with a five- to ten-day rest between each period. During the first ten to fifteen days of treatment, the Wet Cell was to be applied daily for twenty minutes, then thirty minutes for the remainder of the period. Following each treatment, a thorough massage from head to toe was advised, using a combination of olive oil, mineral oil, oil of pine needles, compound tincture of benzoin, oil of wintergreen, and sassafras root. After a rest period of five to ten days, the woman was to take Atomidine internally, one drop daily in half a glass of water. Following the Atomidine treatment, a further rest period of five days was suggested.

After the second series of Wet Cell treatments and massage, 1247 was advised to maintain a diet high in seafoods with seasonings of kelp or sea salt, omitting white bread and potatoes. Cayce also recommended daily applications of the Violet Ray to the areas of the sympathetic nervous system. These were to be applied before bedtime for a period of five to seven minutes, moving the bulb away from the head in a circular motion. To improve eliminations, an alkaline eliminant, such as milk of magnesia, was prescribed along with frequent, gentle enemas.

Hysteria

Hysteria, mainly associated with psychiatry, is a word used to mean different things. Most commonly it is used to refer to those individuals who have a preoccupation with medical and surgical experiences. Hysteria is most common in women in their early and middle adult years.

Edgar Cayce gave two women in their forties one reading each for hysteria. In each case, the basic cause was found to be a type of neurasthenia caused by a highly emotional nature. Neurasthenia is an old term for a group of symptoms which were ascribed at one time to weakness or exhaustion of the nervous system. The readings seem to have used the word in this sense.

Treatment

To encourage relaxation for both individuals with hysteria, Cayce recommended gentle massages along the spine, using alcohol in one case and pine oil in the other. For one woman, Cayce advised an unspecified sedative to quiet the body and relieve the emotional stress. Also receiving one recommendation each were magnetic healing (laying on of hands), blood-building diet, spinal manipulation, and fume baths with witch hazel.

Case History

Case 4060 was a forty-seven-year-old woman who received one reading on hysteria. Her husband's death and her poor financial situation made her extremely nervous and prone to insomnia. Attributing her distress to nervous incoordination, Cayce said, "These are, as it were, the results of the 'batteries' having run down, or the incoordinating of the centers of the lumbar axis, the ninth dorsal, through the brachial centers and the whole area of the cervicals, or the connections between the cerebrospinal and sympathetic systems become short-circuited" (4060-1).

Cayce subsequently advised a series of six to eight spinal adjustments in conjunction with thorough hydrotherapy treatments. These were to include fume baths using small amounts of witch hazel, followed by massages with pine oil.

The woman followed her reading and later reported: "The reading described my physical and mental problems accurately, and after following the treatments as outlined, I was cured."

Impetigo

Impetigo is an acute, inflammatory skin disease, characterized by skin ulcers. Usually caused by staphylococcal bacteria, the source of infection is often another child. Itching is its only symptom.

The only reading alluding to impetigo was case 305 for a two-year-old boy who was suffering from a tonsil infection as well as impetigo. His doctor had given him thirty days to live. The reading indicated that the child was undernourished and that his diet did not supply all the elements needed by his body.

Diet was an important factor in treatment of the child. Pork. beef, and fried meats were to be eliminated from the diet, although beef juice made from lean beef was recommended as beneficial. Sweets were to be eaten only in extreme moderation.

Treatment and Case History

The daily diet suggested was as follows: At breakfast, citrus juices of all kinds could be taken, but these were not to be combined with cereals or milk. Prune and rhubarb juices were to be taken with dry cereal. Coddled egg yolks and toasted brown bread were also part of the breakfast diet. By midmorning, if desired, the boy could drink a plain (not chocolate) malted milk, combining the milk with the yolk of one egg and a few drops of apple brandy.

Lunch was to consist of combinations of juices from fresh-cooked vegetables, such as spinach, carrots, cabbage, and turnips, beans, and lentils. The vegetables were to be cooked in Patapar Paper and the juices removed. To go along with the juices were whole wheat bread and as much milk as possible. In midafternoon, the reading suggested another malted milk or fruits and fruit juices of all kinds, except bananas or apples. Candy was forbidden. Dinner was to consist mainly of the well-cooked vegetables from lunch, best eaten without meats. When meat was desired, lamb with peas, carrots, and onions was recommended. Other possible protein sources were fish, brains, tripe, and pigs' feet.

Medicinal treatments were also recommended, one of which was Atomidine—one drop taken daily in a half glass of water in the morning before breakfast and two drops in a half glass of water before bedtime.

A digestive aid containing iron was also to be taken twice a day—but not with milk.

Additionally, the child was to be massaged each evening using the following compound: two tablespoons mutton tallow (melted), one tablespoon spirits of camphor, one tablespoon spirits of turpentine, one teaspoon tincture of benzoin, and one-half teaspoon coal oil or kerosene. The mixture was to be stirred before each use and kept in a glass container or crock with a top. It was to be massaged into the spine from the base of the brain to the end of the spine, especially under the arms and over the chest, in the groin, and along the ascending colon from the liver downward. The reading predicted that these treatments performed consistently would alleviate the child's impetigo as well as his tonsil infection.

A report from the parents twenty-four years later noted that after some earlier physical problems, their son had grown up to be six feet tall and weighed two hundred pounds.

Incontinence

Incontinence of the kidneys is the inability to retain urine due to stress or an overdistended, flaccid bladder, among other causes. Cayce gave five readings for five individuals on this condition, most of which were for elderly people.

Edgar Cayce's explanation for incontinence varied from case to case. For two, faulty diet had caused acids and sugars to accumulate in the system, causing engorgement of the urethra in one instance. In two other cases, Cayce related the cause to an impingement of nerves arising from problems in the spinal column due to subluxations or to unbalanced chemical reactions affecting the nerve forces. In another case, a man of seventy-two had the condition due to strain in the genital area.

Treatment

Cayce's treatments for incontinence almost exclusively concerned diet, massage and manipulation, and the application of hot packs to the body.

Dietary revisions were outlined in every reading, and generally forbidden were sugar-and-starch combinations and pork and fried foods. Meals containing lettuce, celery, carrots, beets, vegetable soups, and gelatin were encouraged.

In four of the five cases, spinal manipulation or massage

was suggested for relaxation and to relieve the stress placed on the excretory system. The same number of readings gave directions for the preparation and application of various hot packs, mainly Glyco-Thymoline or castor oil, which were to be placed on the abdominal or pubic area for relief of stress on the bladder. In two cases, colonics and internal doses of olive oil were recommended.

Case History

Case 5146 was a fifty-four-year-old woman whose extremely frequent urge to urinate had inhibited her from making social visits or even short trips.

Cayce diagnosed her discomfort as being caused by a superacidic condition throughout the alimentary canal, which was caused by a poor diet. The excess acidity created disorders in the stomach and intestinal tracts, in turn placing stress on the kidneys, which had subsequently become overactive. Cayce's findings also revealed spinal subluxations in the fifth to the ninth dorsal vertebrae.

All sweets, such as cakes, pies, and pastries, were restricted. She was advised to place hot castor oil packs over her liver and abdominal areas for one hour daily for three days, followed by the application of a hot Glyco-Thymoline pack over the pubic area, kidneys, and bladder. She was advised to take a teaspoon of olive oil on an hourly basis until it produced evacuation through the alimentary canal.

To help establish alkalinity in the body, she was also advised to drink three glasses of water daily, each glass containing about five drops of Glyco-Thymoline. Spinal adjustments were recommended to correct the spinal subluxations.

Indigestion and Gastritis

Indigestion is a failure to properly digest food. The usual symptoms include heartburn, nausea, flatulence, cramps, a disagreeable taste in the mouth, vomiting, and diarrhea. Indigestion may also be an accompanying symptom of other diseases. Indigestion and appendicitis frequently display the same symptoms.

Gastritis is an inflammation of the stomach lining and may be characterized by typical symptoms which range from anorexia to hemorrhage, although there may be mild or no symptoms in the case of chronic gastritis.

Cayce gave eighty-three individuals a total of 109 readings dealing with indigestion or gastritis. They ranged in age from nine months to seventy-four years.

Improper eliminations were the major cause for digestive disorders and were cited in forty-eight cases. According to Cayce, the inadequate elimination of excess toxins by the intestines caused irritation to the intestinal lining, resulting in digestive problems, and at times, gastritis.

Poor assimilation was a major factor in the development of digestive disorders in thirty-six cases. The improperly assimilated foods could result in the lining of the stomach becoming irritated and inflamed, which in turn could cause indigestion and the accumulation of more toxins, which could then result in further gastric problems.

A factor in forty cases was nervous system incoordination, which was usually the result of misalignments in the spine which would inhibit proper functioning of the stomach, often producing an excess amount of acid.

Mentioned as a contributing factor in twenty-nine cases was poor circulation, which was possibly another result of an overly toxic system and the consequent overloading of channels of elimination. Anemia and anemic tendencies were closely related factors mentioned in several cases.

Further, glandular imbalances were found to be a contributing factor in seven cases. Although dietary problems were attributed directly to improper diet in only a few instances, the abundance of dietary advice in the readings suggests that this was often a factor. Also mentioned occasionally were adhesions or lesions within the stomach and intestines.

Treatment

Dietary advice was the major treatment suggestion in fifty-four cases. Although Cayce noted that while the dietary practices of these individuals were for the most part acceptable under normal circumstances, changes were necessary to help correct the immediate problem. Easily assimilated foods rich in vitamins and minerals were recommended. Emphasis was placed on fresh fruits and vegetables along with supplements such as beef juice. Also advised were eating on a more regular schedule and regulating food intake more carefully.

In thirty-seven cases, spinal manipulations were recommended. These corrections were to focus on the dorsal vertebrae associated with the stomach and intestines.

In thirty-four cases, stimulation of the eliminations was advised to cleanse the body of excess toxins and relax the intestines. Most often recommended were colonics and enemas. However, stimulants such as milk of bismuth and/ or Castoria were often suggested as well. Occasionally, both internal and external approaches were advised.

Therapy treatments were advised in twenty-eight cases. The most commonly suggested appliances were the Radio-Active Appliance and the electric vibrator.

Digestive aids were suggested in twenty-four cases. Acigest, Al-Caroid, elm water, saffron tea, pepsin, and olive oil each received several recommendations. These preparations were intended to soothe the stomach lining as well as improve both assimilations and eliminations.

Seventeen individuals were advised massages to help relax the body and stimulate various organs to function more normally. Massage substances to be used included olive oil or the mutton tallow and camphor-turpentine formula.

Abdominal packs were suggested in fifteen cases. The most frequently suggested were castor oil or various salt applications, although grapes and Glyco-Thymoline were also mentioned.

Tonics made from a variety of herbs were recommended

for nine individuals to aid the digestion and other functions and to tone the system. Hydrotherapy treatments of either a general or specific nature were advised in eight cases as an aid to relaxation. Suggested in three cases each were Atomidine and Calcios. Other miscellaneous suggestions concerned the therapeutic benefits of rest, sun, fresh air, and moderate exercise.

Case History

Although the majority of those receiving readings on stomach disorders did not report on the outcome of the treatments, reports were received from twenty-two who noted improvements in their condition.

An interesting case which offered no follow-up report was that of 5545, a forty-one-year-old man who received three readings for acute gastritis. According to Cayce, improper assimilations and a sluggish circulation contributed to the development of an overacid condition, which in turn led to lesions in the stomach lining.

To reduce the acidity, the man was advised to go on a diet of alkaline-reacting and easily assimilated foods. Coffee and tea were to be avoided. Additionally, to neutralize stomach acids, the man was advised to take a substance referred to as chalk bismuth (milk of bismuth?). Elm water and mild saffron tea were also suggested as digestive aids, both to be taken before meals.

The second reading recommended spinal manipulations focusing on the fourth, seventh, and eighth dorsal vertebrae to further alleviate the stomach imbalances. Also, daily doses of one teaspoon of Russian White Oil, taken in combination with a teaspoon of Petrolagar, was recommended for eliminations.

The third reading advised continuing the above treatments and suggested that colonics be taken if desired.

Insomnia

Insomnia, the inability to sleep, affects most people at some point in their lives. The cause may be physical,

emotional, or a combination of both. Worry, fear, and other
anxieties are common causes. Sensitivity to certain foods,
too much light, or even the condition of the bed may
be factors. Foods containing caffeine, such as tea, coffee,
and cola, may also deter sleep.

The Edgar Cayce readings contain over 350 references to insomnia. This research deals with seventy-
two individuals, ranging in age from four to seventy-
eight years, who received a total of 79 readings on the
subject. Of course, some of these individuals also had
other physical conditions, reflecting the view that
sleeplessness could be an indicator of the presence of
other imbalances.

Cayce once recommended that the period spent not
being able to sleep be put to good use. Case 2051 asked:
"Why do I have difficulty in sleeping after four o'clock in
the morning, and how may this be controlled?"

Cayce answered: "This is a habit and partly of a
physical reaction. This should not be attempted to be
controlled, but rather used advantageously. If ye are aroused,
use the period of the first 30 minutes, at least, in direct
meditation upon what thy Lord would have thee do that
day. You'll soon learn to sleep more than the next
hour."

Factors contributing to the individual cases of insomnia
varied widely. Emotional problems were a major cause in
approximately one-third of the cases. A combination of
emotional and physical factors was cited in the remaining
cases.

The physical factors involved were quite varied and
included diabetes, menopause, arthritis, aftereffects of surgery, and cancer. The broader category of physical conditions most often listed as factors involved improper assimilation and eliminations. These malfunctions produced
excessive toxins within the body, which often disturbed the
nervous system and, in turn, resulted in insomnia. Pressures on the spinal column also contributed to the disorder
in eight cases.

Treatment

In treating individuals with insomnia, the underlying physical and emotional conditions were generally of prime consideration. Treatments varied with individual needs and cannot be considered specific to insomnia.

The type of physical treatment most frequently advised was electrotherapy, with the Radio-Active Appliance receiving twenty-five of forty-one recommendations. This appliance was intended specifically to balance the circulatory and nervous systems in such a manner as to promote greater relaxation and harmony. According to Cayce, these effects would be enhanced if the appliance was used just before or at the same time as meditation. The electric vibrator was also recommended in a few cases because of its relaxing effect.

Dietary advice was given in thirty-two cases. Although many of these suggestions might improve the quality of rest by providing for a more digestible diet, only one was specific—a glass of warm milk with a teaspoon of honey stirred into it, taken at bedtime.

Spinal manipulation received twenty-three suggestions and was intended to promote relaxation by reducing tension along the spine. Massage was recommended in twenty cases, also as a method to induce relaxation. Various substances were to be rubbed into the skin, including peanut oil, a mutton-tallow combination, as well as other oil combinations.

To help remove toxins from the system, methods to stimulate eliminations were suggested in nine cases. These were in the form of colonics, enemas, and laxatives.

Digestive aids such as Al-Caroid and bicarbonate of soda received seven recommendations. Both, according to the readings, could help the body relax. Other indirectly effective treatments mentioned in up to five cases each were Atomidine, various packs, and hydrotherapy.

In order to help tire the body and promote better rest, ten individuals were advised to exercise. Additionally, the nonphysical aspect of insomnia treatment received some notice and was considered to be of great importance. Pursuits leading to spiritual development, such as meditation and Bible reading, were recommended in ten cases and mental exercises in two.

Case History

Twenty-six individuals followed Cayce's advice and subsequently reported beneficial results. There were no reports in the remaining cases.

One of the instances where Cayce's advice was followed and a follow-up report filed was that of case 515, a forty-year-old woman who received two readings for a number of complaints, among which was insomnia. The insomnia was attributed to nervous system incoordination, which was caused by sluggish circulation and glandular imbalances.

The first treatment suggestion was for an herbal formula containing the sedative valerian. Cabinet sweats were then advised to relieve the body of some of the toxins accumulated because of sluggish circulation. These baths were to be given twice a week for two weeks and were to be followed by a general but thorough massage for twenty to thirty minutes, using unspecified oils and rubbing alcohol.

Daily use of the Radio-Active Appliance was also recommended. This was to be applied during the daily rest period for at least thirty minutes to an hour, or an hour and a half if sleep resulted.

Dietary changes emphasized easily assimilated foods such as fruits and citrus fruit juices. Salads were especially advised for the noon meal. Meats were to be fish or fowl. Also recommended were large quantities of water to help in purging the body.

The second reading given for case 515 noted that myrrh was to be used in the massages and that a heating pad be applied afterward. As an aid to eliminations, internal doses of olive oil were advised.

Iritis (Uveitis)

Iritis is any inflammation of the uveal tract (iris, ciliary body, and choroid). Edgar Cayce occasionally referred to iritis as, or associated it with, neuritis, which is characterized by lesions of a nerve or nerves and which can be an inflammatory condition.

A total of thirty readings were given for eleven individuals who either had a complete case of iritis or a tendency toward this inflammation. One of the individuals, case 538, received a total of sixteen readings dealing with this condition.

The basic causes given by Cayce for iritis varied, but he typically attributed it to at least two of the following: glandular imbalance, general debilitation, cold and congestion, spinal pressures, nonelimination of toxic materials, kidney disturbances, acidity, illness, injury, nervous taxation, poor circulation, and prior treatments which aggravated the condition.

No consistent order of causes is evident, but according to Cayce any of them could result in pressure on the nerves that supply nutriments to the eyes, subsequently slowing the elimination of toxins from the area and allowing inflammation to develop.

Treatment

The treatment most often mentioned—in all but three of the cases—was spinal manipulation and/or massage. Electrotherapy was also frequently suggested, most often in the form of the Wet Cell, the Violet Ray (over the spine), and the Radio-Active Appliance. Diet was stressed in just over half of the cases, with special emphasis on a balanced diet and cleansing foods. Suggested as often were local applications to reduce the inflammation, such as boric acid, Glyco-Thymoline, and cold compresses and eye drops.

Stimulating the eliminations by means of laxatives, colonics, or enemas was suggested in several cases. A few individuals were advised to rest in a dim light and to avoid

straining their eyes, especially after close work in very
bright or dim light.

Case History

Almost half of those receiving readings on iritis reported
some improvement after following Cayce's advice. The
doctor who treated case 934 was impressed with her
recovery. Reports note that when she went to him for
spinal adjustments, she was almost totally blind and that
her eyes were completely covered by white film. However,
after several treatments, her eyes became almost clear. A
little over a year after her first reading, the woman reported
that her eyes had cleared except for a tiny film that was not
noticeable, and that there was no further inflammation.

A typical treatment regimen was given for case 1267, a
fifty-two-year-old woman who was suffering from a general depletion of energies due to a spinal subluxation in the
upper dorsal and cervical areas. This impeded the circulation to her head, which gradually created an inflammatory
condition, dilating and smothering the optic nerve and
thereby impeding the vision in both eyes.

To treat the woman, Cayce first recommended osteopathic adjustments, especially in the affected areas, stimulating all the nerves and muscular forces to the eyes and
coordinating the lower spine to facilitate drainages. These
were to be administered two or three times weekly for
three weeks, followed by a ten- to fourteen-day rest period, another two-week series of adjustments, another rest
period, and then another series.

During the rest periods, she was advised to use the
Radio-Active Appliance, and after each third application
she was advised to use the Violet Ray, applying it over her
head, neck, and entire spine. These treatments were to be
gentle in nature and for only three to five minutes in
duration.

As an eyewash, Cayce prescribed a weakened solution
of Glyco-Thymoline. Additionally, potato poultices were
to be applied over her eyes once or twice weekly just

before retiring. The poultices were to be kept on for at least ten minutes and the eyes cleansed after the poultices were removed.

Colonics were recommended at intervals, using salt and soda in the water every second or third time and adding Glyco-Thymoline to prevent inflammation and assist the eliminations.

Although there was no follow-up information available on case 1267, reports on the woman indicate she was impressed with her reading and planned to use Cayce's advice.

Kidneys: General

The kidneys, a pair of bean-shaped organs each no larger than a human fist, help regulate the normal concentration of blood constituents by the excretion of water and waste products. They contain approximately one million nephrons, which constantly monitor the level of various minerals. It is in the nephrons that the filtering, excreting, and reabsorbing functions take place. Excess sugar, amino acids, and urea, the end products of protein production, are among the substances filtered through the kidneys.

The Edgar Cayce readings contain hundreds of references to kidney afflictions. The Cayce research concerning general disorders of the kidneys focuses on forty-nine readings given for thirty-seven individuals who ranged in age from four to seventy-two years old.

The major cause cited for disorders of the kidneys (and often of the liver as well) was improper eliminations, mentioned in twenty-seven cases. Spinal subluxations, most of which were located in the lumbar, dorsal, or cervical areas, were found to be a factor in seventeen cases. These subluxations interfered with the nerve impulses and blood circulation to the kidneys.

A contributing factor in eleven cases was poor circulation. Improper assimilations, mentioned in nine cases, created a shortage of nutrients to the kidneys, which in turn contributed to a breakdown of the kidneys' functions. Glandular imbalances were cited seven times, with specific mention given to the thyroid, pineal, and prostate glands.

A contributing factor in four cases was general debilitation, which left the kidneys in a weakened state. Neurasthenia, or nerve exhaustion, internal infections, and injuries due to external causes were each mentioned in three cases. A variety of other conditions, including tuberculosis, bronchitis, and pelvic disorders, were occasionally found to be related factors.

Treatment

The treatments recommended for these individuals were fairly consistent. Spinal manipulation was recommended in twenty-six instances. Often the entire spine was to be adjusted, although the dorsal, lumbar, and sacral vertebrae generally received special mention.

Dietary suggestions were made in twenty-two cases, with the intent of supplying what was needed to rebuild the body without putting too much strain on the excretory organs. Fresh fruits and vegetables were the most favored foods. These could be accompanied by foods such as whole-grain cereals, beef juice, wine and dark bread, and plenty of water. Jerusalem artichokes, a natural source of insulin, were recommended in five cases.

Fourteen individuals were advised to use hot packs to help stimulate the circulation, relieve pain, and eliminate excess toxins. Most of the packs were to be placed on the lower back or abdomen. Hot salt packs were those most frequently mentioned, often in combination with Glyco-Thymoline, bicarbonate of soda, or a combination of mutton suet, spirits of turpentine, and spirits of camphor. The duration and frequency of these treatments varied from one case to the next.

Massage was recommended for twelve individuals in order to stimulate the circulation and eliminations. A variety of substances were to be massaged into the skin and at times were to be followed by hot packs. In four instances, to benefit the kidneys a combination of mutton tallow, spirits of camphor, and spirits of turpentine was to be massaged into the base of the spine and/or over the kidney area.

To further aid the circulation, electrotherapy was suggested in eleven cases. The Violet Ray and Radio-Active Appliance were most often suggested.

Colonics, enemas, or laxatives were recommended for five individuals in order to speed the removal of accumulated toxins. Advised in eight cases each were watermelon-seed tea and herbal tonics. Watermelon-seed tea was considered a natural diuretic and kidney stimulant which was a specific for kidney problems. Ingredients in the herbal tonics included sassafras, juniper berries, and sarsaparilla.

Exercise was advised in four cases and Atomidine in three. Receiving two recommendations each were aspirin, Glyco-Thymoline, and lithia water.

Case History

Ten of the fourteen people who responded with follow-up reports noted beneficial results. Reporting beneficial results following the first of two readings was a fifty-year-old man, case 916, who received two readings for a kidney disorder known as nephritis.

The first reading suggested massage of the lower spine with a combination of mutton tallow, turpentine, and spirits of camphor. This was to be followed by hot salt packs placed over the massaged area. The packs were to be topped with a heating pad to further enhance absorption of the massage compound. This treatment was intended to stimulate elimination of metabolic waste products which had accumulated in the kidneys. Colonics, to be given "once, twice, or thrice," were also suggested to increase eliminations.

The man's diet was to consist of food that was light and highly nutritious, including body strengtheners such as beef juice and eggnog.

The man followed the advice contained in his first

reading and reported excellent results. A second reading was requested three and a half years later when the condition recurred. This time Cayce suggested watermelon-seed tea to purify the kidneys. This was prepared by steeping a teaspoon of the ground seeds in two ounces of boiling water. Additionally, general osteopathic manipulations were advised.

While there was no actual report received for the second reading, word was received that the man died approximately three months later.

Kidney Stones

Edgar Cayce gave readings for eight individuals suffering from kidney stones, which form in the kidneys from accumulated deposits. When the stones become too large to pass through the ureter (the passageway from the kidney to the bladder) and the urethra (the passageway from the bladder to the outside), it causes extreme pain and irritation. An operation to remove the stone is the usual medical procedure.

Cayce viewed the cause of kidney stones as a circulatory incoordination between the liver, kidneys, and other related organs. In half of the cases, spinal subluxations were involved, typically in the area of the seventh to tenth dorsal vertebrae. In one case, an injury had produced a lesion in the area, and in two cases an acidic blood reaction to certain foods had triggered the formation of stones. Eating foods cooked in aluminum pots was mentioned as a contributing factor in another reading.

Treatment

Cayce's approach to treating kidney stones involved methods which would help allay inflammation around the kidneys and disintegrate the stone sufficiently to allow it to pass. Among the eight individuals receiving readings, only one operation was suggested, for Cayce viewed surgical procedures as necessary only when there was fever, indicating infection.

Although Cayce's suggestions varied somewhat with each case, some treatments were consistent. Most frequently recommended were complete rest and quiet until the stones had been passed and normal body functions were reestablished. A light diet of semiliquid, easily digested, and body-building foods was advised. This included fruit juices and vegetable broths and beef juice. Once the stone had been passed, the dietary suggestions given were in accord with Cayce's general dietary advice.

Another frequently recommended treatment was the application of turpentine stupes over the kidney or abdominal area. These were to alleviate pain and help dissolve the stone. In three of these cases, the stupes were to be placed over the kidneys, and in another case, over the lower abdomen. In two cases, stupes were to be used twice weekly for at least an hour. In another case, the stupes were to be applied continuously, with a frequent change of cloths.

The stupes were prepared by soaking several layers of flannel in hot water in which spirits of turpentine had been added. The proportions prescribed varied from eight ounces of spirits of turpentine in one and one-half quarts of water, to five drops in a quart of water.

In two cases, both mullein and turpentine stupes were recommended. For one individual, they were to be alternated with one another, while the other reading recommended twelve continuous hours of mullein stupes over the pubic area, with the stupes to be changed every hour.

The mullein stupes were prepared by crushing the leaves and applying them wet between gauze. For one individual, an ounce of mullein tea—prepared by steeping a teaspoon of the flower in a pint of water—was to be taken twice daily.

Osteopathy and massage were also important treatments in some cases. The spinal adjustments were general in nature, with special focus on the dorsal, lumbar, and sacral areas. These were to be administered from one or more daily to about once weekly, becoming less frequent as the severity of the condition decreased.

Massages were to be given on the spine over the kidney area, or from the eighth to the twelfth dorsal vertebrae. In two cases, Cayce advised bedtime massages over the same area, using a combination of equal parts of mutton tallow, spirits of turpentine, spirits of camphor, and compound tincture of benzoin. A cloth was to be placed over the area for absorption and then covered with a hot pad for an hour.

There were a number of less frequent treatment recommendations. Castor oil packs and watermelon-seed tea (a specific for kidneys) were each suggested twice. Other treatments included the Radio-Active Appliance, diathermy, fume baths, Coca-Cola syrup, senna tea, and an herbal tonic.

Case History

Cayce gave a thirty-seven-year-old woman, case 1054, two readings for her condition. In the first, he noted that a past injury had caused a lesion in the eighth, ninth, and tenth dorsal areas of her spine. This lesion, in turn, affected the activity of her kidneys, and due to poor circulation in this area, sediments had been produced.

Her symptoms were pain in the bladder and, at times, through the kidney area and discomfort through the abdomen. Because of her kidney problems, she was also developing toxemia, which would at times alter her heartbeat and cause other discomfort.

Her treatments began with spinal adjustments, the first series of which was to be administered once a week for a month. During this time, she was to take one ounce of watermelon-seed tea daily. At bedtime for this same month-long period, she was to have a massage over the eighth to twelfth dorsal areas, using a combination of equal parts of mutton tallow, turpentine, spirits of camphor, and compound tincture of benzoin. She was to apply only what the body would absorb and then cover the area with flannel and a heating pad for an hour.

After the first month, she was to rest from treatments for three to four days and then resume them again, with the spinal-adjustments routine increased to two to three times a week.

Cayce also suggested that she have mild diathermy treatments once a week during this second month, with the diathermy plates attached to the fourth dorsal and the lacteal duct areas. She was also to drink at least six glasses of water a day and pay strict attention to her diet. Pears and grapes were specified as beneficial fruits.

Between the first and second readings, the woman told the Cayce family that her condition did not appear to have improved. However, she noted that she had not adhered to the treatments as rigidly as the readings stated she should.

Subsequently, in the second reading for case 1054, Cayce determined that she had assimilation problems which had caused blockages in the colon. This, he felt, accounted for the apparent lack of improvement.

This reading recommended a new series of spinal adjustments twice a week, with special attention to the whole length of the sciatic centers or nerve centers of the spine. He also suggested that she continue with rubs, using the formula previously given. Additionally, Cayce advised a series of castor oil packs, these to be placed over the liver and colon areas for a period of forty minutes once a week.

Laryngitis

Laryngitis is an inflammation of the laryngeal mucosa and is due to bacterial or oral infection which results in a partial or complete loss of voice. Hoarseness is the main symptom.

Edgar Cayce gave one reading each for four individuals with laryngitis or a related condition. Those requesting readings ranged in age from twenty-five to fifty-nine years.

Cayce regarded the loss of one's voice as a side effect of

congestion and infection throughout the system which had become sufficiently acute to affect the bronchi and larynx.

A primary cause in all cases was poor elimination, which slowed and overtaxed the entire hepatic circulation, resulting in a buildup of toxins in the bloodstream. As a consequence, congestion and fever would build up in the body, and the throat and larynx would eventually become inflamed. Poor assimilation was at times involved. Too much activity, which had lowered the body's resistance to infection, was another factor mentioned in one case by Cayce.

Treatment

Cayce's treatments for individuals with laryngitis focused on eliminating infectious forces from the system. In each case, an inhalant was suggested to relieve irritation to the throat and nasal passages, ease breathing, and promote expectoration of mucus. The inhalants generally were grain-alcohol based, although in one case a spray was recommended. These solutions contained eucalyptus, or tincture of benzoin, pine needle oil or other substances.

In three cases, to help stimulate the circulatory system and assist in the elimination of toxins, hydrotherapy treatments were recommended. Two patients were advised to bathe their feet and lower limbs in hot mustard water consisting of a half teaspoon of dry mustard to each gallon of water used.

Massages for the feet were suggested in one case and for the upper spine in another. A combination of mutton tallow, spirits of turpentine, and spirits of camphor was to be rubbed into the feet.

Eliminants, spinal manipulation, and a specific diet were also suggested in two cases. The eliminants advised were vegetable laxatives, and the adjustments were to be administered where needed to relax the body. An alkaline and body-building diet was advised, with the emphasis placed on foods that are yellow in color.

Case History

Three of the four individuals receiving readings on laryngitis followed the advice given by Cayce, and each reported beneficial results.

A case in particular was 1100, a forty-one-year-old woman who received one reading for laryngitis. Her condition was attributed to congestion in the blood which was caused by improper eliminations and a lowered resistance to infection. As Cayce explained: "These are acute conditions produced by a general debilitation from...activity, and cold from congestion, which have made for infectious forces through the tissues of the throat, the bronchi and larynx" (1100-7).

Cayce's first recommendations were hot mustard baths for the feet and lower limbs, followed by rubs using a combination of mutton tallow, spirits of turpentine, and spirits of camphor.

To aid the nasal and throat passages directly, the reading advised an inhalant spray containing one-half ounce of grain alcohol, two ounces of distilled water, five minims of oil of eucalyptol, two minims of rectified oil of turpentine, and ten minims of compound tincture of benzoin. This mixture was to be used in an atomizer every two to two and a half hours, with relief promised within twenty-four hours.

Also prescribed were internal doses of Atomidine in water, beginning with one drop taken in the morning and two in the evening, then each day for the next two days increasing each dose by a drop until three drops were taken in the morning and five in the evening of the third day. Following a day of rest, the four-day cycle was to begin again.

The woman's diet emphasized eggs, whole wheat bread, and vegetables. Valentine's Liver Extract was to be taken as a food supplement, and Caroid and bile salts tablets were suggested as an aid to the liver.

To help bring the body back into balance, spinal manipulations were suggested. These were to focus on the upper dorsal and cervical areas, making corrections around the head, neck, ears, and vagus centers.

After following her treatment, the woman reported an immediate improvement in her condition.

Leukemia

Leukemia, a form of cancer of the blood, is a disorder of the blood-forming tissue characterized by proliferation of abnormal white cells. This illness is accompanied by anemia, weakness, pain in the joints, and lymph node swelling.

Edgar Cayce gave readings for twenty-five individuals who suffered either from leukemia or had a predisposition toward this disorder. The following treatment research focuses on ten individuals, ranging in age from early childhood to late middle age. A total of thirteen readings were given to this group.

A major cause cited by Cayce in about half of the cases was disturbances of the circulation, which was triggered by infection, anemia, or chemical imbalances. In fifteen percent, poor eliminations were also involved, implying a toxic blood buildup. In one reading, Cayce described leukemia as arising from "an unbalanced condition in the chemical forces of the body, so active in the blood system in its assimilations as to destroy the plasm that may be said to encase the red blood cell. Thus it is a plasm condition, or lack of the hemoglobin to produce in the effluvia of the plasm the coagulative forces—or the white blood is so intermingled with the red blood as to destroy the plasm" (2699-1).

Also at times mentioned by Cayce were glandular problems. Noted in a few cases was splenomegaly, or engorgement of the spleen, which manufactures red blood cells, indicating a substantial decrease in the number of red cells due to the malfunctioning of this organ.

Treatments

Treatments prescribed by Cayce for leukemia were usually simple. Suggested in about sixty percent were various forms of electrotherapy, including the ultraviolet mercury quartz light, the Wet Cell Appliance, the Radio-Active Appliance, the radium pad, and the infrared light. Cayce specified that the ultraviolet light be reflected through a green "healing" glass plate, which would act as a special filter. The glass was to be positioned fourteen inches from the body, with the lamp forty inches away. The light was to be placed over the back, especially in the area of the ribs and spleen. One reading specified that this treatment be conducted every other day.

The inclusion of blood-building foods in the diet was recommended in fifty percent of the cases. Foods such as liver extract, calf's liver, beef juice, fresh orange juice, and raw vegetables were considered essential to adding new vitality to the blood, and were to be a daily part of the diet.

Blood transfusions were also recommended in forty percent of the cases. This was to remove unhealthy blood and restore fresh, normal blood to the body.

Cayce prescribed a variety of injections in thirty percent of the cases. These included atropine, liver extract and iodine and saline solutions. In more severe cases, both injections and transfusions were called for at times.

The Atomidine dosage was recommended in a similar number of cases. The typical dosage was three to five drops in water in five-day sequences.

Case History

Most of the individuals receiving readings for leukemia were already in the advanced stages of the disease, and available reports usually indicated a negative outcome. However, one individual reported improvements after following Cayce's recommendation. His condition had been diagnosed as lymphatic leukemia, and doctors had given him two months to live. Cayce, however, felt the condition need not be fatal, and seven months after the reading the man was reported to be still alive, although he still had some problems (3616).

A detailed example of a leukemia case treated by Cayce involved a fourteen-year-old boy who received one reading for the condition. The medical diagnosis for case 2488 was acute lymphatic leukemia accompanied by splenomegaly, although Cayce regarded the condition, at least at this stage, as anemia rather than true leukemia. Cayce predicted that if the suggestions given in the reading were closely followed, the blood imbalance could be corrected, provided that the transfusions given proved to be more beneficial than harmful. The readings had expressed concern about the quality of the transfusions, and Cayce's first advice was to take precautions in typing the blood used, as the desired effect had not been achieved.

To improve the benefits from the transfusions, treatments with the shortwave ultraviolet light were advised, with applications to be made in the area of the ribs and spine. These were to be no longer than one minute in duration, using a piece of green glass between the light and the body.

To aid the body structurally and help eliminate the anemia, spinal manipulations were to be given following the light treatments. Rest was indicated, and the child was to be given all the orange juice and liver or liver extract that he could assimilate. Cayce held that the nutritional value provided by food would be better than that derived from vitamins or injections.

Cayce was asked about the phosphorus that the doctors were planning to use on the child, and he recommended that it be used only as a last resort, if there was a rise in both temperature and in the number of white blood cells.

Although the child's mother was pleased with the reading, his blood count was a little higher the next morning, so the treatment with phosphorus was administered. The doctors agreed to use the light and diet recommended by Cayce.

A few days later, it was reported that the boy was up

and walking around. However, the hospital later reported that the child did not respond to any of the treatments and died two weeks later.

Lumbago

Lumbago is a general term to describe rheumatic pains in the lower back or loins (the lumbar region). A total of twenty-three men and women, ranging in age from twenty-one to eighty, sought Edgar Cayce's advice on this problem.

In two-thirds of the readings on lumbago, the cause was attributed to poor eliminations arising from difficulties in digestion. Cayce believed the inability of the body to eliminate toxins would create accumulations of uric acid in the blood, affecting the circulation between the liver and kidneys. Resulting disturbances and the need for eliminations would consequently produce a heavy feeling of pain around the lower back area.

In seven cases where poor eliminations were cited as the cause, uremic poisoning was also involved. Found in many individuals was also a low red blood cell count, or anemia, and this typically contributed to a general state of weariness and overtaxation.

Blood toxicity was also a causative factor in four cases and was due to an imbalance of body acidity and alkalinity. In three cases, spinal lesions or injuries involving the lower lumbar vertebrae were responsible for pressure and strain on the lower back muscles.

Treatment

In two-thirds of the cases, Cayce suggested eliminants such as castor oil, Alophen, Eno salts, milk of magnesia, and olive oil. Also suggested in some cases to clear the intestinal tract were colonics.

Dietary advice was given to eleven individuals with the intent to improve eliminations. Emphasis was placed on fresh fruits and vegetables, occasional cereals, and wheat or rye bread. Several individuals were urged to include more alkaline-reacting foods in their diets. Not advised were pork and fats, and to be eaten in extreme moderation were meats and stimulants.

In over half of the readings on lumbago, massage and manipulation of the affected areas were suggested to ease backache pain and relieve congestion in the lower abdomen. Cayce frequently advised rubbing the painful area of the back with a compound consisting of equal parts mutton tallow, spirits of camphor, and spirits of turpentine, followed by an application of a hot salt pack. In these instances, he also gave specific instructions in eight cases for the use of hot packs saturated with either castor oil or the compound described above, also to be applied to the painful area.

In nine cases, electrotherapy was suggested to help relieve the lower back pain. This was usually the Violet Ray and ultraviolet light.

In addition to physical treatments, Cayce also stressed the importance of attitude, suggesting that "the correct attitudes and the general mental forces be kept in accord with that which is constructive toward all relationships, that there may be kept a more even balance" (348-19).

Case Histories

Two case histories, one for a fifty-nine-year-old man and the other, a woman of thirty-nine, illustrate the variety of readings given.

According to Cayce, the former, case 379, suffered from lumbago due to poor eliminations, which triggered disturbances in the hepatic circulation and accumulations of uric acid in the bloodstream.

The man was advised to wrap his back and abdomen in a hot castor oil pack for an hour and a half during each attack, and at these times to take a tablespoon of olive oil to aid eliminations. His reading also recommended that he eat a raw Jerusalem artichoke every day or two to assist the glandular forces and eliminations.

Seven months later, the man reported that he had obtained good results from the treatments.

The second report, case 1955, the woman of thirty-nine, had a circulatory disturbance between the upper and lower hepatic areas which was creating pressure on the nerve and pain in the lower back.

Diet was Cayce's first treatment, and it was to consist of vegetables; fish, fowl, and lamb; and wheat or rye bread. Not advised were pork, fats, or many starches. On an occasional basis, a high-colonic irrigation was prescribed. Also suggested was the nightly use of the hand Violet Ray, to be administered down each side of the spine. To stimulate the kidneys, drinking watermelon-seed tea twice a week was recommended. The tea was to be prepared by pouring a pint of boiling water over a teaspoon of crushed seed. A series of spinal adjustments was also advised.

The follow-up notes that months later the woman reported feeling completely relieved of lumbago.

Lupus Erythematosus

Lupus erythematosus is a superficial, localized discoid of the skin. In the mild form of the disease, known as discoid lupus, the skin is characterized by red single or multiple plaques on the face. Systemic lupus may affect multiple organ systems and mainly occurs in young women. Symptoms include fever, anorexia, malaise, and weight loss. The course of the disease is characterized by alternating periods of flare-up and remission and may vary from a mild episodic disorder to a fatal illness.

Edgar Cayce gave only one reading on lupus erythemato sus—for 5288-1, a forty-four-year-old woman. The main cause cited was a disturbance in the excretory system which caused a buildup of toxins. Also noted was an incoordination between lymph circulation and certain cerebrospinal areas, which had produced irritating accumulations of fluids under the skin.

The woman's symptoms included skin blisters and

splotches, nausea, headaches, fever, weakness and dizziness, indigestion, poor elimination, occasional coughing, blurred vision, and pressure on the eardrums.

Treatment and Case History

Electrotherapy, using the sinusoidal or shortwave appliance, was the first treatment and was to be administered once a week to help empty the gallbladder and stimulate the kidneys and general energies. Also advised, to improve the general circulation, were twice weekly osteopathic massages.

As an aid to digestion, the woman was prescribed a mixture of three to five drops of elixir of lactated pepsin and a half teaspoon of milk of bismuth in a half glass of water. This was to be taken once daily. If poor eliminations tended to exist one or two days later, a high colonic and dietary measures were suggested.

Further, Cayce counseled the woman on the seriousness of her disorder and advised her to adopt a more positive, less anxious attitude of "creative helpfulness" toward others as well as herself.

One month later, as a result of following her reading, the woman reported general improvements.

Lymphangitis

Eight readings were given for six individuals with lymphangitis, the inflammation of lymph vessels.

In practically all cases, poor eliminations, poor assimilations, and the improper circulation of blood through the affected areas were recurring problems. In some instances, the cause of these disturbances was traced to deflected nerve impulses originating from subluxations and impingements of the spine. In the remaining instances, the causes were not clearly delineated, but poor eliminations, "impoverished" blood, and poor diet were major factors.

Treatment

Although there were consistent factors, treatments varied considerably from individual to individual. In half of the cases, special emphasis was placed on alkalizing the body by having the individual eat more fruits and vegetables and less excessive starches and no fried foods.

Electrotherapy or heliotherapy was recommended in three cases, although in a different form each time. These variously involved the Radium Appliance, the ultraviolet light, and the Violet Ray.

Other readings recommended adjustment of the areas of the spine affected by subluxations, while still others suggested gentle massages of the back and spine, usually on a daily basis.

Eliminants were also suggested and included doses of olive oil, milk of magnesia, and an unspecified vegetable or mineral laxative. Various herbal preparations were also advised, as were various packs. Hydrotherapy, in the form of the Elliott machine, was recommended once.

Case History

Although treatment for each individual varied, case 2643 is one of particular interest. It concerned a thirty-four-year-old woman who suffered from lymphangitis in the digestive tract due to a former back injury. Her treatment included application of hot castor oil packs over the abdomen for an hour a day for three days. On the third day, following the pack, the woman was advised to take three tablespoons of olive oil.

After a day of rest, a series of osteopathic adjustments focusing on the sixth and seventh dorsal vertebrae and the coccyx were to be administered twice a week, and then the packs-and-olive-oil sequence was to be resumed once again. To maintain eliminations, two colonics were recommended during the two-week series of adjustments.

It is significant to note that the woman, who also suffered from Hodgkin's disease, reported a complete recovery from both ailments after following the recommended treatments.

Other reports, largely of a positive nature, were received in two additional cases. One was from a seventeen-year-old boy who had such a severe case of lymphangitis that he couldn't even be helped by doctors at the Mayo Clinic. Among his problems was blindness due to accumulations of lymph in the face, head, and eyes. After following Cayce's treatments, his eyesight was restored, although he did not live long afterward.

Malaria

Malaria is an infectious feverish disease which is usually contracted from the bite of an infected female mosquito. The most common symptoms are chills, fever, and persistent sweating, all in the form of intermittent attacks. Debilitation, anemia, and engorgement of the spleen are also involved. With antimalarials, the prognosis is good for most malaria infections, even with complications.

Four individuals were given a total of nine readings dealing with the prevention and treatment of malaria.

The cause most commonly cited by Edgar Cayce was infection by the malaria bacillus. According to Cayce, the body was made susceptible by other conditions which lowered its resistance, such as improper eliminations, poor circulation, and glandular imbalance.

Treatment

Treatment for malaria included massages, which could serve various purposes. Rubdowns with cocoa butter or peanut oil were recommended to relax the body and to stimulate the circulatory system. In one case, to prevent mosquitoes from biting, a combination of one ounce of cocoa butter and five grains quinine was to be rubbed over the spine, with one hundred percent success reported.

Until the fever subsided, readings for three individuals

gave dietary advice which emphasized semiliquid foods. Also highly recommended were fruit juices and vegetable soups. Pork and fried foods were expressly forbidden.

Other treatments suggested were more individualized. Methods of improving the eliminations were suggested twice and various other treatments only once each.

Case History

Case 608 was a young girl who received five readings for malaria between three and sixteen years. Her most frequent symptoms were fever and nausea, with large lumps appearing occasionally on the side of her throat.

The first reading traced her condition as being related to poor eliminations. The entire hepatic circulation was disturbed, and there was also a substantial strain on the adrenal glands.

To help reduce the fever, spinal manipulations and massages with cocoa butter were advised, with special focus on the lower lumbar and sacral areas. Doses of Castoria were suggested to aid the liver and digestive system. Vegetable soups and chicken broth were advised to help strengthen the body.

Later readings advised continuing the massages and adjustments, and gave further dietary advice. Additionally, the use of other eliminants, such as a combination of sulfur, cream of tartar, and Epsom salts, was prescribed. Other recommendations made during the course of the readings included Ventriculin with Iron (a dietary supplement), Grove's Chill Tonic, and castor oil packs to help clear the gall duct. Doses of Atomidine were also suggested to aid in combating the disease.

A gradual improvement in 608's health was noted over the thirteen years she followed Cayce's advice, and by the age of sixteen, the malaria symptoms were no longer evident.

Two other individuals followed their readings and reported being pleased with the results.

Measles

Measles is a contagious disease caused by a virus which occurs most frequently in children. It is typically characterized by a red rash which begins on the face and neck and gradually spreads to other parts of the body. Other symptoms are fever and cough.

There was a total of ten readings given for eight individuals with measles; they ranged in age from two to thirty-one years.

In five cases, an infectious force in the lymph glands was cited as the cause of measles. Although Edgar Cayce did not specify the nature of the infection, he established in the readings that viruses and infections in the body flourish only under acidic conditions, thus implying that overacidity predisposed the body to measles in these cases.

In two other cases, toxic accumulations in the body, caused by poor eliminations, were a critical factor. In fact, Cayce noted that the skin eruptions could be regarded as the end result of the body's attempt to throw off the infection through the capillary circulation in the skin.

Treatment

Cayce's treatment for measles was consistent, and special emphasis was placed on herbal teas for the assimilations and eliminations, massages to reduce fever and stimulate the circulation, and a balanced diet and laxative substances.

Six readings mentioned frequent doses of either saffron or chamomile tea, given at various intervals. Massages using various combinations of oils were often suggested. This was usually to center on the back and spine. For this purpose, a compound of equal portions of mutton tallow, spirits of camphor, and spirits of turpentine was most frequently suggested. Light rubs with rubbing alcohol were also suggested in some cases to help reduce high fever.

To facilitate digestion and alkalize the system, semiliquid diets were considered necessary during the period of illness. Fruit and vegetable juices, as well as well-cooked oatmeal and other cereals, were strongly advised. Heavy meals and overeating were discouraged.

Frequent doses of Castoria were advised in three cases, followed by a dose of a saline laxative such as Eno salts to completely flush the system.

In several readings, Cayce warned that the aftereffects of measles could be harmful if proper steps were not taken to secure a complete recovery. Frequent advice was to stay in bed, keep out of drafts, keep warm and dry, and avoid bright lights until the measles had passed.

Case History

Case 487, a twenty-three-year-old man, received two readings for a severe case of measles which had obviously been triggered by complications resulting from a bad cold and a glandular infection. There was danger that the infection would settle in the bronchi and larynx and produce a serious bronchitic condition.

To stimulate the eliminations, Cayce prescribed intermittent doses of Castoria. A thorough cleansing of the system with Eno salts or Sal Hepatica was also advised. Saffron tea was to be taken on a daily basis. This was to act as an intestinal antiseptic. Massages using a compound of mutton tallow, spirits of camphor, and spirits of turpentine, followed by hot packs, were to be given over the small of the back to relieve stress on the kidneys.

In addition to maintaining frequent eliminations, the man was advised to stay out of light until he was fully recovered and to avoid cold and dampness.

Several years later, the man wrote to Cayce, informing him that he had "completely recovered" from the measles with no aftereffects and that he had been in excellent health ever since.

Ménière's Disease

Ménière's disease is characterized by deafness, vertigo or dizziness, and tinnitus (ringing in the ears). Other frequent symptoms include nausea, vomiting, sweating, and fluctuating hearing loss, and at times migraine headaches.

Although a number of readings commented on vertigo, only two cases had been specifically diagnosed as Ménière's syndrome. In the summaries that follow, it is evident that Edgar Cayce's treatment not only emphasized the importance of a good diet, but also stressed other important facets.

Treatment and Case History

Case 189 was a forty-four-year-old woman who suffered from toxemia and a tendency toward hypertension, in addition to Ménière's syndrome. Her symptoms included vertigo attacks, severe headaches, and acid indigestion. The reading described the dynamics of this disorder at some length, attributing it mainly to circulatory imbalances which were linked to a shortage of iodine in her system.

When asked about the relationship between the fluids of the ear and the equilibrium of the body, Cayce replied: "It keeps the balance, just like a governor upon an engine, or keeping the balance or equilibrium as if one were on rollers or moving; it aids in keeping the balance in the whole of the system's activity. Hence the dizziness that occurs, the unbalancing in the circulatory forces, and all of these disturbances" (189-6).

Atomidine was recommended to supply the needed iodine. One drop was to be taken in half a glass of water each morning before meals for five days, followed by a five-day rest period, another five days of dosage, etc. Colonics were recommended at intervals to reduce pressures on the liver and heart.

Additionally, a more balanced, less acid, and more laxative diet, with plenty of raw vegetables, was advised. Because of the acidity, citrus-and-starch combinations were to be avoided. During the attacks, the woman was advised to eat only liquid or semiliquid foods and whole-grain sources of B vitamins. Foods containing too much salt were to be avoided.

To counteract nausea, Cayce recommended eating small meals and taking Al-Caroid after eating, especially if greasy foods were part of the meal. Walking was suggested as the best exercise, although other passive forms, such as adjustments and massages, were considered beneficial.

About three weeks later, the woman reported that although she was very active, she felt good. About seven months later, another reading was requested, as she was again (or still) experiencing dizziness and other problems. Interestingly, Cayce said that the dizziness was no longer being caused by Ménière's, but by "the liver in its attempt to work with the pressures being produced in the duodenum, as it empties into the jejunum" (189-7). Her problems were described as partially glandular in origin, implying that menopause may have been in progress.

Treatment measures recommended this time included hydrotherapy, osteopathic massage, Al-Caroid after meals, and occasional doses of milk of bismuth with lactated pepsin. General dietary guidelines were once again given. Two months later, after a number of adjustments, she reported that the dizzy feeling in her head was completely cleared up.

Meningitis

Spinal meningitis is the inflammation of the meninges, or membranes that envelop the brain and spinal cord. Symptoms include fever, chills, headache, nausea, confusion, and back, abdominal, and extremity pain.

Four individuals received a total of five readings on this condition.

One reading discussed the cause of meningitis at length, describing it as the invasion of parasites from outside the body, which attacked the nerve centers in the spine. The reading also gave information on these parasites, "which have taken hold of, or live on the nervous force, or matter [taken] into the body which passed into the system through the sense of smell or through the nostrils, in the air taken into the lungs'' (4814-1).

In the other three cases, the cause was simply indicated as a deterioration of the nerves in the spine by infectious agents. Three out of four of these cases were children under the age of ten years.

Treatment and Case History

Reading 4814-1 also provided a discussion on treating meningitis. Cayce believed that "the effects to use, or reach these can only be through a force which will act on the nervous system, without producing a distortion of the cells." Consequently, relaxation of the spine and muscles was viewed as critical to treatment. This was best accomplished with spinal massages, which were recommended in three of the four cases. Massage substances included full-strength Glyco-Thymoline, diluted Atomidine, cocoa butter, and a combination of mineral oil, cedarwood oil, mustard oil, sassafras oil, and tincture of benzoin. In two cases, relaxation of the body by means of gentle spinal manipulations and adjustments was also advised.

To reduce fever, Cayce recommended a cold pack placed at the base of the brain and on the head. One reading mentioned that this would also reduce attacks of muscular convulsions and spasms.

Unfortunately, most of the readings Cayce gave for meningitis were for individuals in advanced stages of the disease. One young child died before any treatments could be administered.

In another instance, however, improvements were reported following treatment, but no conclusive report is available.

Menopause

Edgar Cayce gave twenty-six readings concerning the physical problems associated with menopause, the cessation of menstruation, which usually occurs between the ages of forty-five and fifty.

These were given for fourteen women, ranging from thirty-eight to sixty-eight years old. The most common symptoms were hot flashes, fatigue, nervousness, insomnia, and muscle pain.

Cayce noted glandular imbalances in each case. These imbalances frequently involved the thyroid gland. Other physical disturbances contributing to the discomfort were nervous incoordination, poor eliminations and assimilation, and poor circulation and overtaxation. Nervous incoordination was involved in seven cases, usually associated with spinal subluxations; poor elimination and assimilation were mentioned in seven and five cases, respectively, producing congestion in the abdominal cavity, and poor circulation and overtaxation were each involved in six cases. Also mentioned at times as contributory factors were poor diet and general debilitation.

Treatment

Electrotherapy was suggested in ten cases, with the Violet Ray being recommended in four cases, diathermy treatments in three, and the Radio-Active Appliance twice. Each treatment was highly individualized, but all were intended to improve the circulation, normalize nervous system functions, and help induce relaxation.

Almost as much attention was given to the alignment of the spine and to dietary instructions. Spinal adjustments were recommended to correct existing problems and to help maintain the proper balance between the cerebrospinal and sympathetic nervous systems. Individual instructions were quite specific, but frequently a general manipulation was recommended for the relaxing quality of the procedure itself. In five cases, rest and relaxation were stressed, particularly before and after receiving the adjustments.

A well-balanced diet was considered important to physical balance. Especially stressed were fruits and vegetables. Generally, in place of red meat, fish and fowl were recommended; fat from red meat was to be avoided completely, as were all highly seasoned foods, fried foods, and starches and large amounts of alcohol.

Diets promoting elimination were recommended for two women. One was given a choice of three diets—the apple diet, the grape diet, or the citrus diet. In each case, only the fruit and plenty of water were to be consumed for a specific time. One reading recommended taking a half teaspoon of olive oil on the evening of the last day of the diet to help cleanse the body of impurities and prevent the formation of gas.

Glandular tonics such as Atomidine and Tonicine were recommended in six cases. Calcios and gold chloride with bromide of soda were also occasionally mentioned to help glandular imbalances. For the relief of hot and cold flashes, herbal remedies were recommended twice. Both contained tincture of valerian, elixir calisaya, potassium iodide, and potassium bromide, with a tincture of capsicum added to one. Male hormone injections, under a doctor's supervision, were recommended twice.

Various forms of physiotherapy were at times recommended, usually in the form of a massage of the cerebrospinal area, using peanut oil in one case. Glyco-Thymoline packs were suggested in two cases for abdominal discomfort. Salt heat was to be applied on top of the pack. The latter was prepared by heating a bag of coarse salt and placing it over the area of discomfort.

Hydrotherapy, in the form of cabinet sweats and fume baths, was suggested in four instances. For the discomfort in the pelvic region, Epsom salt sitz baths were recommended in one case.

For many women, the necessity of maintaining a balanced and positive emotional attitude was stressed, and to this end Cayce prescribed plenty of fresh air and walking and relaxing outdoors. One woman was advised to sing quietly to herself while working for relaxation.

Case History

Case 1540 received four readings related to menopause between the ages of forty-two and forty-four. Cayce attributed her discomfort to glandular incoordination and spinal misalignments. The glandular sluggishness was attributed to deficiencies in some elements and excessive amounts of others.

Cayce's treatments were intended to strengthen resistance and improve coordination between the nerves and glands. His first reading suggested taking Atomidine to purify and stimulate the pelvic organs. The prescribed dosage was one drop daily for ten days in a half glass of water taken in the morning before meals. After a three-day rest period, Calcios was to be taken daily for five days, followed by a five-day rest period and five more days of Atomidine. The series was to be repeated once or twice, as needed. During this period, a thorough osteopathic relaxation regimen was to be administered, with special attention to the coccyx, and the fourth lumbar and third, fourth, ninth, eleventh, and twelfth dorsals and throughout the cervical area.

The woman was advised to refrain from large amounts of sweets. She was to drink grape juice (Welch's or fresh), diluted to two-thirds strength with plain water, about a half hour before each meal and upon retiring.

Hormone injections and pills were not recommended, as they were not being assimilated and were at times more irritating than helpful. If a hormonal stimulant was desired, Tonicine was recommended, to be taken only after at least ten days of Atomidine dosage.

Cayce noted in the next reading that his treatment instructions had not been followed consistently and had created a hardship on the nervous system. The woman, as a consequence, reported headaches and eye aches. He then recommended twice weekly spinal manipulations for a four-week period. This was to be followed by a rest period of two to three weeks and then another series of manipulations. Tonicine was to be taken during both series, a half teaspoon every other day.

Violet Ray applications were to begin after the first week of manipulations, using the rod applicator on the right hand the first day, the left foot the second day, the left hand the third day, and the right foot the fourth day. These were to be given daily for ten days, followed by another series and beginning with two-minute and, later, three-minute treatments.

Vegetables and fruits were to be a major portion of her diet, although lean, well-done roast beef was occasionally permitted. Also recommended were cereals in the morning. To be avoided were fats and carbonated drinks.

To help the woman's emotional attunement, Cayce recommended an attitude of helpfulness, companionship with others, and spiritual attunement.

Those around 1540 were counseled to try to understand her physical and emotional difficulties. Highly recommended were spending time outdoors, keeping the mind and body busy with external things, and rest.

The fourth and last reading noted improvements, and Cayce recommended continuing the Tonicine and having adjustments twice weekly for eight weeks. Also, each evening before retiring, the woman was to apply the Radio-Active Appliance. Prayerfulness in all things was advised.

No follow-up report is available on this case.

Menstruation: Abnormal

Fifteen readings were given for fourteen women, ranging from thirteen years to thirty-eight years, with abnormal menstrual periods. The most frequently recorded complaint was an irregular cycle.

In half of the readings, the cause of the abnormal period was traced to incoordination of the nervous systems—produced by spinal lesions, subluxations, or injuries. Four readings noted such deficiencies in the blood as poor oxygenation or anemia. For both contributing factors, subsequent conditions such as congestion and pressure in the pelvic organs, as well as glandular imbalance were produced, which in almost all cases resulted in the inhibiting of the normal menstrual cycle. Other prominent conditions were poor eliminations and poor assimilations.

Treatment

Edgar Cayce prescribed a variety of treatments in the readings, no two of which are exactly alike. Most frequently recommended, in eleven cases, were manipulations or adjustments of the spine to relieve pressure on the nervous system and to realign misplaced vertebrae. Dietary recommendations were made in seven readings, which stressed more alkaline-reacting foods such as raw and cooked vegetables and citrus fruits and juices. Roasted or broiled fish, fowl, and lamb were also highly recommended. Foods to be avoided were white bread, potatoes, pastries, carbonated drinks, and fried foods.

For six women, the readings gave specific instructions for taking a variety of tonics, generally for the purpose of improving the blood supply. Included among these were liver extract; a beef, iron, and wine tonic; and Ventriculin. The use of electrotherapy was advised in five cases. This was most frequently in the form of the Violet Ray or Radio-Active Appliance.

In four cases, Cayce suggested the use of Tonicine or Atomidine to regulate the thyroid and glandular systems. The women were to take small doses of Tonicine before their period or a drop of Atomidine in a half glass of water twice daily. In addition, three readings suggested the use of Atomidine in vaginal douching with a fountain syringe two or three times a week, using a solution of one teaspoonful of Atomidine in a quart or quart and a half of water at body temperature.

Case History

Reading 625-1 was given for an eighteen-year-old with an abnormally frequent menstrual cycle. Poor eliminations and an unbalanced metabolism had affected the blood, which had become toxic. This resulted in enlarged ovaries and disturbances in the glands and pelvic organs.

Cayce outlined a specific diet as an important part of the young woman's treatment. Breakfast was to consist of cereal or fresh fruits, fruit juices, and dry whole wheat toast. One meal a day was to consist entirely of all raw green vegetables, and dinner was to include well-cooked vegetables served with roasted or broiled meats. Carbonated drinks were discouraged. She was also advised to have two or three osteopathic adjustments a week to coordinate the fourth lumbar plexus with the ninth dorsal plexus area and to correct alignment of the coccyx.

Although no specific follow-up is available in this case, some time after the reading Cayce received a letter of praise from the young woman's mother.

Menstruation: Painful

Edgar Cayce delivered twenty-seven readings on the subject of menstrual pain or cramps for fourteen women, most in their twenties or thirties. Other common menstrual problems discussed were headaches, lower back pain, and occasional nausea.

Various bodily disturbances were found to be responsible for menstrual discomfort. These usually involved the nervous system, glands, and eliminations. In seven cases, the pelvic organs were believed to be directly affected; either the uterus was tipped, or adhesions were found in the vaginal wall, or injuries had caused disturbances in these organs. Poor eliminations, which produced congestion in the pelvic area, were a causative factor in five other cases. And in two cases of painful menstruation, spinal lesions which resulted in improper nerve impulses to the pelvic organs were noted as the direct cause.

Treatment

Cayce paid considerable attention to the alignment of the spine in treating painful menstruation. In many cases, poor alignment was associated with improper positioning of the pelvic organs. In ten cases, spinal manipulation was therefore indicated. Instructions for the manipulations were usually quite specific and involved coordination of the lower vertebrae in the lumbar and sacral areas.

Readings in seven cases advised a well-balanced diet consisting mainly of alkaline-reacting foods and blood-building foods high in protein and iron. Large quantities of meats, starches, and sugar were to be avoided.

Cayce recommended various packs over the abdomen and lower back areas for local relief of menstrual cramps. Most frequently mentioned were hot dry packs of coarse or wet Epsom salts.

Electrotherapy was prescribed in four instances. These readings recommended use of the Violet Ray with the vaginal applicator, to be applied at least once a week. However, the Violet Ray was never to be used during the menstrual period.

To keep the vaginal area clean and free from infection, douching with diluted Atomidine solutions was suggested in three cases. The usual dilution ratio was a teaspoonful of Atomidine to a quart of warm water.

Case History

Cayce's diagnosis for a thirty-five-year-old woman, case 2330, attributed poor eliminations and adhesions and lesions in the pelvic organs, which prevented proper drainage during menstruation, as contributing factors to her menstrual discomfort. She received three readings which outlined a series of specific treatments. Six osteopathic adjustments, with special attention given to the iliac plexus, were to be administered twice a week, followed by two or three general relaxing treatments. Then another series of adjustments was to follow, during which time Atomidine douches were to be given twice weekly. The dilution ratio was one teaspoon to a quart of warm water.

Following the second series of adjustments, Cayce recommended the use of the Violet Ray with the vaginal applicator. This treatment was to be administered for two and a half to three minutes a week, but not during menstruation. For best results, Cayce recommended that the Violet Ray be used after the adjustment and before douching.

Approximately six months later, Cayce gave the woman a second reading which revealed the development of uterine tumors. He also noted that the treatments had not been applied in a sufficiently thorough manner. More corrections were needed through the lumbosacral vertebrae, and six more weekly adjustments were prescribed.

More Atomidine douches with warm water were also suggested, as well as fewer applications of the Violet Ray. The woman was advised not to eat starchy foods or cheeses and to drink several glasses of grape juice every day. To assist in eliminations, frequent teaspoonfuls of olive oil were suggested.

The woman's third reading indicated that she had neglected to follow the prescribed treatments, and her condition was reverting back to its original state. More disturbances were noted in the eliminations and lower back area. A year later, she had a fibroid tumor removed by surgery.

However, excellent results were reported in four cases. In one instance, a woman who had been previously unable to have children gave birth to two babies a few years after following Cayce's recommendations. In most of the other cases, no follow-up reports were available.

Mental Illness

This summary is based on research by James C. Windsor, a professor of psychology, who studied over 350 readings given by Edgar Cayce for people with mental problems. Despite the fact that mental illness in Cayce's time was diagnosed mainly as insanity, current aberrations in behavior are classified in much more sophisticated terminology, among which are schizophrenia, manic-depressive behavior, paranoia, etc.

Typical symptoms shared by those with these mental problems are, however, disorganization of thought, disorientation in time and space, withdrawal and autistic behavior, extremes of mood, hallucinations, and delusions.

It should be kept in mind that many of those who were brought to Cayce for help with mental illness were brought to him as a last resort. They tended to be severely disturbed, and some had been institutionalized for years.

To illustrate Cayce's diagnostic approach, thirty-two cases of mental illness were selected as a sample group. The most outstanding causative factor in these cases was, according to Cayce, physical incoordination, which would then upset the physical and emotional balance. In at least one-half of the thirty-two cases, this incoordination manifested itself as a disturbed nervous system, either as blocked nerve impulses or outright incoordination between the cerebrospinal and sympathetic (autonomic) nervous systems.

Cayce even found a physical cause for a few cases of hallucinations, which are described as synaptic dysfunctions resulting in the central nervous system's receiving messages which were not sent by the sensory system. Other factors involved in mental illness were glandular imbalance (a major factor in itself) and negative emotions.

Noted in at least nine of the thirty-two cases was glandular dysfunction due to such causes as prenatal developmental problems, infections, injuries, and nervous incoordination. The readings frequently referred to the pineal gland and occasionally mentioned the genitive system as well. Cayce implied that the pineal gland is connected to both the involuntary and central nervous systems and serves as a coordinating function.

In at least seven of the thirty-two readings, Cayce found factors related to attitude. These were nervous tension, emotional stress, and overtaxation. He noted that these were at least partially responsible for the physical incoordination. One reading stated that "any individual, who makes destructive thoughts in the body, condemning self for this or that, will bring, unless there are proper reactions, dissociation or lack of coordination between the sympathetic and cerebrospinal system'' (5380-1).

Treatment

Although Cayce's treatment for mental illnesses contained many common elements, each treatment was tailored to a specific individual. The readings emphasized the importance of carrying out the instructions down to the smallest detail. Additionally, it was strongly emphasized that those giving the treatments be sincerely sympathetic. The following information on treatments was abstracted by Dr. Windsor from an unspecified number of readings.

Electrotherapy was recommended in a majority of cases, especially in the form of the Wet Cell or Radio-Active Appliance. The Wet Cell, suggested in a larger percentage of cases, was said to have a rejuvenating effect on the nervous system and was generally to be used with chloride of gold. The Radio-Active Appliance was recommended primarily for those who needed its calming effect.

Other frequently suggested treatments were spinal manipulation and massage, using substances such as olive oil, peanut oil, and lanolin. Also recommended were numerous specific medicines to suit special needs.

Case History

Case 3950 was a thirty-year-old woman. Her mental imbalance was attributed to prenatal conditions, which Cayce felt eventually affected the glands coordinating the nerve impulses. The nerve impulses received by the brain were so distorted that normal mental responses were prevented. Because of the nervous incoordination, the woman experienced periods of depression alternating with periods of extreme nervousness.

Cayce's treatments were designed to stimulate the glands

by creating the elements needed for the system to be balanced and function properly.

To rid the body of its impurities, the mild electrical stimulus of the Wet Cell Appliance was to be applied. The copper plate was to be first attached to the lower spine and then moved upward over a period of time, applying it for five minutes one day in the lumbar region, five minutes the next day in the dorsal, etc. When one cycle was completed, it was to be repeated, this time for seven minutes in duration.

Because of the impurities being eliminated from the respiratory system, salt baths or baths of witch hazel were prescribed. Laxatives were also recommended to help cleanse the alimentary canal and kidneys. As the system became cleansed, the Wet Cell treatments were to be increased to thirty minutes a day, with rest periods of three to five days.

There is no feedback available on this reading; however, other reports received indicated that when the treatments were earnestly applied, improvements were noted.

Mental Retardation

Edgar Cayce gave ten readings for mentally retarded adults who ranged in age from nineteen to sixty. These readings were given between 1910 and 1944. Although his descriptions of the causative factors involved varied in each case, there were several factors that were frequently noted— cerebrospinal misalignments, injury, and glandular disturbances.

Cerebrospinal misalignments which impeded normal physical and mental functioning were mentioned in over half of the ten readings. In three cases, the spinal misalignments were seen as causing physical stress and preventing normal functioning of the nerves and glands. According to Cayce, this dysfunction would tend to prevent normal mental coordination. Reading 499-1 described an extreme condition of total incoordination (and of total dependence of this person on others), where the individual's sympathetic nervous system could not carry out brain reactions, as it was actually disconnected from his cerebrospinal system.

In one of the three above-mentioned instances, there was a lesion at the second and third cervical vertebrae and problems in the last two, or cartilaginous, vertebrae in the coccyx (4711-1). In the second, case 1399, the spinal segments in the coccyx and the sacral and lumbar vertebrae were "too close together." The last case involved the first and second cervical vertebrae (5533-1).

Injury was mentioned as a cause in four of the ten readings. The following are examples as explained by Cayce. A streetcar accident in his early childhood fractured the skull and created brain lesions for case 5234. As a consequence, he became suseptible to epilepticlike seizures when under stress. In another instance, case 1399, a breech birth had produced subluxations in the coccygeal and lumbar centers which in turn affected the glandular system. Injuries in both the cervical and coccygeal areas caused mental and physical abnormalities for case 4712, and the brain deterioration experienced by 5309, a sixty-year-old person, was attributed to injuries and senility.

Disturbance in the glandular system was mentioned in four readings related to mental retardation. An example was reading 5500-1, in which Cayce noted that the glands did not receive the necessary physical elements, perhaps from dietary deficiencies, during gestation and early development. Hence, the person's nerves could not carry the brain impulses that should have in turn coordinated his sensory and sympathetic nerve systems with his cerebrospinal problems.

Treatment

There were many similarities in Cayce's treatments for mental retardation, most of which were fairly specific. He advocated a holistic approach, and his treatments contained mental and spiritual as well as physical elements. Frequently advised for those administering the treatments were a loving and patient approach and a constructive attitude. This positive approach created a climate conducive to healing. In reading 4991-1, Cayce stressed that the one burdened with the treatment responsibility was never given more than he could bear and that it was an opportunity to become stronger spiritually. The treatments "should be kept in an atmosphere and surroundings that are in keeping with those tenets, those lessons of the body, that are *being* taking for the *spiritual* awakening, as well as the material developments" (5500-1).

Since the condition in many instances was long-standing, the treatments suggested were often of a long-term nature as well. Cayce noted there must be "a consistent and persistent application" (1299-1) and that "patience and persistence must be the way to that as would bring aid" (5533-1).

Additionally, Cayce believed that turning to God as the Source of all healing was helpful. Positive-suggestion therapy for healing was recommended for cases 4497 and 5483. Cayce also stressed that, when possible, the retarded individual make an effort on his own behalf to get well.

Overcoming negative emotions and replacing them with positive ones was suggested in all but three of the readings on mental retardation. Some of the negative attitudes to be overcome were worry (4712-1); melancholy brooding over troubles (4497-1); getting excited, angry, or disappointed (5234-1); anger (1399-1); and lack of incentive or confidence (5500-1). For case 5309 to improve, the desire to live had to be aroused, according to Cayce.

Spinal manipulation, mentioned in six readings, was perhaps the most important physical treatment. The manipulations were very individual in nature, although specific areas were at times mentioned. Spinal massage, using equal parts of olive oil and tincture of myrrh, was advised in a seventh reading.

Diet and exercise were also at times part of the recommended treatment. Case 5500, who was eccentric about his foods, was advised to keep a balance; foods high in proteins and minerals such as iron and silicon were

stressed. Another, case 1399, was informed of the importance of a good diet and told to avoid sweets, for diet had
a bearing on his seizures. Case 1399 was also to avoid
sweets. Although instructions for exercises were not specifically given in these cases, two individuals were advised
to get as much outdoor exercise as was practical.

Four additional types of physical treatments appeared in
the readings: the Wet Cell Appliance (five cases), gold
with soda (two cases), the radium pad (one case), and
Atomidine (one case).

Case History

Cayce's explanation on the causes and treatment of
mental retardation given for case 1399, a nineteen-year-old
male, was in many ways representative of other readings
on mental retardation.

A breech birth had caused disturbances in the youth's
coccyx and lower sacral and lumbar regions and had
existed since that time. This condition had retarded the
activity of the glandular systems, creating an imbalance in
the imaginative or sensory responses. Cayce described the
problem as basically physical in nature, although the
mental had been affected. He believed the youth could be
helped through consistent, persistent applications by a
sympathetic person.

To stimulate proper glandular functions, Cayce first
recommended Atomidine taken one drop in half a glass of
water daily before breakfast for ten days, followed by a
three- to five-day rest period, and then resumption of the
same dosage for another ten days.

Following the second rest period, the Atomidine was to
be temporarily discontinued while a series of spinal manipulations began. The adjustments, administered over a two-
and-a-half-month period, were to alleviate the cerebrospinal problems in the coccyx and the sacral and lumbar
areas, coordinating the dorsal and the cervical areas. They
were to be given twice a week, followed by a rest period
of two to three weeks and then a resumption of treatment

for another two and a half months. During this first rest period, there was to be a resumption of the Atomidine and use of the Wet Cell Appliance, which was to introduce gold vibrationally into the system. The Wet Cell was to be used for thirty minutes daily at first and then twice weekly when the adjustments were resumed.

During the period of five to six months, Cayce suggested that the youth have a companion that would help create a regular routine of exercises for him outdoors as well as a schedule for study and recreation.

In summary, Cayce believed that if the recommended treatments were followed, in most cases at least a partial healing could be attained. An exception, however, was case 4991-1, who was "at that stage where little may be accomplished." For others, he predicted that the treatments would bring "the near normal forces to this body" (4712-1), and that they "will bring results" (5500-1). Cayce expected to give further treatments for 1399 (outlined above) and 5333. The reading for 5234, who was subjected to epilepticlike seizures, simply advised dietary caution as well as surgery, preferably at Johns Hopkins or the Mayo Clinic. When someone asked Cayce whether the operation would effect a complete cure, he replied that "it should remove the sources of these pressures."

A questionnaire was sent to the mother of 5234, who had requested the reading, but she did not respond. However, someone acquainted with the case said that the operation was not performed and that the attacks continued regularly.

In another instance, case 5500 was advised to have treatments in a nursing home, but he did not follow the treatments there or elsewhere. In other cases studied, there were no further readings or reports.

Migraine Headache

A migraine, or sick headache, is characterized by sudden intense pain in the head which is preceded or accompanied by sensory disturbances and followed by drowsiness. Occasionally, the headaches are preceded by a short period of depression, irritability, restlessness, or loss of appetite. It is believed that migraine attacks result when the expansion and contraction of blood vessels in the head are disturbed. Migraines, which often begin in childhood, are more frequent among women than men.

Edgar Cayce gave a total of twenty-six readings for twenty-one individuals, most of them women, suffering from migraine attacks.

Characteristically, he regarded migraines as only a symptom of other internal imbalances. Most of the individuals requesting readings had other health problems as well, which according to Cayce frequently had the same root as those that brought on the migraine.

The most common cause mentioned in thirteen cases was an incoordination between the cerebrospinal and autonomic nervous systems due to spinal misalignments, which created an imbalance in almost all of the other systems and organs of the body.

Two other common causes were poor elimination, mentioned in eight cases, and poor assimilation, mentioned in seven. In five instances, all three of these causes occurred together.

Another contributing element, mentioned in ten cases, was poor circulation. General debilitation was a factor in six instances, and occasionally mentioned were glandular incoordination and poor attitudes.

According to Cayce, many migraine headaches began from congestion in the colon, which in turn created pressure on the sympathetic nerve centers and portions of the spine. Cayce further held that the congestion was caused by such factors as poor diet, glandular imbalance, poor assimilation, and nervous stress. In a few cases, spinal subluxations were a cause rather than a result of nervous indigestion and the other factors mentioned. Generally, Cayce believed migraines were the result of colon congestion and nerve incoordination, which would lead to circulatory imbalances and the creation of excess toxins in the blood.

Treatment

Cayce's treatment for migraines were very consistent. He stressed that his treatments be applied in a "consistent and persistent" manner in order to restore a balance in the chemical reactions of the system. Further, dietary improvements, spinal manipulation, and electrotherapy were advised in eleven cases.

In diet, Cayce emphasized foods that were blood and nerve building, such as vegetables, especially leafy green ones, fruits, and whole grains. Advised against were white bread, combinations of starches, fried foods, sugar, red meat, and carbonated drinks.

Spinal manipulation was usually to be administered in specific areas. Electrotherapy most often recommended was the Radio-Active Appliance. This was recommended to improve the circulation.

Colonics, enemas, and gentle laxatives such as olive oil were advised in ten cases. Cleansing the colon to remove mucus and accumulated waste material was considered essential. At times, X-rays were recommended to pinpoint areas where hardened material was located.

Additionally, hydrotherapy, including cabinet sweats, and alkalizers and digestive aids such as Al-Caroid, Glyco-Thymoline, and olive oil were suggested for six individuals. Packs were suggested in five cases, usually in the form of heated castor oil packs which were to be placed over the abdomen. Readings in four cases recommended massage, twice with cocoa butter.

Sedatives were generally not recommended, as Cayce believed they could aggravate the condition. Further, a few individuals were cautioned that some of their treatments might at first appear to aggravate rather than ease their discomfort, but that if they persisted, they would achieve relief.

Case History

There were many reports concerning the readings on migraine headaches, but most were inconclusive. However, many of the individuals reported partial success when applying Cayce's treatments, although few followed them completely.

One of those who received a reading from Cayce on migraine headaches was case 3326, a thirteen-year-old girl who complained of severe headaches. She was given one reading on the problem, during which Cayce attributed the condition to an allergy in the digestive system which had created an inflammation in the intestinal tract and subsequently affected her circulation.

To improve the condition, Cayce recommended colonic irrigations which were to be administered over a period of time, during which she was to avoid eating sweets, especially chocolate, bran, and raisins. Recommended were prunes, plums, cooked apples, and raw vegetables, such as watercress, celery, lettuce, and carrots prepared with gelatin. Highly recommended were six to eight glasses of water daily. Milk could be consumed with wheat germ and whole-grain cooked cereals.

To help cleanse mucus from the colon, at least four or five enemas were suggested. These were to be administered the same time as the colonics or ten days to two weeks apart. During this period, relaxing osteopathic treatments were advised, with special attention placed on reducing a lesion between the sixth and seventh dorsal vertebrae. Cayce warned that any form of sedative would only aggravate the child's condition.

Apparently, the advice given in the reading was followed, for the mother reported that her daughter had had only two migraine headaches in several months, and that this seemed to indicate that her condition was improving.

Miscarriage

Edgar Cayce gave thirty-one readings on miscarriage for ten women who had either experienced miscarriage or who sought preventive measures. The findings in the readings were consistent for both problems.

Cayce noted disturbances in the pelvic organs, especially the uterus, for six women who had either miscarried or who were in danger of doing so. In some of these cases, the uterus was tipped and in a difficult position for childbirth, and in others disorders elsewhere in the body, such as in the nervous or digestive system, had caused problems in the pelvic organs. Weaknesses in the muscles of the pelvic and abdominal areas were also noted as a potential cause for loss of the fetus.

Treatment

Spinal manipulation and massages were recommended to relax and strengthen the body in all ten cases. Cayce also considered exercise, balanced with proper rest, as extremely important to the success of a pregnancy. Especially recommended was walking outdoors in the sunlight and fresh air. Would-be mothers were advised not to stand on their feet too long at one time or to overtire themselves with activity.

Douching with Atomidine or Glyco-Thymoline was also suggested. The recommended dosage was one tablespoon of the solution with a quart of body-temperature water. In cases where proper eliminations and maintenance of body alkalinity were essential to the pregnancy, Cayce generally restricted pork and fried foods and stimulants such as coffee and tea; encouraged were vegetables, fruits, and plenty of water. In some cases, body-building elements such as were contained in Codiron, Calcios, and Beef, Iron & Wine Tonic were prescribed to help strengthen and add vitality to the body.

Seen as extremely important for these women was their basic attitude toward bearing and caring for children. Cayce held that it was necessary to "determine in self as to whether the physical forces are able, or are *willing*," and to realize that "the determination, the *desire*, must *be* within self" (140-33).

Case History

Case 4280, a thirty-eight-year-old woman who had suffered a miscarriage and was anxious about losing her next child, sought Cayce's advice. He found lesions and lacerations in the pubic area which he felt would have endangered future pregnancies, and he subsequently prescribed osteopathic manipulations, especially around the groin and abdomen to strengthen the ability to carry the baby.

Her diet was to consist mainly of fish, fowl, and vegetables. Restricted were heavy foods, tea, coffee, and apples. In order to avoid morning sickness, Cayce advised the woman to take some limewater in a glass of milk before eating.

Several months later, the woman reportedly had a successful birth.

Moles and Warts

Moles and warts are skin elevations which appear as dark spots or skin-colored growths. While most moles are harmless, some may become malignant, whereas warts are generally benign in nature and are more easily treated.

Common warts are known to be caused by a virus whereas moles have other causes.

Edgar Cayce gave a total of seventeen readings for sixteen individuals, ranging in age from five to sixty-two years old, who expressed concern about moles or warts.

According to Gladys Davis Turner, who was Edgar Cayce's regular stenographer during the readings, when Cayce was in a conscious state, he had his own method for removing warts.

"Frequently, Edgar Cayce consciously removed warts from people—he would rub the wart and tell the person to forget all about it; in a few days it would disappear without the person knowing just when or how. Edgar Cayce attributed

Discover the Edgar Cayce way to health and wholeness

	Pyorrhea	Baldness
	Sinusitis	Multiple Sclerosis
	Varicose	Cystitis
Arthritis	Veins	Indigestion & Gastritis
Diabetes	Headache: Migraine	Moles & Warts
Obesity	Constipation	Scars: removal . . .
Psoriasis	Emphysema	plus non-medical
Allergies	Heart: Angina	subjects

Membership Benefits You Receive Each Month

- Magazine
- Home-study lessons
- Names of doctors and health care professionals in your area

- Library-by-mail
- Summer seminars
- Programs in your area
- Research projects

- Edgar Cayce medical readings on loan
- Notice of new Cayce-related books on all topics

Fill in and Mail This Card Today:

Yes, I want to know more about Edgar Cayce's *Association for Research & Enlightenment, Inc.* (A.R.E.®) (Check either or both boxes below.)

☐ Please send me more information. | brc |
and/or
☐ Please send me a trial offer for membership. | N32/PXX |

Trial offer includes: magazine, free book, free research report, member packet. If at the end of 3 months' trial you wish to continue your membership, you need only pay the introductory membership level.

Name (please print)

Address

City   State   Zip

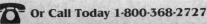 **Or Call Today 1-800-368-2727**

You may cancel at any time and receive a full refund on all unmailed benefits.

NO POSTAGE
NECESSARY
IF MAILED
IN THE
UNITED STATES

**EDGAR CAYCE FOUNDATION and
A.R.E. LIBRARY/CONFERENCE CENTER**
Virginia Beach, Va.

OVER 50 YEARS OF SERVICE

BUSINESS REPLY CARD
First Class Permit No. 2456, Virginia Beach, Va.

POSTAGE WILL BE PAID BY

A.R.E.®
P.O. Box 595
Virginia Beach, VA 23451

785-71

Discover the Edgar Cayce way to health and wholeness

	Pyorrhea	Baldness
	Sinusitis	Multiple Sclerosis
	Varicose	Cystitis
Arthritis	Veins	Indigestion & Gastritis
Diabetes	Headache: Migraine	Moles & Warts
Obesity	Constipation	Scars: removal . . .
Psoriasis	Emphysema	plus non-medical
Allergies	Heart: Angina	subjects

Membership Benefits You Receive Each Month

- Magazine
- Home-study lessons
- Names of doctors and health care professionals in your area
- Library-by-mail
- Summer seminars
- Programs in your area
- Research projects
- Edgar Cayce medical readings on loan
- Notice of new Cayce-related books on all topics

- -

Fill in and Mail This Card Today:

Yes, I want to know more about Edgar Cayce's *Association for Research & Enlightenment, Inc.* (A.R.E.®) (Check either or both boxes below.)

☐ Please send me more information.　　　　　　　　　|　brc　|
　　　　　　　　　and/or
☐ Please send me a trial offer for membership.　　|　N32/PXX　|

Trial offer includes: magazine, free book, free research report, member packet. If at the end of 3 months' trial you wish to continue your membership, you need only pay the introductory membership level.

_____

Name (please print)

_____

Address

_____

City　　　　　　　State　　　　　　Zip

 Or Call Today 1-800-368-2727

You may cancel at any time and receive a full refund on all unmailed benefits.

EDGAR CAYCE FOUNDATION and
A.R.E. LIBRARY/CONFERENCE CENTER
Virginia Beach, Va.

OVER 50 YEARS OF SERVICE

BUSINESS REPLY CARD
First Class Permit No. 2456, Virginia Beach, Va.

POSTAGE WILL BE PAID BY

A.R.E.®
P.O. Box 595
Virginia Beach, VA 23451

785-71

this to a kind of electricity which his hands generated; he said many people could do it,'' she explained.

While Cayce seldom gave specific reasons for moles or warts, his readings suggest that a condition of less than optimal health was the contributing factor.

As he noted in a reading given for an individual with warts, ''It is the accumulation of cellular forces attempting to act themselves. Or, as we see, every atom of the body is as a whole universe or an element in itself. It either coordinates or it makes for disruptive forces by the activity of the eliminating system; and as it accumulates it gathers those things about it and is not absorbed. Hence we have them as moles and warts'' (759-9).

Treatment

Treatments recommended for warts and moles were quite consistent. The major treatment, suggested in eleven of the cases, was a topical application rubbed into the skin at the site of the mole or wart. Castor oil was the most frequently suggested solution, either alone or mixed with baking soda.

Other applications, each suggested once, were a baking-soda-and-spirits-of-camphor combination, a twenty percent solution of hydrochloric acid, and an alum-water solution. Suggested twice was removal with an electric needle by a doctor. Dietary advice was also suggested in two cases.

Case History

In three cases, reports were received on the outcome of Cayce's treatments, and in each instance beneficial results were noted.

An example was case 573, a woman who received one reading concerning moles on her throat and chest. Cayce attributed the growths to poor eliminations which had created an excess of toxins in the bloodstream and which in turn led to the formation of moles.

Castor oil applied directly on the moles was the main treatment suggested by Cayce. This was to be gently applied twice a day.

In diet, whole wheat bread was preferred over white, while most other starchy foods were to be avoided. Fresh green vegetables were especially recommended.

The woman followed Cayce's advice and nine months later reported that her moles had completely disappeared.

Mongolism

Mongolism, or Down's syndrome, is a condition of moderate to severe mental retardation. The mongoloid is usually recognized by his facial features, which include a flattened skull, flat bridged nose, short stature, and squinting eyes. The mongoloid typically exhibits a lack of alertness and initiative.

Six children, ranging from two to twenty years, received one reading each on this condition.

Mongolism was understood by Edgar Cayce as a condition of mental deficiency arising from a number of physiological factors. From the physical viewpoint, mongolism was described in three cases as a severe lack of coordination between the sympathetic and cerebrospinal nervous systems due to prenatal negligence. As a consequence, the glandular functions, especially the glands of growth and reproduction, were seriously imbalanced, affecting physical and mental development.

Interestingly, three out of the six cases of mongolism were attributed to karmic conditions. Cayce believed that the limited state of mongolism was a means for the soul to grow and develop through difficulties on the material plane. The readings strongly indicated that the soul's development would be assisted by receiving love and attention from those in charge, whose task was also karmic in nature.

As Cayce explained in a reading, "Here we have an entity meeting its own self. These [deformities] are not [desirable] and yet it is for the unfoldment and development of this soul entity. . . . Here we find an individual entity born not only to be a charge to the parents but it is needed for the parents as well as needed by the entity'' (5335-1).

Treatment

In all of the cases on mongolism, the parents were urged to provide their child with an abundance of love and care. Although Cayce believed there was the possibility of improvement in five out of six cases, he also cautioned that a great deal of patience and perseverance would be required.

In treating mongolism, emphasis was also placed on electrotherapy, which was recommended in four cases, and massage, which was recommended in three.

Case Histories

To illustrate the variety of treatments recommended by Cayce for mongolism, four have been outlined.

The reading for case 1105, an eleven-year-old boy, recommended the use of the Radio-Active Appliance with gold chloride. Connections were to be made to the alternate extremities and the umbilical area for one hour daily. Cayce predicted that results should be noticeable in two to three and a half years. There is no follow-up report available.

In case 1153, that of a five-year-old girl, the Wet Cell Appliance was to be applied for twenty minutes daily. The small copper plate was to be attached to the brachial center, and the large nickel plate to the area of the lacteal duct. Solutions of gold chloride and Atomidine were to be alternated on a daily basis. When using the Atomidine, the small copper plate was to be attached to the lumbar plexus. A thorough massage with olive oil was to follow each treatment.

The Wet Cell with gold chloride, applied for an hour

before bedtime, was recommended for case 5335, a twenty-year-old woman. The small copper plate was to be attached to the ninth dorsal plexus. Massage with olive oil and peanut oil was recommended immediately following treatment. After three months of treatment, no improvement was noted, and apparently the parents discontinued the procedure.

In the case of 1104, an eight-year-old girl, use of the Radio-Active Appliance was suggested for forty-five to sixty minutes nightly. These treatments were to be followed by a general massage, using a combination of olive oil, castor oil, and petroleum or coal oil. A follow-up report indicated that this procedure was found quite helpful in quieting the child at bedtime.

Mumps

Mumps is an acute infectious disease caused by a virus, and it is characterized by painful, swollen salivary glands and fever. The incubation period is fourteen to twenty-one days. Complications are rare in children, and the entire course of the infection rarely exceeds two weeks.

Edgar Cayce gave one reading apiece for two young children and one thirty-eight-year-old woman who suffered from mumps or related glandular infections.

In each instance, some type of glandular imbalance was involved in the contraction of the disease. In one case, it was caused by a failure to eliminate toxins from the system.

Treatment

Dietary advice was given to each individual as a means of speeding recovery from mumps. The diets were to be light, nourishing, and at times semiliquid, with an emphasis on foods such as milk, milk toast, fruit juices, and plenty of water.

In all three cases, Cayce recommended massages of the

neck and spine, and in one instance he recommended massaging the stomach also. Twice suggested to help relieve congestion was a combination of mutton tallow, spirits of turpentine, and spirits of camphor. The massages were intended to relax the body, stimulate the circulation, and assist the eliminations. In two cases, the use of eliminants was also advised.

In each case, to help reduce the discomfort and speed recovery, the individual was advised to keep the body quiet.

Case History

Case 1208 was a six-year-old boy with an acute case of mumps. He was feverish, irritable, and had an upset stomach.

Cayce's advice was to keep the child as quiet as possible and to massage the back of the neck between the shoulder blades, using a combination of mutton tallow, spirits of turpentine, and spirits of camphor.

Further, in the evenings, the same areas were to be massaged again, and the area around the ear (for earaches) was to be massaged with flannel dipped in kerosene.

The diet was to be alkaline and body building. Sweets were to be avoided.

There was no follow-up reported in this case.

Muscular Dystrophy

Muscular dystrophy is a progressive, hereditary disorder which is characterized by atrophy and stiffness of the muscles. While many forms of this degenerative disease are cogenital and appear shortly after birth, muscular dystrophy may occur later in life.

Edgar Cayce gave ten readings for nine individuals, ranging in age from seven to fifty-four years, who had some form of muscular dystrophy.

In every case, the disorder was attributed to, at least in part, either karmic factors or to glandular imbalances. In general, the readings indicated that degenerative diseases were a result of glandular or chemical disturbances in the body which weakened the nerve impulses.

Although the readings for MS were as encouraging as possible, Cayce made it clear that the treatments would require a long-term effort, possibly years, to reverse the process of degeneration and bring about marked improvements. In the meantime, they were advised to cultivate a spiritual orientation toward life. At least three individuals were counseled to stay hopeful, have patience, and try to understand the nature of the karmic disability.

Karma was mentioned as a direct cause in six cases, and it was strongly suggested that muscular dystrophy and probably other degenerative disorders as well could be mentally, emotionally, and physically inherited. The readings frequently stated that the glandular centers of the body were the direct bearers of karma. Karmic situations were generally regarded as opportunities for soul growth for the parents as well as for the afflicted individual.

Prenatal factors, cited as a first cause in two cases, would also be regarded as karmic, as would injury, which in one of two cases occurred at birth. In such instances, Cayce believed that certain spiritual lessons needed to be learned. One reading on this subject remarked, "In analyzing the conditions here, we find much of this prenatal, yet not that which might be called the sin of the Fathers, nor of the entity itself, but rather that through which patience and consistency might be the lesson for the entity in this experience" (3681-1).

Cayce held that in karmic situations, the attitude of the person or persons involved was vitally important. This was substantiated by Cayce's remark to some individuals seeking his help, that they could recover if they chose to do so. In his view, anyone who was seeking spiritually and trying to be more helpful to others had made that choice.

Treatment

Cayce's physical treatments for these individuals were consistent. In each case, electrotherapy was suggested to help rebuild the nerves and reverse the course of the atrophy. In every case but two, the appliance recommended was the Wet Cell, usually with gold chloride. The gold was to be alternated with other substances, such as silver nitrate and camphor spirits.

Also recommended for each individual were massages, which were to help stimulate the nerve ganglia and restore the ability to respond to the weakened muscles. Massages were to be administered daily over the spine, lower limbs, and other areas, generally immediately after electrotherapy treatment. Peanut oil, usually in combination with olive oil and lanolin, was the substance most frequently recommended for the massage, although cocoa butter was also recommended twice.

In five instances, dietary suggestions were part of the treatments, with emphasis on body-building foods high in vitamins A, D, and B complex. Vitamin supplements were suggested at least once.

To help regenerate the sluggish nerve forces and glandular energies, two individuals were prescribed small internal doses of gold chloride and bromide or bicarbonate of soda. Also suggested in two cases were spinal manipulations.

Case History

Three of the individuals receiving readings followed the advice given and reported on the results. Two experienced good results, and the third noted no improvement.

One of the cases reporting results was that of 3649, a nine-year-old boy who received one reading for muscular dystrophy. He had previously visited the Mayo Clinic, where his condition was diagnosed as hypertrophic muscular dystrophy. The doctors could offer no treatment suggestions. The child's brother had the same disease.

Cayce believed the boy's condition to be a karmic one. Physically, it was attributed to pressures caused by an apparent injury which occurred at birth.

The reading suggested use of the Wet Cell Appliance for approximately thirty minutes daily. Afterward, a thorough massage was to be given with cocoa butter along the spine, proceeding from the base of the head to the soles of the feet.

After following the treatments for a period of time, the boy's father reported, "We are giving the kid the treatment, and he is doing some better."

Myasthenia Gravis

Myasthenia gravis is a chronic progressive muscular disorder which usually begins in the face and throat. The condition is marked by muscle fatigue, with consequent weakness and paralysis.

Edgar Cayce gave only two readings on the disorder, and these were for a thirty-six-year-old man. Cayce indicated that myasthenia gravis was glandular in origin, and aside from specific prenatal factors involved in this instance, he traced the cause to "a lack of glandular activity through the body, which hinders that plasm that forms the structural portion of the muscular forces and tendons of the body" (2207-1).

Treatment and Case History

Treatments focused primarily on purifying and balancing the glands. Beginning just after a new moon, 2207 was to take one drop of Atomidine in a glass of water every morning before meals for ten consecutive days. On the eleventh day, he was to take an ounce of fresh carrot juice with his midday meal and an ounce of cooked beet juice with his evening meal. The two juices were to be taken every day until the next full moon and then the Atomidine was to be resumed for another ten days. (Atomidine and juices were never to be taken on the same day.) In order to achieve noticeable results, Cayce advised that the treatment be continued for a period of at least four to six months.

In the second reading, Cayce placed still more emphasis on the Atomidine treatments and extended them to fifteen consecutive days.

Follow-up indicated that the man had been consistent with the treatments and that some improvements had been noted in the general circulation and assimilations. However, several years after the second reading, 2207 reported that he had not continued the treatments and was regrettably unable to judge their benefits.

Myopia

Myopia, or nearsightedness, is a defect in the vision in which the rays from distant objects are brought into focus before reaching the retina.

Edgar Cayce gave twenty-seven readings for fourteen individuals with this problem.

The cause most frequently cited by Cayce for myopia was strain from overtaxation of either the eyes, the nervous system, and/or the system as a whole. At times, the strain could be attributed to factors such as injury, glandular imbalances, and congestion. Spinal pressures and lesions were also frequently involved, either as initial causes or as results. Nervous taxation in combination with impingements in the cerebrospinal system could trigger disorders such as poor circulation, poor eliminations and assimilations, and toxemia, and as a result hinder vision, according to Cayce.

Treatment

Cayce consistently noted that by treating the causes of myopia, the vision could over a period of time be markedly improved, even to the point of completely discontinuing use of glasses.

Most frequently recommended by Cayce were spinal

manipulations and/or massage, which were mentioned in all but one of the cases. Most frequently mentioned was the importance of exercise, especially that involving the head and neck. General exercise was also stressed, in the open when possible, for both the upper and lower portions of the body.

Discussed in eight cases were diet and electrotherapy, the latter involving the use of the Violet Ray over the spine, face, or eyes. Diathermy treatments were suggested twice. Precautions regarding use of the eyes included avoiding overuse of the eyes in very strong or very dim light, using regular or shaded lenses when needed, and changing prescription of the lenses when required.

Case History

Follow-up reports on cases of myopia are somewhat sketchy, but one case of progressive myopia was gradually arrested, and the vision of three individuals was markedly improved. Additionally, there are three reports from individuals who used the head and neck exercises with success. Two were able to discontinue wearing glasses.

A typical case was 3549, a thirty-four-year-old woman who suffered from arthritis and neuritis in addition to being nearsighted. Cayce's diagnosis was that poor eliminations had upset the coordination of superficial and deeper circulation, thereby affecting the nerves and producing excess toxins in the system. This had caused the neuritic and arthritic tendency and seriously affected several other areas of the body as well, including her eyes.

Cayce prescribed a number of hydrotherapy treatments, including at least two thorough colonic irrigations in the first month. Following this, the colonics were to be given at regular intervals if more were required. These treatments were to include a massage after a rest period.

The diet was to include an abundance of fresh raw vegetables such as celery, lettuce, carrots, radishes, onions, mustard greens, and watercress, making them the main part of one meal daily. Plenty of saltwater fish was also recommended; red meats and sugar were to be avoided.

Cayce believed that the removal of toxic pressures in the system would improve the vision, as would regular head and neck exercises performed morning and evening. He predicted that treatments would bring results in six months.

After three months, 3549 reported that her general health had improved. Her vision was also steadily improving, with flashes of completely normal vision daily. Six months later, she was still reporting progress. However, two years later she was to some degree still nearsighted.

Narcolepsy

Narcolepsy is characterized by episodes of uncontrollable desire to sleep and usually occurs before age forty. Although the sleep is similar to normal sleep, it is apt to occur at inappropriate times. Narcolepsy is more frequent in men than women.

Five individuals, ranging in age from twenty-eight to fifty-seven, received a total of six readings from Edgar Cayce on this condition.

In all cases, narcolepsy was linked to a glandular imbalance reflected in the blood supply. For one individual, narcolepsy was attributed to pressures in structural portions of the body. Noted in two cases were symptoms of stress and overtaxation and karmic conditions.

According to Cayce, "The very nature or type of this disturbance is insidious and subtle. There is the inability to remain conscious of reaction or response between brain and sensory forces. . . . This is a blood disturbance or lack of effluvia in the blood" (986-1).

Treatment

With the exception of spinal adjustments, which were recommended in four out of five cases, Cayce's treatments for narcolepsy did not conform to any set pattern.

Mentioned twice in the readings were dietary improvements, massage, and electrotherapy. In one case, the diet was to consist primarily of foods rich in iron and in vitamins A, D, and B_1; pork and ham were to be avoided. Massages for this same individual were to be part of a hydrotherapy regimen which was to include vapor baths and witch hazel. Electrotherapy treatments were to be administered with the Wet Cell and gold and silver in one case, and the Radium Appliance in the other.

Nasal Catarrh

A catarrh is an inflammation of the mucous membrane which is characterized by the secretion of excess mucus.

Fourteen readings were given for twelve men, women, and children with a catarrhal condition in the soft tissue of the face and head, particularly in the nasal passages. In the majority of cases, symptoms of dizziness, nasal congestion, postnasal drip, and a ringing in the head were reported.

In five cases, the disorder was attributed to deficiencies in the blood, and in four cases, to neural disturbances affecting the sensory organs. The blood deficiencies were caused by an imbalanced circulation of blood through the head, which allowed excess mucus to accumulate in the soft tissue of the face and throat. Anemia was noted in two cases as a causative factor of the circulatory problem, and in two other cases, deficiencies in the blood itself were factors.

In five instances, spinal problems, usually in the dorsal vertebrae, altered nerve impulses to the soft tissue of the face. This condition created an impaired circulation which triggered the accumulation of mucus in the antrum and throat. Many readings noted that the dripping of mucus from the throat and sinus cavities to the digestive tract seriously affected digestion. Additionally, Cayce noted that sympathetic conditions in the circulation were in many cases produced by improper nerve transmission and vice versa.

Treatment

In the majority of the readings, the treatments recommended were consistent. Eleven contained specific instructions for diet, which generally included a high level of alkaline-reacting foods, such as citrus fruits, vegetables and juices, and fish, fowl, and lamb. Red meats, starches such as white potatoes, and fried foods and candy were discouraged. In place of white bread, whole wheat was often suggested.

Six readings contained instructions for an inhalant containing pure grain alcohol and various expectorant substances which were to be prepared by shaking the solution in a small bottle. Twice daily the fumes were to be inhaled through a small tube inserted first in one nostril, then in the other, and finally through the mouth.

Six readings contained suggestions for osteopathic adjustments of the spine. Usually these were to be administered once every week or two, with varying intervals of treatment and rest. To insure proper drainage of the sinus passages in the face, in most cases Cayce recommended correction of the dorsal and cervical vertebrae.

Hydrotherapy was recommended for three individuals, and treatment usually included a cabinet sweat bath, followed by a thorough rubdown and massage with alcohol or equal combinations of peanut and olive oil. The treatment cycle began with two sweats-massages a week for several weeks. This was discontinued for one week and then resumed for three or four more weeks on a once-a-week basis.

For five individuals, elimination of excess toxins in the body was necessary. Three received recommendations for a colonic irrigation once or twice a month, while two were prescribed a teaspoon of Castoria on an occasional basis.

Case History

Although the majority of those receiving readings for nasal catarrhs did not report on their progress, good results were obtained by four individuals, one of whom was a six-year-old girl.

She was given readings 628-2 and 628-3 for her severe running nose, which she experienced each morning upon awakening. Cayce explained that a disturbance in the second and third dorsals was affecting the blood circulation in the head and causing a deflection in the circulation passing through the throat, where accumulations of mucus were found. He recommended an adjustment along the cerebrospinal centers every three or four days, with a rest period after the third or sixth treatment and then the resumption of another series of three or four treatments. To prevent the accumulation of acids in the body, Cayce advised an alkaline-reacting diet for the girl.

Instructions for preparing an inhalant were given. It was to be used in the morning and evening.

Two months after the readings, the girl's father reported that the readings had been helpful for his daughter.

Nasal Polyps

Nasal polyps are small growths found in the mucous membranes of the cavities of the nose or in the upper throat passages. They can produce obstructions if they are large enough.

Four readings were given for individuals with this condition; the causes varied from case to case. In one reading, the condition was seen as a symptom of a nervous ailment, and Edgar Cayce advised having the polyps cauterized or removed. In two other cases, however, digestive disorders producing poor eliminations and assimilations were seen as the cause. In one of the two cases, the difficulty was attributed to poor diet; in the other, to an injury the individual had received in his right back which caused the position of the stomach to tilt, severely impairing the processes of digestion and assimilation. In both instances, the growth and spread of bacteria, which the body was unable to fully eliminate, was stated or implied to be a direct cause of the formation of polyps.

Treatment and Case Histories

Treatments recommended by Cayce for nasal polyps were diverse. Case 349, a young woman whose digestive condition had originated with an erratic and unbalanced diet, was advised to eat three meals a day at regular intervals. These were to contain large amounts of leafy greens and vegetables such as cabbage, celery, and lettuce. Rye, graham, or whole wheat bread were suggested in place of white bread, and vinegar and other acidic seasonings were discouraged. Fish and fowl, eaten in moderation, were also advised. Additionally, a preparation of equal parts bicarbonate of soda, tartaric acid, and salt dissolved in warm water was recommended as a nasal inhalant to relieve the polyps. Cayce believed healing would also be aided by spinal manipulation in the area of the cervical and dorsal vertebrae.

Follow-up noted that the woman reported improvements in her condition within several weeks after her reading and the beginning of her treatments.

Treatments prescribed for case 5511 focused on correcting the tilted position of the stomach, which was contributing to severe problems with digestion, assimilation, and eliminations. Chiropractic or osteopathic adjustments were suggested to coordinate the cerebrospinal centers, giving special attention to the lower cervical and upper and central dorsal vertebrae. Massage of the solar plexus and umbilical areas with an electric vibrator was also mentioned.

Finally, Cayce advised that removal of the polyps would be facilitated by applications of the Violet Ray at unspecified intervals to the soles of the feet and palms of the hands. The second reading given for case 5511 warned against eating when anxious and suggested eating only when relaxed.

The follow-up report here indicated that case 5511 noted improvements in her condition after application of treatments.

Nephritis (Bright's Disease)

Nephritis, also known as Bright's disease, is an inflammation of the kidneys and can occur in acute or chronic forms. One symptom is excess water retention, which causes swelling accompanied by albuminuria (the presence of serum albumin, serum globulin, and other proteins in the urine).

A total of nine readings were given for eight individuals who either had nephritis or were beginning to exhibit some of the symptoms.

Edgar Cayce attributed nephritis to circulatory system imbalances and poor eliminations. However, the related causes were many, including nervous incoordination, spinal misalignments, poor assimilation, distention or prolapsus of the colon, congestion, other forms of kidney problems, hypertension, heart trouble, and negative attitudes.

Generally, poor elimination would lead to circulatory imbalances and a buildup of toxins in the system. The eventual result would be an incoordination between the liver and kidneys, leading to strain on the kidneys and the secretion of albumin in the urine.

Treatment

Dietary observances and cleansing measures were the two most consistent treatments recommended by Cayce for nephritis. The diet was to be light and highly alkaline, and the most frequently recommended foods were fruits, vegetables, and whole-grain products. The individuals were also advised to drink plenty of water. Meat, sugar, and alcohol were to be used only occasionally.

The eliminations were to be stimulated by various methods, including colonics and mineral-based laxatives. Also suggested at times were electrotherapy, rest, and moderate exercise in the outdoors.

Case History

There were no conclusive reports in the majority of the cases, but two individuals experienced marked improvement. In one case, after four days of treatment, a high albumin content was reduced to a trace. Another was the case of a young child whose condition was considered incurable. However, after a week of treatment the mother reported, "Never saw anyone improve like he has."

Although there was no follow-up reported in the following case, the treatments prescribed were typical of those recommended by Cayce for inflammation of the kidneys.

Case 2489 was a fifty-year-old man with tendencies toward nephritis. He also suffered from circulatory imbalances, uricacidemia, plethora (fullness), and prolapsus of the colon, and had a tendency toward coronary thrombosis. Pressures caused by the colon problem were leaving poisons of a uric acid nature in the system and slowing the circulation between the liver and kidneys, contributing to both the kidney and heart problems. Cayce noted that this was a potentially serious situation, as overtaxation could adversely affect the heart.

The initial treatment was colonic irrigations, given in a series, to help eliminate the colon fullness and help equalize the circulation between the liver and kidneys. To avoid strain on the heart, the colonics were to be given gently and expertly at intervals of a minimum of ten days apart. Petrolagor or Glyco-Thymoline was to be used in the last water.

Also recommended were spinal adjustments which were to relax the upper dorsal area and stimulate the spine from the ninth dorsal downward. Although a strict diet was apparently not required, the man was advised to refrain from eating many sweets and starches and was also cautioned against overeating. Rest was strongly recommended, along with moderate activity.

Neuritis

Neuritis is an inflammation of the nerves which results in continuous, often severe pain in particular areas of the body and slow, progressive muscular weakness. In extreme cases, paralysis and sensory system disturbances can result.

A total of twenty-two readings were given to ten individuals with symptoms of neuritis or related conditions. The individuals ranged in age from twenty-two years to the sixties.

In ninety percent of the cases, poor eliminations were cited as the cause of nerve irritations which resulted in neuritis. According to Edgar Cayce, inadequate elimination from the intestines would lead to a buildup of toxins in the system, which in turn would accumulate in the blood supply to the nerves, causing irritation and inflammation.

A related factor in almost as many instances was an incoordination between the cerebrospinal and sympathetic nervous systems, resulting from spinal problems. Cayce believed an overtoxic system, erratic emotions, infection, and strain or spinal subluxations would irritate the nerves sufficiently to cause neuritis. Indicative of this imbalance was that when pain accompanied the disorder, it was basically contained on one side of the body.

In three cases, poor circulation contributed to the neuritic condition. Toxins in the system or general overtaxation of the body would put extra strain on the circulation.

In two instances, spinal subluxations created pressures on the nerves, leading to the inflammation.

Treatment

Although there were consistent factors, treatments recommended by Cayce for neuritis varied from one individual to another. At least one method to encourage elimination of accumulated toxins was given each individual and included enemas and colonics and mild laxatives such as

Eno salts and Castoria. Readings in several instances suggested digestive aids, such as herbal tonics and Glyco-Thymoline, to help alkalize the system.

Six individuals received dietary advice which emphasized alkaline-reacting foods, such as raw fruits and vegetables. Meats were to be eaten only in moderation, if at all, although beef juice was highly recommended. One individual was advised to go on the apple diet for cleansing purposes.

Massages were advised in four cases to stimulate the circulation, usually following a mild sweat. In an equal number of cases, various electrotherapy treatments were suggested. In three readings, packs were recommended, twice using Epsom salts to relax the nerves and relieve pain; spinal adjustments were advised as often—in one case accompanied by heat.

Case History

Cayce gave two readings on neuritis for case 424, a woman in her sixties. At the time, her condition was a combination of neuritis, toxemia, and insomnia, all of which were found to be a result of slowed circulation and poor eliminations. These led to an inflammation of the ganglia which caused pain and restricted movement on the left side of her body.

An herbal tonic, which consisted of wild cherry bark, sarsaparilla root, cinchona bark, prickly ash bark, mandrake root, and buchu leaves, was recommended as an aid to digestion and eliminations. Massages, using a combination of camphor gum, mustard oil, and cedarwood oil, were recommended for the lumbar area and lower limbs.

To remove the toxic accumulations from the body, enemas were advised, and to improve both sleep and circulation, use of the Radio-Active Appliance was suggested.

During the woman's second reading, Cayce prescribed two different tonics to replace the first herbal mixture. One was a combination of oil of eucalyptus, rectified oil of turpentine, tincture of benzoin, essence of wild ginger, and alcohol. The other consisted of syrup of sarsaparilla, tincture of stillingia, essence of Indian turnip, syrup of rhubarb, and grain alcohol.

To aid digestion, raw fruits and vegetables were recommended. Due to their acid-forming qualities, white bread and most red meats were to be avoided.

After following the treatments, a little improvement was noted by case 424, who reported that the neuritis symptoms still existed.

Six other individuals reported improvements in their condition upon following the advice given in their readings. All reported improvements to at least some degree.

Obesity

When obesity, or excessive weight due to accumulation of fat, reaches twenty percent or more of the normal weight for a person's particular age, sex, and height, it can result in heart and circulatory problems, breathing difficulties, and even death.

Two causes of obesity are overeating and metabolic imbalances. Contributing factors in overeating are foods such as fats and sugars.

Edgar Cayce gave 120 readings for obesity, and in ninety-six cases glandular incoordination was cited as the major cause. In eighty-eight cases, poor diet was a cause, and in fifty-four cases, poor circulation was a contributing factor.

Treatment

Alterations in diet were recommended for 102 individuals and usually involved a change to a diet rich in fruits and vegetables and their juices.

Especially recommended was grape juice, as Cayce held that it would supply the necessary sugars without promoting a weight gain. According to Cayce, one to four ounces of grape juice (ordinary purple Concord), often diluted with water, taken about thirty minutes before eating and over a period of time, would normalize the digestive system so as to prevent ordinary foods from being abnormally converted into fat by the body.

Specifically recommended for several individuals were Jerusalem artichokes; fried foods, starches, and sugars were generally to be avoided. Digestive aids or supplements were recommended for ninety-one individuals, with Al-Caroid and Kaldak being mentioned most often. In eighty cases, electrotherapy was recommended, with the Radio-Active Appliance being mentioned most frequently.

Additionally, colonics were suggested for sixty-two individuals in order to help rid the body of toxins, and recommended in sixty cases were massages with various oils and combinations of oils. Spinal manipulations, concentrated in the lower spinal areas, were suggested for forty-eight individuals. Tonics, which varied according to individual needs, were recommended forty-eight times.

Case History

Eighty-one individuals receiving readings on obesity reported beneficial results from Cayce's advice. Two cases, stemming from different causes, are cited below:

The first, case 2579, a twenty-five-year-old woman, received one reading for obesity. Her condition was caused by a glandular disturbance. Also noted was an unbalanced condition in the nerve forces related to her blood supply.

She was advised to first take one drop of Atomidine in half a glass of water each morning before breakfast for five days. This was to be followed by a five-day rest period and then a repeat of the Atomidine. This procedure was to be repeated at least five times.

When the Atomidine cycle was completed, the woman was to take one drop of a solution of gold chloride and two drops of a soda solution in a half glass of water each evening for three days. The gold solution was prepared by adding one-grain-per-ounce solution in distilled water; the latter, by adding three grains of sodium bromide to one ounce of distilled water. After a three-day rest period, the woman was to take the solutions for another three days, then repeat the procedure at least five times.

Following the medication, she was advised to take mild diathermy treatments and general massages at least once a week. The massage formula consisted of one ounce of heated olive oil, one ounce tincture of myrrh, and two ounces of peanut oil added in that order. This solution was to be massaged especially on the joints of the limbs, on the neck, and across the diaphragm.

The woman's diet was to include salsify, or oyster plant, because it contains salts that tend to eliminate hardening centers in the tendons of the body. She was to avoid certain combinations of food because of her allergies. For example, tomatoes could be eaten with potatoes, but she was advised against eating them with corn, peas, or beans. Combinations of starches were to be avoided, and fried foods were not advised.

Cayce counseled that she would not notice much change in her condition until after the electrical treatments and massages had been started, but that she should be patient and persistent.

No follow-up report was received from case 2579.

Another case history of interest was that of 1183, a fifty-five-year-old woman who received one reading for obesity. She had several problems and was told that "there is the form of plasm in the blood supply not being properly balanced . . . this arises primarily from a disturbance in the glandular system. For the assimilations are not proper . . . a balance has not been kept in the proper coordination" (1183-2).

Her poor circulation had caused poisons in the throat, head, and soft tissues of the face, which at times caused enlargements in her joints, muscles, and tendons.

In an effort to stabilize her glandular disturbance, Cayce recommended a specific diet, which began with a breakfast consisting of brown toast or Rye Krisp, an egg (principally the yolk), or cereal. She was not to eat cereal, however, on the same day that she had grapefruit or orange juice. Lunch was to consist of only a raw, fresh vegetable salad, which could be taken with broth, if desired. Fish, fowl, or lamb could be eaten at the evening meal along with vegetables. (Two leafy vegetables were to be consumed to each pod vegetable and three leafy vegetables to each of the tuberous variety.)

Raisins and figs were to be included in the diet to help revitalize the vibratory forces and to assist in the effect created by the osteopathic adjustments, which were also recommended. Grape juice was to be taken with Rye Krisp in the evening or just before the evening meal. In addition to promoting weight loss, the grape juice was to help build up her blood.

To help coordinate her circulation, the Radio-Active Appliance was suggested. It was to be used from thirty minutes to an hour each day, during a period of quiet and meditation for attunement on all levels—mental, physical, and spiritual.

Osteopathic adjustments were to be made to the spine; however, Cayce's advice was not to overdo any of the treatments. The schedule for adjustments was to apply them for two or three weeks, skip them for a week or two, apply them once again for a week to ten days, and then skip them once again. The Radio-Active Appliance was to be applied for a month, stopped for a couple of weeks, and then resumed again for another month.

This woman's follow-up report noted that she "was having treatments as directed and Dr.————said she was getting along fine."

Oophoritis

Oophoritis, inflammation of an ovary, can involve both the ovaries and the fallopian tubes. The symptoms include discomfort or pain in one or both sides of the lower abdominal and pelvic region, accompanied by excess water retention, headaches, and nausea. Vaginal discharge is also often present.

Edgar Cayce gave thirty-three readings for twelve individuals with oophoritis, which he attributed to congestion in the ovaries or tubes and related to the general condition of other organs in the excretory system. Consequently, poor eliminations played an important role in causing the distress. Secondary causes were either kidney or uterine disorders. In half the cases, kidney or liver problems were associated with the inflamed ovaries.

Treatment

Treatment for oophoritis focused primarily on spinal adjustments, which were prescribed to stimulate the excretory organs and correct and relieve pressure due to an abnormal position of a particular organ. In half of the cases, the women received some form of local application to aid in reducing inflammation of the pelvis. These consisted of one or more of the following ingredients: Epsom salt packs, Glyco-Thymoline packs, coarse-salt packs, wet heat, or turpentine stupes. A combination of mutton tallow, camphor, turpentine, and at times other ingredients was recommended as a rub in cases where colds or congestion in the reproductive organs were involved. This compound was to be massaged over the entire abdominal area, particularly the kidneys.

Additionally, suggested in one-third of the cases were Atomidine douches—a mild solution of three-quarters of a teaspoon of Atomidine to one and one-half quarts of water. In one case, this was to be alternated with a Glyco-Thymoline douche.

The readings frequently cautioned that close attention be paid to the progress of the treatments "while those activities may be eliminated without operative forces, if there are again the ACUTE conditions arising—with temperature— then it would be necessary for operative forces to prevent this from producing infection in the areas about the capsule that holds the intestines as well as the lower portion of the abdomen; to prevent peritonitis or such reaction'' (313-12).

In one-fourth of the cases, Atomidine was also prescribed to be taken internally to stimulate glandular activity.

Case History

A series of three readings was given for a woman who had written concerning pains in her abdomen, particularly her right side, which her doctor had pinpointed as the location of her tubes and ovaries. She requested a reading to check on the accuracy of his diagnosis.

In the first reading for case 715, Cayce described ''a congestion in the form of neuralgia of the uterus'' and added that the whole system had been affected sympathetically, with congestion being evident in both the stomach and liver.

Cayce recommended daily use of the Elliott machine, which administered treatments similar to warm douches. Daily abdominal rubdowns, using a combination of mutton tallow, spirits of camphor, spirits of turpentine, coal oil, tincture of benzoin, and oil of sassafras were also suggested, as were hot coarse-salt packs, which were to be placed daily across the abdomen and around the back. This was to be followed by Atomidine douches every two to three days. All treatments were to be discontinued during menstrual periods.

Atomidine was also to be taken internally, one drop before breakfast for five days, then none and then a repeat of the five-day routine. Walking was suggested as exercise.

The second reading noted improvements in the woman's general condition, although she was warned that precautions must be taken so that the oophoritis would not become malignant. The treatments, however, changed somewhat from the first reading. Atomidine douches were to be stepped up to at least three times a week to help prevent infections. Body rubs with an electric vibrator were to be administered over the cerebrospinal system, over the throat and neck, and across the diaphragm and the lower abdomen.

The mixture for this rubdown was to consist of Russian White Oil, coal oil, and oil of sassafras.

The diet was to consist of citrus juices in the morning, broths and fresh green raw vegetables with light meats such as fowl, lamb, or fish for dinner. In between meals, chocolate malted milks using the yolks of eggs were suggested.

The third reading noted that congestion in the pelvis was still causing problems. However, due to improvements in the woman's system as a whole, the treatments were changed again.

Diet continued to be stressed and Ventriculin with iron was recommended three times weekly. An herbal tonic "to work with the blood supply as related to the sympathetic . . . nervous system, especially of the organs through the pelvis" was suggested.

This compound contained essence of wild ginseng, tincture of stillingia, Indiana turnip, and fluid extract of tolu. The dosage was one teaspoon before meals.

Atomidine douches were to continue every other day. Epsom salt packs were suggested in the evening whenever pain was severe, and was to be applied over the abdomen or across the back with a heating pad on top.

One month later, the woman reported that she was carrying out the suggestions outlined in her readings and was feeling better than she had in a long time. A year later, she wrote saying she had not been able to maintain her treatments due to finances and had caught several colds and was seriously ill.

The woman received subsequent readings over the next eight years, during which time it was noted that the discomfort in her pelvic area had eventually disappeared.

Osteocondritis

Osteocondritis, a serious bone disorder characterized by an inflammation of the bone and its cartilage, is often mistaken for rheumatism. In its advanced stages, it leads to a twisted bone structure and crippling effects.

Edgar Cayce gave one woman a total of thirty-two readings for osteocondritis. The readings were given when she was between nineteen and twenty-seven years. The major cause cited by Cayce was an inflammation in her hipbone, which was caused by a dislocation of the hip itself. The right femur subsequently became enlarged, and a disturbance was created in the blood supply. As the disease progressed, her right foot had drawn up five inches shorter than her left, twisting her spine. Her doctors had diagnosed her condition as acute rheumatism and declared it to be completely incurable.

Treatment and Case History

The first reading given for the woman recommended large internal doses of carbon ash added to a half dram to an ounce of distilled water at least once a day. Additionally, she was to have ultraviolet light applications across the clavicle, down to the middle knee, and then upward. Slow improvements were noted, and at this point the woman, case 409, was admitted to the Cayce hospital in Virginia Beach for intensive treatment.

The next ten readings, given during the woman's hospital stay, advised a continuation of the above treatments, with the addition of carbon-lamp and infrared applications. Frequent massages were also recommended, most often using a combination of olive oil, tincture of myrrh, and sassafras oil.

Another reading advised deep spinal manipulations, especially in the lumbar, sacral, and lower dorsal areas. These were to continue for several months. This reading also advised Petrolagar to aid the eliminations and Glyco-Thymoline as an intestinal antiseptic. To aid digestion, an alkaline diet was suggested. Later, hot Epsom salt packs and mullein stupes were to be applied to relax the ligaments, and bicarbonate was recommended to aid the eliminations.

The woman was also advised to begin more exercises.

After nine months of treatments, case 409 received another reading, in which she was told she could leave the hospital but that she should receive further treatments at the hospital every other day. Stressed at this time was the importance of maintaining good spiritual and mental attitudes. Up to this point, her condition had gradually improved, and she was only using crutches as a walking aid. Later readings basically recommended a continuation of the treatments. After a few setbacks, continued improvements were reported.

The results in this case were quite impressive, considering that before she received help from Cayce the doctors had thought her condition incurable and were convinced that the woman would be bedridden the rest of her life. At the conclusion of her treatments, she was able to walk out of the hospital, using no support.

Osteomyelitis

Osteomyelitis is acute or chronic inflammation of the bone due to infection. Treatment is individualized and can include surgery and/or antibiotics.

There were a total of four readings given for three individuals with osteomyelitis. In two cases, Edgar Cayce attributed the infection to improper treatment of a former bone injury or fracture; the reading for the third individual noted a serious case of spinal cancer. In general, the readings, however, stressed that the disease had developed gradually over time due to the negligence in caring for a past damage to the bones, implying that osteomyelitis could have been avoided had an injured bone received the proper initial care.

Treatment

In all cases, the readings stressed establishing stronger alkaline conditions in the body, which would help prevent infections that flourish under acidic conditions. Vegetables, vegetable broths, and blood-building substances such as meat juices were highly recommended.

Surgery was advised in two cases, provided that the coagulative properties in the blood were normal. In reading 3775-1, Cayce discussed in detail a procedure referred to as "trephining" (or trepanning), which involves boring into the bone, using carbolic acid, and scraping and then sealing the bone. This procedure would remove elements in the marrow which could spread further infection, according to Cayce.

In two cases, special therapy was suggested. This was to follow deep manipulations or adjustments for best results and took the form of the Wet Cell with gold in one case and a sunlamp in the other. Other treatments varied.

There are no follow-up reports available.

Paget's Disease

Paget's disease, which is marked by deep bone pain, is a condition in which the bones thicken and soften. Larger bones which support the body are also known to bow and bend through the effects of this disease, which has a strong familial incidence.

The only person receiving a reading from Edgar Cayce on Paget's disease was a sixty-eight-year-old woman. According to Cayce, poor circulation to the ribs had prevented normal structural activity in the bone marrow. Additionally, an injury to the pelvis had produced irritation to the outer layers of the pelvic bones, and her condition had progressed to the point where her bones had become soft and thick.

Treatment

For Paget's disease, Cayce prescribed daily osteopathic adjustments, followed by a thorough massage with a combination of olive oil, peanut oil, and lanolin. To encourage good eliminations, a colonic was to be administered every three or four weeks. Diet also played an important role in treatment, and blood-building foods such as calf's liver, pig's feet (not pickled), and chicken necks, cooked well enough to allow for the mastication of the bones, were highly recommended.

The woman, case 3587, was advised to have a second reading a few weeks after the start of her treatments, at which time a second series of treatments and the use of the infrared light would be explained. However, the woman never requested further assistance.

Paralysis: Facial

Paralysis is the loss of motor function or of sensation caused by an injury to the nerves or by the destruction of neurons. Facial paralysis involves the muscles of expression of the face.

In the three readings given by Edgar Cayce on the subject, he noted the primary causes as being poor assimilations and poor eliminations, which produced congestion in the digestive and excretory organs. In each case, the result was an incoordination between the sympathetic and cerebrospinal nervous systems. Other causes noted by Cayce were circulatory imbalances, negative attitudes and emotions, and infections.

Treatment

Treatment for facial paralysis varied. In one case, Violet Ray treatments were recommended to restore balance to the sympathetic and cerebrospinal nervous systems. Along with the electrotherapy, this individual was to take a sedative containing camphor, gum, muriated iron, and sulfate of morphia. The treatment was designed to correct the nerve and circulatory imbalance and to alleviate symptoms of chills and the tingling sensations in the lips, tongue, fingertips, and bottoms of feet. Holding an attitude of faith was emphasized.

For another individual, Cayce recommended spinal adjustments to aid assimilations and coordinate all the centers of the sympathetic and cerebrospinal nervous systems. Elixir of lactated pepsin was suggested as a digestive aid.

Following the spinal adjustments, a spiritual healer was to place his hands on the person's spine and right side for at least ten consecutive treatments.

Case History

Case 3395, a sixty-three-year-old woman, was suffering from facial paralysis indirectly due to congestion of the liver. The poor eliminations which ensued resulted in pressures in the alimentary canal, which in turn caused a blockage of the nerve supply to the disturbed facial areas.

Cayce's treatment regimen for the woman was to cover a period of time and was to begin with the application of hot castor oil packs over the abdomen for one hour at a time for three consecutive days each week. These were to relieve the congestion in the liver and stimulate the lacteal ducts, thus improving the assimilations and eliminations. After each pack, she was to take one tablespoon of olive oil, increasing the amount over a four-week period until half a teacup was taken.

Following the application of the first in the series of castor oil packs and dosages of olive oil, the woman was to have a mild sweat from a fume bath, using witch hazel. To correct the nervous incoordination and improve her circulation, a massage was to follow, using heated olive oil, tincture of myrrh, and liquefied lanolin. After four weeks of the above regimen, the woman was to have diathermy treatments for three weeks, and then the entire group of treatments was to be discontinued for a period of time and then resumed. Meditation and prayer were also suggested.

In a letter to Cayce written by the woman when she was in her fourth treatment cycle, she reported that she had followed Cayce's advice faithfully and was subsequently recovering.

Paralysis: General

Edgar Cayce gave a total of nineteen readings for ten men and women with various forms of paralysis, which ranged from a sensation of numbness in the limbs to a total loss of the use of the limbs.

The diagnoses in these cases were consistent—paralysis had arisen from a lesion (injury) or subluxation in the spine, causing deflections in nerve impulses to the motor neurons of the limbs. Also noted with regularity was resultant incoordination in the sympathetic nervous system and digestive problems, all originating from nerve impingements. In three such cases, the spinal-nervous disorders were traced to injuries sustained in accidents, and in two cases pelvic infections triggered pressures in the lower back.

Treatment

Cayce's treatment of paralysis was also consistent and focused primarily on restoring proper nerve-impulse transmission, if possible. Regardless of the extent of nerve damage, Cayce viewed no situation as hopeless, and even in the case of 724, an individual who suffered paralysis as the result of a cervical fracture sustained in a diving accident, Cayce said that improvements in the peripheral nerve system were possible, although technically the case was "hopeless."

Since the basis of nerve function is the conduction of minute electrical impulses, treatment concerned the healing of the electrical forces of the body. In all cases, massage was recommended to relax and regenerate the nerves, particularly along either side of the spine. Frequently recommended for the daily massages were combinations of oil, such as oil of cedar, oil of mustard, and Russian White Oil.

Electrotherapy was prescribed in eighty percent of the cases, sixty percent of which involved the use of the Wet Cell battery with gold chloride, at times alternating with spirits of camphor or silver. The attachments of the plates were discussed individually in each reading and depended on the diagnosis. Wet Cell treatments were to take place for specified periods of time in the evening and were usually to be followed by a massage.

In eighty percent of the readings, some of which outlined very specific diets, an alkaline-based diet high in blood-building foods was recommended. In general, fish, fowl, and lamb and, at times, organ meats were advised. Additionally recommended were plenty of leafy green vegetables, citrus fruits and their juices, whole wheat grains and cereals, and soups containing vegetables such as celery, carrots, onions, or leeks and some tuberous vegetables. Combinations of starches, fried or fatty foods, and sweets were to be avoided.

Other recommendations were also made, depending on the nature of the condition, and included spinal manipulations, which were mentioned in three cases, and hot packs using Epsom salts or mud, which were mentioned in two cases. However, the general treatment revolved around massage and electrotherapy.

Case History

Case 724 was a twenty-year-old woman who Cayce thought could be helped by treatment, "though we find conditions rather what may ordinarily be termed hopeless." She suffered a lesion to the base of the brain, at the juncture of the skull to the first cervical vertebra. Although the extent of her paralysis was not discussed in the reading, cervical lesions generally give rise to quadriplegia.

A diving accident several years prior to her reading had caused a fracture in her cervical vertebrae, rendering little or no response in several of the spinal nerves which control movement.

Cayce's thirty-day course of treatment began with the Wet Cell Appliance, using alternating solutions of gold chloride with silver nitrate every other day for twenty minutes a day. Following the Wet Cell application, a massage along the length of the cerebrospinal system was to be administered. The massage formula was to consist of mineral oil, oil of wintergreen, pine-needle oil, cedarwood oil, and sassafras oil added to one-half gallon of unleaded gasoline.

Her diet was to include more blood- and nerve-building substances, such as fresh fruits and vegetables, nuts, liver, tripe, and pig's feet.

There is no follow-up report concerning case 724; however, four of those receiving readings for paralysis reported that Cayce's treatments restored full movement to their paralyzed limbs.

Paralysis: Spine Injuries

Edgar Cayce gave nine individuals with serious cases of spinal paralysis a total of thirty-four readings. Most of the cases involved people who were paralyzed from the waist down and were incapable of any movement or sensation in the lower limbs. In each of the cases, the paralysis had been caused by severe damage to the spine as a result of an automobile accident or a fall.

The majority of those requesting readings were young men and women who had been paralyzed for several years as a result of injuries sustained during childhood play. Although the areas of the spine directly affected varied, in each case the nerves leading to the lower limbs were affected. In two cases, the back had been broken in three places.

Treatment

In all cases, treatments were very similar, with special emphasis being placed on stimulating the nerve impulses by means of electrotherapy and on relaxing the body by means of massage. In four cases, and most frequently recommended, was the use of the Wet Cell Appliance, using a solution of gold chloride or sometimes silver nitrate. It is interesting to note that in two of the four cases, Cayce suggested attaching the copper and nickel plates to the opposite extremities, as is the usual procedure with the Radio-Active Appliance. Treatment durations were twenty to thirty minutes, applied daily or a few times weekly, depending on the severity of the paralysis. Also recommended at times were the ultraviolet light, the Violet Ray, sinusoidal treatments, and the Radio-Active Appliance itself.

Gentle massage of the limbs and back was recommended in eight of the cases and was to be administered immediately following the electrotherapy treatments. Considered important in providing both relaxation and stimulus to the impaired muscles and nerve centers were the various oils used during massage. Combinations of oils, such as peanut oil, olive oil, and lanolin, or olive oil and myrrh, were most commonly mentioned. In some instances, stronger combinations were indicated. Among these were (unleaded) gasoline with oil of cedar, oil of mustard, and oil of sassafras; and Nujol, oil of pine needles, oil of sassafras, peanut oil, and olive oil.

In half of the cases, an alkaline diet, consisting of fruits and vegetables and fish, fowl, and lamb, was advised. Discouraged were fried foods, and in some instances, raw apples.

Fresh air and light outdoor exercises were suggested for four individuals who were capable of some movement with crutches or leg braces. Strain and overactivity were to be avoided, as they would have detrimental effects on the muscles and nerves.

Cayce stressed the benefits of a positive attitude to about half of those suffering from severe paralysis. He noted that a positive attitude would have as much effect on recovery as the physical treatment. Optimism, persistence, and patience were strongly encouraged. In some instances, paralysis was referred to as a needed karmic lesson: "But know that it is SELF ye are meeting" (1212-6).

Finally, readings in three cases suggested gentle spinal manipulations to relieve pressures on the spine and to relax the muscles and nerves.

Case Histories

Follow-up reports varied. In the case of a seriously broken back, Cayce's treatments did not seem to help. In two cases, indications were that the readings were not followed, and in three others, definite improvements were noted.

Case 1215 was a sixteen-year-old boy who had been paralyzed as a result of a severe spinal injury from a driving accident a year earlier. Cayce gave ten physical readings and one life reading for 1215, which attributed the paralysis to a karmic need for the soul to experience suffering. It was explained that as an aggressive Roman soldier in a past lifetime, 1215 had taken pleasure in the suffering of others less fortunate. It was therefore necessary for the soul in its present incarnation to learn the true meaning and value of suffering by experiencing a serious physical disability.

The reading, however, also noted that the youth possessed many positive qualities: an extremely powerful sense of will and determination, as well as the patience and persistence which were so often encouraged in the readings. In fact, the boy's mother was advised that "there is committed to thy care a great soul that may give much to others" (1215-4).

In treating the condition physically, Cayce recommended the use of the Radio-Active Appliance once daily for an hour. Following each treatment, a gentle rub of the back and limbs was to be administered using a combination of mineral oil, cedarwood oil, pine-needle oil, wintergreen oil, camphor gum, sassafras oil, and compound tincture of benzoin. A weak solution of bicarbonate of soda was suggested for removing the oil remaining on the skin after the massage.

During the second reading given for 1215, Cayce recommended changing the massage formula to a mixture of olive oil and myrrh. Cayce also found that the youth could begin using orthopedic braces a few weeks after the treatments began. Positive visualization was also encouraged as a means of preparing the body for improvement. The youth was told to imagine himself getting better and more mobile on the leg braces.

In subsequent readings, gentle osteopathic manipulations were recommended on an occasional basis, provided that care was taken not to irritate damaged areas of the spine. After the first few months of treatment, improvements were observed.

Two years later, the youth's mother reported that he could move his limbs much more easily. However, by the age of nineteen years, he had grown tired and impatient with the Radio-Active Appliance treatments and discontinued them in spite of Cayce's advice to the contrary. Ambitious to become independent, he traveled and eventually moved to California, where he attended a school for the handicapped.

Although Cayce noted that discontinuing the appliance had cost 1215 several years' worth of improvement, through treatment he eventually began to lead an independent life. By the age of twenty-three, he was still unable to walk unassisted, but he had shown remarkable recovery, considering the extent of this injury.

Parkinson's Disease

Parkinson's disease is a form of paralysis characterized by muscular rigidity and involuntary, uncontrollable trembling. It is a condition with a slow progression and is usually found in older people, with the onset occurring in the fifties and sixties.

Of the thirty-four men and women who consulted Edgar

Cayce about the malady, at least twenty-one were above fifty years old. Symptoms mentioned were partial or almost total paralysis, general debilitation, sensory distortion, and virtually constant uncontrollable shaking.

Cayce gave a total of forty-seven readings on Parkinson's disease, which in thirteen cases was attributed to nervous incoordination and deterioration of the nervous system. He believed that Parkinson's disease was caused when the body, in a weakened condition, subjected the nerves to deterioration and the loss of the ability to accurately transmit and coordinate impulses received from the brain.

As Cayce explained: "The breaking down of the nervous energies, and the inability of the locomotory reactions to be normal, comes from the infectious forces that are understood, that are attacking the agitans as it reflects in the locomotory centers. It involves . . . the assimilating system and the nervous forces . . . through their inability to produce, through that assimilated, the proper stamina in the nerve forces" (1870-1).

The reference to "infectious forces" was made in several readings and implies that the body, once weakened by the lack of needed elements, cannot resist attack by bacteria. It is interesting to note that in at least three cases, individuals were found to have foreign metallic elements in the blood, such as mercury, which had greatly contributed to the impairment of the nerve functions.

In another ten cases, Cayce's diagnosis pointed to poor glandular functioning or insufficient glandular secretions. Most of the readings noted that the neural disturbances were a direct result of the inability of the glands to secrete elements necessary to nerve vitality and regeneration. For example, in reading 754-1, when Cayce was asked about the cause of the disease, he replied: "The gland secretions have been disturbed; and thus far have brought for the centers in both the reactions and incoordinations between the sympathetic and cerebrospinal system the incoordination there."

The role of karma, attitudes, and emotions were also mentioned as causes in several cases. Some were advised that their negative attitudes had helped to bring about their bout with Parkinson's disease. One man was told that he had abused his creative abilities in a past lifetime; consequently, in his present incarnation he had been deprived of bodily functions necessary to the creative process of cellular regeneration of the nerves.

In case 3100, Cayce explained a positive aspect of the illness: "The self is being given an opportunity . . . to interpret, to understand and to be of help not only to self but in contributing something to the welfare in all of their stages of development or seeking for physical, mental and spiritual help."

Treatment

Cayce mainly directed his treatments at stimulating and relaxing the nerves in order to encourage better coordination. Readings in twenty-six cases recommended the use of electrotherapy, eighteen of which specified the Wet Cell Appliance. Typical use of the Wet Cell was from twenty to forty minutes daily, using gold chloride as the conducting solution every other day. On the alternate days, solutions such as Atomidine, spirits of camphor, and silver nitrate were to be used. In seven cases, the gold was to be alternated with camphor, and in four cases with silver nitrate. Other forms of electrotherapy recommended were the Radio-Active Appliance, the ultraviolet light, and the Violet Ray. These were almost always designated for daily use.

Massages, recommended in twenty-five cases, also formed an important part of treatment. In each case, massage was to follow the daily electrotherapy treatment. Emphasis was placed on the thorough massage of the spine, back, shoulders, and limbs, using a wide variety of massage preparations. Most frequently advised were combinations of peanut oil and olive oil, olive oil and myrrh, or preparations including substances such as mineral oil, cedarwood oil, sassafras oil, and witch hazel.

An alkaline diet was suggested in one-half of the cases.

Basic dietary instructions included foods such as leafy green vegetables, whole wheat and other whole grains, citrus fruits and their juices, and plenty of seafood. Restricted were starches, fried and fatty foods, and all meats except wild game and lamb.

Hydrotherapy, including fume and steam baths, hot and cold showers, and occasional colonics were advised in six cases. These were to stimulate the circulation and promote good eliminations.

Spinal manipulation was mentioned in five cases as a means of relieving pressure within the spine and promoting better nerve coordination.

Other recommendations included dosages of Atomidine, Kaldak, Calcidin, or prescription medications given under a doctor's supervision. Finally, Cayce strongly encouraged that prayer and meditation be a part of treatment, as they would help the individual to understand and come to terms with the significance of the affliction.

Case History

In the case of 3491, a thirty-two-year-old man, Parkinson's disease was attributed to "hindrances in the abilities of the glandular forces to reproduce themselves," causing subsequent nervous incoordination. He was advised to begin treatments with the Wet Cell Appliance and use it every day for thirty minutes. Gold chloride and silver nitrate solutions were to be used on alternating days.

In making this application, the small copper plate was to be attached to the ninth dorsal plexus and the larger nickel plate, to the area of the lacteal duct or umbilicus. This treatment was to be followed by a thorough body massage with a combination of peanut oil, olive oil, and lanolin.

Osteopathic relaxing treatments, given once a week, were also suggested. In the diet, 3491 was advised to eat foods rich in vitamins B_1 and E and to avoid starches. Regrettably, he did not recover from the disease. However, there was no follow-up or information filed on whether any of Cayce's treatments had been followed.

In other instances, five individuals did follow Cayce's advice, and it was reported that their conditions greatly improved.

Phlebitis

Phlebitis is the inflammation of a vein and is characterized by varicosity or dilatation and knotting in a portion of a vein. Phlebitis may eventually lead to the formation of a blood clot which can break down and create the risk of a blocked vein.

Edgar Cayce gave a total of seven readings for six individuals with phlebitis and related conditions. The persons ranged in age from childhood to seventy-three years.

The major cause cited was a disturbed circulatory system. Four readings mentioned such conditions as infection and congestion in the blood supply and an overtaxed lymph circulation. Contributing factors in three cases were poor eliminations and spinal problems, especially in the lower region. Also involved in two instances were general physical overtaxation and glandular imbalances.

Treatment

The treatments recommended by Cayce varied considerably. Dietary advice was given in four cases, with an emphasis on alkaline, easily assimilated foods such as fruits and vegetables. Meats were to be avoided or eaten only in moderation.

To help reduce the inflammation along the veins, a variety of packs and poultices were suggested for three individuals. Mullein poultices received two recommendations, and plantain and Epsom salt packs were each mentioned once. Other topical applications were also mentioned.

Several other treatments were each mentioned twice. Spinal manipulation and massage were advised to alleviate tension, improve circulation, and generally relax the body.

Electrical treatments such as the Violet Ray were mentioned

as a means of stimulating the superficial circulation. Hydrotherapy was advised to promote the elimination of toxins through the pores of the skin. Homeopathic medicine was found helpful in reducing swelling, with one reading specifying a remedy known as Cimex Lectularius.

Case History

Three of the six individuals receiving readings on phlebitis reported obtaining positive results. However, the following case history, for which there is no later report, did produce success for another who followed the information given in the reading for case 944.

Case 944 was a sixty-five-year-old woman who received one reading for phlebitis. Congestion in the blood supply due to an excess of toxins in her system, along with subluxations in the coccygeal area, caused her phlebitis. Additionally, she was suffering from open sores on the extremities.

Cayce's first recommendation was to take doses of Al-Caroid after meals. This was to cleanse and alkalize the system. Following two days of Al-Caroid after meals and two days of rest, Caroid and bile salt tablets were to be taken in a similar manner for a week. After this, a series of colonics was prescribed.

Following a week of the above treatments, massages of the lower spine were to begin, using a combination of mutton tallow, spirits of turpentine, spirits of camphor, and compound tincture of benzoin. Hot Epsom salt packs were to be applied afterward.

Violet Ray treatments were recommended to strengthen the nervous system and stimulate the circulation. These were to be five to ten minutes in duration each evening. The diet was to be alkaline, with plenty of fruits and vegetables and very little starches and meats.

Skin abrasions were to be treated with a combination of one ounce Iodex and ten grains animated ash. Cuticura salve was also to be applied directly to the infected and bruised areas. The wearing of elastic hose over inflamed veins was also advised.

Pinworms

Pinworms are small nematode worms located in the cecum. The presence of these parasites is characterized by itching around the anus, which causes scratching and, in turn, reinfection.

Fourteen readings were given for one adult and twelve children, ranging in age from one to thirteen years, who had pinworms and related parasites. The most prevalent cause of the condition, mentioned in eight cases, was poor digestion coupled with poor assimilation. According to Edgar Cayce, gastric upsets and other metabolic problems would lower the body's resistance, leaving it open to infestation. Colds and congestion were closely related factors mentioned in three cases.

Cayce held that intestinal worms, like bacteria, are always around us and can proliferate and become bothersome when the resistance is sufficiently low. A form of bacteria then found in raw milk was cited as a contributory element. Consequently, he recommended drinking skimmed or malted milk or heating (pasteurizing) milk before consuming. (With current technology, milk purity is not a problem, and virtually all milk is pasteurized.)

Treatment

Cayce's treatments for pinworms were extremely consistent, with only three major types of treatment offered. Dietary advice was given in eleven cases, with emphasis placed on eating raw green cabbage or lettuce. Cayce considered large amounts of these two vegetables to be a highly effective vermifuge, or worm remover. One reading noted that "one leaf of lettuce will destroy a thousand worms." Other readings suggested eating other raw vegetables and fruits, particularly celery.

For eight individuals, Cayce recommended taking a series of tablets which were typically based on calomel (a purgative containing mercury) and santonin, a substance which acts directly on the pinworms. At times, this treatment involved other ingredients. Cayce generally suggested that these tablets be taken for a three-day period and under a doctor's supervision.

In seven out of nine cases, Castoria was recommended to insure that the pinworms had been properly eliminated and to cleanse the body of the remains of the calomel. Recommended Castoria doses were a half teaspoon every half hour until at least half of the bottle had been consumed, or until it was evident that the entire intestinal tract had been flushed.

Case History

Positive reports were received in ten of the thirteen cases receiving readings for pinworms. There were no follow-ups noted in the remaining cases.

A typical case involved an eight-year-old girl who received one reading for pinworms. A disturbed digestion was cited as a direct cause.

Cayce's first recommendation for case 308 was to keep the body quiet for three or four days. A diet consisting principally of raw green cabbage was suggested, with coffee or tea as a beverage. Following the beginning of the diet, a half teaspoon of Castoria was to be taken every half hour until half a bottle had been consumed. This was to be followed by a dose of calomel and santonin, followed by another in two and a half hours which included nux vomica. At the conclusion of this treatment, the girl was to finish her first bottle of Castoria and take another half bottle.

When a normal diet was resumed, it was to include plenty of milk, with instructions to heat it if cow's milk were used, or to drink dried or malted milk. Citrus juices or stewed fruits and buckwheat cakes were suggested for the morning meal, a sandwich of chicken or lamb for lunch, and cooked vegetables with seafood or calf's liver at dinner.

Follow-up reports indicate that the child's worms disappeared after treatment.

Pleurisy

Pleurisy is an inflammation of the pleura and is usually accompanied by painful and difficult respiration, coughing, and fever.

Edgar Cayce gave one reading apiece for three individuals with pleurisy. They ranged in age from twenty-eight to sixty-four years. Causes noted by Cayce differed in each instance. Two individuals had adhesions in the pleura, which were attributed to lung collapse in one case and to fluid in the lungs resulting from cold and congestion in the other. The third individual suffered from an excessive blood flow which affected the lungs, in combination with a lesion in the dorsal area.

Treatment recommendations for these individuals were fairly consistent. In fact, treatments in two cases were practically identical and included Glyco-Thymoline and Acigest to alkalize the system and improve digestion, Calcios as a nutritional supplement, the apple brandy keg for inhalation therapy, and dietary recommendations which emphasized raw vegetables. No other treatments were recommended more than once.

Case History

Two of the individuals receiving readings on pleurisy reported following the advice given by Cayce with good results. One involved a twenty-eight-year-old woman, case 5097, who had one reading. Approximately two years earlier, she had been afflicted with tuberculosis in both lungs, which resulted in a collapsed lung. This condition caused adhesions in the pleura which weakened the lungs and lowered their resistance to infection.

Use of an inhalant prepared by placing apple brandy in a charred oak keg was Cayce's first treatment for the woman. The keg was to be placed near heat to produce fumes which were to be inhaled. She was also advised to take three drops of Glyco-Thymoline two or three times daily. This was to act as an intestinal antiseptic which would aid in combating infection. Calcios was suggested as a dietary supplement and was to be taken a few times a week and then daily. Twice a week, she was to take a teaspoon of Acigest in raw milk. This was to help improve digestion. Occasionally a little Coca-Cola syrup in plain water was suggested as a diuretic.

Her diet was to contain plenty of egg yolks, raw vegetables, and fruits such as plums, pears, and roasted apples. Fish, fowl, and lamb could also be eaten, provided they were not fried.

To aid the body in its gradual recovery, Cayce advised special exercise sessions morning and evening. These were to begin in a standing position with the arms at the sides, gradually raising them first to shoulder level and then finally up over the head. This exercise was intended to raise the level of the collapsed lung in the body and gradually eliminate the tendency for adhesions in the pleura.

The woman's follow-up report noted: "As for myself, during the past month there has been such obvious change. I feel it, and mentally I am shaking off a lethargy."

Pneumonia

A common though dangerous illness, pneumonia is an inflammatory process in the lungs and respiratory tract and is usually caused by an infection. Fever, chills, chest pains, and a harsh cough are the most common symptoms.

A total of thirty-eight readings were given by Edgar Cayce for twenty-one individuals with varying degrees of pneumonia.

Cited in twenty cases, the most common initial cause of

pneumonia was colds and congestion, which would lower the body's resistance and allow the pneumonia-causing bacteria to take hold. The respiratory passages throughout the lungs and bronchial tubes would subsequently become irritated and inflamed, further weakening the body.

In seven cases, improper eliminations contributed to the illness. Other factors mentioned in a few cases each were poor circulation and emotional stress.

Treatment

A variety of treatments were recommended for individuals with pneumonia. In fourteen cases, in order to speed the body's recovery, Cayce advised changes in diet. Generally, an alkaline, easily digested diet was advised. Also at times, until the worst of the illness had passed, a semiliquid diet was recommended. Especially recommended were fruits and vegetables and their juices and beef juice and meat broths. Eggnogs consisting of milk, egg yolk, and a little alcohol (whiskey or apple brandy) were also believed to be highly nourishing.

Twelve individuals were advised about various methods of increasing their eliminations to help cleanse the body of excess toxins. In five cases, Castoria was suggested at times in combination with Syrup of Figs. Other methods suggested included high enemas, colonics, and Simmon's Liver Regulator (a preparation based on ragweed).

To help relieve congestion and inflammation and make breathing easier, Cayce recommended packs and poultices. Suggested for eight individuals were poultices of crushed boiled onions, which were to be applied over the throat, chest, and abdomen. Antiphlogistine (a special type of mud pack) and a combination of mutton tallow, spirits of turpentine, and spirits of camphor were at times to be used in the same manner. In some instances, more than one type of pack was recommended for the same individual.

Massages were suggested for eleven individuals in order to stimulate the circulation on various parts of the body, such as the feet and spine. Alcohol rubs over the spine were specifically suggested to reduce fever.

Also occasionally mentioned were combinations of substances, such as olive oil and tincture of myrrh, or mutton tallow, turpentine, and camphor combinations.

To reduce pain and inflammation of the air passages as well as to aid expectoration of mucus, some type of inhalation therapy was prescribed in seven cases. Most were alcohol-based inhalants, containing such ingredients as eucalyptus and benzoin. At times, it was suggested to add these substances to boiling water to fill the air with fumes.

Substances to be taken internally for cleansing purposes and/or to strengthen the body's resistance to infection included Syrup of Squill (recommended six times), herbal tonics, onion juice, and Glyco-Thymoline.

Due to its serious nature, several individuals with pneumonia were also advised to get plenty of rest in quiet surroundings. One reading advised keeping the body warm and moist, another keeping the feet warm. Doctors were to be consulted if necessary.

Case History

Reports indicated that in seventeen cases, improvement and complete cures were the result of following Cayce's advice. One individual, however, felt he had not derived any benefits from his reading.

Case 1208, a fifteen-month-old boy, received four readings for pneumonia. According to Cayce, the child had a bad cold which created congestion in the bronchi and led to the respiratory inflammation.

To help make breathing easier, the child's first reading suggested an inhalant preparation consisting of one ounce of tincture of benzoin, half an ounce of oil of eucalyptus, and a fourth of an ounce of oil of turpentine. A teaspoon of this combination was to be placed in boiling water as often as necessary to keep the air full of decongestant fumes.

Osteopathic adjustments focusing on the dorsal area were recommended to improve the nerve impulses to the respiratory passages, and to relieve the heaviness in the chest, ten to fifteen drops of Syrup of Squill were to be given every two to three hours. If these treatments failed to bring relief, Cayce advised that the child be taken to a doctor.

The reading was followed, however, and the boy's condition improved. The second reading advised small doses of Castoria mixed with a little Syrup of Figs to aid eliminations. Additionally, the child was to be given five drops of Glyco-Thymoline twice daily to act as an intestinal antiseptic.

To help relieve congestion, Vicks was to be applied over the throat and chest, and a combination of mutton tallow, spirits of turpentine, and spirits of camphor was to be massaged into the feet and other parts of the body.

The boy's condition continued to improve, and a third reading advised continuing the mutton-tallow-formula massages. At this point, to stimulate elimination through the kidneys, one to three small doses of sweet spirits of niter were recommended. Cayce also advised taking the child outside for sun and fresh air.

Although the boy seemed to have been completely cured, he experienced a slight relapse three months later. A fourth and final reading suggested applying Vaseline to his nostrils to prevent chafing and irritation, and to help reduce congestion the mutton-tallow formula was to be applied over his abdomen, liver, spleen, and colon. A piece of warm flannel was to be temporarily placed over the area.

Fruits, vegetables, egg yolks, and especially citrus juices were recommended. Suggested as a digestive aid was a combination of limewater and cinnamon water. Finally, an enema was advised to help cleanse the system, using Glyco-Thymoline added to water.

Once again the child recovered.

Poison Ivy

Poison ivy is a rash occurring on the skin after coming in contact with the fluid in the poison ivy plant. Symptoms are itching, burning, and stinging. At times, the symptoms can be severe.

Five readings were given for three females and two males.

Although contact with the plant is necessary to cause the rash, Edgar Cayce noted in one case that a lack of proper eliminations, in addition to an acid-alkaline imbalance, had contributed to the reaction.

Treatment

In each case, the common denominator in treating poison ivy was the use of Atomidine and Ray's Solution. In three cases, the Atomidine was to be taken internally—one to two drops daily in a glass of water for four to ten days. Two of the cases were also advised to bathe the affected parts of the body with a weak solution of about a teaspoon of Atomidine in a half glass of water. Ray's Solution applied to the rash was suggested for two individuals. One was also told to take one heaping teaspoon of Eno salts (an eliminant) each morning for eight to ten days.

Case History

Case 1635 was a three-year-old girl whose uncle had wired Cayce for a reading. No mention was made of the child's problem. The reading which followed indicated that there was a lack of proper eliminations and an acid-alkaline imbalance, combined with an acute condition from poison ivy. The symptoms included temperature and a disturbance in the lymph and superficial circulations.

Cayce outlined a varied and detailed treatment, starting with a compound of half a grain of podophyllum, one grain of leptandrin, and one grain of sanguinaria, which were to be mixed and made into five pellets. One was to be taken in the morning and one in the afternoon. Then on the third day, after the last pellet had been taken in the morning, the child was to be given Fletcher's Castoria— one-quarter of a teaspoon every thirty minutes throughout the entire day, or until there were thorough eliminations.

Cuticura soap was to be used to bathe the affected parts and the Cuticura ointment was to be applied after each bathing. Ray's Solution was to be applied after the Cuticura had been used for several days. Dietary suggestions given were to eat raw and cooked vegetables and not too much fruit. No carbonated drinks and little or no meats were advised.

The follow-up report came from the child's grandmother, who noted that she had never seen anything work so quickly in clearing a rash.

Polycythemia Vera

Polycythemia is characterized by greatly increased red cell values and an increase in total red mass. Symptoms may include a dusky redness on the lips, fingernails, and mucous membranes, headache, mental vagueness, loss of hearing, itching, and pain in toes and fingernails.

Edgar Cayce gave one reading each for four individuals with polycythemia vera, who ranged in age from eleven to sixty-five years. The most consistent causal factor noted by Cayce was poor assimilation, which was mentioned in three cases. For two individuals, this involved excessive activity of the pancreas. Other contributing factors cited included nervous incoordination, glandular imbalance, and poor circulation.

Cayce's main treatments for this condition were dietary recommendations and herbal tonics, each mentioned in three instances. In diet, fruits, vegetables, and small amounts of protein sources were recommended, while sugar and starchy foods were to be avoided. In one case, a diet of fruit juices and water was suggested to replace the lost plasma and lower the red blood cell count. To help purify the system and build the blood supply, various tonics were suggested. Electrotherapy received two recommendations.

Case History

Two follow-up reports were received from individuals receiving readings on polycythemia; one noted beneficial results, and the other reported she didn't follow her reading.

The one reporting beneficial results was that of case 674, an eleven-year-old boy who received one reading for the illness. According to Cayce, an injury to the dorsal area of the spine had produced a subluxation that caused the pancreas to become overactive. The liver subsequently became sluggish and the kidneys overactive, resulting in the high red blood cell count.

To correct the disturbance in the pancreas and normalize the blood, two herbal tonics were prescribed. One was a typical version of clary water, and the other contained burdock root, tincture of stillingia, ragweed, honey, and alcohol.

Also recommended were spinal manipulations, to be administered twice a week for three to four weeks, with special focus on the dorsal area. Following a one-week rest period, the adjustments were to continue for another few weeks, followed by another rest period and then further treatments.

The boy's diet was to include citrus fruit or cereal at breakfast, raw vegetables at lunch, and cooked vegetables with fish, fowl, or lamb at dinner. Sugar and highly starchy foods were to be avoided.

Beneficial results were noted after the boy followed the treatments for one month.

Possession

Sixty-six of the Edgar Cayce readings discussed various forms of possession as it was experienced by thirty-two individuals. Hallucinations and unpleasant visions occurred in roughly half of the cases. In other individuals, the loss of physical, mental, and emotional control was so extreme that they had been judged insane and were committed to mental institutions. Common symptoms in these cases included hysterical laughing or crying, the hearing of voices, sudden and uncontrolled bouts of rage, and severe depression.

Four cases involved an obsession with alcohol, characterized by a complete lack of resistance to drinking. Common in all cases was a marked loss of physical, mental, and emotional control, feelings of persecution, and feelings of estrangement within the self and from others.

Cayce believed possession had mental, psychological, (spiritual-emotional), and physiological origins, as the following statement illustrates: "From the viewpoint of the psychiatrist this would be termed a mental condition. From the pathological it would be termed nerve affection. From the analytical it would be termed suppression. From that of the psychological it would be termed pre-possession, or the activity of cosmic forces manifesting in material sense through the incapacity of the mental image to hold self in accord with the physical being" (5506-1). Most of Cayce's diagnoses of possession at least considered its physiological and psychological dimensions.

A severe impairment of coordination between the cerebrospinal and sympathetic nervous systems was the physical cause present in almost two-thirds of the cases. Factors contributing to the unbalanced condition included spinal subluxations, injuries, and glandular disorders. Seven other individuals had become possessed as a result of psychic experimentation which had left them open and receptive to negative psychic influences and mental intrusion by harmful discarnate entities (souls between incarnations). Cayce noted that some of these individuals were quite sensitive and spiritually developed, but had overindulged in spiritual study and practices without proper guidance and preparation.

Cayce explained that their psychic, or glandular, centers had been overstimulated through intense concentration and too much meditation, leaving them open and vulnerable to psychic attack. It is interesting to note that special reference was at times made in these cases to the "leydig" center, which, according to Cayce, governs man's sexual nature through the adrenals and gonads.

Overstimulation of these (lower) centers had resulted in disturbing physical sensations of being attacked or brutalized by horrible creatures, or subjection to peculiar sexual urges and fits of anger or aggression. Other causes implied or stated in a number of readings were negative attitudes and emotions and karmic conditions in which the afflicted individuals were suffering madnesses similar to those to which they had subjected others in past lifetimes.

Treatment

A renewal of the flow of positive, healthy "vibrations" through the mind and body was critical in the treatment of possession. Prayer, meditation, and Bible reading were the most frequently recommended methods of attuning to the healing influence of the Creative Forces. Afflicted individuals and their families were encouraged to appeal to their own divine powers within as sources of healing and inspiration. At the same time, they were advised to abandon all fears, feelings of persecution, and feelings of self-condemnation, as these produced the very weakness and vulnerability which invited interference from negative outside influences. Where Bible reading was suggested, specific passages were often cited. In a few cases, Cayce advised the services of a person such as a professional hypnotist to help the individual come to terms with his own subconscious.

Equally important on the physical level was a reestablishment of the normal coordination of nerve impulses. This was to be accomplished through daily electrotherapy treatments prescribed in various forms in twenty-three cases. Most often recommended were the Wet Cell Appliance with gold, the Violet Ray, and the Radio-Active Appliance. Diathermy treatments were mentioned twice. Duration of treatment with the Wet Cell and the Radio-Active Appliance ranged from twenty to sixty minutes daily, and the Violet Ray was generally to be used for approximately two minutes daily.

In fifteen cases, spinal manipulation was advised, usually in a series of two or three a week, extending over a period of several weeks. In some cases, adjustments were to directly precede electrotherapy.

In twelve instances, massages of the spine or the entire body were suggested, using various combinations of oils. Most commonly suggested were mixtures of peanut oil and olive oil, or olive oil and tincture of myrrh. The daily massages were to be administered for at least twenty minutes, following electrotherapy or adjustments.

Various other external applications were at times suggested to relieve symptoms of physical stress produced by the nervous disorders. They included castor oil packs, Glyco-Thymoline packs, and a rub using a compound of mutton tallow, spirits of camphor, and spirits of turpentine. All of these were usually applied with heat.

Finally, in seven cases, changes in diet were recommended and included more alkaline-reacting foods, such as fruits and all types of vegetables. The only meats to be eaten were seafood, fowl, and lamb. Fried foods, alcoholic beverages, and starchy foods were strongly discouraged.

Case Histories

Case 1789 involved a young woman of thirty-two who was an established artist and painter. She had been committed to a mental hospital when she began experiencing sudden uncontrollable outbursts of hysteria and periods of mental depression. The origins of her condition were twofold: a man had brutally assaulted her, and in her attempt to escape she had fractured her coccyx, causing serious nervous disorders as well as extreme emotional trauma. Symptoms of possession had resulted.

Cayce gave nine readings for 1789, several of which were conducted while she was confined to the hospital. In these, he repeatedly insisted that she be removed as soon as possible, as he believed the hospital environment was extremely detrimental to her condition and would produce further emotional disturbances.

The woman subsequently returned home and was placed under the care of a nurse. Treatments involved surrounding her with love, prayer, and companionship. To correct the physical condition, she had a series of osteopathic corrections of the coccygeal and sacral end of the spine. After three or four such adjustments, daily thirty-minute treatments with the Wet Cell Appliance with gold, extending over a period of six weeks, were recommended. The small copper plate was attached to the ninth dorsal center, and the larger nickel plate to the umbilical area.

After the first several weeks of treatment, results began to be noted. The schedule of Wet Cell treatments was then altered to include rest periods and was made more complex. Following these treatments, body massages with peanut and olive oil were advised, to be administered three times weekly.

Follow-up on the condition of the woman indicated that she had no recurrence of the problem, and in the years following the readings, she was subsequently able to return successfully to her art career.

Near out-of-body experiences prompted case 436, a twenty-five-year-old man, to request help from Cayce. He was given four readings which explained the nature and prevention of this phenomenon, which had arisen from the young man's excessive involvement in spiritual practices. This was a case of overtaxation on the physical and mental level which had opened the glandular centers, making him susceptible to possession by discarnate entities. In addition, Cayce found incoordination existing between the nerve centers of the body, which produced effects of sensory disorientation.

Cayce explained that the young man needed to better understand the dynamics of meditation, which he had unknowingly abused. Some positive and helpful affirmations were given for the use of meditation.

To improve the nerve coordination, osteopathic adjustments and daily use of the Radio-Active Appliance with gold were recommended. Cayce also suggested occasional doses of passion flower fusion, in addition to body-building doses of beef, iron, and wine tonic. Massages of the nerve centers in the spine and head were to be given with an electric vibrator.

Follow-up on case 436 indicated that the readings helped him, and he was subsequently able to continue his spiritual pursuits without further psychic disturbances.

Over a third of those individuals who followed their readings reported beneficial results and that they eventually became free of the symptoms of possession. Other reports indicated that the treatments were not well understood and therefore were not followed.

Pregnancy

A total of sixty-eight readings discussed the health of twenty-nine women, ranging in age from sixteen to thirty, who were in varying stages of pregnancy. Many of the women received two or more readings.

Overall, the readings embody a highly consistent approach toward the care and nurturance of both mother and child during this time. They offer sample instructions for care at virtually every stage of gestation, dealing with normal and, at times, abnormal development in the process.

Treatment

Edgar Cayce attributed the nausea or "morning sickness" experienced by many women during the first three months of pregnancy to the radical changes taking place in the body of the mother. He held that this was a normal condition which could be alleviated in several ways, and the remedy most often suggested was a stomach-settling formula, which was to be taken as needed. The basic formula, which was also recommended in cases of motion sickness, consisted of limewater, cinnamon water, and a weak solution of potassium iodide and potassium bromide.

In some cases, the formula varied; at times the iodide potassium was omitted and in others the formula simply consisted of equal parts limewater and cinnamon water. Extreme moderation was always advised, and in one case the formula was considered more detrimental than helpful.

For some women, Cayce recommended only limewater, either by itself in water or in combination with other substances. Suggested in three cases was adding a little limewater to milk.

Other liquids suggested to counteract nausea were lime juice (or limeade), orange juice, freshly squeezed grape juice, and occasional use of Coca-Cola syrup in plain water. Two women were advised to avoid rising or eating too early in the morning.

The majority of pregnant women, twenty-two in all, received dietary advice, with emphasis being placed on a balanced, alkaline diet of body- and blood-building foods, such as fruits, vegetables, milk, whole grains, seafood, and light meats such as fowl and liver.

In a few instances, Cayce recommended sources of the vital minerals calcium, chlorine, iodine, iron, lime, phosphorus, and silicon, or vitamins such as B complex, A, and D. These sources included carrots, celery, cabbage, Jerusalem artichokes, squash, beans, salsify, onions, and lettuce. The fruits most often recommended were citrus, grape juice, and melons. Drinking plenty of pure water was stressed at times.

During the first trimester, carbonated drinks, alcohol, and coffee were, at times, to be avoided; and during the second two trimesters, red wine (with dark bread), coffee, and tea were permitted in extreme moderation.

Generally, if the mother's health was good, Cayce did not suggest dietary supplements. However, in order to meet the special needs of pregnancy, he recommended Calcios, a source of highly assimilable calcium, in ten cases. Cayce noted that "Calcios is the better manner to take calcium. It is more easily assimilated and will act better with pregnancy than any type of calcium products as yet presented" (951-7).

Calcios, which has about the consistency of peanut butter, was to be taken in an amount that would be thinly spread on a whole wheat cracker. Calcios, which was most frequently recommended during the second and third trimesters, was to be taken about twice weekly with the noon meal.

In three instances, to supply additional iodine and act as a glandular stimulant, very small doses of Atomidine were suggested. Other dietary supplements occasionally suggested included wheat-germ oil, Adiron, White Cod Liver Oil tablets, Ventriculin (without iron), and Codiron.

A large percentage of the readings emphasized the importance of parental attitudes during the course of pregnancy, as Cayce felt these would reflect upon the character and temperament of the child. He repeatedly suggested that the mothers-to-be maintain a consistent cheerful, constructive attitude, avoiding sources of contention, anxiety, and overexcitement.

Cayce encouraged holding a spiritual ideal or, as he explained in one reading: "Keep the attitudes for the mother in the manner in which there may be known that those who bring a soul into activity in the material world have those privileges, opportunities, for the giving of an expression of creative forces in an activated way and manner, that with the development of that soul in the material world may not only make for joy and peace and harmony in the experience of that soul but be an added condition for manifestations of God's love to the sons of men" (575-1).

Cayce held that attitudes influence the innate motivations of the child. One woman was advised that the type of entity attracted would be determined by the types of interests she chose to pursue during her pregnancy, whether these were artistic, mechanical, or financial, for instance. Still other couples were encouraged to hold their desire for a great soul capable of being a blessing to many.

Cayce emphasized the importance of pregnancy and motherhood by noting: "For in the analysis of motherhood, there is nothing above same. And for every act of motherhood is toward that fulfillment of the purposes in life. . . . For in giving to the world, the development of a soul in and through this material plane is adding to the creative forces of the universe'' (140-15).

A physical treatment advised in seventeen instances was spinal manipulation, which Cayce regarded as highly important to keeping the body toned and relaxed during the extra demands of pregnancy. Its primary purposes were to stimulate the circulation, strengthen the muscles of the abdomen and those along the spine, promote general relaxation, and correct specific imbalances.

Primary focus of these adjustments was on the lower back, or the lumbar-sacral-pelvic area. Secondary emphasis was on the dorsal (midback) and cervical (neck) areas. Although frequency varied, a general recommendation during a healthy pregnancy might be once or twice a month. One reading noted that if the manipulations were adhered to, the pregnancy would result in an improvement of the general health.

The type of adjustment generally specified was osteopathy, although neuropathy was occasionally suggested. In fact, Cayce felt the osteopathic approach to obstetrical care would greatly benefit mother and child and advised several women to choose an osteopathic hospital for the delivery of their child.

Massage was recommended almost as frequently as manipulation, at times in conjunction with spinal adjustments but more often in their place. In fact, the purpose of massage was similar to that of adjustments. Generally, the massages were to be administered in the evening or while resting and could be given on a daily basis or less often. At times, focus on specific areas was advised, such as the lower spine, lower limbs, or abdomen. A typical massage formula included olive oil, tincture of myrrh, peanut oil, and cocoa butter.

Cayce held that achieving a good balance between sufficient exercise and sufficient rest was necessary to the well-being of the mother. Consequently, he stressed the importance of daily exercise, especially out of doors. Walking was highly recommended. The length of the walk varied during the course of the pregnancy and depended on the stamina of the future mother and on the weather. Even if there was little inclination for activity, Cayce advocated being outdoors as much as possible, especially during warm weather.

Other types of exercise were occasionally advised and included head and neck exercises, rising on toes and then bending from the waist, circular motions of the lower limbs, stooping, rowing, swimming, and dancing. All were to be done consistently and with moderation.

The need for sufficient rest during pregnancy was strongly emphasized. The readings cautioned against overexertion of any kind, including housework. Activities to be avoided included straining, pushing, pulling, climbing, running up and down stairs, heavy lifting, and standing on one's feet too long. This same advice applied to the time shortly after delivery. Also to be avoided were sources of mental or emotional overtaxation, such as worry and too much excitement.

In several instances, gentle methods of stimulating the eliminations were suggested and were predominantly in the form of enemas or colonics or mild laxatives such as milk of magnesia and those having a senna base such as Castoria. At times, Cayce advised against placing too much strain on the kidneys, especially during the second and third trimesters, and recommended certain foods such as watermelon, cabbage, tuberous vegetables as well as watermelon-seed tea, Coca-Cola syrup in water, and plenty of water. Conversely, during the third trimester, diuretic substances were to be avoided, as they could overtax the kidneys.

Other recommendations during pregnancy were diverse. A few women in the latter stages were encouraged to use a flexible abdominal support, and a few others were advised to have dental care. In several cases, various herbal teas were suggested and included watermelon seed (for kidneys), clover (for the mammary glands), plantain (for a tumor), chamomile, saffron, and slippery elm (for digestion), mullein (for varicose veins), and horehound.

Drugs, including sedatives, were never recommended during pregnancy. Also not generally advised was electrotherapy, although the Radio-Active Appliance was suggested in one case for insomnia.

Breast-feeding after birth, "as all normal ones should" (301-6), was generally recommended and could be continued as long as the mother was healthy and the milk sufficient for the child. There were only three exceptions—one, until deficiencies in the mother's diet could be corrected, and the other two, due to health and perhaps the age of the mother.

Case History

It appears that in the majority of the cases, Cayce's advice was actually followed, and almost all of the pregnancies concluded with a normal delivery of a healthy child.

One woman, who was suffering from an advanced and painful urethral carbuncle, succeeded in giving birth to a normal child (by Caesarean section). She attributed her own life and that of her baby to "Cayce's and God's help."

A case of general interest was 2635, a healthy twenty-three-year-old woman who received three readings from Cayce during her pregnancy. The first reading, given during her third month, noted that conditions were normal and the pregnancy was proceeding satisfactorily.

To assist in the structural development of the fetus, the woman was advised to take Calcios (or another source of additional calcium) within the next two or three months. This was to be taken about twice a week.

She was advised two or three osteopathic adjustments during her third and fifth months. These were to assist in development of the child and were to focus on the third and fourth dorsal vertebrae, extending to and through the sacral area.

Her diet was to include an abundance of body-building foods. Vitamin D could be supplied through Calcios, and vitamins A and C through fresh raw vegetables, which were to be part of one meal daily.

As a good daily exercise, she was advised to walk for thirty to fifty minutes, spending up to an hour and a half in the outdoors. She was to avoid pushing, pulling, straining, or heavy lifting.

Cayce believed the attitude held by the mother during gestation would affect the character of the entity attracted, as well as her own physical and mental development. Advising her therefore to ''keep sweet,'' he continued: ''Keep happy, and keep that expectancy of that character and disposition that is desired in the offspring; knowing and realizing in self as should be in the companionship— that this is being a channel for the manifestation of God's love in the earth. Not as a duty or obligation, but as the opportunity for being a handmaid of the Lord.

''That attitude, that nature of prayer in those periods of meditation and preparation, will keep not only self better, but the attitude of the offspring will be more in keeping with that desired'' (2635-2).

In the woman's second reading, Cayce noted that the child was developing normally. He advised daily walks once again. The woman was to add to her diet a combination of more or less equal parts of carrot and celery juice two or three times a week. This combination was to be part of her diet for at least six weeks, to give more vitality to the nerve forces of the developing child as well as to her own.

The third reading again reported that the baby was developing normally, but she was again cautioned about being overactive. She was to continue taking Calcios for another ten days. Cayce noted that the time for the delivery of the baby was near and encouraged the expectant mother to be prepared, not anxious.

About three weeks later, a healthy son was born.

Pregnancy: General (Monthly Sequence)

Thirty readings were given for thirteen expectant women, ranging in age from sixteen to thirty-seven, and mainly concerned simple, helpful advice on good nutrition, physical well-being, and the necessity of maintaining a positive outlook during pregnancy.

The importance of nourishment for the mother and fetus was emphasized with specific dietary recommendations being made in over three-quarters of the readings. Foods rich in calcium, phosphorus, and silicon were frequently mentioned as essential to the healthy development of bone and muscle and are listed as follows:

Calcium: oyster plant (salsify), carrots, jackets of Irish potatoes, almonds and filberts, turnips, parsley, parsnips, red cabbage, spinach, steel-cut oats, whole wheat, whole rye, halibut, cheese, onions, garlic, rhubarb, milk, raw cabbage.

Phosphorus: raw egg yolk, whole wheat, almonds, walnuts, fish, shellfish, barley, rye, peas, lentils, raw cabbage, milk, steel-cut oats, salsify, brains, liver, lamb, or kidney stew.

Silicon: steel-cut oats, spinach, apples, barley, egg yolk, strawberries, peas, figs, goat's milk, beechnuts, grapes, almonds, walnuts, chestnuts, carrots, shredded wheat, unpolished rice, rye, peaches, cherries, whole wheat, asparagus, cabbage, gooseberries, endive, red wine with black bread, pumpernickel, or whole wheat or sourdough bread.

A balanced diet incorporating the above foods, plus chicken, fowl, and citrus fruits and their juices constituted a healthy diet for pregnant women, according to the readings.

The most important nutrient of all was calcium, and five women were advised to eat a cracker thinly spread with Calcios a few times a week as a calcium supplement. A good balance between calcium and lime was also emphasized.

Advice on exercise was given in two-thirds of the readings, and walking was recommended as the best exercise for pregnant women. Bending over, lifting heavy objects, and hurried activities were discouraged, as well as prolonged standing. It was also important to keep the feet warm and dry and to avoid sudden chills or colds.

Cayce had advice to relieve frequent complaints heard during pregnancy, such as nausea and dizziness during the early months, strain on the kidneys and bladder, and constipation.

To relieve the kidneys, Cayce suggested eating watermelon or drinking watermelon-seed tea to promote eliminations. He was conservative in recommending commercial laxatives and suggested senna tea in some cases, but if necessary, milk of magnesia or Fletcher's Castoria was suggested for constipation. Colonics were suggested in two other cases, but in general Cayce pointed out that if the recommended diet was adhered to, there would be little problem with eliminations, especially if plenty of raw fresh vegetables were eaten. For nausea, the typical recommendation was to drink limewater or limeade or to add a few drops of limewater to a glass of milk.

Massage and manipulations of the back were recommended in about half of the cases to relieve pressure on the spine and lower back, where pain was found to increase during the later months of pregnancy in some women. A light evening massage along both sides of the spine and to the lower limbs, using peanut or olive oil, was suggested in almost half of the cases to relieve muscular tension and strain and to promote good circulation. As pregnancy advanced, keeping off the feet was advised.

The mental outlook of the expectant mother was important to the success and comfort of the pregnancy as well as to the development of the child's own attitudes, according to Cayce. The readings advised the expectant mother to avoid being critical, irritable, and anxious and to maintain a calm, positive outlook, as these traits could affect the development of the child. Reading 711-4 provides a positive affirmation in this vein: "Lord, make me a channel of blessings to others, through their grace, thy mercy, thy love, as manifested in Jesus, the Christ. Let me in my mind and body be always in keeping with thy purposes with the children of men.''

The readings advanced an unusual concept of pregnancy— that the traits and characteristics of the child are most influenced by the mother's thoughts and behavior, particularly during the third and fourth months of pregnancy. On several occasions, Cayce pointed out that if a certain trait in a child was desired, the mother should harbor thoughts in that vein and should surround herself with an appropriate environment to promote the desired trait. If surrounded by classical music, a child would grow to appreciate classical music, or ''if purely mechancial, then think about mechanics— work with those things'' (2803-6). Furthermore, the mother's attitude would clearly impact on the child, so that a tolerant, loving mother would tend to influence the child accordingly, while a judgmental, irritable mother would foster such qualities in her child. As noted in reading 2803-6, ''The spiritual forces—which is the life—is as that projected, and that builded is the outcome of the attitude, and mental forces as well as physical of the body.''

Case History

A thirty-two-year-old woman, case 540, obtained readings 540-6 and 540-7 from Cayce during her first and third months of pregnancy. She had experienced some nausea and constipation early in her pregnancy and was subsequently advised to take fresh limeade for nausea and to improve her diet for help with constipation. She was advised to take milk of magnesia and Fletcher's Castoria only when necessary.

She was advised to maintain a balanced diet, which was to include watermelon, squash, butter beans, and onions. A light girdle was suggested for support, provided it did not cause too much pressure on the abdomen. A cheerful, positive attitude was also encouraged.

In her second reading, the woman was advised to include more calcium in her diet from raw milk, and more silicon and iron. Watermelon-seed tea was recommended for eliminations. Fried foods were to be avoided. Osteopathic manipulations were also advised as needed.

The woman's pregnancy advanced without complications, and she gave birth to a healthy baby boy.

Further follow-up records indicate that where the advice given in the readings was followed, the mothers gave birth to healthy children. In very few instances were any difficulties at birth noted.

Prostatitis

Prostatitis is an infection of the prostate gland. It is generally a sign of other infections in the body, such as urethritis or an active infection in the lower urinary tract. Symptoms include perineal pain, frequent urination, fever, and urethral discharge.

A total of sixteen readings were given for twelve men with prostatitis and related infections, who ranged in age from twenty-eight to seventy-two years.

The main cause cited in every case by Edgar Cayce was poor elimination, especially through the kidneys and bladder. The infection frequently began with cystitis, which would then spread and cause pressure upon the prostate gland. At times contributing to the infection were disturbances of the entire hepatic circulation.

Treatment

Cayce's treatment for prostatitis basically involved establishing proper drainages from the system and reducing the inflammation. Readings for eight individuals advised an alkaline, body-building diet. The men were to avoid pork and foods that could irritate the kidneys, such as alcohol, seasonings, and carbonated drinks.

In seven instances, hydrotherapy was advised, with the Elliott treatment receiving four recommendations. In other cases, hydrotherapy was advised to relax the body and promote elimination of toxins through body pores. Generally, hydrotherapy treatments for prostatitis placed emphasis on sweats, with the one exception being the individual who was advised to take Epsom salt baths.

In seven cases, massages were advised, either directed at general circulation or for particular areas of the body. At times suggested for massages was a combination of peanut oil and olive oil.

Five individuals were advised to have spinal manipulation or to apply packs. The adjustments were frequently to concentrate on the lower spine where most tensions existed, and were intended to facilitate better eliminations and relieve the pressures on the prostate. Most frequently advised were Glyco-Thymoline and salt or Epsom salt packs, which were generally to be placed over the pubic area or the lower spine.

Electrotherapy was suggested in four cases, with the Radio-Active Appliance being suggested twice.

Case History

Only four of those receiving readings for prostatitis definitely followed the advice given, and reportedly each noted an improvement in his condition. However, the subject of the following case history was not pleased with his reading and chose not to follow it.

Case 5162 was a forty-five-year-old man who received one reading for prostatitis. Cayce found a plethora in the transverse and descending colon and noted a poor diet and poor eliminations, all of which he felt contributed to the man's infection.

To avoid putting additional strain on the prostate gland, Cayce's first advice to the man was to abstain from intercourse for a time. To improve sleep and relieve tension, he was advised to use the Elliott machine. A colonic to eliminate toxins from the body was to accompany one of the treatments. Also recommended were hydrotherapy treatments, including fume baths, which were to be followed by gentle massages of the spine, focusing on particular vertebrae to improve the nervous system coordination and eliminations.

Dietary advice emphasized leafy green vegetables. Highly seasoned foods, carbonated drinks, and other substances which would overstimulate the excretory organs were not advised.

Pruritus

Pruritus is a skin irritation involving localized itching or a generalized stinging and burning sensation.

Edgar Cayce gave a total of thirty-five readings on pruritus for twenty-six individuals. A variety of complications, especially related to the nerves, circulation, and digestion, was noted in the majority of cases. In fourteen instances, the cause of pruritus was attributed to poor eliminations.

According to Cayce, the itching sensations and rashes were the result of the body attempting to expel wastes through the skin. Under normal conditions, he explained, waste products are systematically eliminated through the excretory, respiratory, and perspiratory systems. But when the metabolic channels of eliminations are placed under stress, wastes accumulate and become more toxic, producing skin irritations.

As Cayce noted in reading 304-23, "Poisons attempting to be eliminated from the system create an irritation to the epidermis of the skin itself."

For eight individuals, their pruritus was attributed to spinal subluxations or disturbances in the nervous system, which caused a deflection of the nerve impulses to the circulatory or digestive systems. Subsequent difficulty was produced between the hepatic or deep circulation and the superficial circulation beneath the skin, resulting in the irritation and itch.

For the remaining four cases, glandular disturbances, especially involving the lymph glands, were the major contributing element.

Treatment

Cayce's approach to the treatment of pruritus was holistic, and he directed his treatments toward healing the underlying cases rather than just the superficial disturbances. Of primary importance was the establishment and maintenance of equilibrium and harmony in all body functions.

In each case, a series of treatments was advised, and recommended for about two-thirds of the individuals were spinal manipulatons to encourage sufficient drainages and eliminations, correct subluxations, and reduce pressures. These were to be administered about twice a week or when needed and were to be coordinated with other aspects of the treatment.

In about half of the cases, a balanced diet was outlined, stressing highly alkaline foods. Recommended were raw, especially leafy, green vegetables, citrus fruits and their juices, nuts, egg yolks, and all forms of whole grains. Fish, fowl, and lamb and occasionally liver or tripe were included in the diet. Undesirable foods were those high in starch or carbohydrate content, such as white bread and potatoes. Pork and all fried and greasy foods were to be avoided.

In thirteen cases, occasional eliminants and colonics were suggested, with emphasis being placed on natural eliminants such as olive oil or a combination of sulfur, cream of tartar, and Rochelle salts.

In eleven cases, massages were recommended and were usually to follow spinal adjustments or hydrotherapy treatments. Additionally, electrotherapy was suggested for eleven individuals. Recommended in order of frequency were the Radio-Active Appliance, diathermy, and the Violet Ray. Also occasionally recommended were herbal preparations and body-building supplements.

Topical preparations for the immediate relief of itching were advised in about a third of the readings on pruritus. Among the solutions recommended were the D.D.D. in cream or powder, and a body powder containing stearate of zinc with balsam. Hydrotherapy, including sitz baths, cabinet sweats, and fume baths were also occasionally recommended to stimulate and help regulate the circulatory system.

Case History

In the majority of the cases concerning pruritus, no further reports were received. However, eight individuals were grateful for Cayce's advice and subsequent help.

A typical case involved a forty-five-year-old man, who complained of a constant itch and crawling sensation under his skin. During his two readings, his condition was attributed to a poorly balanced circulation due to nervous incoordination.

In the first reading, Cayce prescribed general osteopathic treatments, rubdowns as needed, and a strictly alkaline diet which was to include fruits, vegetables, egg yolks, and fish, fowl, or lamb.

The man, case 436, reported improvements upon following Cayce's advice, but when he deviated from the recommended diet, his pruritus symptoms returned. In the second reading, Cayce emphasized, once again, the need for an alkaline diet and recommended small daily quantities of olive oil to help stimulate eliminations and small amounts of saffron tea to be taken three or four times daily. The osteopathic adjustments were to continue. Stearate of zinc with balsam powder was suggested as a topical application. This time, it was reported the man followed the advice given in the reading, and his itching completely disappeared.

Psoriasis

Psoriasis is a common skin disease characterized by bright red lesions which are covered by thick, dry, silvery scales. The condition is chronic and inflammatory and usually flares up and improves intermittently. It often affects the scalp and the extremities, where the skin is repeatedly stretched.

Edgar Cayce gave a total of fifty-four readings concerning psoriasis. This research focuses on nineteen individuals, ranging in age from sixteen to seventy-four who received a total of twenty-nine readings for this condition.

The primary cause in each instance was found to be improper eliminations, which were associated with a weakness and thinning of the walls of the intestines. Subsequently, the abnormally thin walls would allow a seepage of toxins into the bloodstream, which, in turn, would lead to disturbances on the surface of the skin. In eight cases, incoordination of the circulatory system was noted as a contributing factor. In five cases, spinal misalignments, primarily in the dorsal areas, contributed to the disorder by affecting both the circulatory and excretory systems.

Treatment

Cayce's treatments for psoriasis were aimed primarily at eliminating the excess toxins from the body and restoring the condition of the intestinal walls to normal. In sixteen cases, dietary advice was given, with an emphasis on alkaline, easily digested foods which would not irritate the colon. The diet was to consist mainly of fruits and vegetables and their juices. Sweets, white bread, fats, fried foods, and alcohol were to be avoided.

Various herbal preparations were prescribed for fifteen individuals. These were to help ease the digestive process and strengthen the intestines. Primarily recommended for this purpose were saffron tea (a pinch of the herb to a cup of boiling water) and elm water (a pinch of powdered slippery elm bark in a glass of cold water). Herbal tonics, mullein tea, and clary water were also occasionally suggested.

To help equalize the circulation and nerve impulses, spinal manipulations were recommended in ten cases. These were either to be general or focus on specific areas, often the lower spine. General massages were advised in three cases for similar purposes.

Readings in eight cases each recommended eliminants, electrotherapy, and topical applications for the skin lesions. Colonics were the most frequent eliminant suggested, although a preparation consisting of sulfur, cream of tartar, and Rochelle salts was also mentioned at times. Electrotherapy treatments, which were basically intended to stimulate circulation, included the Violet Ray, the ultraviolet light, and the Radio-Active Appliance. Topical applications varied, and no single one was mentioned twice. They included Cuticura ointment, Resinol, a two percent solution of carbon tetrachloride in alcohol, castor oil, Lenoir's eczema remedy, carbolated Vaseline, Ray's Ointment, and Ray's Solution.

Hydrotherapy to stimulate the circulation and the elimination of toxins was mentioned in four cases. To improve the condition of intestines, doses of olive oil were recommended for three individuals.

Case History

Eight of the nineteen individuals studied definitely followed the advice given in their readings. Six reported at least some benefit from Cayce's suggestions, while two others did not notice any improvement.

Among those noting improvement was case 2455, a twenty-eight-year-old woman who received four readings for psoriasis. Cayce attributed her condition to improper circulation throughout her excretory system, which was caused by a form of strep in the blood supply. This condition brought toxins to the skin surface and caused lesions to form. Glandular incoordination was a contributing factor.

In response to her question about whether there was an absolute cure for psoriasis, Cayce noted: "Most of this is found in diet. There is a cure. It requires patience, persistence—and right thinking also" (2455-2).

His dietary advice was to include two ounces of grape

juice in one ounce of plain water just before meals. Carbonated drinks, white bread, and fried foods were to be avoided.

Cayce also recommended a series of three or four relaxing osteopathic treatments, which were to focus on the cervical and upper dorsal areas, with corrections also given to relieve pressures in the lumbar vertebrae and sacral axis.

With the first adjustment, the woman was advised to begin taking a combination of sulfur, cream of tartar, and Rochelle salts. This was to help purify her system and was to be taken each day for an unspecified period.

After the adjustments had been completed, a series of hydrotherapy treatments was suggested. These were to include cabinet sweat baths using witch hazel and the fumes. Following this, a thorough massage and rubdown was to be administered, using a combination of olive and peanut oils. The sweats and massages were to be administered once weekly for a period of five weeks.

The woman's second reading recommended continuing the treatments given in the first reading. In diet, sources of vitamin B_1 and B_4 were especially recommended. These could be found in all foods that were yellow in color, such as carrots and yellow cornmeal. Yellow saffron tea was suggested two or three times a week and mullein tea twice a week.

As an aid to soothing the skin, the woman was advised to use Cuticura ointment followed by Resinol in the evening after her bath. Violet Ray applications were also recommended to aid in healing the skin lesions, and to assist in eliminating toxins from the body, enemas were to be administered once or twice a week.

The main advice given in her third reading was to use carbolated Vaseline on the psoriasis which had developed on the head, and the topical applications of castor oil and baking soda on other areas. Also recommended were colonics, massages using peanut oil, and juices in her diet. The fourth reading offered no further suggestions.

The woman followed the advice given in her readings and noted a continuous improvement in the condition of her skin. Eventually the psoriasis cleared up and remained that way as long as she maintained a proper diet. Dietary indiscretions, nervousness, or emotional upsets could cause flare-ups.

Author's Note

John O. A. Pagano, D.C., is a cooperating chiropractic physician who has had excellent results using the Cayce suggestions with his psoriasis patients. His treatments have emphasized spinal adjustments, herbal teas, dietary reforms, topical oil applications, and colonics.

Many of his patients have cleared their skin of lesions in three to four months. Most have found that they must stay on their diet, and periodically carry out some of the other measures for a period of six months to a year after their lesions have cleared in order to maintain the results.

Purpura

Purpura is a disease that can involve the blood platelets, clotting factors, and blood vessels. It can also in some way be associated with other diseases or be of unknown origin.

Edgar Cayce gave twelve readings for eleven adults on the condition.

Cayce noted weaknesses in the venous and arterial vessel walls in each reading on purpura. In nine of his diagnoses, he determined that an unbalanced chemical reaction in the blood was a contributing factor. Other factors noted in a majority of cases were poor eliminations, poor circulation, and an overacid condition. In two cases, the individuals involved were obese; uricacidemia or gout was present in other cases.

Treatment

A proper diet was viewed as the most important factor in treatment of purpura, and Cayce established strict dietary rules for seven individuals. All meats, with the exception of seafood, lamb, fowl, and liver, were forbidden, along with heavy starches, carbohydrates, fried foods, and alcoholic beverages, with the exception of red wine.

Highly recommended were vegetables, especially carrots, turnips, rutabagas, and watercress. Also suggested for their nutritional content were whole-grain cereals, egg yolks, citrus fruits and their juices, and dark breads. Occasional recommendations were liver juice or extract and Jerusalem artichokes, eaten once or twice a week.

In six cases, the infrared light, ultraviolet light, diathermy, and the Wet Cell were recommended in an effort to stimulate the system.

Thorough body massages, usually administered with equal portions of olive oil and peanut oil, were prescribed in five cases. Special attention was given to the spine to help stimulate the nerves and circulation.

In order to eliminate the stress noted in the lower intestines, Cayce recommended a series of colonic irrigations. Spaced about a week to ten days apart, these were to clear the alimentary canal of accumulated wastes.

Case History

Case 2623, a man of forty-six, had severe complications associated with a case of uricacidemia. This condition was complicated by poor circulation, which had caused the thinning of venous and arterial vessel walls in the lower extremities, forming purple blotches on the skin. Contributing further was poor nerve coordination resulting from a former injury to the spine.

To treat his condition, Cayce advised a series of approximately twenty to thirty osteopathic corrections of the spine to be administered twice a week for ten to fifteen weeks. During this time, he was also to begin Wet Cell therapy for thirty minutes daily, alternating solutions of Atomidine with spirits of camphor. On the days when Atomidine was used, the small copper plate was to be attached to the lumbar axis and when using camphor, the ninth dorsal plexus; the nickel plate was to remain consistently on the umbilical area.

A diet rich in leafy green vegetables, including celery, watercress, carrot tops, and rutabagas, was also recommended. At the beginning of his treatment, 2623 was also advised to have two colonics about a week apart.

No follow-up was reported.

Pyorrhea

Pyorrhea is the inflammation of the sockets of the teeth and is a disorder characterized by receding and bleeding gums. If the condition persists, it can lead to the loosening of the teeth.

Edgar Cayce gave a total of forty-two readings concerning pyorrhea for thirty individuals between twenty-one and sixty-five years old. Problems which predisposed the body toward gum infection were cited in a number of cases. According to Cayce, a certain condition in the mouth would lead to the growth of a particular bacillus which attacked the gums and teeth. This organism first found a site for growth and multiplication on the film that accumulated on the teeth. The readings noted that the film was caused by deposits left on the teeth from eating an abundance of soft and overcooked foods. The decay of these food particles on the teeth produced an acid condition in the mouth which was in contrast with the normal alkaline condition. The acid condition lowered the resistance of the gums to the attack of the bacilli, which had already found refuge on the film on the teeth. Eating or drinking extremely hot or cold foods or beverages lowered the resistance of both gums and teeth to the attack. Cayce described the shape of the organism as being similar to that of a bedbug but with larger legs.

The readings also noted that where there were accumulations of toxins in the system caused by poor circulation, poor eliminations, or poor assimilations, the mouth was susceptible to an attack, as were other parts, organs, or joints of the body. In short, the body's resistance was lowered because of the acid condition.

Treatment

Cayce's suggestions for the prevention and treatment of pyorrhea were consistent. In every case but two, a compound known as Ipsab was to be massaged into the gums. The name of the compound is derived from the first letter in the main ingredients found in Ipsab—iodine, peppermint oil, salt, and prickly ash bark. (The American Indians referred to prickly ash bark as "toothache bark.") Cayce held that the ingredients in Ipsab would destroy the bacillus and that the massagelike application required would help rebuild and strengthen the gums and increase circulation.

Other treatments recommended were brushing and massaging the teeth and gums with salt and soda (which removes film), rinsing with Glyco-Thymoline (after Ipsab rubs, followed by a water rinse), and unspecified dental repair work.

Dietary advice was given to thirteen individuals, and eating large amounts of raw vegetables was especially advised. Other alkaline-reacting foods were also advised, while red meats, fried foods, sugar, and fats were prohibited at times.

Readings for seven individuals recommended spinal manipulations, frequently focusing on the dorsal vertebrae. Six individuals were advised hydrotherapy treatments, most often in the form of sweat baths with witch hazel. Also advised in six instances were internal cleansing methods such as colonics.

In four cases, Cayce recommended alkalizers and antiseptic aids such as Glyco-Thymoline orally (three to five drops in a half glass of water each morning). Naturally, readings for several individuals recommended visits to the dentist.

Raynaud's Disease

Raynaud's disease is a circulatory disease in which circulation of the hands and feet becomes blocked. The disease is characterized by intermittent attacks of pallor on the surface of the body (lack of color) or cyanosis (a blueness of the skin due to insufficient aeration of the blood). The condition usually first appears between the ages of fifteen and forty-five and is almost always in women.

Edgar Cayce's only reading for Raynaud's disease was given for a forty-five-year-old woman whose hands had become spotted with discoloration and had begun to knot and wither. He attributed the condition to the lack of a chemical element vital to the regeneration of nerve tissue, which resulted in a subsequent loss of muscle elasticity and nervous coordination.

Although the woman's case had already progressed beyond the help of medicine, Cayce outlined treatments which could be helpful if given on a regular basis. Most importantly, it was suggested that the woman, case 3533, attempt to understand the karmic nature of her illness.

Treatment and Case History

To regenerate the woman's nerves, Cayce suggested daily thirty-minute treatments with the Wet Cell Appliance, using a normal charge and daily alternating solutions of gold chloride, silver nitrate, and spirits of camphor. The large nickel plate was always to be attached to the lacteal duct and the small copper plate to the ninth dorsal when using gold, to the fourth lumbar when using silver nitrate, and to the fourth dorsal when using camphor.

Following the Wet Cell treatment, a thorough massage was to be administered over the entire body, using a mixture of mineral oil, olive oil, peanut oil, lanolin, pine-needle oil, and sassafras oil. Cayce suggested that these treatment periods be used as a time for meditation and prayer.

Additionally, an occasional colonic was considered helpful in this case.

No follow-up reports are available.

Rheumatic Fever

Rheumatic fever is a serious illness which mainly affects children and people under fifty. Symptoms are painful inflammation around the joints, high fever, and inflammation of the heart muscles or valves.

Edgar Cayce gave eleven readings on this condition for six individuals, ranging in age from seven to forty. Typical in all cases was the presence of streptococcus bacteria in the blood and lymph circulation, which produced glandular infection as well as stress on the muscles and nerves. In almost all instances, poor elimination was the factor that had allowed this bacteria to multiply in the system.

Treatment

Although there was little consistency in treatments, particular emphasis was placed on a laxative diet and other eliminants in four cases. Colonic irrigations and eliminants such as Castoria and milk of bismuth were considered to be important means of helping the body dispose of accumulated wastes and toxins. Additionally, the diets of these individuals were to consist of easily assimilated foods, especially soups, cooked and raw vegetables, whole-grain cereals, and citrus fruits.

Also recommended in three cases were thorough massages of the spine and back, using preparations such as a dilution of grain alcohol mixed with cocoa butter. Other occasional recommendations included herbal tonics, doses of Atomidine or Glyco-Thymoline, packs of Atomidine or Epsom salts, and diathermy or sunlamp treatments.

Case History

In the case of 2810, a seven-year-old girl, the rheumatic fever was attributed to faulty eliminations which had led to a strep infection and pressures in the spine. To treat this condition, Cayce prescribed an herbal mixture of podophyllin, leptandrin, and sanguinaria which was to be taken once each evening in capsule form for three consecutive evenings. After this, intermittent doses of Castoria were to be taken until at least three good evacuations were produced, followed by the taking of a large dose of Sal Hepatica.

Twice a day, thorough spinal and back rubs were to be administered, using a dilution of grain alcohol to which cocoa butter was added. Her recommended diet consisted of chicken and chicken broth, fruits, cereals, and vegetables, although the fruits were not allowed until after the Castoria treatment.

The child's parents followed the reading completely and reported that their daughter experienced a recovery which enabled her to resume participation in various school activities, including athletics.

Ringworm

Only two readings were given for individuals with ringworm, a condition that is characterized by ringed, scaling lesions, usually located on exposed areas of the body.

Although Edgar Cayce did not discuss the causes in great detail, he noted complications in the blood supply, digestion, and eliminations.

Treatment and Case Histories

Cayce's reading for case 781, one of the two individuals with ringworm, advised skipping a meal and drinking only water. At the next meal, the subject, a seven-year-old boy, was to eat only raw cabbage and celery with a little salt. Four hours later, he was to begin hourly doses of half a teaspoon of phosphate of soda with syrup of sarsaparilla, oil of turpentine, and eucalyptol in a half glass of water.

Up to five doses were to be taken. The expected side effect was nausea, which Cayce felt was necessary in arresting the condition. Enemas were also advised if needed. As a topical application, yellow-oxide ointment, a powder containing zinc stearate, or boric acid was recommended. The diet was to consist mainly of gruel, citrus fruits, milk, meat if desired, and vegetables.

The follow-up report indicated that after two days of treatment, the boy's ringworm disappeared.

The second case history involved case 1446, a forty-three-year-old woman whose condition was diagnosed as "partially ringworm." Again, faulty eliminations were involved.

Cayce suggested applications of unheated castor oil packs. These were to be placed on the affected areas each evening at bedtime. Additionally, it was recommended that the Violet Ray be passed over the length of the affected arm every two or three days until the condition cleared up.

No further reports were received concerning the outcome.

Sarcoma

Sarcoma is a tumorous condition which is frequently highly malignant. Characteristic symptoms are growths or lumps on the body and sensations of pain and discomfort.

Ten readings discussed sarcoma for nine men and women, many of whom were already in the terminal stages of the disease.

In the three most advanced cases of sarcoma, Edgar Cayce did not bother to explain the causes, but concentrated on the means of keeping these individuals as comfortable as possible. In other cases, the disease was attributed to karmic, attitudinal, and psychological factors.

In the karmic cases, the sarcoma was regarded as a condition that had to be faced so that the individual would have the opportunity to attune himself to the "Creative

Forces" through suffering. another individual developed the disease as "the result of unbalanced thinking" (5537-1).

In the remaining cases, physical disturbances such as poor eliminations and infection were diagnosed as the source. In one case, Cayce found that the condition "arose first, primarily, from too much of meats that carried in same an infectious force" (1500-1). In another case, that of a young boy, the sarcoma developed early in life as a result of prenatal conditions and chromosomal defects.

Treatment

In consideration of the terminal nature of their condition, Cayce gave the majority of individuals with sarcoma minimal treatment recommendations. However, electrotherapy or light therapy was considered vital to establishing healthier patterns of vibrations in the body. He recommended the use of the ultraviolet light in four cases. This was to be positioned thirty-seven inches from the body two or three times a week. A sheet of green plate glass was to be used as a filter. Wet Cell therapy was suggested in two other cases, and the Violet Ray and X-ray in one case each.

Poultices made of plantain leaves and cream were recommended in four cases as applications to the tumorous areas. Preparation of the salve consisted of a pint-size container of young leaves of the plantain plant and a pint of cream cooked (not boiled) together until they were thick in consistency. In three other cases, Cayce advised drinking the juice of plantain leaves or using them to make tea.

Other recommendations included massage and dietary changes, suggested in two cases. Easily digested foods, beef juice, citrus fruits, and plenty of drinking water were advised to build up strength and assist in eliminations.

Case History

Case 975 was an eighty-year-old woman whose cancer was described as originating from a nervous disorder.

Doctors had given her only two more months to live when she received her reading.

Cayce prescribed daily doses of an herbal tonic consisting of wild ginseng, stillingia, wild turnip, ginger, cinchona bark, honey, and distilled water. Three times weekly, she was to apply the Violet Ray over her upper torso for three to five minutes each time. Her diet was to include citrus, whole wheat, beef juice, and small amounts of broiled or roasted meat as well as plenty of water. To help build up her blood, she was advised to sip a glass of red wine and eat dark, dry bread once a day. In addition to relaxing massages with olive oil, Castoria or syrup of rhubarb or colonics were suggested to improve eliminations.

A follow-up indicates that the woman adhered to the advice given her in her two readings and outlived the doctors' prognosis by about four years, dying peacefully at the age of eighty-four.

Scarlet Fever

Scarlet fever, an acute infectious disease caused by bacteria in the system, is characterized by the eruption of red spots over different areas of the body, followed by the scaling and peeling of the skin from these areas. Frequent symptoms are nausea, painful swelling of glands—especially around the throat and ears—and congestion in the throat and bronchial tubes.

Edgar Cayce gave a total of seven readings on scarlet fever for five children, ages twelve and under.

Cayce's readings for scarlet fever focused on immediate treatments rather than causes. However, the main cause consistently referred to was the presence of an infectious agent or germ in the body which contributed to a toxic condition and inflammation in the blood and lymph circulation. As Cayce explained, scarlet fever originated from "inflammation of the lymph and emunctory circulation, by or through infectious forces which disturb the circulation, producing a temperature and, reflexly affecting the organs of the body" (415-2).

Treatment

In treating scarlet fever, Cayce stressed the need for reduction and stabilization of body temperature and for maintaining good elminations. Massage of the spine or throat and chest area was recommended in each case. This was to be administered with a combination of equal parts mutton tallow, spirits of turpentine, and spirits of camphor, to which was added Mentholatum or compound tincture of benzoin or both. In three cases, effective reduction of the fever was also accomplished by warm sponge baths followed by a gentle sponging down of the spinal column with grain alcohol or witch hazel mixed with rubbing alcohol. During the illness, a diet of semiliquids or of fruit and fruit juices, vegetables, and blood-building foods was to be maintained.

Strong dosages of Atomidine were prescribed in two cases to counter inflammation of the throat and ear glands, but these treatments were not to extend longer than several days at a time. In addition, to stimulate eliminations, Castoria, Syrup of Squill, or milk of magnesia was also mentioned in two cases.

Case History

The following concerns a most serious case of scarlet fever and, as a consequence, the readings' most thorough approach to treatment. Case 1519 was a twelve-year-old boy who received three readings for scarlet fever, which Cayce attributed to a bacterial invasion. In addition to a high fever, congestion throughout the bronchial tubes, lungs, and throat was evident.

Cayce's first reading advised keeping the boy quiet and his feet warm. To bring the fever down, Cayce suggested bathing him in warm water and then massaging under the arms, around the throat, and over the abdomen and soles of the feet with a combination of mutton tallow, spirits of turpentine, and spirits of camphor. Grain alcohol sponged around the temples in a motion away from the head would also effectively help reduce the fever, according to Cayce.

Citrus juices and liquids were proposed as the bulk of the diet until the worst part of the illness had passed. To provide the body with necessary elements, the child was prescribed Calcidin tablets dissolved in a glass of water. These were to be taken frequently, a tablet at a time. An inhalant was prescribed to help relieve bronchial distress.

By the time of the child's second reading, improvements were noted. To stimulate eliminations, diluted Syrup of Squill was to replace the Calcidin tablets. Milk of magnesia or enemas could also be used if needed.

It became apparent by the third reading that not enough precautions had been taken to ward off a possible glandular infection. The boy's fever had flared up, and the glands around one ear were swollen, causing an earache. To ease the pain in the ear, Cayce advised placing a drop of sweet oil into the ear and covering it with a warm compress. To reduce the lingering congestion in the throat and chest, a massage using wintergreen oil mixed with pine oil and sassafras oil was advised. Ten to twenty drops of Syrup of Squill were to be taken two to three times a day. For circulation, a rub with mustard water, starting at the feet and progressing to the knees, was suggested. Once the inflammation in the bronchi and head had decreased, six drops of Atomidine in water once or twice a day was also suggested.

There was no follow-up as to the outcome of this case. However, in two other cases, complete cures were reported. In the remaining two cases, no further reports are available.

Scars

There were two distinct types of scars defined in the thirty-four readings on scars which Edgar Cayce gave for thirty-one individuals. The first kind resulted from external flesh wounds such as surgical incisions, burns, or injuries. The other type involved internal scars caused by the accumulation of tissue within the body. In the former cases, treatment simply involved the topical application of remedial oils.

However, an entirely different regimen of internal and external therapies was required to relieve and eliminate aggregation of internal tissue. For this reason, two separate discussions regarding treatment are presented here.

Treatment (External Scars)

Edgar Cayce's recommendations for the treatment of external scars were extremely consistent in all eighteen cases and called for the simple preparation of a topical application which was to be gently massaged into the scar tissue at least twice a day.

In nearly seventy-five percent of the cases, camphorated oil was recommended and was to be used either alone or in combination with other oils. Most frequently suggested were sweet (vegetable) oil or a combination of peanut oil and lanolin. A few readings recommended the use of other substances such as heated olive oil and myrrh, olive oil and cocoa butter, or sweet oil and Unguentine. However, comphorated oil was consistently praised by Cayce as being "the best application for removing scar or scar tissue on any portion of the body" (1566-4).

In a few instances, Cayce's approach to the physical healing of scars also touched upon their karmic nature. For example, he advised two women who had received facial disfiguration through scarring that the conditions had manifested themselves on the physical plane as a result of harmful mental attitudes adopted in the past.

In all cases, however, Cayce noted that scarred areas could be healed and the skin returned to at least near its original texture. Required were the treatments and a good deal of patience and persistence.

Treatment (Internal Scars)

Thirteen cases of scars involved the formation of scar tissue in sensitive internal areas of the body. Usually these were attributed to circulatory dysfunctions and/or nervous or glandular incoordination. For example, in case 3661 the presence of scar tissue in the bronchial area was attributed to deflections of the nerve impulses through the cervical and upper dorsal vertebrae, which prevented the proper circulation of blood though the bronchi and trachea, making for "a thickening of the walls of tissue." In some cases, the formation of internal scar tissue contributed to a blockage of the circulatory and other systems. In one instance, the accumulation of scar tissue on the cervical vertebrae was causing a condition of near blindness.

In cases of internal scars, treatment almost always involved massage and/or spinal manipulation of the afflicted areas of the body. The massages were to be given neuropathically or by means of an electric vibrator. Additionally, readings in over forty percent of the cases called for the application of hot Epsom salts or castor oil packs, or simply wet heat, to the portions of the body where the internal scar tissue was located. Electrotherapy was advised in over thirty percent of the cases and usually called for the use of the Violet Ray a few times weekly. Occasional colonics and vegetable laxatives formed an important part of treatment in twenty-five percent of the cases. The purpose of the former, along with an alkaline-based diet recommended in over fifteen percent of the cases, was to insure the proper elimination of the scar tissue from the system.

Case History

Two case histories are reported here, one regarding internal scars and the other external.

The case of external scars involved a one-year-old girl who had accidentally tipped a pan of boiling water over herself, severely burning her face, stomach, and feet. After providing suggestions on how to treat the burns, Cayce advised the parents to begin a treatment regimen within ten days to two weeks to remove the burn scars. A mixture of Unguentine, sweet oil, and camphorated oil gently massaged into the burned areas was prescribed on a daily basis.

Although no results were reported after this reading, the parents of case 2015 contacted Cayce two years later, requesting information on how to remove severe scars which remained from the burns. This time, Cayce suggested massaging the scars with plain comphorated oil or a mixture of camphorated oil, peanut oil, and lanolin.

Some time after following the treatment, the child's parents reported that all scars had disappeared from their child's body.

The other case, that of internal scars, involved a man of fifty-one who suffered from a generally poor state of health owing to the interference of internal scar tissue and adhesions with the normal biochemical processes in the body.

In treating case 1940, Cayce stressed the need to improve eliminations and recommended occasional colonic irrigations and a diet emphasizing raw vegetables and salads. Fried foods were to be avoided. As a dietary supplement, Codiron was to be taken on a daily basis. Also recommended were neuropathic adjustments and massages and the application of hot and cold blankets to the body to break up the scar tissue and adhesions through stimulation of the muscles and nerves.

No report followed this reading.

Sciatica

Sciatica is characterized by pain along the sciatic nerve through the leg due to inflammation or injury to the nerve. Accompanying symptoms are numbness, tingling and tenderness along the nerve to the muscles, and eventual muscle deterioration.

Edgar Cayce viewed sciatica as symptomatic of other physical problems, with the first causes being attributed to spinal subluxations, poor eliminations, or both.

According to Cayce, subluxations in the lumbar-sacral-coccygeal area would impinge on the base of the sciatic nerve, hindering the nerve supply to the extremities and often causing a muscular contraction which made movement of the legs painful. At times, this condition was attributed to an injury, and at other times to internal stress conditions, such as toxemia.

When the cause was attributed to poor eliminations, it was frequently related to factors such as an overacid diet, constipation, overwork, and anxiety. Cayce subsequently felt the resulting buildup of toxins would cause pressure on the nerves, which would in turn deflect the normal nerve impulses through the extremities and at times become a source for more spinal pressures, and other problems.

Other related causes of sciatica cited at times were congestion, infections, negative attitudes, debilitation, and glandular deficiencies.

Treatment

Cayce believed a cure for the sciatic condition was possible, provided his treatments were consistently and persistently followed. Treatments focused mainly on stimulating the eliminations, rebuilding the nerves and general vitality, making corrections in the spine, and relieving the short-term pain.

To aid eliminations, Cayce prescribed various herbal-tonic formulas, colonics and enemas, and laxatives, alternating vegetable and mineral substances. Castor oil packs and hydrotherapy (especially sweats) were each suggested twice. In over half of the readings, a diet of easily digested, highly alkaline foods rich in blood- and nerve-building nutrients was stressed. Particularly favored were fresh and raw vegetables, fruits and fruit juices, as well as meat juices and broths. To be eaten in moderation—or not at all in severe cases—were meats such as fish, fowl, lamb, liver, and wild game, and starches and sugar. A small amount of honey was permitted. Herbal tonics were also prescribed to help build vitality.

Electrotherapy was the main method of rebuilding the

nerves and stimulating the entire system. Various devices were suggested in almost one-half of the readings on sciatica. In order of frequency, these were the Wet Cell, usually with gold, the Violet Ray, the ultraviolet light, and diathermy treatments.

Additionally, in over one-half of the cases, spinal adjustments were suggested. Typically, they were to focus on the lower back, gently and gradually relieving the nerve impingements and bringing the entire spine into proper coordination. Often suggested was a series of adjustments, beginning with the more general, relaxing variety and gradually making deeper corrections. In some instances, the adjustments were coordinated with other treatments such as heat, massage, hydrotherapy, and diathermy applications. Massage alone was also suggested.

Although conventional medication such as aspirin was needed temporarily, Cayce placed more emphasis on local applications for the relief of pain, mainly penetrating heat designed to relax and break up congestion. Most frequently advised were hot salt packs applied over the lower back and sciatic nerve where the nerves and tendons were painful. The application took two forms—a heated pad of coarse table salt (dry), and hot packs of Epsom salts dissolved in water. The salt packs were recommended alone or to be used as an aid to absorption of other substances. A few readings suggested Glyco-Thymoline packs with salt heat. Another reading suggested mullein stupes applied back and front.

Case History

In a typical reading on sciatica, Cayce traced the condition to a past injury in the lower dorsal which had impeded coordination between the sympathetic and cerebrospinal nervous systems and which had slowed the digestive process and caused toxins to gradually accumulate in the system. As a sympathetic response, lesions were created in the lumbar area. The result for case 5017 was pressure and inflammation of the sciatic nerves.

Cayce's treatment for 5017 began with a gradual series of gentle osteopathic adjustments which were to break up the areas of congestion. After three or four of these treatments, diathermy applications were to accompany further adjustments. Colonics were also advised and were to be repeated occasionally as long as mucus appeared in the stool.

For pain, Cayce advised Glyco-Thymoline packs covered with dry salt heat and applied to the ninth dorsal downward.

Following the first eight to ten adjustments, 5017 was to discontinue the treatments for a month (but adhering to other advice given), and was then to repeat another series of eight adjustments. Also prescribed at this time were B complex vitamins to be taken in cycles.

Sciatica and Rheumatism

Sciatica is often regarded as a form of rheumatism, a painful condition in which the joints become stiff and inflamed. In sciatica, the sciatic nerve, which begins at the base of the spine and traverses the leg, is directly affected. Severe pain in the hips, lower back, and legs may cause limping or even the inability to walk. Accompanying symptoms are numbness, tingling, and tenderness along the nerve, with eventual deterioration of the muscles it supplies.

A total of eighty-two readings was given for sixty-six individuals with sciatica, including some who only had a tendency toward this condition. All of the rheumatism-sciatica readings and about half of the sciatica readings were researched for this study, providing a representative thirty readings. Since the causes and treatments in these two categories are so similar, they are viewed here as a whole.

Cayce described the condition as a serious incoordination between the sciatic nerve and the cerebrospinal nervous system, affecting the muscular coordination of the lower limbs. This was in turn viewed as an effect of spinal misalignments in the lumbar-sacral-coccygeal area which had resulted in an impingement blocking the base of the sciatic nerve. This would hinder the nerve supply to the extremities, at times so severely as to cause painful muscular contractions in the legs.

Problems in the lower spine could have a number of initial causes. Although injuries could be a cause, most common was an excess of toxins in the system as a result of poor eliminations, congestion, infection, or related factors. A toxic buildup in the intestines or excretory organs would create pressure on the spine, deflecting the normal impulses through the extremities. Where poor elimination was involved, it was often closely linked with such factors as an overacid diet, constipation, overtaxation, and general debilitation.

In two cases, negative attitudes contributed to the general distress.

Treatment

Cayce also predicted improvement if not a cure for sciatica-rheumatism, providing the treatments he outlined were scrupulously followed. Treatments mainly focused on making corrections in the spine, improving the diet, rebuilding the nerves and general vitality, stimulating the circulation, improving the eliminations, and providing short-term relief for pain until the cure was complete.

In eighteen cases, spinal manipulations were suggested and were generally to focus on the lumbar-sacral-coccygeal area, gently and gradually relieving the nerve impingements and bringing the entire spine into proper coordination. Often suggested was a series of adjustments to relax as well as make deeper corrections. In some instances, these were to be coordinated with other treatments such as heat, hydrotherapy, and massage.

The importance of a healthy diet was stressed almost as often. Emphasis was placed on foods that are easily digested, laxative, alkaline, and blood and nerve building.

Especially noted were fresh vegetables, both raw and cooked, fruits and fruit juices, whole-grain cereals, and meat juices and broths. Starches, sweets, and beef were to be eaten in moderation or, in extreme situations, not at all. Fish, fowl, lamb, liver, and wild game were permitted and pork and fried foods forbidden.

In fourteen cases, to help rebuild nerves, Cayce suggested electrotherapy treatments of various kinds, including the Wet Cell, the Radio-Active Appliance, or the Violet Ray. These treatments were also to improve the circulation and revitalize the entire system.

Massage, recommended in twelve cases, was considered an important means of stimulating the circulation. Applied in the evenings, it would also have a relaxing, sleep-improving function. As in the adjustments, special focus was to be placed on the lumbar-sacral-hip area and the lower limbs. The use of peanut oil or other substances was often suggested. The massages were frequently to be given in conjunction with other treatments such as adjustments, hydrotherapy, electrotherapy, and packs.

Improving eliminations to help rid the body of accumulated toxins was frequently suggested. Typical methods, where specified, were vegetable-based laxatives, such as Eno salts, Rochelle salts, or Sal Hepatica, and flushing methods, such as enemas and colonics. Often, vegetable- and mineral-based laxatives were to be alternated. Herbal tonics, suggested in several cases, could also have a mild laxative effect and improve the assimilations as well. Suggested twice as an alkalizer was bicarbonate of soda in water.

For the local relief of pain, various penetrating heat applicatons were recommended to break up congestion and relax the affected areas. Most frequently suggested were packs of hot salt applied over the lower back and where the nerves and tendons were painful. These took two forms—a heated pad of coarse, dry table salt or stupes made of cloths dipped in a hot, saturated Epsom salt solution. The salt packs could be used alone or to aid in the absorption of other substances such as Glyco-Thymoline. Additionally, mud packs and castor oil packs over the abdomen were each mentioned twice.

Suggested in three cases was another application for acute pain. This involved "painting" the lower back with a combination of tincture of opium and aconite. Heat could then be applied.

Hydrotherapy was recommended in several cases and most often took the form of sweat baths, at times accompanied by hot baths or rubs.

A change in attitude was advised in two instances. One individual was told to be less condemning of others; the other to be more forgiving.

Case History: Sciatica

Follow-up reports indicated that thirteen individuals noted improvements following their readings. Their degree of success, which ranged from some improvement to a complete cure, was largely dependent on how completely the readings were followed.

A case of sciatica which noted a complete recovery was that of 2516, a fifty-six-year-old man whose sciatic condition was so severe that he had difficulty in walking. Cayce attributed his condition to toxins in the system resulting in nerve pressures and spinal subluxations and lesions in the upper lumbar area due to congestion and strain. Impingements at the base of the sciatic nerve impeded the nerve impulses to the legs.

Treatments were to begin with Violet Ray applications, which were to be applied at bedtime for up to one and a half minutes at a time. They were to begin at the base of the brain and move down the spine. If a sedative was needed after the first treatment, Alka-Seltzer or aspirin could be taken.

The next day, he was to have an osteopathic adjustment, with special focus on the area from the ninth dorsal to the base of the spine. In the evening, hot Epsom salt packs (wet) were to be applied over the lower back, followed the next evening by a Violet Ray treatment and the next day by another adjustment.

At this time, a combination of a half teaspoon of Syrup of Figs and Castoria was to be taken every hour until there was a complete evacuation. This was to be followed the next day by two heaping teaspoons of Sal Hepatica in a glass of water. The man was advised to stay off his feet for two days.

Following this treatment, another adjustment was to be made, preceded by heat applications. The diet was to contain plenty of easily assimilated foods, such as cereals, milk, fruit, vegetables, beef juice, and chicken broth.

The man received a second reading which noted improvements, although more were needed. Cayce recommended painting the lumbar-sacral area and the tendons and nerves of the lower extremities with a combination of three parts tincture of opium to one part tincture of aconite. Eposm salt packs were to be applied then, to further relax the area. This was followed by a spinal adjustment.

The man was advised to have quiet and at least two or three bowel movements daily. Further, he was to continue the Violet Ray treatments and maintain proper diet.

Case 2516 reportedly followed Cayce's recommendations until he had completely recovered and was restored to normal health.

Case History: Rheumatism-Sciatica

Case 647 was a woman who was under considerable strain from taking care of a husband who was ill. Her first reading of three indicated gneral debilitation, noting that the greater strain on the system was arising from anxiety and overwork. This had led to poor circulation, poor eliminations, and a tired, heavy feeling, making for pressures in the limbs and other parts of the body.

An herbal tonic containing lactated pepsin, milk of bismuth, elixir of calisaya, and tincture of valerian was prescribed to aid the digestion and calm the nerves. Additionally, to relieve tensions and improve the nerve coordination, at least ten to eighteen general osteopathic massages were recommended. These were to be given about three times weekly or a Swedish massage once a day.

Her second reading ten months later noticed that her condition had not improved. She was still run-down and had developed rheumatism, uremia, and a tendency toward diabetes. Cayce attributed the rheumatism to the accumulation of toxins in the system.

The second reading focused primarily on diet, recommending that the woman abstain from starches and especially sugars, which were aggravating the physical problems. The only sweets permitted were honey in the honeycomb. Vegetables and fruits were highly recommended. Meats were limited to fish, liver, tripe, fowl, and organ meats and were never to be prepared by frying.

At the time of the third reading, given two weeks later, rheumatism was still present and sciatic pains had developed. However, Cayce attributed the pains to a temporary localizing of the toxins in the system, which was caused by the change to a more alkaline diet. Also contributing to the discomfort was the ineffectiveness of her kidneys, which made the sciatic nerve contract.

To relieve the sciatic pains locally, Cayce advised "painting" the lumbar area and lower hip with a combination of three parts tincture of opium to one part aconite. Then heavy packs of hot Epsom salt solution were to be applied. The treatment was to continue until relief was obtained. Also recommended at this time was watermelon-seed tea, prepared by steeping a tablespoon of crushed seed in a pint of water. This was to be taken, a tablespoon at a time, twice a day for two or three days, followed by a rest of one or two days and then a resumption of the watermelon-seed tea. Recommendations made earlier were to be continued.

After following the advice given in her third reading, the woman began to experience relief and unbroken rest. A week later, her son reported that she was much better. Thirty years later, the woman is still living and has led an

unusually active life, free from pain and most of the ills
common among the aging.

Scleroderma

Scleroderma is a rare disease which is characterized by
thickened, hidebound skin with loss of normal folds. An
increase in calcium content within the cells eventually
turns the skin into a immobile, ivory shield. This disease
can also affect the lungs, heart, and various other internal
organs, with organ failure and death as the eventual result.

Physicians who have studied the Edgar Cayce readings
on scleroderma have concluded that the disease originates
as a glandular deficiency, general involving the thyroid,
adrenals, and liver, which creates a lack of nutrition to the
skin. This in turn disturbs the lymph flow, causing nerve
damage that ultimately affects the internal organs and
inflames the lymphatics. Also according to findings in the
Cayce readings, scleroderma is associated with tubercle
bacilli that adversely affect the skin.

Cayce gave thirty-five readings for four individuals,
ranging in age from twenty-two to sixty-seven years. The
central cause noted in each case was a disturbance in the
glandular systems which accompanied the onset of the
disorder. As Cayce noted: "We find that the condition is in
those stages of a form of inflammation of the lymph that
consumes the circulation between the outer, inner and the
still inner skin. While it gives a great deal of disturbances,
it is gradually closing those portions that there is a mal-
formation in the areas that are attacked" (2525-1).

Treatment

Treatments suggested for the four individuals were consistent in several ways and involved the application of
castor oil packs, massage, and dietary changes. The heated
packs were to be placed over the hardened areas through-

out the body, generally three times a week, avoiding direct application to open sores.

The massages, which were intended to stimulate the circulation throughout the body, were to focus on affected areas such as the hips, base of the spine, and lower limbs. Various substances were to be rubbed into the skin, and most frequently recommended was a combination of peanut oil and olive oil. These treatments were typically to take place each evening.

The diet was to consist of raw vegetables, beef juices, and whole grains, which were especially recommended to strengthen the body. Sweets, large amounts of starches, and fried foods were to be avoided.

Readings for three of the four individuals recommended internal doses of Atomidine to help balance the glandular system. Advised in an equal number of cases was the use of Wet Cell Appliance with gold chloride, Atomidine, and the spirits of camphor to help restore the nervous system to normal functioning. Topical applications such as Ichthyol ointment and others were also suggested in two cases to speed healing, as were various eliminants. Additionally, inhalation of the fumes from apple brandy in a charred oak keg was advised to stimulate the circulation and help destroy the tuberculosis bacteria.

Case History

The success rate of these cases was one hundred percent, as all four followed the advice given in their readings and experienced a great deal of improvement. In later years, other individuals have tried these same recommendations with remarkable results.

A typical case from the readings involved a twenty-two-year-old woman who received fifteen readings for scleroderma. Cayce found that a glandular imbalance combined with weakened lymph forces and poor eliminations had permitted the spread of the disease for case 2514.

The woman's first reading offered dietary advice, and strongly advised were leafy green vegetables. The preferred protein sources were fish, fowl, and lamb. Fried foods were to be avoided. To help stimulate the glands to function more normally, Cayce recommended one drop of Atomidine in a half glass of water taken six mornings a week for three weeks. In the evenings, massages were to be administered, using olive oil and peanut oil rubbed thoroughly over the cerebrospinal system.

Following a three-week period, Wet Cell treatments were to begin, using solutions of gold chloride, spirits of camphor, and Atomidine on separate days.

Case 2514's second reading recommended starting castor oil packs. These were to be applied over the affected areas for at least two hours each day. During periods of distress, Ichthyol ointment was to be used. The skin was to be cleansed with Cuticura soap once healing began.

In later readings, Glyco-Thymoline was recommended as a cleansing agent for the skin. Osteopathic adjustments and ultraviolet light treatments were also recommended at this time to aid in stabilizing both the lymph circulation and the glandular system. Calcios was suggested to build the resistance, and Acigest was to be used as a digestive aid.

The woman followed the treatments for a three-year period, during which time she experienced a great deal of improvement and the full use of her body.

Scoliosis

Scoliosis is an abnormal, lateral curvature of the spine. In eight of the thirteen cases of scoliosis in the readings, the curvature specifically occurred at the lower end of the spine, especially in the coccyx. A total of fifteen readings were given on this condition.

Edgar Cayce viewed scoliosis as both a cause and an effect of other bodily disturbances. In at least six cases, subluxations, lesions, or abnormal pressures in the spine were responsible for a variety of sympathetic disturbances in the circulation, eliminations, or assimilations. In four cases, poor conditions in the eliminatory processes had threatened, or already produced, scoliosis in the spine due to unnatural contractions of muscles surrounding the spine. Three readings did not delineate any cause of the spinal curvature.

Treatment

In treating scoliosis, major attention was paid to spinal correction and alignment. Cayce recommended gentle spinal manipulations in ten cases, always specifying whether these treatments were to be given by a chiropractor, neuropath, or osteopath. In two cases, simple hand manipulations of the spinal muscles could be given by a friend or family member.

Spinal and back massages were essential to treatment in six cases. Usually, this was to follow manipulations and, in two cases, a hot bath. Most readings mentioned massage oils, such as peanut oil, olive oil, and myrrh or cocoa butter.

Dietary revisions were recommended in five cases, and the emphasis was on vegetables, especially leafy greens, and citrus fruits and whole grains. Occasionally, broiled fish, fowl, lamb, and at times beef were to be included.

Five readings indicated that the application of electrical vibrations would be useful in reestablishing healthy energy patterns in the body. The Radio-Active and Wet Cell Appliances and the Violet Ray were each suggested once, while two other readings suggested unspecified forms of low electrical currents, possibly referring to the Wet Cell Appliance.

Especially important for four individuals, one of whom was a five-month-old infant, were hot baths and/or the overnight application of hot packs to the spine. These were to consist of either Glyco-Thymoline or a combination of mutton tallow, spirits of turpentine and spirits of camphor.

Case History

Since treatments varied considerably, summaries of two case histories follow.

Case 1503, a man of twenty-seven, suffered from scoliosis at the coccygeal end of the spine, which produced severe pressures in the lumbar region and throughout the cerebrospinal system. In addition, glandular disturbances were present.

He was prescribed six consecutive weeks of daily spinal adjustments, to be administered only by a chiropractor or neuropath. This treatment was to be followed by a two-week rest period and then resumed for another six weeks. Use of the Radio-Active Appliance was suggested for thirty to forty minutes daily. A diet of beef, fish, milk, whole wheat bread, and vegetables was recommended. Starches were to be avoided.

The scoliosis in case 4529, that of a female adult, was attributed to poor eliminations which were causing muscular contractions at the coccygeal end of the spine. She was advised to take hot vapor baths each week, to be followed by a back massage with pure grain alcohol and olive oil. After three or four weeks of this procedure, 4529 was to begin neuropathic treatments to correct impingements and pressures in her spine.

No follow-up reports are available for either case.

Seborrhea

Seborrhea is a skin condition similar to psoriasis which is characterized by dry scales that usually appear on the arms and legs or as dry yellowish dandruff.

Nine individuals received one reading each for seborrheic dermatitis, a form of eczema.

Edgar Cayce held that most skin disorders were the result of uneliminated toxins caused by an imbalance in the eliminations, and in the majority of cases of seborrhea discussed by him, such an imbalance was noted as the cause. In reading 5291-1, Cayce explained the cause as "poisons which should be eliminated through the alimentary canal." Also noted in several instances were factors such as glandular malfunction or nervous system incoor dination.

Treatment

Treatment for seborrhea placed emphasis on internal remedies and physiotherapy. In six cases, Cayce recommended an alkaline-forming diet free of fats, starches, meats, and fried foods. In four readings, he advised assisting elimina- tions with frequent internal dosages of olive oil, saffron, or mullein tea and milk of magnesia combined with milk of bismuth.

External therapies included, in four cases, spinal manip- ulations to relieve nervous system incoordinations. Gener- ally, treatment was to be administered once or twice a week for a specified period of time.

To promote stimulation of the circulation and to relieve tension, spinal and body massages were suggested in four cases. These massages were generally to be administered with olive oil and/or peanut oil.

To reestablish coordination of the eliminations and im- prove digestion, herbal tonics were prescribed in three cases. Generally, they included combinations of tincture of stillingia, sassafras oil, yellow dock root, and syrup of sarsaparilla. As external medication, two readings pre- scribed a salve consisting of plantain leaves cooked in heavy cream.

Case History

Poor elimination was noted as the main factor involved in the case of 4569, a woman with seborrheic dermatitis of the hands and feet.

As Cayce explained, the blotches appearing on her hands and feet were "the effects of an elimination set up through the capillary system that brings distresses to the extremities, in the way the circulation has, in a manner, *stopped*, or caused abrasions. The cuticle itself breaking, cracks, and the tendency of the separation between the dermis and epidermis in the extremities. This is due to an improper equilibrium in the eliminating system'' (4569-2).

Recommended as an internal remedy was an herbal tonic consisting of simple syrup, syrup of sarsaparilla compound, tincture of stillingia, ten percent solution of potassium iodide, elixir of calisaya, tincture of capsicum, oil of sassafras, and balsam of tolu. An alkaline-reacting diet high in green vegetables, fruits, and nuts was also considered an essential part of the treatment. Additionally, manipulations, especially of the limbs, and frequent Swedish massages were recommended.

For immediate relief of the skin irritation, the woman was advised to bathe her hands and feet in rainwater into which plantain leaves had been cut and soaked.

Although three of the individuals receiving readings on seborrhea reported improvement in their skin after adhering to treatments recommended in their readings, there is no indication available whether case 4569 followed the advice given by Cayce.

SIDS (Sudden Infant Death Syndrome, or Crib Death)

SIDS, or sudden infant death syndrome, is the medical term for crib death, the sudden and unexplained death of an infant. Although there are many theories surrounding SIDS, there is no accepted medical explanation for the tragedy.

Edgar Cayce discussed sudden infant deaths in several readings and offered a number of explanations, one of which was that crib death was not an accident, but a deliberate act of will on the part of the soul to leave the body.

Although given as life readings for adults, readings 136-1 and 1648-2 revealed that in previous incarnations these individuals had only ''brief sojourns'' on the earth plane, i.e., they had died suddenly and quickly in infancy. In each of these cases, the incarnation had served as a brief but necessary proving ground so the soul could experience materiality. From this "brief" experience, 136 gained "consciousness of the plane in which the elemental may be manifested through flesh." Similarly, 1648 had reincarnated for only a short time because "the soul sought expression through the unity of activity in the material experience. . . . That there might be those assurances, in spirit, in mind, in truth, of the relationship self bears to the whole." From this it follows that Cayce held that these incarnations were necessary for the soul to experience its wholeness. Once this was accomplished, there was no other purpose for the soul to continue to exist. On a metaphysical level, the brief sojourn was meaningful despite the tragedy associated with the physical deaths.

A second reason for crib death, which was apparent in the readings, was that the soul departed the earth plane after realizing or deciding that its present embodiment was unsuitable for its needs. In readings 480-37 and 480-44, where bereaved parents questioned Cayce about why their baby had died suddenly after birth, Cayce replied, "The soul preferred to stay with its Maker." Obviously, then, Cayce believed that the new entity had the option to leave the physical after having reassessed its new environment as undesirable.

A similar soul decision had taken place in the previous incarnation of case 1177, a twelve-year-old boy. Ironically, Cayce's wife realized, through the information given on the boy's previous incarnation, that the baby had been Cayce's own son, Milton Porter Cayce, who was born and died in 1911. In the infant's life reading, Cayce noted that the length of the child's previous incarnation was only two months, and that the soul departed because circumstances would not have been appropriate for its development. Additionally, the soul was not mentally prepared for another earthly sojourn, "for there was too great a distance in the mind and the experience during that period of gestation for the soul to remain in that experience."

Another life reading affecting the Cayce family was that of 2390-1, a young woman whose previous incarnation was as Edgar Cayce's oldest sister, who died at the age of two and a half.

Her soul had judged its present experience in the physical as upsetting and undesirable, and the baby slowly "wasted away" to its death. Cayce's mother, recalling the child's death, remembered that when the baby was ten days old, her husband had a fit of drunkenness, which so profoundly affected the child that she was never again the same. Disappointment and disillusionment eventually diminished her desire to remain in the family. Also mentioned in the reading was that in her present incarnation, the woman still retained a strong distaste for men who drank, but she had chosen to incarnate again as the daughter of an alcoholic so that she would learn to deal with the situation.

Reading 3391-1, which does not specifically deal with crib death, makes an interesting point regarding the parents of such children. The reading was given for the parents of a two-year-old boy who died of cancer. Cayce explained that the disease was "part of the entity's karma" and that the death was a merciful one, sparing the child from a lifetime as a invalid. Furthermore, Cayce indicated that it was also the parents' karma to lose the baby, as they needed to learn certain lessons from his death.

Cayce, who was aware of the difficulty in accepting his concepts, tried to reassure those concerned in reading 1648-2: "HIS ways are not past finding out. Though to the material mind they may oft be misunderstood, the spiritual mind bears witness as one to another."

Skin Ulcers (Decubitus)

Skin ulcers are a specific type of ulcer caused by prolonged pressures over bony or cartilaginous prominences. They are most often seen in the elderly. Ten readings were given for four individuals with skin ulcers, all of whom had sores on their legs. Two also had varicose veins.

In all four cases, a common cause of skin ulcers was

poor circulation. In three, a contributing factor was tension and worry. In two, improper functioning of the excretory system was involved, and the combination of poor circulation and poor eliminations was sufficient to cause the toxins to be thrown off through the skin, thus causing the skin irritation. In two cases, the poor assimilation of sugar contributed to impurities in the blood and the poor circulation. One individual had spinal problems which affected the blood supply and digestion, resulting in hyperacidity. This acidic condition caused the skin to erupt.

Treatment

Edgar Cayce's treatments were primarily external. One prescribed for relief and healing was the application of mullein leaves to the affected areas. The mullein was prepared by steeping two or three green leaves of the herb in hot water and then applying them directly to the skin. This treatment was recommended for individuals who also suffered from varicose veins. One reading suggested the application of Glyco-Thymoline before and after the stupes.

In other cases, D.D.D. and Iodex were advised as antiseptics. Cayce prescribed a combination of Iodex and animated ash as a topical ointment for one individual, but the combination proved to be too strong, and later readings advised using the Iodex alone.

Spinal manipulation was suggested in three of the four cases and was intended to stimulate the circulation by loosening up the areas where it was restricted.

In the case where the muscles were tight from tension, Cayce recommended massages with a combination of plantain and cream cooked into a jelly. Additionally, in the cases also involving varicose veins, the readings recommended ultraviolet light therapy. One of these individuals was advised to expose the irritated areas to the sun for brief periods.

Internally, various eliminants were recommended in two cases.

Case History

A female adult, case 2714, was found to have impurities in her blood, poor circulation, and a deficiency of vitamin B_1, all of which contributed to her problem with leg ulcers and varicose veins. The ulcers were directly attributed to an infection in her system. As Cayce explained: "As we find, with this body, 2714, while the outward conditions cause the greater distress, the effects arise from infection that is latent within the system. It gives an expression which is indicated in the ulcered conditions that respond little to local applications."

As treatment for this condition, Cayce recommended a tablespoon of dried mullein tea daily in two ounces of boiling water. Also, two or three green mullein leaves, placed in hot water, were to be applied directly over the affected area. As an antiseptic, Glyco-Thymoline was to be applied before and after the mullein-leaf application.

Foods high in vitamin B_1 were to be eaten, and every other day the sacral and iliac plexus were to be relaxed osteopathically, as incoordination in these areas retarded the circulation to the affected areas. The shortwave ultraviolet light was to be used over the back at a later time.

Smoking: Habit

In Edgar Cayce's day, very little research was available on the harmful effects of tobacco smoking. However, it should be noted that cigarettes in general contained fewer additives than they do today, and the readings reflected the importance of this consideration by strongly recommending only those brands which were made of pure tobacco.

A total of eighty-eight readings, given for eighty-one individuals, dealt at least briefly with considerations related to smoking. Usually these appeared in the question-and-answer section that was part of many readings and was not the general topic of the reading. Those requesting information on smoking ranged from fifteen to seventy-nine years, but Cayce's comments on smoking seemed to apply to all, regardless of age.

One of the more controversial aspects of his comments was, rather than finding tobacco smoking to be completely detrimental to health, Cayce basically regarded it as potentially beneficial if done in moderation. However, it must be remembered that the methods of raising and curing tobacco, as well as the manufacture of cigarettes, were far different in Cayce's time and the resulting product more natural.

While the definition of moderation varied somewhat with each individual, the basic recommendation was six to ten cigarettes a day. Cigarettes were specifically preferred over pipes and cigars. If the reference was to smoking a pipe, Cayce advised no more than two or three pipefuls of tobacco a day.

Although smoking in moderation was acceptable to Cayce, it was never regarded as essential to health. The main benefit, as Cayce saw it, was apparently the calming effect of nicotine on the nerves.

A few individuals, however, were advised to quit smoking, and cutting down on the number smoked a day was at times also advised. Where abstention was suggested or where an individual expressed the desire to quit, a clear unambivalent attitude was suggested. The individual was told to bear in mind that it was what he truly wished to do and was not something he was being forced to do.

An "aversion therapy" mentioned in one reading was to rinse the mouth with Listerine after each cigarette.

Spine: General

A spinal wrench or spinal injury was the common cause for a host of symptoms mentioned by individuals seeking Edgar Cayce's advice. The readings indicate that lesions and scar tissue would form over the years after a spinal injury and put pressure on nerve endings, which then could not function properly.

Some of the symptoms mentioned in the readings caused by a wrenched or injured back are hot and cold flashes, especially when resting; tiredness; "distress" through the liver, pancreas, and upper portion of the intestinal tract; neuritic pains to arms and legs; sciatic nerve pain; overactivity of kidney and bladder; constipation; headaches; nervousness; inability to sleep; stomach swelling and gas; and sterility.

Treatment

The most prevalent treatment was osteopathic manipulations—out of six readings, five recommended these adjustments. If the injury was of long standing, then massaging with oil, as well as the application of electrotherapy and packs, were recommended to increase the circulation and break up old scar tissue and improve eliminations.

One individual was to use a hot saturated solution of Epsom salts, placing it on the injured area with heavy pads so that the heat and applications would be of long duration. These were to be placed daily or at least two to three times a week. The packs were to be followed by gentle osteopathic adjustments and then a massage with equal parts olive oil and peanut oil.

Another individual was to use hot Glyco-Thymoline packs to help relax his spine, followed by a massage with olive oil and peanut oil. Osteopathic manipulation was to be administered only after a series of twenty packs had been completed.

The diet stressed by Cayce was raw vegetables and plenty of fruit. Proper eliminations were important, and several readings recommended colonics.

Spine Injuries: Coccyx

Edgar Cayce gave twenty-two readings for seventeen adult men and women who received injuries to the coccygeal region of the spine as a result of a fall or other

accidents. As responses to the injuries, various disturbances were noted, including headaches, low back pain,
sensory disorientation, and excretory problems.

Incoordination between the cerebrospinal and sympathetic nervous systems was diagnosed as a secondary cause
for subsequent disorders in the hepatic circulation and the
pelvic organs. The readings illustrated the interdependence
between the nervous systems and other systems and reinforced a holistic approach to the treatment itself.

Treatment

Cayce's treatment for these injuries emphasized the
correction of misalignment in the coccygeal and lumbosacral regions in order to restore coordination in the nervous
system and to relieve pressures on the lower spine. In all
but one of the seventeen cases presented, osteopathic or
chiropractic manipulations of the spine were advised. These
were to be administered a few times weekly, usually from
sixteen to twenty weeks.

Massage or relaxing back rubs were suggested in nearly
one-quarter of the cases. This treatment was to relax the
affected area and allow manipulations to take place. In
other cases, prior to treatment wet heat was to be applied
to the lower back and to the area to be manipulated.

To restore coordination and equilibrium to the nervous
system, in forty-two percent of the readings Cayce advised
electrotherapy. Mentioned specifically in four of the readings were the Wet Cell or Radio-Active Appliance, which
were typically to be applied several evenings per week for
thirty to sixty minutes in duration. Other forms of electrotherapy, such as the Abrams radionic machine and diathermy, were suggested, but their usage was not specified.

Different kinds of tonics were also prescribed to help
restore balance to the nervous function. Over one-fifth of
the readings recommended an herbal tonic with ingredients
such as wild cherry bark, sarsaparilla root, yellow dock
root, and black root. One reading specified gold and soda
in water.

Colonics and enemas were suggested in seventeen percent of the readings to relieve poor eliminations which resulted from impaired pelvic circulation.

Case History

Among those receiving benefits from their readings with Cayce was a sixty-two-year-old woman, case 4033, who complained of severe pain in one leg from hip to knee, resembling sciatica and which had troubled her for years. Five doctors had been unable to diagnose her condition.

Her symptoms included headaches and a feeling of head congestion.

Cayce's reading revealed an old injury to the lower end of her spine, which had formed a lesion in the coccygeal vertebrae and the ninth thoracic vertebra. The hepatic circulation, affecting liver and kidney function, had been greatly strained through nerve impairment, and a general state of imbalance between the cerebrospinal and sympathetic nervous systems was noted.

Twice weekly osteopathic manipulations were prescribed, to be preceded by the application of wet heat to the lower spine to relax the muscles. This treatment was to be administered for sixteen to eighteen weeks. To relax general tension, a sedative containing bromides was recommended. Massages were also advised to aid relaxation.

Diathermy treatments to coordinate nerve impulses through the lumbar region and in the ninth and third cervical areas were to follow osteopathic treatments. Nerve-building foods such as seafood, liver, beef, and raw vegetables were to be added to her diet.

Her second reading noted improvements as a result of following the advice given in the first reading. If needed, Cayce said that osteopathic treatments and shortwave applications could continue on an occasional basis.

Following her second reading, the woman reported a complete cure from her discomfort. Additionally, four others noted complete cures. Reportedly, two others did not follow their readings, and their condition grew worse over the years.

Sterility: Female

Eighteen women who were unable to conceive approached Edgar Cayce on the problem of sterility and received a total of twenty-four readings on the subject. In every case, sterility was viewed as a curable physical disorder arising from imbalances in the reproductive system.

The causes most consistently apparent in the readings were factors that affected the glands and organs of reproduction. Often cited as causes were incoordination between the sympathetic and cerebrospinal nervous systems, glandular dysfunctions, and poor eliminations, which offset the cycles of ovulation and menstruation. Several women reported menstrual irregularities and discomforts as well as sterility. In at least eight cases, a combination of at least two of the above disorders was involved.

Treatment

In order to achieve proper nerve coordination and proper placement of the pelvic organs, spinal manipulations and osteopathic adjustments were prescribed in fourteen cases, usually to be given once or twice a week for a series of several weeks.

Internal remedies were also part of treatment in eleven cases. Recommended were either herbal preparations, Atomidine dosages, or a combination of chloride of gold and bromide of soda in water (also recommended for men with this problem). The herbal preparations contained a variety of compounds, including elixir of calisaya, tincture of valerian, and essence of wild ginseng. In the three cases where Atomidine was recommended, dosages were to be alternated with a series of osteopathic treatments or other internal remedies. A typical dose of gold and soda was one drop of one-grain-per-ounce gold solution added to a half glass of water, to be taken at least once a day.

Suggestions for dietary improvements were made in five cases. Alkaline-reacting and blood-building foods were highly encouraged. Foods containing fats and grease and meats and starches were to be kept at a minimum in order to prevent acid buildup in the system.

To equalize the circulation and patterns of vibrations in the body, electrotherapy was recommended in five cases, most often in the form of the Radio-Active Appliance and the Wet Cell (in one case, both appliances were used together). However, electrotherapy was not dominant in the treatments and was generally prescribed during rest periods between other more prolonged series of treatments.

Case History

In case 2432, sterility in a thirty-year-old woman was attributed to a glandular imbalance and faulty connection between the cerebrospinal and sympathetic nervous systems. Cayce prescribed a treatment cycle which involved taking Atomidine internally for five days, resting for three days and resuming dosage for another five days, then resting again and repeating the cycle. The dosage was one drop added to a half glass of water, taken every morning before breakfast.

During the periods when Atomidine was not taken, two osteopathic adjustments a week were to be administered, with special attention to the fourth lumbar and ninth dorsal vertebrae as well as the brachial and sacral centers. A total of twelve adjustments was called for in the initial series of treatments. Following this, the woman was then to begin daily dosages of one drop of diluted chloride of gold and two drops of diluted bromide of soda added to a half glass of water. As with Atomidine, this series was to extend for a five-day period, then discontinued for three days, and alternated with the Atomidine dosages for from three to five full rounds.

Finally, after this series, ten more osteopathic treatments

were recommended. In the diet, quantities of sweets and starches, such as candies, white potatoes, cake, and bread, were to be avoided, while fruits, nuts, and vegetables were to be the major portion of diet.

No follow-up report is available in the case of 2432, and although reports were inconclusive or absent in most cases, five women advised Cayce that after following their readings, they had successfully conceived and given birth.

Sterility: Male

Edgar Cayce gave seven men each a reading to determine the cause and treatment of their inability to conceive a child.

In these readings, sterility was generally attributed to a glandular dysfunction and was considered curable in all cases. Many accompanying disorders were present in most cases, including poor eliminations, nervous stress, and blood or circulatory disorders.

Treatment

Cayce placed major emphasis on herbal and medicinal tonics in treating sterility. These were to cleanse the glands and stimulate normal glandular secretions. In three cases, he prescribed a tonic containing varying proportions of distilled water, chloride of gold, and bicarbonate of soda. Several drops of this combination were to be added to water and taken twice daily. Other recommended tonics contained a variety of herbs—sarsaparilla, Canadian balsam, yellow dock root, burdock root, and others. Additionally, wheat-germ oil, Codiron, and Grove's Tasteless Chill Tonic were prescribed to improve glandular functions.

To relieve nervous pressure related to glandular distress, four men were advised to have a series of weekly spinal manipulations. Other suggestions for treatment involved alkalinization of the system through diet and eliminants or colonics.

Case History

The most thorough and extensive reading was given for case 2548, a thirty-six-year-old male. His inability to produce a child was due to a toxic condition in the blood which had given rise to a disturbance affecting the glands. Cayce prescribed an herbal formula with a distilled water base to which were added yellow dock root, burdock root, prickly ash bark, buchu leaves, mandrake root, elder flower, grain alcohol, and balsam of tolu.

The diet was to consist largely of foods rich in vitamin B as well as fruits, cereals, vegetables, and milk. No meat or fried foods were allowed.

Additionally, the subject was to eat a small amount of Calcios spead on a cracker three times a week. Following a three-day rest period, twice weekly osteopathic corrections with special reference to the lumbosacral region were to be administered. During this interval, dosages of Grove's Tasteless Chill Tonic and Bromo Quinine tablets were to form a part of the treatment. A thorough colonic was to conclude this series of treatments.

No follow-up is available on the treatments for sterility.

Sterility: Tipped Uterus

Eleven women, ranging from twenty to thirty-nine, received a total of fourteen readings from Edgar Cayce for infertility attributed to a tipped or malpositioned uterus. Generally, Cayce's readings revealed other factors involved in preventing conception.

In over thirty-five percent of the cases, spinal sub-luxations—usually in the coccyx or the lumbosacral region—created pressure on the pelvic organs which gradually distorted the placement of the uterus. In another thirty-five percent of the cases, a tipped uterus was cited as the reason for the sterility, but its cause was not explained further.

In the majority of the remaining cases, the women's inability to conceive was attributed to congestion and neuralgia in the pelvic region, caused by dampness, cold, and congestion and residual cold and flu germs in the body. In many cases, accompanying symptoms included irregular or painful menstruation, occasional headaches, backaches, and dizziness.

Treatment

Cayce's treatments were designed to help return the womb to its proper position and keep it there. If the treatments were followed, then in no case was an operation thought necessary. Although surgery might be equally effective, it was generally considered worthwhile to avoid the potential risks and resulting strain on the system if possible.

In over sixty percent of the cases, Cayce recommended spinal manipulation to correct the subluxations and nerve impingements in the lower spine. The manipulations were also intended to readjust the position of the womb. Treatments were usually to be administered twice a week over a period of one or two months.

Various packs, applied externally or inserted within the uterus, were prescribed in a similar number of cases. Externally, hot castor oil packs, hot Glyco-Thymoline packs, hot salt packs, and wet and dry heat were mentioned in one case each. These packs were to be placed over the pubic and abdominal areas during rest periods between spinal treatments and before the onset of the menstrual period. Instructions for the internal medical packs were not specified.

To relieve congestion and discomfort in the pelvic region, douches, to be given with a fountain syringe, were recommended in over twenty-five percent of the cases. Diluted solutions of Atomidine (one teaspoon to a quart of warm water) or Glyco-Thymoline (one tablespoon to a quart of warm water) were suggested. Douches were only to be given a few days before a period or during a painful

menstrual cycle. Also, to supply needed elements to the
system, two individuals were advised to take minute doses
of gold chloride and bromide of soda mixed in water.

Case History

Cayce gave case 578, a woman of twenty-four, three
readings concerning her inability to conceive. He diagnosed her condition as a tipped uterus which had been
caused by spinal subluxations located in the coccygeal
portion of the spine.

The primary treatment recommended by Cayce was
manipulation of the entire spine, with special attention
given to the coccyx and the lumbosacral area. These
adjustments were to take place twice weekly for several
weeks, followed by a two-week rest period and then more
treatments.

Regular exercises were suggested to improve the poor
blood and lymph circulation and strengthen the muscles of
the abdomen and pelvis. One exercise was to swing the
lower limbs in a circular motion, with the body supported
by the elbows. An alternative was to do a shoulder stand
for three or four minutes, moving the legs in a bicycle-
pedaling motion. Massage was also advised for poor circulation and dysmenorrhea.

The woman apparently followed Cayce's advice, and
some time later she became pregnant and had a baby.

Streptococcus Infection

Streptococci are a form of bacteria which assume a
chain or chaplet formation and are evident in various kinds
of infection. They are responsible for such illnesses as sore
throat, scarlet fever, rheumatic fever, pneumonia, impetigo, heart infections, and bone diseases.

The most common strep germs are associated with
"strep throat" and impetigo. If not treated and identified,
these conditions can lead to other complications, such as

ear infections, rheumatic fever, and kidney disease. Treatment is generally in the form of antibiotics.

Edgar Cayce gave one reading each for nine individuals in whom a streptococcus infection was specifically identified, although there were a myriad of medical problems in the readings that involved these bacteria.

Cited in seven cases as the major cause of strep infection was improper elimination. The sluggish intestinal system would allow the bacteria to remain in the body long enough to multiply and cause infection.

Contributing factors were poor circulation and spinal subluxations, which were each mentioned in three cases. These complications were often noted in conjunction with improper assimilations, nervous imbalances, and glandular disorders.

Treatment

In every instance but one, treatment for infection included dietary measures. Special emphasis was placed on alkaline-forming foods such as vegetables and fruits and their juices. Other body-building foods occasionally noted included whole grains, beef juice, liver extract, and yeast. Fats and fried foods were not advised.

Massages and rubdowns, usually of the spine, were suggested in five cases. Massage substances included alcohol to reduce fever and to alleviate congestion, a combination of mutton tallow, spirits of camphor, and spirits of turpentine.

In four cases, electrotherapy was advised, twice in the form of the electric vibrator, which was to be used for massage. Spinal manipulation was also advised in four cases, with special concentration on the dorsal area, and in four cases internal cleansing, via colonics or laxatives, was recommended.

Treatments occasionally mentioned included Epsom salt packs applied over affected areas, watermelon-seed tea, Atomidine, inhalation therapy, and topical applications over painful areas.

Case History

Positive results were reported by three of the nine individuals upon following the suggestions given by Cayce in their readings.

A case of interest involved a forty-one-year-old woman who received one reading for a bacterial infection. Overexertion, in combination with a cold, congestion, and poor eliminations, had lowered case 1100's resistance, which led to the infection.

Cayce's first suggestion was to soak her feet in hot mustard water and then massage the feet and lower limbs with a combination of mutton tallow, spirits of turpentine, and spirits of camphor. To help overcome the cold and congestion, Cayce suggested an inhalant spray for the respiratory passages, composed of water, oil of eucalyptus, rectified turpentine oil, and compound tincture of benzoin.

As an aid in building the body's resistance, one drop of Atomidine in half a glass of water was to be taken internally before breakfast, and two drops before bedtime. On the second day, the dosage was two drops in the morning and five in the evening. The regimen was to be discontinued on the third day and then repeated, beginning with the one-drop dosage.

Also suggested to strengthen the body was an alkaline-reacting diet which included corn bread and Valentine's Liver Extract. Spinal manipulations were to be administered, with special attention to the dorsal and cervical areas and around the head and behind the ears.

Case 1100 followed the advice given to her by Cayce and as a result reported that her condition had improved.

Tic Douloureux

Tic douloureux is characterized by sudden, severe pain through one or more branches of the trigeminal, or fifth cranial, nerve, which runs through the neck and face. Also known as trigeminal or trifacial neuralgia, tic douloureux usually occurs in middle or late life and is more common in women.

Six men and women, mostly in their fifties and sixties, received a total of nineteen readings on this disorder.

In almost all instances, according to Edgar Cayce, the causes of tic douloureux were poor eliminations and/or an imbalance in the nervous coordination, which ultimately affected the trigeminal nerve, causing severe facial pain. In both instances, digestive and circulatory complications were noted as reflex conditions.

Treatment

For the treatment of tic douloureux, Cayce consistently stressed the need to establish better "patterns of vibration" in the body, and six subjects were subsequently advised to have electrotherapy treatments. In five cases, the Radio-Active Appliance was recommended. General instructions included using the appliance an hour each day, alternating the attachments between the extremities.

Also advised for six cases were spinal manipulations and general osteopathic relaxing treatments which Cayce considered necessary to relieve impingements and pressures in the vertebrae. Three individuals were advised to have massages immediately after adjustments. Several readings specified that special attention be given to relieving tension in the cervical vertebrae, which conduct vital nerve impulses to the head and face. Among the massage oils mentioned was a combination of olive oil (heated) and tincture of myrrh.

A more alkaline diet was advised in four cases, with emphasis on raw vegetables, vegetable soups, citrus fruits, and occasionally the juices of meats.

To aid intestinal distress, Cayce recommended daily doses of Castoria, Alophen tablets, and Al-Caroid, each being mentioned in four cases.

Case History

Case 5555, a middle-aged woman, suffered from severe facial pain, which Cayce attributed to pressures created in the fifth cervical center by spinal misalignments. Cayce also cited complications in the woman's digestion, eliminations, and blood supply.

A series of treatments was outlined in the four readings given for 5555 in which diet, electrotherapy, osteopathy, and massage were emphasized. The woman's diet was to consist mainly of citrus fruits, vegetables, grape juice or red wine, and other alkaline-reacting foods. Case 5555 was advised to frequently drink small amounts of spirits of frumenty, burned, to which small amounts of beet sugar had been added, or to drink plain spirits frumenty mixed with a cooked egg yolk and milk. Relaxing osteopathic manipulations, administered twice weekly, and frequent back massages, using a combination of heated olive oil and tincture of myrrh, were also advised. Alophen tablets were recommended to improve eliminations, and the Radio-Active Appliance was to be applied for one hour daily across the solar plexus.

There was no subsequent follow-up report to indicate the outcome of her reading; however, one individual informed Cayce that her condition had been cured by following the advice given to her in his reading. In another case, a woman who had recurring problems with tic douloureux reported improvements, but she could not seem to maintain consistent treatments and suffered several relapses.

Tinnitus

Tinnitus is a sensation of noise in the ears or head which may be objective (heard by examiner) or subjective. In a small percentage of cases, it has obvious correctible causes, such as ear wax, middle ear infection, or high blood pressure. However, some individuals with this problem experience little relief. One form of treatment involves the use of masking devices tailored to produce more calming sounds.

There are eleven readings dealing with this condition.

They were given to seven individuals over a period of time.

Edgar Cayce most frequently attributed tinnitus symptoms to circulatory disturbances. According to the readings, lesions, particularly of the external ear canal, can form as a result of poor circulation to the head and face. Toxemia, congestion, and psychological factors (anxiety, etc.) were also cited as related causes, but Cayce's diagnosis mainly emphasized circulatory problems, at times accompanied by spinal subluxations. Some of the accompanying symptoms mentioned in these cases were pressure in the ear(s), head noises, deafness, impaction of the eustachian tube, earwax buildup, earaches, itching inside the ears, and fatigue from lack of sleep.

Treatment and Case History

Seven individuals received eleven complete readings dealing with tinnitus. Readings in five cases recommended osteopathic adjustments, particularly in the cervical and dorsal areas. General massage was also at times suggested to improve the circulation as well as the coordination between the sympathetic and cerebrospinal nervous systems. Also recommended was hydrotherapy, especially in the form of sweats. In several instances, head and neck exercises were suggested to help improve the circulation in those areas. Surgery was suggested in a few instances where the eustachian tube was severely affected.

Two of those receiving readings on tinnitus were informed that some of their symptoms were sensory reactions to psychic events they were experiencing. They were advised to begin a regular meditation schedule and take action to develop their psychic abilities.

In general, the diet suggested in these readings was to consist mainly of raw fruits and vegetables and little or no meat, with the exception of fish and fowl. In one case of toxemia-caused tinnitus, a rigid diet of no more than twenty percent acidity was suggested. Grapes were to be eaten daily.

Of the seven cases, one person did not follow his reading, and four did not send in follow-up reports. However, two reported they were "cured" through the advice given in the readings. One individual also reported that Cayce's treatment had also "cured" him of blindness.

Tonsillitis

Tonsillitis is most frequently a bacterial infection due to streptococci. This discomfort is often characterized by a sore throat, fever, chills, headaches, lack of appetite, and swollen red tonsils.

Although tonsillitis is generally considered to be a childhood disease, it also occurs in adolescents and adults.

Thirty-seven individuals in fifty-one readings received information about the causes and treatments of tonsillitis; the condition was mentioned in many other readings as well. About half of those cases discussed in this report were for individuals seventeen years and older.

Causes and Treatment

Edgar Cayce generally attributed tonsillitis to three possible sources—spinal subluxation or lesions, poor eliminations, and poor circulation. In many cases, a combination of these causes was noted. Additionally, Cayce believed that infections could not occur when the proper acid-alkaline balance was maintained in the body.

In prescribing treatments for tonsillitis, Cayce always took into consideration the seriousness of the infection. If acute, he would recommend removal of the tonsils after the body had been prepared for surgery, and in forty percent of the cases, immediate or eventual removal of the tonsils was recommended. However, many other suggestions were given to ease and cure the condition when surgery was not mentioned.

Readings in sixty percent of the cases recommended that spinal manipulations be given on a frequent basis, with particular concentration on the cervical and upper dorsal vertebrae. Besides relaxing and aligning the vertebrae, the manipulations were to stimulate proper drainages from the throat to prevent further accumulation of toxins in the lymph tissue. Before surgery, manipulations were almost always recommended to insure that the infection would be sufficiently drained before the actual removal of the tonsil. In some cases, the condition improved so much following the manipulations that surgery was no longer necessary.

Massages and rubs were suggested in over twenty-five percent of the readings. These were to be administered with a variety of substances, including alcohol and cocoa butter. Massages of the throat and neck, as well as the rest of the body, were considered particularly important. Cayce informed the mother of a nine-month-old girl that the enlargement of her tonsils and adenoids could be prevented by massage of the neck and cervical area.

Maintaining good eliminations and at times increasing them was stressed in twenty-five percent of the cases. To help relieve the body of toxic substances, saline laxatives, enemas, or colonic irrigations were prescribed. For twenty-two percent of the cases, an alkaline diet was advised and recommended were citrus fruits and juices, green vegetables, as well as other alkaline-reacting foods. Meats and starches were not allowed or only allowed in minimal amounts. In several cases, semiliquid diets and blood-building foods such as liver juice were advised for cleansing the body and building up stamina.

Herbal preparations were prescribed in several cases and most frequently recommended were podophyllum taken with leptandrin and sanguinaria, yellow saffron taken in tea, and garden sage combined with elixir of calisaya and other herbs. Doses were to be taken at regular intervals.

To relieve irritation in some cases, gargles and rinses for

the throat were suggested and included Lavoris, Glyco-Thymoline, and other alkaline antiseptics. A Glyco-Thymoline pack on the throat was recommended in one case to reduce inflammation.

Case History

The majority of individuals or parents of children involved did not send in any progress reports, but six did indicate either a complete recovery or significant improvement.

One child, case 508, had two subluxations in the dorsal vertebrae which caused portions of the lymph glands in the throat to become inflamed. Cayce recommended daily spinal manipulations for five or six days to encourage drainages from the throat. The boy was also advised to take an eliminant. Citrus fruits, vegetables and their juices, and other blood-building foods were encouraged.

The boy's mother, who assisted in his treatments, later reported that her child had recovered completely.

Torticollis

Torticollis is a spasmodic contraction of the neck muscles which usually occurs on one side, resulting in an abnormal position of the head. It is more commonly referred to as wryneck, or "crick in the neck."

Nine women and men with discomfort in their neck sought assistance from Edgar Cayce, who gave eleven readings on this subject.

In all but three cases of torticollis, the cause was attributed to faulty nerve coordination between the cerebrospinal and sympathetic nervous systems, often due to exhaustion and stress. The usual cause of these difficulties was a maladjustment of the dorsal and cervical vertebrae. In the remainder of cases, poor eliminations and assimilations were major causes of the neck problems. Contributing factors in some cases included tension, congestion, and glandular imbalance.

Treatment

Treatment instructions were not always consistent, but there were some important areas of agreement. Typically, they were aimed at relaxing the system, building the body, and making cerebrospinal corrections. Recommended in seven cases was either spinal manipulation, with specific reference to the dorsal and cervical vertebrae, or massage, at times administered with substances such as olive oil, peanut oil, and/or alcohol.

Easily assimilated, body-building foods, such as vegetables, seafood, wild game, soups, and meat juices, were recommended in five cases. Greasy and acid-reacting foods were to be avoided.

Also recommended in five cases was electrotherapy. This treatment was to stimulate the circulation and encourage the proper functioning of organs. In each case, the type of treatment differed but was to be administered once a day for several minutes, for a duration of from five to twenty minutes.

At times, Sal Hepatica, Alophen, Castoria, and Atomidine were recommended.

Case History

Case 52, an adult male suffering with a painful neck condition, accompanied by muscular spasms and convulsions, was advised to have an osteopathic adjustment every day for twenty days, followed each time by application of a sunlamp over the whole cerebrospinal system. His diet was to focus on easily digestible foods.

While there is evidence that case 52, who was diagnosed as having an incoordination between the cerebrospinal and sympathetic nervous systems, expressed enthusiasm about the reading, there is no follow-up report available.

Tumors: Uterus

Edgar Cayce delivered a total of seventy-three readings on uterine tumors, a condition characterized by fatty accumulations which become attached to the fallopian tubes or the uterine wall. These readings on uterine tumors were for ten women, one of whom received sixty readings on this as well as other conditions.

In three cases, the causes were not discussed, for the tumorous growths were quite serious and surgery was advised as soon as possible. In the remaining cases, Cayce attributed the tumors to a combination of disorders within the system.

Cited in four cases were poor menstrual eliminations which had clogged the lymph glands, allowing for accumulations of lymph in the uterus. Other contributing factors were incoordination between the glands and a lack of certain elements in the blood. In two cases, the presence of adhesions and lesions in the pelvic organs was responsible for the formation of the uterine tumors.

Treatment

Treatments were somewhat different for each individual. Suggested in five cases was an alkaline-based diet mainly consisting of raw and cooked vegetables, citrus fruits, and fish, fowl, and lamb. Fried foods, fats, starches, and sugars were to be avoided.

Spinal adjustments to relieve pressure on the pelvic organs and set up better eliminations were recommended in five cases. Here special attention was to be directed to the lumbar and sacral vertebrae, which have a direct link to the pelvic organs.

Also advised in five cases was the use of various forms of electrotherapy, most frequently in the form of the Violet Ray, using the vaginal applicator, and the Radio-Active Appliance.

Douching with a highly diluted solution of Atomidine or Creolin was advised for four women. The usual Atomidine dosage was a teaspoon to one quart of warm water. Recommended as often was the use of eliminants such as olive oil, Serutan, or Epsom salts to improve eliminations. At times, Cayce also recommended massages and gentle rubs with olive oil.

Case History

Case 2330 was a thirty-five-year-old woman with a tipped uterus which had contributed to the formation of adhesions and lesions in the vaginal wall, causing menstrual difficulties and accumulations in the uterus. She received a series of three readings for her condition.

Recommended were a series of six osteopathic adjustments administered twice a week, with special concentration given to the coccygeal, sacral, and lumbar vertebrae. Once a week, preferably on the day after the adjustments, the woman was to use the Violet Ray with the vaginal applicator for a few minutes and then douche with a dilution of one teaspoon of Atomidine in a quart of warm water. Following the reading, a general improvement was noted.

The second reading advised the woman to have six to eight more weekly spinal manipulations in the lumbosacral area. Additionally, more Atomidine douches were suggested, and the use of the Violet Ray was to decrease to once every ten days. During the menstrual period, these two treatments were to be discontinued.

Her diet restricted starches, fats, and cheese, while more citrus fruits, especially grape juice, were encouraged. To improve her eliminations, she was advised to take a half to a full teaspoon of olive oil three to four times daily.

The woman's condition apparently improved temporarily, but within two years after her first reading, the symptoms began to reappear, and she reported having problems with her menstrual periods and eliminations. A third reading called for five to six more osteopathic weekly adjustments in the lumbosacral and lower dorsal vertebrae.

Additionally, treatment with the Violet Ray and douches using diluted Atomidine or Glyco-Thymoline (one tablespoon to a quart of warm water) were recommended once a week each.

Within a year after this reading, it was reported that 2330 had undergone surgery for the removal of a fibroid tumor the size of a grapefruit. According to a report given by a close friend, 2330 had not followed the advice given in the readings and had neglected her condition.

Ulcers: Duodenal

Duodenal, or peptic, ulcers are characterized by superficial sores on mucous membranes which are usually located on the duodenum, the first part of the small intestine leading from the stomach to the middle division of the small intestine.

Edgar Cayce gave a total of fifteen readings for eight individuals with the condition and in at least four of them attributed it to general debilitation of the entire physical system. Poor circulation and emotional problems such as anxiety were mentioned in three cases. Contributing causes mentioned were colds and poor eliminations, and in two cases cancer was also involved.

Treatment

Cayce's treatments for duodenal ulcers focused on alkalizing and otherwise easing the distress in the stomach, and on stimulating the eliminations and improving the individual's general physical condition. The major recommendations, each made in at least fifty percent of the cases, were massage, spinal adjustments, and proper diet. Dietary suggestions were characteristic of the readings as a whole, with emphasis on a highly alkaline diet. Drinking plenty of water was often advised. Each mentioned three times were cleansing herbal tonics, castor oil packs for eliminations, elm water (powdered slippery elm bark in water) as a digestive aid, electrotherapy, and colonics and enemas. Al-Caroid, hydrotherapy, and animated ash were each mentioned twice in the readings for duodenal ulcers.

Case History

The series of three readings given for case 1724, a forty-year-old male, indicated that his condition was the result of aftereffects of intestinal flu which affected his circulation, especially through the intestinal tract. Anxiety and colds were other contributing factors.

To help alkalize the system, Cayce suggested a powdered antacid taken in water. Other suggestions included stimulating the eliminations with monthly colonics and other hydrotherapy, and electrotherapy treatments of an unspecified nature applied across the stomach and spine. The diet was to be balanced and kept free of acid-producing fruits, white bread, meats, and fried foods.

The second reading advised continuing the intake of antacid and increasing the number of colonics to two or three, ten days apart before resuming the monthly schedule. In diet, Cayce suggested less sugars and no coconut, preserves, pudding, and alcohol. However, Coca-Cola with carbonated water was in this case recommended. Spinal adjustments to coordinate the sympathetic and cerebrospinal nervous systems were to be administered at the completion of colonics. Special attention was to be given to the ninth dorsal and throughout the cervical and upper dorsal centers.

After receiving his third reading, the man wrote to Cayce, noting that the readings were accurate and to the point and that his condition was beginning to improve.

Vaginitis

Vaginitis is an inflammation of the vagina which is characterized by severe itching and/or discharge. Edgar

Cayce gave twenty readings on vaginitis for seven women and one baby girl.

According to these readings, vaginitis was caused either by an incoordination of the nervous system which affected the pelvic organs and glands, or by poor eliminations which resulted in excess acidity throughout the system.

Treatment

Although there was little consistency in his methods of treatment, Cayce placed importance on internal therapies. Recommended frequently were spinal manipulations. Prescribed to correct subluxations and impingements responsible for nervous system incoordination, these were to be administered at least once a week.

Cayce also advised frequent douching in four cases and recommended dilutions of Glyco-Thymoline (one tablespoon to a quart of water at body temperature) or Atomidine (one teaspoon to a quart of water at body temperature).

Dietary improvements were advised in three cases, with special attention toward more alkaline-reacting foods. Meat, fried foods, and starches were strongly discouraged.

In two cases, frequent dosages of beef juice and Ventriculin were recommended. Also considered beneficial was the use of the Violet Ray.

Case History

Case 538, a forty-three-year-old woman, obtained thirteen readings for a recurring condition of vaginal itching and rash. She received by far the most extensive and thorough series of treatments given in the readings on vaginitis.

Diagnosis indicated that the vaginitis had originated as a reaction to medication taken for another ailment. The medication had created an imbalance in the body chemistry which affected the capillary circulation, especially in the pelvic organs. The result was poor eliminations and a persistent itchy rash in and around the vagina.

To improve eliminations, Cayce suggested daily doses

of charcoal tablets and small amounts of Eno salts. Frequent douches with a dilution of potassium permanganate and a few drops of tincture of myrrh were also advised. In addition, sitz baths with small quantities of these substances added to the water, along with a small amount of balsam of tolu, were to be taken every other day. The use of the Violet Ray with the vaginal applicator was also suggested.

Improvements were noted by the second reading, which now suggested douching with weak solutions of Glyco-Thymoline or Lavoris twice a week. In subsequent readings, alkalizing the body through diet was recommended, with the emphasis on orange and lemon juices.

A series of three to five spinal manipulations was also recommended, with special attention given to the lumbar area. The Violet Ray vaginal applicator was to be substituted with external use of the bulb applicator applied over the cerebrospinal system and the lower abdomen and diaphragm areas. These treatments were to be administered for fifteen minutes twice a week.

Following improvements in her condition, case 538 experienced a recurrence of vaginitis. Cayce subsequently recommended treatment with the Radio-Active Appliance, with the attachments at the pubic bone and the forth lumbar vertebra. This was to be applied for thirty minutes daily in a four-day series, interspersed with rest periods, until the rash disappeared. In later readings, Vaseline, D.D.D. cream, Cuticura, Resinol, and camphorated oil were all suggested as topical applications to relieve the itching.

Follow-up reports noted a few recurrences of vaginitis, but upon adhering to the readings, 538 later reported that the condition had cleared up and that she was in good health.

Varicose Veins

Varicose veins are dilated or enlarged veins caused by the stretching or breaking of the cells which form the walls of the veins. They appear most often in the lower extremities and are generally attributed to poor circulation and/or blood pressure imbalances in the lower limbs. The veins are usually visible and form bluish-black or even purple discolorations under the surface of the skin. This disorder has a higher incidence in women who have been pregnant.

Edgar Cayce gave thirty-three individuals, most of whom were mature or elderly women, a total of thirty-four readings which dealt partially or completely with varicose veins.

Cayce's diagnoses in these cases indicated one or more contributing factors which led to the enlargement of the veins. In one-half, poor circulation and problems with blood pressure were found to be the major causes. Frequently connected with poor circulation was nervous incoordination, caused by spinal pressures or subluxations which were often responsible for a deflection of the nerve impulses to the legs, resulting in slowed circulation to the lower extremities.

In nearly forty percent of the cases, poor elimination contributed to the circulatory problems, resulting in a buildup of toxins, which would create stress on the venous walls and eventually lead to their deterioration. Evident in twenty percent of the cases was an infection in the system, which could also be associated with a toxic state.

Treatment

Suggestions for treatment were consistent in most cases. In nearly forty percent, Cayce recommended spinal manipulations to remove blockages of the nerve impulses to the lower limbs. Generally, the adjustments were to be given about twice a week for several weeks. In thirty-five percent, thorough massages were advised, at times using combinations of oils, such as peanut oil or olive oil and myrrh. To help create healthier circulation in the lower limbs, the massages were to center on the areas of the feet, ankles, and legs.

Mullein tea or other herbal preparations were to be taken

daily in over thirty percent of the cases. In twenty-five percent, Cayce recommended stupes made of the fresh mullein leaves, which were to be applied over the dilated veins.

More than twenty-five percent of the individuals were advised to wear elastic stockings, especially during periods of activity on the feet. These stockings were intended to provide support and prevent further dilation of the veins due to increased circulation in the lower limbs. Finally, to insure good eliminations and provide the body with needed nutrients, an alkaline diet was advised in twenty percent of the cases.

Case History

Only four of the thirty-three individuals receiving readings from Cayce on varicose veins reported their results, with three noting positive results and one noting no improvement, although there was some indication that he may not have followed his reading.

One case of interest was that of 243, a fifty-four-year-old woman whose left leg was swollen with pain when she had the first of two readings. Cayce indicated that the condition had arisen from poor circulation, which damaged the veins of the superficial circulation in her legs. Poor elimination was also involved due partly to the slow and inefficient circulation through the lower part of her body.

Cayce advised her to wear elastic support stockings, especially when active. Her diet was to be alkaline, and frequent massages were recommended over her back, legs, and abdomen.

The woman apparently followed Cayce's advice and with good results. However, nine years later the varicose veins recurred and another reading was requested. This time, Cayce noted that pressures in the lower lumbar axis were impeding the circulation to the lower limbs. Due to the poor circulation and poor eliminations, a buildup of acidity in the kidneys had also developed.

Treatment this time consisted of a series of osteopathic

adjustments. She was also advised to drink one to one and a half ounces of mullein tea daily, which was to be made fresh every three days.

Mullein stupes were also recommended and were to be applied directly over the varicose veins. Her feet and legs were to be massaged, using weak black coffee made from used coffee grounds.

These suggestions were followed and with positive results once again. However, at a later time other physical complications developed and the varicose veins were again aggravated.

There were no further reports received.

Vertigo

Those who suffer from vertigo frequently experience feelings of dizziness, at times associated with nausea or headaches.

Four adults received one reading each for this condition, which Edgar Cayce diagnosed as arising mainly from overtaxation of the nervous system through stress and overwork. Other disturbances, such as poor eliminations, anemia, toxemia, emotional anxieties, and excess blood in the body, were also present in these cases.

Cayce gave readings for four individuals on vertigo.

Treatment and Case Histories

Since Cayce's treatment was specific for each individual, each will be summarized briefly.

Treatment for case 294 involved massage with an electric vibrator, daily rubdowns with olive oil, and daily doses of Beef, Iron & Wine Tonic. Also advised were frequent sunbaths and drinking six to eight glasses of water a day.

Sunbaths and drinking plenty of water were also recommended for case 87, an elderly man. Also prescribed were spinal manipulations, outdoor exercise, and an unspecified form of electrotherapy, possibly the Wet Cell Appliance.

In the case of 5301, a forty-two-year-old woman, Cayce prescribed a daily teaspoon of Eno salts to be taken for five mornings consecutively, then discontinued for two weeks, followed by a resumption of the dosage. Recommended for thirty minutes daily was usage of the Wet Cell Appliance with gold, followed by a general massage.

In the case of 86, a seventy-year-old woman, treatment consisted of a series of two spinal manipulations a week, in addition to sitting under a sunlamp twice a week. These treatments were to correct spinal pressures and establish healthy body vibrations. Also advised was maintenance of an alkaline diet as well as occasional colonics.

As a result of following Cayce's advice, the forty-two-year-old woman, case 5301, and the seventy-year-old woman, case 86, reported that their conditions had improved.

Vitiligo

Vitiligo is a disease characterized by white blotches appearing on the skin. Found in only one percent of the population, it is caused by the destruction of pigment cells.

Edgar Cayce gave readings on the subject for six individuals and held that inasmuch as the condition had taken years to develop in some cases, the treatments would take several months to a year before they would be completely effective.

In his study of vitiligo through his readings, Cayce believed that the condition was caused by disturbances of the skin pigment in the inner skin layers, caused by waste particles in the superficial circulation which had not been properly eliminated by the body.

Treatment

In treating vitiligo, Cayce placed special emphasis on diet, for he felt it was essential to proper metabolism. All treatments focused on the necessity of an alkaline-reacting, well-balanced diet, emphasizing citrus fruits and green vegetables and excluding pork, fried foods, and many starches.

In four of the cases, use of either the Wet Cell, using gold chloride solution, or the Violet Ray was recommended as an effective means of restoring proper assimilations and stimulating good circulation throughout the body.

For purification and cleansing of the glands, Atomidine was prescribed once a day for varying periods of time. The recommended dosage for three cases was one drop in a half glass of water taken every morning before eating. In two cases, herbal tonics containing ragweed were considered necessary to aid the assimilating processes. Other active ingredients included balsam of tolu, elixir of calisaya, and elixir of lactated pepsin.

The need for eliminants was stressed in two cases in which colonic irrigations were recommended on a frequent basis until improvements in the general physical condition were noticeable.

Case History

In her first reading, case 236 complained that white spots had begun to form on her neck some years prior and were now also appearing on her hands and arms. Cayce's diagnosis revealed that poor eliminations and assimilations had affected the capillary circulation in her arms, changing the pigmentation in the skin's inner layers.

The first reading prescribed an herbal tonic consisting of green ragweed, sassafras root, elixir of calisaya, grain alcohol, and balsam of tolu, prepared and administered according to specific instructions.

The diet recommended was to consist of green vegetables and other alkaline-reacting foods. Lunch was to be omitted. Occasional colonics were also suggested, as well as small quantities of Petrolagar.

Six months later, case 236 indicated that the vitiligo had ceased to spread in the areas already affected. In her second reading, Cayce advised nightly use of the Violet

Ray in thirty-minute intervals. Careful application was to extend slowly over the entire cerebrospinal system for at least four or five passes, then to extend slowly over the brachial plexus and the solar plexus, passing down the sciatic nerve and finally down over the lower limbs. Use of the Violet Ray was to continue for thirty days consecutively, following a five-day series involving the ragweed tonic.

Although good results had been noted at first, after the second reading, the woman did not follow up with further reports.

Xeroderma

Xeroderma is a form of dry skin which affects individuals in varying degrees. The skin is characterized by dryness, roughness, and the pulling off of flakes of skin.

Edgar Cayce gave a total of three readings for two individuals, aged twenty-one and sixty-five, who had xeroderma. Readings for both disclosed that improper eliminations had created a toxic and overacid condition within the body which had a weakening effect on the system. Other contributing factors were spinal subluxations, poor circulation, and congestion.

Treatment

Changes in diet were among the first treatments recommended by Cayce, who stressed alkaline-reacting foods consisting mainly of fruits and vegetables. Massages over the affected areas, using substances such as olive oil and myrrh, or castor oil and peanut oil were also suggested. Additionally, the two were advised to use an alcohol-based inhalant containing expectorant substances such as oil of eucalyptus.

Case History

The advice given by Cayce was followed by only one of the individuals, case 1771, a twenty-one-year-old woman who received two readings on xeroderma. In addition to overacidity, spinal subluxations in the cervical and dorsal areas in conjunction with poor eliminations contributed to her condition.

The first treatment suggested by Cayce was osteopathic adjustments, which were to focus on the lumbar, sacral, and coccygeal areas, coordinating the vertebrae in the lower part of the spine. Ten such treatments were recommended.

To aid in breaking up congestion, an inhalant was to be used frequently. In addition to pure grain alcohol, the ingredients included oil of eucalyptus, compound tincture of benzoin, rectified oil of turpentine, Canadian balsam, and a solution of tolu.

Foods containing sugar and refined starches were to be avoided, while alkaline foods such as fruits and vegetables were strongly emphasized. Also recommended were exercises for the feet and outside exercises involving a circular motion of the muscles of the diaphragm.

The second reading advised continuing the treatments recommended in the first reading. To relieve irritated areas on the balls of her feet, Cayce prescribed massages using a combination of olive oil and tincture of myrrh, to be administered each evening before retiring.

The woman followed the advice given by Cayce and ten months later reported that she had experienced a "complete cure."

Cayce's Pharmacology

Author's Note: Certain portions of the following section have been taken from *An Edgar Cayce Home Medicine Guide*, published by the Association for Research and Enlightenment, Virginia Beach, Virginia. Those wishing more information concerning particular pharmacological matters listed in this book may contact the ARE in Virginia Beach or consult the Circulating Files on specific illnesses. The author also wishes to thank the Heritage Store in Virginia Beach, which supplied additional research for this section. (Keep in mind that specific names of formula products, and product availability constantly change.)

ACIGEST

Acigest, a ten percent hydrochloric acid solution, with each cc containing 11.88 mg of potassium iodide, was recommended by Edgar Cayce as a digestive aid. In each case, it was to be taken in raw milk. Since certified raw milk cannot be purchased in most states, Acigest has become impractical to use and is off the market.

ACNE LOTION (528-2)

This formula was recommended by Edgar Cayce in a single reading, for a case involving acne scars. It is not advised for everyone, although its popularity indicates that it has been used effectively by others.

The ingredients are camphorated olive oil, witch hazel, and Nujol, a mineral oil. The formula acts as an antiseptic and astringent. The reading advised thoroughly cleansing the skin before massaging the formula into the scarred and affected areas.

AL-CAROID

This antacid compound was recommended in about 180 readings for acidity, incoordination between assimilations and eliminations, poor digestion and toxemia, and for related problems such as poor assimilations, poor eliminations, and flatulence. It is no longer available in the powder form preferred by the readings. (See Bisodol.)

ALMONDS

Cayce indicated that, as a food, almonds contain elements vital to a healthy metabolism, supplying phosphorus and iron in a combination that is more easily assimilated than other nuts. Almonds contain potassium, calcium, sodium, magnesium, and sulfur. They are rich in protein and unsaturated fat and are the most alkaline of all the edible nuts.

The best-known references to almonds deal with the prevention of cancer. Three individuals were told that eating one to three almonds every day would guard them against cancer, as a vitamin in the almonds would increase the body's resistance to all forms of the disease.

Almonds were also recommended for anemia because of their capacity to supply iron, and one reading noted that

eating two almonds a day would prevent skin blemishes.
The readings referred to the commonly available sweet
variety and not bitter almonds.

ALPINE RAY–RINO RAY

The above were brand names for sunlamps that are off
the market. Substitutes for these appliances might be other
brands of sunlamp or natural sunlight.

ANTI-NAUSEA FORMULA

This formula contained limewater, cinnamon water, iodide
of potassium, and bromide of potassium and was a typical
formula recommended in cases of nausea, including motion
sickness, baby care, and nausea due to pregnancy. About
one-fourth of the approximately ninety readings did not include the iodide and bromide of potassium in the formula.

ARTHRITIS MASSAGE
FORMULA

Massage was frequently advised in cases of arthritis.
One widely used formula described in reading 3363-1
included Nujol, olive oil, peanut oil, oil of pine needles,
sassafras oil, and lanolin. The readings claimed that regular weekly massages using peanut oil alone could actually
prevent arthritis and rheumatism from developing. As
Edgar Cayce explained: "Those who would take a peanut
oil rub each week need never fear arthritis" (1158-31).
One reading noted that olive oil was one of the most
effective agents for stimulating muscular activity or mucous membrane activity that could be applied to the body.
Oil of pine needles was an ingredient in about twenty-five
arthritis massage formulas, and sassafras oil was also included in about ten of these compounds.

ASPIRIN

Occasional small doses of aspirin were recommended in forty-two readings. These recommendations were most frequently for general sedation and in cases involving colds and congestion, poor eliminations, headaches, fever, and arthritic discomfort. Edgar Cayce remarked more than once that aspirin is one of the least harmful sedatives and is far better than taking narcotics to relieve pain.

Aspirin was always to be taken in extreme moderation and only when needed rather than at specific intervals. Dosages ranged from one-half to two five-grain tablets at a time. In half of the cases, aspirin was to be taken in combination with other substances, such as soda mint tablets, to neutralize aspirin's acidic qualities, or with asafoetida, a digestive aid, or with Alophen, a laxative.

ASPIRIN SUBSTITUTE

As an aspirin substitute, Edgar Cayce offered formulas containing a few drops of substances such as benzoin tincture, rectified oil of turpentine, Canadian balsam, oil of eucalyptus or eucalyptol, and benzosol. The first four ingredients were the most common, and reading 4983-1 gave an explanation of their effect on the body. "These taken internally will aid as an antiseptic, as an expectorant, as an active force on the organs of digestion; especially through the liver, duodenum, and pancreas, making also the tendency to increase eliminations through the activity of the kidneys."

ATHLETE'S FOOT LOTION

This external treatment for athlete's foot is found in reading 291-1. The formula contains Nujol, witch hazel, sassafras oil, and coal oil (kerosene).

ATOMIDINE

Edgar Cayce's Atomidine, which he called "atomic iodine," is a concentrated source of iodine which, according to him, was more active and less irritating to the system than other forms of iodine. As a consequence, Cayce believed this substance could be taken internally in small doses in addition to its use as an external antiseptic. Atomidine supplies approximately six times the minimum daily requirement (MDR) of iodine in a single drop. Atomidine cannot be advertised as a product for internal use except under a doctor's supervision because U.S. drug laws currently limit the maximum allowable iodine content of a single dose of a nonprescription drug or food supplement to 225 percent of the adult minimum daily requirement.

Atomidine was mentioned in 830 readings and concerned a wide range of illnesses. Used externally, Atomidine was considered by Cayce as an effective topical antiseptic, useful in treating cuts, boils, burns, and other surface infections. In some instances, it was to be used full strength, and in others diluted to avoid burning delicate tissues.

Internal doses of Atomidine varied greatly and depended on the nature and severity of the condition. Cayce consistently recommended using Atomidine in cycles: taking the formula for several days and then discontinuing use for a prescribed time. A typical cycle consisted of one drop a day for five days, followed by a rest period of five days and then five more days of the same dosage. After a two-week rest period, the entire cycle could be repeated if desired.

Atomidine was recommended for glandular deficiencies, feminine hygiene, venereal disease, arthritis, blood disorders, assimilations and eliminations, asthma, dental care, and for physiotherapy. Reading 808-5 suggested that Atomidine be used as a flu-prevention measure. Cayce recommended: "Spraying the nasal passages and throat occasionally with a thirty percent solution of Atomidine will insure not getting same; provided the body is kept alkaline with the diets."

Internal doses of Atomidine were not always advised. In some cases, iodine was not needed in the system, as it was receiving sufficient amounts from other sources. Atomidine should never be taken in conjunction with other sources of iodine, such as multiple vitamins or minerals which contain iodine, kelp tablets, Calcios, and Formula 636.

One reading cautioned that Atomidine could cause "irritation" or even nausea if a good diet was not followed. A proper diet would be highly alkaline, containing fruits and vegetables and few fats and heavy meats.

Users of Atomidine are cautioned that when used inter nally it can be harmful if taken in large doses, and it is particularly contraindicated in cases where it might exces sively stimulate the heart. Too much iodine can lead to overstimulation of the thyroid gland, resulting in nervousness, insomnia, and skin rash, as well as rapid heartbeat.

BACKACHES, SPRAINS, STRAINS, AND BRUISES LINIMENT (MUSCLE TREAT)

A massage formula given in reading 326-5 has come into popular use in the treatment of backaches, sprains, strained muscles and ligaments, bruises, and related disorders. The formula contains olive oil, mineral oil, witch hazel, tincture of benzoin, oil of sassafras, and coal oil (kerosene). One reading claimed that a massage with this combination would reduce swelling and alleviate pain. Another reading advised its use in a case of varicose veins.

BALSAM OF SULFUR

A liniment recommended about thirty-five times in the readings, balsam of sulfur was often suggested for such conditions as paralysis, impaired locomotion resulting from arthritis, and misplaced vertebrae. This formula is not available commercially, but may be prepared by boiling sulfur and linseed oil together in the proportion of one pound of sulfur to each pound of linseed oil. The mixture is to be boiled until the resulting combination is "not too wet or too dry," according to Cayce. Since this combination may be extremely volatile, it should be prepared only by a pharmacist.

B BATTERY

The B battery, or dry cell, was mentioned about forty times in the readings as a substitute for the Wet Cell and the Radio-Active Appliance. The battery, which was sold in most hardware stores in the 1930s and '40s, is no longer available.

BENZOSOL

Benzosol, an old term for guaiacol benzoate, contained close to equal parts benzoic acid and guaiacol. It was at times mentioned as an ingredient for inhalants as well as for capsules to be taken internally to stimulate respiration. It is no longer commercially available.

BISODOL

This product was recommended in about twenty readings for the relief of acid indigestion and its accompanying symptoms, such as flatulence, fullness, and headache.

BLACK AND WHITE PRODUCTS

Of the products distributed under the Black and White label in Cayce's day, only two are still available: the soap and the ointment. Manufacture of the cold cream, cleansing cream, vanishing cream, and skin whitener has been discontinued.

BODY POWDER

About fifty readings recommended a special kind of body powder containing Peruvian balsam and zinc stearate. The powder was prescribed for irritations arising from skin rashes and was mentioned in cases of acne, eczema, pruritus (itching), psoriasis, and shingles.

BONCILLA PACKS AND MUDD

Mudd is a substitute available for the boncilla clay recommended in eight readings for use in facial packs. The main ingredient in the boncilla preparation was a special type of clay known as Fuller's Earth Somerset—fuller's earth having a particular spectrum of minerals. It was only available in a particular section of England, and the supply has now been exhausted. Mudd also consists of fuller's earth, but from a different source.

Boncilla was not the only type of clay pack mentioned in the readings, however, for there were over forty references to packs of mud, clay, and fuller's earth. These packs were to be applied over various parts of the body as a part of treatment for a wide range of disorders, including complexion problems, spinal lesions and subluxations, and paralysis.

Mudd packs, based on fuller's earth, or natural hydrated aluminum magnesium silicate, possess a unique capacity for absorbing fats and oils. Clay packs were also valued by Edgar Cayce for their astringent qualities.

CALAMUS OIL

Calamus oil was recommended as a massage ingredient in about eight readings involving a variety of conditions which included arteriosclerosis, aftereffects of birth injuries, epilepsy, neuritis, paralysis, Simmonds' disease, and spinal subluxations.

CALCIDIN

Calcidin was a trademark for a calcium iodide compound containing fifteen percent iodine. It was a source of iodine as well as calcium, and was sold as an aid in loosening thick bronchial mucus. Recommended in about 130 readings, Edgar Cayce prescribed Calcidin for lung problems, particularly asthma and tuberculosis, and also in cases of cold and congestion, coughs and bronchitis.

Calcidin has been discontinued by its manufacturers. However, calcium iodide and iodized calcium, generic substances similar to Calcidin, are still available.

CALCIOS

Calcios was recommended in about two hundred readings. In Edgar Cayce's day, it was a formula that was made from pulverized chicken bones, processed so that the calcium they contained could be easily digested and assimilated. In the present formula, bone meal, which is uniform and sterilized, has been substituted. Calcios is high in protein and is also a source of iodine.

Cayce prescribed Calcios as a dietary supplement for tuberculosis, poor assimilations, pregnancy, and glandular imbalance.

Calcios contains the digestive enzymes pancreatin, pepsin, and hydrochloric acid. Cayce believed that taking Calcios regularly would assist the entire digestive process, improving the body's ability to assimilate nutrients from foods.

CALOMEL

Calomel is another name for mercurous chloride, a white tasteless powder which was formerly used as a purgative and as an alterative and antisyphilitic. Edgar Cayce recommended it to about twenty-five individuals, most often as a worm medicine and eliminant.

Since calomel is a mercury compound, it is extremely poisonous. Today it can only be obtained through chemical supply houses.

CAMPHORATED OLIVE OIL

The readings most frequently mentioned camphorated oil as an ingredient for treatment of scars, either alone or in combination with other oils. Some readings noted that camphorated oil should be prepared from camphor and olive oil rather than the then commercially available camphorated cottonseed oil. The readings indicated that this substance would have a soothing influence on scarred tissue.

The readings also noted that although camphorated olive oil will work quickly on newer scars, it can also be used effectively on older ones, provided treatment is patient and consistent.

As Cayce explained: "If he wants to relieve much of the scar tissue on the left limb, we would use sweet oil (olive oil) combined wih camphorated oil (equal parts). Massage this each day for three to six months and we would reduce most of this" (487-15). Because of FDA regulations, camphorated oil cannot be purchased but can be prepared by heating four ounces of olive oil and adding one ounce of camphor and stirring until the camphor dissolves. It must be labeled as poisonous.

CAROID LAXATIVE

Caroid Laxative tablets have evolved from the original Caroid & Bile Salts, which were recommended in about ninety readings. The formula now contains only two of the original five active ingredients: phenolphthalein, a chemical having laxative properties, and cascara sagrada, a laxative herb.

The original Caroid & Bile Salts were recommended primarily in cases of poor eliminations and toxemia. It was found to effectively stimulate the liver, gall duct, spleen, pancreas, and colon.

Since the formula only contains two of the original ingredients, it no longer offers such a wide spectrum of benefits. The new formula is now only a laxative. As with all preparations of this type, Caroid Laxative tablets should not be taken indefinitely, as this could lead to a dependence on laxatives. The readings suggested that their use be gradually discontinued.

CARRON OIL

Carron oil, which is no longer available, was a liniment consisting of equal parts limewater and linseed oil. Also known as "lime liniment," it was first made in Carron, Scotland, where it was found useful in treating burns acquired by workers in the Carron ironworks. It was an ingredient found in three massage formulas mentioned in the readings.

CASTILE-BASED SOAP
AND COCONUT OIL SOAP

Castile soap was apparently preferred by Edgar Cayce because of its effectiveness as a cleanser and due to its gentleness to the skin. In Cayce's day, it was composed solely of olive oil and sodium hydroxide, but today vegetable oils often replace the olive oil.

Coconut oil soap was recommended in one known reading, which advised "a thorough cleansing with any good toilet soap, preferably that prepared with olive oil, or coconut oil rather than other characters of fats" (3051-3).

CASTOR OIL

Palma Christi, or palm of Christ, is another name for castor oil. Cayce found a great many uses for the oil, although he rarely suggested using it as a cathartic. In fact,

there were only a few cases in which internal dosage was
endorsed, while other readings advised strongly against it. As
Cayce noted: "Castor oil taken internally, and such eliminants
are only purgatives. Hence the castor oil absorbed from the
packs will be better than taking same internally" (1433-6).

Castor oil was given a great variety of external applications, however. A mixture of castor oil and baking soda
was advised for application on calluses of the feet, moles,
ingrown toenails, and warts. In about fifty readings, castor
oil was recommended for use in massage, including application for calluses, cancer (skin and breast), cysts, bunions, ichthyosis, moles, tumors, and warts.

The use of castor oil in the form of packs, however, was
advised most frequently and was indicated for cholecystitis, poor eliminations, epilepsy, various liver conditions,
and scleroderma. It was also advised for headaches, appendicitis, arthritis, incoordination between assimilations
and eliminations, colitis, fever, intestinal disorders, incoordination between nervous systems, neuritis, and toxemia.

The following reading offers general instructions for use of
the packs: "Heat the oil; dropping two, three to four layers of
flannel in same, wring out and apply directly to the body. Well
that dry heat [heating pad] be kept over same during the
period of an hour or the like when the packs are on the body.
Bathe off the body afterwards, of course, with a weak
[baking] soda solution, to cleanse the body from the acidity
and from the natural secretions that arise from same" (1034-1).

Castor oil packs were generally to be applied over the right
abdomen according to specific cycles, such as three days of use
alternated with three or four days of rest. The treatment suggestion was an hour and a half in the afternoon or at bedtime.
A dose of olive oil was generally to be taken on the third day
of each cycle.

CASTORIA (FLETCHER'S)

Castoria is a mild laxative consisting of senna in a syrup
base. It was suggested in approximately 150 readings for

children and adults with sluggish excretory systems.

The readings explained that the active properties in Castoria would be absorbed into the system, thereby sweetening the gastric flow, toning the digestion, softening the lobes of the liver, aiding the gallbladder, and cleansing the entire intestinal tract. Moreover, this cleansing would not cause any undue strain on the system.

Cayce found Castoria useful in congested or toxic systems, where rapid drainage was needed. Other uses include baby care, colds, colitis, liver problems, and worms.

CEREALS

The most frequently mentioned cereals in the readings were cracked wheat and steel-cut oats. Edgar Cayce emphasized that these cereals should be cooked a long time to make them easily digestible and that citrus or citrus-fruit juices should not be served at the same meal as cereals.

CHAMOMILE

The herb chamomile was frequently recommended by Cayce as a stimulant and digestive aid. It was mentioned in about twenty readings dealing with stomach ulcers, psoriasis, and indigestion, among other discomforts. Often chamomile tea was to be alternated with others, such as saffron tea and elm water. All of these herbs were regarded as digestive aids, capable of easing intestinal complaints.

CHARCOAL TABLETS

Charcoal tablets were prescribed in about fifteen readings for digestive problems and flatulence. The brand recommended by Cayce is no longer available. However, other brands of charcoal tablets are a possible substitute.

CHARRED OAK KEG

Part of a rather unorthodox form of inhalation therapy, recommended about fifty times for persons with certain types of lung disorders, involved the use of a one- or two-gallon charred oak keg. This treatment, which was recommended primarily in cases of tuberculosis, pleurisy, and scleroderma, advised placing one hundred proof apple brandy in the keg and then inhaling its fumes regularly.

Inhaling fumes from brandy was considered beneficial, as Cayce believed the inhalations not only destroyed living tubercle germs, but had other beneficial effects as well. These included stimulating the circulation and rejuvenating cells of the lungs.

As he explained: "The activity on this is not only for the destruction of live tubercle tissue, but it acts as an antiseptic for all irritated areas; also giving activity to cellular forces of the corpuscle itself. It acts as a stimuli to the circulation, then, recharging each cell as it passes through areas so affected by the radiation of the gases from this fluid itself'' (3176-1).

Inhalation was also intended to aid in purifying the liver and kidneys, curb coughing, and heal damaged lung tissue.

CIGARETTES

A study of the approximately 120 readings indexed under cigarettes and smoking reveals a complex subject. In the majority of cases, Edgar Cayce condoned smoking in moderation, although he noted that most individuals who developed a need for smoking also developed an addiction.

The readings emphasized that while smoking in moderation would not be harmful in certain instances, excessive smoking would be harmful to everyone.

The readings also found that certain varieties of cigarettes are better than others for the body. Although there were a few instances where a particular brand was recommended, most readings simply expressed a strong preference for cigarettes made from pure tobacco rather than those containing various commercially utilized additives. One reading suggested using cigarettes made from untoasted tobacco.

CIMEX LECTULARIUS

This is a good illustration of the premise that even the most useless seeming creatures in nature may have value. The product, which was recommended about ten times in the readings for dropsy, phlebitis, and nephritis, is a homeopathic remedy made from bedbugs. Cimex Lectularius, which is the scientific name for the bedbug, was mainly suggested for dropsy, a swelling of the feet, ankles, and lower extremities, caused by infiltration of the tissues with diluted lymph fluid. Edgar Cayce found that this product would reduce swelling and also create an adrenal reaction that would be helpful to the heart. This product should be used under the direction of a physician.

CINNAMON WATER

Cinnamon is the dried bark of several species of *Cinnamomum,* which is native to Ceylon and China. It is used as a carminative (digestive aid) and aromatic stimulant. These properties are due to a volatile oil which is the active ingredient of cinnamon water.

Cinnamon water was recommended in over ninety readings dealing with poor assimilations, digestive problems, and especially nausea. It was almost invariably recommended in combination with limewater and frequently with iodide of potassium and/or bromide of potassium as well.

Cayce found that both limewater and cinnamon water would function as digestive aids.

CITROCARBONATE

Citrocarbonate, a granular effervescent salt, was recommended basically as an alkalizer for the alimentary canal. Mentioned in about sixty readings, it was to relieve upset stomach and gas and reduce the body's susceptibility to congestion.

CLARY WATER (5480-1)

This formula was suggested in approximately one hundred cases involving various problems associated with the digestive and excretory systems, including disturbances in the hepatic circulation. Similar formulas were recommended for enlarged or engorged spleens. Clary water was most often recommended for diabetes and as a general stimulant to the system.

This tonic is off the market at the present time, as an important ingredient is ambergris, which is commercially unavailable. For those interested, a typical formula for clary water is found in reading 1739-1.

COCA-COLA SYRUP

Coca-Cola syrup in plain water acts as an alkalizer and diuretic. It was mentioned in about twenty-five readings, most of them cases involving kidney and bladder disorders.

As Cayce noted: "To be sure, Coca-Cola is helpful to the kidneys, but if taken, use the Coca-Cola syrup in plain water—and this to the body will not be very palatable" (2332-1).

The readings advised using pure Coca-Cola syrup. A typical dose consisted of one-half to one ounce of syrup in a glass of water. This was to be taken no more than two or three times a week.

COCOA BUTTER

Cocoa butter is derived from cocoa beans. It was recommended in about 185 readings as a massage ingredient, to be used either by itself or in combination with other substances. It was suggested for a variety of conditions, including baby care. The parents of one child were advised to daily "massage the spine well with cocoa butter; not so much as to become disturbing, but sufficient that the properties may be absorbed by the system. Also massage this down the limbs, especially the underside... This as we find should keep the baby in its correct developing stages" (2289-1).

COCOA BUTTER AND QUININE OINTMENT (5188-1)

This formula was given for a young staff sergeant in the U.S. Air Force during World War Two, who requested a physical reading from Edgar Cayce. One of his questions was: "Have I any trace of malaria; how can it be prevented?"

Cayce responded: "Occasionally do massage along the spine with cocoa butter; that is, an ounce in which there has been put five grains of quinine, mixed thoroughly. Massage this along the spine, under the arms and in the groin. Not only will the mosquito not bite but there will be no malaria. These are not as an omen but are those influences which will keep the body in attune with the infinite" (5188-1).

This product is not commercially available but can be prepared at home by melting an ounce of cocoa butter and stirring in the contents of a five-grain capsule of quinine sulfate.

CODIRON

Codiron was a dietary supplement recommended for a little over one hundred individuals. Its body-building qualities were most frequently recommended in cases of gener-

al debilitation, poor assimilation (and elimination), anemia, toxemia, and congestion.

Presumably this product, which is now off the market,
was a combination of cod liver oil and iron. The name was
later changed to Adiron.

COLDS LINIMENT (2036-6)

In approximately 285 readings, a liniment was prescribed consisting of equal parts of mutton tallow (at
times called mutton suet), spirits of camphor, and spirits
of turpentine. Some variations included the addition of
tincture of benzoin or other substances. This liniment
was suggested primarily in cases of cold and congestion,
poor circulation, and kidney disorders. The readings
explained that the mutton tallow would penetrate the
skin and open its pores, thus allowing the healing
properties of the turpentine and camphor to be quickly
absorbed.

In cases of colds, attention to the feet and lower extremities was particularly stressed. Often the application of heat
in combination with the liniment was advised.

"We would also rub these [substances] over the lower
portion of the feet, bottoms of the feet, toast them, as it
were, before the fire or before any heat that will make for the
drawing of the circulation towards these portions" (304-33).

COLITIS TONIC (2085-1)

This formula for colitis has been found to be typical of
the many readings in which such a tonic was recommended.

The ingredients contained in the formula are wild ginger, wild ginseng, lactated pepsin, and stillingia.

COLONICS

Various methods of cleansing the colon were included as part of treatment in a large number of readings. Colonics and enemas were the method most frequently advised to help increase the effectiveness of other treatments, both in cases of illness and for general upkeep of physical health and balance.

In general, colonics were advised whenever they were needed, and prescribed use ranged from twice a week to once every six months, with the average recommendation being once every six weeks. An occasional colonic was suggested for almost everyone.

Edgar Cayce's recommendation for colonic irrigations was that the water used be body temperature, with the first water containing about a teaspoon each of baking soda and salt to each half gallon of water. A tablespoon per gallon or the same amount per quart of Glyco-Thymoline was to be added to the last water used.

This treatment was not designed to correct the original causes of the imbalances, but to cleanse the intestines, thereby reducing irritation and pressure.

COUGH SYRUP (2431-29)

Cayce recommended this formula to soothe the lungs and bronchial passages, act as an expectorant, and heal the irritations causing the cough.

The formula contains syrup of wild cherry bark, syrup of horehound, syrup of rhubarb, elixir of wild ginger, honey, and alcohol.

As Cayce noted: "The taking of those properties indicated for allaying of cold and congestion—as in the cherry, the horehound—will not only aid digestion but stimulate the circulation for the upper portion of the head and through the bronchial area, thus giving a better flow of circulation for the throat and gums" (808-3).

CRUDE OIL

The Edgar Cayce readings offer hope for the effective prevention and treatment of falling hair by safe and natural methods. Cayce considered both internal and external aspects of the causes and treatment of baldness in a total of ninety-two readings given for sixty-five individuals.

The most frequently mentioned topical applications were crude-oil, Vaseline, and grain-alcohol solutions (generally twenty percent). These were all aspects of the same treatment in some instances and were recommended separately in others.

Other topical applications suggested included pine tar soap (shampoo could be substituted), olive oil shampoo, Listerine, and in cases of female hair loss, hog lard. The use of Listerine as well as the alcohol solutions was in many cases especially recommended for those with dandruff.

Reading 636-1 suggested that a crude-oil treatment be given two or three times a month, following the crude-oil application with twenty percent grain alcohol and Vaseline. This reading also suggested a diet high in iodine to stimulate the thyroid gland.

DANDRUFF FORMULA (2611-2)

This particular formula appeared only once in the readings, although differing versions involving various strengths of diluted grain alcohol were mentioned many times as part of treatment for dandruff.

This formula contained eighty-five percent grain alcohol and pine oil added to distilled water.

D.D.D.

This was a topical preparation recommended in about fifty readings for skin irritations such as dermatitis and pruritus, leg ulcers, psoriasis, eczema, hookworm, insect bites, hives, and poison ivy. No longer on the market, it was available as a liquid, cream, or soap. (See Ray's Ointment.)

DIATHERMY

Diathermy, a treatment that uses a high-frequency electrical current to produce heat in the tissues and organs of the body, was once a common form of electrotherapy used by physicians and hospitals.

There are three forms of diathermy: long-wave, which produces a current of moderately high frequency; shortwave, which uses high-frequency current and produces deep heat in a localized area; and the newest form, microwave diathermy, which is a single beam of extremely high frequency electromagnetic energy focused from a distance on the region to be treated. Both the long-wave and shortwave methods were apparently available in Cayce's day. Because the conventional high-powered form of long-wave diathermy interferes with AM radio reception, production of this type of machine was discontinued by international agreement around 1954.

Diathermy was referred to as "deep therapy," and was recommended in a total of 110 readings. It was advised in cases of incoordination between the autonomic and cerebrospinal nervous systems, spinal subluxations or misalignments, glandular imbalances, impaired circulation, and poor eliminations.

DOBELL'S SOLUTION

Dobell's solution is a sodium borate solution. Cayce recommended its use in six readings as a nasal cleaner, gargle, and eyewash.

DOG-ON-FOOT

This was a foot cream recommended in three cases of athlete's foot. It contained salicylic acid, benezoic acid, and a substance called "thymic acid." Possible substitutes are Ray's Ointment and Cayce's athlete's foot lotion.

DOVER'S POWDER

Dover's powder is a diaphoretic (perspiration inducer) and sedative recommended in readings for forty-five individuals. It is available only by medical prescription and contains ipecac and opium. Ipecac is an expectorant, diaphoretic, and stomachic; opium, a narcotic which dulls pain and produces sleep.

Cayce recommended Dover's powder primarily as an ingredient in particular herbal laxative preparations and as a sedative.

ELECTRIC VIBRATOR

Massages with an electric vibrator were suggested in approximately 375 readings as part of a variety of treatments. The main purpose of these treatments was to stimulate the circulation in sluggish areas and relieve tension and establish balance in the superficial circulation. The vibrator was also used by those following the crude-oil treatment for baldness.

Recommended most frequently in cases of subluxations of the spine—incomplete dislocations or sprains—Cayce said: "To correct the system we only need to produce the vibration necessary to make the equalization of the nerve pressure through muscular forces over the system, and we will correct or bring the normal forces to this body" (4101-1).

ELIMINATIONS STIMULANT
(4288-1)

This herbal tonic was recommended in a reading for a woman with high blood pressure. Cayce attributed her condition to poor eliminations which had created an excess of toxins in the blood and, as a consequence, increased the blood pressure.

The tonic was to stimulate the eliminations and normalize her blood pressure. As Cayce explained: "This is to produce elimination through the kidneys and carry functioning through the system to relieve through the dross, see." This would "give full balance to the system and make the body efficient in its physical force" (4288-1).

This formula contains sarsaparilla root, wild cherry bark, burdock root, mandrake root, buchu leaves, grain alcohol, and balsam of tolu.

ELIXIR OF LACTATED PEPSIN

Cayce mainly recommended pepsin as an aid to digestion and assimilations and in case of incoordination between assimilations, acidity, toxemia, and colitis.

ELLIOTT TREATMENT

This technique was intended to produce a high localized temperature through the use of water, and in Cayce's day it was used medically for certain pelvic inflammatory diseases and in rectal prostatic conditions.

The Elliott machine consisted of a water-heating container, a motor-driven pump, and gauges and valves for the control of temperature and pressure. Rubber vaginal and rectal applicators were placed in the body after enemas and colonics, then the introduction of water would produce a mechanical distension of up to three or four pounds of pressure, or whatever was comfortable for the patient. The temperature would begin at slightly above body heat and rise to 103 or 135 degrees Fahrenheit. Treatments usually lasted half an hour and were given three times weekly. This machine has fallen into disuse today. (See Violet Ray.)

ELM WATER

Edgar Cayce mentioned elm water in about 125 readings, primarily for individuals with poor assimilations, psoriasis, and stomach ulcers. It is prepared by adding a pinch of the powdered slippery elm bark to a glass of cool water and waiting five minutes before drinking. Cayce's advice was, "Do not make the elm water until it is ready or just before it is ready to be drunk, for this is easy to become rancid" (348-6).

The physiological action of the elm bark was to coat and heal the lining of the stomach and intestinal walls.

ENO SALTS

In the approximately 170 readings mentioning Eno salts, Cayce at times recommended the variety containing fruit salts (citric acid). However, only the regular variety is still available.

ERLANGER TREATMENT

This was an electrical method of treating visual disorders about which very little is known. Edgar Cayce once referred to it as a "direct current to the eyeball," and once as a low galvanic current. Another reading recommended the Erlanger treatment to stimulate the nerves and centers of optic impulses in the spine, which suggests that this was a method of stimulating the optic nerve. This method is no longer used. (See Violet Ray.)

EYE TONIC

Edgar Cayce recommended herbal tonics for many and various disorders, and eye problems attributed to poor digestion and poor elimination were no exception. The formula given in reading 3810-1 contains sarsaparilla root, yellow dock root, burdock root, black haw bark, prickly ash bark, elder flower, and balsam of tolu. The reading was for a sixty-year-old woman suffering from toxemia who had been blind for over a year.

While taking the tonic, the woman was advised to have sweat baths, which Cayce believed would distribute the medicinal properties throughout the body. Also suggested were dietary measures as well as use of the electric vibrator to stimulate the system.

This treatment, Cayce claimed, would restore her sight to normal in nine weeks. Reports accompanying a series of readings for 3810 indicated that her condition did improve.

Users of the tonic may prefer to take it cyclically—three weeks on and one week off.

FOOT FORMULA (555-5)

A formula recommended for a man with an infection on his foot contained four ounces of mineral oil, two ounces of witch hazel, one ounce of rubbing alcohol, and three to five minims of oil of sassafras. The formula was to be shaken well and used in small portions at a time. Cayce's advice was to begin with the hips and rub down to the feet. He claimed that the formula would be good for anyone who spent a lot of time standing.

FORMULA 636

This tonic is the only formula of its kind in the Cayce readings. Although it was originally recommended as an aid to restoring natural color to gray hair, based on reports from users, it seems to have a direct balancing and energizing effect on the system, even among individuals who have no complaint about their hair color.

The formula is a combination of herbs and other substances such as lactated pepsin, liver extract, ginseng, and black snake root, that are high in vitamins and minerals.

FOWLER'S SOLUTION OF ARSENIC

Fowler's solution of arsenic is a potassium arsenite solution containing one percent arsenic trioxide. It is a prescription item formerly used in the treatment of leukemia and other disorders, such as malaria, chorea, and skin diseases.

This preparation was recommended by Edgar Cayce in fourteen readings given for eleven individuals. Apparently it was regarded as a blood purifier, useful in cases of poor eliminations, incoordination between the assimilations and eliminations, and poor circulation. Dermatitis and other skin problems were frequently involved in these cases.

Since too much arsenic is poisonous, extremely small doses taken in definite cycles were suggested by the readings. As Cayce explained: "As is understood, arsenic is a slow poison, in small quantities, as this, but it is also an element that will work with the gastric forces in the duodenum, and especially in the lacteal glands" (394-10).

GEMS AND MINERALS

Edgar Cayce believed that gems and stones could be helpful influences in both mental and spiritual respects, as well as on the physical well-being of individuals.

One reading advised carrying a piece of carbon steel in the front pants pocket, claiming that its influence would protect the user against colds, congestion, and mucous membrane disorders.

Lapis lazuli was recommended in several readings as a bringer of health and strength to the body. The stone was preferably to be worn next to the skin.

GINSENG

Wild ginseng was recommended in about thirty-five readings. It is an herb that was never suggested by itself, but always in combination with other herbs, such as in Formula 636 and the colitis tonic. *Wild* ginseng was always emphasized and as Cayce explained: "Wild ginseng . . . [is] an essence of the flow of the vitality *within* the system itself. It is an *electrifying* of the vital forces themselves" (404-4).

GLYCO-THYMOLINE

According to its manufacturer, Glyco-Thymoline is today primarily sold as a cosmetic mouthwash because of FDA regulations. Formerly it was sold as a treatment for mucosity as well as for smoker's cough, sore gums, false teeth or partial dentures, halitosis, superficial cuts, allergies, diaper rash, feminine hygiene, poison ivy, hives, insect bites, and sunburn. The manufacturer reports that the formula has not changed since Cayce's day, although the label has.

In the readings, Glyco-Thymoline was referred to 810 times in a variety of ways, such as an intestinal antiseptic, a refreshing application for tired or irritated eyes, and in the application of packs in a variety of other conditions that included kidney problems, pelvic disorders, spinal problems, injuries, and nasal and sinus congestion.

According to Cayce: "There should be a systematic series of osteopathic adjustments. However, each time before these adjustments are made—which should be twice a week—we would relax the area to be adjusted by applying heavy packs of Glyco-Thymoline" (3157-1).

GOLD CHLORIDE

Gold chloride, at times referred to as gold chloride sodium by Cayce, is a solution of gold chloride dissolved in distilled water and is perhaps best known for its use in conjunction with the Radio-Active Appliance and the Wet Cell Appliance.

Many readings stated or implied that it was best to add gold chloride to the system vibrationally by means of the above-mentioned appliances rather than by injection or ingestion. However, there were also about 190 readings recommending small amounts of gold chloride taken internally in combination with bromide of soda or bicarbonate of soda in water.

The gold-and-soda solutions were recommended most frequently in cases of arthritis. Since gold chloride is poisonous when taken in large quantities, it is recommended that a physician be consulted before taking this product.

GRAIN ALCOHOL
(TWENTY PERCENT SOLUTION)

The Cayce readings mentioned twenty percent grain alcohol solutions five times as a portion of treatments outlined for hair and scalp problems such as baldness, falling hair, graying hair, and dandruff. A twenty percent solution contains approximately one part 190-proof (ninety-five percent) pure grain alcohol to four parts distilled water. It was specified that only grain alcohol be used, never denatured (rubbing) alcohol or wood alcohol.

GROVE'S CHILL TONIC

This remedy, labeled Grove's Tasteless Chill Tonic, appeared around 1900 as a remedy for malaria, chills, and fever. Off the market now, it contained cinchona, or "fever bark," which Cayce recommended as a natural source of quinine, along with iron and lemon flavoring in a syrup base.

Cayce recommended this tonic about twenty-five times, primarily in cases of malaria.

HEADACHE REMEDY

This formula was given in a reading for a person suffering from severe headaches and contained equal parts of spirit of camphor and tincture of lobelia. It was to be applied to the temple to ease the pain.

HELIOTHERAPY

Heliotherapy referred to treatments that used various kinds of light or radiant energy. Shortwave ultraviolet and infrared light are components of natural sunlight, and each received frequent recommendations in the readings. Cayce believed in the health-giving qualities of moderate exposure to sun and recommended light treatments or heliotherapy for similar reasons. In fact, natural sunlight was at times regarded as the first choice and the light treatments as the best available substitute. In these cases, the light treatments were only to be given on days when exposure to the sun was impossible, such as during cloudy or inclement weather.

Shortwave ultraviolet-light treatments were recommended for over four hundred individuals and were most often mentioned in conjunction with treatments for tumors and in cases where there was a predisposition toward malignancies. The treatment was also suggested in cases of spinal subluxations and lesions, blood imbalances such as anemia, tuberculosis, poor eliminations, toxemia, arthritis, general debilitation, and injuries.

Infrared-light treatments were mentioned for a little over one hundred individuals, also for a variety of physical disorders, such as injuries, problems with assimilation, circulatory and bone disorders, nervous system disorders, and general debilitation.

HERBAL SPRING TONIC
(5450-3)

In March 1930, Edgar Cayce gave a formula for an herbal tonic for general-purpose seasonal use. It was designed to purify the system. It is the only herbal formula in the readings that was generally recommended for everyone as a "spring tonic."

The nineteen-year-old female for whom this tonic was suggested was suffering from acne, boils, and other skin eruptions, which Cayce found to be internally caused. The formula contains sarsaparilla root, wild cherry bark, yellow dock root, dogwood bark, dog fennel, prickly ash bark, balsam of tolu, sassafras oil, and tincture of capsicum.

"HONEYIDA" WATER
AND PLUTO WATER

Two mineral salts mentioned in the readings and used as laxatives were Hunayadi (spelled Honeyida in the Cayce transcriptions) and Pluto Water. The former was a purgative mineral water of Hungarian (Cayce said Austrian) origin, named for the locality where it was obtained; and the latter consisted of water to which magnesium sulfate (Epsom salts) and other minerals were added. Pluto Water originated from the French Lick Springs Hotel, French Lick, Indiana, and was occasionally referred to as French Lick Water. Both are apparently no longer available.

Hunayadi Water was mentioned fourteen times in the readings and Pluto Water twelve.

ICHTHYOL

Ichthyol is a particular variety of the substance called Ichthammol, an ointment made by chemical breakdown and treatment of certain types of asphaltic rocks. Considered an antiseptic ointment for skin diseases, Cayce prescribed it about twenty-five times, particularly for bedsores and scleroderma and also in cases of eczema, dermatitis, pruritus, and infections.

INHALANTS (2186-1)

Instructions were given in approximately 225 readings for preparation of inhalant formulas to aid respiratory problems, including asthma, bronchitis, coughs, colds, emphysema, hay fever, pleurisy, pneumonia, postnasal drip, sinusitis, and tuberculosis. Depending on the condition involved, the formulas varied from case to case.

Basically, the inhalants recommended consisted of pure grain alcohol to which small amounts of substances known as stimulating expectorants, which included oil of eucalyptus, rectified oil of turpentine, tincture of benzoin, tolu balsam, rectified creosote, and oil of pine needles, were added. The fumes arising from the solution were to be inhaled as often as necessary for relief.

According to Cayce: "First we would prepare the inhalant, that there may be the antiseptic reaction from the gases for the throat, bronchials, lungs, that not only heal but that prevent accumulations from poor circulation through the muco-membranes of throat, nasal, bronchi, and the forces in the soft tissue of face, from becoming infected from these drosses. But it will aid also in keeping down the tendencies for the circulation to be so active through these portions" (421-8).

The ingredients mentioned in the readings for inhalants are derived from plants. The fumes are most effective when inhaled regularly several times a day. Care should be taken to inhale only the fumes and not the liquid.

INNERCLEAN

Innerclean, an herbal laxative compound, was suggested in about twenty-five readings where improved eliminations were desired. The ingredients of this formula remained unchanged for about fifty-five years, until 1977 when new

FDA regulations forced the manufacturers to eliminate agar-agar and Irish moss from the formula.

IODEX

Plain Iodex, the kind that Cayce recommended, contains iodine in an ointment base. This product was recommended about thirteen times in the readings for boils, carbuncles, dermatitis, bruises, eczema, and bedsores. One reading stated that it would also relieve the tenderness of bruises.

IPANA TOOTHPASTE

Although Ipana brand of toothpaste may actually still be available, the version recommended by Edgar Cayce in seventeen readings is no longer being made. This version contained prickly ash bark, a substance Cayce felt was beneficial to the gums.

IPSAB

Ipsab, mentioned in approximately seventy readings, was designed as a preventive of and remedy for periodontal disease or pyorrhea. As Cayce noted: "The receding gums and those tendencies towards pyorrhea would be allayed by the consistent use of Ipsab as a massage for the teeth and gums. Also these should be treated, some locally, with the dentist's paraphernalia—[as well as] the small wads of cotton saturated with the Ipsab and applied in the areas where the conditions are indicated at the base or edge of the gums" (3696-1).

Many readings prescribing Ipsab also gave directions for making it, with the formulas varying somewhat from reading to reading. A few stated that the finished product should be a paste, but the majority referred to it as a liquid, and a specific formula was given by Cayce for general use. If desired, a paste may be easily made by adding salt in sufficient amounts to the liquid.

The complete Ipsab formula contains prickly ash bark,

salt, calcium chloride, peppermint, and iodine. The primary active ingredient, prickly ash bark, was known to the American Indians as toothache bark, and Cayce at times referred to it by the same term.

JERUSALEM ARTICHOKES

The Jerusalem artichoke, at times known as a "sunchoke," is a native American variety of sunflower which was cultivated by some American Indians. The Jerusalem artichoke is a small tuberous vegetable which looks like fresh ginger, crunches like a carrot, tastes sweet and nutty, and has fewer calories than the potato. One theory explaining its identity with Jerusalem is that it developed from the Italian word "*giragale*," which means "to the sun."

Cayce recommended this vegetable for improving assimilations and eliminations and as an alternative to insulin injections for diabetics. To avoid overstimulation of the pancreas, Cayce advised that children be given artichokes that were smaller in size.

According to Cayce, Jerusalem artichokes were best eaten in salad or cooked, and some readings suggested that these methods of preparations be alternated. When cooking, the readings advised preparing the artichokes in Patapar Paper. Generally, a hen's-egg-size piece (about two ounces) was recommended for an adult at one meal.

KALDAK

Kaldak was a nutritional supplement recommended by Edgar Cayce in about eighty readings. It was primarily to be used in cases of general debilitation and also for anemia, arthritis, and poor assimilations.

Cayce advised its use as a tonic to increase the number of red blood cells by supplying iron, phosphates, silicon, and B complex vitamins to the system. This product was made by the KalDak Company of Lansing, Michigan. It is now off the market. A possible substitute is a vitamin B complex syrup with iron.

LAUDANUM AND ACONITE

Both laudanum and aconite are prescription drugs. The former is another name for opium tincture; the latter an extremely poisonous drug which is a cardiac, respiratory, and circulatory depressant that acts as a diaphoretic, antipyretic, and diuretic. Cayce recommended that these substances only be used externally. In about eighty readings, combinations of the two were suggested as a topical application for the temporary relief of chronic, severe pain.

These medications were advised for a wide variety of disorders, including cholecystitis, sciatica, neuritis, injuries, arthritis, spinal problems, and appendicitis. The place of application varied with the nature of the disorder and the site of the pain.

LAXATIVE CAPSULES

The number of ingredients in these preparations ranged from two to six in various combinations and proportions. The formula given in reading 294-12 contained the four most frequently mentioned herbs—podophyllin (mandrake), licorice, cascara sagrada, and black root (leptandrin). Other herbs mentioned less frequently in such formulas were sanguinaria and senna. These capsules are not commercially available, but may be prepared by a pharmacist.

LIMEWATER

Limewater, a mild antacid, is a saturated solution of slaked lime (calcium hydroxide) in water, which was recommended in a total of about 125 readings, either alone or in combination with other ingredients. (See Cinnamon Water.)

LIQUID LANOLIN

Lanolin in liquid form was recommended in about 165 readings but never prescribed by itself. Rather, it was to be used in combination with other ingredients in a variety of massage and lotion formulas. It is included in the formulas for skin lotions, scar formula, and the arthritis massage formula, among others.

According to one reading, lanolin soothes the skin and, when combined with other oils, prevents them from causing any irritation.

LISTERINE

Listerine, a well-known antiseptic, currently contains alcohol, thymol, eucalyptol, methyl salicylate, menthol, and benzoic acid. It is intended for use in oral hygiene and as a topical application for minor cuts, scratches, insect bites, and infectious dandruff.

Edgar Cayce recommended Listerine in sixteen readings as a hair and scalp treatment and to counteract dandruff, which Cayce attributed to poor circulation.

LITHIA WATER

Lithium is a light, chemically active metal which has reported therapeutic uses going back to ancient Greece, where the water of certain mineral springs, known for their power to soothe madmen, contained high levels of lithium.

Cayce recommended lithia water, or water enriched with a salt of lithium, primarily as a kidney purifier. In the approximately forty readings on this topic, Cayce found this water to be beneficial in cases of poor eliminations and toxemia.

In Cayce's day, lithia water was prepared by dissolving a lithia tablet in a glass of water. This amount was to be taken occasionally or at specific intervals, such as once a month, once weekly, or every other day. In a severe case of ulcers and one of psoriasis, all of the water taken into the system was to contain either elm or lithia, or elm, lithia, or saffron, respectively.

MASSAGE FORMULA (1968-7)

One reading contained a formula for a general all-purpose skin lotion that is one of Cayce's best-used products. The reading claimed that an occasional massage with this formula would stimulate the superficial circulation as well as help keep the body beautiful and free from blemishes.

The original formula contained peanut oil, olive oil, lanolin, and rose water. The commercially available formula is the same, with the exception of the rose water and the addition of a small amount of vitamin E. The rose water was omitted due to the fact that it spoils easily, and when in combination with oils it appears to cause them to grow rancid more quickly.

MILK OF BISMUTH

This digestive aid is a suspension of bismuth hydroxide and bismuth subcarbonate. It was recommended in almost 275 readings, primarily to assist the digestive processes in cases of acidity, problems with the assimilations and eliminations, cholecystitis, colitis, stomach and intestinal problems, liver problems, and toxemia, among other disorders.

The bismuth was generally to be taken in conjunction with other treatments (often alkalizers or eliminants), and was often combined with other substances as well.

MILK OF MAGNESIA

Milk of magnesia, a permanent suspension of magnesium oxide in water, is used as an antacid and laxative. Cayce recommended it in over 170 readings for both of these purposes. There are many brands of milk of magnesia available.

MULLEIN

The herb mullein was mentioned about fifty times in the readings. Edgar Cayce found it particularly valuable as an aid for varicose veins. Either the fresh or dry herb was to be used, but whichever version was chosen was to be taken consistently.

One reading recommended mullein tea in combination with daily walks to help reduce swelling of limbs caused by pregnancy. It was also recommended as an aid to circulation and kidneys.

Mullein leaves were also used in the form of stupes or poultices. In some of the cases of varicose veins, this application was recommended in addition to taking the tea internally.

As Cayce advised: "We would apply the mullein stupes now more to those areas that are the sources from which the limbs receive their circulatory activity, and those portions about the limb to reduce the swelling. Apply these about once a day, and for about an hour" (1541-6).

MUTTON TALLOW

Cayce never recommended the use of mutton tallow alone, but always in combination with other ingredients such as those found in the colds liniment formula. Recently, however, a new use of this substance has been developed by Hazel G. Drexler, Ph.D. After three years of informal observations, Dr. Drexler reported that when pure mutton tallow is applied over the solar plexus area or the entire abdomen, it has a markedly calming effect on both children and adults.

Dr. Drexler noted that she first used the mutton tallow in this manner on herself at the suggestion of Genevieve Haller, D.C. The mutton tallow relieved an aching solar plexus associated with what could best be described as an attack of negative emotions. She was so impressed with the results that she subsequently recommended its use to a number of friends and acquaintances who were under various kinds of stress. The mutton tallow seemed to reduce negative emotions and stress connected with "insomnia, anxiety, irritability, fear, aching solar plexus, pain of hiatus hernia, nervous tension, hyperactive behavior, upset emotion, and obsessive thoughts."

Dr. Drexler's observations were given mention in the ARE Clinic's *Medical Research Bulletin*.

MYRRH TINCTURE
AND OLIVE OIL

Myrrh tincture is an alcoholic solution containing myrrh, a fragrant extract of gum resin from trees in the Red Sea coast forests. A few readings suggested it for internal use, but it was more commonly recommended as a massage ingredient. Cayce believed that myrrh was good for the muscles and stimulated the superficial circulation through its absorption by the pores of the skin. He explained: "Tincture of myrrh acts with the pores of the skin in such a manner as to strike in, causing the circulation to be carried to affected parts [scars, in this case]" (440-3).

Myrrh also received several recommendations as a fume bath ingredient. In massage, myrrh tincture was almost invariably recommended in combination with olive oil. Instructions for preparing this combination were to warm the myrrh in a pan and then add an equal amount of olive oil. Since the combination, once heated, will not keep for more than a few days, only a few ounces should be prepared at one time.

NUJOL

This is an extra-heavy mineral oil which is used medically as a laxative. It is a mixture of liquid hydrocarbons obtained from petroleum, and it is odorless and tasteless at room temperature.

Edgar Cayce suggested this substance for external rather than internal use—as an ingredient in massage formulas. Nujol was recommended in readings for 62 individuals, and its counterpart, Russian White Oil, which is no longer available, for 162 individuals. Since a number of readings at the time suggested Nujol as an alternative to Russian White Oil, these recommendations are summarized together.

The massage formulas of which heavy mineral oil was an ingredient were used to treat a wide variety of disorders. Those most frequently mentioned included spinal subluxations, paralysis, impaired locomotion, multiple sclerosis, poor eliminations, nervous incoordination, Parkinson's disease, glandular problems, general debilitation, polio, neuritis, and problems with the feet.

OCCY-CRYSTINE

Occy-Crystine is a laxative and cathartic which was mentioned in twenty-four readings. The saline combination of sodium thiosulfate and magnesium sulfate (Epsom salts) has both cleansing and alkalizing properties.

This substance was most often suggested to stimulate poor or imbalanced eliminations, improve the assimilations, and stabilize the acid-alkaline balance of the body. These three functions were viewed as being closely interrelated.

Occy-Crystine was generally to be taken until the system was thoroughly cleansed and alkalized. Usually this meant taking it once daily in the morning before meals for a period of several days.

ODORS AND SCENTS

Edgar Cayce often referred to the importance of odors and scents. He once noted that "there is no greater influence in the physical body . . . than the effect of odors upon the olfactory nerves" (274-7).

The impact of odors and fragrances, according to the readings, can be either positive or negative, making for spiritual stimulation or sensual indulgence. However, in general they were regarded as a spiritual force, "For odors are necessary, else would they have been given to the rose, to the violet, to the lilac . . . to those things that show the beauty of a loving heavenly Father? Then they have their place" (1402-1).

Generally, particular fragrances were intended to act as helpful influences or as aids to mental clarity or spiritual attunement. Since the type of influence was apparently determined by past life associations, choosing a helpful odor was naturally regarded as a very individual matter. However, several were mentioned frequently enough that they may have some general application.

Lavender, mentioned seven times, was regarded as a spiritual influence and meditation aid. In two of these instances, lavender was recommended together with orris root to help raise the vibrations.

Sandalwood, mentioned six times, was regarded in three readings as a mental and spiritual stimulant, with two other readings advising against its use.

Orris root was mentioned in five readings as a spiritual or helpful influence, twice with lavender and twice in combination with a violet scent. Oriental incense received four recommendations as a mental or spiritual stimulant or as a helpful influence. Cedar was suggested in three readings for all of the purposes mentioned above.

Scattered references throughout the readings were given to other herbal and flower fragrances.

OLIVE OIL

Olive oil, a light oil pressed from ripe olives, has historically had a variety of uses, among which are as a nutritive food, a laxative, an emollient application to wounds and burns, a liniment ingredient, a fuel, a cosmetic medium, and an ingredient in soap. In medicine, it was formerly used in the treatment of gallstones and as a remedy for intestinal worms.

Cayce recommended olive oil for both internal and external purposes. As a food and internal medicine, olive oil received close to five hundred recommendations. Cayce recommended it as a laxative because it was considered a most valuable food for the intestinal system.

Internal doses of olive oil were recommended for a variety of physical problems, including cholecystitis (inflammation of the gallbladder), poor assimilations, toxemia, epilepsy, intestinal and liver disorders, adhesions, lacerations, constipation, general debilitation, and acidity.

External application of olive oil was recommended close to nine hundred times, making it the most frequently recommended massage oil in the readings. According to Cayce, olive oil not only softens the skin but is also "one of the most effective agents for stimulating muscular activity, or mucous membrane activity that can be applied to the body" (440-3).

OLIVE OIL SHAMPOO

Olive oil shampoo was mentioned about ten times, making it the most frequently recommended shampoo in the readings. It is similar to castile shampoos, which were originally based on olive oil, and some readings used these terms interchangeably. No particular brand was ever suggested.

Olive oil shampoo was at times suggested without explanation; however, other readings implied that it was beneficial to the scalp because the oil opened the pores. As Cayce explained: "For this particular body, use olive oil shampoo, for there is needed the oil for the scalp and the opening of [the pores of] same. Cleanse the scalp with some good cleanser, preferably tar soap, and then apply the olive oil shampoo" (3379-1).

Additionally, a few of the readings noted cosmetic benefits from using olive oil shampoo. One commented that it would make the hair shine, especially if a few drops of olive oil were added to the water as well. Another reading claimed that if the shampoo was used once a week, it would keep the hair light in color.

PASSION FLOWER FUSION

An infusion (water extract) of the passion flower vine, also known as maypop and mayblossom bitters, was recommended in over ninety readings.

Edgar Cayce regarded this preparation as the best sedative for epilepsy and also recommended it in cases of nervous incoordination. Cayce noted: "The passion flower effect is upon the sympathetic nervous system. It is to relinquish the congestions that are produced in the attacks of incoordination at the base of the brain, through the flexure as indicated which is produced through the areas along the spine, and in the adhesions in the area indicated." (2153-5).

According to Cayce, passion flower was non–habit forming and was recommended often as a substitute for sedatives such as Phenobarbital and Dilantin. The herb was also believed to be better for the muscles and capillary circulation as long as a proper diet was followed to avoid congestion in the intestines. Cayce noted that care should be taken to avoid taking passion flower at the same time as other sedatives.

More information was offered in other readings which explained that passion flower influences the sympathetic nervous system, helping to normalize impulses between the glands at the base of the brain and the hypogastric nerve center, which controls digestion and assimilation. In the process, it also affects the blood supply, gall duct, and certain areas along the spine.

Passion flower may be taken as a tea when occasional sedation is desired.

PATAPAR PAPER

Now called vegetable parchment, this product is a nontoxic, tasteless, and odorless sheet of specially processed paper which is grease resistant and keeps its strength when wet.

In readings advising vegetables in the diet, Patapar Paper was frequently recommended for use in cooking, with the vegetables tied in a dampened sheet of the paper and placed in simmering water until done. This method retains valuable vitamins and minerals.

As Cayce explained: "The vegetables that are taken should be preferably cooked in their *own* juices, as in Patapar Paper. This will make a vast difference in the building of resistance" (861-1).

PEANUT OIL

Although there were no mentions of peanut oil for internal use in the readings, hundreds of readings recommended its use in massage, both by itself and in combination with other oils. As of 1948, before the indexing of the readings had been completed, these preliminary statistics were reported: Peanut oil as an ingredient in massage formulas was recommended in forty-nine out of fifty-nine cases of arthritis, in fifty out of sixty-three cases of polio studied, in nine out of fifteen cases of multiple sclerosis studied, and in forty out of fifty assorted cases of paralysis studied.

The readings specified the use of only "pure Peanut oil." Peanut oil massages were advised in a variety of illnesses, among which was the case of a woman suffering from menopausal symptoms. Cayce noted that a rub once weekly would be exceptionally beneficial for her. He also added that those receiving a weekly peanut oil massage need never fear arthritis. Cayce also believed that massages would generally supply energies to the body as well as improve the circulation and relieve tension.

PHOSPHATE OF SODA

Phosphate of soda is sodium phosphate, a colorless or white granular salt used as a mild saline cathartic. It is available in plain or effervescent varieties. In the effervescent kind, citric and tartaric acids and sodium bicarbonate are added to make it more palatable.

Edgar Cayce recommended phosphate of soda in about one hundred readings. Many did not specify a particular brand, but Fleet's, which contained sodium biphosphate and sodium phosphate, was suggested in about twenty-five cases.

Phosphate of soda was suggested as an eliminant in a variety of conditions, including acidity, incoordination between the assimilations and eliminations, bacillosis, and toxemia. For these, Cayce often recommended the use of the plain (presumably noneffervescent) variety. A typical dose was half a teaspoon stirred into a half glass of water and taken in the morning before meals. At times, several drops of syrup of sarsaparilla (five drops, generally) were to be added to this dose. Also, in several cases, the addition of a drop of turpentine oil or a similar substance was to be added either occasionally or every third day or dose.

For cases involving cholecystitis or inflammation of the gallbladder, Cayce recommended Fleet's Phospho-Soda. In these and other instances, it was part of a specific procedure designed to drain the gall duct of sediments and stimulate and normalize all the abdominal organs.

PINE TAR SHAMPOO AND SOAP

Although pine tar soap was recommended in about seven readings, the shampoo was never mentioned, even though in each case the soap was to be used as a shampoo. It is possible that only the soap was available in Edgar Cayce's day and that the shampoo did not appear on the market until a later day.

Because of the antiseptic nature of pine oil, it was most frequently indicated for scalp treatments in conjunction with such applications as Vaseline, olive oil shampoo, crude oil, and diluted grain alcohol. One treatment for dandruff advised application of diluted grain alcohol followed by Vaseline and a thorough cleansing of the head with tar soap.

According to Cayce: "For the scalp [dryness] and for the hair, we find it would be well to have a thorough massage or shampoo with pure tar soap—at least once a week, and then to massage a little white Vaseline into the scalp after such a shampoo. This will materially aid the hair and produce a better condition there" (633-12).

QUININE

Quinine, a white, odorless, bitter-tasting powder, is an alkaloid obtained from cinchona bark. Its major medical use is in the teatment of malaria, although it is also used as an analgesic and antipyretic (fever reducer) for treatment of colds and fevers other than malaria. It is also employed as a bitter tonic in convalescence and as a stimulant to the uterus following childbirth.

The Edgar Cayce readings recommended several different forms of quinine, referring to quinine 16 times, quinine sulfate 10, cinchona or Peruvian bark 23, and calisaya 336 times. Quinine sulfate is the most popular salt of quinine and may be what Cayce intended for those individuals when a particular form was not indicated. Cinchona and calisaya are more natural sources, which were at times preferred for their mildness, as in one reading that described calisaya as "a mild form of sulfate of quinine" (4281-6).

Combining the references, quinine was recommended in ten cases of malaria and in a large assortment of other disorders. Its basic purpose was to stimulate the liver and spleen and assist in the elimination of toxins from the bloodstream, aiding the entire circulation and reducing the effects of congestion. One reading offered a more detailed description of its properties, with a cautionary note: "For the quinine is an active stimuli for a clarification of the blood stream, especially as to fermentations as are produced from any character of pus or bacilli as forms primarily in the circulation, coming directly from the liver or hepatic circulation; but too much of these may be made as harmful as it may be made beneficial" (340-1).

RADIO-ACTIVE APPLIANCE
OR IMPEDANCE DEVICE

An appliance referred to as the Radio-Active Appliance or Impedance Device was mentioned about 455 times in the readings. However, despite one of its names, there is nothing radioactive about it, at least not in terms of today's atomic age connotations. The term "Radio-Active" may have originated from the current or vibrationtheoretically produced between the appliance and body,which was viewed as being comparable to radio waves.

The Radio-Active Appliance, a battery for which many readings supplied construction details, does not by itself generate electrical current, although it was claimed to affect the electrical energies of the body. Edgar Cayce recommended it to improve the circulation and normalize the functioning of the nervous system, thus aiding in relaxing the body. It was suggested as a preventative more than a cure for serious physical disorders, although cases in which the appliance was suggested included the following, in order of frequency: nervous tension and incoordination, circulatory incoordination, insomnia, neurasthenia, debilitation, hypertension, abnormal children, deafness, obesity, and arthritis.

For curative purposes in special cases, a solution jar containing substances such as gold chloride, silver nitrate, tincture of iron, spirits of camphor, tincture of iodine, or Atomidine was attached to the appliance. In this manner, it was believed, certain needed elements in the solution would be transmitted into the body.

Cayce also held that the Radio-Active Appliance could bring renewed energy, improve the memory, and keep the body tuned into the creative forces. As he explained: "[The] Radio-Active Appliance [is] good for *anyone*, especially for those that tire or need an equalizing of the circulation, which is necessary for anyone that uses the brain a great deal, or that is unactive on the feet as much as is sufficient to keep the proper circulation" (826-3).

The readings stressed using the Radio-Active Appliance according to directions, including maintaining the proper attitude during its use.

RADIONICS

Radionics was mentioned in over forty readings and referred to a controversial diagnosis and treatment method involving devices known in Edgar Cayce's day as the Oscilloclast, the Abrams Machine, and (Cold's) etheronics. Its developer, the medical doctor Albert Abrams of San Francisco, devoted many years of research toward the scientific establishment of an "electromagnetic" basis for health and disease.

Abrams' device, popularly known as "The Black Box," could allegedly diagnose illness by contact with the patient or by a simple drop of the patient's blood. It could heal, even over distances, by broadcasting pulses of a type of radionic energy tuned to alleviate the particular disorder.

Abrams' electromagnetic theory closely paralleled Cayce's view of life as vibrational or electrical in nature. He frequently noted that "life is, and its manifestations in matter are of an *electronic* energy" (440-16). Cayce suggested radionics both for research and development and as an aid to physical health, especially in cases involving nervous incoordination.

RADIUM APPLIANCES

Edgar Cayce recommended Radium Appliances for 160 individuals. This type of therapy made use of healing properties in the radioactive element radium. The Radium Appliance consisted of a pad which was wrapped around the body, usually over the solar plexus area, and which could be worn during the day, at night, or both, as needed. The other appliance, Degnen's Lens, was a set of goggles which was worn over the eyes as a treatment for blindness and other eye disorders. Both items were charged with radium. The appliance could be recharged by placing it in strong sunlight.

The company that manufactured the devices is no longer in business, and the items are no longer on the market, although radium is used medically today in the treatment of cancer and other skin disorders. However, the manufacturer and Cayce had a broader concept of its use, recommending it for disorders such as general debilitation, spinal subluxations, toxemia, and some types of cancer and ulcers, as well as eye problems. The readings also recommended it to build the blood, rejuvenate the nerves, and raise the vibrations.

As Cayce noted: "In this body, then, the higher vibrations as would be found in the Radium Appliance, that gives new life, new blood supply to the physical forces of the body—creating a perfect coordination throughout the physical; thus allowing the mental and spiritual forces to manifest in the body" (4735-1).

RAGWEED LAXATIVE

Ragweed, also known as ambrosia weed, was mentioned by Edgar Cayce in more than 125 formulas. It was frequently mentioned as a tonic and laxative, but was also suggested at times as an aid to assimilations and eliminations.

The simplest ragweed tonic suggested was basically a tincture, a medicinal substance in a hydroalcoholic solution. It consisted of a tea made with dried ragweed leaves and distilled water to which grain alcohol was added.

Cayce also believed that a tonic made from fresh ragweed would help reduce susceptibility to hay fever. He explained that ragweed pollen aggravated certain nervous imbalances and that taking ragweed prior to the season when the plant blossoms could alleviate the bronchial and nasal reactions to the pollen.

RAY'S OINTMENT AND RAY'S LIQUID

Ray's products were formulated by a Roanoke, Virginia, chemist, Thomas Ray Wirsing, who eventually became involved in preparing medicines for individuals who had received special formulas in their readings. Ray's medicated products were recommended in about fifteen readings, primarily for cases of eczema, athlete's foot, dermatitis, and poison ivy. The ointment was recommended in the majority of the cases, while the liquid solution was suggested in cases of poison ivy and, in one case, of athlete's foot.

Ray's Ointment contains salicylic acid, phenol, zinc oxide ointment, pine tar ointment, resorcinol, sulfur ointment, petrolatum, and lanolin. Ray's Liquid contains sulfurated potassium, zinc sulfate, salicylic acid, phenol, and alcohol.

SAFFRON

Yellow, or American, saffron (*Carthamus tinctorius*) is an herb used at times as a natural dye and known primarily for its uses in cooking. It was recommended approximately 190 times as an aid to digestion. Cayce explained: "These properties [of saffron in water] as a tonic or stimulant in the assimilating system would produce and keep, with the digestive forces, the proper reactions as to prevent recurrences or disturbing conditions that have been indicated for this body heretofore" (556-16).

The frequency and duration with which saffron tea was to be taken varied from reading to reading. In one case, it was recommended once or twice daily for an indefinite period. Another individual was advised to take it in cycles of several days at a time, alternated with rest days, until conditions in the alimentary canal had noticeably improved.

SALT AND KELP SALT

Kelp salt was mentioned in about thirty readings, and in many of these instances "deep sea salt" could be substituted if preferred. Both salts are high in natural trace minerals, especially iodine. Kelp is a product derived from seaweed. Sea salt in Cayce's day was salt extracted directly from seawater rather than mined from deposits found on land.

The readings noted that kelp salt used as a seasoning for foods (corn bread and vegetables were mentioned) would add valuable elements to the diet and strengthen the body. Kelp salt and sea salt were recommended not only for general use but also in a variety of cases involving a lack of sufficient iodine in the system.

Salt was also suggested for physiotherapy, with hot salt packs being recommended in about eighty readings to relieve the pain of pelvic disorders and other problems. Also at times recommended were poultices of salt and apple cider vinegar for treatment of sprains and bruises. Equal parts of salt and baking soda were highly recommended as a tooth powder.

SCAR FORMULA (2015-10)

The Cayce formula now most frequently used as an application for scars was mentioned in only one reading, although variations of this formula were suggested in some of the other sixteen readings on scars.

The formula, consisting of camphorated olive oil, lanolin, and peanut oil, has been used for the removal of scars from severe burns and the treatment of burns themselves, as well as for the removal of stretch marks. FDA regulations have required that some commercially available versions of this formula be changed to have sightly less camphor and be an ointment rather than a liquid.

SIMMON'S LIVER REGULATOR

Simmon's Liver Regulator was a laxative formula containing ragweed and licorice that was recommended in about seventy readings. This product is no longer available. (See Ragweed Laxative.)

SINUSOIDAL RAY

This was an electric device which, according to one source, was never actually manufactured due to regulations regarding communications systems. It was, however, recommended in about 120 readings. Although there is some argument as to whether or not the sinusoidal was a form of diathermy, it is known that the sinusoidal ray was low in voltage—five volts at two amperes, with an oscillation varying up to a maximum of one thousand cycles. The device had metal plates which could be placed in contact with the skin and could apparently be applied by hand.

It was described in the readings in terms of reverse coil, alternating current, and deep therapy and was most often recommended in treatment of spinal lesions and subluxations. Its purpose was to "equalize and relax and stabilize the nerve impulses that control the muscular forces of the body" (1008-1). A possible substitute is diathermy, which is used by some osteopaths and chiropractors.

SKIN FRESHENER (404-8)

For the woman who asked for a good skin freshener, Edgar Cayce suggested a formula with an olive oil base to which small amounts of rose water, alcohol, and glycerin were added. This solution, which must be shaken well before each use, was termed a "skin invigorator."

SPIRITS OF CAMPHOR

Spirits of camphor is made by dissolving camphor, used medically as an irritant and stimulant, in alcohol. Mentioned in nearly 235 readings, it is probably best known as an ingredient in the colds liniment—in combination with equal parts of mutton tallow and spirits of turpentine. Spirits of camphor was recommended in other types of massage formulas in combinations with such ingredients as sassafras oil, cedarwood oil, Nujol, witch hazel, and olive oil.

Cayce gave spirits of camphor other uses, one being an application for the feet, particularly in cases of bunions, calluses, corns, and ingrown toenails. He explained: "This will tend to make the nails crumble at once or within the month; but then the new nails should come in normally, provided the other applications are kept up as indicated, and the changes wrought in the glandular activity by the diets outlined for the body" (2315-1).

Spirits of camphor was also recommended in the treatment of severe sunburn. Applications were to be made with cotton, followed an hour or two later by a lukewarm bath and the application of peanut oil. Another use was as an ingredient in fume baths.

S.S.S.

S.S.S. is a patent-medicine blood builder which is still available from the S.S.S. Company. Five readings recommended it as a tonic that would help build the red blood cell supply and improve digestion and assimilations.

Specific doses varied, with the general rule being small doses taken daily or less often.

ST. JACOB'S OIL

St. Jacob's Oil, once advertised as "the great German remedy for pain," is an analgesic liniment which was at times recommended by Edgar Cayce for ear problems. The ingredients were probably chloroform, camphor, oil of thyme, camphorated oil, and turpentine.

While this product is still on the market, the original formula has been altered by the omission of one ingredient. It should not be used in the ears.

SULFUR LAXATIVE COMPOUND (5016-1)

This formula, recommended in about forty readings, contains equal parts of sulfur, cream of tartar, and Rochelle salts. Instructions for preparation frequently stressed that the mixture be stirred *thoroughly* and often suggested that a mortar and pestle be used. Some readings suggested the use of Epsom salts instead of Rochelle salts.

According to the readings, the mixture acts as a mild laxative and blood purifier, or as Cayce explained: "This would be taken as a cleanser for the whole system" (1711-1). It was also mentioned in cases of boils and carbuncles, eczema, acne, psoriasis, and dermatitis.

SWEET SPIRITS OF NITER

Sweet spirits of niter is an alcoholic solution of ethyl nitrate known also as spirit of niter and spirit of nitrous ether. The solution was recommended for almost sixty individuals, primarily for kidney and bladder problems. It was recommended almost solely for its diuretic properties, as a stimulant, and as a cleanser which "taken occasionally will tend to clear the activity of the kidneys and the bladder" (601-25).

This product is no longer on the market. A substitute may be watermelon-seed tea, which contains niter.

SYRUP OF FIGS

A laxative preparation known as Syrup of Figs was suggested in over ninety readings. It contained extract of figs and, according to the readings, had a senna base. Because of its gentleness, this preparation was a preferred choice in cases where the eliminations needed stimulating. Cayce also regarded it as a stimulus to the assimilations which would "act with the gastric juices of the system and ...increase the flow through the alimentary canal" (378-7).

This product is apparently no longer on the market. A possible related product, Dr. Caldwell's Laxative (Glenbrook Labs), is available.

SYRUP OF SQUILL

Edgar Cayce recommended Syrup of Squill in about fifty readings, primarily in cases of colds and congestion, pneumonia, and poor eliminations. He also suggested its use as an aid to the respiratory system, as a decongestant, and occasionally as a cardiac stimulant.

Syrup of Squill is a prescription-only item available at pharmacies.

TANNIC ACID

Tannic acid is a yellowish astringent substance derived from several species of plants. Although it is used in tanning and dying, it also has several medicinal uses, one being as a local dressing for burns.

It was recommended for local application in two cases of burns to the face and eyes.

TIM (1800-20)

Tim is a compound which was recommended in about fifty readings, primarily for hemorrhoids, but also in a few instances of skin irritation, such as pruritus, eczema, abrasions, and boils. Recommendations were at times accompanied by instructions for preparation, and the formula given varied somewhat from reading to reading. The version developed for general use contains iodine and benzoin in a base of butterfat and tobacco.

TONICINE

Tonicine was recommended in about sixty readings, primarily for glandular imbalances and for conditions related to the "generative" organs such as menopause and pelvic disorders. This product, which is no longer on the market, was sold by Reed and Carnrick on a prescription basis. Although the ingredients are not known, one reading noted that it was made from "glandular secretions" or "glandular reactions." Formula 636, a glandular tonic, is a possible substitute.

TORIS COMPOUND

No longer on the market, Toris Compound was a laxative preparation recommended in about seventy readings, primarily for inadequate eliminations and toxemia. A possible substitute is Ragweed Tincture.

ULTRAVIOLET LIGHT

Edgar Cayce at times recommended the use of a shortwave ultraviolet light, which should not be confused with black light or the long-wave variety. One type frequently recommended was Burdick's, which was a mercury quartz lamp. In most instances, use of a one-quarter-inch sheet of green plate glass was suggested as a filter to block the ultraviolet rays.

No known source for the glass now exists, although

ultraviolet lights are still available and may be rented. A possible substitute for this treatment is exposure to sunlight. One reading advised reduction of treatments when sunlight was available. (See also Heliotherapy.)

VACCINES

Readings given for more than fifty individuals answered questions pertaining to preventive inoculations. These questions concerned both children and adults. It should be kept in mind, however, that Edgar Cayce's opinions on vaccines were based on those available in his day and might not be relevant to the advanced techniques and formulas available today.

On the question of what age to begin giving vaccinations, the readings generally advised avoiding them in the very young. The exceptions were a few readings recommending immunization against diphtheria, in one case at the age of eight months (in extremely minute doses) and in two cases at the age of nine months or older.

Another reading for a nine-month-old child stated that vaccinations should be avoided until the teeth had been formed. Cayce explained that ''with the disturbances that are produced in the system through the hardening—or the calling on the system for the necessary elements to build this in and for system, these would work [in the form of vaccinations or serums] a hardship on the general system, making for deformities in the teeth themselves. This may be seen in many instances where those of such activities have been given to the very young during such periods. Should there be exposure to such influences, then precautionary measures—or emergency measures—might be necessary. Under general or normal conditions, very much later in the years would be very much better for such in the system'' (299-2).

The age frequently advised for childhood inoculations was four and a half years or later. Immunization against smallpox, diphtheria, and whooping cough was advised for several children of seven and eight years of age.

On the usefulness of vaccinations, Cayce commented: "This is the best that can be said of vaccination—that it turns loose the poisons in the system and, if taken care of properly, may assist anyone having any glandular trouble. With this set loose, and the system set in correct eliminations, the assimilations become natural, see? Take advantage of same" (5566-3).

Comments made to adults contemplating various types of inoculations were more diverse than those for children. Those traveling to other countries were generally advised to accept the preventive measures that were required. In fact, a thirty-five-year-old man was told that if he entered the military service, the inoculations given him would actually eliminate many of his present physical disturbances.

VALENTINE'S LIVER EXTRACT

Valentine's Liver Extract is a liquid extract of edible mammalian liver, approved by the medical profession since 1929 for the treatment of pernicious anemia and related deficiency diseases. It is especially valued for its supply of B vitamins.

The plain version of Valentine's Liver Extract was mentioned in about fifteen readings. Edgar Cayce called it a blood and body builder, suggesting it primarily in cases of anemia and general debilitation.

Valentine's Liver Extract is an ingredient in Formula 636.

VEGETABLE JUICERS

Fresh raw vegetables and their juices were recommended in many readings, and about twenty advised the use of a juicer to extract the juices. The varieties of vegetable juices most often mentioned by Edgar Cayce were beet, carrot, celery, lettuce, spinach, and tomato. Beet juice was specified in some cases involving arthritis, neuritis, and muscular disease; carrot juice for arthritis, the eyes, and toxemia; and celery juice for the nerves.

VENTRICULIN

Ventriculin was recommended in about fifty-five readings, and Ventriculin with Iron in about forty. Both were manufactured by Parke-Davis until the mid- or late 1950s. A substance derived from the gastric tissue of hogs, it was used to stimulate the formation of reticulocytes (a type of red blood cell) and was recommended by the manufacturer as a specific for pernicious anemia. A powdered form that was taken orally, Ventriculin was mentioned by Cayce primarily in cases of anemia and a wide range of other conditions, including scleroderma.

VIOLET RAY

The Violet Ray, as this appliance was termed in Edgar Cayce's day, is basically an ultra-high-voltage, low-amperage source of static electricity. Today this appliance is more commonly referred to as a high-frequency device. It has a voltage output of about 50,000 volts with only a few milliamperes of current. Its frequency of over one million cycles per second makes it a mild form of diathermy, a treatment providing therapeutic heating of tissues beneath the skin.

The Violet Ray consists of a hand-held base into which a vacuum-glass applicator or "electrode" is inserted. The electrical current is diffused into rapidly vibrating sprays of deep violet color, giving the appliance its name.

Mentioned by Cayce approximately 925 times, the cases in which it was suggested as part of treatment were many and varied. The primary function of the appliance was to stimulate the superficial circulation. In the process, according to Cayce, additional beneficial effects could be obtained, including more restful sleep, greater physical stamina, improved eliminations, relief from nervous complaints, and a better balance throughout the system.

The Violet Ray was recommended in cases of eye problems, including cataracts, blindness, and myopia, and in cases of hemorrhoids, anemia, arthritis, pelvic disorders, and related problems, just to name a few. Concerning its use for anemia, Cayce commented: "To bring at the present time the better conditions to the body we would use those of the manipulation as applied by the hands rather than the vibratory forces, still using the electrical forces as would be applied from the Violet Ray, that we may bring more of the blood supply through the nerve reaction in and through the tissue in [the] exterior portion, as well as through the deeper tissue. Apply across the abdomen very thoroughly, that we may awaken the functioning of the liver, spleen, and those portions in the digestive tract" (979-3).

Duration of treatments varied widely from reading to reading and ranged from one to ten minutes. One individual was cautioned against overdoing a good thing and was told that one and a half minutes daily would be sufficient.

VITAMINS

Edgar Cayce viewed vitamins as "that from which the glands take those necessary influences to supply the energies to enable the varied organs of the body to reproduce themselves" (2072-9). Vitamins were recommended in over three hundred readings, although it must be added that in most cases these substances were to be obtained in their natural form, i.e., as food. Under normal circumstances, supplements were regarded as the "lazy way" to incorporate the needed vitamins into the system.

Cayce's manner of recommending vitamins and their sources varied. In some instances, he would mention certain vitamins that were especially needed and then name a number of good dietary sources. In other instances, he would simply name the vitamins without bothering to list their sources. Additionally, there were many more instances where detailed dietary guidelines were given without any mention of vitamins, although the need for certain elements was implicit in these recommendations.

In the instances where vitamin supplements were found advisable, they were always to be taken for limited periods of times, for their purpose was to correct an existing deficiency and stimulate the body's own ability to assimilate and synthesize these nutrients. For this reason, vitamins were generally to be taken in cycles, alternated with rest periods at regular intervals.

The vitamins recommended most frequently were the B vitamins, which received a total of close to 150 recommendations. Cayce valued B vitamins as a source of vital energy, once referring to B_1 as the "exercise or energy vitamin."

Vitamin D was recommended in more than forty readings and was regarded as another valuable source of vital energy to bolster the body's resistance to infection. Cayce regarded vitamin D as crucial to the building and maintenance of teeth and bones.

Vitamin A was suggested almost as frequently as vitamin D and was considered another energy supplier, a "sunshine vitamin" vital to the health of the eyes and kidneys. Additionally, cod liver oil, a substance high both in vitamins A and D, received over one hundred recommendations.

Surprisingly, vitamin C was mentioned only a little more than ten times, although its sources were recommended with great frequency. It was highly regarded as an element that gives the nerves stamina and vitality, helps keep the structural portions of the body healthy and intact, and "supplies the necessary influences to the flexes of every nature throughout the body, whether of a muscular or tendon nature, or a heart reaction, or a kidney contraction, or the liver contraction, or the opening or shutting of your mouth, the batting of an eye, or the supplying of the saliva and the muscular forces in face'' (2072-9).

In several cases, taking a multiple-vitamin preparation was preferred to taking supplements individually. This was to insure that the needs of the body would be met in a balanced manner, with nothing taken to excess.

WATERMELON-SEED TEA

Watermelon-seed tea, made from dried, crushed watermelon seeds, was recommended in the readings about seventy-five times. The readings commented that this diuretic source would help remove toxins from the system, remove water accumulations in the abdomen, reduce kidney and bladder inflammation, aid in relieving disturbances in the ovaries, and help avoid kidney problems from strain during pregnancy and following birth. As Cayce noted about the latter: ''The delivery [of the baby] should be normal, as we find, but there will be trouble with the kidneys unless proper precautions are taken to keep the activities well. Hence very small quantities of watermelon seed tea would be well, soon after the birth of the babe'' (951-7).

Instructions for preparing watermelon tea were to add one teaspoon of dried, crushed seeds to a pint of boiling water and then steep for about fifteen minutes. The tea was to be taken once a week or more frequently and was to be made fresh every few days.

WET CELL

The Wet Cell Appliance is a galvanic battery that produces a small but measurable electric current that is of a type that Cayce felt actually stimulated the growth of nerve tissue and connections between nerve tissues. The appliance was recommended in approximately 975 readings for a wide variety of physical and mental disturbances, including incoordination between the sympathetic and cerebrospinal nervous systems, retardation in children and adults, multiple sclerosis, insanity, arthritis, paralysis, Parkinson's disease, and deafness. As a general rule, the Wet Cell was suggested in conditions where the nerves had deteriorated and rebuilding was needed in order to function.

In most of these cases, specific solutions were to be included in the circuit to supply certain elements to the body through vibrations from the Wet Cell. The solutions most frequently used were spirits of camphor, gold chloride, silver nitrate, and Atomidine.

Cayce explained the workings of the Wet Cell in the following manner: "We find that any such solutions may be given to the body, as we have indicated, through this manner; causing the activity of same without passing through the system itself, for it may be directed to various organs of the system that are in need of such elements" (1800-25).

WHEAT-GERM OIL

Wheat-germ oil was suggested as a dietary supplement in approximately twenty-five readings. Especially valued for its vitamin E content, it was recommended for arthritis and physical alteratiᴏns involving the generative organs, such as menopause

Edgar Cayce believed that wheat-germ oil would be good for the nerves and for building energy when taken in small amounts. Generally, a dosage of one to two drops daily, taken cyclically, was sufficient.

WHITE COD LIVER OIL TABLETS

White Cod Liver Oil tablets were recommended in about fifty readings, primarily for body and blood building and as a dietary supplement for growing children. In a reading

for a child, Cayce advised the White tablets to help build
the body; and in a reading for an individual with toxemia,
Cayce commented that this supplement would add to the
blood, create oxygen in the system, purify disturbed lung
tissue, and aid the digestion.

WITCH HAZEL

Witch hazel is an alcoholic solution made from the
leaves of a particular genus of small tree or shrub. The
solution has mildly astringent properties and is at times
used as a liniment.

Cayce recommended the use of witch hazel in physiotherapy in just over 180 readings. By far the most frequent
recommendation was as an ingredient in fume or steam
baths. Apparently, Cayce found the astringent property of
witch hazel particularly effective when used in this fashion. These treatments were generally to be administered
once a week. The amount of witch hazel used in the
cabinet ranged from a teaspoon to two tablespoons added
to a pint of boiling water.

In several cases, witch hazel was also recommended for
rubdowns, as a topical application for the skin and for use
in packs. One reading described the benefits that would
result from a bath, a rub with a coarse towel, and a
massage using witch hazel and water: "These will aid in
alleviating the tautness as is seen in muscular forces, from
those conditions as have long existed there, and are being
gradually corrected—and this will make all adjustments
much easier. This will relieve the condition to the extent
where, were these given, that there may be the perfect
relaxation just before the body retires, and the insomnia
will disappear and the sleep will be beneficial" (2519-2).

WYETH'S BEEF, IRON & WINE

Edgar Cayce recommended a combination of beef extract, an iron supplement, and red wine in over fifty readings in cases of anemia, general debilitation, and other conditions where a building of resistance was needed. Although no longer available, Cayce recommended Wyeth's Beef, Iron & Wine most frequently. However, there are many other versions of this tonic on the market today.

ZILATONE

This is a laxative compound mentioned in about eighty readings for inadequate eliminations and related problems, such as cholecystitis, incoordination between the excretory functions, toxemia, and cases in which the liver needed stimulating. Its ingredients are bile salts compound, a digestive aid; extract of cascara sagrada, an herbal cathartic; pancreatin, used for its enzymatic action in various forms of digestive failure; white phenolphthalein, a laxative; pepsin, an animal extract useful in digestion of protein; and capsicum, a carminative. There have been no known changes in this formula since Cayce's day. It is interesting to note that several readings mentioned that Zilatone contained a mild heart stimulant. This may have been a reference to capsicum.

Treatments

Aids to Elimination

Poor eliminations were considered a common problem by Edgar Cayce, and he suggested many different treatments to improve them. These included enemas, colonics, laxatives, cathartics, diuretics, diet, exercise massage, spinal manipulation, hydrotherapy, and packs.

The readings viewed disturbed eliminations as a condition that affected the entire body, for the alimentary canal, intestines, colon, liver, kidneys, and perspiratory and respiratory systems are vital to the body's effort to eliminate waste products and toxins. A buildup of uneliminated toxic wastes in the intestines eventually affects the bloodstream as well. This results in the slowing of the circulation, further aggravating the situation.

Consequently, Cayce continually stressed the importance of all the excretory processes to maintaining good health. In fact, he believed that if eliminations and their counterpart, assimilations, were kept normal, life might be extended for a much longer period.

This was one reason why stimulating eliminations was only part of the suggested therapy in the treatment of disease. Cayce pointed out that it was wrong to associate poor eliminations only with constipation. Eliminations can actually be impeded in other parts of the body, even when evacuation of the bowels is regular, he noted.

Enemas and colonics were often recommended methods of internal cleansing, the former removing accumulated fecal matter from the lower bowels and the latter reaching even higher with its cleansing action.

Colonic irrigations cleanse the colon by mechanically pumping body-temperature water, which may contain other ingredients, into and out of the body. One reading stated that every person could benefit by an occasional colonic irrigation. However, the readings also advised against using colonics too frequently. A typical recommendation, under normal circumstances, was once every two or three months. Initially, small amounts of salt and soda were to be added to the water used, with Glyco-Thymoline added to the final rinse water. These substances were at times recommended for enemas as well.

Cayce believed that colonics and enemas helped keep the eliminations adequate through the intestines, and with minimal intervention helped in maintaining a balance between the assimilations and eliminations. They were recommended in a variety of disorders, included apoplexy, cystitis, varicose veins, colds, colitis, and constipation.

Also recommended by Cayce in a significant percentage of the readings were laxatives and cathartics. In addition to removing wastes from the colon, the process at times acted to aid the digestion and assimilations. Laxative preparations and their dosages were specifically tailored to meet individual needs. For example, a formula containing sulfur, cream of tartar, and Rochelle salts was supposed to improve the circulation in the alimentary canal and act upon the liver, kidneys, and respiration. This preparation was recommended for such disorders as acne, psoriasis, and obesity. Other preparations were supposed to act as antacids, gastric stimulants, or provide therapeutic benefits in addition to performing as a laxative.

The readings recommended laxatives with both vegetable and mineral sources, and to avoid strain or irritation they were frequently to be used alternately. Vegetable laxatives suggested included herbal compounds which were either available in drugstores or were to be prepared according to instructions given in the readings. Senna was one herb recommended for general use which is still available as an ingredient in Castoria. Olive oil was also highly recommended as a gentle laxative, as were Syrup of Figs, Zilatone, Innerclean, and ragweed tonics.

Most of the mineral-based eliminants suggested by Cayce are old drugstore remedies. They included Sal Hepatica, milk of magnesia, milk of bismuth, Eno salts, and phosphate of soda. Those prescribed laxatives by Cayce were cautioned to take them only when needed and for limited periods of time. Routine use could create a dependence on them and possibly irritate the system. Laxatives and cathartics were recommended for such disorders as arthritis, cystitis, epilepsy, obesity, bursitis, and indigestion.

Mild diuretics were suggested to alleviate excess water retention, alkalize the system, and stimulate and purify the kidneys. The two most often mentioned were watermelon-seed tea and Coca-Cola syrup in plain water. Watermelon-seed tea was recommended in the prevention and treatment of cystitis as well as other kidney and bladder disorders. According to the readings, watermelon seeds contain a form of niter that helps purify and clean the ducts of the kidneys. Coca-Cola syrup taken in noncarbonated, diluted form was considered a medicine rather than a beverage. Its use was advised for kidney and bladder disorders as well as for other problems. Also recommended was lithia water, a kidney purifier, which is made by dissolving a small amount of a salt from the mineral lithium in water. Also regarded as beneficial to the kidneys was drinking large amounts of plain water daily (six to eight glasses). The readings also recommended water as a laxative.

Despite the laxatives prescribed, Cayce considered a laxative diet preferable to the use of eliminants on a long-term basis. A laxative diet involved eating an abundance of fruits (figs and prunes especially), vegetables, and whole grains. Also recommended were fruit diets (apples, citrus) for those in need of more radical cleansing.

Additionally, various external treatments were recommended to stimulate the circulation and improve eliminations. These were exercise, massage, spinal manipulation, hydrotherapy, and packs.

Exercise was highly regarded by Cayce, as the activity promotes elimination through the pores of the skin. Further, he believed the rhythmic motion of walking could also directly benefit intestinal action.

Cayce basically regarded massages as a passive form of exercise for its stimulating effect on the muscles and circulation, which he believed promoted elimination through the pores of the skin. He also held that the use of oils in massage increased its effectiveness.

Spinal manipulation was recommended in cases where subluxations or lesions of the vertebrae were interfering with the nerve impulses and, hence, circulation to and elimination in certain parts of the body. In some instances, manipulation of the lower spine was recommended specifically for improving drainages.

Hydrotherapy was advised to stimulate the perspiratory system to eliminate toxins through the pores of the skin. This took various forms, including cabinet sweats, steam baths, and whirlpool baths.

Various packs were suggested for particular therapeutic purposes, with castor oil packs being advised specifically to assist the eliminations as well as improve the condition of the abdominal organs. A dose of olive oil was generally to be taken along with the treatment. Castor oil packs were almost a specific in cases of epilepsy, as well as other disorders.

The Cayce readings regarded eliminations as a function of the entire body rather than a single area. Viewed in this way, it is understandable why proper eliminations were regarded as a key to good health and how the various treatments worked together to stimulate particular parts of the process.

Diet

Specific dietary recommendations were outlined in most of the Edgar Cayce readings and form the basis for a diet that is appropriate for general application, both in sickness and health.

According to Cayce, poor diet was one of the primary sources of disease, and as a consequence a nourishing and well-balanced diet was the number-one treatment for many of the illnesses and "dis-eases" which concerned him.

To Cayce, an important aspect of diet was the maintenance of a proper acid-alkaline balance within the system. He held that the normal diet should contain a ratio of eighty percent alkaline-forming foods to twenty percent acid-forming foods, and that a highly alkaline diet could help strengthen resistance to disease and remove systemic toxicity. In fact, he believed that a cold could not exist in the body with a sufficient alkaline level.

Broadly speaking, the list of alkaline-forming foods is composed of vegetables and their juices, fruits and their juices, and milk. The list of acid-forming foods, on the other hand, is composed mainly of starchy foods and protein sources. These include grains and their products (cereals, bread, pasta, rice, etc.), some legumes, eggs, nuts, meat, fowl, fish, and sugar.

These are only generalities, because some foods are more acid or more alkaline than others. A few are actually neutral or in between, and there are exceptions and qualifications in every category.

A major means of adding to the body's alkalinity, as well as supplying roughage and nutrients, is a daily raw vegetable salad. This was preferably to be eaten at the noon meal, and soup, bread, or crackers could be included. Large amounts of lettuce and cabbage were highly recommended means of purifying the bloodstream. Other raw vegetables, including carrots, celery, and green peppers, are also sources of vital nutrients. Gelatin was often suggested as a catalyst which would assist the assimilation of nutrients from salad vegetables. The juices of raw vegetables such as carrots and beets were also at times suggested.

Cooked vegetables were also highly recommended and were generally to be the major portion of the evening meal. Considered especially nutritious were vegetables of the leafy green variety (kale, spinach, turnip greens, beet greens) and those which are yellow (carrots, squash, corn, sweet potatoes). However, basically the whole range of cooked vegetables available could be eaten under normal circumstances, and most, though not all, of these are alkaline forming.

As a general rule, a ratio of three vegetables grown above ground to one tuberous vegetable grown below was suggested. Other highly recommended vegetables were vine-ripened tomatoes, Jerusalem artichokes, and, to purify the blood, cooked onions and beets. Vegetables were preferably to be prepared by steaming in Patapar Paper, a vegetable parchment, to preserve juices and vital nutrients. Often these juices were to be consumed as well.

Fruits and fruit juices are also alkaline forming for the most part, with the main exceptions being cranberries, plums, and large prunes. Citrus fruits and juices were highly recommended—especially orange juice. Stewed fruits (prunes, apricots, etc.) were often mentioned in morning menus. Also specified at times were pears, grapes (especially Concord), all yellow fruits (peaches, cantaloupes, apricots), and watermelon.

In general, all fruits commonly available were found to be beneficial, with the occasional exception of raw apples (these were often to be cooked) and bananas that were not vine ripened. Fruits were to be eaten at breakfast and between meals. At times, a fruit salad at the noon meal was suggested in place of a raw-vegetable salad.

Additionally, Cayce expressed a strong preference for fresh, locally grown vegetables and fruits when possible. Freshly picked produce contains more nutrients than that which loses its freshness through shipping. According to the readings, fresh, locally grown vegetables help acclimate the body to the "vibrations" of a particular area, making a person more in tune with his environment. Of course, even those fresh foods that are not locally grown are usually preferable to those which have been preserved in some manner. If foods are only available in a preserved form, there is evidence that suggests freezing generally retains more nutrients than canning.

Frequently suggested were milk drinks such as Ovaltine, malted milk, eggnog (using only the yolk and a little apple brandy or whiskey), and warm milk and honey at bedtime. Interestingly, honey is alkaline forming, unless in the comb.

The acid-forming foods are equally necessary for health, and their importance should not be ignored. Moreover, large amounts of starch and protein are probably needed during cold weather and when engaging in strenuous physical exercise.

Especially recommended for the morning meal were whole grains and their products in such forms as toast, hot or cold cereal, and pancakes. Of course, bread and crackers could be eaten at other times of the day as well. The grains most frequently mentioned were wheat, oats, cornmeal, rye, barley, buckwheat, and rice. Pasta was not highly recommended. Potatoes, beans, and peas were to be eaten only in moderation and picked fresh if possible. However, potato peelings, and the water in which the potatoes or peelings were cooked, were considered valuable sources of iodine.

Meat was recommended in moderation, most often in the form of the "lighter meats," such as fish, fowl, and lamb, rather than beef and pork. Seafood was especially recommended for its iodine content, which Cayce felt was important to normal glandular functions. Liver and other organ meats were at times suggested as blood builders. For most people, beef was recommended only infrequently or not at all, and generally pork was to be avoided, with the occasional exception of very crisp bacon. On the other hand, homemade beef juice was found to be a valuable body builder. Meats were most often recommended for the evening meal. They were to be served only a few times a week and were to be prepared by baking, broiling, or stewing— never frying.

The acid-alkaline balance was frequently involved in Cayce's rejection of certain foods which he considered health hazards. These included beer, hard liquor in general, carbonated beverages, all fried foods, meat fats, vinegar, refined flour and white sugar, sugar-and-starch combinations (cake, pastry, etc.), and excessive amounts of any stimulant (such as coffee and wine). Cayce believed these foods interfered with the physical balance and eliminating them from the diet could prevent illness from occurring as well as help eliminate existing problems.

So far as the seasoning of foods is concerned, kelp salt and sea salt were preferred to other types of salt because of their iodine content. To avoid losing nutrients in foods, salt was always to be added after rather than during cooking. A little butter could also be added at this time. As a rule the use of black pepper was not advised. Condiments were generally not recommended, nor was vinegar, a highly acidic substance. The most preferred form of sweetener was honey, followed by beet, grape, and raw cane sugars. Sweeteners were always to be used moderately.

Also highly recommended was an ample fluid intake. A general suggestion was six to eight glasses of pure water daily to aid in the elimination of toxic wastes from the kidneys. Cayce also advised drinking half to three-quarters of a glass of lukewarm water each morning on arising to help clear the kidneys. In general, large amounts of water are best taken between meals rather than with them.

One dietary principle often ignored by nutritionists but dominant in the readings concerns the benefits and detriments of certain food combinations. One combination considered beneficial was a small amount of red wine taken with dark whole-grain bread. This was usually to be eaten in the afternoon between meals and was recommended as a blood builder. Also considered highly nourishing at the same time of day was eggnog, prepared by combining a small amount of whiskey with the yolk of an egg before adding the milk. A cooked breakfast cereal containing figs, dates, and cornmeal, known as "mummy food," was recommended as an eliminant and source of essential nutrients.

According to Cayce, serving citrus fruits or juices at the same meal as either cereal or milk (or milk products) was not advised. Citrus fruits, he believed, were more beneficial when accompanied by foods such as eggs and perhaps rice crackers. Of course, other fruits and juices could be served with milk and cereal.

Cayce frequently suggested alternating citrus and cereal days and drinking milk and citrus juices on alternate days. Combining sweets (sugars) with starches was considered especially harmful to the system, and to a lesser degree combining starches with meats or with other starchy foods at the same meal was viewed as harmful. Coffee or tea with milk or cream was not advised.

In particular instances, Cayce recommended special diets, one of which, the apple diet, involved eating raw apples and drinking plenty of water for three days. This was for the specific purpose of cleansing the intestines. The only other substance to be taken during the three days was, perhaps, a little coffee or tea. On the evening of the third day, up to half a cup of olive oil was to be taken to speed the removal of toxins from the body.

Recommended especially for obesity was drinking a small amount of diluted grape juice a half hour before meals and before retiring. This was intended to satisfy the craving for sweets without contributing to stored fat. An alkaline, easily digested liquid or semiliquid diet was emphasized during illness. Especially suggested for individuals with anemic conditions were orange juice, liver (or liver extract), and beef juice.

Proper food preparation was an important aspect of Cayce's preferred diet, which has already been covered to some extent. The frying of foods, especially deep frying, was never recommended, although foods such as eggs might be prepared in a little butter if the heat was not too high. Baking, broiling, stewing, and steaming (preferably in Patapar Paper) were considered the best cooking alternatives. (Cooking in aluminum pots was contraindicated, especially where acid foods such as tomatoes and cabbage were concerned.)

The readings took a somewhat unique position on the question of vitamins, noting that under normal circumstances these nutrients could be supplied through the diet. In those cases where supplements were needed, they were always to be taken in specific cycles of dosage and rest rather than on a continuous basis. According to Cayce, this would help the body make the most efficient use of the extra nutrients without becoming dependent on them to the extent that the body ceases to manufacture them itself.

Fasting

Fasting refers to a complete or partial abstinence from food. The Edgar Cayce readings recommended fasting, both for physical healing and spiritual attunement. Cayce held that true fasting was of the mind and involved a setting aside of self in order to become a clearer channel for creative and spiritual energies.

In his commentary on fasting, Dr. William A. McGarey, M.D., commented: "For prayer and fasting is not what man usually thinks of it—doing without food—but rather it is a man bringing himself to low estate, abasing himself in order that the creative force of God might be made manifest."

Cayce viewed fasting on a physical plane as therapy which could be used to detoxify the body and bring about adequate coordination of the organs and systems of the entire body. Fasting was recommended as treatment for poor diet, poor assimilations, poor eliminations, and incoordination between the sympathetic and cerebrospinal nervous systems. The apple diet was one suggested method of detoxifying the system.

Other related reasons were imbalances or toxins in the circulatory system, improper acid-alkaline balance, glandular malfunctions, and general congestion in the body. Since Cayce believed the diet was responsible for many physical problems, fasting was the logical way to restore balance in the body. According to Cayce: "Fasting means what the Master gave: laying aside our own concept of HOW or WHAT should be done at any period and letting the SPIRIT guide. Get the TRUTH of fasting! To be sure, overindulgence in bodily appetites brings shame to self, as overindulgence in anything. But true fasting is casting out of self any thought what WE would have done in becoming channels for what He, the Lord, would have done in the earth through us" (295-6).

Hydrotherapy

Edgar Cayce's hydrotherapy recommendations range from simple baths to cabinet sweats. Hydrotherapy—basically treatments that use water in various ways—is intended to stimulate circulation and help eliminate waste products, primarily through the perspiratory system, passing off toxins by way of the pores.

Hydrotherapy was also considered a gentle method of stimulating the eliminations, with less tendency toward unbalancing the system than many other methods. According to Cayce, its value lay not only in the treatment of illness, but in the maintenance of good health as well.

The types of hydrotherapy recommended by Cayce include Epsom salt baths, sitz baths, other baths, hot and cold showers, douching, cabinet sweats, steam baths, and fume or vapor baths. These will be explained below. Enemas and colonics might also be regarded as forms of hydrotherapy, but they are included in Aids to Elimination.

*Epsom Salt Baths—this therapy required that the individual be immersed in very hot water, to which Epsom salts had been added, for twenty to thirty minutes. The recommended amount of Epsom salts was usually a pound for each two gallons of bathwater. Hot water was to be continuously added to maintain a temperature as hot as possible without causing weakness. Fresh water was to be prepared for each bath, for the salt was intended to draw out toxins. For arthritic cases, for which Epsom salt baths were frequently recommended, the readings advised that the extremities be rubbed during the bath to further stimulate the circulation. Following the baths, a complete body massage was frequently advised. The residue from the Epsom salts was to be rinsed off prior to the massage.

*Sitz Baths—a form of bath with 110°-120° water, this therapy was intended to provide a localized increase in circulation. Only the hip area was to be immersed in the bathwater. Sitz baths were at times advised in the treatment of cystitis and hemorrhoids.

*Other Baths—these most frequently took the form of soaks for the feet, which were recommended for congestion and a number of other conditions as well. The soaks could be plain hot water or have other substances added. Dry mustard, for instance, was recommended for its stimulating qualities. Additionally, full baths could have various substances added.

*Hot and Cold Showers—this treatment, referred to as hot and cold needle showers at times, was only one facet of a hydrotherapy regimen. The purpose of the showers was to stimulate circulation and leave the body feeling energized rather than enervated, as can sometimes happen with heat treatments. This type of shower uses fine high-pressure jets of hot and cold water, rapidly alternated.

*Douching—a treatment for women involving cleansing the vagina with water or other liquid for the purpose of maintaining feminine hygiene or allaying infection. The substances most often to be added to the water were Glyco-Thymoline, an alkaline wash for excess mucus, and Atomidine, an antiseptic recommended to reduce inflammation and irritation of the glands of the reproductive system. Typical proportions were a tablespoon of Glyco-Thymoline or a teaspoon of Atomidine added to two quarts of warm, body-temperature water. Often these two solutions were to be used alternately. Douching was recommended for many types of pelvic disorders, including cystitis and oophoritis.

For one individual with cystitis, Cayce's treatment began with a mild cabinet sweat using dry heat, later adding witch hazel to boiling water to create a fume bath. This was to be followed by a hot and cold shower and then a thorough rubdown, using a combination of olive oil and oil of pine needles.

*Cabinet Sweats—these were referred to by several different terms, which are more or less interchangeable. All were means of inducing perspiration. A cabinet sweat could technically refer to the use of either dry or wet (steam) heat. However, Cayce expressed such a marked preference for wet heat that this was generally what was intended.

*Steam and Fume Baths, or Vapor Baths—these terms generally refer to one of the types of cabinet sweats mentioned by Cayce. Frequently, small amounts of various substances were to be added to the water so that they would vaporize and create a fume or vapor-bath effect. Substances recommended for this purpose included witch hazel, Atomidine, wintergreen, pine oil, Epsom salts, and others. Each had particular uses. For instance, witch hazel was the substance most frequently recommended in cases of arthritis.

This form of hydrotherapy was to be administered with the patient sitting in a cabinet which surrounded his entire body except for the head. If a steam cabinet was used, 110 degrees was the maximum temperature, and at times lower ones were required. A typical treatment duration was about ten minutes, although this could vary. In circumstances where cabinet treatments could not be obtained, alternatives which could be arranged at home were at times suggested. These involved sitting in a small, enclosed space, such as on a stool under a plastic blanket, and using a pan of boiling water on a hot plate to produce the fumes.

When high-temperature hydrotherapy was prescribed by Cayce, he sometimes cautioned the patient that the procedure should be carefully monitored by an attendant watching for signs of dizziness, fainting, or heat strain. Experts caution against the use of hydrotherapy involving high heat for the old or debilitated, or for those with high blood pressure or advanced heart conditions.

All hydrotherapy treatments were generally recommended in conjunction with other treatments and were often intended to facilitate their effectiveness. This was especially true for massage and manipulation, for the relaxing nature of hydrotherapy was considered ideal preparation for such treatments.

Cayce advised hydrotherapy as part of treatment in a wide variety of disorders. For instance, a series involving Atomidine therapy, Epsom salt baths, and massage was consistently recommended in the treatment of arthritis.

Hypnosis

Edgar Cayce called hypnosis "the subjugation of the mental-physical" (4506-2) or the "subjugation of the normal activity of the body" (567-2), a condition that was brought on in response to suggestions made by others or by suggestions made by the self.

Cayce recommended hypnosis and suggestion in over twenty-five readings as aids in healing various physical and mental problems. Generally, he recommended that hypnosis be induced under the guidance of a professional hypnotist, but noted that the individual could give the suggestions to himself or have them given by a close family member.

However, Cayce stressed that hypnotism or suggestion be given only with the very best of intentions for the subject. Cayce warned against self-aggrandizement and ego gratification, which can be manifested in those adept in mentally manipulating others. His treatment instructions were therefore very specific, and in one case he recommended hypnosis only by "one of the people that has a clean mind themselves" (4506-1).

The procedure required a sincere desire to heal and a

quiet meditative period. Generally, the suggestions were to be given at bedtime, when the subject (frequently a child) was drifting off to sleep. For Cayce, himself, who suffered from headaches, the readings gave the following suggestion, to be repeated: "The circulation will be equalized so as to remove all strain from any and every portion of the body. . . ." (294-4).

In reading 146-3, Cayce advised the mother of a deaf-mute, who was also an epileptic, to massage her child gently, making suggestions that his disturbances would be removed and that he would eventually become normal. Cayce told her to repeat, "May the self, the ego, awaken to its possibilities, its responsibilities, that, as I speak to you, in the normal waking state you will respond in that same loving careful manner that is given to you." It was not necessary to follow his words exactly; those giving the suggestions could develop their own, but to Cayce the important factors were to "appeal always to the inner being" (146-3) and to harbor no intention other than that of being helpful.

The subject's disposition was always critical in determining whether or not to use hypnosis or suggestion. In many readings, Cayce strongly advised against the use of hypnosis in healing because the subject was not mentally ready to receive the therapy. An example was case 567, who was undergoing electrotherapy; the combination of treatments being used for his body was not conducive to hypnotic therapy being added.

Massage

The Edgar Cayce readings recommended the use of massage in a large number of instances to promote health and healing. It was one of the most frequently mentioned treatments, recommended to stimulate the circulation, break up congestion by improving drainages, and relieve pain and tension by inducing relaxation, especially of the muscles along the spine. This physical therapy was also suggested to help maintain muscle tone and stimulate the glandular centers.

Depending on specific needs, a massage could be relaxing or stimulating and could either accompany a spinal adjustment or sometimes even take its place. The readings suggested that a massage could actually be viewed as a gentle form of manipulation, and some even recommended a combination treatment referred to as an osteopathic massage. Readings recommending a rubdown could probably be understood as a brief and stimulating treatment, whereas massage could be viewed as being relaxing and soothing.

Generally, the entire body was to be massaged, with special focus on the cerebrospinal or back area, where the circulation affects the nerve flow feeding various parts of the body. Cayce held that increased circulation to the spine by massage helped to stimulate the nerves to function normally. Often, specific areas were designated for special attention. For instance, for a person with head congestion, extra attention would be paid to the neck area.

To assist the normal flow of blood through the body, the motions of the massage were almost always directed toward the heart. Exceptions were made in cases of apoplexy (stroke) and some cases of arthritis, where the direction was away from the heart and toward the extremities. When massaging the spine, the use of a circular motion was often indicated.

Generally, massages were only one aspect of a complete treatment program, and were usually to be administered cyclically and often on an alternating basis with other therapies. Treatments viewed as more complementary to the functions of massage were usually other forms of physical therapy and included adjustments, hydrotherapy, heat, and electrotherapy. A massage could increase the effectiveness of an adjustment by relaxing tense muscles associated with stress and misaligned vertebrae. A massage could also be effective following hydrotherapy treatments such as sweats and steam or whirlpool baths. Heat treatments could also take the form of various kinds of packs applied before and after a massage. A relaxing rub was at times indicated after the use of an appliance such as the Radio-Active Appliance or Wet Cell.

An important aspect of massages was the variety of oils and other substances used during the treatment. In addition to providing necessary lubrication and keeping the skin moist and supple, some oils were found to have specific therapeutic purposes. Some were used as mild stimulants, some as counterirritants, and others to supply energy to the body. The most frequently suggested oil was peanut oil, which was to be used either alone or in combination with other substances. A specific use was in the prevention and treatment of arthritis. Olive oil and lanolin were other favorites, making the general-purpose olive oil, peanut oil, lanolin formula the most often recommended combination for massages.

Cayce also recommended other massage formulas for specific treatment programs, such as the formula given in two readings for the treatment of backaches, sprains, strains, swelling and bruises, and varicose veins. This formula contained olive oil, Nujol, witch hazel, tincture of benzoin, oil of sassafras, and coal oil (kerosene). A formula frequently suggested to relieve congestion and problems associated with the kidneys contained equal portions of mutton tallow, spirits of camphor, and spirits of turpentine. Another formula, this one widely used in the treatment of arthritis, contained mineral oil, olive oil, peanut oil, oil of pine needles, sassafras oil, and lanolin. A combination of olive oil and tincture of myrrh was recommended for a number of disorders, and other formulas containing camphorated olive oil were advised for scars. Many massage formulas were unique, and instructions for their use were quite specific.

Not every massage substance recommended by Cayce can be classified as oil, however. An unusual stimulating body rub was salt glow and involved rubbing the body with salt. This type of massage was at times suggested in the treatment of syphilis. It was to be preceded by a fume bath, using oil of wintergreen.

Only the amount of oil needed for the massage was to be poured into a saucer. This was to avoid contaminating the rest of the oil by contact with the skin. Instructions were to leave the oil on following the massage so it could be further absorbed by the skin. Any excess could be removed with towels, alcohol, and water.

Resting after a massage was strongly advised. In fact, the readings regarded bedtime as the ideal time for massage, as massage was considered a more beneficial manner of inducing restful sleep than drugs.

In a number of instances, massages using an electric vibrator were suggested. Cayce believed the vibrator could provide many of the same benefits as a manual massage. According to the readings, vibrator massages could help restore normal alignment of the vertebrae when applied along the spinal column. Additionally, Cayce believed the vibrator could stimulate and balance local circulation, aid the coordination of the assimilations and eliminations, as well as help coordinate the nervous system.

According to the Cayce philosophy of health, massage was a helpful addition to treatment programs for virtually every type of disorder.

Medicinal Herbs and Tonics

A variety of herbal remedies were frequently part of Edgar Cayce's treatments for a diversity of conditions. The Edgar Cayce readings had specific uses for certain medicinal herbs, some of which appear in herbal lore and others of which are quite unique. This section describes some of those herbs which received the most frequent recommendations and talks about their internal uses. Some of these were to be taken as a tea and others in tonic forms that contained four to eight different herbs.

Among those frequently recommended, which are mentioned in the pharmacology section of this book, are mullein, a common herb which was basically prescribed as a tea, especially in cases of varicose veins; ragweed, or ambrosia weed, recommended as a laxative, digestive aid, and tonic; Simmon's Liver Regulator, a proprietary laxative; yellow, or American saffron, mentioned as an aid to digestion; chamomile, suggested as a digestive aid; clary water, a tonic for problems involving the assimilations; and the passion flower herb, which was sometimes referred to in the readings as maypop or mayblossom bitters and was prescribed as an antispasmodic.

Others often recommended were senna and slippery elm bark. The former was often prescribed to those in need of a mild laxative. Medicinally, this herb promotes action in the bowels and acts as a vermifuge (to expel parasitic worms) and a diuretic (to increase secretion and flow of urine). According to the readings, senna is more than a laxative; it also stimulates the action of the kidneys, liver, and perhaps other systems of the body as well.

Senna was recommended both as a tea and as an ingredient in various laxative preparations. It is the active ingredient in Fletcher's Castoria, a proprietary children's laxative that was suggested in numerous readings for adults as well as children. A preparation containing senna pods, pumpkin seeds, Rochelle salts, alcohol, and honey was stated to be a good eliminant for anyone, any age.

Senna was recommended in readings dealing with a variety of disorders. In some cases of toxemia, senna was advised to increase the flow of lymph through the alimentary canal and thereby cleanse the system. For an individual with cystitis, senna was found to aid the digestion in such a manner as to affect the hepatic circulation.

Another herb widely recommended by Cayce was slippery elm bark, the inner bark from the slippery elm tree. According to herbalists, this acts as a mucilaginous (soothing to inflamed tissue) substance, which is useful externally as an emollient to relieve inflammation. Cayce basically recommended slippery elm bark internally, however, to soothe the stomach and aid digestion. It was suggested primarily in cases of poor assimilations, psoriasis, and stomach ulcers. In a few instances, pieces were to be chewed and dissolved in the mouth. For one individual with psoriasis, this activity was intended to benefit the pylorus, duodenum, and salivary glands. The more frequent suggestion was to drink elm water prepared by stirring a pinch of the powdered bark into a glass of cool water, letting it stand for three minutes before drinking it. Depending on the need, this could be taken once a day, or elm could be added to all of the drinking water.

The readings recommended a number of different herbal tonic formulas in the treatment of colitis, and typically these contained extracts of wild ginseng, wild ginger, valerian, stillingia, and other ingredients.

Cayce's herbal remedies may be unique and unusual, but their simple effectiveness makes one recall that a century ago, before modern "miracle drugs" came into existence, almost all physicians recommended or practiced herbal medicine!

Packs

The readings recommended a variety of packs for a number of therapeutic purposes and utilized different substances, some of them quite unusual.

Mentioned with perhaps the greatest frequency were packs of castor oil, Epsom salts, pure salt, salt with apple cider vinegar, and Glyco-Thymoline. Although each pack had its own special uses, packs in general were recommended to facilitate the absorption of beneficial elements into the system, relax the patient, ease pain, stimulate circulation, and break up congestion.

An explanation of the packs mentioned above follows:

*Castor Oil—this pack is prepared by saturating three or four thicknesses of cotton or wool flannel with heated castor oil. General instructions were to place this pack over the abdomen and cover with a piece of plastic or oil-resistant cloth to prevent the oil from soiling clothing and linens. Heat was to be applied, usually with an electric heating pad. According to Edgar Cayce, the heat increased absorption of oil by the pores, and subsequently, many were advised to keep the packs as hot as possible. General instructions included cleansing the skin with a weak solution of bicarbonate of soda following each pack.

Castor oil packs were most frequently to be applied for about an hour and a half at bedtime and were generally to be applied in a series, such as three days on, three off, and three on. To assist in the elimination of wastes, an internal dose of olive oil was frequently to be taken on the third day of the series.

According to the readings, castor oil packs gently stimulated the organs of elimination and helped them to function more normally. Apparently, the packs also stimulated the lymph glands, thereby increasing the circulation, which in turn aided in removing toxins from the system. In general, castor oil packs were recommended for conditions involving poor eliminations, incoordination between the assimilations and eliminations, and nervous incoordination. Recommendations were also made in more specific types of disorders, such as epilepsy. In certain conditions, such as scleroderma, the packs were to be applied over areas other than the abdomen. Cayce advised against using castor oil packs during menstruation or during three-day apple diets.

*Epsom Salts—this pack is prepared by soaking a coarse towel in a hot, saturated solution of Epsom salts and then applying it, as hot as possible, to the affected areas. To help contain heat, Cayce advised placing another towel over the pack, which was to remain in place until it cooled.

Epsom salt packs were generally recommended to relieve pain and increase the circulation in particular areas. Hot, local packs were part of the treatments suggested for relieving the pain of arthritis and bursitis. In the treatment of arthritis, Epsom salt packs were at times recommended to relax the spine prior to adjustments.

*Pure Salt—these are made by filling a cloth bag with salt and then heating it in the oven prior to use, taking care not to scorch the bag. As with Epsom salt packs, hot salt packs were to be applied over the affected areas to relieve pain. In the treatment of cystitis, a salt pack was to be applied at times over both the lower spine and abdomen following a massage using a compound of mutton tallow, spirits of turpentine, spirits of camphor, and compound tincture of benzoin. Used in this manner, the hot salt was intended to aid the absorption of the massage compound by the skin, stimulating the circulation and alleviating local congestion.

*Salt and Apple Cider Vinegar—this combination was recommended either as a pack or rub in the treatment of bruising, sprains, and torn ligaments. In these recommendations, either the salt was to be moistened with vinegar or the vinegar was to be saturated with salt. Salt and vinegar was perhaps the most common application advised in the treatment of fractures or sprains. An individual with a fractured knee was advised to alternate salt-and-vinegar rubs with a combination of oils.

*Glyco-Thymoline—this is a mouthwash and treatment for mucosity which had many other uses as well and was suggested by Cayce for a variety of conditions. In these recommendations, a cloth was typically saturated with warm Glyco-Thymoline and then applied over the affected area. In some cases, heat was not needed, and in others the pack was to be kept warm, using an electric heating pad or other type of heat application.

To help reduce inflammation in cases of tonsillitis and sinusitis, Cayce suggested the application of an unheated Glyco-Thymoline pack. This procedure involved soaking two or three thicknesses of cotton cloth with Glyco-Thymoline and then wrapping the pack about the face and throat. In the case of an infant with acute colitis, Cayce recommended applying a Glyco-Thymoline pack over the abdomen two or three times daily, making it as hot as could be tolerated and leaving it on until cooled. Reportedly, this brought quick relief.

To relieve the discomfort of cystitis, one individual was advised to place Glyco-Thymoline packs over the pubic area, keeping them warm by means of a hot salt pack. Glyco-Thymoline packs could also be applied over the eyes (diluted) to relieve fatigue.

Spinal Adjustments

The Edgar Cayce readings frequently recommended mechanical manipulation of the spinal vertebrae and occasionally other bone groups as a method of restoring balance and normalcy to many parts of the body.

Osteopathy and chiropractic are two schools of therapy which focus treatment on the spine. Although there are differences in training between the two, as well as differences between schools in the same profession, the treatments themselves are similar in many ways.

The central rationale underlying spinal manipulation is that each vertebra in the spinal column is the site of nerve pathways to particular areas of the body. When a vertebra is out of proper alignment, it can block normal nerve impulses, causing poor circulation and discomfort in the area normally supplied by those nerves, as well as in the spine itself. A misalignment in one part of the spine can lead to problems in other vertebrae as well as increased muscle tensions. The purpose of spinal manipulation is therefore to restore the vertebrae to their proper positions and to relieve pain and tension at their source.

Spinal adjustments were suggested as part of a treatment regimen in more than two-thirds of the diseases reviewed. Treatments were usually to be administered cyclically and were to be given at regular intervals for specific periods of time. They were always recommended in conjunction with, or were to be alternated with, other treatments such as light therapy, hydrotherapy, heat applications, massage, and electrotherapy.

In long-standing or more serious conditions, the adjustments were often to begin gradually at first, becoming more complete and more stimulating as healing progressed. The readings cautioned that while initial treatment might alleviate the pressures, a balance of nerve flow could not be achieved unless structural alignment was maintained over a period of time. This was the reason a series of treatments was often advised.

Spinal adjustments can have far-reaching results in the system. According to the readings, these treatments can correct structural abnormalities (subluxations) in the spine, stimulate and balance the nervous system, increase circulation, coordinate activities of various organs, induce relaxation, encourage healing of injuries, and stimulate the activities of assimilations and eliminations.

Spinal manipulation was also claimed to alleviate the need for frequent massage, although a treatment referred to as osteopathic massage (part adjustment and part massage) was at times recommended.

Cayce found that spinal manipulation could be an important facet of treatment for many different disorders, such as apoplexy, anemia, varicose veins, arthritis, diabetes, epilepsy, angina, hydrocephalus, colitis, constipation, asthma, emphysema, obesity, and sinusitis.

Stupes and Poultices

Stupes and poultices are external treatments intended to bring temporary relief at the site of local pain, swelling, or discomfort. Since they have similar uses, Edgar Cayce at times used the terms interchangeably.

By definition, a stupe is a soft cloth which has been dipped in hot, often medicated liquid, with the excess moisture squeezed out, and applied to the body to relieve pain; a poultice is a soft, moist mass of some substance applied to a sore or inflamed part of the body. To act as a counterirritant and to aid absorption of medicinal substances by the skin, heat is at times applied over the applications.

In the readings, stupes and poultices took many forms, of which a few will be mentioned here.

One of the best known were mullein stupes, which are, technically, poultices since the mullein leaves are used themselves rather than the liquid they are steeped in. The mullein application is prepared by bruising and softening fresh mullein leaves and placing them in a glass container and soaking them in hot water. The leaves are then placed over the affected area and covered with a piece of gauze or other cloth to keep them in place. Duration and frequency of application varied.

In herbal literature, mullein is considered a vulnerary, or application, for minor external wounds. One of the main recommendations for the leaves was in the treatment of varicose veins. The instructions were to place them either over the affected area or directly above the swelling, if the obstruction was attributed to edema. If desired, the stupes could be placed on the part of the body supplying circulation to the swollen area.

Cayce Documented
Today

The medical testimonials included in the following section vary in their details, but are the result of surveys conducted by the Association for Research and Enlightenment in Virginia Beach or research by the ARE Clinic (4018 North Fortieth Street, Phoenix, Arizona, 85018). Also included in this section is correspondence received by a health food store in Virginia Beach which specializes in the Cayce formulas, and oral or written correspondence received by the author.

Many included are not comprehensive and as such only present a sampling of the opinions of some of those who feel they have been helped by the Cayce medical readings. Others, such as those supplied by the ARE Clinic, are detailed.

The specific remedies and treatments mentioned in this section are explained in the section of the book devoted to pharmacology.

The "Black Book" referred to in several testimonials is the *Individual Reference File of Extracts from the Edgar Cayce Readings,* which is published exclusively for members of the Association for Research and Enlightenment.

Those wishing further research on a particular illness may contact the ARE, P.O. Box 595, Atlantic Avenue, at Sixty-seventh Street, Virginia Beach, Virginia 23451, and ask for details on membership.

Accident Injuries
Post-Reading Case History #1

(The following is extracted from the *ARE NEWS*. For more details, see the November 1983 issue, volume 18, number 11.)

A recent case study at the ARE involved a young woman who was injured in a motorcycle accident. She approached the ARE Therapy Department and asked for their help in obtaining the full use and total growth of her left leg which had suffered extensive trauma originating from an accident in 1979. She had been fighting to save it for 2½ years.

The motorcycle she was on had been swiped by an automobile. She was consequently left with only one muscle in the lower part of her leg, multiple fractures of the tibia and fibula, a compound fracture of the femur and between 75 to 80 percent skin loss to her lower leg.

When she approached the ARE Therapy Department in August of 1982, Dr. William McGarey of the ARE Clinic in Phoenix, Ariz. was in Virginia Beach and helped set up a workable program which included meditation, prayer, affirmations, visualization, castor oil packs, scar massage and diet.

The physical part of the program involved the application of castor oil packs for four consecutive days, discontinuing for three days, and then a continuous repeat of this pattern. She was advised to take supplements which contained vitamin B and C and zinc and iron. Three times a week she was to exercise her leg, either by swimming, biking or walking.

Her diet was to be 80 percent alkaline-producing and 20 percent acid-producing, as suggested by the readings.

Mentally she was to visualize her leg as whole and perfectly healed; spiritually she was to meditate at least once a day.

During meditation she was to seek an attitude of healing. She was also placed on the ARE Glad Healpers prayer list.

After eight months on the program, the following results were noted: physically her leg began to show change. The edema around her ankle and kneecap had virtually disappeared. There appeared to be an increase in tissue thickness on the back portion of the leg and increased flexibility in the graft area under the patella. The calf muscle had more tone, and there seemed to be tissue growth extending from that muscle down the leg.

Additionally, there was a decrease in pain, an improvement in all areas of the leg in tone and a fading of scarring.

Accident Injuries
Post-Reading Case History #2

A woman on the West Coast was injured in an automobile accident in which the bones of her right leg were smashed. Part of the medical treatment she received involved putting plates and pins in the leg and helping rebuild her bones with bone putty mixed with chips of her own bones so that the bones would grow together.

Because of her age when the cast was removed, her bones hadn't formed completely together. She was subsequently advised to have a bone graft last summer. "I asked how much more time they would give a young person and was told another month or two. I told them I wanted the maximum time."

As a member of the Association for Research and Enlightenment, she was familiar with Edgar Cayce and his readings. She began applying the Impedance Device to her leg overnight and the scar massage each evening before retiring. Also, when her leg was giving her discomfort, she applied Egyptian Balm. (Now called Egyptian Oil.)

The results were positive, for she recently had surgery to remove most of the metal, at which time she was told that her leg had healed almost a hundred percent. "There was only one soft area," she said. "The nurse couldn't get

over how thin the scar was, it is only a thin pencil line,"
she said, explaining that her injury had been a compound
break involving the tibia, fibula, and ankle bones.

She credits the advice she received from Cayce via his
readings with her recovery, which she feels was special—
shortly after the accident there had been a chance her leg
would have to be amputated.

Alcoholism
Post-Reading Case History #1

(The following case history is reprinted from *The Edgar
Cayce Products—Ten Years of Research,* published by
Heritage Publications, Virginia Beach.)

I have been a heavy drinker for ten years. I lost nearly
all of my friends, and my family's support through my
drinking habits.

I always felt I had a good time when drinking, but everyone
always said that I was totally obnoxious. They said that I was
mean, crude, very loud and impossible to deal with. But I
couldn't see any reason to stop drinking because I like it.

One day I found out about Edgar Cayce's cure for alcoholism. At that point, I had come to the conclusion that I was an
alcoholic, that I used alcohol to escape my problems. I said I
would try the cure. I was told by a knowledgeable friend that
I was probably "possessed" when drinking, as discarnate
entities would sometimes attach themselves to people who
drink. It is easier to take over a person's body when under the
influence of alcohol as their resistance is lowered. As crazy as
this sounds, I believe this. When I drink, I would often reach
a point where I'd feel a certain "click" within me. After that
click I blacked out and could not remember anything until
waking up the next morning. I would be appalled, to say the
least, when someone would tell me what I had done the night
before. My personalities between sobriety and drunkenness
were so completely different, that I seemed to be two
different people.

Anyway, I started doing some of the things Cayce recommended. One was to use the Violet Ray on either side of the spinal column. However, I feel the main "cure" was using the gold chloride cycle. My "desire" for drinking has dropped tremendously. It is amazing. For ten years I was used to drinking at the very least 12 beers a day. Now my intake has lowered [to] from one to two beers a day.

The one time I did drink a lot since starting the cycle, I was so sick for the two days following I couldn't get out of bed. I vowed "never again!!," but due to a very stressful situation recently, I found myself imbibing again...but was pleased and amazed that I did not undergo the usual blackout period.

Thanks to gold chloride and prayer, I am a new person! I'm always me. My friends and family have noticed a total change in me, and I have too....

Alcoholism
Post-Reading Case History #2

(The following report was submitted by a practicing Virginia Beach chiropractor who uses treatment programs suggested in the Cayce readings in his private practice.)

Twenty-six-year-old male with a four-year history of alcoholism.

Treatment program used which was suggested in the Cayce readings was a prescription to deter drinking: one drop oil of eucalyptol; one drop tincture of benzoin; one drop tincture of valerian. Prescribed dosage: three tablets taken in one week.

Results: This patient recovered completely from alcoholism and has not had a drink since the time of treatment two years ago.

Arthritis
Post-Reading Case History #1

(The following is reprinted from *Pathways to Health*, March, 1983, volume 5, number 1, a publication of the ARE Clinic in Phoenix, Arizona. William A. McGarey, M.D., is director.)

Helen came to the Clinic's Temple Beautiful Program in March 1981 with the above diagnosis (arthritis: polymyalgia rheumatica). It is a form of arthritis which produces chronic pain in the muscles throughout the body and is thought to be autoimmune in nature.

The pain she had begun to experience in her hips a year before had progressively worsened, spreading through her legs, neck, and shoulders. She experienced temporary relief from chiropractic manipulations, cortisone shots, and a daily dosage of prednisone. But as an R.N., Helen was not comfortable with the medication and was concerned she would be "crippled for the rest of her life. . . ."

During the seventeen-day program, Helen's regimen included the Cayce arthritis diet, castor oil packs, Epsom salt baths, Atomidine, vitamin and mineral supplements, exercise, manipulations, medication, prayer, and dreamwork. She received various therapies: colonics, acupuncture, massage, biofeedback, and ETA sessions.

Not only did Helen progress physically during the program, but she learned to recognize and release tension, to truly relax, and visualize healing in her body.

Nine months later, Helen wrote us to say she was feeling "great." She was continuing the program regimen at home, had been able to reduce the prednisone dosage and was as active as she wanted to be. She knew she would not be "a cripple for life."

Arthritis
Post-Reading Case History #2

(The following is reprinted from the February 1976 issue of *Fate* magazine and is a portion of an article I wrote for the publication titled, "Cayce Cures Still Baffle Science.")

... Dr. John Peniel of Birmingham, Ala.... a general practitioner, recalls that in March 1969 he considered his arthritis incurable. "I went through the conventional cures with a rheumatologist, a medical man specializing in arthritis," he explains. "Nothing helped." His treatment included tranquilizers, Ascriptin, and Butazolidin-Alka, which had the potentially disastrous side effect of pulling his white blood count down to dangerous levels. "Buta-zolidin-Alka is supposed to be an anti-inflammatory drug for reducing swelling and pain," Dr. Peniel comments.

Despite these medications Dr. Peniel slowly was becom-ing bedridden. Walking from his bedroom to the kitchen was an ordeal. "I was told I had to live with it," he says. "I had to discontinue my active medical practice."

In the midst of all his discomfort Dr. Peniel started praying. "Up to this point I had been a strictly orthodox medical man. I found God and learned he never had been lost."

Things began to happen—slowly at first. Someone intro-duced him to the healing effects of herbs and he began taking ginseng to regain his strength. Then he read a book about Edgar Cayce and the remedies he had given during trance readings. Dr. Peniel went to Virginia Beach, Va., and spent two weeks doing research in the Cayce files at the Associa-tion for Research and Enlightenment. On the basis of his findings Peniel began using Cayce's Wet Cell Appliance, his impedance device, and some of the solutions recommended to go into them. He also began taking doses of Atomidine and gold chloride with sodium bicarbonate orally.

"I could tell a difference right away," he remarks. "Before that I had to stay in bed all day except for maybe four hours. If I pushed too far one day, I had to stay in bed

two days. After three months of following the Cayce
prescriptions I could stay up 12 to 18 hours a day."

Although Dr. Peniel describes himself as spiritual rather
than religious, he feels he was guided to the ARE "through
prayer and faith. I saw the ARE in a dream before I visited
Virginia Beach for the first time in 1972," he states. "I
could describe it from that dream."

The Wet Cell Appliance and the impedance device used
by Dr. Peniel are only a few of the many remedies the late
Edgar Cayce recommended while in trance. . . .

Arthritis
Post-Reading Case History #3

(The following is an excerpt from a letter received by a
health food store in Virginia Beach specializing in the
Cayce formulas.)

. . . like my mother, arthritis, bursitis, and neuritis [were]
setting in. Sometimes my hands actually looked deformed.
All my hinges felt like they needed a good oiling, and
that's exactly what they needed! Faithful massages with
peanut oil and they were as good as new. A friend of mine
was using a cane because of arthritic hips. He was becoming more and more incapacitated and feared being confined
to a wheelchair. I told him about peanut oil and now he
thinks I am a saint because he's getting around like he did
ten years ago. I never miss an opportunity to share my
Edgar Cayce knowledge with anyone with ears. . . .

Arthritis
Post-Reading Case History #4

(The following report was submitted by a practicing
Virginia Beach chiropractor who uses treatment programs
suggested in the Cayce readings in his private practice.)

For the past three months, Mrs. C has had pain in her knees, fingers, and toes.

Treatment program used which was suggested in the Cayce readings were adjustments with a peanut oil massage and Atomidine—one drop in a glass of water every other week for two weeks.

Results: All joint and bone pain went into remission. If joint pain returns, it is controlled very well by a course of Atomidine.

Arthritis
Post-Reading Case History #5

(The following report was submitted by a practicing Virginia Beach chiropractor who uses treatment programs suggested in the Cayce readings in his private practice.)

Sixty-eight-year-old patient was hospitalized in 1975 and was unable to feed herself because of the severity of symptoms. Abnormal physical findings: pain and inability to move joints of fingers and shoulders. Pain on ambulation.

Treatment program used which was suggested in the Cayce readings was massage, adjustments, Wet Cell with Atomidine, colonics, Epsom salt baths, Epsom salt packs, and fume sweats.

Results: This patient's symptoms have been managed fairly well for the past three years using the above treatment program. Flare-up did occur which required the use of cortisone, as well as pain medication. However, considering she had been hospitalized, we consider the results to be good.

Arthritis
Post-Reading Case History #6

(The following is an excerpt from a tape-recorded interview August 27, 1980, with a Virginia Beach chiropractor who discussed his successes with the treatment program suggested by the Cayce readings.)

* * *

Lyme disease is a rare kind of rheumatoid arthritic condition. It is caused by tick bites in the area of Lyme, Connecticut. The type is viral, it is chronic, and it is characterized by exacerbations and remissions. In the case of this particular patient, there were very few remissions. She had joint pain in her hands, knees, and low back. . . .

According to the Cayce readings, arthritic conditions are basically caused by metabolic imbalance, so I approached it from that point of view, and I gave her a diet which was low in fat, low in refined carbohydrates, and high in vegetable matter and high in whole grains. She followed the diet closely. I gave her chiropractic care. I also advised her to start using Atomidine, and she responded remarkably. Eighty percent of her symptoms were in a state of remission after three weeks.

Arthritis
Post-Reading Case History #7

(The following is reprinted from *Pathways to Health*, September 1980, volume 2, number 7, a publication of the ARE Clinic in Phoenix, Arizona. William A. McGarey, M.D., is director.)

Thank you for sending the requested "preliminary report" on the arthritis (rheumatoid) study. . . . The report was interesting for me for a special reason—In March of 1976, I was diagnosed (blood tests and all) as having rheumatoid arthritis and gout. I immediately wrote for the circulating files and began very seriously working toward the changes needed (without realizing that you at the Clinic were doing the same thing for patients at the Clinic—same time). I have been persistent and consistent.

This year at my annual physical checkup, the doctor noticed there are no more symptoms, and wanted to run another set of blood tests ("arthritis profile" I think he called it). He was very impressed and called me a few days later to say that the results of the tests were quite negative—no sign of any rheumatoid arthritis or any arthritic related diseases at all. He said, "Whatever you're doing, keep doing it." I know I was led to working in the right direction toward eliminating detrimental things in my life (attitudes, diet, etc.) and in building up the more positive aspects which I've known all along, but had become in a stressful rut, and had neglected at times. Anyhow, thanks again....

Asthma
Post-Reading Case History #1

(The following are excerpts from a talk delivered by a former Virginia Beach chiropractor on January 21, 1981, detailing his success with the Cayce treatments. In addition to his doctor of chiropractic degree, he has a B.A. in economics and a B.S. in human biology.)

The first case is a . . . female age twenty-six. When she came to me, she had been to the emergency room three times that week with . . . substantial difficulty in breathing, unable to sleep at night, taking epinephrine. . . . [She] had a shot the day before [in] the emergency room. It had gotten so bad that it just wasn't helping her. This would have been her third shot that she had had that week. . . .

We began utilizing colonics . . . [and] a totally milk-free diet. Put her on an alkaline diet. When I say milk-free, all milk products. I began instituting manipulation and treated her for about six weeks. She got over the crisis period in about a week of therapy. Treated her regularly for about six weeks, twice a week [three colonics in that time]. . . .

[When] she told me she had followed the diet rigidly . . . the frequency of the treatment . . . dropped to about once every two weeks and after a period of time, once a month . . . for about two years. . . . Following the diet and using Inspirol, she did not have any more asthma attacks for that two-year period. . . .

The [next] . . . case is a young woman . . . from Cleveland,

Ohio, who had attacks of asthma on a yearly basis. It may
well have been an allergy. . . . She came to me interested in
the Cayce material, wanting to follow the suggestions in
the Cayce material, which we did. . . .

We followed therapy for approximately a year, and after
that point . . . she occasionally visited me, possibly every six
to eight weeks . . . for an adjustment. [She] followed the diet
very well. . . . For three years after . . . therapy, she . . . never
had a crisis, whereas prior to the therapy she would have a
period every year . . . where she would have repeated attacks.

Inspirol was used in the . . . asthma cases. A diet that was
totally free of milk and milk products and an alkaline
diet was used. Manipulation and colonic therapy was used.

Asthma
Post-Reading Case History #2

(The following is an excerpt from a letter received by a
Virginia Beach health food store which specializes in the
Cayce remedies.)

. . . finally joined the ARE in 1973. The first file I asked
for was "asthma" for my third child. She was diagnosed
as bronchial asthma at age 3 weeks, and for nine years was
almost continuously on medications that caused many
fungus infections and also bleeding of the lower bowel. I
ordered the Inspirol Inhalent [sic], followed the diet and
worked up the courage to see our first chiropractor. She
has not had an attack for seven years now. . . .

Balding
Post-Reading Case History #1

Although there was little feedback on the results of
Edgar Cayce's readings during his day, there have been
recent positive reports from those who have used the
advice found in his readings.

An example is one formerly bald man who has even supplied sketches to illustrate the dramatic regrowth of his hair. After using Vaseline, crude oil, and Atomidine for two years, he reported that his sideburns had widened and that there was thin new hair all over the top of his head where he had been bald before.

In 1972, an independent researcher analyzed the survey responses of forty-five of those who used crude oil to stimulate hair growth. Eleven percent reported considerable to complete hair restoration, and another forty percent, little to moderate restoration.

Balding
Post-Reading Case History #2

(The following letter was received by a Virginia Beach health food store specializing in the Cayce remedies.)

About eight years ago . . . 50 percent of my hair fell out and the remaining hair broke off at the neckline. Following the Cayce readings, I applied Crudoleum for about six months time. The result was that my hair grew in much thicker than it had been previously, which is really rather remarkable because my hair is extremely thick to begin with, and I didn't think it would be possible to get even thicker after I had lost so much of it!

Balding
Post-Reading Case History #3

(The following is a portion of a letter received by a Virginia Beach health food store specializing in the Cayce formulas.)

Following my hospitalization in 1965, I started to loose [sic] my hair at an alarming rate. I did everything every hairdresser told me but still went from a hairpiece to a full wig. After a shower and shampoo I had to vacuum my towel and rake the tub.

Olive oil shampoo actually stopped the fall-out at the first use. The situation reversed itself and I now have a full head of healthy hair. I depend on it. . . .

Balding
Post-Reading Case History #4

(The following case history is reprinted from *The Edgar Cayce Products—Ten Years of Research*, published by Heritage Publications, Virginia Beach.)

. . . [My husband's] most exciting thing of course is the Crudoleum results. He is 40 years old and becoming slightly thin on top. Following surgery (sympathectomy) his hair naturally began to fall in bunches. I convinced him to let me try Crudoleum treatment—nothing more. . . . So, I started a twice a week five-minute massage with the Crudoleum, followed by an olive oil shampoo. In the 10-week period since we started, we have had rather dramatic results. All of the hair, including the bald spot on top, has filled with new hair. The front view now shows short but thick hair. The quality of the hair has also improved 100 percent and the new hair is a soft brown in color. In fact the improvement in so short a time has convinced one of my co-workers to start work on his hair also. In one week his falling hair has stopped—period and there is a dramatic improvement in the texture.

As for myself, I have found the Crudoleum treatment has done lovely things for my hair. I have no more problems with itchy scalp, dry hair or whatever. Of course Formula 636 probably deserves to be applauded in that area also. Although the gray streak has not vanished (what can you expect in five months?) there is great improvement. . . .

Balding
Post-Reading Case History #5

(The following letter was received by a chiropractic student in 1981.)

* * *

A young man I know has suffered for the past 17 years with the distressing problem of premature baldness. It began when he was only 17, when he started losing his hair in spots roughly the size of a silver dollar. Then it progressed into typical male pattern baldness, though his scalp remained oily throughout this period rather than being dry and flakey as happens in so many such cases.

After trying several commercial preparations with no results, he finally was persuaded to experiment with a bottle of Crudoleum. To his great surprise and pleasure, his hair started growing in again before the first bottle was used up. He ran out of the Crudoleum some time ago but reported to me that his hair was still growing in and that the silver dollar size spots were now a good 50 percent smaller in diameter....

Cancer: Cervical (Tendencies)
Post-Reading Case History

(The following is a case profile from the ARE Clinic in Phoenix, Arizona. The ARE Clinic is a nonprofit Arizona corporation dedicated to providing the best available medical care, utilizing conventional and holistic therapies. Medical research—finding better methods of healing and regeneration—is an important part of the clinic's mission. This report is part of a series of publications intended to keep medical professionals and the general public informed of research findings that might give hope to persons struggling with illness. Those who wish further information may send a letter of inquiry to: Medical Research Inquiry, The ARE Clinic, 4018 North Fortieth Street, Phoenix, Arizona 85018.)

The following report concerns a twenty-nine-year-old woman who had a tendency toward cancer of the cervix. She achieved and maintained normal Pap smear tests after five days of Cayce therapy. Follow-up after three months showed continued normal lab results.

According to the report, the woman's "primary concern was repeated evidence within the previous three months of abnormal cell development, consisting of mild and moderate dysplasia—Class II—on four Pap smears and a culposcopy-directed biopsy, a technique in which the cervix is examined microscopically and samples of tissues taken from the most abnormal areas. Cells from the cervix showed structural abnormalities considered to be precancerous by her doctors. Cryosurgery (the destruction of tissue by application of extreme cold) was done, but a follow-up Pap smear done one week before coming to the ARE Clinic still showed mild dysplasia."

The subject had a history of obesity, asthma, hay fever, and food allergies. Further, she had had three abortions, was on birth control pills, and had smoked for the past five years.

The clinic designed "a treatment program which included castor oil packs; Glyco-Thymoline douches on Mondays and Wednesdays; Atomidine douches on Tuesdays and Thursdays; Glyco-Thymoline—five drops in four ounces of water four times daily to alkalinize her body; castor oil—five drops by mouth at bedtime to rid her body of toxins; vitamin C—six thousand mg per day; Atomidine—one drop on Monday, increasing by one drop per day to five drops on Friday for three weeks on and one week off; a special 'cancer diet' with cytotoxic serum test restrictions; no further smoking; exercise; massage; meditation; prayer; dream work; biofeedback; ETA treatments; and visualizations."

During her five ETA (electromechanical therapeutic apparatus) treatments, the woman "learned to become more aware of how her emotions produced physical symptoms in her body and how to release both emotions and symptoms." Other treatment included a laying-on-of-hands healing group, during which time she learned that the "blockages" of energy she was feeling could be released. She also experienced a lightening of the "heaviness in her torso area," and a dissipation of "flashes of sharp pain in the left side of her cervix."

One month after the woman left Phoenix and received Pap smears classified normal (Class I), she remarked,

"I've learned that once I get my mind straightened out, my body will follow."

Cancer: Skin
Post-Reading Case History

(The following case history is part of a membership survey project conducted by the Association for Research and Enlightenment in Virginia Beach in January 1984.)

A "firmly diagnosed" case of nonmalignant skin cancer was successfully treated with a combination of castor oil and baking soda, according to a report from a middle-aged man. The castor oil was applied to the skin and then topped with dry baking soda.

The cancer, which was diagnosed by a dermatologist, was treated by the health-care specialist with liquid nitrogen, but the cancer areas, which were located on the temple just below the hairline and the earpieces to his eyeglasses, would return three to six months later. This occurred three or four times until he decided to try castor oil and baking soda, which he did every evening for four or five nights for one hour each time. "The only discomfort was the itching," he said.

Although his dermatologist is skeptical, the man is pleased with the results, for out of four locations on his face, two of the cancerous areas have disappeared, one is still sensitive, and the fourth, "I'm not sure yet."

The subject feels that castor oil increases the blood flow to the area and, as a consequence, he uses it for other skin eruptions.

Cataracts
Post-Reading Case History

(The following is a portion of a letter sent to a Virginia Beach health food store specializing in the Cayce formulas. It details an individual's success with the treatment program for cataracts suggested in the Cayce readings.)

. . . I have studied the files on cataracts and am improving my vision slowly. When I took the test for a driver's license about a year ago, I was given a license for only three years instead of four. Recently when I had my eyes examined, the physician told me that my vision had improved. He added that had I taken the test when my eyes were as relaxed as they were when he tested me, I would have been given a four year license.

Charcot-Marie-Tooth Disease
Post-Reading Case History

A recent case was that of a forty-four-year-old woman who was a patient of a Virginia Beach chiropractor. The woman's problem was apparently connected to a twenty-foot jump she made at the age of thirteen, in which she landed flat on her feet on hard ground. She was subsequently unable to walk for a few minutes.

Despite the fact that she was still quite mobile and able to run, a year later she developed a flat-footed walk. However, at the age of thirty-three, she lost the use of some of the muscles in her left leg and foot, developing a condition known as drop foot (peroneal muscular weakness). She tripped and stumbled and could no longer run.

Over several years, the woman visited different physicians and followed their suggestions, but the condition only grew worse. Eventually, her right foot became paralyzed, and she walked with a limping gait, using a cane. Both legs were a purple-gray.

The chiropractor's examination revealed that her muscles responded normally, except for those on the back and outer sides of her legs. Her treatment program, based on a number of Cayce's readings on paralysis, included spinal adjustments, especially in the coccygeal area; a special dietary program which included nutritional supplements;

corrective exercises and arch supports; occasional colonics; massages with oil—over the entire body and specifically over the legs and feet—along with castor oil packs over the abdomen; Wet Cell and sinusoidal electrical treatments; and a change to a more constructive thought pattern, which included prayer and the recording of dreams and a willingness to work with her disorder on physical and other levels.

The woman responded rapidly to the treatments, and accordingly, after several months she was able to walk without a cane and to spend considerable time on her feet. After six months of treatment, it was reported that her physical stamina had increased to the point that she was able to hold a part-time job.

Colitis
Post-Reading Case History

(The following report was submitted as part of a recent survey project on the results of healing concepts, principles, and specific modalities and formulas mentioned in the Cayce readings. The research was conducted by the ARE.)

Prior to beginning his treatment for colitis as recommended in the Circulating Files, this subject was on Donnatal and Donnagel and was forced to avoid many foods.

Upon consulting the files, he began a regimen of castor oil packs followed by doses of olive oil in a cycle of three days on, four days off, and a repeat of the cycle for about four times. He reported that "later I could eat and drink anything." To maintain his condition he uses the packs three times every month to six weeks.

The results he has termed "excellent" and notes that he originally became acquainted with the concept of castor oil packs through Dr. Harold J. Reilly's book *The Edgar Cayce Handbook for Health Through Drugless Therapy* (Jove).

However, despite the fact that he has been using castor oil packs for five years, he feels the need to use them on a regular basis "due to stress. If I don't continue use, I get a relapse within six months."

Cyst: Ovarian
Post-Reading Case History

(The following report was submitted by a practicing Virginia Beach chiropractor who uses treatment programs suggested in the Cayce readings in his private practice.)

Patient was diagnosed as having an ovarian cyst December 1982 with ultrasound. Abnormal physical findings, a palpable mass, abdominal wall on the right side.

Treatment program used which was suggested in the Cayce Readings were castor oil packs over abdomen, five times the first week; two times the week after. Adjustments—five times the first week, two times week after. Massage the spine daily with oil. A colonic after first five days of treatment.

Results: Subjective—pain and discomfort in the pelvic cavity were reduced by 70 percent. Objective: Palpable mass was gone after about ten days.

Cyst: Pilonidal
Post-Reading Case History

(The following case histories are part of a membership survey project conducted by the Association for Research and Enlightenment in Virginia Beach in January 1984.)

This report is from a woman who had two pilonidal cysts removed by surgery. In both instances, it took years before she could convince a physician of its presence, as he was initially unable to detect the mass when she came in for an examination. When she called for an appointment, the mass was evident; when she arrived for her examination, "it went down."

According to the woman, it took fifteen years to detect the first pilonidal cyst and seven years, the second. Both were accompanied by severe or migraine headaches.

Six months after the second cyst was removed, her headaches began to return along with swelling, pain, and drainage. At this time, she had become familiar with castor oil packs and heating pads from a Cayce book she had read in 1982. "Rather than hassle with doctors, I started the castor oil packs," she said. She applied the packs in the area of the cyst for five consecutive nights for one-half hour before bed and continued this routine for a couple of months.

"Once the headaches left, I knew [the cyst] was gone!"

Damaged Knee
Post-Reading Case History

On July 4, 1976, a woman in Tucson, Arizona, underwent four hours of emergency surgery following an accident on a motorcycle. The surgery was performed at the Tucson Medical Center. Following surgery and due to cartilage damage, fluid would continually collect around the knee, requiring removal by medical procedure, which the woman described as "very painful."

Despite the removal of the fluid, the condition kept recurring and eventually the woman's orthopedic surgeon put her leg in a cast, immobilizing it for six weeks.

When the cast was removed, the fluid subsequently returned. Since she could not afford to undergo any more expensive surgical procedures, she began applying salt-and-vinegar packs to the area in an attempt to reduce the inflammation and fluid. "My friend looked it up in the files to see what Cayce suggested," she explained.

At first, she applied the packs a couple of times every twenty-four hours; later she reduced it to just once a week for five or six weeks, in durations of fifteen or twenty minutes, "or longer if I had the time," she said.

"I was told it would take a couple of months at least. . . . The thing amazed me . . . it worked almost immediately."

The young woman feels she has gone a long way from sixty-seven stitches in the knee area and the fear of having to have her leg removed at the knee. "I walked at first with crutches, then later a cane and now, for years, nothing."

In fact, she hasn't had any symptoms since 1977, not even after working all day and going out later at night.

Depression
Post-Reading Case Histories

(The following are excerpts from a talk delivered by a former Virginia Beach chiropractor on January 21, 1981, detailing his success with the Cayce treatments. In addition to his doctor of chiropractic degree, he has a B.A. in economics and a B.S. in human biology.)

I became interested in depression and read all of Cayce's files on depression. I had . . . three outstanding cases in which the patients, one . . . attempted suicide, two of them . . . talked about it or felt that way. In one case, the patient was experiencing extreme paranoia, was afraid to go out, was afraid to be around people. . . .

In all three of these cases, the Radio-Active Appliance was used, manipulation, and in two of the cases some colonic therapy. I found that in these cases there was a bit of stasis. There was a problem of low blood sugar. . . . I recommended vitamin therapy, the Radio-Active Appliance, a strict alkaline diet. . . .

The Radio-Active Appliance was used with gold chloride on the ninth dorsal in each . . . case. In these three cases, the responses [were] very favorable. I know all three of these people are presently out functioning again in a very normal fashion and have lost the depression. . . .

Diabetes
Post-Reading Case History

(The following report was submitted as part of a recent survey project on the results of healing concepts, principles, and specific modalities and formulas mentioned in the Cayce readings. The research was conducted by the ARE.)

The subject reported that prior to applying the principles found in the Edgar Cayce readings, he was on twenty units of insulin daily and a 1,300-calorie diet instituted by a nutritionist at a hospital. Additionally, he was restricted to no intake of sugars. He noted that results obtained from this regimen were poor.

Upon consulting the Cayce Circulating Files, he began the grape juice diet and followed the general diet suggested by Cayce in the Circulating Files.

He rated the overall results as excellent and noted that he lost twenty-five pounds and was able to reduce his insulin from twenty units to none in a period of three months. At the time of the report, he had been insulin-free for several months.

Diarrhea
Post-Reading Case History

A woman from upstate New York reported excellent results obtained from using Formula 208 tonic for ulcerative colitis.

While hospitalized for diarrhea and after undergoing a series of tests, she was informed that she had ulcerative colitis and that there was no cure for it. A diet was advised.

Later she had the opportunity to read about Formula 208, learning that it was supposed to cure simple diarrhea. She decided to give it a try, and after one and a half bottles she found her bowel movements "were perfectly normal."

Since her physician was "completely amazed" at her improvement, she gave him a bottle, which she feels he sent out to be analyzed.

In the meantime, she said she has passed the information on to others who have also had "good results."

Diverticulitis
Post-Reading Case History

(The following is part of a recent survey conducted by the ARE in Virginia Beach.)

A woman writes that she feels she has prevented attacks of diverticulitis by eating a high-roughage diet and by applying castor oil poultices over the affected area and covering it with a heating pad.

Her system is to apply the castor oil poultices for a few hours three or four days in a row at the first sign of symptoms.

She also finds getting colonics helpful too at this time and reports that since starting applying the castor oil she has not had to miss work due to diverticulitis.

Eczema
Post-Reading Case History

(The following case history is reprinted from *The Edgar Cayce Products—Ten Years of Research,* published by Heritage Publications, Virginia Beach.)

* * *

In 1971 I first developed an itch on my stomach, which was treated at the Portsmouth Naval Hospital. Initially they tried the standard treatment for scabies, which only made the problem worse. A biopsy was then taken, and my case was diagnosed as similar to psoriasis or eczema. Next a dermatologist gave me around 150 cortisone shots directly into the sores on my back, which bled and required a bandage over my entire back. This slowed down my symptoms for about four days. I used Synalar (a prescription topical steroid), both in the ointment and liquid forms, for at least the next two years, with no results. The problem spread over other areas of my body—elbows, chest, knees, shins and ankles.

Finally on the advice of a friend I turned to the Cayce treatments for skin problems. Around March of 1976 I took about two-thirds of a bottle of Sulflax in capsules and used half a bottle of Ray's Ointment externally. In ten days my skin condition had cleared up except for some minor welts in the scalp area. In October of 1976 I suffered a minor relapse with itching at the base of the spine. I then repeated the Cayce treatments and everything cleared up, including the welts on my scalp.

Epilepsy
Post-Reading Case History #1

(The following are excerpts from a talk delivered by a former Virginia Beach chiropractor on January 21, 1981, detailing his success with the Cayce treatments. In addition to his doctor of chiropractic degree, he has a B.A. in economics and a B.S. in human biology.)

Two cases of epilepsy. One was a male, approximately age thirty-two. . . . He had his first seizure at age twenty-four, when he was a senior in college. There was no history of it in the family. It was listed as psychomotor epilepsy.

He was put on phenobarbital, which he did not respond favorably to. After awhile he was put on Dylanton and phenobarbital. In both cases, the seizures continued with a frequency of about once every month or occasionally once every two months. However, the side effects of the drug or drugs left him feeling very foggy . . . not able to concentrate and frequently fatigued. He was dissatisfied with the . . . medication.

He was put on . . . an alkaline diet, given manipulation— as a sedative he was given passion flower fusion. He had stopped [other] medication prior to being given the passion flower fusion . . . before seeing me for treatment. The Radio-Active Appliance was used. After the beginning of treatment, he went approximately two years with no seizure and with no other than occasionally . . . passion flower fusion . . . and diet and manipulation. . . .

The second case of epilepsy that I treated was a young girl who began having seizures at the age of approximately twenty-four. They were . . . psychomotor or hysterical. That was never determined. . . . She was driving a car and had an automobile accident, and after this the frequency of the seizures was much greater.

She also had substantial headaches and . . . a lot of body and joint pain, and it was difficult to tell whether they were related to the aftereffects of the seizures or not. She had visited . . . quite a number of medical doctors. Her husband was retired from the Navy. . . . They had her on several medications. . . . None of them seemed to help, and at the time that she came to my office she was having as many as ten seizures a day. I put her on an alkaline diet, began giving colonic therapy, manipulative therapy. She was transferred to passion flower fusion as a sedative. She voluntarily went off [other] medication.

She also complained about . . . not having mental control while on the medication. . . . In this . . . case, she was put on the Radio-Active Appliance. When she followed therapy . . . the number of seizures were reduced from as many as ten to twelve a day while on medication, down to one or two a week. . . .

Castor oil packs were used in both of the cases mentioned, and the diet played a very big part in the therapy. They were taken off any form of alcohol, tried to reduce the amount of caffeine or any kind of stimulant ... [and] both ... responded well; however, there was never a complete cure in either case. ...

Epilepsy
Post-Reading Case History #2

(The following case history is part of a membership survey project conducted by the Association for Research and Enlightenment in Virginia Beach in January, 1984.)

A young woman who had her first "stress-related" seizure as a child of four has been able to control her epileptic attacks with diet, meditation, and prayer.

After her initial attack as a child, the seizures returned in 1972 when she was in her early thirties. She was placed on medication by a physician, which was to be taken on a regular basis.

Concerned that the medication might become habit-forming, she began to look back on her life and delve into the Cayce materials.

Now maintaining a calmer outlook on life, she has been seizure-free for several months and attributes it to daily meditation, prayer, and nutrition. Her low-carbohydrate diet consists mainly of turkey, chicken, fresh fruits and vegetables, salads, eggs, etc. She avoids all pork and beef and includes fish in her diet once a week.

Eyes: Vision
Post-Reading Case History

(The following letter was received by a Virginia Beach health food store specializing in the Cayce formulas.)

I want to report on the amazing results of my 12-year-old daughter Jennifer's treatment with Optikade for her eyes.

This past summer (1983) she started having more and more problems with her eyes. She would have headaches, and if she read too much, her eyes would water and ache. We took her to an ophthalmologist who prescribed glasses. We began to think seriously about getting glasses for her but decided to try Optikade first to see if it would help.

Just before she started taking Optikade in the fall we measured her eyes, using an eye chart and the standard procedure. We found her right eye, which is the weaker one, to be 20/50 and her left eye to be 20/40. A month after starting the Optikade there was a slight improvement, with the right eye measuring 20/40 and the left eye 20/40. A month later we measured them again and the right eye was better than 20/20!—but the left was still 20/40. After one more month . . . the right eye measured 20/10 and the left eye, 20/15, better than perfect!

I should add that while Jennifer was taking Optikade she also had about one chiropractic adjustment a month, ate two or three raw carrots a week and did the head and neck exercises almost every day. I think this is a really striking testimonial to the effectiveness of Cayce's treatments and one I'm personally very, very happy about.

Flu
Post-Reading Case History #1

(The following case history is reprinted from *The Edgar Cayce Products—Ten Years of Research*, published by Heritage Publications, Virginia Beach.)

My child had been ill all summer. It started with a simple cold, went into his ears, and the massive doses of oral antibiotics and shots threw him into a siege of diarrhea and vomiting that threatened to dehydrate him and did in fact leave him weighing two pounds less after the weekend of July 4th than he had on June 2nd, a considerable weight loss for one so small (he's 2).

After four rounds of oral antibiotics, two shots of

penicillin, a round of sulphur [sic] drug, and many con-
comitant decongestants to keep the mucus from pushing
out from his nose to his ears and infecting them further, I
had spent almost $200, had visited our three pediatricians
an average of twice a week for six weeks, and woke up
one morning to my child's coughing and coming down
with another cold when I decided to go back to Cayce, dig
around and see what I could come up with.

I ordered "Medicines for the New Age" and used it to
make my decisions about what to order. . . . I started giving
cocoa butter massages—and added Campho-Derm massages as soon as the first order arrived, plus started letting
him inhale from the Inspirol and take one-third adult dose
of the 636 formula. You would not recognize him as the
same child about two weeks from the beginning of my
cocoa butter rubs and a week on the . . . medicines which
arrived last week. He's gained weight, has enormous
energy, his nose has cleared up—and though the Mother
Earth Cough Syrup just arrived today—I doubt he will
need it now—because he is no longer coughing. . . .

Cayce's treatments seem so simple it is hard to see how
they could possibly work—and I was frankly afraid to risk
using them with my child until I got desperate—or when
everything our doctors did so obviously failed. . . .

Flu
Post-Reading Case History #2

(The following is an excerpt from a tape-recorded interview on August 20, 1980, with a Virginia Beach chiropractor who discussed his successes with the treatment
program suggested by the Cayce readings.)

Patient number fourteen . . . with classic viral syndrome
flu symptoms—muscle ache, sinusitis, inability to breathe
as well as congestion in the chest. . . . I suggested the
Inspirol as well as the Mother Earth cough syrup, and the
patient said that she was given considerable relief, not just

symptomatic relief, immediately upon the use of those products.

Glaucoma
Post-Reading Case History #1

(The following letter was received by a Virginia Beach health food store specializing in the Cayce remedies.)

A neighbor of my bookkeeper read in Dr. [Harold] Reilly's book about potatoes being good for eyes. She was scheduled for an operation for glaucoma but didn't like the idea. For about two weeks, twice a day for about an hour, she put potato packs on her eyes. When she went for her next examination, the doctor said he couldn't explain it, but she no longer needed the operation.

This happened in the fall of 1982. . . .

Glaucoma
Post-Reading Case History #2

(The following case history is reprinted from *The Edgar Cayce Products—Ten Years of Research,* published by Heritage Publications, Virginia Beach.)

I am nearsighted to the point of needing glasses constantly. Late in 1977, I went to my eye doctor because I could hardly see out of my right eye. He diagnosed a pressure of 24 in my left eye and said 25 would require medication for glaucoma. He also found the beginning of a cataract in my right eye.

Three or four months later, one night I dreamed of an herbal formula, but couldn't remember anything but "balsam of tolu." . . . A few days later [I] happened to look at a bottle of Optikade and noticed that it had balsam of tolu in it. I went and read the Cayce reading on the product and decided to try it since it was a formula for the eyes. I subsequently took about eight (8 ounce) bottles of the tonic over the next year.

Other dreams that I had during this period recommended eating carrots—raw with gelatin or cooked, lettuce and kelp powder, along with spinal manipulation of the cervical area. I also used castor oil packs, and potato poultices over my eye area, as well as getting steam baths and massages.

Late in 1978, I had another eye test and found that my eye pressure reading had dropped to 18, close to the normal level of 16. I also have noticed that the vision in my right eye has improved substantially.

Gum Disease
Post-Reading Case History

(The following letter was received by a health food store in Virginia Beach specializing in the Cayce products.)

Ipsab and Calcios are two of my favorite Cayce products and I'll tell you why. In 1973 I was referred by my dentist to a periodontist due to deterioration of my gums. The disease process in my gums had progressed to the point that oral surgery was required to remove the decayed tissue. The surgery was performed and the periodontist doubted that I would be able to keep two of my molars beyond a year as so much of the supporting gum tissue had been removed.

According to my periodontist, oral surgery was a procedure to allow the patient to either maintain the status quo of the mouth or merely slow down the disease process. At this time I read what Cayce had to say about caring for your teeth. As a result of my reading I began using Ipsab and eating a fresh salad daily. When I turned 30 I also took the recommended Calcios treatment in accordance with the "teeth-change" cycle.

Each six months I have returned to my periodontist for an oral evaluation where he measures any change in gum tissue. With each exam there has been continuous "regrowth" of gum tissue. After a pregnancy at age 34, a check-up at the periodontist's office showed that my gums had completely regrown to a point where my mouth was healthier than when I first visited him. Moreover, I have all of my teeth today and don't intend to lose any!

My periodontist is somewhat baffled yet pleased by my progress. Probably because of his long training period as a periodontist he is able to view my cure only as being a result of "unusual circumstances and skill in surgery." As I mentioned before, his other cases either maintained the status quo of their mouths through surgery or slowed the disease-process down. . . .

To conclude then, I highly recommend the above mentioned products for anyone with gum disease. They're also beneficial to anyone else (diseased or not) who desires to maintain a healthy mouth!

Headaches: General
Post-Reading Case History

(The following is a portion of a letter received by a Virginia Beach health food store specializing in the Cayce remedies.)

I had originally ordered it [Glyco-Thymoline] for my migraine headaches which were bilateral and felt like hand grenades going off in my head. Sometimes I would have a temperature as high as 106 degrees with them. My vision was blurred and my hair would hurt for days afterward. . . . What grateful relief the Glyco colonics brought. I also found that a compress, wet with Glyco, and applied to the forehead brought an end to almost every kind of headache.

I have applied it to various skin rashes and itches and, diluted, as a compress to eyes irritated from chlorinated swimming pools. . . .

Hematoma–Hemangioma
Post-Reading Case History

(The following is reprinted from the December 1983 *Medical Research Bulletin* [volume XII, number 4], published by the ARE Clinic, 4018 North Fortieth Street, Phoenix Arizona 85018, Copyright 1977 by the ARE Clinic, Inc. Reprinted by permission.)

Somewhere in the middle ages, a perceptive individual called the castor bean plant the "Palma Christi," apparently because of the shape of its leaves, although it may have been because of the healing quality of the oil taken from the beans of the plant. In any event, the castor oil—as applied in the pack—has become so much of a symbol of healing in our experience with our patients and with our own family....

We recently received a letter from one of our correspondents that tells another story of healing that is quite remarkable. Phil's mother was disturbed the day after he was born because of a knot on his head about the size of a golf ball. The pediatrician assured her that this was not unusual— "newborns' heads look funny." However, each day the size of the tumor grew larger until the doctor finally X-rayed the child's head, found it to be most likely hematoma (accumulation of blood under the scalp) or a hemangioma. He told the mother that it would continue to grow until he was age one or two and that nothing could be done until then. The mother continues the story: "The swelling grew daily—the growth was noticeable and my concern grew, being a new mother. My mother... called me in Iowa one day and said to try the castor oil packs. (At that time, the tumor was almost the size of his head.) The next day I started them—by that evening I thought the tumor was getting smaller, but then I thought it might be my imagination, too. By the next afternoon it was definitely noticeable that it was going away. I continued the packs for five days and the swelling was gone, except for a very small knot that disappeared in three weeks.

"His doctor was amazed and took several pictures of the 'after' and requested pictures of the 'before,' although he laughed when I told him of the packs. . . ."

Hepatitis
Post-Reading Case History

In November 1982, a woman began traveling with her husband in India. In June 1983, she began to feel weak and had no appetite and began to experience nausea almost constantly. During this time, she lost ten pounds.

She visited a doctor in India who noted a tender liver. In Japan, her regular doctor diagnosed hepatitis and prescribed pills and injections. The doctor took her blood count once a month. After three months of treatments, she was considered cured and left for California. Two months later, she began to experience a relapse and decided to try some of Cayce's recommendations. A month later, after daily applications of castor oil packs, the symptoms once again disappeared.

Hernia: Hiatal
Post-Reading Case History

(The following is an excerpt from a letter received by a health food store in Virginia Beach specializing in Cayce formulas.)

Cold-pressed castor oil has been used for many things by my family. I use it as a pack on my abdomen for hiatal hernia when the condition becomes spasmodic and I can't stop vomiting. It has a soothing, relieving quality to it, and I usually end up relaxed and asleep. We have used it for sprains, to relieve constipation (in abdominal packs) and other related ailments.

Herpes
Post-Reading Case History

(The following case history is reprinted from *The Edgar Cayce Products—Ten Years of Research*, published by Heritage Publications, Virginia Beach.)

My first herpes outbreak occurred in August of '76. To my satisfaction, and from visual observation, from the use of Ray's Ointment, Slippery Elm Tea and Sulflax I have experienced no more herpes outbreaks. I used Sulflax for five days. I have continued daily with Ray's Ointment and drinking one to two cups of Slippery Elm Tea, which I enjoy with orange blossom honey. Ray's Ointment does stop the sting and itch mentioned, but not the inner pain.

Hodgkin's Disease
Post-Reading Case History

(The following case history is reprinted from *The Edgar Cayce Products—Ten Years of Research*, published by Heritage Publications, Virginia Beach.)

I think it important that I believed I was going to get well from Hodgkin's Disease before I ever came to Virginia Beach or got involved with the readings. But prior even to the believing was a willingness to turn the whole thing over to God with the understanding (gained from a reading of the New Testament) that somehow He would redeem (i.e., make sense of and transform) my present state of health and consciousness about it and my life.

I had tried all I knew, doctors (and very fine ones) had tried all they knew and there was simply nothing else to be done but to say, "Okay, God, you must know something I don't about this whole thing, and there must be something good about it that you'll let me know about when you get ready to tell me or when I'm ready to hear or understand it." . . . You pray to God and then you listen to Him. I started it. Very soon I experienced ineffable peace. . . .

I began to get well (my dosage, Leukeran, was reduced from three pills every morning to two) and paradoxically getting well was no longer what mattered most. It was this new understanding of God and me that most consumed my attention. Later (and ostensibly unrelated to all this) I moved to Virginia Beach on a temporary basis. I had planned to leave after several months to take up another commitment, but somehow that all got changed as I began to understand that following my intuition might be more important in some cases than "living up to" my word. At Virginia Beach I was introduced to the readings on Hodgkin's Disease, met the Doctors McGarey and decided to go to their Clinic in Phoenix the following summer (1971). I had already met a woman who had been cured of cancer at the Clinic, and had made up my mind to be willing to do exactly what they told her to do. My conversations with her were the clincher on my commitment to go ahead and flow with it and see what happened. Certainly orthodox medicine had by that time failed to give satisfactory results with the Hodgkin's healing.

I spent two weeks in Phoenix, loved every minute of it (loved going to the doctor???!!!) and in addition to colonics and massage and the "Normal Cayce Diet" (which I'd already started after meeting the McGareys) I took up drinking chaparral tea each day and inhaling apple brandy from a charred oak keg. How romantic! I was really "getting into" this healing business, having picked my own tea in Phoenix. [Dr. Bill McGarey gave me a map to go into the desert and get it—not really into the desert—I was already there—but I pretended I was going further into it when I went to that abandoned field to pick the chaparral.] . . . How much nicer than the death-like stillness and the ominous whir of the cobalt machine. In addition to those therapies, Dr. McGarey recommended osteopathic adjustments, and castor oil packs applied to the abdomen, which I still do, and almonds, which I still eat.

By the time I went to Phoenix, my hematologist at Duke University Medical Center in Durham, N.C., had already stopped the Leukeran altogether, and when I went back to him in the fall I saw him in the hall before I'd even gotten my clothes off for the examination and he said, "What's happened to you? You look wonderful." I'd been seeing him regularly since the Hodgkin's Disease was diagnosed in August of 1966. Since June of 1971 there have been no active signs of it, and I know I am cured. I believed that this doctor, along with many people, was a channel for the healing I experienced.

Kidney Infection
Post-Reading Case Histories

(The following are excerpts from a talk delivered by a former Virginia Beach chiropractor on January 21, 1981, detailing his success with the Cayce treatments. In addition to his doctor of chiropractic degree, he has a B.A. in economics and a B.S. in human biology.)

In one case . . . a woman . . . approximately age thirty-five . . . had recurring kidney conditions. She had been treated repeatedly by medical doctors . . . in which the kidney infection would simply recur and it began to affect her whole lifestyle. She would have very bad stomach pain and back pain . . . would be given . . . medicine, and the kidney condition usually would respond. However, it would simply recur in a matter of six months. . . . It went on for about seven years.

In this case, we used an alkaline diet . . . watermelon-seed tea, and manipulation . . . she got over the acute stage and was told . . . to visit occasionally and to maintain the alkaline diet. She went for approximately a year and a half before having a recurrence of the condition, at which time therapy was reinstituted and she responded again favorably. . . .

. . . I have treated quite a number of people with recurring kidney infections, and the response has always been favorable in changing the diet, utilizing colonic therapy, increasing the eliminations, getting on an exercise program. I have never had an unfavorable result with kidney problems. . . .

Kidney Stones
Post-Reading Case History

In 1968, a man living in St. Louis, Michigan, had a kidney stone in his left utheter removed by a process known as transvesocularutherodomy. This left scar tissue at the utheter-bladder junction. In 1971, he had the same process on the right.

In 1973, due to a persistent back pain, he consulted an orthopedic specialist. Previous examinations by a urologist showed nothing in the kidney, but the back X-rays showed another kidney stone, this time in the left kidney, as well as an accumulation of blood in the thoracic vertebra which was characterized as a hemangioma or birth mark in the vertebrae.

The only treatment he subsequently received from the orthopedist was the advice "Live with it." The urologist wasn't much more optimistic, and since he had been operated on twice for a similar condition, he wasn't too hopeful himself.

In 1974, he researched the Circulating Files on kidney stones and found that one of the readings (1054-1) covered all his symptoms. After obtaining the necessary ingredients suggested in the reading, he began his treatments. Then shortly thereafter, he took a motor trip to Florida, and the stone dropped from the kidney to the utheter. He consequently altered the treatments in accordance with the readings and his condition. X-rays a month later confirmed that the stone was gone. His urologist said that the stone probably passed without his feeling it until the man reminded him that a retrograde cystogram was impossible in 1973 due to scar tissue at the utheter-bladder junction.

The man notes in his letter, "Needless to say ... that prayer also had its part in my success story."

Laryngitis
Post-Reading Case History

(The following is a portion of a letter received by a Virginia Beach health food store specializing in Cayce remedies.)

Camphoderm is a constant in our house. Many times in the winter mornings I have awakened with a raspy throat, later showing signs of laryngitis which was rapidly spreading. Usually one rubbing of the Camphoderm on my throat is enough. My son insists it should be heated, but I have had excellent results by just shaking it well, and rubbing it on at the first sign of discomfort.

Lumbago
Post-Reading Case History

(The following report was submitted by a practicing Virginia Beach chiropractor who uses treatment programs suggested in the Cayce readings in his private practice.)

Patient had lumbalgia and came with moderately severe low back pain as well as some pain in her shoulders, which she had had for about three weeks. Among abnormal physical findings: straight leg raises 70 degrees on right; 60 degrees on left.

Treatment program used which was suggested in the Cayce readings was castor oil packs over the liver and colon on right, two times a week for three weeks, "broken doses" of olive oil, six times a day on alternate days. Fletcher's Castoria to flush system, once a week. Chiropractic adjustments, once a week.

Results: Pain running down leg completely gone. Pain in

lower back, eighty percent relief. Halitosis relieved. Yellow "tinge" in sclera of the eye gone. More energy.

Lupus Erythematosus
Post-Reading Case History

This case history concerns a sixty-three-year-old woman who had been diagnosed as having lupus erythematosus in 1955 and was treated for it at the ARE Clinic in Phoenix, Arizona. She displayed advanced skin symptoms along with fever, headaches, insomnia, muscular infirmity, anemia, and leukopenia.

At the clinic, she received massage therapy and osteopathic manipulations. Additionally, she was given a therapy program to follow when she returned home, which included internal doses of Atomidine, Epsom salt baths, Wet Cell treatments, a special diet, exercises, and castor oil packs. She was also counseled to adopt a constructive attitude.

Later, in a letter, the woman expressed the feeling that the change in attitude was instrumental in the healing she had experienced. During her visits to the clinic, she developed a new understanding of the disease, accompanied by a sense of faith that a cure was possible.

Her next medical checkup found that she no longer had lupus. Doctors confirmed that although it was evident that she had had the disease, it was no longer visible on her body. She expressed faith that the same power which had helped cure her lupus could also relieve the aches and pains that remained where the disease had damaged her body.

Malabsorption Syndrome—Megacolon
Post-Reading Case History

(The following is reprinted from *Pathways to Health*, March 1984, volume 6, number 1, a publication of the

ARE Clinic in Phoenix, Arizona. William A. McGarey, M.D., is director.)

. . . Throughout his early life, Edgar Cayce's dream was to help children—to become a doctor. That was not to be, however, probably for divine reasons. He was intended to be what he is remembered as being—one of the world's best known and most gifted seers or psychics.

In August, 1980, Beth's mother brought her to the Clinic as a "last resort." She was malnourished due to a defect in her assimilations which had been called a "malabsorption syndrome." She also had a "megacolon"—the large bowel was tremendously enlarged. Her abdomen was swollen, and she looked for all intents and purposes as a child who was starving to death. After a fall down the stairs two years prior, she thereafter gained no weight at all and developed the syndrome just described.

The staff of the Clinic set up a program of therapy which was aimed at helping her change her approach to life, and helping the physiology of the body recover from the shock of the blow in the solar plexus which staff doctors felt was the primary cause of her difficulty. Castor oil packs, magnetic field therapy, massages, a special diet and all other special approaches found in the Temple Beautiful program gradually made a change. Beth started to blossom like a flower. Whereas she had not gained an ounce in two years, she gained three pounds in 17 days. When asked how long it would take to make her well—just before the end of the program—she retorted "six weeks!" She did just that, and before the end of the year, she was running around like any little girl would, who is filled with vibrant life. . . .

Today, Beth is 7 years old, is going to school and showing forth some of the tremendous potential which all of us at the Clinic recognized in her during her stay here. Recently, her granddad wrote to Doctor Bill McGarey and in a few words showed how the Edgar Cayce legacy has changed lives for the better all around the world.

These were his words: "I am the Grandfather of the

4-year-old girl that came to your clinic for help and you
opened your heart and gave us life. I would call it a
miracle.''

Meningitis
Post-Reading Case History

(The following is a portion of a letter received by a
Virginia Beach health food store specializing in the Cayce
remedies.)

My daughter was suffering with severe neck and shoulder pain. The physician diagnosed it as a simple form of
meningitis. His remedy was Valium for the pain and
complete bed rest.
She took the Valium for a week as prescribed and stayed
in bed throughout. The pain was there when the Valium
was removed and she worried about becoming addicted to
it. My son taught her husband how to make a castor oil
pack which was applied several times a day with a heating
pad, to her neck and shoulders. Within a week she was
able to sit up and maneuver without the help of the
Valium. Improvement continued steadily after that, with
the help of the castor oil pack. At the same time as she had
this, another friend of hers had the same thing. She didn't
use the castor oil and a year later was still doctoring for
pain.

Menopause
Post-Reading Case History

A fifty-year-old Virginia Beach woman began experiencing trouble with her periods, which at times were
preceded by spotting for about thirty days before a normal
flow set in.
In some instances, these "normal" periods were marked

by an extremely heavy flow, which almost made it impossible for her to continue with her day's work.

In December 1983, she once again began the annoying spotting, and after two weeks she remarked to a friend that she did not know how she was going to go through another thirty days of spotting followed by the heavy flow. Her friend suggested that she try a castor oil pack topped with a heating pad on her right side.

She applied the pack for thirty minutes one afternoon, and almost immediately thereafter her flow began in earnest. Although it was a bit heavy, it was not as heavy as she had been experiencing. Since that time, she has had no preamble of spotting, and her periods have become less in intensity.

Menstruation: Abnormal
Post-Reading Case History

(The following is an excerpt from a letter received by a health food store in Virginia Beach specializing in the Cayce formulas.)

My menses was giving me a great deal of trouble when it bothered to come at all. I would bleed so heavy that if my legs didn't have me flat in bed, my period would have. I shouldn't say "flat" for I was practically standing on my head in an effort to avoid a hysterectomy.

I had ordered Formula 545 as a spring tonic, I needed a good "vitamin" but they made me sick. . . . 545 gave me the lift I was looking for but the surprise side effect was what it did for my period. It gradually returned it to normal; better than normal! I know it was the 545 because every time I didn't order it fast enough the heavy flow returned, and stayed, until I started the 545 again; I took it for two years. Now I use it as prescribed "as a spring tonic," and that is what it is.

Mongolism
Post-Reading Case History

A favorable report was received in 1975 from an ARE member who had given her mongoloid child daily massages under the supervision of a cooperating physician. Immense improvements were noted in both the child's physical condition and behavior as a result of this regimen, which the mother had read about in the Circulating File on mongolism.

Muscle Strain
Post-Reading Case Histories #1 and 2

(The following reports were received by a Virginia Beach health food store specializing in the Cayce formulas.)

I was a runner (7 miles a day) and have always had pain in my knees and ankles. . . .

Recently at the urging of a friend I tried Muscle Treat on my knees and ankles and was quite surprised to find total pain relief within one half hour. The relief lasted for four days. I say surprised because I'm not a believer in Edgar Cayce but am beginning to believe in Muscle Treat since it also worked for my bursitis.

In the spring I strained the muscles in both elbows working with hardwood trees. After three months, the pain sensations were still there. I used Muscle Treat morning and evening and within three days my arms were completely healed. Not only is this product effective, it has a nice smell and feel.

Muscle Strain
Post-Reading Case History #3

(The following is an excerpt from a tape-recorded interview, August 20, 1980, with a Virginia Beach chiropractor who discussed his successes with the treatment program suggested by the Cayce readings.)

Patient number four had considerable problems with aching joints of her shoulder and elbow as a result of playing tennis. She was fifty-eight years old and refused to quit playing tennis. She used castor oil packs on her shoulder and elbow twice a week for about five weeks, with remarkable results. She can now play tennis without difficulty.

Narcolepsy
Post-Reading Case History #1

A case reported in the ARE *Medical Research Bulletin* was that of a forty-year-old woman examined in the clinic who had suffered from narcolepsy for four years. She experienced cataleptic or trancelike seizures which were triggered by vigorous laughter.

Since Edgar Cayce consistently attributed narcolepsy to glandular disturbances, it was decided to give this woman internal doses of Atomidine, although this was not reflected in the narcolepsy readings, which did not mention Atomidine. In this case, the doses were gradually increased over a month's time to ten drops daily for five days out of the week. During this time, the patient also used castor oil packs and kept up an exercise program of walking and yoga.

According to a report from the woman, she experienced immediate relief from the seizures and after four months had regained a feeling of well-being and energy that she had not enjoyed for many years.

Narcolepsy
Post-Reading Case History #2

(The following is a portion of a letter detailing an individual's success with the treatment program suggested in the Cayce readings for arthritis. This excerpt concerns the person's use of Atomidine for treatment of narcolepsy. The letter was received by a Virginia Beach health food store specializing in the Cayce formulas.)

... And finally, and very important, I began to take Atomidine, and later prescription 636, for the research convinced me that I have a glandular deficiency, and also a form of narcolepsy, characterized by uncontrollable attacks of sleepiness. I fought sleepiness while driving by turning down all the windows. Sometimes I would have to get out of the car and swing my arms. Then one day with no warning at all, I dropped off to sleep while driving. The steering wheel turned quickly to the left. The jar woke me up. Atomodine is helping.

Now I am not only free of arthritis, but I have better health, more stamina and energy than most women, many younger than I. (I am 81 and a half.) I notice this particularly at square dancing and table tennis when many of the women have to sit out after a game or two, while I am able to continue playing....

Nausea
Post-Reading Case History

(The following is a portion of a letter from a nurse received by a health food store in Virginia Beach specializing in the Cayce remedies.)

... Another of my constant companions was nausea; Yellow Saffron Tea took good care of that.... Yellow Saffron also stopped my chronic hiccoughs like a magic potion. I am never without this tea for myself as well as my family. I also keep a little jar of it at work for my patients. I know I have saved many a patient from a post-op Paralytic Ileus.

Nephritis (Bright's Disease)
Post-Reading Case History

(The following is a letter received by a Virginia Beach health food store specializing in the Cayce remedies.)

In the summertime of 1977, the results of a urinalysis had come back positive (showing symptoms of disease)... there was a trace of albumin, a slight amount of blood. . . . I had hyaline casts showing up in the urinalysis test. The doctor who told me this wanted me to get treated at Mount Sinai Hospital, but I decided to order products that were recommended in the Edgar Cayce readings for kidney problems. I experienced *immediate* beneficial results from using them. The Campho-Derm and watermelon tea relieved me of fluid retention, but the lithia water actually did the most good for me in clearing out my kidneys. I was helped immediately upon my first drink of lithia water. My condition could have developed into a serious case of Bright's Disease, but it didn't.

Anyway, I was tested again for my kidney ailment in June 1979 and February this year [1980] and I show absolutely no trace of kidney trouble. . . .

Plantar Wart
Post-Reading Case History

(The following is a section of a letter received by a Virginia Beach health food store specializing in the Cayce formulas.)

Castor oil came into my life with my daughter's planters wart. It had been treated by the pediatrician with acid for eight weeks without results. As it was very sore to walk on he recommended surgery. I will do anything to avoid surgery! It took three months of a drop of castor oil on a bandaid twice a day; but the oil kept it soft so she could walk without discomfort, until it turned black and fell out like a little stone. This is the standard treatment for warts in our house now. Most of them just take a few weeks. . . .

Pneumonia
Post-Reading Case History

A young woman may have avoided a bout in the hospital with pneumonia because a friend agreed to try to help her with some of Edgar Cayce's advice.

To combat the pneumonia, her doctor had treated her with antibiotics for five days, and she did not respond. He told her that if she did not improve in three more days that he would have to admit her into a hospital.

According to a report received by the ARE, the woman was given an enema to cleanse her system and then Calcidin and beef juice every hour and B complex vitamins. Her back was massaged at night with peanut oil so that she could get her rest.

After the first day's treatment, the woman, who did not as a rule eat properly, was ready to eat. Her friend continued treating her, and by the second day she was walking around the house. She considered herself well by the third day and, as the report was received, was continuing to improve.

Pruritus
Post-Reading Case History

(The following is an excerpt from a tape-recorded interview August 20, 1980, with a Virginia Beach chiropractor who discussed his successes with the treatment program suggested by the Cayce readings.)

Patient number eleven (twenty-seven-year-old female) . . . with symptoms of muscle twitching and severe itching preventing sleeping for periods of the preceding three weeks and intermittently for six months preceding that. Suggested what is considered the Cayce normal diet, which is no refined carbohydrates, no greasy foods, knocked out the . . . pork and beef. Prescribed because the pruritus files . . . suggested citrus breakfast, massage with peanut oil and olive oil on the feet and backs of the knees and lower spine to promote eliminations through the kidneys, and olive oil, one to two tablespoons, in a vegetable salad, and chiropractic care over five days. After three visits and fifteen days care, the patient reported remarkable improvement with no problems of itching and sleeping throughout the night instead of waking up twelve times a night.

Psoriasis
Post-Reading Case History

In October 1983, a sixty-year-old woman with patches of psoriasis on her nose, under her eyes and mouth, and in her ears sought relief through the use of Cayce's remedies. She purchased a mixture of cream of tartar, Rochelle salts, and sulfur and took a teaspoon once every morning. Following cleansing of the areas, she topically applied Ray's Ointment. "I drank a lot of water . . . and I did not eat red meat," she added.

She noted an improvement the next day, and by the following week all indications of the psoriasis had disappeared. Although she has not had any recurrence of the psoriasis, when areas of her skin begin to feel dry, she applies the Ray's Ointment as a preventive.

Pyorrhea
Post-Reading Case History

(The following letter was received by a health food store in Virginia Beach specializing in the Cayce formulas.)

* * *

Sometime last June or July I experienced a bad toothache and upon investigation and dentist's diagnosis, discovered that my gums were sore and receding i.e., pyorrhea.

As my dental habits were very good... I could not understand how this could have happened.

The dentist recommended cleaning the teeth and gums with a toothpick, getting braces and doing skin grafts from the inside gums to the outer, receding ones after the braces....

In August I began a regime of trying to have one raw salad a day, brushing frequently and vigorously and rubbing my gums with Ipsab for five minutes every other day....

This went on for seven months until one day, quite unexpectedly I brushed and *there was no pain*!

I now use Ipsab about once every three days.... I still am amazed when I brush my teeth and where once there was so much tenderness and pain there is *none*!...

Ringworm
Post-Reading Case History

A 1974 report indicated that the use of the castor oil pack, peanut oil rubs, healing suggestions, and the application of Atomidine successfully removed ringworm in a ten-year-old boy.

Scars
Post-Reading Case History

(The following is a verbal report received by a health food store in Virginia Beach which specializes in the Cayce formulas.)

...In April of 1983 a young woman was involved in a truck wreck which threw her out of the vehicle and scraped her along the pavement. "I was dragged along the pavement on my front and the bone was exposed on my cheek, left side of my face, and left knee and nose," she said. In addition to these injuries, the large side-view mirror went into her right leg about two and a half inches just above her kneecap. An operation was performed on the knee at North Carolina Memorial Hospital at the University of North Carolina at Chapel Hill to remove glass fragments.

Afterward, a plastic surgeon at the hospital proposed three or four plastic surgery operations on her face and knees. That same day, a friend brought her a bottle of Scar Formula to use and rubbed some on her. "The nurse went crazy because she was afraid of infection. She called the plastic surgeon and he did his best to dissuade me from using it and warned me about infection and getting it in my eyes . . . even threatened to cancel the plastic surgery if I persisted, which, of course, I did." At that time, she also alternated using vitamin E with the Scar Formula but found the massage formula more effective. . . .

On the sixth day, the plastic surgeon came to check on her condition, and at the time she happened to be rubbing the scar on her nose. "To my surprise and his amazement, the entire nose scab came off in my hand. I thought my nose had fallen off when the surgeon's mouth dropped open. He stared at me for thirty seconds with his mouth open and then sat down and asked me in more detail exactly what I'd done since my nose was almost healed." Later, she continued, he had a secretary take down in shorthand all of the details on exactly how she had used the Scar Formula and any other medication she might have used.

"As of August 23, 1983, all of my facial scars are at least ninety-five percent gone, while the scars on my knee where I used the Scar Formula are almost eighty percent gone," she said, explaining that her right knee was so scarred that people found it difficult to look at it. "One little girl started crying after seeing it," she added.

"Needless to say, I have canceled the plastic surgery,

and I have given the Scar Formula to several friends. I am still using it every day."

Sciatica
Post-Reading Case History

(The following is an excerpt from a tape-recorded interview made on August 27, 1980, with a Virginia Beach chiropractor who discussed his successes with the treatment program suggested by the Cayce readings.)

Patient number twenty-five...with sciatica, inflammation of the sciatic nerves, as a result of displacement of the sacrum on the ilia, two pelvis bones that it rests between. It had been intermittent for the previous three weeks. At that time, he couldn't sleep as a result of the pain. I did the chiropractic care, and I suggested the use of massage with olive oil and peanut oil. I suggested a sitz bath which is contiguous with the readings. He recovered completely, quickly in two or three days.

Scleroderma
Post-Reading Case History

(The following is reprinted from the February 1976 issue of *Fate* magazine and is a portion of an article I wrote for the publication titled, "Cayce Cures Still Baffle Science.")

...Another desperately ill man who sought help from the Cayce files was Sidney Kalugin, the man who was "turning to stone." In July 1972 Kalugin was tagged a "walking miracle" by a Virginia Beach journalist. The 50-year-old Kalugin was a senior court officer in New York state when in 1968–69 he began to notice strange swellings around his ankles.

"The swellings were peculiar," he explains. "They felt like clay and when I put finger pressure on them, the hole just remained. The flesh didn't spring back."

Doctors in New York's Montefiore Hospital diagnosed his illness as scleroderma, hardening of the skin. Extremely rare, the illness has no known cure. Cortisone was recommended but had to be discontinued after Kalugin became ill from the side effects. Then he took Vitamin E with no results. By now the hardening had progressed up to his torso and his legs were worse. He sought help from a specialist on muscular ailments at Mt. Sinai Hospital in New York. Tests there confirmed the diagnosis of scleroderma.

Scleroderma not only produces uncomfortable hardness of the body but when Kalugin fell down instead of bruising his body would chip! "I was literally turning to stone," he remarks.

Through a chiropractor friend who had vacationed at Virginia Beach, Kalugin learned of Edgar Cayce and that the clairvoyant had prescribed cures for scleroderma while in trance. Kalugin immediately purchased the well-known book, *There Is a River* by Thomas Sugrue, and began to acquaint himself with Cayce. During the first few moments with the book, he wrote, "My thumb stopped at a page and lo and behold, there in front of my eyes was the word 'scleroderma.' . . ."

He began to use some of Cayce's recommended cures such as olive oil, castor oil and peanut oil massages. He noted a gradual softening and a lightening of the abnormal beet-red skin he had grown accustomed to. Later Dr. William A. McGarey of the medical research division of the Edgar Cayce Foundation in Phoenix, Ariz., told Kalugin to contact Dr. Frank Dobbins (now deceased) of Staten Island, N.Y. Dr. Dobbins, who had been recommended in the Cayce readings, suggested Kalugin take Atomidine. Kalugin also began to use the wet-cell and to inhale fumes supplied by apple brandy in a charred oak keg—another Cayce cure.

Although this combination of treatments is unorthodox, today Kalugin feels he is completely cured of his "incurable" disease and he enjoys an active healthy life.

Seborrhea
Post-Reading Case History

(The following letter was received by a Virginia Beach health food store specializing in the Cayce formulas.)

... I am 68-years old and for four or five years have been troubled with redness on both sides of my face, like where a mustache would be worn. Whether I shaved with an electric razor or a blade razor and no matter how carefully I would shave, there would be a red, irritated look that never really went away—also my forehead had an area that always looked irritated. The skin behind my ears and included the lobes were scaley.... My family doctor said it was a seborrhea condition....

Awhile ago I had purchased from you a bottle of "Dermaglow" but hadn't really used it. I saw it in my medicine cabinet and thought why don't I try this, what do I have to lose. To my surprise after six treatments with "Dermaglow" my skin condition on my face, forehead and behind my ears has improved at least 90 percent.

Seizures: Infantile
Post-Reading Case History

(The following is a case profile from the ARE Clinic in Phoenix, Arizona. The ARE Clinic is a nonprofit Arizona corporation dedicated to provide the best available care utilizing conventional and holistic therapies. Medical research— finding better methods of healing and regeneration—is an important part of the clinic's mission. This report is part of a series of publications intended to keep medical professionals and the general public informed of research findings that might give hope to persons struggling with illness. Those who wish further information may send a letter of inquiry to: Medical Research Inquiry,

The ARE Clinic, 4018 North Fortieth Street, Phoenix, Arizona 85018.)

The following report concerns a four-year-old boy with severe infantile seizures who obtained significant gradual reduction of symptoms during two years of therapy derived from the Cayce readings and related sources, including a complete withdrawal from large doses of anticonvulsant medication.

According to the report, the child was brought to the clinic when he was ten months old. The boy had contracted spinal meningitis when he was three months old and subsequently developed severe infantile seizures. After seeking help from some of the best orthodox centers in their home state of Hawaii and receiving seven months of tests and medical treatment, the child was still having thirty to forty seizures a day, with pain-related behavior, such as screaming and chewing on his fists.

The report further states, "The large doses of anticonvulsants made him drowsy, but did not stop the seizures. The mother was told that institutionalizing [the child] would be wise, as his prognosis was bleak. Unwilling to accept that path, she went to several medical centers in California, including the Center for Child Study at UCLA. . . ."

Eventually the child was brought to the clinic, where he obtained beneficial results after one week of therapy. The mother and child then returned to Hawaii. A year later, the parents brought the child back and, following two weeks of therapy, decided to move to Phoenix.

When the child was first brought to the clinic, evaluation showed very limited sensory processing. "[He] took notice of visual, auditory, or tactile stimuli only occasionally and then very briefly—one to five seconds attention span. His eyes demonstrated a light reflex, but he had no central eyesight, relying entirely upon sporadic peripheral vision. Coordination and mobility were poorly developed, but he was of normal size for his age and a handsome boy."

The treatment program at the clinic included:

*ETA therapy—electrotherapy for half-hour sessions was initially conducted every day, then evolved gradually to one to two sessions per week.

*Castor oil packs—used initially every day over the abdomen, then gradually these were applied on an "as needed" basis.

*Cranial and spinal manipulation—started in Hawaii and continued in Phoenix, with frequency of treatments at the direction of the practitioner.

*Music therapy—to promote sensory integration and, when used during massage, to relax.

*Massage—[he] was fortunate to have a father who was an accomplished masseur, specializing in the Hawaiian Lomi-Lomi massage. Both full-body and spinal massage were administered daily.

*Passion flower fusion—an herbal tea preparation recommended often by the Edgar Cayce readings for reducing seizures.

*DMSO—administered topically over the entire body at the direction of Dr. Jordan at the University of Oregon.

*Patterning—administered through the Center for Neural Development Studies at Arizona State University and the National Academy for Child Development, as a process of stimulating neurological organization through repetitive physical and sensory exercises.

*Masking—breathing exercises to develop increased oxygen supply to the brain by using a plastic mask, a therapy devised by the Institutes for the Achievement of Human Potential.

*Counseling—an ongoing process of discussion and supportive caring with parents.

Progress was noted by both parents and staff at the clinic. Eventually he was taken off phenobarbital and his Dilantin dosage gradually decreased. "With each change in replacing drugs with 'natural' therapies, the pattern of his seizures changed," the report continues.

Following the initial two weeks of therapy, the child began sleeping better and having fewer seizures. Additionally, the boy's father noted that his son made sustained eye contact for the first time since the seizures began.

During the course of treatments, improvements continued to be noted. Eventually the child was "weaned" off all anticonvulsants. Now approaching four years of age, he is presently "enjoying his best health since the onset of the infantile seizures.... His parents and friends report how affectionate and loving [he] has become—he interacts with others much more now. No longer are his fists clenched, and the bouts of screaming have all but disappeared. The seizures are now much less frequent and severe.... His physical, emotional, and mental development continues to delight his parents."

Sinus
Post-Reading Case History

(The following is a portion of a testimonial received by a health food store in Virginia Beach specializing in the Cayce formulas.)

I used to have a terrible sinus condition. I had one operation on my nose which produced little relief. My surgeon is one of the outstanding men in his field in the Southeast and he said my nose was one of the two worst he'd ever seen.

I had to try to decide whether to have another operation which would involve a great deal more cutting in a delicate area. I eventually decided to have the operation based on what I read in the Cayce reading—that medication and treatments could do a lot for problems with cartilage, membrane lining and drainage—but little with bone structure.

In the time during which I was making up my mind, I used Glyco-Thymoline the way I'd read about it in Jess Stearn's book and also on the directions. It helped a great deal, but not satisfied with that, I ordered the original readings on sinusitis and Glyco-Thymoline and found that Cayce had recommended a much more specific treatment using the Glyco-Thymoline with heat and then finishing off with an ice pack. For sinus drainage this cannot be beat! I would have horrible headaches any day I didn't follow this treatment.

After a year and a half, I decided to risk the second operation—which was successful—possibly even more so because with the treatment I'd been able to keep down sinus infections. I still use Glyco-Thymoline for a number of things, and I've since moved to Florida because Cayce sometimes recommended another area of the country—which seemed to say to me that a change of location to a more benevolent climate could be a more natural way to treat a problem.

I do think the message in this is that one should always peruse the original readings and attempt to see just what Cayce did advise—in detail, and follow those details to the letter.

Spine
Post-Reading Case History

In 1966, a young man in the military injured his spine while attempting to remove a rock buried in the ground. At the time, he said, he was sitting on the ground and tugging at the rock, which he discovered was stuck deep in the soil. As he tugged, he heard a "cracking sound" in his fourth lumbar area, following which he was unable to walk. "I almost had to crawl back into the house," he added.

What followed was a diagnosis from the military doctor who told him that he would require an operation to fuse his spine.

Later, upon being discharged, he visited three other physicians who agreed that an operation would be necessary. However, still not satisfied, he delayed surgery and in the meantime moved to Virginia Beach so that he could be near the Association for Research and Enlightenment.

Following the advice found in the medical readings, he started administering treatments with the Wet Cell Appliance and Radio-Active Appliance, the former in the morning and the latter in the evening, as prescribed by Cayce, according to the man.

This treatment continued for three to four years, bringing temporary relief. Later, during his research at the Cayce library, he discovered a volume written by a chiropractic doctor from California and found his symptoms were more sympathetic to those mentioned in the book as the result of problems with the sacroiliac. The book gave a series of yoga-type exercises designed to relieve the condition, which it did, he said.

Although twinges of the discomfort return intermittently, performing the simple leg exercises relieves them.

"I don't know what I would have done if I had had my operation and found out later that it wasn't necessary."

Tachycardia
Post-Reading Case History

(The following is reprinted from the June 1981 *Medical Research Bulletin*, volume X, number 1, published by the ARE Clinic, Inc., 4018 North Fortieth Street, Phoenix, Arizona 85018. Copyright 1977, by ARE Clinic, Inc. Reprinted by permission.)

... A lady correspondent reported on her experience with palpitations several months ago. She had been ill as a child with rheumatic fever and thinks this may have caused her palpitations about eight years ago, when she was 27. Medications were given (Inderal) and this produced some response. She was free of symptoms for two—three years, but then it recurred. The second course helped again, but did not clear up the condition completely. Then, nearly three years ago, she came across the Cayce Readings and on the recommendation of several of her friends, started taking the Herbal Tonic 545, which Cayce said would be an excellent spring tonic for anyone.

Just half a bottle later, the palpitations had decreased by 75 percent, and shortly thereafter, the condition was gone.

They recurred once, after she had stopped the tonic, but when she started again, they once more disappeared.

The formula is found in the reading 545 and contains several ingredients. Sarsaparilla root, wild cherry bark and yellow dock root are found in a variety of readings together and seem to be dealing with poor eliminations, incoordination between assimilation and elimination, acting as a stimulant to the pulmonary system and bronchial passages, stimulating the flow of gastric juices and aiding the liver in clearing the blood of toxins. Prickly ash bark stimulates the liver, gallbladder, pancreas and spleen. Other herbs in this tonic include dogwood bark, dog fennel, balsam of tolu, sassafras oil and tincture of capsici.

One wonders if we don't often miss the forest for the trees or vice versa—in looking at the organ that is malfunctioning instead of the causes that lie behind the malfunction. Cayce suggested in readings given for the radioactive appliance, that some portions of the body have excess electrical charges and some have too little. The appliance was given to aid in the correction of many of these imbalances. But herbs that cleanse the vital organs may bring about the same type of response in allowing the body once more to function normally.

Perhaps it was in this way that simple herbs cleared up a very distressing condition for this woman.

Tumors: Breast
Post-Reading Case History

(The following case history is part of a membership survey project conducted by the Association for Research and Enlightenment in Virginia Beach in January 1984.)

"I had a golf ball sized oval lump in my breast—three doctors recommended surgery," one woman noted in her report. After deciding against immediate surgery and that she wanted to live, she began to treat the condition using some of the advice found in the Cayce readings.

"I alternated putting my breast in cold and then hot water and then applying a mixture of peanut oil and castor oil," she said, explaining that the packs were predominantly castor oil. "Cayce said these two oils are absorbed through the skin and have healing qualities."

She made her packs by soaking a tissue in the oils and then covering with plastic wrap. When she began her treatment, her lump was large and sore. It took her four months to effect any radical changes, but as she explained, "I figured it took a long time to get big."

Although change was gradual, after the first two months, the pain had lessened considerably and "I gradually stopped using ice." (Which was part of the pack when she was uncomfortable.)

She also changed her diet and eliminated caffeine and chocolates or sugar. She also ate foods rich in vitamins B and A. "I also worked with color ... wore a blue-green nightgown. ... Cayce said green was healing."

Underlined for emphasis in her report are the words, "The lump is gone!" followed by the explanation that "although the tissue is somewhat [granular], the doctors say this is considered normal."

Tumors: Fibroid
Post-Reading Case History #1

(The following report was submitted as part of a recent survey project on the results of healing concepts, principles, and specific modalities and formulas mentioned in the Cayce readings. The survey was conducted by the ARE.)

After refusing to schedule surgery to remove fibroid tumors diagnosed by her physician, a young woman consulted the Circulating Files and began a regimen of castor oil packs, five days on and three days off; took internal doses of Atomidine according to the files, three days on and two days off; and douched twice a week with Atomidine and Glyco-Thymoline.

She later returned to her gynecologist, who once again examined her. His response on her condition was, "Why were we considering surgery? Your tumors are now quite small."

She rates the results of following the advice given in the Circulating Files as "excellent" and notes that despite the fact that small tumors may be still evident, "mid-menstrual-cycle bleeding has stopped. So has all talk of surgery."

At the time of her report, she had been using the treatments "faithfully" for six months. "I now use castor oil packs quite regularly, but have stopped [regular] Atomidine and douching."

Tumors: Fibroid
Post-Reading Case History #2

(The following is part of a recent survey conducted by the ARE in Virginia Beach.)

After being diagnosed as having fibroids in the uterus, a woman began Edgar Cayce's castor oil packs. However, she found the messiness of the oil and cover, plus lack of time to stick with it too demanding, so on the third night she switched to just rubbing castor oil on her uterine area each morning and night.

She also endeavored to visualize the area as healthy. Following a few weeks of the procedure, she went to her gynecologist and took a sonogram test. There was no trace of the fibroids.

A week later, she returned to her physician for a final determination based on the tests, and the former opinion was confirmed: there was no trace of the fibroids.

Although she initially began to follow the readings in the conventional manner, she reports that she has to attribute her progress to just rubbing in the castor oil, using no cover. She applied it once during the day and just before going to bed.

Tumors: Uterus
Post-Reading Case History

Encouraging results were obtained more recently by a member of the Association for Research and Enlightenment who told her story to the ARE Clinic. This woman had a long-standing problem with uterine flooding and had had two D & Cs performed over an eight-year period. She was subsequently diagnosed by two physicians as having a fibroid tumor the size of a baseball on the wall of her uterus. A hysterectomy and another D & C were recommended.

At this point, the woman studied the readings for 2330 on fibroid tumors and decided to use alternating Atomidine and Glyco-Thymoline douches as suggested. After applying these regularly, she found that the iodine did not agree with her and discontinued the use of Atomidine. On the advice of another doctor, she began using castor oil packs, applying them over her lower abdomen. After a week of applying the packs daily, she had a menstrual period with an unusual amount of mucus. She began flowing heavily and although she was scheduled for surgery in a few weeks, after a two-day delay was admitted to the hospital, where she was immediately taken to the operating room. Following surgery, she was informed that there had been no tumor, just a mass of clots that had been misdiagnosed as a tumor. She later asked the doctor if fibroid tumors ever eliminate spontaneously and was told that it never happened.

Although nothing could be proved, the woman felt that if she had not used the castor oil packs, she would no longer have her female organs.

Ulcers
Post-Reading Case History

(The following case history is reprinted from *The Edgar Cayce Products—Ten Years of Research*, published by Heritage Publications, Virginia Beach.)

As a child, I was sickly and underweight. I grew to the five-feet, eight-and-one-half inches that I am now by the time I was 13-years-old. Due to growing so fast, my pelvis had a tilt of three inches, according to my family doctor, which left me in pain most of the time. Nothing was done about the tilt because the doctor said I would "grow out of it." By the time I was 17, I had what he called "pre-ulcers." All I knew was that my stomach hurt and when I sat for any length of time, I couldn't get up because my upper legs would cramp. I got to college and discovered alcohol, but I found that every time I would have a gin and tonic, I would be in agony. A doctor prescribed . . . stomach relaxers.

Once out of college, I was not troubled by the pains until the summer of 1974. I was in Florida vacationing at the time. I had no warning other than an excruciating headache that went on for days. I took my little girl to a pool two blocks away. While at the pool, I started having very sharp pains in my stomach. I headed back to the house and had to send my daughter ahead because, by the time I was half a block away, I could no longer walk. That night I found out what "writhing in pain" meant. The next morning, I went to my mother's family doctor who was also a surgeon. Needless to say, he wanted me in the hospital. I was terrified of surgery, and decided that, as long as I was conscious, I would say "no." He agreed to treat me at home as long as I called him at least twice a day. I was given, once again, an antacid and some other drugs to stop the bleeding.

The bleeding did stop and two weeks later, I came to Virginia Beach. A very good friend of mine drove to Florida to pick me up, and brought with him the Cayce

Circulating File on ulcers. I remember craving a tomato, and this was a definite "no no" on the doctor's diet. Cayce, on the other hand, recommended it to one of his cases. I still remember how wonderful it tasted.

When back in Virginia Beach, I started bleeding again. This time it was worse. I called all the doctors I could think of in the area. At the time there had been a rash of malpractice suits against doctors, and all of the ones that I called refused to see me unless I was admitted to a hospital. In panic, I referred back to the Cayce Readings, this time studying them with a lot more fervor. After all, he was the only "physician" who I could consult with.

Saffron tea was invaluable. I kept a lukewarm cup of the tea brewing all the time. The lime and cinnamon water helped the vomiting. Contrary to the doctor's recommended diet, I ate no bread, grains or milk products other than a little yogurt, and the bleeding stopped. I felt that the illness had ended, but I was frustrated. Still bed-ridden, I could not understand why I was not beginning to feel completely well and strong. That very same friend intervened once again asking me if I had read all of the readings. When I said I had read them four or five times, he then proceeded to read them with me. It was then that the "miracle" began to happen. I had followed the diet, and all of the suggestions except one. At the end of the Cayce Readings, he reminded the people to pray. I had been following the diet, but I had continued to lay there and worry. The very minute I substituted the positive energy of praying for my negative worrying, I felt a difference. The pains began to subside and in two days I was walking again.

Once I was well enough to get there, I started chiropractic treatments with a friend. He found that because of my pelvic tilt, the parts of my spine that related to my stomach region were out of alignment. He worked on me and now, four years later, I am healthier and stronger than I ever was. I have no back trouble. I have no stomach problems. The best part of all is that I still have my stomach.

I am very thankful to Edgar Cayce and my friends.

Cayce Documented Today:
Part 2

The following section of Cayce Documented Today is a review of some current medical theories and opinions which generally hold the same philosophies as suggested by Edgar Cayce while he was alive.

The research and findings mentioned in this section were made independently of any effort to document the Cayce therapies.

Alcohol

"Alcohol in moderation is well for MOST bodies. But too great a quantity taken...[can] cause a slow congestion in the liver area. But alcohols taken evenings—very well" (877-13).

Also indicated was the suggestion that a glass of red wine once or twice a day as a food would be helpful, and that an excessive amount of hard liquor could be devastating to the gastric flow. (875-1)

Supporting Cayce's recommendation for wine once or twice a day is research by Dr. Brian Mishara and colleagues of the Harvard Medical School, who reported that when elderly patients at a nursing home were allowed up to two drinks of spirits, wine, or beer a day, they became friendlier and were more active and happier. They slept better and complained less about their health and living conditions.

According to Dr. Mishara in the March 1978 *Moneysworth*, patients in the study began to take "more control and responsibility for their own lives and make more demands upon both the environment and each other."

The March 24, 1979, issue of *Executive Fitness* published results of the U.S. Government's Second Report on Alcohol and Alcoholism, revealing that moderate drinkers outlive teetotalers, and that abstainers outlive excessive drinkers.

Also in the report were the results of a study conducted

by Arthur L. Klatsky at the Kaiser-Permanent Medical Center in Oakland, California. It was found that among 120,000 people evaluated, those who drank moderately were thirty percent less likely to have heart attacks than teetotalers.

Although it can be said that teetotalers may be more "uptight" than moderate drinkers, Professor William J. Darby, a biochemist from Vanderbilt University and president of the Nutrition Foundation of New York, feels it involves something else: "There is also growing evidence that moderate alcohol intake elevates the amount of high-density lipoproteins (HDL) in the blood." And this is good, the article notes, for HDL helps keep arteries clear of cholesterol.

"It's not the most potent drug in the world," added Dr. Jonathan O. Cole, head of psychopharmacology at McLean Hospital in Massachusetts, "but I think alcohol has a mild anxiety-relieving, mood-elevating effect on a fair number of people."

Despite the anxiety-relieving effects, Cayce felt that some individuals could not tolerate alcohol in any quantity. He noted that for some, alcohol could weaken the aura within the body, making that person open to possession. Because the body would be depleted, lower entities would be attracted, he believed.

Nearly all mental hospitals have patients who run amok when they drink alcohol, according to Dr. Frederick Gibbs, professor emeritus of neurology at the University of Illinois in the January 1979 *National Medical Bulletin*. In the same article, Dr. Alberto A. Marianacci, also professor emeritus of neurology, who has developed a method to test alcohol intolerance, noted, "The person who is made dangerous by alcohol is a walking time bomb."

His testing of alcohol intolerance was measured by an electroencephalograph (EEG), and brain waves were measured three times while the patient was sober and then under the influence of six ounces of alcohol in the bloodstream.

"Normal brain waves showed up like a calm sea, but

abnormalities triggered by alcohol came across like a
raging ocean," according to the article.

The cause of alcohol intolerance could be attributed to
an accident, a birth defect, or even an infection during
pregnancy, all of which could have resulted in early brain
cell damage, Dr. Marianacci said.

Alzheimer's Disease

"Cook not in aluminum but rather in enamel or glass-
ware. NOT in aluminum for with this condition, aluminum
becomes poisonous to the system. Do not use aluminum
ware in any form where this body takes food from." (1223-1)

In the January 1980 issue of Huxley Institute CSF
Newsletter, Dr. A. Hoffer, a psychiatrist who practices
orthmolecular medicine and psychiatry, reported that high
levels of aluminum were found in the brains of patients
who suffered a nerve disorder related to senility, or
Alzheimer's disease.

The authors of an article in the April 18, 1980, issue of
Science, the publication of the National Association for the
Advancement of Science, also noted that their findings
seemed to show that there is an association of aluminum
with damage to the brain cells. The research team was
from the University of Vermont College of Medicine and
the National Institute of Environmental Health Science.

Further, the *New England Journal of Medicine* published
a letter from a reader who noted that when he cooked in
cheap aluminum pots while he was in medical school, he
noticed signs of corrosive pitting and whitish powdery
deposits around the pits. His advice: throw away all
aluminum pots and pans.

Arthritis

The causes attributed to arthritis in the Edgar Cayce
readings were poor assimilation and elimination, impaired

circulation, glandular malfunction, karmic and psychological factors, previous treatments, and spinal subluxations and injuries.

Poor assimilation and elimination were noted as the first cause in thirty-seven percent of the cases defined as arthritis. Cayce believed that improper eliminations triggered excess acid, which decreased the function of the lymphatic system. The liver, in turn, became less active and did not produce the enzymes needed in the digestive process.

Poor assimilation resulted in a decrease of rebuilding forces normally needed to stimulate regular eliminations. Consequently, it was held that some foods actually became poisonous in the system because they could not be utilized properly. The trapped waste materials were picked up again by the circulation, resulting in a surplus of toxins in the blood.

Among the foods to be avoided, according to Cayce, were beef and fried foods, and recent medical findings note that low-fat diets can contribute to a decrease in inflammation of the joints.

Dr. Charles F. Lucas, chief of endocrinology and metabolism at Harper-Grace Hospitals, Detroit, has reported that a diet low in animal fats will ease rheumatoid arthritis pain. "Some of our patients who tried the diet reported that pain and stiffness nearly disappeared. Swelling in joints decreased markedly," he said.

Further substantiating Cayce is a study conducted by the Department of Medicine at Wayne State University in Detroit, Michigan, which reported (*Clinical Research*, volume 29, number 4, 1981), "fat-free diets have been found to produce complete remissions in six patients with rheumatoid arthritis."

Cayce also recommended internal doses of gold-and-soda solutions in fourteen percent of his readings for arthritic cases. In an issue of *Health* magazine, an article on apheresis, a blood-cleansing technique used by some physicians as a possible treatment for rheumatoid arthritis, noted that the most impressive results using apheresis were obtained by patients who also used "long-acting medications such as gold."

Two pain-relieving treatments mentioned in one percent of the readings were cobra and bee venom. Although a bit unorthodox, they have recently attracted new interest from medical science as possible treatments for arthritis.

According to Cayce in reading 3561-1, the bee venom would produce immunity to certain poisons and would stimulate the lymph flow, which had become impaired. As part of this treatment, the person's limbs and joints were to be thoroughly massaged following the injection of venom. Supporting Cayce here are recent experiments in Great Britain which have isolated an antiinflammatory agent in bee venom. This agent is apparently nonpoisonous and has produced no harmful side effects. In the United States, it has been found that bee venom injected into painful joints activates natural cortisone production in the bones, thus relieving the pain of arthritis and rheumatism.

Research with cobra venom is being conducted in India and Belgium. However, due to the obvious danger involved with cobra venom, these tests have been extremely limited and restricted.

Attitudes and Emotions

Medicine is beginning to accept the theory that people can and do die of grief, although research hasn't proved how this occurs. However, one recent study at Mt. Sinai Hospital in New York, described in *"Behavioral Kinesiology Report,"* noted that six bereaved widowers were more susceptible to infection due to depressed lymphocyte activity, which depends on the health and activity of the thymus gland, which reacts adversely to emotional stress.

Cayce spoke frequently of the necessity to balance the emotions as well as the need to balance the diet. In many readings given for physical disturbances, he suggested a change in attitude as a possible treatment for the discomfort. Ulcers, hypertension, asthma, and high blood pressure are only a few of the physical ailments that medicine now recognizes as linked to the emotional state.

Medicine has noted that an emotional upset can cause the stomach to secrete the hormone gastrin, sending it into the bloodstream. This hormone causes the stomach to produce extra amounts of hydrochloric acid. An excessive amount of hydrochloric acid tends to irritate and possibly inflame the lining of the stomach.

Other findings today that tend to support Cayce's theory on attitudes and emotions were noted in a study in which over one thousand adults were given information concerning high blood pressure. They were invited to attend lectures and discussions and received information in the mail. Later they were compared to a control group which had received no special attention or information. The results suggested that ignorance is bliss, for those not overly concerned (overinformed) about high blood pressure had lower blood pressure readings.

This was substantiated at the Ninth Annual Scientific Meeting of the International Society of Hypertension in Palm Springs, California, in which Vincent DeQuattro of the University of Southern California Medical Center in Los Angeles noted that high blood pressure patients experience significantly more anxiety and repressed anger than persons with normal blood pressure.

American Health magazine (November-December 1983) in its article "Anatomy Of a Laugh" notes that "laughing can lighten stress, anxiety, depression and pain. . . . In laughing, we may arouse enzyme secretions that aid digestion and might even work as a natural laxative."

Cayce believed that the body was the temple of the living God and that it should be treated, physically and mentally, as such. He said: "Keep the mental attitude in the constructive force that make for knowing that the body is not only good but good for something" (906-2).

If attitudes and emotions were important, so was love, according to Cayce, who held that sudden infant death syndrome (SIDS) was linked to the absence of love and due to the soul deciding to leave the body.

An article in *Psychology Today* (May 1981) suggests

that maternal emotions during pregnancy have both an immediate and long-term effect on a child. The article, "Prenatal Psychology: Pregnant With Questions," notes: "A healthy 17-year-old girl gave birth to an apparently normal baby boy after a medically uncomplicated pregnancy. Twenty hours of normal infant care followed, with mother and child side by side. Then the baby vomited fresh blood. He was examined and still appeared healthy and vigorous, but his vomiting continued, and one hour later, the baby died. Postmortem examination revealed three peptic ulcers."

The tragedy raised the question of whether the mother was under enough stress while pregnant to transfer it to her unborn child. Discussions with the mother revealed a stressful pregnancy, especially in the last trimester.

In line with this suggestion is a recent book, *The Secret Life of the Unborn Child* by Thomas Verny with John Kelly (Dell, New York, New York, 1982), which notes evidence that even a four- or five-month-old fetus is sensitive to the mother's experiences and responds to them.

Blindness: Tendencies

Edgar Cayce gave fifty-three readings for twenty-nine individuals suffering from varying degrees of loss of vision. He generally concluded that the loss of vision could be attributed to a variety of physical imbalances, including poor or depleted circulation.

Findings reported in the March 1981 issue of *Discover* suggest that damaged blood vessels can block nourishment to the eye, thereby impairing the vision.

Additionally, Cayce said that direct light into the eyes should be avoided. According to an article released by the Vitamin Center of Eye Research, "Light shining into the eyes can trigger a photochemical reaction that results in the production of chemicals shown in laboratory experiments to be damaging to the eye lens." The findings were attributed to Dr. Shambhu D. Varma, director of eye research at the University of Maryland.

Cancer: Breast

One of the causes of illness in general, and cancer in particular, given by Cayce was poor eliminations. Although his diagnosis was a bit unorthodox at the time, it was not new, for doctors around the beginning of the twentieth century blamed many diseases on constipation, believing that it caused a toxic-waste buildup which entered the bloodstream.

However, this theory was discontinued when research at the time failed to substantiate it. Now two physicians at the University of California have noted that women who have few bowel movements per week have four times the risk of breast disease than women who have one or more bowel movements each day.

The physicians Nicholas L. Petraskis and Eileen B. King studied more than five thousand women. Dr. Petraskis noted in *The Lancet*, "We found that five percent of women having one bowel movement per day would have abnormal dysplastic cells, while 10 percent of women having fewer than one bowel movement a day would have this abnormality. . . ." However, he added that this supposition should not be allowed to create the fear of breast cancer in women who are constipated.

Cancer: Diet

Some researchers have reported that if a person eats properly, in some instances cancer may be avoided.

Those foods which they feel should be avoided were those frequently mentioned in the Edgar Cayce readings as hazardous to the health. These included fried or fatty foods, beef, and highly seasoned foods.

Foods recommended by Cayce were fruits and vegetables—in short, an alkaline diet.

As an example of recent research, studies have indicated that persons who consume foods high in vitamin A have less lung cancer. One such indication comes from the National Cancer Institute, whose research has shown that various vitamin A compounds can prevent cancerous transformation of human and animal cells in the test tube.

In another study, it was noted that animals that were fed heated vegetable oils developed malignant tumors, while the other fats did not have such an effect, according to the *Vegetarian Times* (November 1982).

Additionally, an article in *Reader's Digest* (February 1983, "At Last, An Anti-Cancer Diet,") reports "[In] studies made in different parts of the world, the incidence of breast, colon and prostate cancer is significantly lower among people who eat lots of vegetables."

In line with this thought, Cayce, who did not always recommend immunization against contagious diseases, believed that "if an alkalinity is maintained in the system—especially with lettuce, carrots and celery, these in the blood supply will maintain such a condition as to immunize a person" (480-19).

Concerning meats, Cayce's advice was to "avoid too much of the heavy meats not well cooked. Eat plenty of vegetables of all characters. The meats taken would be preferably fish, fowl and lamb; others not so often" (1710-4).

The National Research Council Committee of the National Academy of Science notes: "Foods rich in carotenes (deep-yellow fruits and vegetables and dark-green vegetables) or vitamin A are associated with a reduced risk of cancer." However, authorities warn against taking large doses of vitamin A over a long period of time, as these can become toxic. Although Cayce mentioned vitamins in over three hundred readings, in most instances he recommended that they be obtained in their natural form, i.e., food. Under normal circumstances, supplements were regarded as the "lazy way" to incorporate the needed vitamins into the system.

Cayce's advice on vegetables was to "have at least one meal each day that includes a quantity of raw vegetables; such as cabbage, lettuce, celery, carrots, onions, and the like. Tomatoes may be used in their season.

"Do have plenty of vegetables grown above the ground; at least three of these to one below the ground. Have at least one leafy vegetable to every one of the pod vegetables taken" (2602-1).

A physician with the NCI's Division of Cancer Cause and Prevention says he encourages his family to eat either raw or cooked carrots every day, a vegetable especially valued by Cayce, who recommended eating "that portion especially close to the top. It may appear the harder and less desirable, but it carries the vital energies" (3051-6).

Diet: Nutrition

In the years since Edgar Cayce's death, there have been numerous scientific findings that substantiate some of his dietary suggestions found in the readings. The benefits of raw apples in the form of a three-day diet of only raw apples were suggested by the readings.

Pectin, an ingredient in apples, has been found to be extremely valuable in reducing cholesterol levels in the blood by blocking absorption of fats, and when diarrhea-causing bacteria join with pectin in the digestive tract, they are eliminated from the body.

Researchers have found that fifteen grams of pectin given to adult volunteers once a day lowered blood cholesterol by thirteen percent and raised excretion levels by thirty-five percent. The apple diet was just one recommended method of eliminating fat and cholesterol from the body. In nearly all of the readings where an alteration of the diet was suggested, Cayce stressed the need to eliminate sweets, fatty foods, and fried foods. Research over the past twenty-five years has proved the damaging effects of these foods.

Eating foods high in fat, such as rare beef, slows down the eliminations, prevents the proper assimilation of other foods, and impedes circulation. These problems, alone or collectively, contribute to many diseases of the body.

One study headed by Richard Shekelle of Chicago's Rush-Presbyterian-St. Luke's Medical Center was described in the 1980 *New England Journal of Medicine*. In 1957, nutritionists asked 1,900 men, aged between forty and fifty-five, to tell about their eating habits. They were then measured for their serum cholesterol. The highest levels coincided with the fattiest diets. The nutritionists surveyed not only the cooking methods employed in their homes but also the subjects' eating habits outside the home.

A year later, the research was conducted again, with the cholesterol intake being averaged and the men divided into three groups according to their fat and cholesterol intake. Nineteen years later, the death rate from heart disease was thirty percent higher in the high-cholesterol group.

Another bit of nutritional advice from Cayce concerned eggs. He recommended that they be soft-boiled and that only the yolks be eaten. Substantiating his advice was a study conducted in the late fifties which noted that fried or hard-boiled eggs produced the highest serum cholesterol levels in rabbits; soft boiled, the lowest. The white of the egg is known to be high in albumin—a hard-to-digest substance.

Diet: Figs

Once in a dream state, Edgar Cayce was visited by a mummy who came to life and translated ancient Egyptian records for him. He was told of a preparation said to be "spiritual food," consisting of black or Assyrian figs, Assyrian dates, and a handful of cornmeal or crushed wheat, which were to be cooked together.

Modern science has discovered that the pineal organ produces a hormone called melatonin through the action of an enzyme on the chemical serotonin. One of its functions is to inhibit sexual development and to increase or enhance intelligence. (This may account for the theory that the most intelligent human beings seem to be late developing sexually.)

Figs have been found to be exceptionally high in serotonin. It is interesting to note that the bo tree (*Ficus religiosa*), under which Gautama Buddha sat for almost thirty years, produces figs, providing food for the master during those years.

Diet: Roast Beef

Edgar Cayce recommended avoiding all red meats, especially rare red meats: "Keeping away from meats that are of red or rare meats—though meats are not harmful that are WELL cooked, save hog meat" (641-5).

At a talk presented by William B. Knight of a New Jersey food products company at the Sixty-second Annual Conference of Central Atlantic States Association of Food and Drug Officials at Ellenville, New York, on May 24, 1978, Knight told the group that rare roast beef was the cause of over two hundred reported, and possibly thousands of unreported, outbreaks of human salmonellosis (food poisoning due to salmonella bacteria) in the summer of 1977. To prevent a reoccurrence, the USDA "enacted overnight emergency measures prohibiting the manufacture and processing of commercially prepared roast beef which did not reach a minimum temperature of 145 degrees in all parts of roast."

Diet: Sugar

Possibly the most widely used suggestion from the Edgar Cayce readings is his basic diet, which recommended that eighty percent of a person's daily food intake consist of alkaline-forming foods such as fruits, vegetables, both from above and below the ground, juices of all kinds, some dairy products and approximately eight glasses of water.

Twenty percent of the diet should consist of acid-forming foods such as whole-grain cereals; meats such as fowl, fish, or lamb; and dark breads.

Cheeses, potatoes with skin, and desserts of custards, cooked fruits, ice cream, or cookies were to be eaten about three times a week. Foods containing an excessive amount of sugar were to be avoided entirely.

In recent years, sugar has received a great deal of attention from the medical world. Dr. John Yudkin, a British nutrition specialist, explained that "the increasing consumption of sugar in affluent nations is now suspected of being causally related to a number of phenomena intimately associated with health of the Western peoples in modern times, including growth acceleration, diabetes mellitus, atherosclerotic cardiovascular diseases, obesity, cholelithiasis (gallstones), dermatoses (skin diseases), periodontal (gum) diseases, dental caries (decay), peptic ulceration, and hormonal imbalances."

According to a report presented to the Optical Society of America by Ben C. Lane, optometrist and nutritionist, eating excessive amounts of sugar can worsen nearsightedness. The consumption of refined carbohydrates, such as sugar and overcooked protein, is known to deplete the body of chromium and calcium. Dr. Lane discovered a link between the body's deficiencies of these substances and nearsightedness.

Another study, this one by Drs. Ringsdorf, Cheraskin, and Ramsay at the Department of Oral Medicine of the University of Alabama Medical Center, has shown that sugar will lower the body's ability to resist any type of bacterial infection. A major defense against bacterial invasion is the presence in the blood of white cells, which engulf invading microorganisms and chemically destroy them. This protective activity has been found to be reduced by fifty percent or more as a result of a typical rise in blood sugar from twenty-four ounces of soft drinks (April 1979, *VIM Newsletter*).

Dr. Howard Lutz, in the lecture "Why We Are Falling Apart," sponsored in 1979 by the Prince William Extension Services, concluded from his investigation that "the acid-alkali imbalance in the diet was the major cause of most fatigue symptoms and 'lack of resistance' such as repeated infections," according to an issue of *Preventive Medicine Forum*. This acid-alkali imbalance was repeatedly noted by Cayce during his medical readings and was frequently listed as a cause of specific illnesses.

Diet: Wild Game

"Meats should be preferably fowl, fish, lamb, rather than beef or other meats. Wild fowl are, of course, the better" (1153-1).

Orville H. Miller, Ph.D., anthropologist and pharmacologist at the University of Southern California, became scientifically interested and personally involved in American Indian and Afro-Asian medical folklore while seeking a cure for his son's acne in the sixties.

According to his findings, the key nutritive factors exhibited by the wild animals are the mucopolysaccharides (MPS). MPS in the broadest sense include all polysaccharides with mucoid or gelatinous properties. They are found in all fluids such as connective tissue, tendons, cell walls, blood vessels, and in joints and intravertebral disks, mucous membranes, skin, etc.

The list of well-reported pharmacological activities for mucopolysaccharides found in the wild game includes treatment of infection, stimulated antibody production, increased resistance to toxins, improvement in arteriosclerosis and scleroderma, improved complexion, to name a few benefits.

Elimination

The National Institute on Aging and the National Digestive Diseases Clearinghouse have suggested that Americans should "avoid taking laxatives if at all possible." To help combat constipation, the experts advise eating fresh fruits and drinking liquids. Laxatives, they note, disrupt normal bodily rhythms.

The federal health experts warn that it is easy to become dependent on laxatives and consequently, "The natural muscle action for defecation will be impaired."

Cayce, who felt that good eliminations was necessary to maintain a healthy body, noted: "Correct [your eliminations] better by diet than by taking eliminants, when possible. If not possible to correct otherwise, take an eliminant but [alternate] between one time a vegetable laxative and the next time a mineral eliminant. But these [elimination problems] will be bettered if a great deal of the raw vegetables are used and not so much of meats" (3381-1).

Exercise

Dr. Grant Gwinup, chief of the Division of Endocrinology and Metabolism at the University of California, considers walking "the one exercise that does everything." Edgar Cayce recommended walking for various reasons, which included boosting spirits and exercising the heart and lungs. He considered walking to be the exercise that everyone can do and which under normal circumstances will not strain or injure the body, as other exercises might do when done in excess.

Cayce noted: "To over-exercise any portion not in direct need of same, to the detriment of another, is to hinder rather than to assist through exercise. Exercising is wonderful, and necessary—and little or few take as much as is needed, in a systematic manner. Use common sense. Use discretion" (283-1).

Research, which began in 1950, disclosed a link between exercising and heart disease. British investigator Professor J. N. Morris found that those who walked suffered fewer heart attacks as compared with those who did not.

Further, a three-day Conference on Exercise in Aging,

held at the National Institutes of Health in Bethesda, Maryland, in 1980, which drew physicians from around the world, concluded that walking is the safest and most efficient form of exercising for the aged.

Cayce's advice on how to spend the day included: "After breakfast, work awhile; after lunch, rest awhile and after dinner, walk a mile."

Hemophilia

Edgar Cayce reported during his readings for patients concerned with excessive bleeding that hemophilia was due to a chemical defect in the blood which inhibits effective coagulation.

According to information included in the September 1979 issue of *Bestways*, "Vitamin K is an essential element in the production of prothrombin which is one of the clotting factors produced by the liver." Vitamin K is manufactured in the large intestines, and any interference with the bacteria in the intestine or a liver disease which would block it from being absorbed could cause bleeding, the report continued.

Massage

Massage was frequently part of treatment for many illnesses and disturbances. Edgar Cayce advised massage for a wide variety of illnesses—for example, to help relieve hiccups, to improve memory, to remove scar tissue, and as drugless therapy, to cite a few instances.

Promoting drugless therapy, he noted: "For the hydrotherapy and massage are preventive as well as curative measures. For the cleansing of the system allows the body forces themselves to function normally, and thus eliminate poisons, congestions and conditions that would become acute through the body" (257-254).

The National Capital Area Chapter of the American

Massage and Therapy Association has noted that "massage can aid in digestion and elimination or restore good tone to the body. As an alternative to drug therapy, massage can ease stress and relieve fatigue, quiet and soothe tension and promote relaxation."

The association also claims that massage therapy can help lower back pain, migraine headaches, and arthritis. Cayce advised massage treatments for sixty-three percent of his arthritic cases, for he believed that massage, properly administered, was especially beneficial for those whose systems had become especially sensitive to treatment.

Moderation

Edgar Cayce felt the balanced life—or everything in moderation—contributed to longevity, and research today on extended life span gives support to that theory.

Among the data collected by the committee for an Extended Lifespan in San Marcos, California, in which information was collected on one thousand Americans who had lived a hundred years or more, was "nothing in excess." Those who drank did so in moderation, smokers did not inhale, and few of those interviewed were overweight, suggesting that there was moderation in their eating habits.

Other research, from a survey of a thousand Japanese over one hundred, noted as the common factor—moderation. The percentage of those who stopped eating before "getting full" was 54.7, while 52.4 percent attributed their longevity to their ability to limit unnecessary worry and 46.3 percent said they felt a "regular life-style," or a normal quiet life, counted the most.

Cayce's prescription for a balanced life, in part, was "plenty of brain work, but the body is supposed to coordinate the spiritual, mental and physical. He who does not give recreation a place in his life, and the proper tone to each phase—well, he just fools self and will someday— as in his body in the present—be paying the price. There must be a certain amount of recreation. There must be certain amounts of rest. These are physical, mental and spiritual necessities. . . .

"Do that and live a normal life, and you'll live a heap longer" (3352-1).

Music

Edgar Cayce believed that music was good for mental illnesses, and a recent program at a New York center for neurological impairment has substantiated this theory.

Music was turned on in one section on July 15, 1978, playing continuously during the day, and during alternate quarter hours from 8:30 P.M. to 7:00 A.M. Improvements in some patients were noted by the end of August 1978, with seventy percent of the staff reporting "definite qualitative improvements in residents' behavior." Another twenty-five percent thought there was "possible improvement."

According to another report, music is an effective treatment for tension and chronic pain, as well as for mental illness. A study at the Royal Victoria Hospital in Montreal noted that terminal cancer patients required fewer painkillers when listening to classical music.

However, researchers have found that pitch, the number of vibrations produced by sound waves, has an effect on the autonomic nervous system, with high pitch creating tension and low pitch, relaxation.

As Cayce noted: "For music is of the soul, and one may become mind and soul-sick for music, or soul and mind-sick from certain kinds of music" (5401-1).

Obesity

A familiar suggestion given by Edgar Cayce as part of a weight-reduction plan was to drink diluted grape juice one-half hour before meals. While the popular belief holds that it acts as an appetite suppressant, the readings hint at a biochemical relationship between the grape juice and loss of weight.

According to *Perspective* (volume 5, number 5), a monthly research service published by the ARE, "In discussing the causes of obesity, Cayce described an abnormality in some of the intestinal cells that absorb digested food into the system, whereby they turn most foods into sugar. This condition apparently develops through long-term poor eating habits which engender a physiological need for the fattening nutrients. As a result, the dieter may find his or her body fat level sustained despite calorie reduction."

Some researchers now describe a similar notion, that those who are overweight tend to process food in a way that seems designed to sustain fat cells. Accordingly, the researchers hypothesize "that the body has a 'set point,' a narrow weight range which is (or has come to be) normal for that body. . . .

"Dr. John D. Brunzell, metabolic specialist at the University of Washington in Seattle, reports that in patients who have lost a lot of weight, blood levels of the enzyme lipoprotein lipase (which works to promote storage of fat in fat cells) are markedly high. Thus the body's chemical profile reflects a continuing physiological mechanism to restore the fat that has been lost."

However, in research with rats, those put on diets as well as exercise schedules developed a higher percentage of muscle and a lower percentage of fat.

Cayce had another hopeful theory. While those on diets learn more healthful eating habits, drinking grape juice will help hold fat storage tendencies in abeyance: "Then, over time, the intestinal cell which learned to turn most foods into sugar will be gradually replaced with new cells formed under the influence of good eating habits."

Possession

Thirty-two individuals consulted Edgar Cayce concerning various forms of possession, some of which were accompanied by hallucinations and unpleasant visions. Symptoms most marked were loss of physical, mental, and emotional control, feelings of persecution, and feelings of estrangement within the self or from others.

Substantiating the theory of possession are many such cases reported today. Occult researcher Ian Currie, author of *You Cannot Die* and a lecturer in sociology and anthropology at Guelph University in Toronto, Canada, has investigated some fifteen possession cases and witnessed "powerful effects produced by entities that are not of this world."

Currie adds that there are many spirits "hanging around. Most are confused, some are evil. The majority don't even know they are dead."

Cayce's advice to an individual thought to be possessed was to "begin and read the 30th of Deuteronomy.... Then read the 19th of Exodus and the 5th verse, and know it applies to self" (3380-1).

Psoriasis

Edgar Cayce stated that psoriasis was due, in part, to a "toxic overload" resulting in inadequate elimination through the kidneys.

Supporting his theory is Dr. William A. McGarey of the ARE Clinic in Phoenix, Arizona, who reported in the 1978 *Medical Research Bulletin* (volume VIII, number 9) that patients with psoriasis improved with osteopathic manipulations; eliminative teas; a basic diet eliminating fats, sweets, and pastries and adding a great deal of fruits and vegetables; having colonics; and taking salts. Many of these treatments have the effect of cleansing the blood, subsequently clearing up the surface skin of eruptions and irritations.

Kidney dialysis is a method used to cleanse the blood of patients whose kidneys are no longer functioning adequately. According to reports from University of Missouri researchers, patients who used the kidney dialysis machine who had previously suffered from psoriasis found improvement in their psoriasis after three weeks of treatment on dialysis.

Sex During Pregnancy

Edgar Cayce recommended abstinence from intercourse after the third month of pregnancy for a woman requesting a reading, and recent studies have shown that mothers who had intercourse up to the time of delivery risked giving birth to babies who might develop severe breathing problems and jaundice.

Newborns may even die as a result of infection suffered by mothers who had intercourse during pregnancy, says a study of 26,000 pregnancies conducted by Dr. Richard Naeye of Hershey, Pennsylvania. Dr. Naeye noted that "mothers who reported coitus [intercourse] once or more per week during the month before delivery had more frequent amniotic-fluid infections before 33 weeks of pregnancy than did those who reported no coitus."

Sleep

In several readings, Edgar Cayce referred to the old-fashioned remedy of a glass of warm milk before bedtime to cure sleeplessness. Sleep has become a major interest of study over the last decade, and interestingly enough, one of the findings has been that a glass of warm milk before bedtime may have some scientific validity. In one study, it was found that when amino acids, which are found in milk, were given in large doses to volunteers, they produced a sedative effect.

Also, another inducement to sleep, as reported in the September 1979 *FDA Consumer,* was exercise, a pastime which Cayce heartily recommended. As noted by the

FDA, "Exercise during the daytime, especially if followed on a routine basis, has a beneficial effect on sleep."

Stress

Dr. John Diamond of Valley Cottage, New York, president of the International Academy of Preventive Medicine, says that classical music can reduce stress, strengthen muscles, and reduce pain. One of the reasons he attributes these healing qualities to music is that "it's the closest sound to the pulse beat of the heart."

In reading 933-2, Cayce states that "the rhythmic vibrations of the body, as to music, set the electrical forces of the physical body."

Stuttering

Stuttering has historically been considered the result of an emotional or psychological problem or disorder, and the treatment recommended has often been psychotherapy.

However, the underlying cause in five of the six case readings given by Edgar Cayce on the condition was some injury or imbalances in the nervous system. In every case, osteopathic or chiropractic adjustments to the spine were suggested for treatment.

Supporting Cayce's theory is a recent report on a meeting of the American Academy of Neurology: "New evidence, reported by neurologist David B. Rosenfield of the Baylor College of Medicine in Houston, suggests that in a significant number of cases, stuttering may result from a failure of the neuromuscular system controlling larynx function."

Although it was noted that emotions can aggravate movement disorders, Rosenfield added that psychotherapy could only help alleviate symptoms. "Psychotherapy never cures stuttering," he concluded.

Teeth and Gums

Edgar Cayce suggested that today's "soft" foods, as opposed to what he termed "detergent" foods such as lettuce and raw carrots, were a cause of teeth and gum disorders. He also said that "keeping such teeth cleansed with an equal combination of soda and salt at least three to four times a week will cleanse these of this disturbance.... Use any good dentifrice once or twice a day" (457-11).

Dr. Paul Keyes, clinical investigator at the National Institute of Dental Research, said he had never seen periodontal (gum) problems in patients who used salt or soda dentrifice with any degree of regularity.

Dr. Robert Nara, a dentist, explains in his book *How to Become Dentally Self-Sufficient* that baking soda will neutralize the acids in the mouth which produce bacteria from sugar on the tooth surfaces. Dr. Nara also notes that the capacity of salt "to act as a hypertonic and draw water (fluids) from tissues—should be kept in mind" as a medicine for an affected tooth, which may be so affected due to a buildup of fluids. After all, he questions, "Wouldn't it make sense to use a 'medicine' which helped reduce this fluid pressure?"

In support of Cayce's admonition against today's soft-food diet, Dr. Weston Price, author of *Nutrition and Physical Degeneration*, notes that decay and imperfect mouth structure are related to Western diets that require no chewing, thus inviting destructive bacteria to live in the mouth.

Additionally, Cayce was almost consistent in recommending that his patients avoid drinking carbonated drinks. A recent explanation of what occurs in the mouth when a carbonated drink is ingested reinforces his prohibition. Accordingly, when a carbonated liquid is taken into the mouth, carbon dioxide gas is released from the liquid-forming bubbles, which break as they reach the surface of the liquid. Since surface-tension forces are involved in the formation and breakup of gas bubbles, the results are powerful impacts against the enamel of the teeth, which can possibly cause minute cracks in the surface.

Afterword
by Randall A. Langston, M.D.

Years after the event, Jess Stearn was to recall the nadir of Edgar Cayce's career in his classic book, *Soulmates*. The story goes that in 1931 he was arrested in New York City by undercover policewomen and charged with fortune-telling. The policewomen had entrapped him by joining the Association of Research and Enlightenment and then requested a reading. This reading was given at no charge to them. The case was thrown out by the judge who considered it to lack merit. Nevertheless, the incident distressed Edgar Cayce. He asked his wife Gertrude why God had not made him a doctor if he wanted him to help people. His gentle soulmate replied, "Then you would be simply a doctor like any other." Here, indeed, was a man who was not a doctor like any other.

As a scientifically oriented and trained physician, I was asked to look at this large and comprehensive work. I knew that we were examining the fruits of a rare interface between the metaphysical and scientific worlds. The metaphysical portions, of course, were the readings themselves given in a hypnotic trance. And yet the diagnoses and therapies given fell into the scientific realm. They were certainly consistent with the knowledge of the day and some knowledge that didn't exist in that day. And even forty years after Cayce's death we are left with more questions than we have answers.

The facts of Edgar Cayce's life are well documented and we know to have been verified during his lifetime. There were many physicians and scientists who witnessed the readings with the purposes of discrediting Edgar Cayce only to say in essence, "Keep doing what you are doing— some day we will catch up." They realized that the anatomical and physiological facts coming from the mouth of this man who was in a trance were accurate. They could not discredit the trance information and they could not understand it, and so they merely stated, "Keep on doing what you're doing—some day we will catch up."

Let us review some of the known facts that may aid us to take a somewhat scientific look at the health readings. That is, we will have to progress from what we know to what we do not know. Number one, we know the readings were given by a man in an altered state of consciousness. This altered or hypnotic state was such that he had no waking conscious knowledge of the content of the readings. Fact number two is that the depth of scientific knowledge that flowed through the readings could not have been possessed by the awake Cayce. For example, he could not have obtained medical textbooks and simply memorized anatomy, physiology, and pharmacology. Medical texts were closely guarded in those days. A layperson could not simply walk into a book store and obtain a textbook. And even if he had obtained such books, the pathophysiology or the causal mechanisms of disease often were at variance with the traditional teachings of the times. And often the causes of illnesses were not even known to medical science at the time the readings were given. A good example concerns advice given regarding Alzheimer's disease. Reba Karp has described this very beautifully in this book. For example, the only therapy or help suggested for Alzheimer's disease advised against the use of aluminum cookware in cooking. Now, we certainly do not know all the factors associated with this dread disorder, but Reba Karp has noted two studies suggesting a possible causal relationship between aluminum and Alzheimer's disease. One is in the 1980 April issue of *Science,* an article entitled, "The Association Of Aluminum And Damage To Brain Cells." The authors were from the University of Vermont College of Medicine and the National Institutes of Environmental Sciences. The other was by Dr. A. Hoffer in the 1980 Huxley Institute CSF Newsletter. The article was entitled, "High levels Of Aluminum Found In Brains Of Alzheimer's." Today, there is some debate on the use of antacids that contain hydroxide and the use of deodorants that contain aluminum. The astounding fact is that the suggestion that aluminum is somehow associated with brain damage was not appreciated by the scientific community until many years after Cayce's death.

Another good example concerns pellagra in the early 20th century. Pellagra, due to vitamin B_6 deficiency, was particularly rampant in the South at that time. At the time of the readings, the B vitamins had not yet been identified, nor the cause of pellagra. What did the readings advise? The therapy given was green leafy vegetables, which were a good source of vitamin B complex, and indeed this therapy did ameliorate the symptoms of pellagra. It is rare to see this condition today in industrialized countries. We marvel at the fact that the treatment given in the readings was accurate. What was the source of this information? It certainly was not in any textbook of the day.

The readings recognized the totality of each person. The person was not just a body with a physical ailment to be treated in isolation from his mind, the manifestations of personality, and even his soul. So we see variations in the causal mechanisms for the same disease in different patients. A cold must have a virus, as we all know. But what causes one person to catch a cold and not another? Today,

we know it is due to alterations in the immune system.
Well, what causes those alterations? We now know that it
can be associated with stress, anger, chilling, fatigue,
dietary indiscretions as noted in the pages of this work, or
problems with eliminations and assimilations. The readings seem to stress a balance to maintain or regain health.
Doesn't that sound current and very modern? And, what is
it that today's scientists are saying about diseases such as
cancer and heart disease? They are saying there is evidence
to connect lifestyle choices, such as diet, exercise, environmental exposures, and emotional characteristics to the
contracting and course of these diseases. For example,
people with a type A hard-driving personality are more
prone to heart attacks. Women who have had breast cancer
who are aggressive about their disease have much better
survival rates than those who simply give in and are
passive. And what about diet? Food in the American south
of Edgar Cayce's day was usually fried with plenty of
grease. I am sure this is the diet that he grew up with on
the farm. Yet the dietary recommendations in the readings
are consistent with the most recent thinking. When you
pick up a magazine, what do you see? You see—avoid
sugars, sweets, and refined carbohydrates. Avoid fried and
fatty foods. Avoid red meat such as pork and beef. Eat
large amounts of complex carbohydrates with little meat,
and the little meat preferably being fowl, fish, or lamb.
Edgar Cayce stressed these diets be in proper alkaline/
acid
balance. The high roughage diet recommended in the
readings was not generally recommended even when I was
going to medical school in the late 1950s and early 1960s.
Dr. Burkitt, a medical missionary to Africa, noted that the
natives on their poor but high fiber diet did not appear to
get the degenerative diseases so common in the West.
There were such varied conditions as arthritis, heart disease, cancer, adult onset diabetes, gallbladder disease, and
on and on. A good example of the readings being somewhat ahead of conventional medical thinking concerns the
management of the painful inflammation of the pouches
extruding from the large intestine, called diverticulitis.

When I was an intern and general surgery resident, we put these patients on "bowel rest." That meant they received no roughage in order to rest the bowel while it was healing. Today's therapy is more in line with the readings. In fact, it is generally believed that high fiber diets may prevent not only diverticulitis but the development of the pouches which we call diverticulosis. So we can see that what may have been anathema to scientists in Edgar Cayce's day appear to be the treatments of choice today.

The treatments recommended were from many disciplines. Often the treatments were from osteopathy, chiropractic, homeopathy, physiotherapy, as well as traditional medicine and surgery. Many of the therapies may seem curious or archaic to the modern. I have no way to make value judgements on many of them. But the reader must remember that many of these therapies were given before the advent of wonder drugs, such as the antibiotics and some of the anti-tumor therapeutics. The therapies were really aimed at bringing the body back into homeostasis, or balance. That is, a body that is in balance both psychologically and physically is less likely to contract this or that disease. Certainly, I think we would all agree with that in this day and time. But more than that, the fact remains that the therapies seemed to help. The usages recorded in the recent testimonials are most impressive. That is, the people today are experimenting with the therapies, and they seem to help. I'm going to cite one example that Reba Karp mentions, and that was the use of scar massage cream to get rid of scars from a terrible accident by a patient at Duke University Hospital. The fact was that the scar massage cream worked to rid the lady of her scars. Now, we do not need a double blind study to verify such a therapy. It's plain as the nose on the lady's face. Another case not mentioned in this book was that of a runner relieving his "runner's" knee pain with peanut oil. This was after other therapies had failed.

In the final analysis, we in the scientific community cannot explain from what source or sources these readings came. We only know that they did occur and that the scientific contents of many of them were extremely accurate. The cures or advice were often extremely helpful. And let us note that in the advice for many diseases there was no cure or therapy offered. For example, patients with terminal illnesses were often told that they were terminal and that they should prepare themselves spiritually. Doesn't that sound a great deal like the hospice movement of today? We can only observe the failure of many to discredit the readings by submitting the names of nonexistent patients. In those cases when Edgar Cayce would go into trance, there would be nobody found and no reading would occur. So that is another clue that we were dealing with a real and genuine phenomenon. And finally, we can only observe the helpfulness of the readings to the thousands of people both then and now. Indeed, there is enough potential research material in these readings for many investigators for many years to come.

Keep doing what you are doing—some day we will catch up.

Randall A. Langston, M. D., 1985

THE WONDERS NEVER CEASE WITH
"AMERICA'S GREATEST SEER"* EDGAR CAYCE

27 million Americans can't read a bedtime story to a child.

It's because 27 million adults in this country simply can't read.

Functional illiteracy has reached one out of five Americans. It robs them of even the simplest of human pleasures, like reading a fairy tale to a child.

You can change all this by joining the fight against illiteracy.

Call the Coalition for Literacy at toll-free **1-800-228-8813** and volunteer.

Volunteer Against Illiteracy. The only degree you need is a degree of caring.

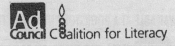

Ad Council Coalition for Literacy